Arab and Muslim
Science Fiction

CRITICAL EXPLORATIONS IN SCIENCE FICTION AND FANTASY

A series edited by Donald E. Palumbo and C.W. Sullivan III

Earlier Works: www.mcfarlandpub.com

Arab and Muslim Science Fiction

Critical Essays

Edited by
HOSAM A. IBRAHIM ELZEMBELY
and EMAD EL-DIN AYSHA

CRITICAL EXPLORATIONS IN
SCIENCE FICTION AND FANTASY, 74
Series Editors Donald E. Palumbo *and* C.W. Sullivan III

McFarland & Company, Inc., Publishers
Jefferson, North Carolina

LIBRARY OF CONGRESS CATALOGUING-IN-PUBLICATION DATA

Names: Elzembely, Hosam A. Ibrahim, 1968– editor. | Aysha, Emad El-Din, 1974– editor.
Title: Arab and Muslim science fiction : critical essays /
edited by Hosam A. Ibrahim Elzembely and Emad El-Din Aysha.
Other titles: Critical explorations in science fiction and fantasy ; 74.
Description: Jefferson, North Carolina : McFarland & Company, Inc.,
Publishers, 2022. | Series: Critical explorations in science fiction and fantasy ; 74 |
Includes bibliographical references and index.
Identifiers: LCCN 2021057480 | ISBN 9781476685236 (paperback : acid free paper) ∞
ISBN 9781476643175 (ebook)
Subjects: LCSH: Science fiction, Arabic—History and criticism. | Science fiction,
Middle Eastern—History and criticism. | BISAC: LITERARY CRITICISM / Science
Fiction & Fantasy | LITERARY CRITICISM / Middle Eastern | LCGFT: Literary criticism.
Classification: LCC PN3433.5 .A73 2022 | DDC 809.3/8762089927—dc23/eng/20220210
LC record available at https://lccn.loc.gov/2021057480

BRITISH LIBRARY CATALOGUING DATA ARE AVAILABLE

ISBN (print) 978-1-4766-8523-6
ISBN (ebook) 978-1-4766-4317-5

Front cover illustration by Tithi Luadthong (Shutterstock)

Printed in the United States of America

*McFarland & Company, Inc., Publishers
Box 611, Jefferson, North Carolina 28640
www.mcfarlandpub.com*

A Dedication

To our nation, the Arab Muslim Civilization, to the good people all over the world. To the memory of Nehad Sherif, the father of Egyptian sci fi. To the memory of James Gunn, one of the most eminent sci fi writers of the Western Civilization.

To the Egyptian, Arab and Muslim youth, the only hope for a change in our civilization. A civilization destined to be in the middle of the world. The multi-dimensional meaning of the word "middle" is truly pivotal in our civilization and inspiring to all of us.

To the sci-fi readers, writers, critics and academics all over the world with whom we share the passion and dreams of pushing further the boundaries of science and the imagination.

Ahhh! The Sky, Heaven and Hell…. Those three words were known in the East…. Once you take them out of our earthly world, the whole world will fall apart … all the masterpieces we have made would sound and look platitude.

I know the West now is an object of admiration for its science and discoveries but what does it worth judging by the greatest discoveries that were found in the east?!

Verily the West is exploring the Earth and the East is exploring the Sky.

—Tawfik Al-Hakim

Quote taken from "توفيق الحكيم," *Goodreads.com*, https://www.goodreads.com/quotes/462856-ahhh-the-sky-heaven-and-hell-those-three-words-were-known.

Table of Contents

Section III—A Literature in Appraisal

Acknowledgments

This book would have been an impossibility without the dedicated help of the following individuals and groups, and were it not for their other commitments they would have surely contributed to and enriched this book beyond all measure—Jörg Matthias Determann, Orkun Uçar, Ola Diab, Jaymee Goh, Ahmed A. Khan, Phenderson Clark, Iraj Fazel Bakhsheshi, Hussein Rashid, Hacen Ahmed Chekkat, Jaroslav Olsa, Jr., Harris Durani, Amalia A. Mokrushina, P.A. March-Russell, Melanie Magidow, Nada Faris, Bodhisattva Chattopadhyay, Malak Mohammed, Timothy James Dimacali, Margaret Litvin, Hugh Nicol, David Stanford, Jill Abahussein, William Melaney, Tendai Huchu, Geoff Ryman, Chuah Guat Eng, Gina Yap Lai Yoong, Eve Shi, Shaharzad Akbar, S.A. Chakraborty, Lauti Nia, Jenniliisa Salminen, Mazi Nwonwu, Bilimkurgu Kulübü, SEA SFF, the Malaysian Writers Society, the African Science Fiction and Fantasy Reading Group, Bahrain Poet Society, and Southeast Asian Writers & Poets.

We evolve through science fiction.
—*Hosam and Emad*

Preface

HOSAM A. IBRAHIM ELZEMBELY

This is a book dedicated to filling in the gap once and for all in the production and dissemination of knowledge about Arabic and Muslim science fiction. There are notable works on the topic, but all told from the singular perspective of a foreign expert, invariably an academic, who is not intimately acquainted with our cultural perspective and values or the exact nature of the problems we all face in our various settings as authors, researchers, publishers and translators.

This book is the brainchild of the Egyptian Society for Science Fiction (ESSF), the first organization of its kind representing the plight of SF and fantasy authors in Egypt, with plans from very early on to reach the rest of the Arab world and tackle and forever change the culture and environment of SF in the Arab world, a very antithetical culture that belittles science fiction and stymies its ability to organize and make a contribution to the Arab literary scene. The ESSF was formed in 2012, in the glorious aftermath of the Arab Spring and the January 2011 revolution in Egypt specifically. Sadly the events of 2013 brought a halt to our activities, when we were at our zenith as a group, having published four short story anthologies, with three that year alone. By 2017 it became clear the political situation was not going to improve so we resumed our activities with a new sense of mission and a new philosophy. We wanted to reach outwards to the world entire, through the vehicle of the English language. We began contacting like-minded individuals and groups in formal fashion in countries as far afield as the United States and Turkey and Malaysia, Iran and the Gulf Arab states and from there Russia and Central Asia and Australia. Previously, despite our clear pan–Arab focus, we always relied on informal contacts to bring in friends and counterparts from Yemen and Morocco and Syria and Somalia, but we never, ever ventured out further, till now.

By 2018 we'd accumulated enough contacts, and enough confidence, to take this to the next level. As a scientist, a medical doctor and also a human development expert, I think of books as pure science. To me everything is an example of value-added, an enzyme that speeds up chemical reactions and interactions and leads to a critical mass and cascade effect from the simple raw materials that have always been there, people and ideas and publications. That is what the Arab and Muslim sci-fi world is in dire need of. A stimulant that can fill the gap once and for all in international knowledge of the nature, genesis, history and challenges facing Arabic and Muslim science fiction—who is writing, all those less well known youthful names, and what they hope to accomplish and on whose shoulders from past generations they are resting, the heroes who got the ball rolling.

2 Preface

This book is our gift to the world as Arabs and Muslims and we hope that it will be a thoroughly enjoyable as well an informative gift. It has something for everyone, whether an avid non-expert reader of SF or an academic or publisher or translator or advocate of the cause. It is the least we can do for our colleagues of the future to break down barriers and build cultural bridges once and for all in that neglected field of Arab and Muslim futurism.

Introduction

Marcia Lynx Qualey

I first met Arabic literature in translation as a teenager, through Zayd Mutee' Damaj's *The Hostage,* translated by Christopher Tingley and May Jayyusi; Ibrahim al-Koni's *Bleeding of the Stone,* also translated by Tingley and Jayyusi; and Yusuf al-Qaid's *War in the Land of Egypt*, translated by Lorne and Olive Kenny, also with Tingley. They were all published through Interlink Books' Emerging World Writers series. I don't know which book I stumbled across first, but soon I was scouring library shelves and bookshops for the little Emerging World Writers logo that looked like a cancelled postage stamp, and sucking them down like candies. I have always liked literature that de-centered and expanded my world; made me feel I was just one small, odd creature in a very large universe.

I first met science fiction in seventh grade, when a teacher who wore a polyester pantsuit and a wig that sat askew assigned us a thick, faded packet of stories; it looked as though, each year, the packet was photocopied from the previous year. I don't remember who any of the authors were, but I still remember the thrill of terror at futuristic landscapes of inexplicable aliens and empty smart homes. And the frustration when a line was missing because of some accident with the photocopier.

It didn't occur to me, back then, to study either Arabic literature or science fiction; perhaps I didn't even realize they were things one could study.

For a very short time, I had the sort of proper office job where one neither read Arabic literature nor science fiction. In 2001, I fled the suffocation of it for Egypt, where the sky was open and where I was fairly certain Mahfouz's characters, as well as al-Qaid's young Masri, were lurking somewhere, just around a corner.

It was years still before I learned about the Egyptian science-fiction community, which isn't as visible as those in English, which now has well-established literary prizes and is covered by the mainstream literary community. I also slowly learned about writers in Syria, Iraq, the Emirates, Kuwait, and Algeria who worked in the genre. Although literature is often depicted as a solitary passion—and in some ways, it is—literary communities, diwans, and discussions, such as those held by the Egyptian Society for Science Fiction, are essential for the flowering of new literary forms. Because of interruptions, science fiction has had a difficult time taking root in Arabic; still, passionate readers means it persists.

Genre literature is often disdained by Arabic literary critics, the genres—horror, romance, fantasy, speculative fiction. And yet *joy* is essential for drawing in a wide variety of new readers. Any time I feel weary at literature, I can always turn up a speculative-fiction story and remember the weird, wonderful spark that brought me to books and keeps me here.

Thus this volume is doubly important; it uplifts science fiction as the serious literature that it is, while also spotlighting what is going on in an oft-neglected part of the global literary landscape. Most of the critical and academic attention given to science fiction has been to the literature produced in North America and Europe, which misses out on the rich landscape of science fiction in other languages, and the ways in which it fuses with other literary and cultural traditions. Some critics and writers have been too quick to declare an Arabic novel "dystopic" when it is meant to reflect a current reality; others have been quick to declare there is no such thing as Arabic science fiction at all.

This volume goes to the source: seeking the views of practitioners, authors, translators, scholars, patrons, passionate readers, and others who are deeply involved in the universes of Arab, Arabic, and Muslim science fiction. This is an excellent start to building our knowledge of a genre and a discipline that will yet have many things to say.

Dividing Lines

The World-View of Science Fiction

Adapted from *The Science of Science-Fiction Writing*

James E. Gunn

> Humankind is being led along an evolving course,
> through this migration of intelligences,
> and though we seem to be sleeping,
> there is an inner wakefulness
> that directs the dream,
> and that will eventually startle us back
> to the truth of who we are.
> —Rumi

Fred Pohl recalls that British writer John T. Phillifent once wrote to him that he had discovered that what set science fiction writers apart was that they used the science fiction method—but he died before he could say what the science fiction method was. So we are left groping for what distinguishes SF from other kinds of fiction and like the blind men fumbling around the elephant find ourselves dealing with one aspect or another but never quite encompassing the whole beast. Fred goes on to speculate that what his friend had come up with had something to do with the way in which SF writers look at the universe. There may be something to this.

Certainly SF, like science itself, is based on the assumption that the universe is knowable even though the greatest part of it may be unknown and may be destined to remain mysterious for the life of any of us, or, indeed, the life of all of us, by which I mean the human species. The knowable universe has no room for the supernatural, or those experiences that by their very nature can never be "known." To bring experiences of the transcendent or the ineffable into the natural world is to destroy one or the other. Thus we have a basic distinction between fantasy and science fiction and even, though, it is not immediately apparent, between mainstream fiction and science fiction.

I would like to suggest, however, that the worldview of science fiction can be narrowed even further. The relationship between science fiction and Darwin's *The Origin of the Species* long has been apparent. We know, of course, that modern science fiction began with H.G. Wells. Wells seems contemporary and everything before Wells seems quaintly historical, Mary Shelley, Poe, even Verne. *The War of the Worlds* can be updated, and has, repeatedly to great effect. But *Frankenstein* and *From the Earth to the Moon* can only be produced as period pieces.

Shelley and Poe and Verne were influenced by blossoming science and an awareness that the world was being changed by it and by its child, technology, but Wells had the benefit of the publication of *The Origin of Species* in 1859. At an obvious level, Darwin's theories of evolution were the most important elements in Thomas H. Huxley's career in biology, and his relationships with Darwin and the defense of his theories in debates across the English countryside are well known. Almost as well known is the fact that the young Wells spent his first year of college studying biology under Huxley and recalled it as a shaping influence, and the fact, as Jack Williamson demonstrated in his doctoral dissertation published as *H.G. Wells: Critic of Progress*, that the early (and most important) portion of Wells's SF writing was a coming to terms with evolution. Not quite so apparent is the fact that Darwin's theories underlay what we now point at as science fiction.

I've always felt that naturalism and SF have a lot in common—that SF, say, is fantastic naturalism, or naturalized fantasy, or simply that which hasn't happened yet, that we know of, treated naturalistically. Maybe it goes farther than that. C. Hugh Holman, in *A Handbook to Literature*, defines naturalism as "a movement in the novel in the later nineteenth and early twentieth centuries in France, America, and England," and "in its simplest sense … the application of the principles of scientific determinism to fiction…. The fundamental view of man which the naturalist takes is of an animal in the natural world, responding to environmental forces and internal stresses and drive, over none of which he has control and none of which he fully understands. It tends to differ from realism, not in its attempt to be accurate in the portrayal of its materials but in the selection and organization of those materials, selecting not the commonplace but the representative and so arranging the materials that the structure of the novel reveals the pattern of ideas—in this case, scientific theory—which forms the author's view of the nature of experience. In this sense, naturalism shares with romanticism a belief that the actual is important not in itself but in what it can reveal about the nature of a larger reality; it differs sharply from romanticism, however, in finding that reality not in transcendent ideas or absolute ideals but in the scientific laws which can be perceived through the action of individual instances. This distinction may be illustrated in this way. Given a block of wood and a force pushing upon it, producing in it a certain acceleration: Realism will tend to concentrate its attention on the accurate description of that particular block, that special force, and that definite acceleration; Romanticism will tend to see in the entire operation an illustration or symbol or suggestion of a philosophical truth and will so represent the block, the force, and the acceleration— often with complete fidelity to fact—that the idea or ideal that it embodies forth is

A portrait of the dearly departed Dr. James Gunn (courtesy of the artists, Srinivas Mouni and Gandhi Mouni).

the center of the interest; and naturalism will tend to see in the operation a clue or a key to the scientific law which undergirds it and to be interested in the relationship between the force, the block, and the produced acceleration and will so represent the operation that Newton's second law of motion (even on occasion in its mathematical expression— $F = ma$) is demonstrated or proved by this representative instance of its universal occurrence in nature. In this sense naturalism is the novelist's response to the revolution in thought that modern science has produced. From Newton it gains a sense of mechanistic determinism; from Darwin (the greatest single force operative upon it) it gains a sense of biological determinism and the inclusive metaphor of the lawless jungle which it has used perhaps more often than any other; from Marx it gains a view of history as a battleground of vast economic and social forces; from Freud it gains a view of the determinism of the inner and subconscious self; from Taine it gains a view of literature as a product of deterministic forces; from Comte it gains of view of social and environmental determinism…" (Holman, 1973: 337–338).

Most of Holman's description of naturalism could be applied to science fiction with only a few reservations. The reason for this is partly because both are the products of modern science and in particular of the theory of evolution. Darwin produced naturalism and science fiction applied naturalism to the fantastic. In other words, science fiction takes the unusual, the remarkable event that has not happened, and presents it as part of the natural world. More important, the naturalistic story treats human beings as part of the natural world, as a product of their environment, and their failures and successes (primarily their failures) as a result of their environment rather than their characters or decisions, but as captured in that moment like fossils embedded in limestone. Science fiction, on the other hand, treats human beings as a species that has evolved as a result of environment but, and this is the crucial distinction from naturalism, as a species upon whom the evolutionary process is still at work.

Science fiction, then, deals with people as if they were creatures as adaptable as the protoplasm from which they emerged. Change the conditions and humanity will change. The first premise of SF is that humanity is adaptable. To that premise, however, science fiction added another that naturalism never had: Although humanity is as much a product of its environment as the other animals, it possesses a quality that the other animals lack—the intellectual ability to recognize its origins and the processes at work upon it, and even, sometimes, to choose a course other than that instilled by its environment. In naturalism such recognition at best leads to a sense of tragic loss.

One of the best statements of this SF worldview is contained in Isaac Asimov's *The Caves of Steel* and *The Naked Sun*—his 1950s Robot novels. In *The Caves of Steel* people have become so accustomed to enclosure that they all suffer from agoraphobia; for them even the possibility of going outside the roofed city is unthinkable. The murder mystery that drives the action of *The Caves of Steel* is based upon the agoraphobia of its citizens, and a major factor in its solution is Lije Baley's ability to think the unthinkable.

Moreover, a subplot of the Robot novels involves the plans of some Spacers to push the short-lived, disease-ridden, agoraphobic Terrans into expanding into what will later become the Galactic Empire, but that depends upon Terrans conquering their agoraphobia and being able to set off in spaceships for distant suns. Baley not only fights his own fears of open spaces in *The Naked Sun*, he organizes a group to help others do the same.

These two basic principles, it seems to me, create that difficult-to-define something by which we identify science fiction, and if it doesn't involve them we may feel that it is *like* SF but it doesn't quite have the right stuff. At least that is true of American SF. New Wave SF, for instance, tended to describe the environmental aspect of human behavior but, like naturalism, stopped at that. Or, rather, it assumed that people are moved more by obsession than rational choice, and that crippled their ability to cope with change. J.G. Ballard's stories and novels are good examples, with their characters paralyzed by change rather than adapting to it or moved to action by it. A good deal of non–English-language SF does not have the second premise (the ability to act other than the way one is conditioned to behave), either, and when I was researching stories to include in *The Road to Science Fiction #6: Around the World* I found a great many stories that involved the naturalistic recognition of humanity's evolutionary past but not as much of the human ability to recognize that fact and rise above it.

This is not to say that there is anything inherently right or wrong about belief in the power of rationality over conditioning. Most of the time people do behave as if they were programmed, but occasionally they act as if they had free will. American SF has focused on the few problem solvers who have done the most to change life and society, and thereby, according to American SF, people themselves. Other SF, Forster's "The Machine Stops," say, as opposed to Campbell's "Twilight," may have based its beliefs about people on the more common kind of behavior.

In "The Machine Stops," for instance, humanity has been reduced to total dependence on the machine and not only does not recognize that fact (except for one aberrant individual) but does not even notice when the machine begins to fail. In "Twilight" humanity has lost its curiosity because of the lack of competition, not because of the machine, but at the end a visitor to that far-distant future instructs a machine to create a curious machine, making it the inheritor of humanity's mission to ask questions of the universe.

Mainstream fiction seems to do without Darwin entirely. As a matter of fact, in a mainstream story the origins of humanity, if they enter at all, are more likely to be Biblical than evolutionary. If evolution enters, the story is transformed into science fiction.

Mainstream fiction's preoccupation with the present reflects an apparent desire to freeze reality in its current state, and a belief that everything that has happened or is likely to happen is of little importance except as it reflects upon the present. Mainstream's preoccupation with the reactions and reflections of individuals who have little influence in their own times and no historical influence suggests that reality is less important than the way people feel about it. To put it another way, the concentration by mainstream fiction on social interactions seems to incorporate the conviction that the most important, if not the only important, aspect of existence is the ways in which people relate to each other.

Science fiction, on the other hand, incorporates a belief that the most important aspect of existence is a search for humanity's origins, its purpose, and its ultimate fate. Mainstream fiction may seem more "real" because it reflects the reality that most people deal with in their everyday existence: the social world and our interactions with it and our feelings about it. But is the evolution of humanity less real because it is less quotidian?

The shape of mainstream fiction is dictated by its belief in what is important. It is dense with character not because that is what "good fiction" concerns itself with but because that is what mainstream fiction is about. Science fiction, which has often been criticized because of the thinness of its characterization, is similarly the result of SF beliefs. When one is concerned about the way in which people are the products of their environments and how one can free oneself to act in ways other than that one has been conditioned to do, the feelings of the characters about their situations, or even aspects of individual character or reactions to the general predicament, seem of little moment.

Similarly, mainstream fiction has minimized or discarded plot as "mere incident," while plot remains at the heart of science fiction. This suggests that for the mainstream what happens does not really matter; nothing new is going to occur, and the only proper concern is how character should react to repetition. Science fiction, on the other hand, exists in a world of change, and the focus is on external events: What is the change and how are humans (or aliens) going to respond to it?

The science fiction method we could say is this appreciation of change. The author of science fiction is never satisfied with the world as it is today. His is the striving for continuous change. Change for the better, we hope, but being able to discern the contours of these transformations, of what governs change and how man goes along with it. Darwin taught us to accept this eventuality of life, that it is ultimately for the better, part of the natural history of the world and man. Wells was the first to introduce this perspective to science fiction, changing the genre forever.

It is always refreshing to see this designation taking root somewhere else. One could surmise that Arab and Muslim authors have been struggling like the blind men and the elephant each forming his own impression as to what the genre is for their own good time, just as we have. They are the latest generation of fantastical naturalists, making sense of the changing world around them and the prospects it opens up for them and the laws that ultimately govern the process—technological, social, biological. We can only wish them luck and hope that our story with science fiction can lend a helping hand.

Work Cited

Holman, C. Hugh. (January 1973). *A Handbook to Literature, Based on the Original by William Flint Thrall and Addison Hibbard.* 3rd edition. Indianapolis: Odyssey Press. https://archive.org/details/in.ernet. dli.2015.88999/page/n6.

• NORTH AFRICA •

The Continuum

Four Waves of Egyptian Sci-Fi

HOSAM A. IBRAHIM ELZEMBELY

In the past, traditional art was based on making manifest what is enduring in man, like love, jealousy, hatred, envy, and greed…. Today art has to look again at these unchanging qualities, because society is no longer unchanging. It is up to art today to show us what has become of these unchanging qualities in a world which is moving and changing.

—Tawfik Al-Hakim[1]

The story of science fiction in Egypt is very much like the story of science and life. You have individual actors, brilliant people who are ahead of their times, trying desperately to make a difference but no community as a whole made up of those actors that can really get things done. I resolved to correct this situation with the founding of the Egyptian Society for Science Fiction (ESSF), with many other related projects and initiatives.

My own story with science fiction began with my tender years, as a teenager in the United Kingdom, when the Star Wars series came out. I was captivated with the genre from the word go and pressed my father, Dr. Abdelhamid Ibrahim, to put me in touch with family friends who were also distinguished Egyptian SF authors themselves—Dr. Mustafa Mahmoud and Nihad Sherif. Mustafa Mahmoud was a fount of wisdom and Nihad Sherif was the gentlest person I ever saw. Both exerted their influence on me to this day, although I hoped to outdo them with my own brand of Islamic-Arabic science fiction, beginning with my first three novels: *The Great Space Sage: The Half-Humans*, *The Planet of the Viruses: The First Dialogue with a Microscopic Civilization*, and *America 2030: The Story of the End of the World*. While science fiction authors in Egypt in the past were no doubt influenced by Islam as a religion and moral system, they did not necessarily write science fiction that can be designated as Islamic. They did not necessarily set their stories against a backdrop that was culturally Arabic and Muslim, going through a fabric woven of the customs and traditions and religious practices of our peoples.

I tried to remedy this situation with my writings and also with the Egyptian Society for Science Fiction. We want to do more than write science fiction, as Muslims and Arabs and Egyptians. We want to promote the culture of science fiction in our countries, to promote scientific literary and fight ignorance and superstition, and we want to resurrect our Islamic-Arabic civilization and engage in dialogue with the other and reconcile differences, at home and abroad.

A Personal Case Study

It will surprise you to know that my three novels, while published in Egypt in 2001, I actually wrote while I was in the United States completing my doctorate in ophthalmology. The atmosphere in Egypt is very stifling for creativity. It's not just the workload, I was busy with my studies in the U.S. and yet it never got me down. You can't hardly drive in the roads in Egypt without being honked at or finding terrible and inexplicable things happening in front of you that could cost your life, or at least your sanity. It is very off-putting to the creative and aesthetic drive. That, and the work load and responsibilities of marriage and family life, and having two clinics, one in my home town of Minia in the south of Egypt with the other in Cairo in the North. My ten years' experience in working with the American University in Cairo (AUC)'s School of Business, Executive Education unit was both enriching and demanding. The concepts of quality and management infiltrated my life through that experience.

All I have written since returning to Egypt is short stories. In fact, thank heavens, I did my novels early in life. I would send them to my father in Egypt to get them published. Here is what I hoped to do with my novels and how they came into existence.

The Half-Humans

As someone who wanted to pioneer a fourth wave of science fiction in Egypt—please see the diagram below—I dreamed like many of my generation of a single, prosperous, unified Arab-Islamic civilization. This novel articulates our dream of a single, united nation that is scientifically advanced and equally participating with Western civilization and other human civilizations to boost the advanced path of mankind.

The Union of Muslim States, modeled on the European Union—democratic and egalitarian—has helped in terraforming Mars and Venus and is now leading the first manned mission to Titan, the mysterious moon of Saturn that scientists have long wanted to explore. While there, the two Muslim astronauts are interdicted by an alien intelligence (the half-humans) that places them on a rescue mission that they cannot refuse, because of their principles and ethics as Muslims.

The Planet of the Viruses

While I was doing research at Louisiana State University in 2001, my mentor was Professor H.E. Kaufman, one of the pioneers in finding novel medications for viral corneal ulcers. His research team used to have a weekly scientific meeting where they discuss their research issues. Attending these meetings inspired me to write the novel within the context of my plans for the fourth generation of sci-fi writers in Egypt; i.e., the fabric of the novel was authentic as regards the cultural and civilizational aspect.

Again there is the democratic and constitutionally governed Union of Islamic States, working diligently to find a cure for a viral infection threatening to rob humankind of the power of sight. Rival teams of scientists compete but if they had cooperated with each other the stunning discovery made by the Muslim scientists would have taken place much earlier. And it is up to the Muslims now to represent humanity in its dialogue with the "microscopic" civilization they stumble on in the story.

America 2030

The fear of dictatorship is present deep inside our psyche (residents of the developing world). This fear is exaggerated when it comes to major powers like the USA. My presence in the United States from 2001–2002, and witnessing George W. Bush's dogmatic attitude, sparked my fear of the USA (as a great power) falling into the hands of a dictator. The novel visits such scenarios and it's near future genre, and just before 9/11.

As dazzled as I was by how advanced the country was, I felt there was something wrong, a sense of consternation brewing behind the scenes. I gave vent to this in my novel, the closest thing I have written to a dystopia, where the country slowly turns into a dictatorship where people, on the surface have rights, but do not pursue them in practice, distracted as they are by material wealth and materialistic pleasures. The consequences of this for the rest of the world are even more harrowing, which is why the novel is subtitled "The Story of the End of the World." Today, and after about two decades of the publication of the novel and the appearance of (Trump's Controversiality) the theme is even more threatening with the same trajectory.

With the coming of the 2011 January revolution in Egypt and the hope for democratic transformation, I saw an opportunity to introduce a fourth wave in the path of Egyptian science fiction. I had tried to instigate with my books and stories. Hence, the birth of the Egyptian Society for Science Fiction in 2012 and the beginning of our publications with the first volume of Shams Al-Ghad (Sun of Tomorrow), also in 2012.

But before we can go into that, an account of the Egyptian Society and its mission statement, goals and modus operandi, we must recap on the history of science fiction in Egypt. As a scientist, I will present it in diagrammatic form.

An illustration that shows the four waves describing the evolution of sci-fi in Egypt (courtesy of the artist, Ammar Al-Gamal).

Charting the Four Waves: Characteristics and Transformations

The list below should not be seen as exhaustive. There are too many authors to list here for such a populous country as Egypt, the leader of the novel and the short story in the Arab world, as well as realism and science fiction. The authors listed in the table are the leading lights of the genre; names are by date of birth to give a chronological sense to history of contemporary Egyptian SF.

In the First Wave (the Exploring Wave) (sporadic with blurry borders), covering the 1950s and 60s, the field was dominated by major literary figures who made their names outside of the sci-fi realm in theater (including radio plays), literary criticism and philosophy. The names include: Tawfik Al-Hakim (1898–1987); Yousif Ezz Al-Din Issa (1914–1999); Yousif Al-Sibaie (1917–1978); Mustafa Mahmoud (1921–2009); Fathi Ghanem (1924–1999). Another dominant feature of this period is that many of the works by these authors were borderline, often blurring between fantasy and science fiction. Finally, this writing in this period was "sporadic" in nature. There was no concerted effort to keep writing science fiction once this era came to a close. The inspiration for this phase was in fact the space race between the superpowers and the prospect of landing on the moon. It was not an internal thirst of maturity on the part of the readers or the critics and publishers that drove this wave and so it did not last.

The Second Wave (the Founding Wave), 1970–80s, involved many more names fortunately: Saad Mikawi (1916–1985); Nihad Sharif (1921–2011); Anis Mansour (1924–2011); Mohammad Al-Hadidi (born 1926); Sabri Musa (1932–2018); Raof Wasfi (born 1939); Hussien Qadri (born 1934); Omayma Khafagi (born 1960). Again most of the names were established figures in literary life in Egypt. But the number, diversity and quality of writing improved, and particularly with the entry of Nihad Sharif, who was the first fulltime SF writer in Egypt and the Arab world, and an inspiration to all who followed him. Sabri Musa also did what is often considered the first Arabic Utopia-dystopia novel, *Al-Sayyid min Haql al-Sabanakh* (The Master from the Spinach Field). There was much more hard sci-fi in this period too. Mohammad Al-Hadidi wrote a novel about a brain transplant operation and Omayma Khafagi a novel on genetic engineering. There was also the space opera and adventures series first written by Raof Wasfi.

The Third Wave (the Spreading Wave) came in the 1990s and extended, critically, to 2011. This was an arid period, sadly, with only a handful of prominent authors: Mohammad Naguib Matter (born 1953); Nabil Farouk (born 1956); Ahmed Khaled Tawfik (1962–2018); Hosam Elzembely (born 1968). Nonetheless, it was a fruitful period and prefaced what came next, thanks to the heroic efforts of Nabil Farouk and Ahmed Khaled Tawfik and their hugely successful pocket book series, in science fiction and other genres fictions not always deemed popular, successful or critically recognized in Egypt—action-adventure, spy fiction, horror and the paranormal. These two authors broke all the taboos, and records, and birthed an entire generation of readers who later became writers in the fourth wave.

Finally, from 2011 to the present there is the Fourth Wave (the Authenticity Wave). Here the Egyptian Sci-Fi started to taste more Egyptian, more Arabic and may be more Islamic with an abundance of Islamo-Christian interactions. This is quiet unique, which supports the claim for authenticity or originality. In Egypt, an Arab Muslim country with a large minority of Christians we noticed that the safety valves against inter-religious discrimination or even hatred are not present. We as the Egyptian Society for Science Fiction (ESSF) do not clearly have constitutional or legislative influence. So, we decided to create those safety valves within the fabric of the ESSF and through its works. We encouraged diversity. "Diversity is a Right" is one of our core values. It is the most numerous by far and the most diverse, in terms of subgenre, subjects, and the backgrounds of the authors (gender, education, career, place of birth). Here are but a few names to ponder: Emad El-Din Aysha (born 1974); Basma Abdel Aziz (born 1976); Mustafa Seif Al-Din (born 1977); Majid Jahin (born 1977); Majid Shahin (born 1977); Wael Abd Al-Rahim (born 1978); Mohammad Rabie (born 1978); Mohammad Al-Naghi (born 1979); Mahmoud Abd Al-Rahim (born 1981); Ahmed Badran (born 1984); Moataz Hassanien (born 1991); Ahmed Al-Mahdi (born 1991); Ahmed Al-Sayyid (born 1995); Ammar Al-Masry (born 1996); Mohammad Abd Al-Aleem (born 1996); Egyptian Society for Science Fiction (established 2012).

I should add that the members of the third wave continued to write in this period, intensifying their efforts and guiding contribution. Muhammad Nagib Matter is writing more than before, novels and anthologies as well as non-fiction on science and science fiction. As for myself I am editing and writing short SF with a mix of reality and preparing for a project to write a novel. And Nabil Farouk stopped doing spy stories to focus more on horror and SF. Ahmed Khaled Tawfik, sadly passing away in 2018, finally helped us all reach an international audience with the translation of his full-length novel *Utopia*. Shams Al-Ghad anthologies are the landmark of the Fourth Wave as the main literary group product of the ESSF.

Under the Spotlight: The Composition of the Fourth Wave

A more detailed exposition of the members of the fourth and latest wave of SF authors is called for here to give the reader an idea where Egyptian SF is going and what has changed over the years. Here is a biography of the contributors to our first two volumes of our *Shams Al-Ghad* anthologies.

Mustafa Muhammad Seif Al-Din, in addition to being an author with several published works to his credit, is also a noted blogger.[2] He attained his bachelor's in pharmacology in 2000 and his publications include fantasy and drama as well as science fiction. His most notable SF publications are the anthology *Al-Daw Al-Aswad* (The Dark Light) and *Jedala* (an eBook with two of his first SF short stories, and the book itself is named after one of those stories); he also participated in two collective works and *Box of Crayons*, an eBook.

Amal Ziyada, by contrast, is a lawyer, as well as a journalist and author. She covered the January revolution as it took place in Egypt. She has seven books to her name, a mixture of fantasy and science fiction with an epic feel, such as her novels *The Cave* and *The Mountain of Legends*, along with a number of romance novels and social dramas that also deal with science, such as *Blood in Foreign Lands*. Mohammad Abd Al-Alim works with Egypt's Olympic committee and is a writer of both science fiction and horror, winning several horror awards in Egypt, including the Nabil Farouk contest. Mohammad Al-Naghi holds a bachelor's degree in business from Port Said University. He is also a political columnist and won the Ministry of Youth's 2009 award for short fiction and the Ihsan Abd Al-Qudus Award in 2012, also for short fiction.

Lamyaa Al-Said, a law school graduate from Cairo University, and also a student of English law, grew up reading Nabil Farouk and Yehya Haqi. She has six novels to her name and many, many short stories, a mix of science fiction and horror. She's a blogger and journalist and has written about science fiction.

Majid Al-Qadi, a science graduate from Cairo University in 1995, and now a professional author with a historical novel and two science fiction novels (*We the Past* and *A Cosmic Visitation*), a blog (political and cultural commentary), and many short stories to his name. Ahmed Mahmoud Badran, a law graduate from Ain Shams University in 2005, a legal consultant and novelist who writes both science fiction and horror. Majid Jahin, from Alexandria, an arts graduate from Alexandria University (2001), followed up by a master's from the same university (2010) in animation and 3D effects. He's taught and worked as an Art Director at university and worked in television and indie cinema.

As you can see, one of the most distinguishing features of the fourth wave of Egyptian SF is the growing number of female authors. This is a deliberate policy on the part of the Egyptian Society for SF, I will have you know. We have distinguished women authors in our publications, including Manal Abd Al-Hamid, Hebatallah Ahmed, Abeer Mufti, Yusra Ahmed Hassan, Doaa Ahmed Shukri, and Nadia Al-Kilani. Lina Kilani, a distinguished Syrian SF writer, has also graced the pages of our publications more than once. Special mention should also go to Sadia Abd Allah Shirah, from Somalia. Al-Samidoun (volume 5 in the Shams Al-Ghad series) enjoys a 14:9 ratio of men to women, a marked improvement from our previous editions, and with new entrants. Al-Mostakbaloun (volume 6 in Shams Al-Ghad series) is the first sci fi anthology dedicated to children and written for them. Al-Moukawemoun (volume 7 in Shams Al-Ghad series) is a Sci Fi anthology specialized in stories of resistance. The latest one is Al-Ektesadoun (volume 8 in Shams Al-Ghad series) is a Sci Fi anthology specialized in stories of economic theories of the future.

The reach of the authors is also broader. Many of the younger generation in Egypt have grown up in or worked in the Gulf Arab states, a privilege that the three previous generations of Egyptian SF authors did not enjoy. This gives authors a broader perspective and access to more resources than we enjoyed in our day. It's all very refreshing and portends well for things to come, but without a place for all these people to gather together and a helping hand marshaling them in the right direction, all that youthful energy could be wasted.

Which brings us to the ESSF, circa 2012.

Pooling Resources: The Egyptian Society for Science Fiction

My chief career is in medicine, at the university level and in clinical practice, but I am also captivated by the human development, quality and management sciences.

In the immediate aftermath of the 25 January 2011 revolution in Egypt the whole of Egyptian society was in a state of renewal and was also on an achievement model as the morale was very high. We as a group of Egyptian sci-fi writers decided to participate in creating what I may call a "Civilizational Tsunami" that would change our countries and our nation dramatically. The Egyptian Society for Science Fiction started in the year 2012 with several cultural salons and several books of short sci-fi stories. The experience was unprecedented in our country and in the region.

The philosophy of ESSF is inspired by a book called (Al-Wasatya) by Abdelhamid Ibrahim, my father. This ideology puts the ESSF in the middle stream of the Egyptian-Arab-Muslim people spectrum. Somewhere between far-left communists and secularists and far right Islamists.

The vision of the ESSF is: "We are going to be the main engine that drives forward science fiction both in Egypt and the Arab world."

The mission statement of the ESSF is: "We are here to deliver and boost cultural activities related to science fiction both in Egypt and the Arab world."

The core values of the ESSF are three:

First; Diversity is enriching.

Second; the right to Disagree is fundamental.

Third; Respect: as the fabric of all relations within and around the ESSF.

The objectives of the ESSF are as follows:

1—Contacting and keeping up to speed with fantasy and science groups all over the world.

2—Planning for integration in the Arab world in the realm of SF, in preparation for a pan–Arab society for science fiction. (We are Arabs, at the end of the day, and what helps or hinders SF in the Arab world by extension affects us.)

3—The discussion of the literary works of the society's members on a monthly basis.

4—To establish a publishing house dedicated to science fiction by the end of 2020.

5—Simplifying sciences for the lay audience is another function of the society, facilitated by the fact that we have several scientists and medical doctors in the membership.

6—Keeping up to speed with the latest publications in the genre, globally, and critical analysis and discussion.

7—Translating the latest science fiction and fantasy publications.

8—Contacting TV, theater, radio and cinema producers to break the barrier between Arab literary SF and popular art.

9—Organizing an annual conference on science fiction.

Professor Abdelhamid Ibrahim: "One of the founding fathers of the Faculty of Dar Al-Oloum, Minia University, and the author of *Al-Wasatya Encylopedia*."

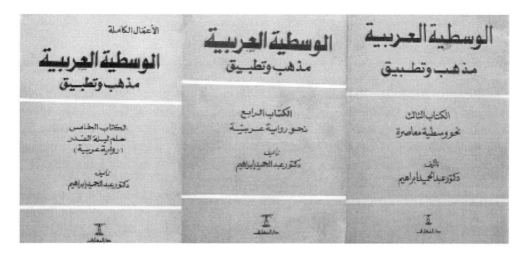

A select list of Professor Ibrahim's publications.

Among the first participants to the society were Mohammad Al-Naghi, Mohammad Ali Abd Al-Hadi, Mohammad Abd Al-Alim, Mustafa Seif Al-Din, Yassir Abu Al-Hasab, Majid Al-Qadi, not to forget Mouad Byd from Morocco and Riadh Mrihil from Tunisia. Our focus is always pan–Arab, as you can see. (Riadh has just received his Ph.D. in Tunisia as we speak, and his thesis was in science fiction no less.)

This was in 2012, of course then came 2013. It was a setback when the military took over the country. Of course we are not anti-military but we are pro civic engagement and governance. We decided to cocoon till just last year, 2017, when the butterfly decided to leave the cocoon, starting a renaissance for the Egyptian Society for SF.

To give you an idea of the enormity of the problems you must see that in 2013 alone, before the bureaucracy interfered, we published *three* anthologies in a single year. Please understand that our contributors are not financially reimbursed for their efforts and yet we had more and more contestants for each successive anthology.

Since then we have resumed all our activities in earnest and are finally reaching out to like-minded individuals and groups in the region and internationally, whether fellow authors, academics, journalists, translators and—last but not least—publishers. We have reached international recognition, with our own Wikipedia page and mentions and interviews and reviews and articles on websites like *Islam SciFi*, *ArabLit in English*, the *FAA* (the Future Affairs Administration, in China) and the pioneering research of Jörg Matthias Determann on Arabic science fiction—my three novels and the work of the Egyptian Society for SF included (Determann, 2018). As he says in his post:

I am deeply thankful to Alena Kulinich for inviting me to give a lecture at Seoul National University on Tuesday, May 15, 2018, at 4pm. My lecture is entitled "Space Aliens, Islam and Politics in Arabic Science Fiction." The event will take place as part of the Seminar in West Asian Studies in building 4, room 308. In my preparation of this lecture, I have benefited greatly from an exchange with science fiction authors Hosam Elzembely and Emad El-Din Aysha in particular. The lecture will be the first presentation of my new book project with the working title Islam and Extraterrestrial Life: Astrobiology and Science Fiction in the Muslim World. In this project, I am very fortunate to have the support of several talented research assistants. They include Fajr Aamir, Haldun Faruk Gümüş, İrfan Batur and Mosammat Samiha Sadeka. Fajr, İrfan and Samiha are part of the student employment program of Virginia Commonwealth University in Qatar.

We are also a key point in his forthcoming book: *Islam and Extraterrestrial Life: Astrobiology and Science Fiction in the Muslim World*. This is his latest posted on *Facebook*:

I greatly look forward to participating in the World Congress for Middle Eastern Studies (WOCMES) in Seville, Spain, next month. I am very thankful for the opportunity to give a presentation titled "Lord of the Worlds: Islam, Astrobiology, and Science Fiction in the Middle East." My panel, titled "Scientific culture in the Middle East," will be in room 113 on July 19, 2018, between 11:30am and 1:30pm. I am very excited to talk about the surrealist art of Ayham Jabr and about the Egyptian Society for Science Fiction—الجمعية المصرية لأدب الخيال العلمى, among other topics.

I have been invited to the APSFCon (Asia-Pacific Science Fiction Convention, 19–20 May 2018), sitting on two panels of an event that hosted representatives from 20 countries, including China, Japan, Korea, the U.S., Canada, Australia, New Zealand, Singapore, Philippine, the Czech republic, Russia, Poland, India, Malaysia and Vietnam (Elzembely, 2018).

During the APSFCon the ASFA (Asian Science Fiction Association) was established and I was chosen as the national liaison for Egypt and the vice president of the ASFA for the region.

The American University in Cairo picked me as a representative of the Egyptian Society for Science Fiction (ESSF) for a workshop (Global AI Narrative Project) that was held in Cairo 13–14 October 2019. The fore-mentioned project was jointly organized by the Leverhulme Centre for the future of intelligence (University of Cambridge) and the access of knowledge for development center (American University in Cairo). The Global AI Narrative Project aims to establish new connections between academics, artists, writers, designers and technologists working on AI in different regions of the world.

The key questions that were issued during the workshop: "How is AI portrayed in the Middle East and North Africa?/What are the 'local' understandings of AI?/What is the relationship between the Islamic thought and AI?/What is the perspective of women working on AI in the region? Is there an Arab Futurism?"

These were on Day 1, "HISTORY AND MYTHS IN THE FUTURE" with Dean Francis Alfar, Dr. Hosam Elzembely, Dr. Ramkishan Bhise and "BETWEEN GREECE AND CHANG'AN: THE BELT AND ROAD INITIATIVE AND SF" with Dr. Srinarahari, Kim Bo Young, Volodymyr Arenev. Also present at the conference was Francesco Verso, editor-in-chief of *Future Fiction*.

The only remaining thing to do, aside from getting cooperation from the government on promoting science fiction in Egypt, is to get Arab television and movie producers interested in SF. This is the real game changer that will get SF the mass support it needs to flourish and become self-sustainable here in the Arab world.

NOTES

1. Quote taken from "Tawfiq al-Hakim Quotes and Sayings—Page 1," *INSPIRINGQUOTES.U.S.*, https://www.inspiringquotes.us/author/2704-tawfiq-al-hakim.

2. Mustafa Seif Al-Din's blog is called 'Tyr Al-Ramad': http://6eyr-elramad.blogspot.com/.

SUGGESTED READINGS

"Egyptian Society for Science Fiction." (27 June 2020). *From Wikipedia, the free encyclopedia.* https://en.wikipedia.org/wiki/Egyptian_Society_for_Science_Fiction.

"The Pioneer of Moderation in Literature… The Literary Critic Dr. to Al-Jazirah." (17 May 2001). *Al-Jazirah.* http://www.al-jazirah.com/2001/20010517/cu3.htm [Arabic].

Zayed, Abdu. (19 January 2016). "Islamic Literature… And the Middle Path of Moderation of Dr. Abdelhamid." *International League of Islamic Literature.* https://adabislami.org/news/2340 [Arabic].

WORKS CITED

Determann, Jörg Matthias. (15 May 2018). "Space Aliens, Islam and Politics in Arabic Science Fiction." Seminar in West Asian Studies, Seoul National University. http://asia.snu.ac.kr/bbs/board.php?bo_table=52&wr_id=61.

Elzembely, Hosam. (19 May 2018). "Asia-Pacific Science Fiction Convention." *Future Affairs Administration, Beijing.* http://www.apsfcon.com/day1/.

Mapping the Maghreb

The History and Prospects of SF in the Arab West[1]

KAWTHAR AYED

Be kind to your sleeping heart. Take it out into the vast fields of light....
And let it breathe.

—Hafez

My story with science fiction, it will not surprise you to know, began during my childhood. This was in the 1980s, when my brother and I stumbled on Nabil Farouk's famous *Future File* series from Egypt. I've stocked up his pocketbooks since those early days and am a proud owner of the whole set, from start to finish.

My next formative experience with SF came at high school, when I wrote a script for a theater contest. It was very clearly in the sci-fi genre, with a disenchanted alien that wants to destroy our Earth because of the havoc we humans have wreaked, waging endless wars and polluting our own world. Fortunately two scientists talk him out of it, saying that there is still hope that humankind will reform itself and change its ways. I am quite proud to say that I got the first prize, and was even able to produce the play myself!

Of course, that was then and this is now. I was too young at the time to know what the critics had to say about Nabil Farouk, and Ahmed Khaled Tawfik's own pocketbook series, was that it was popular literature and so not "proper" art. Be that as it may, it is still science fiction in the proper sense of the world, and since when did the critics of sci-fi in the Arab world distinguish between proper fiction and pulp fiction in the genre?

To them *all* science fiction was pulp, whatever format it took, and so was not worthy of the Arab literary palette. To cite one early example of this, and from Egypt no less, we have Naguib Mahfouz. He described science fiction as a literature that was severely lacking in "depth" and served no true function. Serious literature, by contrast, was the kind of literature that puts forth human experiences. Instead SF tries to imagine what the future of technology will be and so what effect this will have on human beings, in this imagined future. If this future world became a reality, argued Mahfouz, then the anticipatory power of the original literary work loses its value. And if it does not come true then it is pure imagination and man is concerning himself with things of no value.

This prompted the great Moroccan author Abd Al-Salam Al-Baqali into an equally severe reply, as printed in the 1986 edition of his classic novel *The Blue Flood*. He argued that such a summary abrogation of such a creative field, ipso facto, was uncalled for and downright cruel. Such a great literary figure as Mahfouz was placing restraints on the human imagination and it is *this* creative faculty specifically that distinguishes human-kind from God's other creations.

Anyone who reads Jules Verne and H.G. Wells and Isaac Asimov and Ray Bradbury and Arthur C. Clarke, the classic authors who made this genre into a fine art, would not make such claims. Al-Baqali added that the issues raised by science fiction were some of the most noble of human concerns, including the threat of global war, the pollution of everything—air, water, soil, food, not to forget atomic pollution—and the subjugation of man to machine and the silent bomb that is the population explosion. Science fiction is to be cherished and promoted, not put down, he insisted.

To cite an Egyptian SF author, Sabri Musa, science fiction is precisely the literature that is closest to humankind's daily concerns and lived experiences. It is just that these worries and anxieties are *contemporary* experiences, so they look foreign and superfluous to the untrained eye.

But, more to the point, Musa argues that science fiction should be wholeheart-edly embraced because the genre opens up tremendous opportunities for the writer. It allows for the author to test new literary strategies and revolutionize the arts and push the boundaries of the human consciousness. SF allows for the author to create a new aware-ness in people of new issues that previously were not on their mind, not to mention pre-dicting the near future by taking a long hard and critical look at the facts of the world today.

That is the position I adhere to and I am eternally grateful to the likes of Nabil Farouk and Ahmed Khaled Tawfik for reaching out to the wider readership, through so-called pulp sci-fi, and getting the literary ball rolling for the rest of us.

In these pages I will attempt to catalogue the contribution made by the Maghreb[2] to the literary corpus of Arab sci-fi. The story is full of surprises and the contributions made by authors from the Maghreb, not least my native Tunis, cannot be properly gauged and understood without looking at the broader history of Arabic sci-fi—a history of missed opportunities, for the most part.

Paradoxes of Place

Tracing the history of Arabic science fiction is a daunting task. There were a great many works penned from the 1950s and 1960s but none of them were "classified" as sci-ence fiction, even by the publishers and authors themselves. These works were merely described as a new genre of fiction to the uncomprehending Arabic reader. The term khayal 'ilmi (خيال علمي), or scientific imagination, only seems to have been used openly in Arabic in 1978. More common terms were (أدب الإستشرافي), the literature of anticipation and, of course, (أدب طوبوي) or utopian literature.

Science fiction has always been on the verge of taking off in Arabic literature, but some indefatigable force always holds it back. There are many precursors of science fic-tion in Islamic history and Arabic literature that show a keen imagination and need for flights of fancy that transcend mere escapism and are grounded in scientific possibility.

The great Muslim geographer and historian, Al-Mass'udi's, recounts a story in his 9th century *Prairies of Gold and Mines of Jewels* about Alexander the Great with a subma-rine, centuries and centuries before one ever existed or before Captain Nemo. Even the *1001 Nights*, as full of magic and sorcery as it is, contains an oft neglected story about a flying machine, an ivory and wooden horse built with buttons to control altitude and acceleration. And between the 5th and 10th centuries, the Arabic literature was captivated by the genre of the marvelous and the strange (al-'adjib wal-gharib, العجيب والغريب).

Looking at the typology of such works of proto-science fiction in the modern period, you begin to notice a change however. You can see this in the subspecies of Utopian literature in contemporary Arabic history. One of the first Arabic novels in this genre was *Forest of Truth* (1865) by Syrian author Francis Marsh (1836–1873). The inspiration for the book, as stated in the text itself, came from the emancipation of the slaves in the United States with the civil war, beginning in 1861. There were also journalists and literary figures from Lebanon like Adeeb Ishak (1856–1885) and Farah Antione (1874–1922) who wrote stories in this field, imagining a secular future devoid of sectarian division and devoted to rationalism and progress. (Ibn Rushd or Averroes is mentioned, along with Al-Farabi, but so are Karl Marx and the great French socialist thinker Saint Simone. And there is an explicit concern with familiarizing the Arab reader with the Western world and its formative experiences.)

The most explicitly science fictional of this early generation of contributors was the Syrian author Michelle Al-Saqal (1824–1885) with a novel set on Venus and the Moon, but governed by the same considerations. The influences and themes are distinctly non–Arabic and non–Islamic. Many date Arabic science fiction to Musa Salama in early 20th century Egypt, on account of his 1924 novel *Introduction to an Egyptian Utopia*, with a story set in 3105 AD with Egypt becoming a land of pleasure and plenty. But even this novel was not as authentically an Egyptian text as it first appears. It was strongly influenced by Ottoman Utopianism, itself a potent mixture of Turkish nostalgia and modern Western literary influences.[3]

The Arabic history of science fiction, then, is older than we think. Older, deeper, more diverse and more colorful than many imagine it to be, but is also sporadic and prone to relapses and periodic obscurity as it struggles up against other genres and the literary establishment. It is also not nearly indigenous enough. The same holds true, to a considerable extent, of science fiction in the Maghreb, including my own native Tunis.

Some of the accounts below are abbreviated, given that I am more familiar with some Maghribi countries than others, and because of there are more knowledgeable writers contributing to this book on their respective nations. So let me begin with Tunis.

Tunis

The first Tunisian, if not Arab, author of science fiction was Sadek Rezgui (1874–1939) who, towards the end of his life, wrote (and never finished) his pioneering novel *The Lost Continent*. (He died before he could complete it, his son published it in 1939 after his death.) In it he clearly anticipated the laser and the mobile phone, and nonstop electronic surveillance. The story was set in an idealistic utopian cityscape with a global cast of characters with invented futuristic names. This brave new world is made up of two powers, Anasia and Anasfica, the second being an amoral imperialist power dedicated to reconquering and destroying the first, a nation built on the highest of moral principles.

Then Altayib Alturki published an anthology under the title *The Sindibad of Space* in 1978. Needless to say, Alturki imitated the seven journeys of Sinbad of old, just set in outer space with modern technology, including artificial intelligence, with the usual dangers in the outermost reaches of space. This book has been optioned as a school text, combining the delights of the old and the new. Mahmoud Tarshuna's 1998 novella "Sin-bad's Eighth Journey" is a quite a different affair though, with Sinbad journeying back-wards and forwards through the ages thanks to a time machine, also allowing him to meet people he'd encountered during his previous fantasy journeys. He also makes it to Mars, meeting its people and almost taking refuge with them, after Earth has become inhospitable in the 22nd century thanks to nuclear fallout and human technological folly.

The most important contemporary SF writer in Tunisia by far, however, is Al-Hadi Thabit, who began writing in 1999. He is quite a phenomenon if only because of the simple fact that he is the only one to specialize in the field. He has four novels and a mul-titude of short stories to his name, he has also translated SF into Arabic, and he makes it a point to identify his work as SF, on the front cover no less: "a novel of science fiction" (رواية في الخيال العلمي). This not a practice Tunisian publishers encourage and its thanks to Al-Hadi Thabit that we really have a sci-fi genre in our country. The titles of his novels are *Ghar El Jin* (1999), *Djebel Alliyine* (2001), *If Hannibal Returned* (2005), and *The Temple of Tanit* (2012).

His works are full of scientific innovations that take the world by storm, including test-tube babies, genetic engineering and the enhancing of human intelligence by leaps and bounds from the cradle to the grave. One of his storylines focuses on the people of Qanmandiya, technically "aliens" but of human origin. Their distant ancestors left Earth, disgusted with life there, and dedicate themselves to improving themselves from that point onwards. All are hallmarks of hard core science fiction, although Thabit's concerns tend to lay at home, with tongue-in-cheek reference to the current state of Tunisia in Uto-pian and dystopian settings.

Other Tunisian names worth mentioning are Abdelaziz Belkhodja's novel, *2103: The Return of the Elephant* (2005). Here Tunisia has once again become a superpower, on the model of its glory days at the time of Carthage. This is a lopsided world where the economics of the Western nations collapse and illegal migrants come to our shores looking for jobs. The hero, in fact, is a young American studying in Tunisia, eager to find out what the secret of our success is. He learns that the old order of the republic of Carthage has been reaffirmed, politically and socially, with some updating. Technologi-cally, self-sufficiency and renewable energy, relying on the waves of the sea and the sands of the desert, is the key. The hero is just a plot instrument for the reader to learn about himself and what his people are capable of, if they really put their mind to it.

There is also Mustafa Al-Kilani *Mirror of the Dead Hours* (2003), a dystopian, night-marish novel set in 2725 in a Third World country polluted by nuclear waste. People can't even go outside and breathe the air without wearing facemasks and scuba gear. The North is dedicated to remaining spotlessly clean and so dumps its waste down South, something that the authorities in the Third World go along with, leaving their populations feeling more alienated and stranded than ever.

There is Zafir Naji's anthology *The Things* (2006), with a story set in 2092 where the U.S. government has become the world government, or the government of the "free world." Here religious distinctions have been completely wiped out and people are forced to obey, everything from how they eat to how they dress to how they think. Arabic has been outlawed, seen as a "terrorist" language, with the Arabs not being allowed to leave their controlled zone and where free thought is an act of betrayal.

The list goes on and on, with Ezz Al-Din Madani and Ahmed Al-Fani and Radwan Al-Kawni. No more than a few years go by before a new sci-fi title comes out, with little innovations in terms of format or subject matter. Ezz Al-Din Madani's works actually include a theater play and an anthology of children's SF stories.

But before moving on to the fellow Maghribi countries it is important to take stock of the Tunisian experience. You will notice, I hope, a large gap between the very first novel, in 1933, and the next major work in Tunisian sci-fi in 1978. This was no coincidence and sadly such genre gaps exist across the Arab world. The interlude between those two dates was the period of the independence movement and the building of a modern Tunis. Science fiction was put on hold, as it were, which is a tremendous shame since science fiction is specifically one of the ways of agitating for independence and building the future.

Algeria

Algerian science fiction begins officially with Mohammad Dib's 1962 novel *Qui Se Souvient De La Mer* [Who Remembers the Sea]. Mohammad Dib was already a well-established author and surprised his readers with a work of science fiction, written during the darkest days of the Algerian revolution. Here the French are transformed symbolically into heartless machines from another world, resisted by a rebellious few armed with nothing but handguns. Nonetheless, the rebels make their presence felt.

Another early contribution in Algerian SF is Safia Ketou (1944–1989), a female author that specialized in children's stories and poetry but someone who also wrote *La Planète Mauve et Autres Nouvelles* [The Mauve Planet and Other Stories], a compendium of her writings between 1962 and 1978. Sadly, this book has not been republished and not, to date, been translated into Arabic. An English translation of the title story and sci-fi work in the collection has only recently come out thanks to the tireless efforts of Dr. Nadia Ghanem, *Arab Literature in English*'s Algeria Editor (Ghanem, 2018).

Then came Ahmed Manwar's short story "The Great Lake," a children's story that nonetheless won the Sharqah literary prize in 1999. Faycel Lahmeur, author of *Amin Ulwani*, goes without saying. There is also Nabil Daduwa, winner of the Algerian short story prize in 1998, who is both an author and someone who has written about the genre, beginning with his novel *The Beautiful Words* (2008), about a trip to Venus. He's also a publisher, journalist and the initial president of the Algerian science fiction club in 1994 in a very explicit attempt to stir up the tepid waters of Algerian literature.

The club was set up by Faycel Lahmeur and Nabil Daduwa, primarily, but also Aras al-Awadi, Boukfa Ziryab (author, famously, of *Tomorrow Is a Day That Has Passed*), Ahmed Qartoum and Muhammad Al-Saleh Darwish, Lamnour Massoudi. Several of these authors, after making the headlines in 1996 with the issue of the club's periodical *The World of Culture*, have completely disappeared from the literary scene. The club itself fell apart shortly afterward, a tremendous shame since the very institution that was meant to make science fiction sustainable in Algeria itself was not sustainable.

According to Nabil Daduwa, speaking at the time, the club was set up during a delicate period in Algeria's political history, trying to break the stranglehold on Algerian literature, as he put it. This encompassed both the tyranny of the classics as well as the attempt by the Islamists to Islamisize literature and all walks of art. But the story of Algerian SF is not over. Far from it. In 2008 there was a theoretical presentation of a sci-fi play, *Tower of Fire* by Abd Allah Hamil, which itself was derived from *Fahrenheit 451* (Ayed, 2009: 20–21).

The play was showcased during the festivities of "Algeria the Arab Cultural Capital" at the time. And in 2010, Cherif Arbouz published a four volume sci-fi saga, albeit in French (Ghanem, 2018). But the going is still tough, as it is for all of us.

Morocco

The first to write science fiction in Morocco was Abd Al-Salam Al-Baqali, a distinguished author and poet who penned his first SF works in 1957 with his short story "Pioneers of the Unknown," which won the Morocco Prize in 1955. Then came Ahmed Al-Bakri Al-Sibai with "The Melting Pot of Life" in 1966, and Mohammad Aziz Al-Ahbabi's 1974 novel *The Elixir of Life* (Campbell, 2015) and Al-Baqali's dystopian classic *The Blue Flood* in 1976 (Campbell, 2017).

In 1985 there was Ahmed Afzaran's anthology *Tomorrow*, his 152-page anthology, I should say, consisting of 18 stories. It has a preface and introduction but, more importantly contains an appendix at the end explaining the esoteric terminology in the book, along with some scientific facts. The titles of the individual stories alone are indicative of the breadth and depth of his scientific and technical concerns and passions. They include "The Electronic Dress," "The Organ Farm," "Guest on Earth," "The Superman Club," "When Robots Fall in Love," "The Amphibious Flier," "Bacteria in the Service of Cleanliness," "The Moon Greets You," and "For the Black Hole."

Not to be outdone, Al-Baqali also penned his novel *The City of the Deep* in 1987. In 2008 Abd Al-Samad Al-Ghazwani, only a young man, published a novella named mysterious *H*. The story is set in 2182, with computerization and detailed programming allowing machines to take over everything, including our thought processes. Then in 2009 Khaled Al-Yaaboudi wrote *Return to Granada through Sagittarius*, with its similar Andalusian references—the hero is a Morisco[4] and with the great Muslim historian Ibn Khaldun as a central character in this time-travel epic, through a black hole!

Libya

Only two to date: Yousef Al-Quawri in 1966 with his novel *Diary of an Unborn Man*, and Abdulhakeem Amer Tweel with his 1988 anthology *A Problem of Faith*. I will refrain from saying more given that there is a Libyan contribution to this book.

Mauritania

To date there is only one Mauritanian author of science fiction, Moussa Ould Ebnou, one of Mauritania's most distinguished writers, a professor at the University of Nouakchott in Mauritania and the cultural advisor to the president of the republic. His SF works include *L'Amour impossible* (1990) and *Barzakh* (1994) and *Fragments de Futures* (2015), a short story anthology featuring everything from alien invasions to individuals who email their past selves. (Not to forget his short story "Voyage dans l'outre-temps" in the 2017 issue of *Galaxies*).

Moussa Ould Ebnou's original field of specialization is historical novels, so this may seem like a break from the usual for him. Not so. Many of his works are borderline, splicing myths and fantasy with futuristic settings and concerns, along with older forms of narrative technique (Qader, 2002). This comes out most clearly in his planned three-part epic on the Hajj (pilgrimage to Mecca), beginning with *La Mecque païenne* (2016), set in pre–Islamic pagan Mecca with all its glories and contradictions—a world of genies and poetry and love. The second novel in the trilogy is set in the present and the third, reportedly, in the future, looking at the trials and tribulations of each era and how much life has changed over the years (Brahim, 2017).

The author is an interesting phenomenon in his own right, not only for its overnight success but the fact that his novels were written originally in French and then Arabized (Ould Moulay Brahim, 2000). He has since begun translating his own novels and before the original French texts hits the bookshelves, taking Arabic into consideration while penning the French.

A Perpetual Culture

To change a culture towards science fiction it is prudent to study past successes for science fiction in that culture. In my native Tunis, I can say without a shadow of a doubt that Nabil Farouk's *Future File* is the very epitome of success. It is the most widely read sci-fi series in the whole country, appealing to young and old alike. That is the way to go.

We said above that one of the advantages of science fiction, compared to other genres and modes of literary expression, is that it allows for the changing of people's consciousness, pushing it in a more scientific and critically analytic direction. And there is no reason for science fiction to be seen as an aloof discipline that is not representative of people's wants and needs and problems and anxieties. It is representative, just not in a way that is readily acknowledged. Who of us does not suffer from pollution or overpopulation or the interference of technology, and the state, in their everyday lives, often without them even knowing about it? Who does not have existential dilemmas? Who does not live in a world teetering on destruction or on the edge of becoming a dystopia? Who would not like Hannibal the Great to come back and pass judgment on our current state of affairs? Who wouldn't want to go backwards in time and meet ibn Khaldun, the sheikh of the historians, and get his advice on how to fix our modern world? Who is not influenced, in some way or other, by the vestiges of multinational corporations and developed nations interfering in our domestic affairs, in our livelihoods, in the very food we eat and air we breathe?

The trick is to make people aware of what is already there right in front of them that they cannot see, and education and language are two modes for actualizing this. Medhat Al-Jayar also argued that the way to promote science fiction and broaden its cultural influence is through language. SF must have its own lingo encapsulating its own little world—present-day scientific terminology about physics and the cosmos, future terms and expressions embodying new technological capabilities. Words like warp speed and black hole and teleportation and cloning and wormhole and dark matter are household terms in the West, and in part thanks to such legendary works of SF like *Star Trek*.

Something like that has already happened, on a smaller scale, in the Arab world thanks to the *Future File* series, which is precisely why my colleagues and I are so eager to add these pocketbooks to the school curricula in our home country, and at the primary level, engaging in a long and continuous conversation with school teachers to get them on board.

This is our own little trek outwards to the worlds of sci-fi, and eastwards towards the origin of much Arabic science fiction, in Egypt and the Levant. The end results are still not in but the early indicators are encouraging. Will keep you posted in the meantime!

NOTES

1. Translated by Emad El-Din Aysha.
2. Morocco, Algeria, Tunisia, Libya, and Mauritania make up the Arab West, or Al-Maghreb Al-Arabi as it is called in Arabic. For the benefit of English speakers, the word Gharb (West) in Arabic comes from ghurub, the setting of the sun. The East, by contrast, is the Sharq, from the shurouq of the sun, its rising.
3. For my earlier research in this regard, please see (Ayed, 2015).
4. The Moriscos were descents of Spanish Muslims who were finally evicted by the Spanish authorities in 1609, long after the fall of the last Muslim enclave in Granada in 1492.

WORKS CITED

Ayed, Kawthar. (July 2009). "Science Fiction Literature in the Arab West." *Science Fiction.* (12): 12–25. [Arabic]

Ayed, Kawthar. (1 June 2015). "Science Fiction Literature in the Arab World." *Al-Mawqif Al-Adabi.* Issue No. 530. http://archive.sakhrit.co/newPreview.aspx?PID=2968424&ISSUEID=18042&AID=406918: 64–76 [Arabic].

Brahim, Elhadj. (28 April 2017). "The Mauritanian Novel … Narrative Opportunities Lost_Full Text." http://rightpencil.blogspot.com/2017/04/blog-post.html [Arabic].

Campbell, Ian. (March 2015). "Science Fiction and Social Criticism in Morocco of the 1970s: Muḥammad ʿAzīz Laḥbābī's *The Elixir of Life.*" *Science Fiction Studies.* 42:1 (#125): 42–55.

Campbell, Ian. (March 2017). "False Gods and Libertarians: Artificial Intelligence and Community in Aḥmad ʿAbd al-Salām al-Baqqālī's *The Blue Flood* and Heinlein's *The Moon Is a Harsh Mistress.*" *Science Fiction Studies.* 44:1 (#131): 43–64.

Ghanem, Nadia. (13 August 2018). "Safia Ketou: The First Algerian Sci-fi Novelist of Post-independence Algeria." *Arab Literature (in English) Blog.* https://arablit.org/2018/08/13/safia-ketou-the-first-algerian-sci-fi-novelist-of-post-independence-algeria/.

Ould Moulay Brahim, Mohamed Lamine. (2000). "The Mauritanian Novel and the Duality of Origin." *Alif: Journal of Comparative Poetics.* (20): 77–102.

Qader, Nasrin. (Fall 2002). "Fictional Testimonies or Testimonial Fictions: Moussa Ould Ebnou's Barzakh." *Research in African Literatures.* 33(3): 14–31.

The Mechanics of
Writing Algerian SF
Resistance to the Speculative Tools of the Trade[1]

Faycel Lahmeur

A man goes to sleep in the town
where he has always lived, and he dreams he's living
in another town.

In the dream, he doesn't remember
the town he's sleeping in his bed in. He believes
the reality of the dream town.

The world is that kind of sleep.
—Rumi

An Ode to Aldous Huxley

Almost thirty years ago to this day, when I read Aldous Huxley's *Brave New World*, I felt ecstatic. I said to myself that this was exactly what I want from life, from writing, and from science fiction. Looking back on it, it is hard to believe that it was science fiction that had accompanied my readings and from my earliest days. What an odd coincidence that the first books ever placed in my hands at preparatory school were works of science fiction. The French teacher gave me *The Last Castle* by Jack Vance, while the Arabic teacher loaned me *Tomorrow's World* by Tawfik Al-Hakim. This unexpected occurrence in turn led my father, God bless him, to break his cardinal rule to never celebrate birthdays (because of a painful memory that happened to him during a birthday). My reward was Robert Louis Stevenson's *Dr. Jekyll and Mr. Hyde* at my next birthday party. And this was despite the fact that my father's education was in French; he barely spoke Arabic.

Being greeted by this jolt of genre literature so early in life would leave you thinking that there was nothing out there worth reading but science fiction…. A path in life that was further reinforced in my encounter with Aldous Huxley's novel.

There were also some important Arabic literary influences on me in my formation years, most prominently Nihad Sharif and Tawfik Al-Hakim from Egypt, especially Tawfik Al-Hakim. I found the latter's works, those related to science fiction, resonated well with what I was looking for personally. That is, philosophical assumptions, the mental dimensions of the process of writing, the focus on writing as a workshop for brainstorming and fine-tuning your mental skills; not just a source of shallow entertainment, something that has never interested me.

Alas, when it came to the influence of fellow authors from the Maghreb (Arab West) and particularly Moroccan authors, early pioneers of Arabic SF like Abd Al-Salam Al-Baqali (author of *The Blue Flood*), I'm afraid I must admit that their presence in the Algerian arena was very limited. French was the bigger influence. I immersed myself in French-language literature to fill in all the gaps in my knowledge.

Faycel Lahmeur on the streets of Algeria during its own reboot of the Arab Spring (author photograph).

Fresh out of school, some literary friends and I decided to fill the world with talk of science fiction, preoccupying everyone we met with the subject. We were young and at university at the time. Some ears were eager to listen to what we had to say while others deliberately *ignored* us…. The question that was posed to us, repeatedly, at debates, seminars, interviews and press conferences that reverberated in the halls of the Algerian cultural scene … the question that came to us from the streets, bloodied and full of determination: "How can you talk about journeying to the planets while people are dying around you every single day?" We tried, in vain, to convince them that someone, anyone, who wants to prevent his mind dying, to keep away the death on the streets, had to train his heart to travel in space and time….

No one listened to us, but we listened to ourselves enough.

My Story, Algeria's Story…. A Tortuous Trek Towards SF

My story with writing science fiction began at university, perhaps because university life fuelled my creativity. University also revives your instinct to question everything around you, an instinct we are born with and enjoy thoroughly when we are children, an inclination that sadly becomes dormant just before you go into higher education. In point of fact, everything important to me in the world of writing began at university. This is when I began my journalistic career and started publishing in literary and educational supplements for journals…. That being said, I was very fortunate to be at university in the early 1990s, when Algeria witnessed a tremendous revolution in the world of journalism at this delicate stage in the history of the country. The period from 1991 to 1995 was distinguished by political openness, ideological experimentation and artistic pluralism.

I was also inclined towards writing, even before university, when I was at high school. My whole handling of books was "professional," especially for a young man of 15 or 16. I would read all night long and jot down notes in a ledger on all the books I'd read. I would also correspond with my lifelong friend Nabil Dadwa, a distinguished author in his own right, engaging in lengthy discussions with him over my readings, exchanging opinions and learning to accept the criticisms of others, to question assumptions, and so on and so forth.

At that stage in my life I also began to keep a diary, something essential for a novice at that age. A diary on the model of the books I had in my family's library: the diary of people like Julian Greene, General De Gaulle, Che Guevara and Anaïs Nin, to name a few.

I should add that I'd pursued several careers before settling down into university life, something which is fully in line with the imagination of the science fiction writer. It's a milieu where you remain immersed in the world of books and close to the world of the imagination by supervising university work in this genre…. As for my life prior to university, the careers I'd led included: construction work, painting the buildings I helped build, pizza preparation, a shop salesman, working at a bakery, a private tutor, used clothing vendor, a translator, journalist in several newspapers, advertising…. Most of these were odd jobs, to help make a living on the sidelines of my studies.

Finally, after making the transition to university life, we formed the Algerian Science Fiction Club in 1995, in Constantine. It was essentially an informal club, not so much a proper organization, that worked mainly on the ordering of written texts and coordination of efforts in that field. It was a very active group and helped promote creativity in all walks of literature but its activities were soon swallowed up by the work team for the newspaper that I'd established with my friends—"The World of Culture," meant chiefly to promote science fiction in Algeria. The newspaper's three main pages were devoted to science fiction, covering everything in the genre from translation, publishing, criticism, introducing the field and defining it, etc. The newspaper could have gone far, if it hadn't been for the financial hardship it faced a year and a half after its appearance. The publication also fell afoul of the personal ambitions of its owners.

One of the goals of the newspaper was to create a publishing house of the same name focused on works of science fiction, whether local or in translation. To this day in Algeria publishers just sell SF among their other lists of novels, without any special regard for the genre, not even showcasing the front covers of SF works in a way that might draw readers to them.

Getting to the Bottom of SF … as Complicated a Story as Man Himself

People never seem to agree on a single definition for anything, let alone science fiction. I've struggled with this quandary myself for the past quarter century. Looking back on it now you realize that "science" isn't as key a factor as we think. The literature tends more towards the imaginative, exploring the possible, of what could be, but dealing with it with the point of a scalpel. Logic, scientific method, facts, all of that can be in there, but so is ideology and satire. My preferred way of defining SF is to look at it as a repository of topics that are associated in some way or another with this octopus-like genre. You can just as easily rebel against prophecies of what is to come and the superior knowledge posed by science as delve into the possibilities and consequences of movement through time, the exploration of space, first contact with alien life-forms, the end of the world, weapons of mass destruction, the life of scientists and their discoveries, embodying the inner psychological life of man through plot and characterization and the world you build ... *any* mode of storytelling that deals with such related notions counts as sci-fi as surely as skepticism about these topics.

Robert Scholes describes SF as a species of "fabulation," a fictive form that "offers us a world clearly and radically discontinuous from the one we know, yet returns to confront that known world in some cognitive way" (Scholes, 1976: 47). He adds, cryptically, that in "works of structural fabulation the tradition of speculative fiction is modified by an awareness of the nature of the universe as a system of systems, a structure of structures, and the insights of the past century of science are accepted as fictional points of departure.... It is a fictional exploration of human situations made perceptible by the implications of recent science" (1976: 54–5).

As for the torturous relationship of SF with literary and artistic "realism," it is wrong to think of science fiction as escapism and anti-realism. On the contrary, we could almost call it *hyper*-realism. A simulation of realty that is both fantastical and yet completely convincing to the point that you can't tell fact from fiction anymore. This is realism in its purest form, tackling reality head on, but at a deeper, invisible level. Exploring what lies *behind* reality, the hidden causality responsible for the phenomena we see right in front of us (more on this below).

This negative predisposition towards the genre has changed completely, at least in the rest of the world. Science fiction has become one of the most creative aspects of literature, with literary professionals depending on it more than any other genre to usher in a vision of the future. As one of those experts, Said Yaktin, says, SF is the literature of "renewable" energies, constantly recreating itself as it progresses towards the future. It is the only branch of literature that is *forward*-looking, whereas all the other branches are backwards looking and satisfy themselves with reminiscing on the past, as J.G. Ballard argues, a contemporary of Kingsley Amis. This makes science fiction special, forcing us to be especially attentive to all the developments in the Arab arena, in general, and the Algerian arena in particular, in this genre. For nearly thirty years now works of science fiction have been emerging, nonstop, without garnering much attention. The critics prefer works that simply rehash familiar topics.

Personally, I have always been partial to the multidimensional view of science fiction that Americans adhere to. To quote Lou Anders, who argued that it is more appropriate to define SF with reference to the content than the overall form, SF is:

> always easier to identify at its center than at its edge, and I feel strongly that definitions need to be descriptive not prescriptive, talking about what it does rather than what it isn't [quoted in Hayden, 2010].

Lou Anders himself cited sci-fi legend Frederik Pohl on this same tricky issue. What makes for good SF is also what makes SF *unique*. It informs of us of things we were woefully ignorant of, it opens up new possibilities or future states of being, that it allows us to perceive ourselves in an objective and informative way (facilitated by looking at ourselves through the eyes of an extraterrestrial, for instance), and so and so forth. Style alone is not the only criteria but "content."

In the process, science fiction has become a culture in its own right, with derivatives in fashion, invention, film production, home decor, tattoos, wall paintings and all modes of popular expression—the very concept of beauty itself. And in writing SF has become *avant-garde*, a label that has fallen out of favor recently but signifies how it is experimenting with the most courageous, and least popular, modes of writing.

Confiscated by the Other ... How We're Expected to Be....

The resounding success of two recent works in Algeria, *2084: The Tale of the Last Arab* by Waciny Laredj, and *2084: The End of the World* by Boualem Sansal, could have been a useful occasion in Algeria specifically to look closely at this genre of writing with its unique futuristic credentials. What genre other than science fiction tries to anticipate the world of tomorrow, reading the present in detail with an eye on the future, hoping to give birth to that future? It was also a tremendous opportunity to address our aesthetic convictions as genre writers, an issue that has never been raised in earnest. It is enough to point out that there are no books on this topic in the Algerian arena, despite the revival of the publishing industry over the past few years and the great deal of journalistic attention given to this genre. The one exception so far is a book by the distinguished researcher, Dr. Lamia Aitou, *Faisal Al-Ahmar's Narrative of Science Fiction* (2013), in which she discussed my experience with the genre.

What is actually going on in our cultural life, which we insist is "ill," is its fear of everything new and unconventional. There is a dangerous cult of worship for what we are used to, our pre-existing tastes. We can add another very serious problem that I had talked about previously in a number of seminars. I expressed it through a word game that garnered the approval of many of colleagues, namely, that the Arab author is, essentially, a monkey!

The bottom line is that I was discussing some issues I raise in my novels during a seminar held in the Republic of Georgia and one of the attendees, a Frenchman who happened to be a publisher, struck up a conversation with me afterwards:

"Do you write in French? And what do you write?"

I said yes. I explained that, in fact, the vast majority of what I wrote was science fiction, adding that I have a philosophical novel written in an unusual way employing experimental stylistics. I depict the life of a writer, in the near future, where I pose philosophical questions about literature, elitism, the role of thought and literature, governing institutions, the meaning of culture, etc.

The friendly individual stopped me at that point, with a peculiar grin on his face, and said: "Do not go too far.... We in France, if we want philosophy, experimentation, intelligence and science fiction, we don't need to get these things from Algeria. Why don't you just write about the realities of the situation in Algeria? About the security crisis there and the problems facing the Islamic world that everybody is talking about?"

This is the dilemma facing Arab science fiction due to Orientalism—conform to the Western stereotype or live in obscurity (courtesy of the artist, Ammar Al-Gamal).

I replied, politely: "We'll see."

In short, the opinion of this individual is that the role of the Arab writer is to be a monkey in a cage. A monkey that has a clearly allotted job in life, one function to serve that he should never deviate from: a Western view of an exotic oriental world, with set features already predetermined beforehand dating as far back as *The 1001 Nights*.

In the current century, it is the image of the bearded terrorist desperately seeking slave girls—Osama bin Laden in the form of the historical Turkish soap opera Hareem Al-Sultan.

Philosophy…. My Other Story

So, once again, what is science fiction about and why am I so attached to it? Mental renovation, in a word.

Changing the way we think…. Reviewing our knowledge of ourselves, the assumptions we make about ourselves, that is … and our convictions about the world and everything in it…. Renewing our connection to history…. Looking at what we want and how to attain it…. That is what you believe in if you grew up on a steady, healthy diet of SF, and that is what we have to aspire to.

If I had to choose the salient features of my literary life, I would choose science fiction first and philosophy second. This choice is not accidental, since science fiction and philosophy are age-old brothers. The very act of telling stories about our perception of the future dissolves the line between them.

Paul Ricoeur (1913–2005) highlighted this unexpected aspect of SF, the philosophical and structural role that the very process of narration plays; a process that varies with different narrative styles. The more you utilize methods not employed previously by works of literature, the greater the expanse for literary experimentation. Narration creates a world you live in. The text is not a closed thing, but a prospective universe independent of the universe in which we live.

We can contemplate, here, the narrative engine that moves Mary Shelley's *Frankenstein*, which is the resurrection to life of the dead body through the electricity from a lightning bolt. This is a clear and distinct event that highlights the scientific construction of this world, its reliance on logic and the rational faculties of the mind, despite the impossibility of this act of resurrection actually happening. Hence, the magic of narration and its philosophical power.

We have to recollect here the classic novella *Micromégas* (1752), Voltaire's own little contribution to space travel. It is worth noting how the work came in the wake of the furor over the publication of a philosophical treatise by Voltaire—a scathing critique of society—that did not go down well at all with the "Mufti" of Paris. (The term "Mufti" is Voltaire's, a reference to the patriarch of Paris, and not my own jaundiced reading of his intellectual career.) … What we're up against, all over again, is the age-old war between Reason and the Church … between the scientific, materialistic interpretation of things and the religious reading, which depends as it does on dogma and received wisdom. Blind faith takes the place of factual analysis and experimental deduction.

At the same time, it is necessary to understand the fact that the idea of science fiction sprang from the incubator of the fantastic, the literature of the miraculous. One of the most prominent French-language critics out there, Jacques Sternberg (1923–2006), entitled one of his key texts on the topic *Une Succursale du Fantastique nommée Science-Fiction* [A Branch of the Fantastic Called Science Fiction], published in 1958. It's a title that rests heavily on us, true enough, but that does not detract from the truth of its message. He insisted on straddling the line between fantasy and science fiction, seeing one as originating out of the very essence of the other.

For his part Roger Caillois (1913–1978) argued that the fantastic represented a breach in the order of the universe, a supernatural intrusion into a world governed by laws of nature (Caillois, 1975: 14).

Science fiction, however, does not take the same approach, explains John Searle since it represents continuity with the present. It creates its own internal coherence, which convinces you of its plausibility. If, for example, the subject involves anticipating the future, we can see that there are a number of elements that combine (rationally, scientifically) to create as specific effect (Searle, 1975).

There are those who consider science (the natural sciences) to be a philosophy itself, a philosophy that explains the phenomena that surround humankind. It is worth pointing out here that fantasy is not just a means of entertainment. Fantasy is also a philosophical tool par excellence, explains Gilbert Hottois in his classic *Philosophy and Science Fiction* (2000). All philosophers, from Plato to Heidegger, filled their books with thousands of little stories that helped illustrate (and very effectively) points they were making about the world around them, explaining and simplifying complex phenomena to normal readers. It is the very proximity of reality that makes it hard for us to see it properly, which is precisely why we need stories to represent this reality *for* us, to take it apart, expose its salient features. Otherwise we would be lost, failing to comprehend something before our very eyes, simply because we are too close to it.

All of this brings us back to the very kernel of science fiction, which is "What if." It is this notion that allows us to construct theoretically plausible worlds that are logically consistent and food for thought, highlighting possibilities and salient features of reality we were previously unaware of.

Man, from the very beginning, was drawn to fantasy, to the question "what if," to the unknown and to life's many mysteries. In the domain of literature this came out first in the form of fantasy and fairy tales, a prelude as it were to science fiction, a more productive species of literature that tries to construct logical, comprehensible futures. Science fiction is the literature of the possible whereas fantasy is the literature of the "impossible." What distinguishes science fiction is that it posits possible worlds, from the mind of the author, grounded in logic, constantly returning in some fashion or other to the possible and to the known and recognizable. The connection with the real world is never severed entirely, unlike the case with pure fantasy. Both the author and the reader are connected to the real world, taking it as a springboard for the imagination, constructing worlds that do not exist but are possible nonetheless.

Fantastical literature is the ancestor, the very appropriate and urgent ancestor of science fiction, but making this distinction is necessary because science fiction is not fantasy, and each has its own characteristics. Of course, they both belong to the imaginative species of fiction but each has its own set of laws. Science fiction is the literature of the possible while fantasy properly conceived is the literature of the miraculous, of what is truly impossible. Science fiction is characterized by suggesting images of worlds created by the imagination of the writer based on logic, with a rich and varied reference to the world of the real as it is now, of the known and the possible—convincing you it is possible, with enough thought and contemplation. It is a literature that always takes the *initiative*, that takes virtual worlds ready to be actualized and makes them real (Turner, 1979: 256).

Science fiction stands in a healthy relationship with the real world. Science fiction gives us the theoretical energy we need to explore dimensions that are absent from the circle of the senses, to engage in abstract theoretical thought, the kind utilized both by the great scientists, and the artist. It is this kind of imagination that allows civilization to advance by leaps and bounds, the imaginative powers that Galen, Archimedes, Ibn Al-Haytham, Ibn Sina, Al-Khwarizmi and Abbas Ibn Firnas used to great effect. Not to forget Galileo, Tortachelli, Pasteur, and Einstein.

My Career with Science ... and Speculative Fiction

To me science fiction is more an adventure in writing than a set way of talking about ... people's concerns about the near future and the technological developments that besot us today, and the ever accelerating pace of change.

Sci-fi is an adventure in "writing," specifically, because it opens up *so* many possibilities for the author, stylistically. After all, isn't the basic premise of science fiction ... the very stuff of fiction, to disassemble reality, breaking it up into small pieces, then rearranging those pieces in accordance with a given strategy?

In England, beginning in the 1960s, the literary vanguard launched a new reading of the label SF, rephrasing it as "Speculative" Fiction instead of *Science* Fiction.

Recollect Einstein's maxim that imagination is more important than knowledge. Speculation, something you do in the stock exchange, is precisely what science fiction writers do. They take imaginative risks, using philosophy, ideology, politics, environmental concerns, natural disaster warnings, scientific research, and so on and so forth as raw materials to build a storyline. The author tries to imagine what will happen, for real, if this or that scientific discovery is made or this disaster prediction comes true. It is fantasy but a realistic exercise in fantasizing.

In my very first scientific fiction novel, serialized in "The World of Culture" in 1997, I imagined a world divided into three spheres: America, China, and "Islamia" (the title of the novel). Now look at the world today, twenty odd years after I wrote my story, and we're living through a similar epoch to my imaginings. My sense of the opposition coming from the East was strong at the time, although all regional transformations at the time were indicative of the emergence of a new European pole (I'd written the novel in 1994). Even so, it seemed to me that the role of the Orient, both China and the Muslim countries, would one day outweigh Europe, and the world today has endorsed my vision.

Literature, like politics, is the art of the possible ... and science fiction gives us the opportunity to look at a whole range of possibilities in thought, language and beauty.

My second SF novel (entitled "The Day the Heavens Comes," to be printed by Dar Al-'Almaiya) was written in 1997 and has a very strong Sufi orientation. It is a journey in outer space ... in search of the self.

My Sufi education worked away on the contours of the novel, as Sufis believe in the *inner* journey, and that traversing the heavens to reach the holy spheres is in truth a diving into the deepest caverns of your own soul....

The novel also has a strong environmental dimension, lamenting the destruction route by technology on the lower strata of society, the earth itself, and nature, the fragility of animal life, the plants that we do not see as useful thanks to the logic of the marketplace.... I did not head out to green movements around the world to work out my novel, however. Instead, I found that it was enough to head back to two areas in the Algerian countryside, one of which was where I was born, while the other was a rural town where I spent some of the best years of childhood.... *They* were the true source of my inspiration.

The following novel, the one I consider to be the most complete of my works of science fiction, is *Amin Al-Alwani*. (The novel was written between 1999 and 2001 and then published in 2007, then in 2011 with Dar Al-Maaref, and then with the Egyptian publishing house, Al-Ain, in 2017.) ... It was this novel that bunched together so many different narrative formats.... Biography, poetry, video documentary, literary venues, short fiction, critical theory.... All in the framework of a transfer of someone's life to the reader, a distinguished author by the said name Amin Al-Alwani who exists in the future. It is a reflective, philosophical tale that tackles the very core of literature and art, and fate, the complex links between the literary text and history, man and words. It reflects critically on the very function and role played by literature in human affairs, notions that have undergone severe shocks in the 20th century.

It's an experimental novel because it toys around with the process of writing itself, rewriting the very rules of the novel. For too long now we have taken the rules of novel writing as sacrosanct, as if they never change and are never replaced.

Amin Al-Ilwani, for me, expresses the tremendous potential for literary expression lying at the heart of science (or speculative) fiction. I want to push the fold as far it would go, trying to prove just how open to experimentation the genre really is.

Science fiction, at the end of the day, is the voice of tomorrow. Isn't futurist literature one of the most popular definitions of SF? This is both literally and figuratively true in *Amin Al-Ilwani*. The novel afforded me the opportunity to toy with the basics of the imagination, the very foundation stone of fiction, since I imagined that the person the novel is about would, some day, chance upon the book himself and read it. Then I tried to envision how he would react upon reading a work that charts out his life in detail. I even fancied that Mr. Al-Ilwani would become captivated by the experience and start digging up information on the failed author (with delusions of grandeur) of this work, the said Faycel Al-Ahmar, and begin writing about him. In the process I created a game of mirrors, with both writers constructing images of each other, each in his own timeframe, coupled with the commentary of the narrator—a third person entirely who is the true author of the biography of Amin al-Ilwani.

I now convey to you words from the preface to my novel because it sheds light on what I wanted to do, the kind of spirit that animated the whole work, and what drives my experience with scientific fiction in general:

> To write a science fiction novel means to face up to reality and never evade it.... It means to be careful, because the reality in the world of science fiction is always on the move, shifting and changing. It's a living, breathing thing.... For too long now reality has suffered from stasis, and its inability to speak for itself, at the hands of the so-called "realists." That reality is nothing more than a photograph frozen in time, and a picture can be anything except for the reality it is picturing. Reality, in truth, is made up of layers of tangible realities, and levels of consciousness of those tangible things, and the many, many ways of interpreting what the senses and the conscious mind perceives.... And realist literature is incapable of translating these things.... That is the domain of science fiction.

Nietzsche spoke of multiple realities as a means of countering the over-confidence of the Enlightenment mode of thinking which presumes that it can comprehend everything, from metaphysics to the sensible world which itself is made of many things we cannot detect. Nowadays we talk about the multiplicity of reality itself.... Is reality what *we* think is real?

Is reality what we experience while awake or is being awake itself an illusion, an unreal situation we dive into whenever we get out of bed, a reality we assume is presented to us truthfully, a reality that isn't deceitful in itself? ... Or is reality what the drunkard perceives or the mentally ill or the hallucinating junkie? ... What is the genuine reality when a group of people live through the same set of circumstances and yet each sees it his own way? Who of those conscientious individuals is aware of reality as it is, while the others are the ones who are sorely mistaken?

Science fiction, and the more philosophically oriented speculative fiction, is the only genre that can answer these questions....

To write a science fiction novel means to be brave and exhibit a certain boldness because you have to be prepared for disappointment over what you imagine to be the shape of the future. You have to be ready to be exposed to the very probable absurdity of your imaginings, the weakness of your imagination itself.... Never an easy task for an author.... The only consolation for such a writer, who becomes a laughing stock, is often death! It's a twilight reality in its own right, after all!

Couldn't it be that "reality" is what awaits us after death, and that all life is a dream—a fantasy game that revolves around a fictional land called "Earth," for example?

To write a science fiction novel means not to wait for recognition from your surroundings because the digestion of SF, by readers and critics, and for nearly two centuries now is difficult, more often than not. Rarely has a serious work of SF garnered the recognition of readers and critics, especially in your immediate vicinity as an author.... You have to console yourself to that delicious pleasure you experience as a writer in this genre, the enjoyment an SF author experiences as he peels away the layers of reality in his imagination. Try to visualize that pleasure as I open a gate in my head to the only reality that exists in it, the reality which no one else knows. The reality which has been hidden until I choose, for whatever reason, to expose to others. The reality I labored and enjoyed to write and describe, narrating its contents, one by one, as if describing a piece of art. A pleasure that can last for a whole year or more of writing, till it takes its final form, the very book you hold in your hands!

Well, perhaps there is "one" other consolation, namely, the quest for *glory*. (Didn't Aristotle say we have an instinct of glory?)....

The writer must work in silence, strive to be faithful to his novel, to flaunt taboos and exceed the limits that he sees as stupid and stifling.... To be honest with himself and with others.... To love his work and love others and write, keeping in mind that his only vocation in life is to reach out to his family. (Not just his household and relations but to every reader out there, potential or real, who could be as far off as Japan, or living two or three centuries in the future.)

To write a speculative novel—finally—is to be crazy, one of those breed of people who can defy the law of gravity and the impulse to conform to the supposedly rational multitude, and ignore the vestiges of power and politics. It means being an expert at going backwards, as Ibrahim Ramadan does, the hero of my story "Crazy" (from my sci-fi anthology *The Happenings of the Other World*, 2002). It means being oblivious to the sycophants and the temptation of just getting ahead in life and pleasing those in power.

It means only having respect for the truth, a truth that always stands up to evil and injustice and lies; from the very beginning of creation, without compromise or negotiation or searching out a common ground.

Next to Amin Al-Ilwani I have a whole other work of "experimental" science fiction, a short story collection entitled *Proceedings from the Other World* (published in 2003 by Ibda'a Publications). The stories are about the usual fair in science fiction, such as travel in time and parallel dimensions, the mad scientist, and a world headed towards disaster if current trends hold…. But with a distinct slant, philosophical concerns that haunt me as a writer who can't refrain from thinking…. Concerns like: the role of freewill, the will to freedom itself, the human spirit and the need to raise above things, genius and its social milieu, absolute power in the hands of humans … beings who are ultimately limited by their impulses, madness, existential crises and how they are connected to the necessities of society, and conflicts over power and hegemony and the like.

A Parting Word

I can't go any further in my testimony here without touching on my own translation of *Brave New World* by the Englishman Aldous Huxley (published in 2009 in Algeria and then in 2016 by Damascus University). This novel belongs to the so-called anti-utopia or dystopian genre, which paints a gloomy picture of the future, cautioning people to the risks that lay just round the corner if they walk down certain paths and not others.

It is a novel positively saturated with meaning, reflecting well the penetrating mind of the philosopher who authored it. Aldous Huxley, the amazingly cultured man that he was who could cut through the surface of things to the reality lying beneath, a man gifted with a picturesque and all too humorous imagination.

That is the speculative vocation of the true author of science fiction.

Note

1. Translated by Emad El-Din Aysha.

Works Cited

Caillois, Roger. (1975). *Images, images*. Paris: Stock.
Hayden, David Alastair. (2010). "An Interview with Lou Anders." *Redstone Science Fiction*. http:// redstonesciencefiction.com/2010/05/interview-lou-anders/.
Scholes, Robert. (1976). "The Roots of Science Fiction," in Mark Rose, ed. *Science Fiction: A Collection of Critical Essays*. Englewood Cliffs NJ: Prentice-Hall: 46–56.
Searle, John. (1975). "The Logical Status of Fictional Discourse." *New Literary History*. 6.2: 319–332.
Turner, Georges. (1979). *Encyclopédie visuelle de la science-fiction*. Paris: Albin Michel.

Libyan SF

A Short Story in the Making[1]

ABDULHAKEEM AMER TWEEL

> Civilization is in a race between education and catastrophe. Let us learn the truth and spread it as far and wide as our circumstances allow. For the truth is the greatest weapon we have.
>
> —H.G. Wells[2]

It has been said that the very first Libyan to write science fiction was Yousef Al-Quawri, who penned the novel *Memoirs of an Unborn Man* circa 1966. This book was most definitely a work of science fiction, a time-travel "story" that took the protagonist (and the reader) to the year 2600. (It's more a series of "reports" about the future and how advanced technology is and doesn't really have a continuous narrative with a beginning, middle and end, with a dilemma and climax.)

But does it really count as "Libyan"? Yousef Al-Quawri grew up and received his education in Egypt and all his literary influences were Egyptian likewise. The Libyan story and novel and Libyan poetry and the whole Libyan environment exerted no influence on him, to my knowledge. He was much more part of the Egyptian literary scene, and maybe that's for the better, given how long it has taken for science fiction to emerge, indigenously, in this part of the Arab world called Libya. I am, without bragging, the only Libyan author of science fiction. This is something I am "proud" of, introducing my country to this profoundly important—and enjoyable—genre but it's not something I am terribly *happy* about.

Libya from the 1990s onwards, like much of the Arab world, is awash with youngsters from the IT generation. If anyone is going to ignite the flash of SF in our country, and across the Arab world, it's them.

Sadly, from my personal experience as an ex-instructor in our polytechnics, it is *this* generation that is specifically being muffled, having its creative instincts trampled into the ground, and by our education system no less.

A Literature in Childhood

I first began publishing my short stories in 1998 in the Kuwaiti magazine *Galaxy*, a monthly publication issued by the Kuwaiti Science Club. The editorial board was especially jubilant about my work, I'm glad to say. The other venue I published in was the seventh issue of *The Scientist* magazine in Saudi Arabia. Note that they were both scientific publications, not literary magazines as such. I should have understood this before I began, naively, sending my stories to proper literary journals in Libya and the Arab world. All of my stories got turned down, without anyone telling me why. It seems they thought I was writing children's stories!

That is actually an all too common response across the Arab world when it comes to the critics and publishers, and even quite a few authors. They don't see SF as "proper" literature, which is why I had to resort to an anthology, which was published by the Majlis Al-Thaqafi Al-Aam al-Libi (the General Council for Culture in Libya).

How ironic the charge of children's stories is. As any science fiction author will tell you, they got *hooked* at an early age, either from reading SF or from television. That is certainly my story with SF. My father, after returning home from his work, would always shower me with translated books, coming from Egypt and Lebanon to Tripoli's bookshops, of Jules Verne and H.G. Wells. There was also *Star Trek* on television, on our first foreign channel in Libya during the 1950s and the 60s, then the "European" TV channel during 1980s, and also nature programs, science shows and SF adventure stories on the radio. My late aunt Fawzia also made it a habit to bring scientific books with her when visiting us, from Tripoli bookshops coming from Egypt, and so I became familiar with the name Mustafa Mahmoud, positively devouring his novels—*The Spider* and *A Man Under Zero*—in no time at all, spending the rest of the week staring at the wall, going over what I'd just read. Mustafa Mahmoud became one of my icons, the great Islamic thinker that he was, and a great deal of who I am today is because of him.

In short, the young are the people to go after if you want to usher in a generation of SF writers. Therefore, how "tragically" ironic the situation the Libyan youth are in thanks to the many, many cultural factors working against them, at their age, when it comes to scientific flights of fancy. Here is a *list* of hurdles.

Libyan literature, needless to say, is obsessed with *realism*, and gritty realism at that, talking about poverty and suffering. It's a heritage bequeathed to us from the old days of occupation and imperialism and the early days of independence, before the oil bonanza. Even people who didn't grow up poor themselves seem to be influenced by this austere way of thinking, influenced by their relatives and friends who are or were poor at one point in time. Our very subconscious, as Libyans, in grounded in realism. We seem to revel in it, identify with it. But that is not an excuse. We've been living the good times for the past 50 years, well, until the Arab Spring in 2011, but even so, that period of prosperity and national unity did not dent our enthusiasm for the mundane in literature and the epiphany of suffering.

Worse still, we made no connection between poverty and suffering and the "underdevelopment" of our nation as part of the Third World, and the *need* for science fiction. Who else is going to build the future but scientists and engineers, come out with solutions for our problems and improve the standard of living and set us on the right course?

Why else would I be so dedicated to popularizing science? My book, *Can You Believe it? Nuclear Power Is in Your Home!* (1991), was written in a journalistic format, with chapters like separate articles that could be read in isolation, in as non-technical and (I hope) exciting a way as possible, dispelling all those sensationalist myths surrounding nuclear power.

Another problem, and this will surprise you to no end, is that fantasy is considered to be *unmanly* in Libya! All our young toughs consider "frowning" to be a requirement of manhood, and disdain the life (and posture) of contemplation. Our upbringing is very harsh, admittedly, but this could be counteracted if we had an education system that fosters and encourages creativity and the pursuit and love of knowledge.

This is the final and most daunting factor holding back the young. The science curricula at our polytechnics are just as hard and just as "crammed" as those at university level, and this is inexcusable. The very graduates of these technical places of learning come out hating all walks of science and technology, thinking of it as boring and, even more inexcusably, impractical. In the modern world, polytechnics and science classes are *fun*. They are full of exploration and history and experimentation and practical applications that engage the pupil and make him crave more and more knowledge, while also letting his imagination run wild.

The critics and the publishers merely reinforce this jaundiced way of not doing things when it comes to science and literature.

It goes without saying that writing SF is hard because it demands of the novelist and artist some scientific or technical background, but I know several scientists and engineers who are men of letters, poets and short story writers, who have never ventured even once into the realm of writing SF. Things are *that* bad, which is why I am the lonely one waving the banner of SF in the wilderness, let alone the situation today with my country on the verge of continuous collapse.

A Nationalist in Time

There are many problems besetting the Libyan author in general, and not just the SF writer. A profound lack of "cosmopolitanism" is one of these. We think of our problems and our problems *only* and even think that our problems are the problems of everyone else. We are not connected enough to the outside world when it comes to literature and art, and no wonder then science fiction suffers as well.

Libyan authors, likewise, have not tried to make us feel, as Libyans, that we are citizens of the world, that what is true of humanity is true of us. The Libyan author has not tried to upgrade us as a people and feel that we are destined for more than merely living, but living on a par with other better off nations in the world. Education, again, is partly to blame. People who go into the sciences study foreign languages at university, but people who go into literature do not. Translation is weak in Libya as well, with few Libyan works translated into foreign languages, and not much foreign literature translated into Arabic.

This does not just go for science fiction. All walks of genre literature suffer, such as horror and detective fiction. All are treated as cheap entertainment, pulp fiction and children's adventure stories. Anything that detracts from social drama and misery and suffering and the disempowerment of the individual, anything that involves actually "thinking" for yourself while you read, is anathema. It is a problem we share with our Arab brethren but I would wager that it is more pronounced here.

Science fiction is the thinking man's genre par excellence. Alas, the genre does not speak to the daily needs and worries of the average Arab reader—putting food on the table, getting married, finding a place to live in, political troubles—but focuses instead on philosophical, ethical and even religious questions that concern humanity as a whole. It is the supreme literature that connects man to the world. The catch is that the writer, and reader, are also connected to a world where the loaf of bread you eat is a little cleaner and the political horizons you operate in are a little broader, not the kind of world the "average" Arab reader subsides in. This has consigned the Libyan author to merely transferring the reality he sees to the reader, who already sees and lives in it, and in such a way that there is not the faintest glimmer of hope!

Political isolation is also partly to blame. I was very, very fortunate as a child, because my family were so open to the literature of the world. By myself I would not have been able to find so much on the bookshelves. And I am not just talking about Western or foreign-language science fiction. It took me inordinately long to find books, works of SF, written in the Arab world in our bookshops. It was only when I was a fully grown man that I first came across Taleb Omran, the great Syrian SF author. Apart from him there was Tawfik Al-Hakim, a household name all across the Arab world, but little else. And it was mainly through my annual visits to international book fairs that were held in Libya, and my "web" travels around the Arab world that I was just able to become familiar with the names writing in the genre, without actually finding their works, I'm sad to say.

This is all the more amazing in a country like Libya that was, for so many years, captivated by Arab nationalism. You would think that we would at least be in tune with our neighbors in Egypt and their literary produce. Then again, Arab nationalism in my country was a chimera all along.

Apart from SF I am also dedicated to playing up the cosmopolitan history of Libya, a history that has been deliberately down sided. Hence, my book on the great Protestant cemetery of Tripoli, which existed in 1830 during the rule of the Libyan Qaramanli Dynasty (1711–1835) and all the way till 1917. Tripoli was a city buzzing with activity, its shores open to people of all walks of life and from all over the world, and one of the things I did in my book was to dispel the myth concocted by the previous regime that the cemetery was originally a graveyard for the conquering Americans!

Repairing the mistakes of the past is as much a vocation for me as nuclear power. I'm a founding member of the Law 88/1975 Victims Assemblage. The law in question was passed by the Qaddafi regime to confiscate the personal holdings of Libyan businessmen, supposedly as a first step in the drive towards socialism, borrowing from Abdel Nasser in Egypt.

Pan-Arabism and Arab nationalism has run its course, and with all due respect to the great man, it still would have been nicer to borrow Nihad Sharif. Writing about history and digging into the past is one avenue to repair this heritage of mistakes, but so is science fiction.

Problems of Cosmic Proportions

I am from Libya, a country where the dominant language and culture is Arabic. The Libyans themselves, however, are a mix of Africans, Asians and Europeans—a melting pot of everything that is Mediterranean.

In the past, the Arabic-Islamic past, this mix was a fact and Libya thrived as a consequence. The history of Tripoli by itself is evidence of this. The city reached its high point in the Qaramanli period when it became the capital of Libya, an entire country run by a dynasty of Turkish origin, much like modern Egypt at the time of Muhammad Ali and his progeny (1805–1952). I say Turkish here loosely because the founder of the Qaramanli dynasty was born in Libya and spoke Arabic with a distinct Libyan accent; his own ancestor came to the shores of my country in 1551, an Ottoman seafarer, while his female ancestors were all native Libyans. To add to the irony, it was in this period Libyization of laws took place and the Arabization of official documents in Libyan slang; previously everything was written in Turkish, including diplomatic communiqués.

Not to forget that the retinue surrounding the Qaramanlis were Libyans to a man, and of mixed heritage—Africans, Asians and Europeans. This is when the modern borders of Libya began to take shape, a polyglot Libya that opened its arms to all.

Hence, the Protestant cemetery, housing the deceased of officials and their family members working at the foreign consulates and corporations. And that is not to discount or forget the Jews, who were native Libyans and from before the coming of Islam to the country in 641 AD. They were later joined by Jewish refugees from Al-Andalus in 1609. Sadly, many left to Israel in 1948 and then again in 1967. Only a smattering of them remain, mostly women, either converted to Islam or married to Muslim men.

What better place than science fiction to discuss these antagonisms, and what better genre to engage the reader and help him make up his own mind about such things? I am not going to fall into the trap of social drama and realist literature and *tell* people what to think.

What I hope to do is impress upon the Arab and Libyan reader our broader humanity, the fact that we as a people have so much in common with the other nations of the world, poor or otherwise, and that we will grow closer in the future as we develop. We all live on the same planet and share the same problems, such as the degradation of the environment or the energy crisis or corporations ruling our lives, and raw materials.

You can see this in my story "The Greatest Weapon," where I talk about a recreational resort in outer space, built like a dark pyramid, where humans mingle with aliens, but where the humans are clearly in charge. As one old geezer drinks away, he informs his nephew of how an Earth invasion force was able to subdue an entire planet, during a 200-year long war. There was only one enclave left on this world, on the ocean floor, an entire sophisticated city living under a dome made out of transparent metal that could withstand everything, and with a cloaking device and forests of seaweed to hide them as well.

It was only betrayal that led to the eventual human victory, nothing to be proud about with this extinction of a great civilization at the hands of very inhumane humans.

That being said, my primary concerns are with my own people and their extended family, as Arabs and Muslims, and the chief source of my inspiration and literary identity is still Arabic and Libyan. While most of the characters in my stories aren't necessarily Arabs and Muslim, I make a habit of touching on Arabic and Islamic settings and personas in my stories whenever I can. I want to correct multiple imbalances that operate in the world of SF. There simply isn't enough Arabic science fiction out there and a great deal of the SF written by Arabs is set in outer space with non–Arabic characters behaving in a very Western way. I am very explicit that I do not want the science I write to be a pale imitation of Western SF, with all the respect that is due. And there are not enough Arabs and Muslims in Western SF either, another imbalance I am trying to correct.

What is more, Arabic names and settings should not be seen as restrictive. It is all a question of subtly. The "Greatest Weapon" does not have Arabs and Muslims in it, but nonetheless resonates with the concerns and history of our part of the world—foreign conquest and internal betrayal.

In another story I talk about old-fashioned means of travel and communication and how a young couple feel terrible having to travel to a planetoid in something like 20 minutes instead of being teleported there instantaneously. The man they seek, a very old man indeed who has isolated himself from modern communications, warned them that teleportation may increase your physical vitality but it saps your soul, making life too easy. Wisdom is not only in the destination but in the journey itself, and in the suffering. (In an interview I once described the internet falling on top of our heads like a tidal wave, something I still haven't entirely digested, unlike the IT generation.)

What I also try to do with my stories is find *solutions* to our problems in Libya, modern solutions presented in a modern literary format. And these aren't just the usual mundane problems we face, economically, politically and socially. They are also existential problems brought on by modernity. They may not be here right this minute but we will grow into them sooner or later like the rest of the world.

The place of religion in the future is a case in point, as highlighted by the title story of my anthology, "A Problem of Faith." Here I have a tall, handsome boy going to a building and taking his shoes off, in the usual fashion of entering a mosque. I don't tell the reader it is a mosque straight off, however. The people on the inside, who are there in droves, almost seem like university students—evidence that religion is still popular in the distant future and that knowledge and faith are not and have never been anathema to each other. Certainly in Islamic tradition. Even the walls of the mosque from the outside replicate that of an Ivy League university in the West—I had plants growing on the walls. On the inside you have a forest of pillars, a common architectural type from Islamic and especially Andalusian history, with glorious carpets on the ground that look like they were there before the pillars were put up, almost a landscape in their own right.

The young man is introduced by a saintly looking person to an old, old sheikh who wants to impress the newcomer even further with holographic projections of nature's bounty—God's handiwork— but the young man insists on getting straight to the point. He explains that he has never been impressed by religion his whole

Ghost and the machine, an Islamic appraisal-rejoinder to classic sci-fi dilemmas concerning the nature of consciousness, the soul and morality (courtesy of the artist, Ammar Al-Gamal).

life. He fasts all year round and sees no need for religion when it comes to moral guidance, since he is a medical doctor who set up an entire charitable institute offering treatment for free to anyone, rich or poor, old or young.

The sheikh praises him and then the young guest explains that after this, with his staff doing all the hard work of curing people, he began to think through the meaning of his life and how religion, such an archaic thing that it is, anticipated everything he has been able to do. So maybe there is something to religion after all. What bothers him is if God will accept him as a believer. The sheikh says of course. His good deeds alone are enough. All that he has to do is openly declare that he believes in God and Muhammad as His Messenger, then the big surprise comes. The young man is in fact an android, and he doesn't know if he has a soul and so if God will accept him as a Muslim and believer.

I end the story there, leaving it open to the reader's interpretation, on purpose. Can a machine have a soul and deserve to enter the pearly gates of heaven? Are good deeds enough? Having religion persist, and thrive, in the future is not enough. We have to admit to morality elsewhere in the world, and as a product of the very modernity we both crave and disdain. Just as the future will not be for the West alone, it will not be for the Arabs alone either. They have to learn to respect others, cultures and religions and civilizations, just as they request of others to respect and acknowledge them.

Science fiction can prepare us for this future as much as it can help us create it. We need to go through scenarios in our head as to what the world will look like and how people will interact with each other and what new customs or modes of conduct will emerge, and what moral pitfalls await us as human beings and what dangers lie ahead for our planet, whether home grown or alien.

So there is nothing anathema about being an Arab and a SF writer. It's all a question of how you "see" yourself as an Arab.

Future Imperfect

I would like to say that science fiction is my vocation but it isn't and for obvious reasons. It is my love and part of my mission in life, but it does not put bread on the table. It is also not a coincidence that I became a tourist guide, and one of the first in my country's contemporary history. The country was always open to foreign tourists, whether during the Italian occupation (1911–1943) and also during the monarchy after independence (1951–1969). It was a big and successful industry and individual tourist guides had their own offices.

Then, when Qadafi came to power in the 1969 coup, he closed the country off, claiming that the tourists were all spies hell-bent on destroying the country.

It was only in the mid–1990s that tourism resumed, in Qadafi's half-hearted attempt to prove to the world that he was not a terrorist. (It was also during this period that many NGOs were set up, including the ones I've joined or helped found. Civil society flourished till members of Qadafi's clan muscled in on individual NGOs, either shutting them down or taking them over.) Not that tourism thrived, mind you. All the tourist companies were kept under the purview of the security apparatus and getting permits became a bureaucratic nightmare. Be that as it may, it did bring in money. But, as you can imagine, tourism has all but come to an end, due to the political and security situation. It has given me more time to write science fiction, though.

I am also still at my old job, the Libyan Nuclear Research Centre, in Tajoura, the eastern suburb of Tripoli. I'm a first-ranking specialist there, a word that has almost lost its meaning in the Libya of today. Still, it's one of the new places in Libya that's still up and running.

Publication, on the other hand, has come to a standstill. And not just books, but magazines and newspapers too. Facebook has taken their place, and satellite news. I haven't given up, though. I'm working on publishing two new anthologies, equally sized—12 stories each—like my first story collection. I hope to add some illustrations this time round, but it's all a bit iffy if you know what publishing is like in an Arabic country. We will see. A fourth anthology, same size hopefully, is also on the drawing board. The only thing slowing me down, apart from the terrible situation in the country, is my sense of scientific veracity. I'm making sure all the scientific facts and theories in the two forthcoming anthologies are in fact accurate.

I don't want to make any slip ups. I have my reputation as a nuclear engineer to think about, not forgetting the reputation of Libyan science fiction!

NOTES

1. Translated by Emad El-Din Aysha.
2. Quote taken from "H.G. Wells," *Goodreads.com*, https://www.goodreads.com/quotes/107797-civilization-is-in-a-race-between-education-and-catastrophe-let.

The Survival Guide to Egyptian Dystopia and Apocalypse

Post–Arab Spring Sci-Fi Comes of Age

Ahmed Salah Al-Mahdi

The stars had only one task: they taught me how to read.
They taught me I had a language in heaven and another language on earth.
—Mahmoud Darwish, (2013: 85)

Egyptians and Arabs have always loved telling stories, and listening to them, especially fictional tales. Epic and folktales are a big part of our society such as *The 1001 Nights* and epics like Sayf ibn Dhi-Yazan, Baibars, and more. I was raised in Upper Egypt, and I used to hear the folktales from my grandmother, full of Magic, Jinn and mythical creatures. I also used to see older people hanging around a narrator playing the Rababa and singing the Epic called Taghribat Bani Hilal. It is fascinating seeing all these people engaged in such a tale, their emotion shaped by what they are hearing. You can see the happiness, sadness, or anger; you can say that Egyptians are emotional folk, and they for sure love a fictional tale.

But Egyptians did not know the modern form of telling stories, which is the "Novel," until the 20th century. Some critics may consider that *Zaynab* by Muhammad Husayn Haykal, published in 1913, to be the first modern Egyptian novel ("Mohammed Hussein," 14 June 2020). Thus, we didn't have much time to develop in the different fields of novel fictional narrative, especially science fiction and fantasy, and by the time we had Novels, the whole world was turning away from Romanticism toward Realism after the French revolution, and it was the time that Egypt was facing the British occupation and fighting two world wars. Even Romanticism in poetry was faced with harsh criticism by Abbās al-Aqqād, Ibrahim al-Mazini, and Abdel Rahman Shokry, which resulted in The Apollo Poetic Society closing its doors.

After World War II and the 1948 Arab-Israeli War, the army overthrew the king of Egypt and his son, and established a military rule and a new regime that was heavily inspired by Soviet and Chinese socialist regimes. And these regimes were known for fighting fiction. In revolutionary China they banned cinema and even after allowing it kept on banning science fiction movies like *Back to the Future* and *Ghostbusters*! ("Film censorship in China," 12 July 2020).

In Egypt at the time, the official voice of the government was about the fear of the return of feudalism, and the new enemy at our door, Israel, so everything was about the reality of Egyptian society and the peasants—cinema, poetry and novels. The best example for this are the novels of Naguib Mahfouz, who won the 1988 Nobel Prize for Literature, as his novels revolve mostly around Cairo's streets and alleys, and the best example is the Cairo Trilogy. Another excellent example also is *The Land*, which is a 1969 Egyptian drama film directed by Youssef Chahine, based on a popular novel by Abdel Rahman al-Sharqawi. The film narrates the conflict between peasants and their landlords in rural Egypt in the 1930s.

In that atmosphere that is fraught with the fear of war and feudalism, there was no place for fantasy or science fiction, save some works of children's literature that had the elements of folktales like magic and mythical creatures. Every fantasy work was considered child literature in the eyes of the critics. That is why, *despite* the nature of the Egyptian people who love fantasy and epics, we didn't see that transformed into novels.

But all that changed with one man, Nihad Sharif, who is considered the first "real" Egyptian and Arabic science fiction author. He was born in Alexandria in 1932, and graduated from Cairo University's Faculty of Arts History Department ("Nihad Sharif," 2020). His first novel was *The Lord of Time* about a scientist possessed with the idea of immortality who finds a way to freeze humans for many years. It was published in 1972 and was transformed into a big screen movie in 1987 by the director Kamal El Sheikh and starring big names in Egypt like Athar El-Ḥakim, Nour El-Sherif, and Gamil Ratib.

Nihad Sharif paved the way for the Egyptian science fiction authors that came after him, mainly Dr. Nabil Farouk ("Nabil Farouk," 2020) and Dr. Raouf Wasfi. Both wrote for the Modern Arab Association publishing house's Egyptian Pocket Novels (Rewayāt Masreyya Lel Gēb) series ("Rewayat," 2019). Dr. Raouf Wasfi wrote many science fiction novels, including his main series Nova; received international literary awards; and taught at various universities ("Raouf Wasfi," 2020).

Dr. Nabil Farouk is best known for his two main series, Ragol Al Mostaheel (The Man of the Impossible), espionage novels about an Egyptian Central Intelligence agent named Adham Sabri, and Malaf Al Mostakbal (The Future File), science fiction novels that take place in the near future. The Future File series began with his 1984 novella "Death Ray," which focuses on the fictional exploits of the Egyptian Scientific Intelligence Agency (ESIA). The heroes of this series are Nour El Deen Mahmoud (of Scientific Intelligence) and his scientific team, who apply their police and scientific

The apocalypse Egyptian style with lone survivors battling against past demons as much as future dilemmas (courtesy of the artist, Ammar Al-Gamal).

skills to solve mysteries concerning robots, artificial intelligence, cities under the ocean or on the moon, and many more. However, the series took a huge shift beginning with no. 76, *Invasion*, in which an alien warrior race from the world of Glorial occupies the Earth. After the issue the series was expanded beyond planet Earth and focused more on the planetary wars and dangers far beyond our galaxy. That's why the fans of the series differentiate between Pre-Invasion and Post-Invasion when discussing the series.

A Change of Pace

Up to that point, Egyptian science fiction was about imagining a better future for the country, a future where Egypt is advanced and maybe the leader of the world. But at the beginning of the 21st century the state of the country looks more grim than ever; people die in train crashes and sunken ships, news about cancerous food is everywhere, police brutality increases noticeably, with a decline in human rights and the obliteration of freedom of speech. The presidential election was manipulated so that Hosni Mubarak could stay in his position until his death, and there was a plan for his son Gamal Mubarak to inherit power. These events occurred under the Emergency Law that was expanded many times since the assassination of Anwar Sadat, the previous president, in 1981.

All this led to the Egyptian revolution of 2011, but there were many signs along the road. One of the most important events was the Egyptian general strike at Mahalla, on 6 April 2008, by Egyptian workers, primarily in the state-run textile industry, in response to low wages and rising food costs. The strike was shut down by government force; a series of uprisings and military reprisals turned the city of Mahalla, about two hours north of Cairo, into a conflict zone. The 6 April Movement was formed in the wake of the uprisings which fed revolutionary sentiment and helped lead to the 2011 revolution.

It was in the year 2008 that Egyptian author Ahmed Khaled Tawfik wrote his dystopian novel, ironically named *Utopia* ("Ahmed Khaled Tawfik," 12 July 2020). The novel depicts a bleak Egyptian society in the year 2023, where the upper classes live in the gated city compound of Utopia on Egypt's north coast that is guarded by American Marines. Here everything is permitted, from sex to drugs. The lower class live outside its walls, allowed to enter only as workers and servants. Their life is miserable. As one of them described their life outside the walls saying: "I used to say to them: 'You dogs. You've slipped so far down that you eat dogs yourselves. Hadn't I warned you a thousand times? I'd told you the theories of Malthus and Jamal Hamdan, and the prophecies of Orwell and Wells, but every time you doped yourselves up with hashish and cheap liquor and dozed off. My fury with you is like the rage of the Prophets of the Old Testament on their peoples…. I curse you.' But what truly terrified me was their apathy. They're just looking for the next woman, the next round of tobacco, and the next meal, oblivious to the state they've reached."[1]

Utopia was a new experience for the Arabic reader who was used to reading dystopia in foreign environments only. It was the first "Egyptian" dystopian novel. The novel is very disturbing with many descriptive scenes of sex and gore, which was unusual for A.K. Tawfik, and the ending left no place for hope. However, it was exciting as a new Arabic experience and it opened the door for many dystopian novels to follow.

Utopia wasn't the only dystopian novel by A.K. Tawfik. He wrote a novel named *Like Icarus* that was published in 2015. The novel takes place in the near future of 2020, and extends to the future and returns to the past. It refers to Egypt as a police state, speaking about military coups and about a nuclear war that destroys human life in the future that's leads to life ruled by giant cockroaches while the humans have turned from the hunter to the prey. Another dystopian novel by Tawfik is *In the Tunnel of the Rats*, a re-telling of one of his Pocket Novels, the "Land of Darkness" published by the Modern Arabic Association in a series named "Ma Waraa Al Tabiaa" (The Paranormal). *In the Tunnel of the Rats* is more mature and deeper than "Land of Darkness." In both novels, the Earth is shrouded by dust after a meteor crash, which prevents sunlight from reaching the surface, and so the world drowned in darkness and begins to fall apart. There are people who believe that the darkness is holy and should not be defiled by light, and the rebels who try to bring light to the Earth again.

Tawfik's last novel prior to his death was *Shaäbib*, which in Arabic means the first drops of rain that are few and far between. And like the previous novel, this one is also a re-telling and expanding of "Jonathan's Promise," one of his Pocket Novels in the series called "Fantasia." In the novel the Arabs are scattered in the world, the Arabs of the Diaspora as it is said in the novel. These Arabs face persecution and hate crimes, they are vulnerable migrants. They cannot protect themselves and their families from harm, nor return to their country, as the novel takes place at a time when the Arab world is poor, devastated and one cannot live there with dignity.

One of the most eminent Arabs scientifically and culturally emerged to dream of making a promised land for the Arabs. He was obsessed by the idea that he could falsify a history for the Arabs in the distant land of Papua New Guinea. He uses his connections to convince his friend, the American vice president, of the dream, and begins to implement the project, which attracts the Arabs of the diaspora to dream of a new world.

Tawfik's novels became darker with every new novel, and as if he says in this novel—as he sometimes said in real life—that there is no more hope, and any hope we see is a false, unreal, fragile, and cannot withstand the reality that became harsher every passing day.

Just as Nihad Sharif paved the way for Egyptian science fiction, A.K. Tawfik paved the way for dystopian novels, especially after the failure of the 2011 revolution in which the youth were a major part. They were struck by a deep pessimism, and the future appeared more grim than ever. The young author Moataz Hassanien told me: "As the revolutions of the Arab Spring turned into a bloody fall, destroying the dream of an ideal world, there was a necessity for the birth of new literature to monitor what had happened, and predictably what would happen, the new generation of writers decided that there was no need for equivocation and symbolism" (Hassanien, 2016).[2]

A New Genre Is Born

Hassanien is the author of the dystopian novella "2063" that takes place during the year 2063, where reading books is a crime punishable by the law, like the world that reeked of kerosene in Ray Bradbury's *Fahrenheit 451*. In the novella, the Library of Alexandria is turned into a huge dormitory where the citizens are subjected to "satisfaction" tests (measuring happiness) while secret organizations invite you to join the lost Paradise.

Other novels written by Egyptian young authors like *Mercury* or "Otared" (after the planet closest to the sun, not the substance mercury) a dystopian/post-apocalyptic novel by Mohamed Rabie that was published in 2015 by Al Tanweer publishing house. It reached the short list of the 2016 Arab World Prize for Arabic Fiction, the Arabic version of the International Booker Prize for the novel. In this novel, the author tells the story of "Otared," a police officer who witnessed the fall of police power during 28 January 2011, and the aftermath that followed that, in a grim dark future of Egypt, where there is no place for hope. In an interview the author said: "Hope blinds us, obscures the facts, and I think that any attempt to get out of what we are in now lies in looking at things rationally, completely abandoning dreamy romanticism, knowing how we were defeated, and using a more ferocious technique to defeat the opposing side. This side sees us as an enemy that must be eliminated, and it does so with a strange boldness, while we still remember the days of peaceful demonstrations with endless nostalgia!" (Rabei, quoted in Hashim, 24 March 2016; my translation).

As I told Hupov (n.p.), "Another notable work in the Egyptian dystopia is *The Queue* or 'Al-Taboor' by Basma Abdel Aziz, that was published in 2013 also by Al Tanweer publishing house. The story takes place in a nightmarish atmosphere about the control of authority represented by the 'Gate.' It describes the life of citizens, where circumstances forced them to stand in front of The Gate in a long queue waiting for it to be opened for them to be able to obtain the necessary permits to pursue their life.

"The novel reached the long list of the best literary translated work, BTBA, which is one of the three most important awards in the United States of America for translated works."

The Listeners or "Al-Mustamieun" by Ibrahim El-Saed is a unique dystopian novel mixed with elements of espionage and cyberpunk. It takes place in Egypt in the near future after a devastating civil war, which resulted in a psychologically distorted generation of war children. Then came the idea of The Listeners, people who had programs planted in their minds that made them forget what they heard, making them an ideal choice to unload that negative energy gathered in the hearts of post-war people.

However, another group believes that the idea leads to the increased isolation of the people and their straying from the reality rather than facing it, and they seek to eliminate the program listeners.

The novel added a spin to the Egyptian dystopia and may be considered a Techno-Thriller with all the programming, hacking, espionage, and cyberpunk elements.

A Personal Touch

I myself was affected by these dystopian and post-apocalyptic works. When I was very young I thought that the future will be awesome, we will all have flying cars and live in cites under the ocean or on the moon, and we will conquer the galaxy and build new human civilization on many planets. Until I read *The Time Machine* by H.G. Wells. I was still young at the time; I read it in the series Awaldna ("Our Kids") that was published by

Dar El Maaref, one of the oldest publishing houses in Egypt (since 1890) which is dedicated to translating world literature into Arabic and simplifying for the young reader. I was impressed by the idea of the grim future and the life of two human species of Eloi and Morlocks. Thus my idea of the beautiful future was shaken. It was not *shattered* yet, but was cracked, until I read other novels translated by A.K. Tawfik, like *1984*, *Fahrenheit 451*, and *The Running Man*. I realized that I was a naïve child.

It wasn't just only novels that affected me. Movies played a big part too, like the original *Mad Max* trilogy and *I Am Legend* with Will Smith (later I read the novel) and many other dystopian and post-apocalyptic movies. Videogames played a large role also. As a teen I played many post-apocalyptic games like *Wasteland*, *Fallout*, and *Red Alert*. I was looking for any media related to dystopia or post-apocalypse. At this time, I was old enough to understand politics and economics. (I joined the 25 January Revolution myself).

I began writing at a young age, because I was a voracious reader. My first novels were about magic and fantasy worlds, but they were silly attempts. Then I wrote my first dystopian novel when I was in the last year of high school. My novel was about a society in a highly advanced city (Cairo in the far future) and the people who lived outside in the poor districts. The government is kidnaping babies from a hospital to create super assassins and the protagonist, after killing his target, realizes the truth and goes outside to search for his family using his super abilities and facing his former assassin colleagues. Later, while I was at university, I ditched the idea of the super assassins. I made new Cairo surrounded by a Dome and people outside live in nuclear wastes, under the rule of the ruthless hunters "Sayaadin" who rule the wastes with an iron fist.

After that, I ditched the whole idea of the high-tech city, and focused on the wastes and the life after the apocalypse, thus was born my first published SF novel *Malaz: The City of Resurrection*. The story is set in a distant future Egypt, after modern civilization as we knew it has collapsed in a cataclysmic nuclear war over oil and other scarce resources. The climate is completely different. It's cold, even in the daytime. Egypt is shrouded in clouds, leftovers of a nuclear winter. The water of the mighty river Nile is tepid and yellowed now. The only safe heaven, in the North, is the aptly named city of Malaz. A walled-in Medieval city ruled by the warrior class, the so-called Hunters, people who live off the civilian population—protection money, forced labor in the mines and fields and rock quarries, exploiting the outlying villages.

The hero, Qasim, is a disgruntled youth who—despite his poverty—can read and write. He knows things weren't always this way and busies himself ignoring people's feeble lives, through his inventions. He's an expert mechanic and self-taught metallurgist. His only friend, Uways, is the local blacksmith, and puts up with Qasim's eccentricities. He's also the only one who consoles him whenever he gets roughed up for defying the Hunters. Qasim's grandfather is practically the only Muslim there, praying and reminding Qasim of the importance of faith.

The novel was met with a positive response from the readers and the critics alike; it was discussed in the Egyptian Society for Science Fiction monthly cultural salon, and the national newspaper *Al Ahram* wrote about it.

Dr. Emad El-Din Aysha (Ph.D. in international studies, University of Sheffield) wrote: "I've only recently discovered Ahmed Al-Mahdi's work but I'm already a fan, and Malaaz is a treat. It's quite fast paced and doesn't bog itself down in unnecessary details. This gives it a youthful flavour, especially compared to the usual narrative style prevalent among Arabic authors, with excess linguistic flourishes at the expense of pacing, atmosphere and mood. The opening chapter, 'The Lone Wolf,' tells you everything you need to know about the daily life of the Northern city and the kind of inverted ecological system Egypt has found itself in. But it's not just the geography of Qasim's world that is mapped out in bits and pieces. It's the themes and characters as well" (Aysha, 13 February 2018).

Dr. Melanie Magidow (Ph.D., Middle Eastern languages and cultures, University of Texas at Austin) wrote: "Ahmed Mahdi is a new talent in the Arab World. His books provide great suspense, enchanting world building, satisfying storylines, and compelling characters. The plot was unpredictable in the beginning. It surprised me more than once! The protagonist character learns, grows, and succeeds. I enjoyed the imaginary, futuristic Egypt. In a sequel, I would like to read even more about the landscape. At the end of this book, I want more! I hope to see a sequel some day! However, I would highly recommend this book to anyone interested in an imaginative, fun story. It includes adventure, revenge, coming-of-age, and a hint of romance!" ("Melanie's Reviews," 2017).[3]

Mr. Khalid Gouda, one of the literary critics of the Egyptian Society for Science Fiction, said during the discussion: "*Malaaz* brings back to us the narrative of history through the construction of an uncivilized tribal life in which the bonds of religion have been weakened, or through the instrument of made up pagan faiths. In an effort to predict the future and to issue a warning call about the danger of technical progress if it is used by the greedy warmongers whom pursuit domination and power, and spread like a cancer at the expense of others" (Gouda, quoted in Al-Mahdi, 2018: 7).

After the success of *Malaaz*, many of my readers asked for a prequel that takes place during the apocalypse itself, the disaster that led to the destruction of civilization. The idea was in my mind already, but I hadn't put it on paper yet. During this time I watched more movies like the latest *Max Max* and read works like "The Machine Stops" by E.M. Forster and *The Sky So Heavy* by Claire Zorn, and also played new videogames like *Metro: Last Light* and *The Last of Us*. I began to think about the novel, and it came to me naturally—*The Black Winter*. It was the fastest novel I finished, only taking me three months to write and edit. And it was my first novel to be published outside of Egypt, as it was published by Amnah for publishing and distribution in Jordan.

The story centers on a brother and sister duo, Ziyad and Farida, living a carefree life in Assuit (in southern Egypt) sometime in the near future. Their father, Dr. Seif Al-Din, is a medical doctor at the local hospital, and their mother, Dr. Somaya Alam Al-Din, is a distinguished geneticist working with the government. The Western seaboard in the U.S. is hit by a massive nuclear strike from North Korea, with an appropriate response following that strike. Ziyad and Farida are promptly told to head off home; school and university are cancelled for the foreseeable future. Then Ziyad receives a mobile phone call from his mother to stock up on food and other essential items because she's been recalled to Cairo. The local supermarket is swamped with people and the proprietor makes the best of the opportunity and pushes up prices. Then the mobile networks crash and the TV transmission blanks out, leaving them in the dark in more than one way.

As with its predecessor, it was met by positive responses from the readers and the critics, and it also was discussed at the Egyptian Society for Science Fiction's monthly salon. Dr. Hosam Elzembely, director of the Egyptian Society for Science Fiction, wrote: "Ahmed Al-Mahdi succeeds in drawing a grimly realistic picture of the events that may very well transpire in the event of a black (nuclear) winter enveloping Egypt. It left a distinct impression on one's mind, like the After-Image on the retina. Long after putting down the book and going back your daily routine, the harrowing, frantic way goings on appear before you, haunting your imagination, leaving you with a mixture of anxiety and pleasure. Ahmed Al-Mahdi is etching a prominent position for himself among the writers of the fourth wave of the Arab sci-fi authors in Egypt; this novel is Egypt's own equivalent to Isaac Asimov's classic of classics, *Nightfall*" (Elzembely, quoted in Al-Mahdi, 2018: 6).

Khaled Gouda wrote: "The novelist Ahmed Salah Al-Mahdi is famous for his intriguing narrative, drawing the reader into his story through plotlines woven from a fertile imagination that describe the adventure of post-apocalyptic world following a nuclear disaster. A world flooded in darkness, radioactive contamination and utter horror. It seems so real that it is a warning call for what could come, warning that man in this world is far more dangerous that the apocalypse itself, an all too disturbing prophecy of a dark, foreboding future, where flowers are buried under the snow in the novel's own words. But the flowers remain there, longing for freedom and equality" (Gouda, quoted in Al-Mahdi, 2018: 7).

Aysha wrote: "It's thrilling stuff, and it's always refreshing to see that Egyptian and Arab authors can take on Western genres so effectively, pushing their own brand of such tried and test themes as the end of the world and what lies after the apocalypse. The breakdown of civilisation is almost a luxury in the Western world and so their works in the genre aren't nearly as deep or convincing as what is being produced here, and we're on the brink of collapsing into barbarism 24-hours a day as it is! It was a very sobering novel in that regard. You kept wondering if something terrible like this would happen, a war that apparently doesn't concern us—the Korean peninsula—affecting us over here. Could our admittedly comfortable life, with all its ups and downs, suddenly fall apart? How would we cope? Could we stand to go back to a primitive existence, like our forefathers, and have to chop up wood to stay warm and arm ourselves? Could we survive it all, psychologically, recover from the state of shock like Farida? Would we lose it and become as nasty as Ziyad in key scenes? These questions clearly haunt Ahmed Al-Mahdi and they came to bug me too with their plausibility" (Aysha, 25 February 2018).

I'm glad to be part of the science fiction society in Egypt and the Arab world, to add a stone to the wall of this art of dystopia and post-apocalypse, and wish to see more scenarios from other writers, and maybe in Egyptian cinema also. And I hope our works translated into English and other languages, reach a wider audience, and from there—as Aysha said: "...the sky is the quite literally the limit. Especially if you can't break through the radioactive black cloud cover!" (Aysha, 25 February 2018).

NOTES

1. This is my own translation.
2. This internet item has been blocked in Egypt due to its political content.
3. Melanie Magidow has nurtured Arabic literature in translation, and formally is a patron of Marcia Lynx Qualey's Arablit.org, and a distinguished translator and academic researcher herself. Please check out her website—*Marhaba Language Expertise*, https://www.melaniemagidow.com/.

Works Cited

"Ahmed Khaled Tawfik." (12 July 2020). *From Wikipedia, the free encyclopedia.* https://en.wikipedia.org/wiki/Ahmed_Khaled_Tawfik.

Al-Mahdi, Ahmed Salah. (2018). *The Black Winter.* Amman: Dar Amna Publishers, Jordan [Arabic].

Aysha, Emad El-Din. (13 February 2018). "BOOK REVIEW—Apocalyptic Aftermath: Ahmed Al-Mahdi's *Malaaz* (2017) takes on *The Road Warrior*, and Beats Him!" *The Levant newspaper.* http://the-levant.com/book-review-apocalyptic-aftermath-ahmed-al-mahdis-malaaz-2017-takes-on-the-road-warrior-and-beats-him/.

Aysha, Emad El-Din. (25 February 2018). "BOOK REVIEW—Back to the Future: Ahmed Al-Mahdi Charts a Course through the Arabic Winter of Discontent!" *The Levant newspaper.* http://the-levant.com/back-to-the-future-ahmed-al-mahdi-charts-a-course-through-the-arabic-winter-of-discontent/.

Darwish, Mahmoud. (2013). *Unfortunately, It Was Paradise: Selected Poems.* Berkley: U of California Press. 6th Edition. Translated by Munir Akash, Carolyn Forché, Sinan Antoon and Amira El-Zein.

"Film censorship in China." (12 July 2020). *From Wikipedia, the free encyclopedia.* https://en.wikipedia.org/wiki/Film_censorship_in_China.

Hashim, Muhammad Hamdi. (24 March 2016). "A Special Talk with the Novelist Mohamed Rabei." *Ibda'aat.* https://www.ida2at.com/ttt-pessimistic-mercury-hope-blind-us-and-obscure-facts/?fbclid=-IwAR3VNRM2gv2tmCj-W7hmd2AAMDVNz0zv43odqYiskOlLmTn5aQJYGlOUBEw [Arabic].

Hassanien, Moataz. (13 April 2016). "Dystopia: Morbid Futures in World Literature." *Noon Post.* http://www.noonpost.org/content/11238 [Arabic].

Hupov, Darius. (28 February 2020). "Egyptian Panorama." *Galaxia 42,* https://galaxia42.ro/english/non-fiction/sff-panorama/egyptian-panorama-2958.html.

"Mohammed Hussein Heikal." (14 June 2020). *From Wikipedia, the free encyclopedia.* https://en.wikipedia.org/wiki/Mohammed_Hussein_Heikal.

"Melanie's Reviews > ملاذ: مدينة البعث." (9 July 2017). *Goodreads.com.* https://www.goodreads.com/review/show/2054745642.

"Nabil Farouk." (21 June 2020). *From Wikipedia, the free encyclopedia.* https://en.wikipedia.org/wiki/Nabil_Farouk.

"Nihad Sharif." (30 March 2020). *From Wikipedia, the free encyclopedia.* https://ar.wikipedia.org/wiki/%D9%86%D9%87%D8%A7%D8%AF_%D8%B4%D8%B1%D9%8A%D9%81 [Arabic].

"Rewayat." (29 December 2019). *From Wikipedia, the free encyclopedia.* https://en.wikipedia.org/wiki/Rewayat.

Mending the Egyptian Gap

A Case Study in the Problems
Facing Arab-Islamic Science Fiction[1]

Emad El-Din Aysha

> The stage is a magic circle where only the most real things happen, a neu-
> tral territory outside the jurisdiction of Fate where stars may be crossed
> with impunity. A truer and more real place does not exist in all the
> universe.
> —P.S. Baber, *Cassie Draws the Universe* (2010: 204)

Two anecdotes help introduce the central topic of this contribution, over the fluid and problematic status of science fiction in Arabic literature, using Egypt as a test case. The first relates to the passing away of a very distinguished literary critic and author, Yousef Al-Sharouni, who died at the ripe old age of ninety-three in Cairo, Egypt (Sayed, 2017).

Yousef Al-Sharouni, you see, was one of those rarities in Egypt—a great *patron* of Arab sci-fi. His story with SF began in 1971, as he outlined in his own book on the genre *Science Fiction in Contemporary Arabic Literature* (2002), when he first met Nihad Sharif who handed him an unpublished manuscript of his forthcoming SF novel—*Qahir Al Zaman* or *The Lord of Time*. He admitted that he wasn't even planning on reading the book, just browsing through it and jumping to the end, but once he began reading in earnest, he couldn't put the novel down. He contacted Nihad Sharif the following day, straight after finishing the novel, determined to get the thing published as soon as possible. Al-Sharouni finally enrolled Nihad Sharif in a literary contest, paying the fees himself. The novel won the first prize with the unanimous agreement of the six judges, and all that same year.

Qahir Al Zaman was published the following year, and so began the career of Nihad Sharif—a history graduate originally—one of the most distinguished Egyptian SF writers to this day. This brings us to the second anecdote. I had the good fortune of asking Alaa Al-Aswany—world famous author of *The Yacoubian Building* (Buchan, 2007)—about SF and the overemphasis on realism in Arabic literature (Al-Aswany, 2010). His reply was that SF had already been given more attention than it deserved and explained that many an author had written stories on things like what it felt like to be a potted plant. His preference was for realism since every Egyptian citizen was a walking, living, breathing novel waiting to be written about, with the weight of the

For every man a novel, or for every common-day problem a novel, goes the wisdom of conventional Egyptian literature (courtesy of the artist, Ammar Al-Gamal).

world lying on their shoulders. (Note that he's clearly coupling science fiction with magic realism and surrealism).

This attitude is all the more amazing given that Alaa Al-Aswany is an avowed fan of Gabriel Garcia Marquez, hardly a gritty realist. (SF is also regularly conflated with fantasy and fairy tale literature like *Harry Potter*; see below). Frequenting legally-licensed bookstores and unofficial bookstands here in Cairo, you find that SF, after making significant strides straight after the January 2011 revolution, began to disappear again. More than that, genre confusion has set in with SF being swallowed up by a curious rival and newcomer to the Arabic literary scene—horror. You ask for SF, and you're asked in return: "are you looking for horror?" You get the same response repeatedly with many an accomplished SF writer, like Dr. Nabil Farouk, also switching increasingly from SF to horror.

The two genres have been intimately linked since the publication of the very first SF novel of all time, Mary Shelley's *Frankenstein*, but the kind of novels you find in Egypt are grisly detective novels about serial killers or supernatural scare stories, not SF at all.

All this means that an old, old pattern of literary neglect is reasserting itself. There are many reasons for this, some more broadly cultural, some literary and internal to the realm of Arabic SF writing itself, and some more purely economic and demographic, but there are lessons to be learned here—on Egyptian soil—of relevance to Arabs and Muslims and SF fans everywhere. Not least of which is the fact that SF cannot thrive without the help of critics like the dearly departed Yousef Al-Sharouni who are willing to dish out money from their own pockets to liven up the arid fields of contemporary Arabic literature.

I propose a three-pronged analysis of the problem. The first deals with defining science fiction and how this fits into Arab literary traditions and preferences. The second focuses on cultural problems rooted more in Arab-Islamic history when it comes to narrative and other forms of drama that have a surprising bearing on the topic of science fiction. The third deals with the economic problems facing the publication of science fiction in Egypt, contrasted to some promising Arab examples, problems that need resolving if the dilemmas outlined in the above anecdotes are to be surpassed once and for all.

Defining the Indefatigable

In all fairness, such genre confusions abound all the time, especially outside the Anglosphere of literature. A Chinese friend once used *Harry Potter* as an example of SF while French author Pierre Boulle famously wanted to dissociate himself from the screen adaptation of his novel, *Planet of the Apes*, seeing the novel as one of his "inferior" works (IndieWire, 2014). The important thing to catch onto is how, and why, Arab readers—including authors, critics and publishers—automatically drift towards the fantastical end of fiction, leaving science and technology trailing somewhat behind in the intellectual rally races.

Our colleague Ahmed Al-Mahdi, while an accomplished SF author, has always found fantasy more endearing, if only because of his upbringing, fed on a steady diet of bedtime stories harking back to Arab legends and myths—an all too common occurrence in Arabic culture. To add to this, he confirms that most Arab "critics can't differentiate between fantasy and SF and consider every [imaginary] work a Sci-Fi work" (Al-Mahdi, 2017).

Hence, the quip above with Alaa Al-Aswany and magic realism and surrealism. This is all the more troublesome once you realize that Al-Aswany is originally a dentist, placing him firmly in the bracket of science and technology.

Yousef Al-Sharouni stumbled onto this tendency in his own pioneering research, noting how the great Egyptian author and playwright Tawfik Al-Hakim (1898–1987) took such an arms-length attitude towards SF. This was in spite of the fact that Al-Hakim was one of the first in the Arab world to introduce the genre, through short stories and plays he penned as early as the 1950s. In one of his plays an Egyptian medical doctor discovers a way to regenerate organic material in living tissue and so chances onto the elixir of life, so to speak. He is later employed by a powerful politician to cure the man from a life-threatening illness and return him to his youth, but things go badly wrong because the politician's colleagues and own family don't recognize him and presume he's been kidnapped, and killed, by political rivals.

Tawfik Al-Hakim then extracts himself from these moral dilemmas, route on by the advance of science, by having the doctor give the politician an antidote that will age him again, only for us to discover in the end that it was all a dream. (More on this play below). Yousef Al-Sharouni concluded that this was a copout of sorts, especially since many an Egyptian science fiction writer used similar fantastical ploys. He uses the example of a story where people travel forwards in time to see what has become of humanity, without any explanation provided as to *how* this time-travel device came into being or the societal implications of being able to see the future and whether such technologies should be pursued to begin with. Another story in this genre had people travelling backwards in time, becoming younger and disappearing into their mothers' wombs, to get an opportunity to see their nostalgic notions of the past but, again, without any explanation as to how this can happen.[2] Other stories listed by Al-Sharouni include mythical tales of children before birth, living in a hereafter-type existence, who get to see what the world of the living and what their fates will be like. These authors, then, aren't interested in the science itself, seeing it only as a plot device to talk about morality. And conventionally-conceived notions of morality at that.

I came across the same melodramatic technique in a far more contemporary story written by Dr. Khalid Tuwkal bearing the controversial title "The President and the Clones" (2012). The story is of a father struggling with corrupt bureaucrats in his everyday life and being informed that such-and-such a recalcitrant official is a clone of the president, only to return home and find the same problem there. In the penultimate dramatic scene where his wife, a clone herself, attacks him, he wakes up and finds it was all just a bad dream.

The only thing that jolted Tawfik Al-Hakim into venturing into the sci-fi realm to begin with, adds Al-Sharouni, was the Space Race with rocket launches making the headlines everywhere.[3] Things went back to normal as the Space Race became old news, it seems, resuming the curious coexistence of realism with fairy tales that have continued to dominate literature. It was only with Nihad Sharif that you got proper scientific discoveries and technological advances coming to the forefront of the storyline. And, sadly, in today's literary scene there's only so much room at the top in Egypt, with fantasy and horror displacing sci-fi—at least for the moment.

Theater Is the Impossible

Such gaps in Arab and Islamic literature, then, appear all the time. An even older and more revealing example of this was, interestingly enough, "theater." As Tunisian literary critic Muhammad Aziza explains in his seminal *Islam and Theatre* (1990), past generations of Arab and Muslim poets and storytellers had no excuse for not developing their own brand of theater in the Islamic Golden Age (8th to 13th century) if only for the simple fact that they had ample "access" to the literary masterpieces of ancient Greece, along with the Indian epics. And yet the royal translators of the past skirted over the likes of Aeschylus, Euripides, and Sophocles.

More than this, even a rationalist philosopher like Ibn Rushd (Averroes) balked at translating Aristotle's books on Tragedy and Comedy. The words he used, taken from Arab poetical genres, were Madih (praise, a kind of propaganda poetry) for Tragedy, and Zaam (polemic, also a kind of propagandistic form of Arabic poetry) for Comedy. How is it that someone of Ibn Rushd's philosophical credentials, the scholar of Aristotle that he was, couldn't fathom the basics of Greek theater? Muhammad Aziza rejects Orientalist claims that it is the anti-visualist ethos of Islam that is responsible, with religious restrictions on depictions of holy figures, since there are plenty of examples of visual arts developing in Muslim history along with the existence of a great many non-holy figures that could be easily depicted. His own critique is much deeper, relying on an analytic understanding of the nuts and bolts of Greek tragedy and theater itself, all of which center round *conflict* and struggle. There is "vertical" conflict pitting human free will against the will of the gods. (Prometheus is the classic exemplar, stealing the secret of fire from the gods and handing it to man). There is a "horizontal" conflict putting man up against the social order (as in *Antigone*); a "dynamic" conflict pitting man against fate itself along with the direction of history.

Finally, there is an "internal" psychological and moral conflict in the soul of the protagonist, the tragic figure who knows that he will be punished by fate for having the audacity to stand up to the gods, and yet insists on going down this path nonetheless. This applies to everybody from Prometheus to Oedipus to Achilles and Hector. But how could you transfer this to a Muslim *setting*? It's not that Islam as a religion forbids any of these speculations or that theater was seen as somehow blasphemous, but that Muslims at first couldn't *comprehend* the enormity of such a metaphysical system. A pagan Greek would have no problem seeing the universe as riven with conflict since that was what paganism is all about; gods fighting each other and setting man against man in the process, the story of Troy in all its enormity. Muslims, as good monotheists, then, were essentially suffering from "culture shock."

Aziza adds that a contributing factor to this story of Arabic neglect was, ironically, the fact that Europeans themselves had turned their backs on Greek theater and tragedy in the Christian era, when the Arabs first began translating the heritage of the Greeks (Kamal Al-Din, 1975: 11). Again, the medieval institution of the church saw in these tragic plays a moralistic travesty and skewed metaphysics of the world. (Muhammad Kamal Al-Din, cited here, actually does a great deal to repair the reputation of Arabs as regards theater, but most of the proto-theater traditions he cites are Persian, Turkish and Sufi in origin, in addition to the Shiite examples used by Muhammad Aziza himself; Kamal Al-Din, 1975: 12–16, 19–20).

To their credit, modern advocates of science fiction in the Arab world recognize these self-same Greek elements in SF, which is the whole reason why they *love* it. To quote Egyptian journalist, author and translator of science fiction, Ragi Enayat, the fulcrum of science fiction is "man's struggle with the creations of his own two hands in his drive towards improving his life … and this itself is the modern extension of that struggle between the classical hero and his written fate, as advancement is our permanent fate" (Enayat, 1984, 8). Science fiction is the result of the two-way confrontation between rapidly changing circumstances and man reflecting on himself; the world around him and what it is to be human. Hence Enayat's maxim that we must know ourselves before we dream and that we must dream first before we devise plans to modernize ourselves.

Other literary critics and authors, however, handle these topics with kid gloves in line—you could almost say—with the example of Ibn Rushd. The abovementioned play by Tawfik Al-Hakim is a case in point. While experiencing his youth in this (apparent) dream the politician also grows weary with the "boredom of immortality" and comes to realize that real youth isn't in the body but in the soul, and that there is nothing worse than having an aged soul trapped in a youthful body. The politician's sense of weariness also comes from knowing the future, what lies in store for him and his loved ones, observing that knowing the future makes one a prisoner of these prophecies, adding that true "freedom" lies in the ignorance that we live with "in the present." My students at the American University in Cairo told me the same thing after watching *The Curious Case of Benjamin Button* (2008), saying that the past and future always seem better but in fact it was the present that was best.

We should add that the format used by Tawfik Al-Hakim is recognizable to Egyptians. There are many, many Egyptian black and white movies where the hero is granted all his wishes by a genie in the lamp, only to find himself even more miserable and begging the genie to return everything to the way it was before. So even fantasy proper suffered from this fatalist sense of stunted imagination.

It seems, then, that authors like Tawfik Al-Hakim and many others of the earlier generation of Egyptian SF writers simply shied away from the metaphysical implications of science that could genuinely turn the tables on fate and society and personal morality all in one go. They did this just as their ancestors shied away from the horrendous implications of Greek tragedy and theater and laughing in the face of fateful adversity. And is it a coincidence that the doctor who finds the aging cure himself has an *American* medical researcher friend?

The Economics of Opacity

One suspects, then, that the same thing is happening now, with fantasy and horror being seen as safer outlets for people's creative energies than proper hardcore SF. To cite Ahmed Al-Mahdi again, even the fantasy novel is a new genre itself, despite the Arab world's long heritage of fairy tales. It was the success of the *Lord of the Rings* and *Harry Potter* series that got the ball rolling, he adds. Not to forget the example of Ahmed Khaled Tawfik's *Paranormal* series with a whole generation of authors modeling themselves on him.

This analysis is hardly surprising if you make casual inquiries about the nature of the publishing industry in Egypt and how nonchalant they are about market research and sales drives. Established publishers also focused on established names, while small, new publishers try to shift the burden of advertising onto the struggling author. Even mainstream authors like Naguib Mahfouz suffer from the Egyptian book market if only because the "way the print business model works is that stores take books on consignment" (Ashraf Maklad, quoted in Qualey, 2014). This leaves publishers in the dark as to the success or failure of their works. It also makes it too expensive and too risky to distribute across the Arab world, leaving young authors particularly badly hit. (See also Qualey, 2013). A friendly book publisher, without naming names, lamented how there were only "three" major bookstores in Cairo that were *also* printing presses, allowing them to corner the marketplace. In the process the "system" put in place to pay authors was based on monthly sales. Everybody was suffering, including the textbook sector, with historical texts dumped onto the marketplace—without any new edits and revisions—along with archaic science and history textbooks and translations and reprints of foreign textbooks.

A friendly owner of a fledgling bookstore adds that the person who gets the least out of publishing in terms of monetary returns is the lowly author. Another young SF author I spoke to confirmed this, adding that even the publisher doesn't do so well. When a bookstore buys a book from a publisher for 40 L.E., it sells it for 100 L.E., pocketing that extra 60 L.E. for itself. And that's not discounting the influence of politics in all this. The said unnamed author wrote a dystopian novel about a future post–Arab Spring Egypt, and persistently failed to get a publisher willing to handle it, despite his successful track record in the fantasy realm. (He'd also written online reviews of other dystopian novels and the articles were later "blocked").

If you talk to publishers, especially the less friendly variety, they will tell you that distribution is their responsibility, *not* sales—it's the authors.' What they mean by that cryptic phrase is that bookstores pick and choose what they accept from a publisher, relying on established names and genres. And that's not discounting "connections" (nepotism and favoritism). The only way to get around this Catch-22 situation is for the author to find a way to get his name in the papers to advertise his latest publication, such as a signing ceremony at the Cairo International Book Festival or getting his novel adapted to screen.

Another rule of thumb they pursue is to make novels as "small" as possible, so as not to put off readers. The manuscript itself can be as long as you like, but you have to *compress* it with a tiny font to shrink the number of pages. They also cut costs with the cheap quality paper and ink they use—especially now with the dollar crisis, making good quality imported paper too expansive—and with front covers swiped off the internet. (They don't have proper art departments and illustrators the vast majority of the time, with graphics people paid pennies. Even in non-fiction books, you find the printing used is a "photocopy"). Speaking to older authors in the field, you discover that the publishing industry as a whole is a shambles. Except for academic publication, there is almost no role for the editor, and proofing has to be done by the fiction author himself. (Even a giant like Jules Verne couldn't do without the advice of publisher Pierre-Jules Hetzel, who insisted that Verne make his novels lively and avoid tragic endings). This does nothing to gain the authors critical acclaim, let alone international respect in the Arab marketplace, and can put off readers too with too frequent typos and plot loopholes and bad typesetting (see below).

The key to profitability, you hear, is "distribution." Certain bookstores/publishers span the whole country, while others you can only find in a posh neighborhood of Cairo like Zamalek. Also, since bookstores make the lion's share of the money, the only printing presses that can make serious money are the ones that own bookstores too.

Even established authors face problems, regardless of genres. Fishing around in shop after a shop for the latest novel by a very distinguished author and member of the Writer's Union, I was eventually told by a shop clerk that this author made the mistake of publishing with different print presses instead of signing an exclusive contract with one only. Publishers *punish* such authors by printing only so many copies and not doing new editions.

In this unhealthy context it is no surprise that horror, again, is seen as a safe bet. A young horror novelist told me that writing in Egypt is always captivated by "fads"; for a time it was romantic literature, so everybody hopped onto that bandwagon. Now it's horror, with young authors trying to distinguish themselves by playing around with popular subgenres. (Vampire novels have made their way into Egyptian writing, although vampirism is not part of the Arab-Islamic heritage but the Gothic tradition). He cited the example of the novel *Warm Bodies*, which is in the Zombie subgenre, with the proviso that the hero is a zombie!

Conclusion—The Arab Springboard to Success

Working and succeeding in the Arab sci-fi realm is an uphill struggle but, fortunately, there's nothing *inevitable* about this, from a cultural-religious perspective. Muhammad Aziza himself says the hostility to theater in Muslim history was in "Sunni" Islam, whereas Shiites took it up eagerly and made it a basis for their passion plays and participatory religious rituals. Theater is now universal in the Arab world and Greek tragedy is taught everywhere. And there is no theological prohibition of SF any more than there is a forbidding of theater.

Ragi Enayat, Nihad Sharif and Nabil Farouk aren't heretics by any stretch of the imagination while Yousef Al-Sharouni himself was a good Christian and a pan–Arabist at that, having worked as a cultural consultant in Oman and penned a book introducing Omani literature to a wider Arab audience. His love of SF from Nihad Sharif onwards also coexisted quite nicely with his own brand of realist short fiction discussing the problems facing the Egyptian village. So, if anything is perpetuating this metaphysical fog of miscomprehension in the sci-fi realm, it's the critical establishment's refusal to lend a helping hand to the SF writers of the Arab world.

We can add here that the Writers' Union in Egypt is traditionally biased against SF, making sure not to give any of its serious prizes to the genre's authors. This position has mellowed over the past few years with a special section in the Union set up for science fiction, reveals an older SF author. But the same author adds that favoritism is rampant in the Union, with prizes being dished out to specific authors, regardless of literary merit or if what they write even counts as sci-fi. On one occasion the author read an SF novel that had won the first prize. It was only 120 pages and he found 140 typos in it!

The charged political atmosphere has not helped either, he adds, since anyone mentioning religious rituals in their work is looked at suspiciously—as a closet Islamist that needs to be ferreted out.

Nonetheless, young authors like Ahmed Al-Mahdi are optimistic. Egyptians "love imaginative fiction, and fairytales and epics have always been part of Egyptian folklore," he said. The problem, again, were the critics who considered any piece of imaginative fiction to not be "real literature." His recipe for advance: "We need real prizes for the SF and Fantasy like 'Hugo and Nebula' in the West to encourage the youth to write in those fields, also translating their works into English to be known worldwide" (Al-Mahdi, 2017).

The movie industry also needs to make a contribution since SF in Arab countries is not divided into subgenres such as cyberpunk or space opera, despite the popularity of the *Star Wars* series. If there were Arab SF movies such specialized sets of readers and writers would develop of their own accord, he added.

My advice is to replicate the example of Yousef Al-Sharouni. Writers and publishers have to make a living like everybody else and they can't be expected to re-educate the fans into understanding what SF is, and how significant it is, all by themselves. *Patronage* is the key to slaying the unruly dragon of unpublishable priorities. And political shackles themselves are a driver for SF.

It was the patronage of the state in the 1960s, interestingly enough, that helped overturn many of the older hostilities towards theater, reveals Sharouni in another work of his on Egyptian literature (1973). The patronage came almost by accident, he adds, since this is when television came online in Egypt, creating a ready-made market for playwrights. Still, there are lessons to be learned even from this positive development. This is because theater became *so* successful in fact that it caused a temporary dip in the burgeoning world of the novel, drawing many an author away towards playwriting, while plays published in book form became an important competitor to the still fledgling novel (Al-Shourni, 1973: 8–9).

So, it's never over till it's over, and not even then.

NOTES

1. Special thanks to Rebecca and Hugh.
2. According to Michael Cooperson, Arab time-travel literature goes as far back as the 1880s, with the proviso that the preference was always towards going *backwards* in time to the highpoints of Islamic history, again with no scientific explanation of how the time-traveling takes place (Qualey, 2011).
3. The same holds true, ironically, of Arabic poetry (Abu Ghali, 1995). There was a flurry of utopian poetry during the Space Race, imagining idealistic cityscapes in *industrial* terms—technology, smokestacks—along with the usual motifs of sweet smelling places (gardens and flowers). What these poets attempted to do, in their own little way, was to reconcile the industrial city with their more romantic notions of city life, and by doing this, remind modern man that love and an attachment to nature was called for in addition to material gains that came from the conquest of nature (Abu Ghali, 1995: 286, 289, 296–297).

WORKS CITED

Abu Ghali, Mukhtar. (April 1995). *The City in Modern Arabic Poetry*. Kuwait: Al-Majlis al-Watani lil-Thaqafa wal-Funun wal-Adab [Arabic].

Al-Aswany, Alaa. (13 April 2010). "Present Culture in Egypt." Seminar Lecture delivered (in Arabic) at the American University in Cairo, Downtown (Tahrir) Campus.

Al-Mahdi, Ahmed. (17 June 2017). "Islam and Sci-Fi interview of Ahmed Al Mahdi." *Islam and Science Fiction: On Science Fiction, Islam and Muslims*. http://www.islamscifi.com/islam-and-sci-fi-interview-of-ahmed-al-mahdi/.

Al-Sharouni, Yousef. (1973). *The Contemporary Egyptian Novel*. Kitab Al-Hilal Series 268, April. Cairo: Dar Al-Hilal [Arabic].

Al-Sharouni, Yousef. (2002). *Science Fiction in Contemporary Arabic Literature: Till the End of the 20th Century*. Cairo: General Egyptian Book Organization [Arabic].

Aziza, Mohammad. (1990). *Islam and Theatre*. Cairo: General Egyptian Book Organization. Translated from the original French by Dr. Rafik Al-Saban [Arabic].

Baber, P.S. (2010). *Cassie Draws the Universe*. Bloomington: iUniverse.

Buchan, James. (17 February 2007). "A Street in the Sky." *The Guardian*. https://www.theguardian.com/books/2007/feb/17/fiction.featuresreviews.

Enayat, Ragi. (ed.) (1984). *The Curse of the Dark Star... and Other Stories*. Cairo: Dar Al-Shorouk.

IndieWire. (10 July 2014). "Best to Worst: Ranking the 'Planet of The Apes' Movies." http://www.indiewire.com/2014/07/best-to-worst-ranking-the-planet-of-the-apes-movies-274629/.

Kamal Al-Din, Muhammad. (1975). *The Arabs and Theatre*. Kitab Al-Hilal Series 293, May. Cairo: Dar Al-Hilal [Arabic].

Qualey, Marcia Lynx. (9 July 2011). "Q&A with Michael Cooperson, Translator of Shalaby's 'Time Travels.'" *Arab Literature (in English) Blog*. https://arablit.org/2011/07/09/qa-with-michael-cooperson-translator-of-shalabys-time-travels/.

Qualey, Marcia Lynx. (23 October 2013). "Muhammad Aladdin: 'The Central Problem was—and is—Book Distribution.' Interview of Egyptian Novelist Muhammad Aladdin." *Arab Literature (in English) Blog*. http://arablit.wordpress.com/2013/10/23/novelist-muhammad-aladdin-the-central-problem-was-and-is-book-distribution-2/.

Qualey, Marcia Lynx. (25 February 2014). "Major New Arabic Ebookstore Could Be Publishing Game-changer." *Arab Literature (in English) Blog*. http://arablit.wordpress.com/2014/02/25/major-new-arabic-ebookstore-could-be-publishing-game-changer/.

Sayed, Nesmahar. (2–8 February 2017). "A Rebellious Gift—Obituary: Yousef Al-Sharouni (1924–2017)." *Al-Ahram Weekly*. http://weekly.ahram.org.eg/News/19559.aspx.

Tuwkal, Khalid. (2012). *The President and the Clones: Stories*. Dokki: Arab World for Studies and Publishing [Arabic].

Morocco, Then and Now

The Struggle for Arabic Science Fiction[1]

Mouad Bouyadou

I will not serve God like a labourer, in expectation of my wages.
—Rabia Al-Adawiya

Imagination: A concept known to man since the dawn of history, a power that he came to realize was his alone among all living things....

So he worked to harness this power; he imagined and dreamed, and then planned and executed his plans to build his homes and fortifications, using this faculty to make his tools and plant his land and achieve all that he needs and desires....

It was from this that he understood that were it not for the imagination, he would not have been able to achieve anything.

We, his grandchildren, also know that without the imagination the stories of ancestors would not have reached us, drawn on the walls of the caves, and carved on walls and obelisks....

To this day we have followed the exploits and achievements of generations past and gone through the imagination.... Likewise, it is thanks to the imagination that we have risen to live in today's world with all its advances and the prosperity we enjoy in all walks of life.

As we progressed, we came to understand the sheer vastness of the imagination, dividing it into many smaller branches. We grew up to realize that the most furtive field of the imagination was in the arts, and especially literature. And so we have:

Social drama
Travel literature and adventure....
The literature of fantasy and myth,
Science fiction and detective fiction....
Horror and parapsychology....

Today, however, we are going to talk about science fiction, which we know all too well originated in and developed in the West....

Nonetheless, the Arabs also made a contribution in this area, beginning with the middle of the previous century, and they are still contributing, to this point in time. And they are doing this despite the lack of support and scarcity of scientific sources *of* support, and the difficulties faced in publication and the lack of appreciation, and the reluctance of young people to read, especially in this field.

I will summarize my talk here about my country, Morocco; how science fiction emerged and its first manifestation; and the subsequent attempts of Moroccan writers.

As for *my* story with sci-fi, or khayal ilmi ("imagination" and "scientific") as we call it in Arabic, it began in my childhood, watching movies. I say this despite the fact that my father wrote poetry. He was a teacher of Arabic and a respected school director, and a published poet and essayist, writing from the 1960s to 1980s, in newspapers. (He wasn't able to break into book publication, unfortunately, as hard as he tried). My mother loves literature too and the whole family is very artistic; my sisters write poetry as a hobby. For some reason, though, I was never exposed to the classics of literature.

My first experience with "reading" science fiction, however, came when I was 10, when I stumbled onto a novella from the famous pocketbook series (روايات مصرية للجيب) for Dr. Ahmed Khaled Tawfik and Dr. Nabil Farouk, and Sherif Shaweki. I wasn't able to keep reading this series from Egypt, though; they weren't always available in Morocco. It was only when I was 16 years old that an Egyptian friend found a bookstore on the internet and got me the sequels to that novella.

From then on I began reading SF in earnest—my favorite authors are Isaac Asimov, H.G. Wells, Philip K. Dick, Ray Bradbury and Arthur C. Clarke—and became captivated by this branch of the imagination.

I have been there ever since, despite the many bumps along the way, for both me and my country, let alone the Arab world at large.

Resume of a Nation

The person usually credited with penning the first work of science fiction in modern Morocco was the poet and author Abdel Salam Al-Baqali (1932–2010), with his famous novel *The Blue Flood* (1976), envisioning a modern utopian scientific city. Here a group of brilliant scientists came together to help save the world from utter destruction, pooling together and recording for posterity all of mankind's genius and knowledge and heritage in one place, stored in the memory banks of an invention of their own. (They lost control of this invention themselves, which places them and the human race in jeopardy).

In actual fact, novelist, playwright and critic Ahmad Bakri Sibai (1937–2002) had preceded Al-Baqali with his novel *The Crucible of Life* (1966). Although it was the earlier text, the critics downplayed it for the longest time on account of its admixture of the novel format with the biography of the author himself.

Then came Muhammad Aziz Al-Hababi (1922–1993), a philosopher, poet and writer, who authored the equally famous Moroccan novel *The Elixir of Life* (1974), combining as it does science fiction with myths.

From the current generation, we mention young Moroccans who have been engaged in the writing of science fiction literature, and who also moved into the realms of electronic publishing, such as Abdul Samad Ghazouni. He published his novella *H* in eBook format in 2008. This was in preparation for its eventual publication, on paper, in slightly modified fashion in 2013.

Then there is myself, Mouad Bouyadou; I began my SF writing career in 2009. That is, my career was launched with the electronic publication of my novella "The Elite of the Unit: The Contestants," in the space adventure and military sci-fi genre. The "elite" in question are what the Arab and Muslim world have to offer up against an invading alien force;

they are united in my vision of the future. (It was the first book in a series. Sadly, a computer crash got in the way of the sequel).

Later, in 2012, I published my short story "Who Conquers Us" in an old-fashioned print anthology *The Circle of the Unknown*, with three authors from Egypt. The story is about a man who tells his story from a prison cell. He behaves bizarrely and talks about the people who arrested him … until he fights them in the end, and the truth is revealed.

Then came my anthology *World D-2112*. The book contains five whole novellas as well as five short stories, mostly in the sci-fi adventure genre…. The remaining stories are in the post-apocalypse subgenre as well as detective and spy stories.

I can't tell you why I'm attracted to writing this particular brand of SF…. I didn't grow up reading it by itself and I positively love *all* SF…. I suppose Military SF allows me to invent military tools and weapons systems, and gives me wide space for action and battles…. I try to present alien invasions in an innovative way, not the old and traditional way.

And religion is always a theme with me…. My human characters are Muslims but they vary as persons depending on whether they are heroes or villains. I don't try to force characters into a predetermined mold, though I obviously want the Muslims to win and the Arab world to be united and prosperous.

Did I mention that *World D-2112* won a grant from the Arab Fund for Culture and Arts (Afaq), in the literature category?

Alas, that's as far as the anthology got. It has yet to be "published" due to the postponement of the funded project for a mixture of reasons—personal, technical and administrative.

This is what happens to many writers—not just in Morocco but in the Arab world as a whole. There are always difficulties stemming from the surrounding environment, which is non-supportive of this genre.

A Deadlocked Genre

What SF *needs* is sources of support as well as scientific institutions to fall back on, to answer the sci-fi writer's questions. The state has to chip in, too. The "concerned" agencies have to lend a helping hand by the establishment of competitions and events in support of the dissemination of both science and the culture of science fiction.

What the SF writer, or any writer for that matter, does *not* need is institutions that positively fight authors and prevent them from publishing if they touch on sensitive political topics, like those in power, no matter how indirectly.

As for the role that publishers are supposed to play, they should take into account the financial difficulties us youthful authors face and make allowances to help keep the cost of publishing as low as is humanly possible. On the contrary, they actually *impose* fines on you to cough up cash, no matter how trashy the work in question.

The important thing for them, their only consideration, is profit, even if it means scamming the novice writer….

As if art became a matter of commerce, and an asset to be bought and sold and bartered, not a mission and a lofty task that requires every effort to be exerted on its behalf.

As for the critics, they must abandon the policy of *excluding* science fiction literature, and considering it only literature for children and adolescents. It is time to change their attitudes, because science fiction is deeper and nobler than they can fathom. It addresses the problems and concerns of the individual and society and the world, all in one go.

Without science fiction, humanity would not have reached its scientific, technological, medical, environmental and economic progress. And what the Arab and Islamic nation needs today is this fine art, which ignites the desire for progress and gives hope for a better and prosperous tomorrow.

Abdul Salam Al-Baqali himself argued that the novel was a key instrument in the unification of the Arab world, creating a uniform set of expectations and common set of cultural precepts between the different and disparate Arabic countries.

Without literature the Arabs would remain a set of isolated peoples, and the differences between them will grow and grow with time....

We can add that this genre makes untold millions in the West, in the United States and Western Europe, and that it will sweep towards the Arab world and take captive the Arab reader, once he grows familiar with it and becomes convinced both of its entertainment value and seriousness.

I now live in Switzerland. From my personal experiences, environment is so, so important to writing SF.... There is a culture of science here and people are conscious of the importance of SF. There's even an SF Museum close by!

That helps a lot. I don't wish to contribute to the brain drain in the Arab world, with

In today's Morocco, only the young are propping up the forgotten project of science fiction (courtesy of the artist, Ammar Al-Gamal).

a whole new dimension to it—draining the Arab brain of its science fictional imagination—but what can you do.

I didn't just leave because of the economic situation. There's no freedom of speech, no democracy, and no future for a science fiction writer, which is reason enough to leave, a decision that still weighs heavily on my heart.

I can't believe how I coped as an SF writer back in Morocco. You have to find inspiration for your writings where you find it, and for me, I get it from science books and news, movies, documentaries, and from my own personal experiences and from the world and the universe around us.

A Conclusive Word

The word *khayal* or imagination that we affix with science in the genre does not in any way mean pursuing delusions in a knowledge vacuum, phantasms and sheer nonsense that have no practical bearing on your daily life.

On the contrary, this literature was and is still written by a significant number of scientifically and technically literate authors, not to mention many who are scientists themselves. The list includes the likes of H.G. Wells, Isaac Asimov, Roger Zelazny, Ray Bradbury, and many, many others. All of their writings deal with issues of the utmost importance to humanity and the future, no different in principle than the pressing issues dealt with by social drama and realist literature.

It was Jules Verne and Wells who prepared the Western world for what we see today, the tools of civilization and progress like the telephone and television, and space travel. Today's science fiction writers are preparing today's generations for the future world to come, inspired by current inventions and their impact on the rhythm of life and by extension the impact on the society of the near future.

In conclusion, I hope that other Moroccan authors will appear and sometime soon, contributing to its growth and diversity, putting it on the literary map, and in spite of all the difficulties and obstacles that exist.

Science fiction deserves it. Deserves that you spend all your life savings on it … because it is a distinctive and sophisticated literature, and is an expression of humanity at all times and in all places.

Appendix—The Egyptian Society for Science Fiction

I first learned of the Egyptian society in 2012, through my Egyptian colleague, the writer Yassin Ahmed Said.

He invited me to join the association's page on Facebook. I hesitated at first because I am Moroccan, but asked the founder and director of the group (Dr. Hosam Elzembely), and he responded warmly to the idea. More than that, he was positively enthusiastic that I join—any Arab science fiction writer was more than welcome in the society.

A few days after joining, I was tasked by Dr. Elzembely with a magazine project, a publication specializing in science fiction. I was in charge of designing the magazine cover and coordinating its content.

Sadly, technical and logistical problems got in the way and the project was postponed, indefinitely....

What took its place was the issuing, on a regular basis, of an anthology for the society under the title Shams Al-Ghad, the Sun of Tomorrow.

The series is still going strong to this day. The volume *The Futurists* is dedicated to children's science fiction.

To this day, the Egyptian Society for Science Fiction is still giving, thanks to the efforts and enthusiasm of its founder and its members, contributing to the dissemination of the literature and culture of science fiction not only in Egypt, but in the entire Arab region.

NOTE

1. Translated by Emad El-Din Aysha.

Interview with Ziane Guedim

Prospecting the Next Generation of Algerian SF Writers

EGYPTIAN SOCIETY FOR SCIENCE FICTION

> It is not true that people stop pursuing dreams because they grow old, they
> grow old because they stop pursuing dreams.
> —Gabriel García Márquez (quoted in Welton, 18 April 2014)

ESSF: Your favorite authors growing up? Favorite subgenres?

My eclectic reading habits that reflect on my writing extend well beyond the SF realm and lead me to unexpected literary discoveries.

I like the organic way the real and fantastic mesh in Gabriel García Márquez's work. I like J.D. Salinger's misfit protagonists, James Joyce's dense language. Kafka, Haruki Murakami….

I'm devouring the texts right now of China Miéville, whose speculative fiction defies categorization.

For science fiction, I find myself naturally leaning more towards soft than hard science fiction, and subgenres that favor character development and social commentary, such as magical realism (which lends itself perfectly to science fiction), cyberpunk, post-apocalyptic fiction, the weird, and alternate history. I have tried my hand at some of these genres.

ESSF: Are you a fan of Philip K. Dick, by any chance?

I can't call myself a fan of his but, sure, I've read some of his work. You can't cut across the SF field without stumbling on PKD!

ESSF: Has he exerted any influence on your writing? And has PKD been translated in Algeria?

I don't think so. I haven't read that many of his texts, short stories for the most part. I remember how I discovered PKD. It was via the 1980s classic film *Blade Runner*. When I learned that the movie was based on the novel *Do Androids Dream of Electric Sheep?* I read it, and liked it more than the cinematic adaptation. I don't know of any PKD translation in Algeria. I just read him in his original language.

ESSF: Did you grow up reading comics by any chance? Is there a large comic book readership in Algeria and are there any local brands of Algerian superhero, for instance?

I grew up "listening" to stories, mom's stories, which have speculative bits and all.

Maybe that's what awoke the storyteller in me. Some protagonists in these stories had to overcome, foes, ogres, and monsters, and triumph against other insurmountable odds. So, they can be regarded as superheroes. Comics weren't widely available to a child living in a small town, but I read some. I remember reading issues of *Spiff and Hercules*, human-like dog and cat respectively. There were a few Algerian magazines aimed at children and storybooks, about folklore characters. Anime series and cartoons were more accessible. Spiderman was my favorite superhero. I'm still a fan, but of comic movies, especially the Marvel Cinematic Universe.

ESSF: How long have you been writing SF? Do you intend to make a career out of it? Do you write in any other genres?

First and foremost, I want to make a career as an established and recognized writer and I'm inching my way toward this goal. Having said that, I don't want to put myself in any genre's pigeonhole.

I started writing general fiction, which I think can be considered "mainstream" in Algeria and maybe the Arab world as a whole. Then, speculative elements, including SF, started popping up out of the blue, and I just readily succumbed to the lure and went with the flow. For example, I wanted to write a story about Algerian history, the unavoidable era of French colonization, which left indelible scars. What would I say that hasn't been said already? I don't want to rehash "history"! In this story, under the working title "*Nostalgeria*," history shakes its cobwebs off. It sheds that "read-only" tag and becomes more malleable. Set in the 1930s, this alternate history story—whose narrative is woven around two girls, an Algerian and a Norwegian—makes up the longest chapter in the book. *Nostalgeria* was also the most challenging piece I've ever done, writing-wise.

ESSF: Give us the lowdown on your short story "A Slice of Heaven" in The Worlds of Science Fiction, Fantasy and Horror Volume II *(2017)? You're the only Arab in the whole book. How does that make you feel?*

"A Slice of Heaven" appeared first in French under the title *Un soupçon de paradis*. It was one of ten short stories selected by *The Institut Français* in Algiers after running a nationwide literary contest. This anthology book was published back in 2015, coinciding with the book fair of Algiers of that year.

This contest was centered around the theme of "environment," which happens to be one of my pet topics, and the stories had to be "fantastic," which is a broad speculative umbrella. My winning text was the story of an Algerian-born American citizen, named Al, which works as both a short form for his Arab name "Ali" and a common American name, Al. The construction of the name itself, Al(i), refers to how this character is torn between a past he can't come to terms with and a present he doesn't have a firm grasp on.

But there's a catch. I first started writing the story in English, before I even heard of that contest, and I also didn't get to finish it. When the contest was announced, I took it from there and wrapped it up, in French. Then, another literary contest, in English this time, came my way and it just happened that "A Slice of Heaven" fits. I sent it, and a couple of days later the editor, who's from Australia, contacted me offering to buy it. I sold it, and the book was published. As to your question about me being the only Arab, I think there are a lot of capable Arab writers. It did feel great, though! I proved to myself first that I can do it. It also got me some exposure; after all this is what let you know that I exist and here we are!

On a related note, the rights of "A Slice of Heaven" have reverted back to me. A re-edited version will be a chapter in my coming novel, with some twists.

ESSF: Is religion a theme in your writing? What about politics?

There may be no way around religion, both in real life and fiction, especially with its political lining, and more so in the Arab world. But I'm neither a political militant nor a preacher. I've never adhered to any political party, or even a fraternity at college, and I've never voted before. I might be more of an anarchist than I thought. And, let's put it this way, I always have a bone to pick with "stupid believers."

As a writer, I don't approach religion or politics as a theme to be hammered home, or as the focal point around which the plot and characters revolve. It's the other way around—politics and religion could be ingredients in the narrative's recipe.

ESSF: Have you published in "Arabic" before? Is it easier working with foreign English-language publishers?

I do write in Arabic, but no, no published pieces yet, and not for lack of trying. As you certainly know, getting published, and getting paid, as a writer in itself is at least challenging anywhere in the world, but it is unfortunately harder to be a writer in the Arab world, Algeria included. Compared to English, for example, or even French, there are far fewer publishing opportunities in Arabic. That's why I made the conscious choice to seek publishing, first in French because there's a substantial readership in that language in Algeria, then in English that has the world's doors wide open. I have to make a name for myself, then I'll write in any language and do as I please.

An example to illustrate my point, while we're speaking of it, is my story "A Slice of Heaven." Robert Stephenson, the editor of the anthology, was prompt to reply (as in the same day I submitted my text) and also to pay me. I think most Arab editors, no matter which language they work on, fail to handle both tasks. However, I'm sure many professional and passionate Arab publishers are out there.

ESSF: Are you a member of any sci-fi associations or book clubs in Algeria?

I'm working toward getting the SFWA membership (Science Fiction & Fantasy Writers of America); I just need some more published material in English. I will also get the professional artist card, hopefully soon, from the Algerian National Council of Arts and Letters. Both memberships come with some perks that'll help me boost my writing career.

ESSF: Do Algerians only read SF written in France, or also in other Arab countries, like Egypt and Morocco? And how old, or young, is the readership?

I don't have access to any stats in that regard, and I can only make some guesses on this one. I assume most of the SF readership in Algeria is Francophone because it's perhaps more available. However, other than the Arabophone, there's growing Anglophone readership, which is a healthy sign.

ESSF: Is there a large female readership of science fiction or fantasy in Algeria?

I think female readers in Algeria are more, let's say, "engaged" than their male counterparts. You get a feel of this in libraries and book fairs. By nature, women are more receptive to speculative literature.

ESSF: Is "dystopia" popular in Algeria? The novels 2084: The Tale of the Last Arab *by Waciny Laredj, and* 2084: The End of the World *by Boualem Sansal spring to mind. Is the dating "2084" a reference to George Orwell's* 1984?

Yes, both of them bear a reference to George Orwell's novel. Waciny Laredj said he wanted to project himself a century into the future (1984–2084), and was quoted as saying he was surprised by the resemblance between his book and Sansal's.

However, the similarity stops here. While Waciny wanted it to be somehow a wake-up call for Arabs to take matters into their own hands, Sansal, on the other hand, went pretty much the opposite way. There's a rising dangerous trend in France, and in Europe in general, that of Islamophobia, and some writers, like Sansal and Michel Houellebecq, want to cash in on this. Houellebecq's novel *Submission* is set in 2022 when an Islamic party wins the French presidential elections. You may remember the Charlie Hebdo shooting that left 12 people dead. Some reports linked the terrorist attack with the cover the journal released days before, and which featured Houellebecq saying he'll be fasting during Ramadan 2022, the year his novel is set in.

Dystopia as a literary genre is enjoying popularity all over the world, especially in the U.S. where there's been a surge in dystopian fiction sales, including Orwell's own *1984*, after the election of Donald Trump. The reason may be simple: the world feels a tad dark already, and dystopian books offer an escape into darker worlds. If many stories, like those of Laredj and Sansal, can be categorized as dystopias, each hinges on different mechanisms and offers its own takeaways that it wants you to have.

ESSF: Tell us something about Edgy Labs.[1] The range of topics is quite broad—black holes, water conservation, surgery, cryptocurrency. Is the promotion of scientific "literacy" in the Arab world one of your prime objectives?

Let me first start by expressing my regards to the guys over at Edgy, my fellow writers, the editors, and the development team, especially Alexander De Ridder, the co-founder, and Krista Grace Morris, our editor-in-chief. Edgy Labs LLC is a company based in Texas (USA) that runs a blog and provides SEO services, Artificial Intelligence and Virtual Reality solutions, among other things. I did a lot of writing gigs as a freelance writer before, but with Edgy Labs, I found a sound platform with adequate resources and continuous support. I get to say what I have to say about some hot topics and issues, looked at using a scientific prism. You find the gamut of my articles running from soft to hard science facts, which brings a needed counterbalance to my fiction phantasmagorias.

I like the scientific spirit and the essence of science. I firmly believe that the "decivilization" of the Arabo-Islamic world, which once served as a bright beacon for humanity, is due to us abandoning the first part of the equation, the Arab, i.e., the thinker, the scientist, the artist ... the human. We just kept a "loose" grip on the second part, religion, and we see where things ended up. That "change the world" spirit is not what drives me, but would my writing make any difference? Here's hoping.

ESSF: Is the "blogosphere" in Algeria geared towards literature, science fiction included? Do regular media outlets—newspapers, TV channels—pay any attention to either SF authors or young authors like yourself?

As far as I know, there are no publishers in Algeria specialized in speculative fiction. They mostly pick works that speak to their heart and they deem fit, regardless of the genre. The same goes for any newspapers, literary magazines or ezines.

ESSF: Is science fiction popular on television and in the movie theaters in Algeria? Is Japanese animie known there?

Yes, I guess so, but these are more of a niche market. Japanese mangas and animes were popular when I was a kid and they gained even more popularity since. An international comic strip festival takes place in Algiers every year.

ESSF: Have there been any attempts to make SF movies in Algeria?

Not that I know of. But there could be as I don't keep up to date with local cinema. But I think SF remains out of reach of all Arab filmmakers for a simple reason. Not that they lack creativity or skills. I think it's mostly because they lack funding, money! In general, SF, especially hard SF, and other speculative fiction films need a varying amount of special effects that are costly and technically challenging. Writing a scene describing the landing of an alien spacecraft is something, visually rendering it in a proper way will be a whole new ball game.

ESSF: Finally, a speculative question. If you were the minister of education or culture in Algeria, how would you promote science fiction in your country?

First, this would be a laudable undertaking, no matter who tackles it. Science fiction literature is inspiring; it provokes a sense of wonder, and stirs up curiosity and existential questioning. And not only that, it also helps us envision the future and think out of the box. Promoting science fiction passes through classrooms; it's there that you'll find future readers and writers. Right off the bat; reading classes, bringing guest readers, launching regular writing contests, awarding prizes, recognizing talents, encouraging children to keep daily journals so they develop the habit of writing, … there's a lot that can be done. Then over time, things will just take their natural course.

NOTE

1. For a profile of Ziane Guedim at Edgy Labs, please follow this link: https://edgy.app/author/zed.

WORK CITED

Welton, Emma. (18 April 2014). "Gabriel García Márquez in quotes." *The Guardian*. https://www.theguardian.com/books/2014/apr/18/gabriel-garcia-marquez-in-quotes.

Science Fiction Literature

A Very Personal Journey[1]

TALEB OMRAN

> Three thousand stadia from the earth to the moon,—the first station. From thence to the sun about five hundred parasangs…. Marvel not, my comrade, if I appear talking to you on super-terrestrial and aerial topics. The long and the short of the matter is that I am running over the order of a Journey I have lately made…. I have travelled in the stars.
>
> —Lucian of Samosa

There is no doubt that the mind that provides humanity with its creative energy and the ability to fly in the heavens, sometimes in the realm of pure fantasy, is what raises the status of the human being between all living beings…. Through the imagination humankind can journey in the universe and bathe in the ether, and fly among worlds invisible…. Imagination for the human is his own magical world, circling the universe until he can almost hear the sound of atoms colliding with their electrons and nuclei, till he can almost feel the chill of the most distant, indefatigable planets, or the heat of the closest planets to a star….

The unique power of the mind and its ability to imagine is what gives birth to geniuses and the great in history. Each word that is written down has its own special magic, its own unique impact…. Sometimes we can feel that great vitality, and at other times we only feel its superficiality and triviality from works of the imagination. It is the imagination of the filmmaker, the playwright or radio director who determines the magnificence of a movie or play or radio drama…. Depending on his creativity, he can transfer his imagination to the spectator or the listener, the events as his mind was able to contemplate them, within a stream of expressive images, or sensational sound effects … which determine the depth of his imagination and his success in influencing the spectator or the listener….

When a child builds a sand castle, it is his imagination that portrays it as a real building to him, to the point that he can see himself living within it in his own little worlds. The girl imagines that her doll is in fact a beautiful girl who hears her messages and obeys her demands.

The imagination of the young man in love, his mad longing for his beloved sweetheart, catapults him into a world that is all happiness and passion…. Life is short, and not to be measured by the age of the universe. From the moment of the formation of the fetus and its growth and transformation from child to young man to an aged elder to a person's

There is still room for Arab-Islamic civilization in outer space, once dusted off and rebooted for the future (courtesy of the artist, Yahya Salah Abul Ghait).

death and his burial … it is all the mere blinking of an eye to the universe, of no significance whatsoever.…

As long as we have reason, and we possess our infinite powers of imagining, how can we combine the two and imagine the future within our rational faculties?

By deploying our imagination we can picture ourselves living years into the future, but with the help of reason this can extend this indefinitely into the future, even if we are separated from this future by decades or centuries or even millennia.

Within the confines of these sometimes exhausting questions, science fiction tries to find an outlet for us. So how can we delimit the science-related imagination?

All too simply we can say that the imagination can move across the horizons of time on the wings of a dream that is reinforced by the accumulated knowledge of science. More often than not knocking on the door of the future involves making open-ended prophecies; science entering the world and extracting from the imagination of the author a stream of events that will pull you into the distant future, or the faraway past.

In all cases, it ignites the mind and dazzles you. The mere association between science and fantasy is framed and coherent, and whosoever writes in this field cannot succeed without a scientific background using that knowledge to weave the events of his stories and novels.

To highlight the importance of science fiction it suffices to mention Isaac Asimov and his argument that of every 100 readers of science fiction, at least 50 are interested in science and keep up to speed with the latest discoveries. And out of those 50, at least 25 are children dedicated to pursuing a career in science, and at least 10 of those will go into higher education—and out of that 10 at least one scientist will rise…. Therefore, out of 100 children who read science fiction, America will be rewarded by at least one scientist … quite a larger proportion….

Perhaps the era we are living in is the age of technology, because technology enters into everything and is used by man in all his works, even in the management of the household and the construction of the house itself, and in the various fields of life….

With scientific development, this technology has turned noisy machines into quiet machines. We can "feel" their movement without being disturbed by the sounds that in the past caused us a chronic headache…. With the increasing reliance on silent computerization that programs everything in life around us….

Science Fiction and My Stubborn Beginnings

It goes without saying that with the species of being called man, your childhood and everything that happens in it are important factors in shaping one's mature personality.

For sure, my childhood was different. My father emigrated to seek out a living and left for us many long years alone with my mother. We were two girls and two boys, and as fate would have it, my mother became ill and my elder sister had to take on many of the responsibilities of adulthood when she was only 14 years of age. We lived the life of orphans while there was no one there to pity us…. My uncles were, most of them, merchants and they were not concerned with how we were living, although my father's money continued to flow into their pockets….

That period of my life, and I had not reached the age of twelve, pushed me into the circle of reading until the book became my permanent companion. I was especially interested in adventure books, works about space and history books that investigate previous civilizations.

Additionally, there was poetry. I began to delve into all modes of Arabic poetry, classical and modern, and thankfully our Arabic teacher organized a weekly session for poetry and creative writing. Unlike my colleagues, I did not waste my time copying other people's works. I wrote my own and this prompted our teacher to proclaim, in front of everyone: "You are the only who writes creativity and in the future you will have a place of distinction between the writers."

Of course, such compliments were no more than pep talk to encourage me to continue writing, and of course I did not stop it, writing having become an important part of my world. This prompted me to send my first article on the universe to the *Military Magazine*, a serious monthly publication concerned with scientific and military affairs…. I was surprised afterwards to find it accepted and published very speedily, without too much editorial correspondence … and so began my trip with publication early on in life, when I had not yet reached the age of eighteen….

My articles followed, especially after I moved to the capital in pursuit of my studies at the University of Damascus, writing in university magazines and newspapers, until the university theater performance of my first play—*The Deluge of Blood*…. Then I was put in charge of editing the scientific page of the *Baath* newspaper. That is when I began writing science fiction stories in earnest and I received the approval of a number of critics…. This is when I encountered the distinguished poet and playwright Mohammed Al-Maghout, then editor-in-chief of the *Police* magazine, a popular periodical. I reluctantly handed him one of my SF stories and was surprised to find him publishing it. Shortly after he told me: "You are singing in a world where there are no authors like you in our country. I am sure you will soon be presenting us with outstanding creations."

I heard the same thing from the great playwright Saad Allah Wanus, which is what drove me in 1976 to hand over my very first book to the Ministry of Culture, hoping it would be accepted among its many prestigious publications…. About a month later the Committee of Authorship and Translation got back to me. I walked into the office of Dr. Najah Al-Attar, the head of the committee, who later became the Minister of Culture and then Vice President of the Republic…. Nervously I asked about the book, and I found Dr. Najah asking me if I was the father of the author Taleb Omran!

She liked the book very much and said that the Ministry had approved it and placed a reasonably high price tag on it too. Then I told her who I was and she got up and shook my hand, saying: "You're a young man and you have many years of contributing ahead of you. And I'm pretty sure they will be years of great creativity." She added, "I have been keeping up to speed with your science fiction stories and I see a bright future ahead of you."

I do not deny that publishing my first anthologies was fraught with terrible problems, especially since I approached the famous publishing houses in Syria, the most important of which were the Ministry of Culture and the Union of Arab Writers. If it were not for the help of Antony Makdessi in the Ministry of Culture, and Dr. Hossam Al-Khatib and Zakaria Tamer in the Writers' Union, I may not have succeeded.

One noteworthy incident involved the rejection of my anthology, *There Are No Poor on the Moon*, by one of the referees passing judgment on the work. Thank heavens, Dr. Hossam Khatib, who was a member of the Executive Office of the Arab Writers Union, was also a referee. He explained at great length that this was a new breed of literature for us as Arabs, admittedly, but that it was important literature nonetheless. He insisted that this collection was distinguished.

The author who had rejected my works stuck to his guns, charging that my book was political. Dr. Khatib replied that it was not, with its exclusive focus on the future and not the present.

At his insistence the collection was finally published … to great accolades and popularity.

Zakaria Tamer also promoted my novel *Those Who Passed Behind the Sun*, sending it to the printing press among the other works of the Arab Writers' Union, and also despite the objections of many of the referees.

It was a set of circumstances I suffered because publishing houses were simply not accustomed to the idea of publishing stories and novels of science fiction. There wasn't a single person in the publishing industry in Syria willing to venture and publish this type of literature….

Signposts Along the Path of My Creative Career

Science fiction, in the vast majority of its examples, takes the future as its central focus, with all its implications, discussing human aspirations, problems and concerns in the years, decades or even centuries to come.

It is a literature that has a direct and intimate relationship with science and its future prospects.... And the authors of SF are divided into two different categories:

1. a class that focuses on fantasy, with space monsters and invaders from other worlds and adventures like the fairy tales and myths of yonder, merely using science to fabricate misleading exaggerations that have nothing to do with humankind and the accumulated concerns of his future.

2. a class concerned with the strategies of scientific development and the prospects of scientific advance and the direct relationship of this to people's lives and concerns ... and dreams, and even diseases and disasters....

Such human concerns were the chief focus of all of the writings that began to pour forth from my pen and I will begin by speaking about some of them:

Hard Times: a novel about a trip to a distant planet, only for the pioneers to return to earth to find that an atomic war has taken place and humanity is in its worst crisis.... The novel ends with the hero standing in front of a flower bed that has defied the destruction and germinated....

On a Planet Like Earth: a novel about a trip to a planet like Earth, whose inhabitants have evolved into a fully integrated social system that works, builds and develops. It is a system that cares about the creatures on that planet, their worries and concerns, how its inhabitants love and form families, how they cope with illness and death....

Pioneers of the Red Planet: talks about a trip to Mars, the pioneers heading there encounter the remains of a former civilization scattered on the asteroid of Uros that explain the destruction of the fifth planet lying between Mars and Jupiter, where nuclear weapons were stockpiled and a devastating war broke out to explode the planet into fragments remaining in the expanse between the two planets....

The Fifth Dimension: talking about man's hidden powers, and the future of bio-energy, in solving human problems and treating diseases....

The Young Learners and their Journeys of Explorations: about how the Arabs discovered America in the 10th century AD. A perspective on history based on the words of famous historians, but written in a science fictional setting.... With time-travel and time tunnels....

I have presented many works but the futuristic novel in its rational form charged with human concerns was especially clear in my following novel.

The Dark Times: a novel about a conceptualization of a century, the horrific features of which began with the events of September 11th, stretching from the freemasons to the entry into the terrifying world of tomorrow to the time of programmed rodents and epidemics and worms of death ... stations where I talk about the times that our world subsists in today, with the rising tide of ruin....

In *The Dark Times*, I present what is happening in the world now and what could happen in the coming years, until the year 2040. Where the second phase of events continue until the end of the century....

From wars of utter destruction to Masonic societies that control the world, and then to Guantanamo, where prisoners are experimented on ... with cloning, organ theft, viral infections and transplant operations....

I followed up on many of these concerns in my new novel *Mezoun*, an epic novel that also talks about the future, in its final chapter (the tunnel of future events) about what could happen to the region thanks to the waves of pollution and ruin that could occur if everyone does not rush to save what can be saved.

*   *   *

Science fiction draws a strategy for the future of humankind. Suffice it to say that at the end of this brief talk in the sea of winged fantasies, that those who determine the world's policies for the coming years will rely heavily on the authors of science fiction.... Such authors reveal in reading *into* the future, relying as they do on scientific logic and its infinite possibilities in the coming years....

NOTE

1. Translated by Emad El-Din Aysha.

Interview with Jeremy Szal

Global and Local Imperatives
in Lebanese Science Fiction

EGYPTIAN SOCIETY FOR SCIENCE FICTION

This place where you are right now
God circled on a map for you.

Wherever your eyes and arms and heart can move
against the earth and the sky,

The Beloved has bowed there—
knowing you were coming.
—Hafez

ESSF: Please give us the ABC of your background and education? How did your parents end up in Australia? What drew you to SF, and how many languages do you speak?

My mother was born in Australia, but her parents immigrated from Lebanon a few years before that. My father was born in Poland and spent most of his childhood behind the Iron Curtain. There's a lot of history there, but the highlight is him escaping to Germany when he was only 16, and then coming to Australia a dozen years later. So with my feet planted in very different continents and backgrounds and cultures, I'm very much a mongrel and happy to be one. I do speak German as well as English, although my Polish and Arabic are pretty abysmal.

My mother is a teacher, so I was homeschooled for most of my childhood education (along with my sister), but spent my final few years in school. It was my mother who got me interested in reading—I still remember her giving me Enid Blyton books to read during holidays when I was a boy. When I devoured them all, she'd take me to the bookstore and help me pick out anything that struck my fancy. I didn't differentiate between genres back then. I liked stories that were dark, fast-paced and had a strong element of mystery and suspense, so that's what I read. I read everything I could by Michael Grant, Eoin Colfer, Stephen King and George R.R. Martin. It wasn't until I was 14 or so that I found myself enjoying the fantastical and the weird so much more. I got a much greater kick out of anything set in space or an alternative reality, and loved anything to do with aliens, monsters, beasts, futuristic megacities or starships. So, with my mother's help, I stumbled on the likes of Iain M. Banks, Karen Traviss, Brandon Sanderson and Joe Abercrombie. I've never looked back, and today I'm writing my own SF stories.

To summarize: I blame my mother for the whole thing.

ESSF: You grew up in the mid–1990s and early 21st century. Were books, or television and cinema more important to your literary upbringing?

Television, not so much. But video games and books were pretty fundamental to my literary upbringing. I know a lot of people tend to scoff at the notions of video games being a medium for self-expression and exploring ideas, but I'll never forget the summer months I spent exploring vast fields and searching mountain caves in *Skyrim*, or juggling between moral decisions in *The Witcher 2*, or getting a heavy dose of cyberpunk and (slightly terrifying) government conspiracies in *Deus Ex: Human Revolution*. Where I was already reading books, it was the interactive nature of those video games that showed me the full scope and narrative potential of speculative fiction.

ESSF: In your own online bio you say you were born in the Australian outback, and quite literally raised by dingoes.[1]

I wasn't raised by dingoes, as my parents would probably be quick to point out. That's just my very Australia, very self-depreciating humor shining through. Our country is one big British prison. Making fun of ourselves is basically a national requirement.

ESSF: Transhumanism, in your stories "Walls of Nigeria" and "Dead Man Walking" where you have biotech spacesuits and body-armor that fuses with the flesh or plays around with brain chemistry, as in "Inkskinned." What attracts you to such subgenres and what themes do you explore?

I love a bit of horror in my fiction, and there's nothing quite as intimate and frightening as body-horror, because the source of the horror doesn't come from an external source. It's internal. It's, quite literally, a part of who you are. There's no escaping it, just like there's no escaping your own skin. The body is an organism that's attractive on so many levels—physiological, sexual, psychological, biochemical—so to me it's the ultimate and most personal tampering tool.

And in a world where we're all so close and intimate with our technology, I've found exploring the use of technology to merge and tamper with the body and brain in horrific ways to be a literary niche that's very relevant (and very fun) to write in. We're seeing people spending so much

A transhuman body armor suit that lives and breathes as it turns its host into a lifeless machine. Is this what the future has in store for us? (courtesy of the artist, Ammar Al-Gamal).

time on their phones they might as well be glued to their hands, and we're hearing about bio-implanted tattoos, chip-implants that could render keys obsolete.

I choose body suits and power armor because they're things that have always attracted me to science fiction. Being obsessed with technology and gadgetry, I love the idea of having my own hyperadvanced power suit, literally wearing and being encased in a personal piece of technology. So, of course, I had to figure out how this could go wrong. I got the armor to grow into human flesh, meshing through wounds and stripping out organs, not just because it's an incredibly creepy image, but because it tells us so much about the relationship between humans and technology, between metal and steel and flesh and body chemicals. Armor is awesome, and I love the idea of it, but I wanted to show the flipside of it, too.

In everything I write, I try to provoke the reader on a visceral level. I want to display something that causes a reaction, that penetrates consciousness. Whether that's grinning, cringing, or squirming, although I'd be very happy with all three. I'm not interested in passive readership—I want to engage with the reader on a deeper level. Writing fiction that makes the skin crawl is just my favorite method of doing so.

ESSF: Is the war on terror a concern in your stories? Terrorism is explicitly mentioned in Inkskinned?

Yes and no. I don't go out of my way to write about terrorism or the war on terror. I am interested in writing about mass-scale conflict, and about how the individuals involved are impacted on a personal level. Terrorism is just another source of conflict, albeit one that's unfortunately very present in modern society.

"Inkskinned" is very much a story about two civilizations clashing, and the continued conflict that occurs when the war is supposed to be over and these two groups have to learn to live with each other. One side has strong reservations from allowing their former enemies to live among them, and the other side has to deal with the prejudice and cultural adjustment as they move into new territory. "Inkskinned" isn't an allegory or a metaphor; I don't write stories that are grandiose parables that exist to tell another story between the lines. That feels very cloying to me. "Inskinned" is a story at face value about the conflict between humans and aliens. But you only need to look at the hot-button issues orbiting immigration and refugees to see where I got inspiration to say certain things.

ESSF: On the topic of names, you're also very fond of using Biblical and Quranic names. In your story "These Six Walls" you have a character named "Mikael" and in "The dataSultan" you have robots called "Djinn."[2] Do you feel more comfortable using such cultural references, or are you trying to create a new brand of SF and introduce this cultural background to an international audience?

When I write stories set in a specific culture, I want the reader to be fully immersed in this culture, as you would with any other world-building. "The dataSultan" was set in the Middle East, so everything about it, especially the technology, had to be rooted in Middle-Eastern culture. It wouldn't have made sense (or terribly interesting) for the AIs to be simple bundles of conscious data. They were created in the Middle East, so it made sense to fashion the AIs after Islamic mythological beings. It makes more sense from a cultural perspective, and if it lends international readers a deeper insight into another culture, that's even better.

ESSF: You're also very cosmopolitan in your stories. Is this second nature to you, coming from such a polyglot society as Australia, or is it on account of having Lebanese blood in your veins?

We ask because you mention Phoenician trading vessels in "DataSultan," while the coffee shop in the opening scene has a gun-slinging Wild West feel to it, the saloon motif which is common is Australian literature too. And Alexander the Great was the man who united East and West during his glorious if brief reign; the hero is called Sikandar.

More so growing up in Australia, rather than being Lebanese. I have a massive extended family from backgrounds in over a dozen countries, and I've grown up in a very ethnically multicolored city and had access to foods, languages and cultures from all over the globe. It's little wonder that the same diversity and cultural assimilation has bled into my work. I've written a novel called *Stormblood* that takes place on an asteroid that's been hollowed out and colonized and divided into hundreds of floors and subsections, each with their own cultural setting and background, from Chinatown to a Latin quarter to a modern European metropolis. It's incredibly fun to take what I've known all my life and hyper-expand it into a wide-screen, exaggerated setting.

I'm not a futurist, though, and I'm not attempting to predict which planets humanity will colonize in the future or how they'll do it. I'm more interested in taking these ideas and settings and combining them together in extravagant ways to see what comes out of them.

ESSF: One of our contributors, Sami Ahmad Khan, complained that in the movies alien invasions always seem to happen in the U.S. and not the Third World. Is this a point you set out to rectify in "Walls of Nigeria"?

Very much so. Whenever the aliens come to visit in the movies, it's always over the White House, or some other major American landmark. But the aliens have just as much chance of landing in Nigeria, or any other country, as they do in America. It's what impressed me so much with *District 9*, and gave the film such an authentic feel. I wouldn't say I went out to "rectify" anything with my story, but I wanted to write an alien invasion story through a Nigerian lens, and have had a number of Nigerian readers write in to say how pleased they were to see a story set in their country, and how much it's inspired them. I couldn't be happier with a response like that.

ESSF: The theme of friendship is clearly important in your stories, and also defiance—characters going up against the authorities to save friends. Is this a personal preference or a common trait in Australian literature and society?

Purely a personal preference! I'm not really interested in reading or writing stories about the lone hero, the singular, isolated and tortured individual who will batter his way through half the world because of honor or riches or duty. There's certainly a place for those stories and readers for them, too. But for me, it's characters who make or break stories. Characters and their relationships and interactions with their friends and loved ones and how these relationships evolve and change over the course of the journey. I want to care about the characters I read about on an intimate level, and so I write characters who are friends, friends who are willing to butcher their way through hell and back to save each other. It's much more interesting than people saving the world because they don't want to die (presumably, none of us do). There's so much you can play with, with friends bonding over traumatic experiences or drifting apart over a major disagreement, or just have fun making their way through epic set-pieces. It adds an intimate level that, for me, is missing from the majority of classic science-fiction.

ESSF: Colonization and human "occupations" of other people's lands is a frequent occurrence in your stories, most explicitly in "Dead Men Walking" and also in "Ark of Bones" (with drones and paramilitaries and secret extermination plans). Is the "No-Safe Zone" in "These Six Walls" a reference to the Green Zone in Iraq?

I didn't draw my influence from a specific event or situation—I tend to look at multiple examples and steal bits and pieces from all over the place. It's healthier to have lots of diverse influences for the sake of literary fertilization, and it prevents my work from becoming direct allegories. The Green Zone in Iraq was part of the influence but not the sole one.

For "Dead Men Walking," I looked at colonial occupation and the process of foreign, hostile troops on alien soil and the hostilities that would arise on both sides. "Ark of Bones" was very much inspired by *District 9* and the relationships between humans and aliens, two sides that are meant to be enemies. It was important to me that the human protagonist and the alien protagonist were good friends, that at the end of the day, their friendship triumphed over any barrier or walls or colonial occupation. I'm quite a believer of the human spirit enduring despite all odds, and work it into my fiction whenever possible.

ESSF: The gangster who hunts down and tries to slice off Sikandar's fingers. He's a bad man but he also has a justifiable grudge against the dataSultan, because of the robots that ran riot in Istanbul, killing some of his loved ones. Is the gangster and the "punishment" he meets out to Sikandar a reference to ISIS, by any chance?

The torture techniques spelled out in the story are reminiscent of Abu Ghraib. (Sensory deprivation is used in your story "Inkskinned" and you talk about a bomb-shelter destroyed by the Kichi, which also sounds like the famous shelter destroyed by American smart-bombs during the Gulf War).

Again, I tend not to go for a singular influence so my stories don't become direct allegories or metaphors. I soaked up what I could from looking at torture techniques used by kidnappers and gangsters, both in the real world and in fiction, although I didn't seek out these examples; they tended to just come up in what I was reading (obviously, I tend to read darker stuff).

I'm more interested in what the torture and use of pain says about the one doling it out, rather than what it signifies. The gangsters in "DataSultan" were full of rage and uncontrolled violence, so they wanted to do something fast and brutal, to dole out pain as efficiently as possible. So poor Sikandar got strapped to a chair and his fingers cut off. Whereas in "Inkskinned," the Atlas' enemies were crueler, more sadistic, more interested in torturing him psychologically over a long period of time, of which they had plenty, so they locked him in a sensation deprivation room for a year, knowing his own mind would torture him to a deeper level than any physical kind could. It says a lot about what the characters are able to endure, how they survive, and how they change when they come out the other side.

Of course, it's also fun to mistreat characters. Being an author means I get to indulge in this very frequently.

ESSF: The chief Djinn-robot is named Shamhurish. Is that a name from The 1001 Nights?

Very much so! You're the first ones to catch that reference. It's been out for more than a year, and no one's called me on what's decidedly a very weird and specific name for an AI. I unapologetically stole that name from 1001 Nights.

ESSF: Would you say that one of the advantages that Lebanese SF writers, and Lebanese authors in general, have is how international they are? Different languages, cultures and literary traditions to draw on. There's Amal Al-Mohtar and Saladin Ahmed in North America, Sara Saab in England, Kassem Kassem in Lebanon itself, and you in Australia.

There's more of us than people realize, yes. Being in Australia has allowed me to snatch pieces of inspiration from all over the place, especially with so much fiction being readily available, and the push for more diversity has broadened the genre's horizons.

ESSF: How "connected" are Lebanese expatriate writers and foreign-born Lebanese authors? Do they keep tabs on each other, compete and cooperate, pool resources?

How connected are they to the literary scene in Lebanon itself? Are there any online forums and directories for Lebanese SF and fantasy?

Unusually, no. At least not that I'm aware of. I was speaking with Amal Al-Mohtar at last year's WorldCon in Helsinki, Finland, where she said it was disappointing that there's no online community for Middle Eastern or Lebanese authors, not like there is with Asian or African writers. There's plenty of cultural groups that are regularly in each other's circles and have opportunities to get special, personal insight into the specifics of their niche. But there's no such thing with Middle-Eastern authors. I find that disappointing, too.

ESSF: Two of the famous anthologies you contributed to are Shades Within Us: Tales of Migrations and Fractured Borders, *and the award-winning* People of Colo(u)r Destroy Science Fiction.

Do you consider yourself a "citizen of the world"?

Absolutely. I've lived in both Thailand and Austria, speak two languages, visited five continents, have cultural backgrounds with over half a dozen nations, and my family speaks eight languages between them. I'm Australian, first and foremost, but I'm less interested in drawing lines at borders than I am in investing in what the whole world has to offer.

I find it amusing in the most dour sense that so many Americans are interested in diversifying and reaching out to more cultures, while educating everyone else to do so, and yet most of them couldn't tell you the first thing about the features of a foreign country. Or, in some cases, find them on a map. I find that very odd.

ESSF: It's great to see East Asia finding its voice in the world of genre literature, and Australia playing a part of this, being such a diverse country. One of our contributors is Kristine Ong Muslim, who also contributed to People of Colo(u)r Destroy Science Fiction. *Do you know Timothy James Dimacali, another upstart Filipino SF author?[3]*

I don't know James Dimacali personally, but I've certainly heard about his work and his excellent science reports. The world could use more writers like him.

ESSF: Are such cultural and geographic groupings the way to get recognized on the international scene? Would you encourage Arab and Muslim authors and publishers to do the same, and publish in English?

Publishing in English is pretty much essential, if you want to get noticed on an international scale. If you're not stationed in the U.S., or even the UK, it's very hard to make the right connections and get your work in front of the right people. But if you can write a good story, and are good with networking, geographical barriers should matter a lot less.

ESSF: You've also distinguished yourself as an Editor of the StarShipSofa *podcast for the past four years, working with a number of genre legends, including George R.R. Martin and the late Harlan Ellison. Please fill us in on the details.*

As the editor, I make all decisions on the fiction. The type of stories we play, the authors we have on the show, the length of the stories, everything. This means I (along with my assistant, Ralph Ambrose) read the unsolicited stories sent through slush.

I'm also in charge of soliciting stories from authors and sorting out audio rights. I also collect the story files, the author's bio, the narrator's bio, the place of publication, the links to all the necessary websites, and put them in the show notes. There's a lot of organizing, a lot of file sorting and formatting involved. I also have the job of assigning the stories to narrators. They do all the actual audio producing, but it's my task to decide which narrators are appropriate for which stories, their styles, their voice types, preferences, gender, how long they're going to take, the sort of background that they have, everything. You could just easily toss any given story to any narrator, but you won't get the same quality if you carefully consider each narrator on a case-by-case basis. So I make sure to make the best pair that I possibly can with each given story.

I also edit authors' work on occasion. I throw out my own personal voice and try to inhabit the author's voice, style and approach as much as possible. I'd write some of these stories completely differently, so I make sure I leave my own personal approach at the door and work to bring out the best of the author's work.

In the case of George R.R. Martin, we published his story "The Men of Greywater Station" in audio. Originally published in the 1970s, the story has been out of print for almost forty years and had never appeared online before. When I reached out to Mr. Martin, I wasn't expecting him to even answer the email, let alone give us the green light to produce an audio adaptation of his story. This man is essentially a celebrity in both fandom and mainstream media. But not only did he respond, he gave us the audio rights to play his story. Keep in mind this was all happening while Season 5 of *Game of Thrones* was playing on HBO—and came under heavy fire for controversy. I'm still shocked he responded at all. Then we discovered that "The Men of Greywater Station" was not actually available to grab online. I went back to Mr. Martin and he offered to post a carbon copy of the story by snail mail to me. We got a copy of the story and sent it to our narrator, Nick Camm, and released it on June 4, 2015. Again, Season 5 of the TV show was playing at the time. We knew the episode would be big, but we had no idea just how big. Everyone was talking about it. We were all over the moon at *StarShipSofa*. Within hours the downloads were in their high thousands. All the official fan outlets (Westoros. org, A Song of Ice and Fire forums, etc.) posted about it, too. It's not everyday that an out-of-print story written in the 1970s reappears in audio, especially when it's by GRRM. It was a nice surprise when George R.R. Martin himself blogged about it, adding that he thought we "did a nice job." It was an even nicer surprise when I met the man himself at WorldCon in Finland, where he recognized me by name and remembered how we adapted "Greywater Station" for our podcast, and said again how he loved what we did with his story. Which was pretty huge for me, considering I grew up reading (and watching) the *Game of Thrones* series.

Harlan Ellison is another case entirely. I posted a letter asking to reprint his story "How Interesting: A Tiny Man." Two months later, I get an email with his phone number and an invitation to call. So he knew I was calling and what I was calling for. I'd expected to speak with an intern, assistant, his wife, anyone.

I was not expecting the man himself to answer the phone.

I gave my name, said I was looking to reprint "How Interesting: A Tiny Man" for *StarShipSofa* in audio. Ellison didn't even pause; he launched straight into the thick of it. He told me he was totally cool with us doing it. He asked how we were planning to reprint the story in audio, ("cause it has two different endings, y'know?"). Admittedly, I had a brain breakdown as I'd forgotten that fact, but told Ellison that we'd record both and let the viewers decide ("we've never done split endings before, so it'd be cool to do it for our capstone show"), I vaguely remember saying.

"Huh." Was all he grunted in response. I didn't get called a moron or retard, so I assumed he was satisfied. "But there's an issue with the contract," he told me, and I could hear the (I assume) creak of his chair as he sat up. "The … uhh, obscenity clause. I dunno if some asshole is going to take offense at the word 'I' and I don't wanna be dragged out in court again. It's happened before and I don't want them digging up my body for the next two hundred years to put my bones on trial."

So naturally, I responded with "assuming we get to two hundred years."

And he chuckled. I don't consider myself particularly masterful in the world of comedy, but if I can make the man who got fired from Disney on day one for making Rule 34 jokes about cartoon porn *laugh*, then that's all the validation I need.

The rest of the conversation went smoothly, mainly regarding more confident matters and technical details about the show. But near the end, Uncle Harlan gave his consent and the go-ahead for us to talk more about reprinting and playing his Nebula winning story, how we'd produce it, etc. Again, the man doesn't miss a beat. Old age hasn't made those gears rust one bit. And seeing how he was in a good mood, I opted to tell him that I've been reading him since I was eleven years old, I'm a fan and super stoked to be talking with him now.

"Heh, all right kiddo, thanks for letting me know," was the friendly grunt of a response. By this point I wasn't sure whether I wanted to be chewed out or not, just so I could say it happened, but so far I'd probably lasted longer than a lot of others folks have. "You have a good evening," he ended up saying.

"I'm calling from Australia, actually," I said, thinking that I'd just contradicted Harlan Ellison.

"Ahh. Australia," he drawled out. "I know that place. Too goddamn hot and the people suck, but I love your koalas."

Hand on heart, the author of "I Have No Mouth, and I Must Scream," said those exact words to me. I guess I should have said something witty, but I'm not that smart and we said our goodbyes and the convo ended there.

A few months later, the audio adaptation to "A Tiny Man" went live. I never found out what he thought about it, and with his unfortunate passing, I may never know. But I got to speak with Harlan Ellison on the phone, who to this day remains the only author who's invited me to call him to discuss business, and I consider myself very fortunate I got the chance.

ESSF: StarShipSofa *also provides an audiobook service. Audiobooks are* very *popular in the Arab world, both with the sci-fi fans and authors themselves. Needless to say, it is much easier to listen to a book than read it. Would you say this is a growth market and an effective means for popularizing new and rising authors—like Arab and Muslim SF writers—internationally?*

Absolutely. Distribution is very easy, and anyone of any location or background can launch a podcasting service that can be reached in any corner of the earth. We're based in the UK, and get downloads all over the Middle East. No doubt, there's podcasters doing the same and reaching listeners both locally and internationally.

ESSF: On your website you say you are represented by the John Jarrold Literary Agency, and The Gotham Group for movie and TV rights. In the Arab world, literary agencies are unheard of and we're desperately trying to find people and agencies to represent us to an international audience. Any advice on the delicate art of finding, and keeping, a literary agent?

To get an agent, you need to write a good novel. There's no way around it. All sorts of people on the internet will tell you there's some secret handshake, that you've got to know somebody important first, or you need to already have an established body of work, or you've got to name-drop your contacts, or you've got to perform a special ritual with the blood of a dragon. Or anything else that isn't writing a good book. But that's all there is to it: you need to have written a good book that an agent can not only be personally invested in, but can sell to a major publisher. The book needs to be similar to what's being written today. There was once plenty of room for pulpy, gung-ho Heinlein-esque stories, but it's not 1955 anymore, and no one wants to read that anymore. Agents won't represent something that doesn't click with them on a personal level, nor will they represent something they don't think they can sell. It's what my agent has told me during the many times when I doubted the strength or salability of my work.

First, you need to find an agent that connects with your specific project. Look up established agents, research the types of books they represent, how many books they've sold, how many clients they have, what their approach is to editing, and see if they're a good fit. You could have written the best book of the year, but send it to the wrong agent. I sent my book to John Jarrold because he published and edited several of Iain M. Banks' space opera books, and believed he'd be a good fit for my space opera novels. And it turned out to be a hit.

So: revise and revise and polish your novel until it shines, and then find the agent who fits it best. It's a very hard and very long slog, but I'm living proof that anyone can do it.

ESSF: We're also desperate to get our stories and novels adapted to television and the silver screen. We all believe that this can be the force multiplier that will make science fiction really take off in the Arab world and become sustainable. Is it enough to get scripts adapted to screen, or do you need the legal foundations sorted out first via firms like The Gotham Group?

I leave the complicated verbal dueling with Hollywood to my agent and my extended film agency. But as far as I know, it's almost impossible to sell a straight screenplay to Hollywood on-spec (which means, not written on request). Especially if you don't have prior credentials. I'd say it's probably easier to sell a novel and get the interests of screenwriters and producers in hopes that they can sell it to a Hollywood studio. I've had interest for some of my work, but it's never come to fruition, and I'd certainly never dare attempt to get it done myself. There are exceptions, but 99 percent of the time, a film agency who knows what they're doing is pretty much required to get your work on the silver screen.

ESSF: To finish off, a small side question. Many believe that the "saw" scene in the Watchmen *graphic novel—between Rorschach and one of his victims—originally came from the closing scene in the first* Mad Max *(1979) movie. Can you confirm this?*

I can, indirectly. I was at a panel with James Wan and Leigh Whannell (the creators of *Saw*) where they said the sawing-hand scene in the original *Mad Max* inspired them to utilize a similar "sawing" scene in the *Saw* movies (and inspired them a lot, since they literally named a franchise after it!), which also inspired *that* scene in the Watchmen comic. So *Mad Max* has done a great deal for pop-culture!

NOTES

1. Jeremy Szal's Galaxy Blog, https://jeremyszal.com/.

2. Mikael is the Arabic pronunciation of the archangel Michael and Djinn are genies. Sikander (or Iskandar) is also the Oriental pronunciation for Alexander the Great. There's also a character named Roxanne in "These Six Walls," perhaps named after Alexander's famous Central Asian wife.

3. Timothy James Dimacali or TJ is an MIT graduate, broadcaster, scientific journalist and SF writer, author famously of the *Skygypsies* Filipino SF comic and a contributor to *The Sea Is Ours: Tales from Steampunk Southeast Asia* (2015), *Philippine Speculative Fiction Volume 5* (2012) and *Alternative Alamat: Stories Inspired by Philippine Mythology* (2011).

The Arabs Haven't Given Up on Utopia Just Yet

The Nano-Ethics of Heaven on Earth

Fadi Zaghmout

What strange beings we are! That sitting in hell at the bottom of the dark, we're afraid of our own immortality.

—Rumi

In April 2010, while I was on a trip to Chicago, a close friend of mine asked me to get him that month's issue of *GQ* magazine. I remember flipping through the copy in my hotel room and reading the headlines, when I noticed an article with a title that said human beings may soon be able to live up to a 1,000 years and beyond. It was an interview with Aubrey de Grey, the famous English gerontologist who came up with a roadmap for how to defeat aging. At the time, I didn't know about the scientist, neither was I aware of his work, but the possibility of living a very, very long life hit me hard, as dying from old age has always been something we as Arabs believed is impossible to change.

The new revelation gave me hope. And believing Aubrey's words, I started to imagine: What will life be like when this happens? How will it affect our lives, our morals, and our society? Would it be really like the heaven we dream of when we push death away from us?

A Story in Transition

Putting those imaginings into writings wasn't an easy task. At that point in 2010, and after a few years of blogging about body rights and sexual freedoms, I was still working on my first novel, *The Bride of Amman*, a feminist novel that takes a sharp-eyed look at the intersecting lives of four women and one gay man in Jordan's historic capital. I was, and still, consider myself to be a gender activist. I fell under the influence of the writings of Nawal El-Saadawi in my late teenage years and have always believed that gender equality and more freedom and tolerance of different gender expressions would make our societies healthier. *The Bride of Amman* was published in January 2012 and became a hit in Jordan, but I finished writing it earlier in the spring of 2011 and couldn't stop my urges to start working on *Heaven on Earth* immediately. While no stranger to controversy in my writings and my career, the process of writing a feminist contemporary story is *very* different than writing a futuristic speculative fiction. I have always had an interest in science fiction; I read Egyptian pocketbooks of Nabil Farouk's "The Future File" as a teenager and excelled in math and physics in my high school. To be honest, before starting my blog, language hadn't been an interest for me; I was more into numbers and science. I did my bachelor's degree in computer science and at one point I had a wish to study genetic engineering. Never too late, no?

Anyway, being an activist and using my blog to communicate my ideas taught me the importance of language. At one point, I came to realize that numbers can be limited in comparison of the spaces that language can open. I also realized that telling stories is the best way to convey one's ideas. In a nutshell, I had this interest in science, my language skills that were improved and refined by years of blogging, and my wild imagination. Nevertheless, I had no idea how to write a science fiction novel, and I had no one to guide me.

At the beginning I wanted to set the plot of *Heaven on Earth* into two different times. The first set in a near future to imagine people's reactions when the age-related cures start to show up, and the second set in the far future when curing aging becomes the norm, and life becomes more of a utopia.

I was nearly halfway through writing the story when I realized, from the feedback of some close friends, that it wasn't going in the right direction. I threw it all away and decided to start again from the beginning. That was in early 2013 and at that point, after the success of *The Bride of Amman*, I was doing my Master of Arts in Creative Writing and Critical Thinking at University of Sussex in the United Kingdom. In the first term of the MA, we had to complete a module entitled "Utopia and Creative Writing," which was an eye opener for me. I had to read some major classical works in the genre, including *The Time Machine* by H.G. Wells, Aldous Huxley's *Brave New World*, and George Orwell's *1984*. Huxley's novel inspired me the most, and I wanted to write a braver new world for our century, one that will be shaped by even more technological advancements and disruptive unprecedented discoveries—and all from an Arabic perspective.

I started writing *Heaven on Earth* again while doing my MA and finished it in the summer of the following year, 2014. Once I finished, I sent the manuscript to Dar Al Adab, the prestigious Lebanese publishing house, which replied back to me in August with a full report showing their interest in the story and their intention to publish it.

It came out in Arabic in November 2015, and we had the launch event at Sharjah's annual book fair in the UAE. After only two years, in summer 2017, it came out in English as well, published by Signal8Press from Hong Kong and translated by Sawad Hussain.

An interesting incident that is worth mentioning here is that in 2016, Aubrey de Grey gave a talk at Cafe Scientifique in Dubai, the city I had moved to two years earlier. It was like a dream for me to meet the man who was promising us a longer life, and there was no way I would have missed that event. I went there and met him and told him how he inspired me to write the book. I emailed him a few months later when the English translation was ready and asked him if he would be interested in writing me a book blurb, which he did:

> In this valuable novel, Fadi Zaghmout puts a personal face to the world we are all longing for (some of us more secretly than others). It is an interesting and realistic read, showing humanity as it has always been but with a new dawn of life where the infirmity of old age is a choice.— Aubrey de Grey, Chief Science Officer, SENS Research Foundation

For my "Utopia and Creative Writing" module term paper, I had the opportunity to explore what I call the "Utopian Age" in three major phases of human life: childhood, youth and old age. Writing that term paper helped me shape the plot of *Heaven on Earth*.

The Right Age Group for a Utopia

We go through different stages of life during our lifespan that can be categorized into three main phases: childhood, youth, and old age. I would say that middle age can legitimately claim to be a fourth category, especially today with the extension of the human lifespan, but I can also see that its characteristics can be divided between youth and old age. The same goes for teen age, which can be an extension of childhood and early youth.

Each main stage of a human life feels eternal on its own when lived. Children feel that they would never grow up, young people refuse to let go of their youth even after years of accumulating damage, and the elderly know that their time has run out but cannot grasp the notion of departure.

All of the three phases carry different Utopian aesthetics, and also a dystopian side in different conditions. I am going to explore each stage in relation to Utopian literature and see if there is a specific age that best fits all and can bring happiness and comfort to everybody.

Childhood Dependency

Nurtured in a protected, secured, and loving environment, children do often give the impression that they live in their own Utopian bubble. They do not think if they are happy or not; they just live happily. Perhaps it has to do with the state of limited knowledge/intelligence children bear or the state of dependency they abide by.

H.G. Wells outlines clearly both of these states in his own Utopia, *The Time Machine* (1894–5). He takes us on a journey to a "world in the remote future" where human beings have turned into child-like creatures:

> …little pink hands feeling at the Time Machine….
> Their hair, which was uniformly curly, came to a sharp end at the neck and cheek….
> The mouths were small, with bright red, rather thin lips, and the little chins ran to a point.
> The eyes were large and mild…

Wells goes on to describe the futuristic world in which these creatures live, describing it as a world that has evolved to become a big garden full of wonderful flowers and exotic fruits, one where many animals have gone extinct and where human beings lost their appetite for meat and became strict vegetarians:

> You who have never seen the like can scarcely imagine what delicate wonderful flowers countless years of culture had created….
> Fruit, by the by, was all their diet. These people of the remote future were strict vegetarians….
> At first I was puzzled by all these strange fruits, and by the strange flowers I saw, but later I began to perceive their import…

Wells rationalizes that after countless years of living in a secured and safe environment, humanity's physical and mental powers became obsolete. Human beings evolved to lose capabilities that are no longer needed. Qualities such as the strength of a man and the softness of a woman are only necessitated by the age of physical force; thus, in a utopian state, it disappears, and a childhood state dominates:

> Seeing the ease and security in which these people were living, I felt that this close resemblance of the sexes was, after all, what one would expect; for the strength of a man and the softness of a woman, the institution of the family, and the differentiation of occupations are mere militant necessities of an age of physical force… [Wells, 2004].

These child-like creatures have an intellectual level that does not exceed that of a five-year-old in the year 1895 AD, according to Wells. Knowing that he wrote *The Time Machine* more than 100 years ago, that level of intelligence he describes can be of a child of a younger age today after all of the technological innovations we witnessed in the past century: "Then one of them suddenly asked me a question that showed him to be on the ·intellectual level of one of our five-year-old children—asked me, in fact, if I had come from the sun in a thunderstorm!"

Looking back into historical texts, we can see that Wells is not the only one who seems to believe that Utopia entails a human childhood state. Preceding him by almost 1900 years, The Bible tells us that Jesus called a little child among a crowd and spoke eloquently: "Truly I tell you, unless you change and become like little children, you will never enter the kingdom of heaven" [Matt. 18:3. The NIV Study Bible]. He proceeded to articulate the "lowly position" of the child to be highly regarded in heaven.

In the King James Version of the Bible, the words turn into "humble himself." Christianity teaches a sense of humility attached to childhood and related to the Christian relationship with God, childlike humility in relation to the parent, the humility of dependency: "Therefore, whoever takes the lowly position of this child is the greatest in the kingdom of heaven" [Matt. 18:4. The NIV Study Bible]. And also: "Whosoever therefore shall humble himself as this little child, the same is greatest in the kingdom of heaven" [Matt. 18:3. The KJV Bible].

That state of dependency is required for a childhood Utopia. A higher power ought to maintain the system and keep those unintelligent, dependent creatures safe and happy. The Christian vision is arguably more Utopian than *The Time Machine* with the higher power being a loving God, while Wells's vision is more of a Dystopian one with the higher power being the demonic Morlocks:

> The Upper-world people might once have been the favored aristocracy, and the Morlocks their mechanical servants; but that had long passed away. The two species had resulted from the evolution of man were sliding down towards, or had already arrived, an altogether new relationship. The Eloi, like the Carlovingian kings, had decayed to a mere beautiful futility. They still possessed the earth on sufferance: since the Morlocks, subterranean for innumerable generations, had come at last to find the daylit surface intolerable.

Nevertheless, both of these Utopias keep their citizens in fear of the wrath of their higher powers.

I explored this aspect in the novel by introducing a scientific step ahead when we can reach a point of being able to reverse engineer body cells in a calculated manner, allowing human beings to go back in age beyond their youthful state and into their childhood one. At one point, and due to his sadness about his mundane relationship with his long-married wife Janna, Zaid decides to go on this journey back to his childhood. He thinks that he was the happiest in his life when he was a child and wants to replicate that phase of his life, a complication that adds to the storyline.

Along the same lines, I criticize religious fanatics, Christians this time in the book rather than Muslims, who read the Bible literally. With the possibility of going back to their childhood, they come to believe that if they apply the Biblical verse literally, then heaven will open to them. A trend that takes over the Christian population in Jordan.

Youth When It Lasts

There is nothing that feels as Utopian as eternal youth; a life of everlasting beauty, power, health, and independence. Each characteristic has been glorified on its own in contemporary culture to set eternal youth as the ultimate dream of a human life. This dream that is as old as humanity was pursued by Alexander the Great in his quest of the Land of Darkness. *The Greek Alexander Romance*, one of the most long-lived and influential works of the late Greek literature according to its Penguin Classics introduction, tells us about a spring of immortality that brings life back to the dead in contrast with the tree of immortality that is mentioned in the book of Genesis of the Bible. Alexander, like Adam and Eve, was unfortunate and failed to sip from the water of life. On the other hand, his cook was lucky enough to do so:

> The whole place was abounding in water, and we drank of its various streams. Alas for my misfortune, that it was not fated for me to drink of the spring of immortality, which gives life to what is dead, as my cook was fortunate enough to do… [*The Greek Alexander*, 1991: 121].

This longing for eternal youth is not just old but is also gently set as the Utopian age of the second largest believed Utopia in the world today—The Islamic Paradise. This is a place where humans, no matter at what age they die on earth, are resurrected with the eternal youth of a 33-year-old man. This age is mysteriously connected to Jesus's own age of resurrection and his eternal image of youth and beauty. Though it is not written in the Quran, the words of the Prophet Mohammed were narrated by Mu'aadh ibn Jabal and passed through Jami' Al Tirmidi—one of the great compilers of Islamic hadith. It was published in English in a book called *Islam: Questions and Answers—Basic Tenets of Faith (Belief)* by Mohammad Saed Abdul-Rahman:

> "The people of Paradise will enter Paradise hairless, beardless with their eyes anointed with kohl, aged thirty or thirty-three years."
> Narrated by al-Tirmidhi, 2545. Classed as saheeh by al-Albaani in Saheeh al-Jaami', 7928… [Abdul-Rahman, 2003: 421].

Youth can still be seen as Utopian in literature even if it is not eternal. Aldous Huxley shows us in *Brave New World* that youth and health are maintained until the age of sixty, and then people drop and die without having to go through the hardship of old age:

> All the physiological stigmata of old age have been abolished….
> "Along of them all the old man's mental peculiarities. Characters remain constant throughout a whole lifetime." [Huxley, 2007: 47].

Huxley proceeds with subtle sarcasm to pinpoint the dystopian side of killing off the old: the loss of abstinence, reading, and thinking that accompanies old age when our bodies become frail and our physical capabilities become limited:

> "Work, play—at sixty our powers and tastes are what they were at seventeen. Old men in the bad old days used to renounce, retire, take to religion, spend their time reading, thinking—thinking!"....
>
> "Now—such is progress—the old men work, the old men copulate, the old men have no time, no leisure from pleasure, not a moment to sit down and think..." [2007: 47].

The childhood utopian state of dependency comes in contrast with the youth's utopian state of independence. Dependency can be utopian when the higher power is omnipotent and all good, while independence can be utopian when the independent subject is omnipotent in itself. This can't be achieved with merely the characteristics of youth; it entails some aspects of old age wisdom.

This can be clearer if we move from the individual age perspective into humanity's age perspective.

For many years, humanity was stuck in a childhood state and needed a higher power—a God-like figure—for its utopian ambitions. It matured recently after the industrial, technological, and informational revolutions to reject the figure of a higher power and believe in its own capabilities and independence. This independence falls short of a utopian state with many problems around the world still begging for answers. It pushes for more scientific achievements to take humanity into its next phase of evolution, towards its maturity and so-called old age.

In the novel, I explored the possibility of eternal youth, when it becomes easily available for most of the population who can afford to buy a golden pill containing thousands of nanobots. Nanobots will swim in the blood stream and help the immune system clean all of the cellular junk accumulated by metabolic daily activities to keep people young and healthy. After reaching 75, Janna, the protagonist, and her husband Zaid get the chance to take the pill and rejuvenate their bodies like many other people of that time in the near future.

As the solution of old age comes in a *near* future, the characters in the book are still living in a time where they inherit current social values, religious beliefs, and economic systems. It is a shifting time, where a drastic scientific revolution begins to drive social changes and beliefs such as the status of marriage when life becomes much longer or the way the general public look at death and old age when the cure becomes available for nearly everybody. It is not an "entirely" Utopian state here but an interesting era of gaining more human power that entails giving up old systems and exploring new ways of life.

Some of the ironic systems I mention in the book that seem to endure in the coming 70 years or so is the Jordanian royal family and the failure of the state to come up with a representative modern election system. The same applies to the status of women in society and the shameful state of honor killings that still persist today, and in the future, despite the huge technological advancements. And sadly, the Palestinian cause, which has been an unresolved conflict for more than 60 years and remains the same in the book.

The Old Age of Gods

A Utopian old age is a tricky concept. It is certainly tied to wisdom and power, but it is not easy to draw a clear line between the notions of wisdom and power and the notion of "old" as being in existence for a long time, or "old" as in the state of the human late stage of life and all of the physiological characteristics related to it. In the former sense, someone living eternally in a youthful state can logically be described as being old, yet culturally speaking, it is hardly linked to wisdom. In the latter sense, old age entails a frail body that is neither utopian nor powerful.

I would say that only God can make old age utopian. It requires an omnipotent power to transcend the physical and mental peculiarities of old age while maintaining the foundation of wisdom. This has been the case historically with the mainstream image of the Christian God transcending the characteristics of the old-looking Greek Gods: old with white hair and a long white beard, omnipotent and omniscient.

With the rapid development of artificial intelligence, biotechnologies that promise to defeat ageing and extend the human life span indefinitely, and the potential convergence between man and machine, one can't help but to connect the dots and conclude that humanity is on the verge of its greatest evolutionary leap towards its old age: the Godly species.

For thousands of years, we have created our own gods, whether human-looking ones, spiritual ones, or hybrids. We have longed for someone to take care of us. Recently, we matured to be able to take care of ourselves (to a certain extent). A trend hit the globe to reject the notion of dependencies. But it has been hard to break out of the long history of our cultural heritage. We still long for dependency, and we are heading toward a future where we are re-creating gods—either from our own selves or through artificial intelligence.

The premise of Utopia is there in all of the three main stages of a human life. Each can be utopian on its own, but maybe the ultimate Utopia would be conserving all of the three states. My Utopia may not be yours. A choice of age sounds like a good utopian dream for me.

One More Word

The book has been well received since it came out in Arabic in November 2014. A month after that, I did a book launch for it in Jordan at Princess Sumaya University for Technology Auditorium during Alef's conference. I was the main guest and presented the idea behind the book and its story on stage to an engaged young audience. In the same month, and for three months afterwards, it hit the best-seller list on Jamalon (Jordan's Amazon equivalent for buying books online). It also became a best seller in Readers Bookshop in Amman during the same year. The book generated many good reviews as it shows in its Goodreads page.[1] It was translated and published in English in September 2017. One of the best reviews came from the famous Egyptian literary critique, Dr. Salah Fadl, who cited it as the only example of science fiction literature in the Arab world in his book, *Ansaq Al Takhayyol Al Rewa'e* (*Types of Imagination in Arabic Literature*). Another review that is worth mentioning was published in the famous *Strange Horizon* magazine for science fiction literature, where Gautam Bhatia hailed it as an "accomplished novel" and a "richly satisfying read."

> *Heaven on Earth* confronts—and deals with—fundamental transformations in an entire way of living. The result is a crowded canvas in which not everything is given the attention that it deserves, but whose ambition and boldness makes for a richly satisfying read [Bhatia, 2018].

However, *some* people didn't like it. You can see some negative reviews on the Goodreads page as well, with people ranking it with a one- or two-star rating.

Literary critics were all positive … thankfully.

For my part I wasn't sure about its success because it was a different genre than my first book. Everyone expected a sequel to *The Bride of Amman* or something like it. Science fiction is not that popular in the Arab world yet.

NOTE

1. https://www.goodreads.com/book/show/23454409.

WORKS CITED

Abdul Rahman', Muhammad. (2003). *Islam: Questions and Answers—Basic Tenets of Faith (Belief)*. London: MSA Publication Limited.

Bhatia, Gautam. (12 March 2018). "Review of *Heaven On Earth*, by Fadi Zaghmout, Translated by Sawad Hussain." *Strange Horizons*. http://strangehorizons.com/non-fiction/reviews/heaven-on-earth-by-fadi-zaghmout-translated-by-sawad-hussain/.

The Greek Alexander Romance. (1991). London: Penguin Classics. Translated by Richard Stoneman.

The Holy Bible. (1611). King James Version, Cambridge Edition. n.p. [publication details unavailable].

The Holy Bible. (2011). New International Version, Biblica. n.p. [publication details unavailable].

Huxley, Aldous. (2007). *Brave New World*. London: Vintage.

Wells, H.G. (2004). *The Time Machine*. Project Gutenberg. http://www.gutenberg.org/files/35/35-h/35-h.htm.

The Story of Syrian SF

The Struggle for a Voice of Its Own[1]

Mohammed Abdullah Alyasin

Without a family, man, alone in the world, trembles with the cold.
—André Maurois

A long time ago in a galaxy far, far away....

—*Star Wars*

Writing *about* science fiction in an Arabic country is as much an uphill task as writing science fiction itself in the Arab world. This is what I learned, the hard way, when I did my master's thesis on Arabic SF.

I'd signed up for the Master of Arts program in the Department of Arabic Language and Literature, Faculty of Arts and Humanities, Al–Baath University, and everything was going fine at first. Then my thesis supervisor got a posting in Egypt, and I had to search for another supervisor. All of the professors I spoke to declined to work with me as none had any experience with science fiction. I complained, straight to the dean of our college, Dr. Ghassan Mourtada, and he explained that he could not force a professor to supervise a thesis, adding that he himself did not know much about the field. I then asked Dr. Ghassan to supervise my thesis and insisted that I would be responsible for gathering all the reading material and writing everything, and he agreed. After imprisoning myself in the library for a prolonged period of time, I completed my thesis in 2008, which was approved at my university in 2009.[2]

I now live in the UAE, working as a teacher and a librarian, but I haven't lost interest in the genre and am even penning SF and fantasy short stories and preparing them for publication. If it weren't for my work duties and my planned PhD—nothing to do with SF this time—I would have begun writing SF in earnest.

My PhD program was originally with Damascus University, but the political situation that developed with the Arab Spring in 2011 led to a cancellation. But I have resumed my doctoral studies with Sharjah University in the cultural center of the UAE.

It will cost an arm and a leg but I am hopeful that I may receive a scholarship. Wish me luck!

Drawn to the Field

It may surprise some that I, a student of Arabic literature, chose SF as the topic of MA thesis. My planned PhD is actually about prose literature in the Abbasid era.

Nonetheless, I wanted to break new ground and be one of the first to survey the genre in the Arab world. I've been reading SF since I was a child, and loved the *Spectacular Phenomena* program on Syrian radio. I also encountered Syrian SF authors early in my life, which piqued my interest more and more. Even more fortunately, while working on my MA, I was able to meet with Dr. Taleb Omran at the Syrian television building and found that he was gracious and very helpful.

Afterwards, in 2016, Damascus University decided to publish my thesis in book form and, thanks be to God, it has been showcased in several venues, including the 2016 Sharjah Book Festival. While I was there I had the good fortune to hand over a signed copy to the distinguished Emirati author Noura Al Noman, the pioneer of SF in the UAE.

In the meantime, I became a regular contributor to Syria's own *Science Fiction* magazine (see below), with Dr. Omran himself as Editor in Chief, along with an impressive and very pan–Arab list of staff members. These include Riad Nasaan Agha, the head of our board of directors and the Syrian minister of culture (at the time), and our consultants: Nihad Sharif (from Egypt, now deceased), Dr. Hosam Al-Khatib (from Palestine), Abd Al-Salam Al-Baqali (from Morocco), Dr. Muhammad Al-Hadi Ayad (from Tunis), Dr. Qasim Qasim (from Lebanon), Tiybah Ibrahim (from Kuwait), Dr. Mahmoud Karoum (Syria), and Dr. Kawthar Ayed (a Tunisian residing in France).

Samples of a Short History

Many date Syrian science fiction to the days of the Roman Empire, with the 2nd century AD author and satirist Lucian of Samosata, or Lucian the Syrian as we call him in my country. Many believe him to be the first science fiction author; he was a man who satirized everything from magic and superstition to the gods themselves—a clear advocate of a scientific world perspective grounded in rationally discernible laws. These are the foundations of science fiction, and he was of Syrian origin, if a "Hellenized" Syrian.

Others date the Syrian concern with science fiction to Islamic history, with such wondrous works of fantastical fiction such as *The 1001 Nights*, *Hayy ibn Yaqzan* and other folk tales. I am of a different opinion, and my colleagues will have to forgive me on this count. Some of these can be seen as precursors to science fiction, given that mythical beasts like the Rokh (and Pegasus) stand in for man's desire to break the barriers of distance and see the world, but I insist on my position because I do not find a *continuous* line stretching from these classic works to contemporary works of SF written in Arabic, whether in Syria or Egypt or elsewhere. Another case in point is Utopia. We have *The Virtuous City* by Al-Farabi and some legends of magical cities in our literature, but the modern utopian-dystopian city in Arab SF is clearly derived from the cities and worlds of Aldous Huxley and George Orwell, among others, a point returned to below.

This is a tragedy, of course. We had a glorious scientific past in the heyday of Islamic civilization, but decline and then colonialism has profoundly changed our taste as authors and readers. Fantasy, in the pure escapist sense, unencumbered by facts and logic and scientific experimentation, became popular in this period of decline and disempowerment. No wonder that it took science fiction so long to set down roots in the Arab world, not least in Syria.

Science fiction in Syria, as in much of the Arab world, came to the country in the form of translation. We were very fortunate as Syrians to have high-quality translations by Abd Al-Halim Mahmoud and Mohammad Badran. They translated, respectively, *The Weigher of Souls* by André Maurois in 1946 and *Food of the Gods* by H.G. Wells in 1947 (and also Huxley's *Brave New World* the same year). Other distinguished translators include Mohammad Jamal Al-Fandi and Jabir Abd Al-Hamid Jabir (who translated a work of Isaac Asimov's in 1965). The Ministry of Culture also took it upon itself to translate many works of science fiction, although the names of the translators employed were never printed in these books.

You will see from the names and the period of translation that this was during the golden era of science fiction in the Western world, the 1940–50s, a pattern that holds true for Arabic science fiction in general. The biggest names were translated and passed into the corpus of Arab SF, which itself began in the 1950s. Even older texts were taken up in the flurry of this era, such as Maurois's novel, published originally in 1931, and *Food of the Gods*, circa 1904. Other influential authors in translation are Jules Verne, George Orwell, Yevgeny Zamyatin, Stanisław Lem, Arthur C. Clarke, Edgar Allan Poe, and Ray Bradbury. There are other, far more contemporary Western authors who have exerted their influence on Syrian and Arab SF, but I will mention their names below as need dictates. And that is not discounting cinematic influences on Arab genre authors either.

As for the writing of science fiction in Syria specifically, this really began in the 1980s, with Dr. Taleb Omran, a distinguished scientist, university professor, broadcaster, and a man dedicated to popularizing science. Two other names worth mentioning are Diab Eid (although not an SF author originally) and Mohammad Al-Hajj Saleh. This is not an exhaustive list but they are the writers that I am most familiar with and have studied, and their works are representative of what is written in Syrian SF. It must be understood here that, as a latecomer to the genre, Syrian SF is also not as easily organized into phases as it is elsewhere in the Arab world, so it is best to talk of individual authors. The school of thought writers adhere to is essentially the same in my country, as are their literary influences. The main differences are the individual styles of the writers and how they handle certain topics and motifs.

Dr. Taleb Omran's works are too numerous to list but two particular novels are representative of his faith in science and his concerns as an Arab author. The first is *Space as Wide as a Dream* (1997). The story has Arab scientists heading to Mars to investigate a strange phenomenon—the fact that the apes and monkeys they send there come back five times smarter than when they left. The human crew, when in the planetary orbit, encounter the giant gravitational field of another, hidden plant, and find themselves rubbing shoulders with multitudes of beings made of pure energy. These creatures have given up their corporeal forms and materialist lusts a long time ago, so war and borders, countries and the family have all become things of the past. Everyone is happy, and these creatures dedicate themselves to the pursuit of knowledge, specifically celestial mathematics, the art of predicting the future. The language they speak is the language of music.

They provide the human visitors with everything they need, such as oxygen and protection against harmful radiation, then invite them to come and stay with them, giving up their bodies for the life of pure energy. The humans agree, except for one, as he has family back on Earth. When he returns home, however, he finds everyone has aged—thanks to time dilation. Feeling a stranger in his own world, he returns and becomes a spirit being like his comrades.

Dr. Taleb Omran is well known for portraying aliens and first contact in the best way possible in his writing, in marked contrast to the alien invasion and abduction scenarios

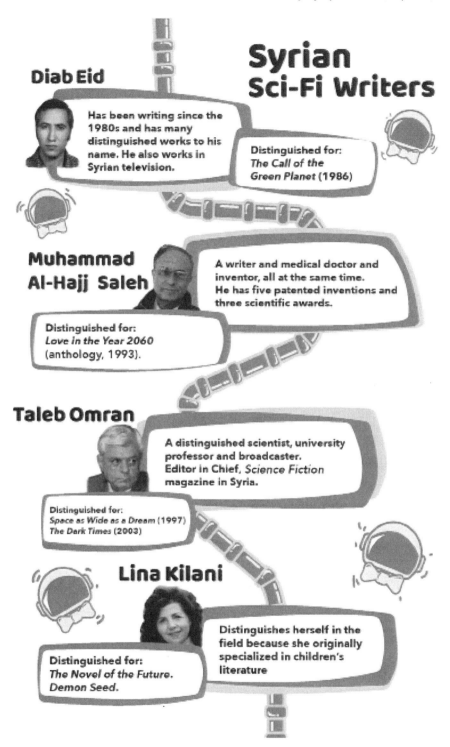

Syrian Sci-Fi Writers

Diab Eid

Has been writing since the 1980s and has many distinguished works to his name. He also works in Syrian television.

Distinguished for:
The Call of the Green Planet (1986)

Muhammad Al-Hajj Saleh

A writer and medical doctor and inventor, all at the same time. He has five patented inventions and three scientific awards.

Distinguished for:
Love in the Year 2060 (anthology, 1993).

Taleb Omran

A distinguished scientist, university professor and broadcaster. Editor in Chief, *Science Fiction* magazine in Syria.

Distinguished for:
Space as Wide as a Dream (1997)
The Dark Times (2003)

Lina Kilani

Distinguishes herself in the field because she originally specialized in children's literature

Distinguished for:
The Novel of the Future.
Demon Seed.

The big names in Syrian sci-fi, an incomplete list for an as yet unfinished trek (courtesy of the artist, Yahya Salah Abul Ghait).

prevalent in the West. For him, alien worlds are an escape from our world, where power insists on monopolizing the world of scientific investigation and perverting the noble message of science.

The second novel I would like to explore here is *The Dark Times* (2003), a long novel with a fair amount of narrative innovation in it—with two time frames, past (2018) and future (2040)—set on Earth and about the world after the cataclysm of 9/11. The central character is Dr. Qasim, an Arab scientist who is returning home from the West. He wanted his homeland to benefit from his knowledge, but typically, he distinguished himself far more as a scientist while abroad. He is kidnapped by a terrorist organization calling itself the Freemasons, one of the many secret cabals that rule the world. They force him to use his skills to produce genetically engineered reptiles, throwing their eggs into the river of his home village in Syria, where the creatures hatch and wreak havoc on the villagers, even killing his mother.

Dr. Qasim later takes revenge against the organization, using the same methods against its members, but is captured and handed over to the Americans. After a quick and unjust show trial by the U.S. military, he is imprisoned in Guantanamo Bay and horrendously tortured. Fortunately, one of the guards there is a personal acquaintance and helps him escape before it is too late. This novel is unique for Dr. Omran because of the level of gritty realism, but it still resonates with his other works because of his profound commitment to the responsibilities of scientists and how powerful men abuse this scientific trust.

Diab Eid, born 1944, has been writing since the 1980s and has many distinguished works to his name. He also works in Syrian television, and his main claim to fame in the genre is his novel *The Call of the Green Planet* (1986), which he wrote before moving into televised drama. The story is set in 2047, when Earth's international space agency receives a distress call from a far off world, the planet Stephani, in the Proxima Centauri system. They answer the call, despite the tremendous distance. It takes seven to eight years to get there by Earth time, given time dilation. On board the space agency's nuclear-powered ship (Salam-1, or Peace One) is a crew of four, the very best of the best that Earth has to offer: Yuri from Estonia, a Brazilian named Peter, Qays from the Arab world, and Eza from Uganda.

Once they get to Staphani, they are shocked to find themselves in a giant forest with massive trees and dinosaur-like reptiles. If they hadn't been trained for all eventualities and were armed, they would have perished immediately. They decide to take a safer approach, flying over the planet, which seems to consist of a never-ending forest, until they find themselves over an open patch of land. That's when they find some old constructions and a windmill that generates electricity, like those on Earth in the 20th century. They stumble on an alien there, and he looks perfectly human. Their robot translates his harsh words, and they discover that he thinks they are "Northerners," from his own planet. Afterwards he befriends them and falls in love with Eza. He explains that the planet is split in two, an industrial North and the South, half of which is covered by savage jungle called Randa.

The North, ever hungry for raw materials, has declared war on the South and devastated much of Randa. Making their way to the North, the human astronauts find themselves being welcomed warmly by the scientific community. It was the scientists, in fact, who had sent out the distress call when they were temporarily in charge of the North, before they were overthrown by the Northern mega-corporations that run things behind the scenes. These corporations were the ones launching the imperialist war of terror on the South, using weapons of mass destruction on the jungle to dominate it and subjugate the resisting population of the South. At this point in the narrative, Qays falls in love with one of the scientist's assistants, a woman with green eyes and blonde hair. The scientists convince the human crew to return to their own world, confident that things will eventually get sorted out in Stephani. The dark-skinned Eza stays while Qays' new love goes with him.[3]

Dr. Mohammad Al-Hajj Saleh (born 1946) is a writer, medical doctor, and inventor, all at the same time. He has five patented inventions, three scientific awards, many scientific publications, as well as numerous SF works, including his anthology *Love in the Year 2060* (1993), which I will talk about here. In one especially interesting story about the end of the universe, humankind is spreading to the galaxies in the distant future, only to learn that the power of the big bang—or the cosmic egg, as the author puts it—is petering out and that the universe will collapse inward on itself. The story focuses on the sheer terror and panic that takes over humanity when they learn of this eventuality; it is as if judgment day has come upon them. The same energy that went into giving birth to the universe will be compressed and reversed into an equally violent death, or so they think.

Most people board spacecraft and flying saucers, escaping their planets, thinking there is somewhere they can go. Others resign themselves to their fates and remain planet-bound. Then the surprise comes: the planets and star systems and galaxies do not in fact collide into each other. All the scientific predictions were wrong, and the universe takes a static oval shape, about half the size and mass of the original universe. The focus, thematically, is not predicting what the world will be like millions of years into the future—technology and medical sciences—but what people are like and how they react differently to dire circumstances. The story is a giant experiment in human affairs.

As for the title story for his anthology, "Love in the Year 2060," humanity is suffering from infertility due to a virus and the hero, a scientist named Ghassan, is struggling to find a cure for this disease. Ghassan, as might be expected from a protagonist, is the odd one out in society. He's in love with his colleague, Zaina, in a world that does not even admit to such sentimentalities. In this future, nothing has any meaning any more. People take no pleasure in music or the gentle chirping of birds, and everything is looked upon with nonchalance and apathy. Creativity and the power of imagination no longer exist; in tandem with this neutralism are disdain for archaic concepts like love. Worse still, the world is ruled by scientists who are opposed to Ghassan's efforts—they don't believe in reproduction—forcing him to inject the medicine secretly into his sweetheart Zaina. The cure is a success, and she slowly regains her humanity, and her femininity, although poor Ghassan is captured and tortured by the most harrowing—and scientifically pristine—means possible. Fortunately, he infected quite a few women with his cure, and humanity slowly begins to wake up from its emotionless stupor. The real surprise, however, comes in the end, when it is revealed that the infertility virus is of extra-terrestrial origin. An evil alien species wants to take over the Earth, and the best way to do this is to de-populate it.

As said above, this is not an exhaustive list. The simple fact of the matter is that Syria does not have many science fiction writers, and it is better to study those whose depth is indicative of what is going on in the genre in the country. Now a deeper critical analysis is called for of the works cited, in a comparative fashion where the general state of Arabic science fiction is taken into consideration, along with an appreciation for the "outside" influences on the literature in Syria.

Searching for a Vision

It is a truism in writing that the author is influenced in what he writes by what he reads, the authors he takes as a guide to his own writings, the literary works he holds up as an example to other writers. This is true of the author of science fiction as it is of any field of literature, but doubly so in the case of Arabic science fiction.

Nihad Sharif, the great Egyptian SF author, has a novella called "The Thing," a clear allusion to the black and white UFO movie classic *The Thing from Another World* (1951). His novella "Number 4 Commands You," where Martians try to prevent Earth from blowing itself to smithereens through nuclear war, is very close to Leo Szilard's "Calling All Stars" (1949). Even his classic Utopian novel, *The People of the Second World* (1977), incorporates elements from Aldous Huxley's *Brave New World*, since education in the underwater city involves indoctrination, with children learning to memorize scientific facts through hearing a recording over and over again in their sleep. His novella "The River" was also heavily influenced by *The Weigher of Souls*, just as Tawfik Al-Hakim's novella "In the Year One Million" and "After a Million Years" by Raouf Wasfi match Ray Bradbury's "The Million Year Picnic" (1946) and *The Boat of a Million Years* (1989) by Poul Anderson.

For Syrian examples we have Lina Kilani's two novels, *The Novel of the Future* and *Demon Seed*, which seem to be derived from *The Novel of the Future* (1968) by Anaïs Nin and *Demon Seed* (1973) by Dean Koontz. Kilani distinguishes herself in the field because she originally specialized in children's literature. Taleb Omran's first contact story "An Encounter of the Third Kind" is akin to the movie *Close Encounters of the Third Kind* (1977), and Lem's *Solaris* (1961) has also exerted a considerable influence on his work.

The range and depth of influences is tremendous, from subject matter to stylistics to motifs to titles and names of characters to the narrative format. Most Arabic science fiction, Syrian included, follows a traditional linear format with a beginning, middle, and end. Flashbacks and narrative tricks are rare. The emphasis is on a crisis at the opening of the story to grab the interest of the reader, with the storyline attempting to resolve this crisis. The story proceeds to the crescendo, with a moment of climatic enlightenment (or tragedy) at the end.

This is not a problem in itself, although narrative innovation and originality are always preferred, but mistakes crop up in the meantime as Western texts are transferred into an Arabic frame.

One notable example of this is Wasfi's story "The Revolt of the Robots," which is essentially copied from Isaac Asimov's classic short story "Reason" (1941). In Asimov's story, the human duo of Powell and Donovan argue fruitlessly with the robot Qt-1 that refuses to obey the orders of inferior creatures like human beings. In Wasfi's story you have more or less the same dialogue, but with the human characters of his story confusing the points of view of Powell and Donovan. Another important example is Sabri Musa's classic dystopian novel *The Lord from the Spinach Field* (1982), since the heroes in the novel, for instance, extol the virtues of traditional marriage in contradistinction to the decision by the ruling council to ban marriage and natural birth, moving toward artificial insemination and cohabitation. Nonetheless, the monologue concerning marriage and traditional family life feels forced and unconvincing, out of place with the foreign feel of the novel.

The defense of family bonds and human sentimentality goes hand in hand with religion and the conservative values of traditional society, but there are no Arabic or Islamic customs, characters, or themes evident in the construction of this world. Note that the two rebellious characters themselves are named Homo and Proof: Homo for Homo Sapiens and Proof for scientific evidence, logic, and empirical facts.

No surprise, then, that much of the content and imagery of the novel comes from Yevgeny Zamyatin's *We* (1924). In Sabri Musa's novel, the human population lives in a giant translucent plastic dome, protecting them from the radioactive wasteland that the Earth has become thanks to a long distant nuclear war. This setting bears a remarkable resemblance to the world of Zamyatin, with its crystalline domed city. And there is a heroic duo in the Russian novel as well.

Stereotypes from Western and international SF also creep into Arabic sci-fi on occasion. One such example, I am sad to say, is Syrian. While obscure writer Omar Haswa has a story where the central character is a terrorist, in typical fashion he is the bearded Muslim fanatic. The fact that he can use modern science and technology and invent new and better weapons does not detract for the Western portrayal of Arabs as locked in the past, always donning traditional Arab dress along with the trademark beard.

Arabizing the names and places in novels taken from foreign sci-fi texts is meant to mask over many of these borrowings, but it does not always work. (The same goes for giving spaceships and star bases and scientific cities Arabic and Islamic names, since stock phrases from English and other languages creep in unabated). What are absent are Arabic "themes" and the cultural and religious setting.

Such crossovers with foreign science fiction are not for any lack of creativity or lack of writing skill on the part of Arab authors, we must highlight. Nihad Sharif's "The Thing" is a very benign story about first contact, unlike the original movie which was in the horror genre, and Sabri Musa was a distinguished writer and literary figure in his own right. The pyramidial power structure in Sabri Musa's novel is actually more democratic than in *We*, and even the two-way TV sets of Orwell's *1984* are used in humorous fashion in *Lord from the Spinach Field*, with Homo's wife spying on him while he exercises.

The real problem, however, is a lack of *confidence* on the part of Arab authors. They are all too painfully aware of how new and alien SF is as a genre in the Arab world and are afraid they will not be able to draw the attention of the Arab reader, so they ape the titles and themes and techniques of headline grabbing novels and stories from international sci-fi.

Other problems develop in the Syrian fold as a consequence. Dr. Taleb Omran's writing style, for instance, is heavily influenced by his work in broadcasting. He has the listener in mind when he writes, not the reader, and this does not allow for the level of depth needed for characterization. The tone of voice of the broadcast or actor in question takes the place of narrative voice in a novel and detailed descriptions of people and places. When the protagonist is forced to do something against his principles in *The Dark Times*, for instance, no major transformation takes place. His conscience "bothers" him while he is putting the eggs into the river but nothing more. He only has a guilt-ridden awakening afterwards. Omran's commitment here is to simplification, his desire to popularize science fiction as much as possible to as wide an audience as possible.

This was equally true of Ezz Al-Din Isa and Tawfik Al-Hakim in Egypt in the early days of Arabic science fiction in the 1950s, since both relied heavily on radio plays to popularize this fledging and thoroughly foreign genre to the Egyptian audience. But, and this is critical, this problem was more or less surmounted in the Egyptian experience but still dogs our efforts as Syrians, being latecomers to the field.

The same problems beset *Call of the Green Planet*, and that is in spite of the fact that Diab Eid is a skilled and accomplished writer, and was so long before he ventured into sci-fi. The novel is very well written and full of intrigue and excitement, but it ends rather abruptly to the point that the reader feels that he has not really learned anything he did not already know. The wild forests and dinosaurs of the southern hemisphere and the cold, calculating world of science in the North are clear allusions to *our* world. The mega-corporations in the North are the multinationals of today, and the overthrown scientists proof positive that the North is not nearly as democratic as it thinks it is. The barren patch of land in the South where the heroes encounter a Southerner sounds very much like the giant desert that is the Arab world.

Another more generic problem suffered by Arabic science fiction is the overreliance on archaic terms. Just as Arabic labels are inserted into SF works in an attempt to make them more culturally authentic, one finds that Ihab Al-Azhari, for instance, begins one of his stories, which is set on Mars, with this opening phrase: "It Will Be in Future Times." In Arabic fairy tales and stories, we say, "*Kaan Ya Maa Kaan fi Qadim Al-Zaman*" (Once it Was, A Long, Long Time Ago). His attempt to modify and modernize this phrase is confusing to the reader. Then he has a character address a "king" with the usual Arabic stock titles of "Your Highness" and "Majesty," which puts the reader back in the frame of mind of the *1001 Nights*. You can almost "see" the king, sitting on his throne, with two slave girls on either side of him, dedicated to his pleasure. And this is on Mars!

The storyline is pushing in both directions, future and past, at the same time, an all too common problem in Arabic SF, leaving the reader with an uneasy and untenable synthesis of fairy tale phantasmagoria and hard-core SF. Even the imagery in the *Lord from the Spinach Field*, with Homo walking among the giant spinach leaves, has a fairy tale feel to it, akin to Dorothy in the Land of Oz.

There is nothing wrong with using fairy tale techniques from our rich and varied literary history in a new fold, but it has to be done properly and with moderation. Syrian SF hasn't entirely left this heritage behind, I am sad to say, a subspecies of the larger problems facing the Arabic species of SF.

Politics and Government Incentives

The fight for science fiction in the Arab world is a hard fight, no doubt, but being a Syrian has its advantages. Syria is unique in the Arab world since it is practically the only country that encourages science fiction outright. The Syrian magazine *Science Fiction*, which has been going strong for 11 years now, even in light of the civil war in my country, is published by the Ministry of Culture and Damascus University. There are a number of programs, both on television and radio, about science fiction.

The ministry of culture also hosted the very first conference for Arab science fiction authors in 2007. It was held under the title of Lucian of Samosata, the honorary Syrian who is said to have gotten the ball rolling, so to speak. During the colonial period, Syria was subservient to France, which brought us in touch with French science fiction, not only the marvelous works of Jules Verne (1828–1905) but also André Maurois (1885–1967). And as a socialist country pitted against the forces of Western imperialism, Syria also had ample access to science fiction from the Soviet Bloc, not least of which include Lem and Zamyatin.

The confrontation with imperialism is another advantage, to be honest. Most Arabic science fiction skirts over strictly political matters, and even when it deals with politics, it does this implicitly. In one of his stories, Egyptian author Raouf Wasfi has a Union of Arab States—the term is modeled on the USA—and so Arabs are leaders in space exploration and scientific research. Other writers are not nearly as optimistic and sneak in political commentary to talk about bureaucracy and corruption and freedom, and so on and so forth.

Politics in Arabic SF, and much of Arabic literature, can be summarized in three overriding concerns: the internal situation in Arabic countries; the Zionist occupation of Palestine; and the relationship of the Arab world with the United States of America. But, again, in most Arabic SF—barring the Syrian variety—these are dealt with indirectly, with a few notable exceptions. You have stories with an advanced future where the Arabs are united with no mention of Israel, although Arab unity is not really feasible with Israel dividing the Arab world geographically into two. It is just "assumed" that Israel no longer exists and so the Arabs have advanced. Even Youssef Al-Sibai (1917–1978), the great Egyptian novelist and member of the Free Officers[4] movement, who dealt with the Palestinian cause in several seminal literary works, only touched on the issue in his SF novel *You Are not Alone*. Instead of talking about the Arab-Israeli conflict directly, he implies it through the alien world that is visited in the story, where nations regularly trespass on each other's territory, and war and occupation are the thing of the day. While commenting on these wars, mostly for raw materials and material wealth, the narrative voice talks about a particular patch of land that was taken over by a handful of people from different parts of the planet, using the excuse that they originally lived there in the long distant past. The inhabitants of the country, needless to say, are all booted out.

This is an allusion to the Palestinian cause, but the Earth-bound conflict in the Middle East is hardly ever dealt with directly. Contrast this with Dr. Taleb Omran's novel *The Dark Times*, where a direct line is drawn between the events of September 11, 2001, and the 2003 invasion-occupation of Iraq under the mantra of the War on Terror. The United States is the Great Satan or Evil Empire here.

Of course, subtlety is the anvil of the artist, and we saw above how aliens can be used either as a stand-in for human aspirations or a symbol for imperialist intervention. Still, Syrian science fiction enjoys a unique status to this date. However, I am perfectly happy for this distinctiveness to abate with time and for other Arab SF authors to deal more explicitly with political issues that concern us all as Arabs.

But that is about as far as the good news goes. Syria is a small country and can only do so much by itself, and the number of Syrian authors is limited. What holds true of most Arabic countries also holds true of my country, to a considerable extent. Our countries are backward countries when it comes to science and technology. This does not encourage authors and intellectuals to pursue this path in the world of literature, and the same holds true of publishers and readers. There are no literary prizes for science fiction at the level of the Arab world, and science fiction is not part of the educational curricula in Syria any more than it is anywhere else. In all my years in university, studying everything written in Arabic history from the time of Jahili (pre–Islamic) Arabic poetry to modern Arabic literature, and with all the studies we have conducted on comparative literature, I did not once attend a seminar lecture or lesson on the topic of science fiction.

The Arabic reader is profoundly ignorant of the genre and so shies away from genre works on the bookshelves. As a consequence, the average Syrian—and Arab—author of

SF works "harder" than most authors, but garners *less*. This is dampening to their aspirations and incentives, needless to say.

In Conclusion

Syrian and Arab science fiction is still in its infancy, with all that entails in terms of style and content and the aping of tried and tested formulas from European and Western SF. To add to our worries, there seems to be a backlash against science fiction everywhere in the world.

The world of science fiction is more popular than ever, in cinema and television in the West and internationally, but you feel that *written* science fiction, where the genre itself began, is suffering. The tyranny of the image over the written word in the world of info media and the global village, you could say, is responsible. Education, the writing and reading and scholarly study of science fiction, can counter this, but we have already extolled the problems faced in this regarding Syria and the Arab world, and we are worse off because we do not even rate as contenders in the world of cinema and television.

To my knowledge, the only science fiction movie ever made in an Arabic country was *The Lord of Time*, an Egyptian production starring Nour Al-Sharif and Athar Al-Hakim, adapted from the novel of the same name by Nihad Sharif. While it does have a surprising plot twist in it, taken from the cheap thriller format, it has no special effects, nothing at all to dazzle the Arab audience, although Arabs do thoroughly enjoy Western sci-fi cinema and American blockbusters.

Nonetheless, I am an optimist. I feel that there is a golden age of Arabic science fiction just around the corner. The fact that I am writing an essay for this book is a good portent for the future.

Again, wish all of us luck!

Notes

1. Translated by Emad El-Din Aysha.
2. I passed with distinction receiving an 82% grade, I am proud to say.
3. Qays, for those who do not know, is the legendary romantic poet in Arabic history, who was later portrayed as the Majnun (madly in love).
4. For the benefit of the Western reader, this was the Egyptian movement that overthrew King Farouk in 1952 in light of Egypt's defeat in Palestine in 1948.

Exiled to the Future

Mental Hurdles on the Road Towards Palestinian Science Fiction[1]

EMAD EL-DIN AYSHA

The artist is always engaged in writing a detailed history of the future because he is the only person aware of the nature of the present.
—Wyndham Lewis[2]

The cat sat on the mat is not a story. The cat sat on the other cat's mat is a story.
—John le Carré[3]

A not too humorous anecdote will help explain the subject and pertinence of this contribution. When I had come back to Egypt from England immediately after completing my post-graduate studies in 2001, I was rummaging through my things from my former life and found my old university school bag. (I'd served a freshman year at the American University in Cairo in 1993 before getting an opportunity to study in the UK). Bags weren't nearly as space-aged and comfy as they are now, so I had no intention of using the thing again, but, stickler for detail that I am, I went through its contents to make sure there wasn't anything usable or important in there. I found some papers, I think an AUC newsletter, that I'd used to jot down some notes on. At first, I didn't recognize the cryptic phrases I'd scribbled down all those years ago. There were weird "dates" among the writing. Then I remembered.

It was a "timeline," a plan for a science fiction story outlining the prospective future of a free and independent Palestine. I'd penned the notes shortly after the euphoria of the Madrid Peace Talks and even imagined Hannan Ashrawi as the future Palestinian president, if circumscribed to the West Bank and Gaza (and Jerusalem). I was *so* depressed when the flood of memories came back to me that I tore up the notes and threw them away.

That's a rarity for me. I keep *everything*, specifically scribbles. Those scribbles are what you are, surely? They are your past, a record of what you can't readily remember with your mind. That prefaces the tragedy we are all in as Palestinians and Arabs, living in the past, recording things we did and collecting books about what others before us did, and said, and wrote, and not *planning ahead*, working to construct a better future for ourselves and our nation. One giant, gaping hole in Palestinian literature is science fiction,

If the history of Palestinian science fiction was a film reel, it might look something like this (courtesy of the artist, Ammar Al-Gamal).

the literary species of future studies. We have *adab muqawama* (resistance literature), we have poetry, we have short and long fiction, we have realist fiction, we have "surrealist" fiction—and *very* surrealist fiction at that—and travel fiction, and even some half-decent detective fiction.[4] But what of SF and futurist fiction? Even the recent winner of the very prestigious Arab Booker Prize, Ibrahim Nasrallah's *The Second War of the Dog* (or *Dog War II*), has not been classed in the domain of science fiction. It's set in the future all right but is not "about" the future, according to Nora Parr, a Canadian scholar at the School of Oriental and African Studies (SOAS), University of London (Parr, 2018).

The techniques employed to explore this blurred future-present world are not scientific, after all, but surrealistic. Speaking to a literary activist who's surveyed the latest generation of Palestinians authors, he only knows of one youthful writer who was planning a SF novel, but nothing came of it—without naming names. The literary scene among Palestinians, it seems, is as recalcitrant as it is among Iraqis. No wonder then that Comma Press took such a long time to find a handful of authors to pioneer the Palestinian sci-fi cause with *Palestine + 100* (originally *Nakba + 100*), following on from their groundbreaking *Iraq + 100* (2016) anthology (Aysha, 2018).[5]

It "seems" the literary focus in Palestinian literary circles is either on gritty realism or surrealism, pigeonholing potential authors before they even put pen to paper. Most of the Palestinian literary figures I spoke to while writing this paper were *not* keen on Palestinian SF and knew of no examples of Palestinian SF authors themselves, in spite of the shining example of Palestinian-Jordanian author Subhi Fahamawi and his novel *Alexandria*

2050 (2009). I only came across his novel by accident myself, long after completing the first draft of this chapter. Mr. Fahamawi has a lot of literary devotees here in Egypt, but I had never heard his name before. Most SF buffs in Jordan haven't heard of Fahamawi either.

Again, the tyranny of surrealism and gritty realism. Both literary tendencies, incidentally, are clearly evident in *Alexandria 2050*. I've only read an excerpt, but it left my head spinning, with a hundred year old man having his memories recorded by an electronic, eavesdropping device as he breathes his last, recollecting his trip to Alexandria in 2050 and how the technological wonders on display are as shocking to him as his experience as a ragamuffin Palestinian when he first arrived in Egypt to get his high-school education. Even while onboard the hydrogen powered balloon ship taking him from the UAE to Egypt (in forty minutes flat), he still feels that the flying wonders in *The 1001 Nights* were more advanced, and the computer stewardess agrees with him. Worse still, his son is a geneticist, married to a coldly efficient German woman, and they parent a "green" human being, splicing plant DNA into the human species to create a new, passive, non-troublesome breed of Palestinian. In its own way, it's not unlike *The Second War of the Dog*. Reviews of his novel struggled to classify it as SF, fantasy, or magic realism.

Still, ignoring such a minor classic as *Alexandria 2050* is inexcusable. All the more reason to develop an entire sci-fi project for Palestinian literature in an effort to push history forward. This has been a long time coming, mind you. In his classic *Returning to Haifa* (1969), author and activist Ghassan Kanafani has a Palestinian man and his wife heading off to Haifa, after 20 years, in search of their infant son who was stranded there during the 1948 war. They find that he's been taken in by a kindly Jewish family and raised as a Jew himself, loyal only to Israel and disdainful of his real parents. In the dramatic climax, the father explains that he came here to dust off his memories, only to find more dust, wondering in the end what it is that makes a homeland a homeland, adding, "We were mistaken when we thought the homeland was only the past." Then he explains that his other son, Khalid, wasn't like them at all; to him the "homeland is the future…. Men like Khalid are looking toward the future, so they can put right our mistakes and the mistakes of the whole world" (Kanafani, 2000: 187).

That's precisely what I propose to do here: explore the future history of the Palestinian people in every relevant domain of their lives as it "could" and *should* be in the world of tomorrow. But first, a little trip down memory lane.

Boundaries Between Fact and Fiction

The story of my education and career in the social sciences is intimately tied up with my reading of science fiction. Growing up in Kuwait, there isn't that much to do, especially if you can't abide the atrocious heat and are not the athletic type to begin with. That was the case with me, although I came to heavy-duty reading of fiction a bit later than I should because I was transitioning from English to Arabic. Fortunately, in the meantime, I busied myself with reading up on ancient history and watching a whole lot of TV, enjoying a scientific upbringing at the hands of Carl Sagan, Dr. Mustafa Mahmoud, and David Attenborough. I'd resolved early on to become a scientist, and my favorite genre in cinema and television, not surprisingly, was SF. There was *Max Headroom*, *V*, and the first season of *Star Trek: TNG* to enjoy on television in Kuwait (along with Japanese cartoons), and before that, *Blake's Seven* back in England, and videos of *Predator*, *The Terminator*, *Star Wars*, *Enemy Mine*, *The Last Starfighter*, and *Robocop* to trade with friends. (My brother was an early gamer, and the walls of our bedroom were covered in posters of SF movie-game adaptations too). But I still hadn't got into "reading" SF just yet.

Apart from some fantastical texts we came across at school like *The Wizard of Oz*; *The Lion, the Witch and the Wardrobe*; *The Phantom Tollbooth*; *Mrs. Nisby and the Rats of NIMH*; Roald Dahl's wonderful books (*The BFG*, *The Witches*, even *The Twits*); and Orwell's not nearly as wonderful *1984*, my independent novel-reading really began with Isaac Asimov's *Second Foundation*, the third book in his initial Foundation trilogy. In this future world, the pioneer of psycho-history—the branch of mathematics that predicts human behavior—Hari Seldon built two foundations, at opposite ends of the galaxy, in an effort to speed up the process of rebuilding human civilization after a dark age ensues. (I later finished the whole series while I was sitting out the Gulf War in Egypt). The book came just in the nick of time too, since we'd begun to take IGCSE economics at school in Kuwait. The two subjects, SF and social science, fell into play in my teenage imagination, and I've been more or less there ever since.[6]

That being said, SF is far more "flexible" than social science. SF is more flexible even than the natural sciences. H.G. Wells, you will be shocked to know, wasn't able to publish his views on the relationship between space and time in serious academic publications; that's why he wrote *The Time-Machine* (1895) instead. In the process, he gave birth to an instant classic that spawned a whole subgenre that has haunted writers and readers alike for time immemorial. No surprise then that Wells was one of the early pioneers of futurology, before the discipline even had a name, anticipating many of futurology's most important tenants and lessons: the centrality of change; standards for measuring the passage of time (long, short, medium run); delineating the exact remit of human agency in making history compared to fate; the ethical responsibilities of one generation towards the next; arguments over the progression of time and cyclicality in history; the meaning of material wellbeing and man's growing material, and spiritual, needs; how to measure the success-failure of a policy by setting targets over time, and that kind of thing (Khalaf, 1986: 20).

SF does things like this all the time, and Wells helped get the ball rolling, not to mention that good old H.G. anticipated Einstein's space-time continuum long before the great physicist himself. Science, then, by itself is never enough. Science fiction functions as a *safety valve*, the last refuge of outlandish ideas that otherwise would never have been written down because they went against the grain of what people thought they knew about the world.

Outlandish ideas that might actually turn out to be right and push history forward. Such was the case with the dream of atomic power and weapons helmed by H.G. Wells himself, and journeying to the moon by breaking the escape velocity of the Earth's gravitational field circa Jules Verne. The same goes for social science, doubly so in point of fact. Everything you can say and do in the world of social science will be held against you in a court of public opinion, so to speak, with promotions, tenure, publication and financing all hanging in the wind. Everything done in social science is of some relevance to society; everything in social science has policy implications of some sort or another. The paradox that results is that these societal and political concerns feed back into the knowledge-making process and *stymie* it, since political opponents are afraid that research in this or that field of social science will somehow unseat them or delegitimize their policy proposals. So, again, you need fiction to wriggle out from underneath these ridiculous restrictions, and social science is all the better for it.

Social science always draws on literature and art, but the same is not always true in reverse. And what you can't achieve in the world of academia and policy, you can achieve in the zany netherworld of fiction. The methods employed by social scientists are akin to those in the arts: thought-experiments, counter-factuals, role-playing and conflict scenarios, to name a few. (Don't take my word for it. The name H.G. Wells shows up side by side with the likes of Herman Kahn, Aldous Huxley, and Arthur C. Clarke; Neumann and Øverland, 2004: 262). It's hard to do experiments in the real world of people so you have to try and "imagine" what the consequence of a certain action will be, and "What If" is the most basic question that SF is premised on.[7] Constructing a fictional world is exactly like doing an experiment, where you control for all the external factors governing a phenomenon, and vary a factor you believe to be the key force responsible for the phenomenon. The science fiction novel, amazingly enough, can outdo the realist novel at its own game since the world constructed can be supremely plausible, allowing you to tease out the relations of cause and effect in human behavior (Williams, 1958). That was Raymond Williams' famous argument, and he was about as much of a literary realist as you can get, being a Marxist. Science fiction involves flights of fantasy, true enough, but without breaking laws of human nature and history, just as surely as fundamental laws of physics and the cosmos. Even so, you can still get what you want done just through an act of will-power and the proper deployment of what you know and have trained yourself to learn. In the process, fiction becomes a guide for the real world, giving you policy options, as it were, that are applicable in the sardonic world of recalcitrant facts.

As luck would have it, that's what I ended up doing, inadvertently, with my very first published science fiction story: "A Detour in Space" (Aysha, 2017). It starred an unnamed Palestinian, in outer space no less, trying to resurrect the memory of Salah-u-Din, with and without the help of many an Arab party. He's on Mars taking a (Lebanese) taxi cab to the Syrian neighborhood of the Arab city on the recently terraformed and colonized planet—the Arabs came late to the party, as usual. He finds that there are in fact "several" Syrian neighborhoods, as warring families have carved out their little enclaves in an already too little quarter in the single Arabic city on the red planet. (Don't think it's just the Syrians who are prone to this factionalism. I queried at a Palestinian NGO once if they helped expatriate Palestinians get married, and a woman there—can't remember her name—told me point blank that getting married Palestinian style was hard because it was a clan-based thing. We *really* need to get our own house in order.)

The Egyptian residents fare better, doing great work on the Martian soil, but are too busy filing lawsuits against each other over land disputes. In the meantime, the Israelis have built three cities and are encircling the Arab colony with a chain of Kibbutzim turning the deserts green. (Whenever I describe the story to fellow Palestinians, they chuckle at this repeat of Arab history on somebody else's turf). Fortunately, the other Muslims on Mars—Malaysians, Turks, Iranians—are doing great, opening up options in an otherwise bleak state of affairs.

The story was meant to be a one-off satirical piece, lampooning the current situation, but the germ of an idea grew in my head, transforming the story into a prelude for an entire novel where the Arabs turn the tables once and for all, thanks to their presence on the red planet. (The novel is called *The Algeciras Chronicles*, a name derived from *al-jazeera al-khadraa*, the green island, a city built by the Arabs in Muslim Spain;

Hussein, 2018). I put everything I am—my knowledge of international relations, economic development, sociology, and history—into the novel, trying to produce a manual for the present-day world on how to extricate ourselves out of the situation we have found ourselves in as Arabs, whether in diplomacy and the affairs of state or technology, agricultural science and renewable energy. Not to mention all those other factors operating below the social science radar, such as translation, poetry, architecture, the romance of a planet and the heart of a woman, the power of the spirit, the guiding hand of God behind the scenes and, interestingly enough (see below), the role of the "ears" in the human psyche.[8]

Science fiction has a revelatory function as much as it helps anticipate and create the future. We need to know what we are capable of, the realities of our own souls, if we are ever to build a better future. I class myself in the social science SF subgenre, along with Asimov (typically) but also Robert Heinlein and John Brunner. And that's how I see my mission in literary life: to help construct plausible futures that both the policymaker and the romantic can recognize and find legible, and to help the average Arab reader realize what he is capable of if he has a reasoned understanding of how the world really works, and how nations rise and fall, and rise again.

Contours of a Culture of Resistance

Something like this has actually existed in Arabic literary history, in larval form, thanks to resistance literature or *adab al-muqawama* (أدب المقاومة), something that Arab poets helped pioneer in the past through (شعر الحماسة) the poetry of enthusiasm, (شعر الفداء) the poetry of sacrifice, and (شعر البطولة) the poetry of heroism.[9] Now Arab SF writers are increasingly becoming the torch bearers to this tradition (Aysha, 2019). Lamis Jadid, a Syrian rights activist residing in England, adds that we have for too long as Arabs thought of resistance in strictly militaristic terms (Jadid, 2019). Violence, even legitimate violence, is a double-edged sword, and self-restraint and self-critique and learning from other nations' experiences are all paramount—with literature as an indispensible tool in this regard.

Querying Ibrahim Nasrallah on resistance literature and realism at a book signing event in Cairo, the audience was told point blank that literature *is* resistance and that in the case of Palestine, there was resistance literature *before* there were any actual acts of physical resistance (Nasrallah, 2018).[10] The literature anticipated as well as agitated for the reality, adding that resistance literature helped put together the Palestinian identity more than realist literature did. Note that Ibrahim Nasrallah began his literary career with *White Horses* (2007), a Palestinian epic stretching from the late Ottoman period through the British mandate to the Nakhbah, using the life stories of martyrs in the war for Palestine to tell the tale of a nation forlorn. Since *White Horses*, he's written a whole series of such historically attuned novels, but even someone like him concluded, with time, that history wasn't enough. A futuristic setting was called for: "We must imagine the future in order to understand what is happening now" (Nasrallah, quoted in Parr, 2018).

Nora Parr adds that *Dog War II*, "despite its cruel characters, its acute portrayals of violence, and the dark world it inhabits, at least there is an open future within which we might be able to imagine something different" (Parr, 2018). This is a very SF-type sentiment, if you've ever read Philip K. Dick's *A Maze of Death* (1970). The story has colonists on a planet being bumped off, one by one, only to wake up at the end and realize they're playing a collective game, onboard a doomed spaceship. They actually prefer the virtual world because there was at least the chance of escaping it, whereas in the real world they're all going to die, lost in space. (In the end, they go back to playing the same game, minus one of them who has mysteriously disappeared. He was rescued by a supernatural entity they dreamed up for the virtual world!)

An even better example of skating on the edge of sci-fi is Palestinian author Samir Al-Jundi. I chanced upon him at the 2018 Cairo International Book Fair while looking for Palestinian travel literature. He convinced me to buy his own novel, *Phantasia* (2016) or *Flights of Fancy*, which could be best categorized as "surrealist" travel fiction—assuming that category even exists. (I almost didn't buy it, having used up most of my loose cash, without an ATM machine in sight. But I got it nonetheless—it was as if it was *meant* to happen.) The novel's stated goal, it turns out, is to construct a "new Palestinian." In the story is a man with a reasonably stable life (good job, income, family) looking for his sweetheart, a thinly disguised Palestine, holding conversations with her when she is not even there. She persuades him to *change* who he is, to assume a different name and identity and travel from city to city, in Palestine first then across the Arab world. This affords the protagonist the opportunity to reassert his identity as a Palestinian, and as an Arab, but also to "rethink" his identity.

Walking the streets of Palestinian cities and villages, chief among them Jerusalem of course, like a ghost who can travel unencumbered, he lives the lives of others and learns from their experiences and suffers their different trials and tribulations. He is both no one and everyone. He learns what it is to be a Palestinian and how they do not all have the same problems and how some can learn from others. In each location, he searches for his sweetheart, and she is different each time: her complexion, her eyes, her hair, her dress, etc. There are *so* many "Palestines" out there to fall in love with, the Palestine of the countryside and the city and the hills, etc. No one Palestine holds precedence, nor should it.

I had a tremendous time reading that early phase of the novel and for personal reasons too. I'm only "half" Palestinian and was raised abroad in a very Englishy time-zone, and so I finally had the opportunity to learn what it *felt* like to be a Palestinian, how they eat, drink, decorate their houses, and mingle with the lovely and fragrant environment. (Their sense of color is especially refreshing, with different shades of green, gold, and silver, along with bright reds and dark browns and deep blues.) The hero's travels across the Arab world are not nearly as colorful, but they are just as "enlightening." Here the hero learns self-criticism of the Arab condition. Yes, we are divided, we suffer from oppression, we are being assaulted from the outside world, but most of our problems lie at home. We did this to *ourselves*; we opened ourselves up to foreign conspiracies that mean to drive us apart. All the foreigner did was take advantage of our pre-existing paranoia and grudges. And if there is any hope for the future, it also lies at home.

Samir Al-Jundi goes to great lengths to disown the claims that Egyptians and Palestinians are at war with each other and makes sure to show how Arabs all greet the Palestinian traveller warmly, especially now that many of them have fallen afoul of foreign occupations just like the Palestinians. Special mention should also go to the two chapters set in Tunisia, and partly for personal reasons—I've also got a chapter set in Tunis in my planned *Algeciras* novel, with similar themes, and experienced the same joy in reading that portion of *Phantasia* as I had in writing my chapter. Not coincidentally, those two chapters were the most optimistic. In one nice scene there is a simple Tunisian proclaiming proudly, "My president is my head!" meaning that *he* takes the important decisions in his life, not the glorious leader at the top of the bureaucratic pyramid running the country. Women hold a special role in the Tunis chapters too—I do the same thing in my storyline—since they are assertive, well-educated, cosmopolitan, and know their rights.

Women often represent land and nation in Arabic literature, and all literature to be honest, so why not have them building the future too, by some means other than procreation and child-rearing? Who would have thought fantastical literature could address so many real-world problems? Realists are mostly content with describing what already exists, describing who we *were*, and not who we want to become. This is understandable since we want to preserve our past, our heritage that the Israelis are so busily trying to wipe out, but it must be understood that identity is not solely based on memories and past accomplishments. But what kind of future do we want, exactly, and how do we intend to get *there* from here? That's where science fiction comes to play. Fantasy points us in the right direction, but the scientific imagination helps us actually get there, fleshing out the details.

The agenda implicit in *Phantasia* should be the explicit agenda for Palestinian science fiction. The status of women as nation-builders, pooling cultural resources in the Palestinian territories and reconciling old and outdated differences, learning to be open to what the world has to offer, not placing all the blame on external forces, understanding that our fate is tied up with our Arab (and Muslim) brethren—whether we like it or not—and remaking ourselves as well as preserving the past. Operationalizing these themes is what science fiction is all about, certainly the kind I'm writing. "A Detour in Space" began as a diatribe against the Arab condition but ended up as a call to intellectual arms in order to progress the Arab cause—and it's only two and half pages long. A whole little world grew in its pages that I expanded on exponentially afterwards, enmeshing Palestinian with Arab and Islamic themes. There is the pan–Arab space agency after all, and its Egyptian director, the so-called Controller, with his forceful personality and his tenuous relationship with the Arab financiers of his ambitions. (Not to forget his even more tenuous relationship with the more scientifically advanced Islamic perimeter around the Arab world).

Not that we can't add a theme or two to the surrealist agenda outlined above. From my brief excursions into Palestinian science fiction, two additional concerns emerge that, to my knowledge, have not been addressed nearly enough in the corpus of Palestinian literature. One is language; the other is time. Rethinking what it is to be a Palestinian and creating new and multiple Palestinians must involve some linguistic revaluation and a temporally stretched out plan.

I didn't have this explicitly in mind when I wrote "A Detour in Space" in 2016—it came out a year later—nonetheless, you can't help but notice that the equally pan–Arab Palestinian hero in my story hides his accent in the Lebanese taxi cab as part of his cover. Later you will learn that, in his earlier life on earth, he speaks with a *pidgin* Palestinian accent, allowing him to be true to his roots and mingle with other Arabs at the same time.[11] Not to forget that he's practically a native speaker of English and as cosmopolitan as they come and a bit of a musician like the late Edward Said, and a part-time translator to boot. (Edward Said is a guiding light in my story "The Cymbals of Progress" too.) The female element was lacking at first, the stand-in for the sought after homeland, but I fixed that in the prospective novel—a work that itself is spawning a whole world of short story spinoffs and prequels where I develop this pidgin linguistic identity further.[12] And even his soon-to-be sweetheart speaks "Iberian" as opposed to Spanish, a rich mix of all the dialects and languages of the Iberian Peninsula, which are already full of Arabic words.

Palestinians, as Arabs and Muslims, are part of a bigger linguistic context, and classical Arabic is the great unifier of Palestinians among themselves and with their Arab and Muslim kinsmen. And linguistic xenophobia is to be discouraged at all times. Nonetheless, there is something to be learned about the relationship between language and "remaking" yourself. To follow the lead of sci-fi classic *Native Tongue* (1984), that is, where the underground movement of feminist linguists remake language from male to female-dominated. So far, the contours of linguistic resistance have either come in the form of maintaining local dialects or speaking in strict classical Arabic. Palestinians, even in Israel itself, speak with hometown accents. But why not up the ante and do something completely different? Build a Palestinian dialect from the bottom up, incorporating local dialects into a common, accepted Arabic fold.

It's like the question of Palestinian cuisine (Sen, 2019). Instead of focusing on what it has in common with Lebanese cuisine, we should emphasize local delicacies that are not held in common with the Lebanese and their refined tastes, or the Jordanians with their way too down-to-earth tastes. Something like this already operates with world-famous Palestinian dress, since each town has its own distinctive patterns but as part of a common set of threads. We need an equivalent in the acoustic spectrum, and science fiction is a way of exploring this through the development of a whole "sound technology."

That is something I pursue in the world of my planned Mars novel and my "neuro-acoustic" stories. By the same virtue, we need our own distinctive tunes in music too that capture what it is to be a Palestinian, whether in the countryside or in the city or under occupation or in a refugee camp. The great signer and musician Abd Al-Wahab did this in Egypt, breaking away from Turkish instrumental music, while also—at the exact same time—modifying and *modernizing* Arabic music, incorporating foreign tunes and concepts of harmony and polyphony. And music has to match a tone of voice, which brings us back to language.

Language in turn allows us to deal with a whole set of interrelated themes, such as "cosmopolitanism" and national unity, as well as coexistence (with host nations) and pan–Arabism. Palestinians are quite a cosmopolitan lot, living all over the world as they do, but that doesn't mean they necessarily recognize this fact about themselves and cherish it. There are problems between the 1948 Palestinians and the Palestinians from the West Bank and Gaza and the Diaspora Palestinians. ("Diaspora Affairs," that's a good title for an anthology or a literary journal). I don't think Palestinian literature, to date, has dealt with these problems. SF is a way of transcending these acoustic-linguistic problems altogether. You can have a scenario where such problems are mentioned in retrospect, an archaeological relic almost, with modern day Palestinians (in the future) looking back fondly at that ridiculous period when we allowed such small things to divide us.

That's the beauty of SF. You can *acknowledge* your problems without letting them weigh you down. Problems turn, as if by magic, into solutions, whether technological solutions or policy options. And part of this optimism, this decoupling from the problems of the present, is futurology—changing your whole disposition towards time, leading you to look for your solutions in the future.

A Final U-Turn

Arabs think of Utopia as something belonging in the past (Ghadanfar, 2018). This is doubly the case with Palestinians, having lost their country, their little slice of heaven on earth (Yaqub, 2012). But were things really that good in the not too distant Palestinian past? The realist writers, to their considerable credit, helped expose and analyze what was wrong in the countryside, where the bulk of Palestinians ultimately live. In Ghassan Kanafini's novella عن الرجال والبنادق (*On Men and Rifles*, 1968) there are tobacco and tourism monopolies under the British Mandate that push out local producers, with quite a few Palestinians taking advantage of this situation. Another novelist, Rashad Abu Shawar, was even more critical. He exposed how a jaundiced feudal system existed in many locales in Palestine as certain tribes—Arab nomads from outside Palestine altogether—took over land and commandeered crops and squeezed taxes out of the peasantry, selling their services first to the Turks and then to the English and then to you-know-who (Abdallah, 1989: 263).

So, the past was never all it was cracked up to be, and it's about time we realized that if we are to move on with our lives to new and better things. Just look at what's happening on the artistic scene, such as the Chapter 31 Exhibition gallery displaying futuristic images of Palestine, a Palestinian utopia. One of the artists in question, Rafat Asad, called his painting *Eltifaf* or *Bypass* (a word after my own heart), depicting an "alluring landscape almost entirely enveloped by an advertising billboard." The argument is that "any viable vision of a future Palestine beyond occupation cannot rest on a nostalgic image of an idealized and resilient past, bypassing the difficulties of the present" (Murphy, 2016). Utopian SF, moreover, isn't just about values, but how we pursue them practically in the real-world. It asks a myriad of questions: How will we manage the economy after independence? What will be our most important sources of wealth—industry, agriculture, human capital, commerce, oil, or gas?

Agriculture was the great redeemer for the Zionist project, turning Jews into productive individuals instead of people who lived off savings and usury, with the Kibbutzim being the incubator of the new Jew, and early Israeli literature certainly followed suit (Abdallah, 1989: 250–251). In Palestinian literature, the concern was different, more to do with cataloguing the life of the peasant in an effort to preserve his memory and expose exploitation. However, there's no reason why we cannot build our Utopia on educational foundations set in the countryside, relying on our own history and resources. (I rely on the kutaab, old-fashioned Quran schools, and the heritage of movements like Ikhwan Al-Safa and the Sufi Ribbat).

Then there's the status of women in this future Utopia to consider. I don't just mean equality at the voting booth or in divorce law. What about the bigger picture? Look at what family life was like at the time of Moses (PBUH), with the *girl* choosing the boy for marriage!

Why not recapture that lost world? Not to forget that having Hannan Ashrawi as president would have spared us a lot of trouble from the likes of Mahmoud Abbas, and even Yasser Arafat, respectfully. And then there's the political system, and social equality and neighborly relations. I don't just mean a confederation with Jordan, but dealing with internal issues that have so far been off the table, such as sectarianism and tribalism. (Not to forget clans and marriage within the family and town loyalties). These factors need to be acknowledged and picked apart, if not pecked to death, but in a futuristic format that gives us some hope. We should be mindful of the fact that many early Zionist writers penned novels "about a future Jewish state, among them B.Z. Herzl's depiction of a future Jewish utopia in *Altnoiland* (written between 1899 and 1902) and those other fictive visions of his from the 1890s which are usually regarded as having served as a 'blueprint' for Israel (see Lea Hadomi's study of Herzl and cognate authors)" (Ben-Yehuda and RMP, 1986: 65).

As grim as many of the stories in *Iraq + 100* were, some did hold out hope for the future, with an Iraq both liberated from American dominance and from the dependency on easy money provided by oil, a proud and brilliant people building their own future through invention and social organization. No reason Palestinians can't do the same, at the very least in their fiction, as the first step on a long road to be reconciled with themselves while still in exile.

To end from where I began, I really shouldn't have thrown away those scribbles in a moment of melancholy despair, if only because those scribbles were about my "future" self, as the proud member of an independent, democratic, and egalitarian Palestine. Fiction's a safety valve, like I said, and charting a future course is a sure-fire way to counter depression and desolation. For me, writing about the future of the Palestinians does more than keep me sane.

Without exaggerating, it's the only time I feel *whole*.

Notes

1. Special thanks to Claire and Marcia. Not to forget the agents of the second-hand book market in Cairo—including Shindi Ibrahim Ahmed and Mohammad Salah Al-Shami.

2. Quote taken from "Wyndham Lewis Quotes and Sayings—Page 1," *INSPIRINGQUOTES.U.S.*, https://www.inspiringquotes.us/author/2403-wyndham-lewis.

3. Quote taken from "John le Carré," *Goodreads.com*, https://www.goodreads.com/quotes/13504-the-cat-sat-on-the-mat-is-not-a-story.

4. For detective fiction, please see Abad Yehia's *A Crime in Ramallah* (2017). The pioneer of Palestinian surrealism was Emile Habibi (1922–1996), someone who had to live an unreal existence as a 1948 Palestinian. Nonetheless, he did more than any other Palestinian author to catalogue the geography of Palestine, particularly in the countryside, preserving the memory of villages long demolished by the Israelis (Fadl, 2018: 197–223; Abdallah, 1989: 254–261).

5. The nakba or "catastrophe" is what Palestinians call the 1948 War. Without bragging, I've been involved in *Nakba + 100* from the very beginning and still prefer the original title (Qualey, 2017; 2018). The contributing authors are Talal Abu Shawish, Selma Dabbagh, Emad El-Din Aysha, Samir El-Youssef, Saleem Haddad, Anwar Hamed, Majd Kayyal, Mazen Maarouf, Ahmed Masoud, Abdul Moti Maqboul, and Rawan Yaghi.

6. The same is true of Nobel Prize winning economist Paul Krugman, who fell in love with economics as a teenager reading Asimov's Foundation trilogy (Briggeman, 2013: 400). Fortunately, I also fell in love with the mind-bending science fiction of Philip K. Dick as a toddler, through a freak accident involving Asimov if you must know. In the process I learnt to be skeptical early on and use art as a rejoinder to social science run amok. That, and my math skills are terrible.

7. Here's proof positive, a special issue of the prestigious *Foreign Policy* journal in the U.S. entitled "Debating a World without Israel" (2005). Yes, the question was posed by several top foreign policy hacks in the U.S. and elsewhere: Brian Klug, Mouin Rabbani, Ilan Pappe, Juan Cole, Anatol Lieven, Fouad Ajamiand, Josef Joffe. That is, would the Middle East be a better, or worse, place if Israel had never existed? This is what is called *alternative history*, in sci-fi speak. Admittedly this is one of the few times that social science is ahead of science fiction, as evidenced by this contest: "Other Covenants: Alternate Histories of the Jewish People," https://chizinepub.com/other-covenants-alternate-histories-of-the-jewish-people/.

8. My first sojourn into what I call "neuro-acoustics" began with an accidental contribution to a Canadian sci-fi anthology about Donald Trump, with my story "The Cymbals of Progress." (Please see http://www.darkhelixpress.com/fiction/trump-utopia-or-dystopia-anthology/). I've since turned that story into a series and yes, the hero, again, is a Palestinian. An English-speaking Palestinian with an Iberian (read Andalusian) wife, that is. The premise is built on the work of media theorist Marshall McLuhan, applied

to subjects like extremism and violence. Culture shock, amazingly enough, applies to the 'sound-scape.' Unfamiliar sounds can be hostile and disturbing, and the more you cut yourself off from others the more you *hear* what others say in hostile terms, even if its' your own community. Sound becomes a measure of *alienation.*

9. Some of the poets and literary figures—including Sufi mystics and prominent public figures—involved in this process include (in Arabic): عنين ,البهاء زهير ,الحسن الجويني البغدادي ,ابن سناء الملك ,العماد القيسراني ,ابن الجويني .السيد البدوي إبن مماتي ,الصفدي ,العكاوه ,الشهاب محمود ,ابن مطروح ,الدين إبراهيم لقمان فخر ,ابن

10. This talk was *long* after I'd written and proofed the initial draft of this essay, I'm glad to say.

11. Pidgin, a kind of hybrid language that emerges out of the interaction between two or more languages, the kind of cosmopolitan language they speak in the sprawling metropolis in *Blade Runner* (1982). The first time I came across the word was, it won't surprise you to know, in a science fiction novel: *Native Tongue* by Suzette Haden Elgin. That book had been recommended to me when I was a freshman at the AUC by an African-American psychology professor who'd given a talk on the mind-body problem at the Philosophy Club. (I was a founding member!)

12. One of my Mars spinoffs has in fact finally been published—"Lambs of the Desert," in *The Worlds of Science Fiction, Fantasy and Horror Volume IV*, https://www.smashwords.com/books/view/917584. Two others have been published since.

Works Cited

Abdallah, Mohammad Hassan. (1989). *The Countryside in the Arabic Novel*. Alam Al-Marifa Series. November, 143. Kuwait: Matabi Al-Siyasa [Arabic].

Aysha, Emad El-Din. (1 May 2017). "A Detour in Space." *Reconnecting Arts*. https://reconnectingarts.com/2017/05/01/a-detour-in-space-by-emad-el-din-aysha/.

Aysha, Emad El-Din. (17 May 2018). "*Iraq + 100* (2016): A Test Case in the Still Tortuous Evolution of Arabic Science Fiction." *The Levant*. http://the-levant.com/iraq-100-2016-a-test-case-in-the-still-tortuous-evolution-of-arabic-science-fiction/.

Aysha, Emad El-Din. (23 January 2019). "A Dialogue with my Friend the Resistance author!" *The Levant newspaper*. http://the-levant.com/dialogue-friend-resistance-author/.

Ben-Yehuda, Nachman, and R.M.P. (1986). "Sociological Reflections on the History of Science Fiction in Israel." *Science Fiction Studies*. 13.1, March: 64–78.

Briggeman, Jason. (2013). "Paul Krugman [Ideological Profiles of the Economics Laureates]." *Econ Journal Watch*. 10.3, September: 400–410.

"Debating a World without Israel." (2005). *Foreign Policy*. 147, March-April: 56–65.

Fadl, Salah. (2018). *Narrative Techniques in the Arabic Novel*. Cairo: General Organization of Cultural Palaces [Arabic].

Ghadanfar, Ahmad Adel. (24 February 2018). "Resistant Women in Ali's *Shadows of the Pomegranate Tree* and Ashour''s *Granada Trilogy*." Paper delivered at the *Resist! In Memory of Barbara Harlow, 1948–2017*, conference held at the American University in Cairo, Tahrir Cairo Campus.

Hussein, Donia. (25 April 2018). "Al-Masaa Al-Araby in Conversation with British-Arab author Emad El-Din Aysha." *Al-Masaa Al-Araby*. http://www.mesaaraby.com/view_news.php?id=35641 [Arabic].

Jadid, Lamis. (4 February 2019). "Towards a Broader Conception of Resistance." *Shujun Arabiyaa*.

Kanafani, Ghassan. (2000). *Palestine's Children: Returning to Haifa and Other Stories*. Translated by Barbara Harlow and Karen E. Riley. Boulder: Lynne Rienner.

Khalaf, Hani Abd al-Minim. (1986). *Futurology… and Egyptian Society*. Kitab Al-Hiala Series 424, April. Cairo: Dar Al-Hilal [Arabic].

Murphy, Sinéad. (8 August 2016). "Utopian and Dystopian Palestines: From Literature to Art and Back at the 'Chapter 31' Exhibition." *ArabLit (in English) blog*. https://arablit.org/2016/08/08/utopian-and-dystopian-palestines-from-literature-to-art-and-back-at-the-chapter-31-exhibition/.

Nasrallah, Ibrahim. (23 November 2018). "Book Signing Ceremony for *Second War of the Dog* by the author Ibrahim Nasrallah," held at Tanmia Bookstores, Cairo, Egypt.

Neumann, Iver B., and Erik F. Øverland. (2004). "International Relations and Policy Planning: The Method of Perspectivist Scenario Building." *International Studies Perspectives*. 5.3, August: 258–277.

Parr, Nora. (27 April 2018). "Five Things You Need to Know About 11th IPAF Winner *Dog War II*." *Arab Literature (in English) Blog*. https://arablit.org/2018/04/27/5-things-about-dog-war-ii/.

Qualey, Marcia Lynx. (9 May 2017). "*We the Aliens, Nakba + 100*, and Palestinian Science Fictions." *Arab Literature (in English) Blog*. https://arablit.org/2017/05/09/we-the-aliens-nakba-100-and-palestinian-science-fictions/.

Qualey, Marcia Lynx. (18 December 2018). "Future-focused *Palestine +100* Wins PEN Translates Award." *Arab Literature (in English) Blog*. https://arablit.org/2018/12/18/future-focused-palestine-100-wins-pen-translates-award/.

Sen, Mayukh. (4 February 2019). "A Writer Describes Palestinian Cuisine, and the World Around It." *The New*

York Times. https://www.nytimes.com/2019/02/04/dining/yasmin-khan-zaitoun-palestinian-cookbook.html?fbclid=IwAR1yC3e_W2h9EdHEt9_p50sR6XNQPtDBxtjX4WNQhOewteFMdSksFpI2yC8.

Williams, Raymond. (1958). "Realism and the Contemporary Novel." *Universities & Left Review.* 4, Summer: 23–24.

Yaqub, Nadia. (2012). "Utopia and Dystopia in Palestinian Circular Journeys from Ghassān Kanafānī to Contemporary Film." *Middle Eastern Literatures.* 15.3: 305–318.

An Eye on the Past, an Eye on the Future

Charting an Independent Course for Iranian SF

Zahra Jannessari-Ladani

> He who becomes the slave of habit, who follows the same routes every day, who never changes pace, who does not risk and change the color of his clothes, who does not speak and does not experience, dies slowly.
>
> —Pablo Neruda (quoted in Dahl, 21 February 2020)

As a member of the English Language and Literature faculty of Isfahan University, a translator and sometimes poet, I came late to science fiction. My first encounters were with Stanley G. Weinbaum as a translator, and then John W. Campbell and Robert A. Heinlein as an academic researcher. I came even later to Iranian science fiction, but I have been making up for lost time ever since. Little did I know that Iran has produced a formidable corpus of science fiction that has, almost from the beginning, tackled issues seldom dealt with in mainstream Western sci-fi, and in new and original ways. Iranian SF has introduced motifs and themes and literary techniques that rate as just as innovative and challenging as any of those produced in the European birthplace of the genre. Sadly, Iranian SF has not garnered the popular attention and critical acclaim it deserves, either internationally or within Iran itself, which is why it has taken so long for academics in my profession to stumble on it. Iranian science fiction not only has its own merits, morally and aesthetically, but can be taken as a new perspective that allows non–Iranian audiences to become acquainted with Persian culture and history and appreciate Iranian ways of looking at things. In the event that the works of Iran's SF authors gain international recognition and enjoy critical analysis and appreciation, these works will contribute new motifs and ideas to the main body of science fiction.

In this chapter, I will first render a brief overview of Iranian science fiction and then try to focus on the main reasons that held back the proliferation of the new genre with its many distinguished early contributions in Iran. From there, I will provide the reader with a detailed reading of several works from contemporary Iranian science fiction, both literature and (most recently) television.[1]

Transplanting Iran's architectural heritage onto another world is not so tall an order given the country's long and proud scientific and fantastical heritage, at variance with much of the Near East (courtesy of the artist, Ammar Al-Gamal).

I. A Story of Birth, Stasis, and Resurrection

Iranian science fiction might strike SF scholars and critics as somewhat new and unrecognized as no Iranian SF work has been seriously introduced or discussed internationally. There are controversial views on the beginning of SF narratives in Persian literature. Iranian SF critics and scholars have recently recognized, for example, parts of Ferdowsi's great epic *Shahnameh* (11th century) to be science fictional. The first group of critics and historians of literature date it back to the 10th and 11th centuries when Ferdowsi (935–1020 AD), the great Iranian bard and chronicler of the Persian kings, took it upon himself to write a fantastical story of the flight of King Kavous to the heavens by means of domesticated and trained eagles to enumerate the stars and visit the sun and moon (Ghassa, 2014; Mirabedini, 2008); or when Avicenna wrote his narrative mystical treatise titled *Hay the Son of Yaqzan* ("Hay" means alive and "Yaqzan" means awake) in which Hay—allegory for reason—sets off on a spiritual journey (quest) from Jerusalem (the east/the locale for pilgrims in the quest of truth/the world of reason) to find his father. The second group of critics believe that these ancient narratives may contain SF elements, but since they belong to a different tradition, they cannot be categorized as SF. They argue that these ancient works came into being at a time when no such genre as science fiction existed and that they had not been written based on motives and mechanisms that emerged since the 19th century and led to the burgeoning of a great body of literature concerned with matters of science, scientific extrapolation and speculation, and techno-logical progress.[2] The latter group believes that Persian science fiction emerged as a result of the influence Western writers such as Jules Verne and H.G. Wells exerted on Iranian fiction writers (Arianpour, 1993: 277). Based on this view, the beginning of science fiction in Iran follows the translation of SF works written by non–Iranian writers, and this trans-lation movement was partly indebted to the efforts of Zabihollah Mansouri, whose free translations acquainted the Iranian audience with the classic works of Jules Verne (Tooy-serkani, 2005: 66). Against the views of the second group, the first set of critics, especially Ghassa, argue that the ancient science-fictional narratives flourished in Iran due to the advancement of natural sciences during the Golden Era of Islamic Civilization (particu-larly the 10th and 11th centuries) and waned as those scientific achievements declined. The decline endured till the last half century when, once again, a serious incorporation of the sciences into the new educational system occurred and paved the way for the emer-gence of SF stories in Iran. Given that the production of science fiction highly depends on the progress of science and technology, the revival of this mode of writing inevitably con-curs with Iran's recent techno-scientific advancements. In other words, the first group's verdict is that the SF mode of writing in Iran has been merely disrupted due to a decline in the course of techno-scientific history, and thus its obscurity on a(n) (inter)national level does not necessarily mean that it was totally absent.

Despite their disagreement on a starting point for Iranian SF, both groups agree that "modern" Iranian SF began under the influence of Wells and Verne. So, I put aside the question of the ancient Iranian science fictional mode of writing or pseudo-scientific works because it would require a separate chapter; this chapter, therefore, will concen-trate on modern Iranian SF. Towards the last years of the 1950s, besides the works of Wells and Verne, Karel Čapek's *The Absolute at Large* (1922) and Voltaire's *Candide* (1959) and *Micromegas* (1952) were translated into Persian. Around the same time, Tooyserkani translated John Christopher's *The Tripods Trilogy*. Alongside these translations, visual media also contributed to the boom; several TV series, including *Tin*, *UFO*, *Star Trek*, *Six Million Dollar Man*, *Bionic Woman*, *Beyond Horizon*, and *Space 1999* were broadcast nationally (Tooyserkani, 2005: 68).

These initial efforts mostly comprised translations, movies and TV series, and comic strips based on non–Persian movies and novels. The first true Iranian SF novel, how-ever, was written before 1950, i.e., *Rostam in the Twenty-Second Century* (1934) by Abdol-hossein San'atizadeh Kermani. The novel was first published in the footnote section of a newspaper but later came out in book form.[3] It recounts the story of an American sci-entist who travels to Sistan (a southeastern city in Iran believed to be the birth place of Rostam, the Iranian mythological hero in Ferdowsi's great epic 11th century poem, *Shahnameh*), to bring the great hero back to life by gathering the remains of his body from his burial place and feeding it into a machine. The novel can be categorized as an invention story, one which extrapolates a new method of resurrection and ends with the conclusion that each human being, Rostam included, is fit for his/her own era, and that a triumphant hero in one era might simply turn into a flop in another. San'atizadeh's other work, *Ālame 'Abadi* (*The Eternal World*) (1938), bestows a unique cast on its didactic mes-sage by mingling science fiction with ontological questions. It creates great suspense by bringing together several scientists who set out to fight senility and death by trying solu-tions such as transplanting the organs of the dead into the living, discovering the artificial heart, and in vitro fertilization. The science fictional side of the story is sustained by the mental journey of a hotel chef who is witness to the wars and triumphs of Alexander the Macedonian in search of the elixir of life.

In a note on San'atizadeh's *Rostam*, Mohammad Ali Jamalzadeh, the father of the Persian short story, maintains: "Nowadays, anyone who writes and publishes a book in Persian language should be lauded, particularly those similar to the respected writer of this book possessed of a strong imaginative faculty, a free mind and an eloquent, sweet and simple language" (First Iranian SF Novel, 2017). In addition, Mirabedini (2008) distinguishes San'atizadeh's works as serious science fiction bearing the mark of invention and differing from the fantasies and romances written in the past. The book is based on a number of inventions like the resurrection machine, television, radio, voice recorder, cinematographic photography, and thought/imagination recorder. In fact, the merit of San'atizadeh's science fiction is that it conjoins the elements of ancient Persian culture and modern Iranian life by highly imaginative techniques and by displacing prominent Iranian figures and examining them inside new and bizarre contexts. Actually, San'atizadeh practices what Darko Suvin terms as "estrangement" by building new worlds to recast the already familiar mythological and cultural issues (Suvin, 1979: 49).

Another outstanding figure at this time is Sadegh Hedayat, famous author of *The Blind Owl*, who also wrote four short and long SF stories: "S.G.L.L." (1933), "The Fathers of Adam" (1933), "Mount Damavand's Monkeys" (unknown), and "Buried Alive" (1930).[4] "S.G.L.L." adopts SF elements to postulate philosophical thoughts on life and death, art and the process of artistic creation, as well as love and lust. This experimental story gains a genuine aesthetic status. In Hedayat's fictional world, two millennia later, techno-scientific progress has made it possible to gratify man's bodily and material needs. In this world, man is relieved but remains vain, and becomes fed up and sickened with his fruitless and empty life and, thus, finds redemption in death and suicide. As a solution, Hedayat's scientist invents the S.G.L.L. serum to destroy lust in men as well as to abolish the human race. He injects this serum into everybody but, by virtue of a mistake in the laboratory, the public goes mad and starts to commit suicide. According to Pedersen (2002), the surging despair in the story signifies "Hedayat's dread of his contemporary society," a society devoid of emotion whereby "the story's Utopia becomes an *Outopia* ('a non-existing place')" (89). Milani (1992) elaborates further by remarking, "City and city life equal modernity … [but] city in Hedayat's works is nothing but misery, wretchedness, and desolation … and modernity, despite its seemingly forward-moving progress, has brought no significant melioration to the human circumstances … in 'S.G.L.L.,' science and citizenship triumph, but people are disgruntled and in greater pain than before" (559). Hedayat cannot reconcile himself with institutionalized modernity and deems the absolutist monarchy to be incapable of making any fundamental change in the Iranian society.

A contemporary writer with similar works is Abbas Arianpour Kashani whose *The Machine of Life* (1937) sets its narrative in 2500 CE. The machine invented in this novel turns the old into youths; the invention, nonetheless, ends up in unexpected crises: famine, sterility, etc. Here, the scientists' attempts to restore man's power of fertility and bring the dead back to life become exclusive and are applied only to those who once were great agents of constructive change in the course of human history, particularly philosophers and poets such as Khayyam and Rumi. But eventually, the scientists decide to hurl the resurrected men into the void of nonbeing for the frustration and vexation they cause by their endless disputes and idle chatter. Again, this novel is an instance of invention story with gadgets and devices—"life machine," "gas of nonexistence," "remedy of life," and "machine of resurrection"—to answer socio-philosophical questions and solve the current problems. Like San'atizadeh, Abbas Arianpour is concerned with the creation of odd situations and removing the borders of time and space to render the negotiation between past and present possible. Arianpour's speculative outlook also coalesces matters of Persian culture and literature into science fiction, taking full advantage of its scientific as well as philosophical potential, his primary concern being national rather than universal issues and motifs. The readers outside Persian culture can get acquainted with Iranian culture and literature by reading Arianpour's and San'atizadeh's works.

Seemingly, Iranian SF writers from San'atizadeh to Hedayat perceive man's scientific advances as doomed, balancing their protagonists' horror and desperation against the most recent scientific achievements. They reveal their concern and anxiety about the current situation so much so that miseries are found in their utopian works as well. Nonetheless, they benefited from the allure of science fiction as a means to represent typically boring subjects in a fresh and innovative fashion.

Dr. Zahra Jannesari-Ladani with the bust of famous modernist poet Mahdi Akhavan Sales (courtesy Dr. Jannesari-Ladani).

The cynical ending of these novels has its roots in the dualistic view many Iranian intellectuals had adopted toward modernity. This view is an amalgamation of attraction and repulsion: attraction toward the acquiring of Western knowledge and technology, and repulsion from new civic thoughts and institutions and from the dark side of modernity that objectifies man. In other words, there is a repulsion following from the phobia of abandoning tradition to join modernity, and from the inquietude resulting from a loss of traditional self-assurance and a struggle against the confusions of modern life conditions, particularly because the advent of modernity in Iran was concurrent with Russian military advances against Iran and the threat of invasion by other colonizers. "Talbof was one of the first theorists who perceived the hidden but potential conflict between modernity and national identity.... He cautioned against the Neverland promised by western civilization, so that one could sense 'the evil stench' of this concept which later became current through its propagators" (Vahdat, 2001: 153–53). In a similar vein, during the post–1931 years, in a series of articles published in *Shafaghe Sorkh* since March 1932, Ahmad Kasravi, the most prominent Iranian critic of European civilization, posited his religious and moral perspective by maintaining that European civilization not only has brought no progress to human society but also has stifled man in guilt and corruption. Put differently, the end of the path taken by Europeans is nothing but man's ruin. Kasravi (1933) deems the mechanization of life in Europe to be the reason for the disturbance of harmony and equilibrium, and with a romantic outlook, commends the old ways of life and desires a return to soil and ploughing, since he believes that materialistic progress has not actually brought comfort to man but has sharpened his pain and made the world a more horrendous place to live in. Both Talbof and Kasravi see Iran as a developing country on the verge of becoming a replica of Europe in terms of the sacrifice of human society to the machinery of technology.

The above-mentioned works of fiction were written prior to the 1970s when the Iranian literary market and television were witness to a translation boom and frequent broadcasting of SF movies and TV series respectively. It is odd that before the boom, original stories and novels had already started to be written, but during the 70s and even later decades, no significant original SF corpus came out. What could possibly be the reason for this halt in the process of the creation and development of a nascent genre in Iran? Tooyserkani relates this impasse to political, social, and economic conditions in Iran at the time. First, the Pahlavi regime (the two monarchs Reza Shah and his son Mohammad Reza) seemed to advocate the advancement of intellectual activities and circles, but in reality, writers from such circles were under suspicion and prone to prosecution by the government's intelligence agency, SAVAK, since the activity of these writers could trigger social unrest and political protests. Second, literacy rates among the public were low and thus, published materials were read only by the educated and those in academia. The third reason is a consequence of the second: commonly, no more than 2,000 copies of a book were published, among them for instance, the translation of Verne's *Twenty Thousand Leagues Under the Sea*, Wells's *The Time Machine*, and Clarke's *2001: A Space Odyssey* (Tooyserkani, 2005). Economically, therefore, publication did not enjoy good prospects, whether original or translated SF.

Tooyserkani's set of reasons for the non-proliferating genre of SF in Iran is very insightful, since it is based on his individual life experience of translation as well as magazine editorship and publication. His observations gain greater credence and depth once additional details are given about the social and political history of Iran at this time. I would like to shed more light on Iran's historical and political context when it was pushed toward modernization agendas that directly affected the Iranian attitude toward SF. The year of 1941 coincides with the coronation of Mohammad Reza Pahlavi, son to Reza Shah (the Iranian monarch during 1925–41). Reza Shah had set out to modernize Iran in many directions since 1925: large road construction projects resulted in a great expansion in the building of highways as well as transportation by roads and railways; the University of Tehran was established and higher education in its Western academic fashion became available to Iranian scholars; industrial plants also increased in number. All this meant that the Iranians had to realign their traditions and religious codes with the modern conditions surrounding their life. One of the ramifications of this modernization was the "Unveiling" project that Reza Shah intended to consolidate, which led to public protest, since the project was in direct opposition to the Iranians' Islamic beliefs. A closer look into the modernization project manifests that things had been arranged by the British imperial power to use the country as a springboard for reversing the advances made by the Russian Revolution in 1917. By 1920, Iran had become a battleground for Russian and British forces. Under Reza Shah's regime, Iran was to become a British satellite to control the Middle East. Thus, Iran's modernization did not impact the literati in a positive way, a major reason for the notoriety of techno-scientific advancements in Iranian speculative fiction up to 1941 (the year of Reza Shah's deposition and abdication as well as Mohammad Reza's coronation).

The year of 1941 precisely falls in the period famously referred to as the American SF Golden Age (roughly 1938–1946), and precedes the British one, which did not come until the 1960s. Iranian writers could have no such optimistic views on scientific progress as American writers had during the first four decades of the 20th century. The American maverick culture and pulps exerted a great influence on the development of SF as a new genre.[5] Techno-scientific discourse in the daily life of Americans was further entrenched with the ascendency of the American corporate system. While World War II brought a halt to the production of American SF, it established the U.S. as a superpower in the world and pushed SF into new directions. Compared to this, no such optimism imbued British SF during this time. Still, British writers added to the large SF corpus they had started to produce earlier than their American counterparts. In contrast, Iran neither experienced such SF pulp explosions, nor had figures such as H.G. Wells or J.G. Ballard to promote the genre. Things were no better in Mohammad Reza Pahlavi's reign. The technology imported from other countries was entirely controlled and manipulated by foreign agents, so much so that no Iranian could possibly learn how to handle, maintain, or repair machines. Where Iranian technicians were present, they were still only secondary to their foreign counterparts in industrial plants, remaining uncouth, inexperienced, and dependent, suffering various degrees of colonization in their own country.

This situation is not comparable to the dominant scientific atmosphere in America and the Continent where mavericks, scientists, and inventors progressively worked through their genuine ideas in techno-scientific terms. In addition, the two Pahlavi monarchs suppressed progress of any sort among the public by emaciating and keeping talents in control, imprisoning reformists and dissidents, and especially revolutionaries, torturing and murdering them. A case in point is the demise of Mohammad Mosadegh—the prime minister of the time who was committed to the nationalization of the Iranian petroleum industry—and his replacement with General Fazlollah Zahedi to suppress the former's project. Nonetheless, Mosadegh's popularity remained intact and protests led to the coup d'état of 1953. The protests gained momentum and were carried on to the next two decades when they exploded into a full-fledged Islamic Revolution led by Leader Khomeini. The post–Revolution phase saw political and economic turbulence due to hostilities on the side of both domestic and foreign adversaries of the Revolution. Iranian resistance against these hostilities made adversaries think of an extended war against Iran and, thus, Saddam Hussein was chosen to operate the plan. Hence, an eight-year war (1980–88) broke out between Iran and Iraq.

The post-war era in Iran was devoted to reconstruction and the exploration of new ways of progress in all directions. Iran was now an emancipated nation after 2,500 years of being torn to pieces and harassed by monarchs and colonizers. The Iranians proved that their revolution was earnest, that they would never again wish to be ruled by kings, and that their Islamic republic would provide them with opportunities to restore their identity and participate in the building up of their nation's future. The Iranians had a great historical, cultural, and social heritage, part of which had been lost in the hands of undeserving kings. The Iranians required time to revive this treasure, but this seemed difficult in the context of global sanctions imposed on the country. Of course, these sanctions were not new. They had started after the 1979 Revolution, expanded in 1995, and intensified once more in 2006. The post–Revolution era, however, has been techno-scientifically crucial, mostly in terms of indigenous achievements.

I would like to suggest that written speculative fiction after 1941 in Iran never became a focus of attention possibly for several reasons. In the period of 1941–1979, Iran was still ruled by a monarchical system dependent on imperialists; thus, practically, the nation was colonized. Life priorities in a colonized nation are not the writing of SF or any other genre unless it serves to encourage decolonization by means of an ideological critique of the *status quo*. As a result, the Iranians could not possibly think of traveling to the moon or other extraterrestrial alternatives while their territorial integrity was still uncertain. Neither could they think of such things because they were not colonizers; the idea of traveling to other planets was mostly cherished in countries that had a long colonial experience in diverse parts of the world; i.e., countries with anxieties concerning "economic and cultural inundation of the postcolonial world" (Rieder, 2008: 148). For these reasons, the Iranians could barely think of inventions in their stories, since they had been kept backward for such a long time. Great scientists like Abu Rayhan Biruni (973–1048), Avicenna (980–1037), Omar Khayyam (1048–1131), and Sheikh Bahaei (1547–1621) belonged to a golden past in Iran's history and to discover, educate, and patronize such geniuses required proper socio-economic and political grounds, which were lacking during this phase. Since SF was no priority among Iranians at this time, scholarly work in the SF field, too, was palpably lacking. Perhaps few Iranian scholars felt the necessity of looking into, recognizing, and crediting this new genre, or perhaps the task was too costly for scholars to afford. Ghassa's view in this regard is noteworthy; he believes that three crucial factors had led to this condition: lack of a professional institute or magazine for the flourishing of this genre; lack of written SF stories in opposition to the growing interest in the translation of foreign works; the adherence of Iranian writers to formal and stylistic features of western writing as a gesture of enlightenment and as a refutation of backwardness. Indeed, Iranian SF found its real voice as soon as Iranian writers welcomed their indigenous values and foregrounded their national identity in their fiction.

Ghassa adds that the Iranian new wave in SF actually began in the 1980s when the translation of SF novels and short stories into the Persian language was gradually resumed after a break of two years caused by the Islamic Revolution (1979). This led to the publication of two to five translated titles annually for several years. One magazine promoting this movement was *The Scientist*, publishing a special issue on SF in addition to several translations. Some of the most prominent translators in this line are Peyman Esmaeelian Khameneh, Mohammad Ghassa, Naser Baligh, Hossein Ebrahimi (Alvand), Hooshang Ghiasi, Hassan Asghari, and Shahriar Behtarin. According to Ghassa, there were also some publishers contributing to this progress, e.g., Ofogh, Shaghayegh, Noghteh, Pasargad, and Bonyad.

During the last two decades, however, we have been witness to the writing and publishing of more SF novels and short stories as well as the production of TV series and movies. Novels such as Mohammad Ghassa's *The Leap of the Next Day's Memories* (1998), Rasoul Hosseinli's stark satirical SF *Tehran under Achilles' Heels* (1999), and Iraj Fazel

Bakhsheshi's *Men and Supertowers* (2006), *A Message Older than Time* (2007), and *The Guardian Angel* (2008), all incorporate national and indigenous elements as well as Eastern and Islamic tenets.

Works written by other writers have been published in an electronic magazine by the Speculative Fiction Group (SFG), a professional club of (mostly young) writers, critics, translators, and fans. Formerly known as the Fantasy Academy, SFG was founded in 2004. Meeting weekly to discuss science fiction, horror, fantasy, and detective genres, the club encourages young talents to write creatively. SFG also bestows the annual Persian Speculative Fiction Art and Literature Award to the best writers, translators, critics, publishers, and promoters of the genre. Furthermore, SFG is the founder of an online magazine as well as an encyclopedia, *Shegetfzar* and *Persian Speculative Encyclopedia* respectively. SFG is also responsible for having held three SF and fantasy and two fan fiction writing contests at diverse venues to celebrate great SF writers such as Robert A. Heinlein, Isaac Asimov, and Ray Bradbury; SFG members have translated over seventy SF stories into Persian and written over eighty Persian SF and fantasy stories and fifty interviews, reports, and essays related to SF and fantasy. They have reviewed over thirty SF books and films; SFG has published a Persian book as well as six translations on SF. As a pioneering force, SFG has attracted writers from different parts of Iran and continues to welcome more members each year. Some of the best stories published in *Shegetfzar* include "The Movement" (2011) and "The Warning" (2012) by Habibollah Kalantari; "Gospel in the Words of the Military Man" (2007) and *Mona* (2011–12) by Arman Selahvarzi; "Teleporter" (2008) and "The Lovely Horror" (2011) by Ebrahim Taghavi.[6]

Contributing to this promising progress in the last two decades, some successful cinematic productions are worth mentioning: Rambod Javan's comic series *The Travelers* (2009), Masoud Abparvar's TV series *Black Intelligence* (2010), Behrooz Afkhami's *The Fox* (2014), and Javad Ardakani's series *Nooshdaru* (2012–2013), among others. A thorough examination of the mentioned works within this chapter is impossible and should be held up in future research. However, for the purpose of this chapter, three works will be reviewed and analyzed: Iraj Fazel Bakhsheshi's *A Message Older than Time* and *Guardian Angel* and Javad Ardakani's series *Nooshdaru*.

II. Iraj Fazel Bakhsheshi: A Hallmark in Iranian SF

Iraj Fazel Bakhsheshi is one of the best SF writers of our time, with six novels and two collections of over fifty-two short stories, signifying a hallmark in the history of SF in Iran. He was born on 19 April 1965 in Mashhad. He studied at the University of Tehran and graduated as a mining engineer in 1989, and now he works in the mining industry. His novels and short story collections include *Men and Supertowers* (2006), *A Message Older than Time* (2007), *Guardian Angel* (2008), *Patient in Chamber 320* (2009), *The Sun's Sons* (2011), *Yellow River Mine* (2013), *Mr. Fourth Generation and Other Stories* (2014), *Travel to Planet Tera* (2016), and *52 Short Stories* (2017). Only a few of his stories, i.e., "Murder," "Sorrow and Mirth," "World in World," and "Lilith" have been translated to Russian and Kazakh and published on some social networks such as Facebook. His science fiction has been appreciated for investigating and foregrounding human issues, culture, and the influence of techno-scientific progress on society. His characters usually have no names; this means that they can be understood universally, but simultaneously he shows his commitment to national and indigenous concerns by incorporating them in his fiction so skillfully that the Iranian reader will immediately recognize them. Fazel Bakhsheshi's amazing imaginative power encapsulates local/regional incidents and events, vocational matters, and social concerns in such unfamiliar fictional coordinates that the effect is almost always thought provoking or even shocking.[7]

Fazel Bakhsheshi distinguishes SF as a convenient subgenre for developing themes, since it outstrips conventional or mundane settings and is capable of creating greater suspense. In an interview, he explained that he had been reading SF since childhood, including the works of Jules Verne and Isaac Asimov. While what he has read might have shaped his fictional world, there is no particular SF writer that he considers as a model for his writing (Hosseini, 2011). Time travel, space travel, invention stories, alternate history, and social and anthropological science fiction are the major categories found in his works. For instance, time travel and alternate history are major devices in *Guardian Angel*, where a detective travels back to the time of Cyrus, the great Iranian king, to save the Cyrus Cylinder (c. 538–539 BC) from destruction and oblivion. Space travel is the subject of *Travel to Planet Tera*, *A Message Older than Time*, and *The Sun's Sons*. And social and anthropological concerns do appear in almost all of his fiction, particularly *A Message Older than Time*, *Men and Supertowers*, and *The Patient in Chamber 320*. Here, I would like to select two of Fazel Bakhsheshi's novels for discussion in greater detail: *A Message Older than Time* and *Guardian Angel*.

A Message Older than Time shows Fazel Bakhsheshi's great concern with matters of (d)evolution. The novel examines the reasons for the perishing of the advanced civilization of the semi-cartilaginous species living before the Paleolithic era. This species enjoys the greatest degree of evolution due to its biological privileges lacking in other species. They have three hands and three legs: two pairs osteoid and one pair cartilaginous. In fact, they are somewhere between invertebrates and vertebrates, but compared to these two species, the semi-cartilaginous are more evolved because their hands and legs grant them higher speed and maneuverability over the uneven surface of the earth. These creatures live in advanced constructions built into caves near salt waters, and their scientists have been able to achieve technological breakthroughs, building spacecraft as well as decoding messages into energy and back, messages that move across time, and can be fed into the brains of other species and understood by them regardless of their language or means of communication. The race's life is, nonetheless, threatened by a gigantic meteorite approaching the earth. As the narrator, White-Head-Fifty-Five-Moles-In-The-Third-Hand (Five-Moles), reveals in the course of his message to the geologist and mining engineer in our era, the problem is not actually the meteorite which is going to destroy parts of the earth and change its atmospheric features, but the corrupt and basically racial/hierarchical ideology that dominates the society of the semi-cartilaginous. They prepare to travel to a new home world—Earth II— before the meteorite strikes the earth, but then again, they apply a very stratified method in the selection of the fittest to travel first in the best spaceship, leaving others behind to travel in spaceships with little chance of survival due to their greater size and smaller fuel store. The narrator does not mention whether the travelers of spaceships with smaller chances of survival could escape the Earth in good time or not, but he allows us to know that he himself was responsible for the destruction of the first spaceship that was supposed to carry the first-rank citizens to Earth II. During the flight, the semi-cartilaginous biologist presses a button that hurls the spaceship into the magnetic orbit of the meteorite where it strikes the colossal germ and explodes. The biologist actually determines to put an end to the semi-cartilaginous species to prevent their colonization of Earth II as well as transplanting their racist attitudes in building a second civilization. The escape ironically materializes in self-annihilation and extinction of a whole species.

The astronomical findings at the time of Five-Moles indicate that after the Earth rotates around the sun a million times, the chances are high that a meteorite will strike the Earth again (Fazel Bakhsheshi, 2007). So before leaving the Earth, the biologist records a message for later species who might have the chance of survival, to caution them against the approach of another meteorite. The message advises the later species, particularly the human race that has evolved from anthropoids and possesses a greater chance of survival due to its higher mental powers (despite its more vulnerable physique), not to repeat the fatal flaws of the semi-cartilaginous race and their elitist and disintegrationist approach toward their ilk and other life forms. Indeed, more than just a message, it is a critique of the semi-cartilaginous civilization and can be taken as a deftly devised allegory of man's civilization. This novel, moreover, can be categorized as a biological (evolutionary) fantasy, one which bears resemblance to Stanley G. Weinbaum's "The Lotus Eaters" and "The Mad Moon," where the author focuses on diverse species and places them within the context of possible civilizations. By deploying this SF subcategory in the writing of *A Message Older than Time*, Fazel Bakhsheshi actually renders his pessimistic view of man's civilization and proposes reformist steps towards real evolution (that is, humanitarian perfection rather than biological fitness). In his view, man's physical and intellectual evolution does not necessarily mean social and psychological improvement; rather, he thinks highly evolved societies are more vulnerable to extinction unless they adopt a philanthropic and altruistic approach in solving their problems: "The opportunities you will lose in the course of your evolution due to your narrowmindedness and the time you spend on fighting others or imposing your beliefs on them are irretrievable. You must believe that you and your ilk as well as other creatures on earth have mutual interests and that lack of respect for the rights of others ends in annihilation" (Fazel Bakhsheshi, 2007: 72).

If Fazel Bakhsheshi's *A Message Older than Time* mostly focuses on universal issues, *The Guardian Angel* examines national history and the status of Iran as a harbinger of peace among the nations of the world. In this novel, the Cyrus Charter is stolen from a museum. The Charter is an object from ancient times in Iran made of clay upon which statements in the Babylonian language have been written. The cylinder was first believed to have belonged to the monarchs of Babylon and Assyria, but further investigation indicated that it dated back to 538 BCE and was crafted after King Cyrus the Great (530–550 BC) commanded so upon his entrance into Babylon. It was found in the excavations of the ancient city of Babylon in 1879 in the Mesopotamia region, but the barrel-shaped cylinder has been damaged in the course of history and thus part of the written script on it is indecipherable (Fazel Bakhsheshi, 2008). The Cyrus Charter is the most ancient manifesto on the rights of man discovered to date and is considered as a document of honor for the Iranians, since it attests that the Iranians were pioneers in honoring the beliefs and thoughts of other nations. Below is part of Cyrus' declaration engraved on the Cylinder:

> When I entered Babylon with no war and bloodshed, all people welcomed me happily…. Marduk (the Babylonian god) attracted the pure hearts of the Babylonians to me for I honored them. My great army entered Babylon peacefully…. I never allowed any affliction to be suffered

by the civilians. The domestic condition of Babylon and its holy places tore my heart. I struggled for peace. I abolished slavery. I put an end to their wretchedness and sorrows. I commanded that all people be free and undisturbed in the worship of their gods. I commanded that
no civilian be killed. My great God was content.... I commanded that ... all closed temples be
reopened. I replaced all gods to their temples. I gathered all the people from their ruined neighborhoods and rebuilt their houses. I granted peace to everybody [Fazel Bakhsheshi, 2008: 22].

The theft is revealed to be more complex than it initially seemed. The narrator,
a dexterous detective from the special police bureau, discovers that the thief took his
orders from a mediator connected to extraterrestrial enemies who have failed so far to
overtake the Earth, but wish to attack it once more, this time with the hope of conquering it through the channel of history. They have stolen the cylinder to test it in the lab
and estimate its date of production. They have also equipped their earthly agents with
time machines to get back to the time of Cyrus the Great and kill him before he commands the Charter to be made. In this way, they will try to forestall the writing of the
first and most ancient manifesto on peace, which implies that, in case they succeed,
there will be no Charter at this juncture in the history of man that can inspire later peace
manifestos. As a consequence, later peace manifestos will not be written, and the Earth
will be the site of bloodshed and war, a planet no more indomitable; hence, the extraterrestrials will be able to conquer it eventually. This plot, however, is nullified by the
detective who accidentally finds the time machines and is thrown into the era of Cyrus.
He cleverly changes the course of the operation by preventing the murder of Cyrus and,
thus, saving the Charter.

The narrative hints at the significant point that the slightest change in the course of
history will lead to a drastically different future (the butterfly effect) whether positively or
negatively; *The Guardian Angel* can be recognized as a very intelligent piece of alternate
history (allohistorical) fiction. According to Hellekson (2000):

The alternate history as a genre speculates about such topics as the nature of time and linearity,
the past's link to the present, the present's link to the future, and the role of individuals in the
history-making process. Alternate histories question the nature of history and of causality; they
question accepted notions of time and space; they rupture linear movement; and they make
readers rethink their world and how it has become what it has. They are a critique of the metaphors we use to discuss history. And they foreground the "constructedness" of history and the
role narrative plays in this construction [254–55].

Hellekson (2000) goes further to underline the significance of alternate history
as a unique genre in literature which "playfully subverts reality while discussing the
underpinnings of how we construct reality, foregrounding history's (and reality's) arbi-
trariness" (255). She believes that alternate history "foregrounds the importance of the
individual in bringing about history" (255). Closely connected to these remarks is Fazel
Bakhsheshi's perception of history as an entity capable of being shaped as well as shaping the course of things. In an interview, he points out that he wrote *The Guardian Angel*
as a response to the movie *300* (2006), a historical fantasy in cinema, the details of which
he deemed totally misleading and wrong. Far from having chauvinistic intentions, Fazel
Bakhsheshi wished to say that the Cyrus Charter affected things in the whole world, and
that if it had not been made, man would, for instance, never achieve scientific progress
as we know it today. That is why the aliens are going to destroy the Charter; indeed,
their main goal is to bring man's scientific advancement to the point of stagnancy (Hosseini, 2011).

Bameshki (2016) argues that three different historical accounts in three parallel worlds are to be identified in *The Guardian Angel*: first, the world in which Cyrus spreads his message of peace among mankind by ordering the Charter to be made; second, the world of the extraterrestrials in 2150 CE where Cyrus is killed and his Charter is destroyed; and finally, the world of the protagonist, i.e., the detective who battles the deputy of the aliens on earth and prevents the murder of Cyrus as well as the destruction of the Cyrus Charter. The novel conjoins "counterfactual history" and "time travel," both building blocks of the possible worlds theory. Indeed, Fazel Bakhsheshi's *The Guardian Angel* fits Joseph Collins's third and fourth categories of alternate history fiction, i.e., parallel worlds and time travel alteration (Collins, 1990). Or if you wish, it also conforms to Hellekson's "nexus story," which includes "time travel" and "time policing" stories whereby a policeman travels to a different era to correct past wrongs or "deliberately alters a time line in order to bring about the preferred happenings" (252). The alien deputy's dialogue with the detective in *The Guardian Angel* confirms the rationale behind this policing tendency to reform things:

> Savagery and brutality should overtake the world and supplant friendship. Much the better if Cyrus's corpse symbolizes this. Next morning, they'll find you [the detective] here but won't understand your language and you won't be able to explain things to them. So they will arrest you for regicide and kill you in the worst possible way to make an example of you. This savagery will be recorded in history as a good substitute for the Cyrus Charter [Fazel Bakhsheshi, 2008: 81].

In *The Guardian Angel*, Fazel Bakhsheshi takes advantage of alternate history's capacity to change history to shape a different reality, which is what science fiction does in terms of the speculation and extrapolation of the present condition to shape an imaginary future. Fazel Bakhsheshi's major concern with alteration and reformation is to a great extent understandable when the unjust accusations against Iran as a propagator of terrorism are reinforced through media at a global level. This anti–Iranian attitude, therefore, becomes a motive for Fazel Bakhsheshi's counternarrative as well as other Iranian reactions such as the one we find in Javad Ardakni's *Nooshdaru* series, the subject of my discussion in the next section.

III. Sanction SF in Javad Ardakani's *Nooshdaru* Series

Nooshdaru (2012–2013), a TV series directed by Javad Ardakani, was produced at the time of sanctions against Iran. In the course of twenty episodes, the series depicts the critical circumstances in which Iraq-Iran war veterans and ex-construction soldiers, accompanied by a group of experts and scientists, are working hard to find a way out of sanctions in the petroleum industry.[8] In this project, they are going to produce a "liner hanger" part used in the petroleum extraction process. Indeed, without this part, the extraction process is impossible, the knowledge of the production of liner hanger systems being exclusively at the disposal of the United States and the United Kingdom. The part, moreover, is one of the items on the list of sanctions, among others, so Iran cannot purchase it from other countries. Undoubtedly, the part has to be produced inside the country, which means that the knowledge of this technology has to be achieved and made domestically in the first place. After all efforts to purchase the part from diverse dealers crumble, a team of metallurgists and manufacturers start to work on the project in highly confidential circumstances and eventually triumph after frequent disruptions. The domestic production of a "liner hanger" means that Iran no longer needs to import or purchase it, and the sanction on this part is automatically nullified by means of its indigenization; consequently, Iran can increase its oil extraction rates.

The technique adopted for the scenario narrative integrates the past and present effectively, with epiphanic moments of disclosure and discovery at each step taken toward the achievement of the finished product. The gradual unraveling of the puzzles and mysteries and the resolution of conflicts are embedded in the total extrapolative framework of the narrative, creating strong suspense till the last episode. This technique is achieved through flashbacks and flashforwards causing two parallel plotlines: first, the 1980s, when war-struck Iran suffered strict sanctions as well as economic deprivation, a decade in which construction soldiers were actively involved in the production of equipment and goods necessary for operations and battlegrounds in general. For instance, the series refers to the manufacturing of the "hog missile valve," a part highly resistant to great temperature variations. The story depicts the success of the construction soldiers, now much younger, in producing the valve despite its being under strict sanctions. The triumphs at war greatly depended on this achievement. The second is in autumn 2009, when the main story in the present—the manufacturing of "liner hanger" to nullify the sanction—occurs. The connection between these two plotlines and their parallel progression in similar but distant contexts leads to the point where we perceive that the narrative of the series is actually a historical continuum rather than two diverse periods of time; put differently, the narrative proceeds through an extended context, partly pre-war, partly post-war, but the essential facts about this traumatic situation remain: 29 years of sanctions and the nonstop efforts of the characters to transcend this seemingly un-removable barrier is the reality that never changes. Whether during the war or after it, the role of the characters as "construction soldiers" is kept intact, pushing their scientific, social, and political status to the background.

What makes this series specifically a work of SF is the speculative and extrapolative nature of scientific-experimental scenes towards the indigenization of parts such as "liner hanger" and "hog missile valve," a process one could similarly see in the SF written by Golden Age SF writers such as John W. Campbell and his stable of writers who made hard science fiction a cornerstone during the 1930s and 40s. For instance, in the second half of *Nooshdaru*, the audience is exposed to the concentrated and hard work of the researchers in diverse laboratories and workshops as well as the scientific explanations for the failure or success of each step in the production of the alloys used in the "liner hanger." Metallurgical details and processes are rendered and causes and effects are clarified. But then, what I would like to propose is that this series go beyond pure SF and feature national, ideological, and political questions. Here I should stress that the scenario does not encourage any bizarre version of politics and religion like what we see in the *Dune* series, where the author Frank Herbert imbues his text with Eastern and pseudo-Islamic ideology, Islamic names, and motifs.[9] Rather, Ardakani tries to put techno-science at the service of religion and politics. The soldiers considered the war a holy one and were ready to sacrifice their lives in the battle; according to Islamic tenets, a soldier killed during the war in defense of the Islamic community is a martyr and his death is a holy one. One may notice the fact that some of the characters in *Nooshdaru* have been modeled after the martyrs of the war. In an interview, Ardakani admits, "A significant part of the series was inspired by the life story of martyr Razavi and martyr Aghasizadeh, and we specified some of the episodes to martyr Razavi where the audience see a sequence related to him; we also have shown his photo on some occasions. I do not claim that we see a lot of their photos but their life was a great influence" (Ardakani, 2013). Seyed Mohammad Taqi Razavi and Hassan Aghasizadeh were both civil engineers and bridge builders; the former graduated from Mashhad Institute, the latter from University of Toronto. Both participated in war as construction soldiers and served in crucial projects that demanded a great deal of knowledge and expertise. Similarly, the series has also been dedicated to the memory of martyr Hossein Sherkat, a student of theology and a commander of infantry operations for construction purposes, who after a short time proved his great talent and was granted the rank of military engineer. These details prove that the series invests greatly in religious/ideological as well as scientific and technological matters and their mutual reinforcement.

The Islamic set of beliefs related to the characters of the story, accordingly, not only remains intact in the interval between the two periods but is strengthened when matters of national integrity and political independence are raised once again as vital criteria for abolishing interventionist tendencies on the side of adversaries. Here, science and technology are more than pure science fictional factors and become mandatory in Iran's anti-imperialist struggle and signify further advancements. Thus, Iran's indigenization of technology will provide the country with an opportunity for economic competition among other mighty rivals in the global market, as well as political credit and prowess. The point is that *Nooshdaru* has been successful in introducing the issue of "sanctions" and "anti-sanction projects" as a new type of motif into SF film, not sufficiently explored before, perhaps because no writer or director ever worked in this direction. The series investigates how the balance of power in the world could be altered by means of corporate efforts towards the expansion of knowledge and the progress of indigenous techno-science. I would like to propose that *Nooshdaru* be taken as a new subcategory in science fiction studies, i.e., "(anti)-sanction" SF. One might argue that SF is essentially after alteration in the *status quo*, resolution of problems in difficult conditions, or progress in a certain direction, and all these can be found in *Nooshdaru*. I would argue that most SF written with the above purposes in mind has been produced in advanced countries, countries that never had to tackle the problem of sanctions, and the motivation for their writing bears on discovery and invention, corporate agendas, individual ambitions, or colonial dreams. In contrast, *Nooshdaru* concentrates on full-fledged and sustained sanctions on all sides against Iran, whereby anti-sanction aspirations turn into the motivation for its production. This motivation for indigenous technology no longer bears on corporate, individual, or colonial purposes but is emergent, compulsive, and national. Mohammad, the main scientist in this series, does not think of any financial gain after he chooses to participate in the project of the production of the "liner hanger;" rather he sacrifices his money, job, house, and even his family. In return, despite the many industrial lapses and disruptions brought by the economic and technological siege placed on Iran, the sanction on the "liner hanger" eventually paid off and had the merit of forcing the country toward autonomy in the petroleum industry; finally, this particular sanction also caused the addition of one more successful series to the resumé of Iranian cinema.

Concluding Remarks

Besides American and British science fiction—well-established, daily produced, reviewed and discussed in popular and academic venues—fewer known types of indigenous SF are emerging and gradually finding their voice. In this context, Iranian science fiction might be noticed as a newly emergent branch of literature, though not yet constituting a significant body or corpus to attract the attention of the Iranian audiences and consequently not known outside Iran. Science fiction ebbs and flows with the status of science and technology in a society, but science fiction also has a life of its own and is capable of breathing life into the world of science and technology in a so-called underdeveloped country. Iran has long been a pioneer of both science and fantastical literature; its accomplishments in the past in literature and human thought have been duly recognized. Its contemporary contribution, however, has not. Part of the blame lies at home, this is no doubt true, but the internal situation is fast being corrected, opening up potentials for the appreciation, critical analysis, and international mark of recognition Iranian SF rightly deserves. The agenda of international literature will be impacted as more and more indigenous SF is produced in the developing world, bringing new ideas, themes, and techniques to the world of SF. It is also hoped that Iran can, once again, play a major role in Islamic civilization, and Islamic science fiction is one avenue in which the country can excel and help put Muslims once again on the international scene as guardians and leaders of civilization.

A furthering of institutional bonds between SF societies in the Muslim world, and Third World, coupled with translation of Iranian SF into international languages—English, French, Spanish—and regional languages—Azeri, Arabic, Turkish—are recommended. (It is tragic that Iraj Fazel Bakhsheshi's works have not been translated into English). The furtherance of cinema and TV production, in line with domestic accomplishments, such as *Nooshdaru,* and Iran's international acclaim in cinema with its Oscar wins, are also recommended. There is no need for Iran to become a replica of Europe to be modern any more than there is a need for Iranian SF to mindlessly ape Western conventions. It is the very distinctiveness of Iranian art that has earned it respect in the world, and it is hoped that this accomplishment will be repeated in the field of SF for Iran and for all nations of the so-called developing world.

NOTES

1. Unless otherwise stated, all translations from Persian are my own.
2. Included in the second group are Yahya Arianpour and Mehrdad Tooyserkani.
3. The title of the newspaper was *Shafaghe Sorkh* (*Red Twilight*).
4. The date "Mount Damavand's Monkeys" was written is still not known by scholars of Hedeyat.
5. For instance, Eric M. Drown (2001) argues that Gernsback's magazines embodied "liberal republicanism," educated amateurs outside the walls of the university, and encouraged them to build the future through imagination, perseverance, praxis, self-reliance and commitment (63).
6. See http://www.fantasy.ir or https://en.wikipedia.org/wiki/Speculative_Fiction_Group.
7. I have a work on this topic—see detailed reference below—"Eco-Heroines and Saviors in Iraj Fazel Bakhsheshi's *Men and Supertowers* and *The Sun's Sons,*" my contribution to Douglas Vakoch's collection *Ecofeminism and Science Fiction.*
8. Construction soldiers are a group of soldiers that participated in the war as engineering forces that engaged in construction projects and made equipment necessary for operations.
9. These are *Dune* (1965), *Dune Messiah* (1969), *Children of Dune* (1976), *God Emperor of Dune* (1981), *Heretics of Dune* (1984), and *Chapterhouse: Dune* (1985).

Works Cited

Ardakani, Javad. (2013). Interview. *Young Reporters' Club* [جوان خبرنگاران باشگاه. مصاحبه]. [online] Available at: https://bit.ly/2JBCrM2.

Arianpour, Abbas. (1938). *The Machine of Life* [زندگانی ماشین]. Tehran.

Arianpour, Yahya. (1993). *From Saba to Nima* [نیما تا صبا از], 2nd vol. Tehran: Zavar.

Bameshki, Samira. (2016). "Parallel Worlds and Narrative Semantics" [روایت شناسی معنی و موازی های جهان]. *Naghde Abadi (Literary Criticism)*. 9(34): 91–118.

Collins, W. J. (1990). *Paths Not Taken: The Development, Structure, and Aesthetics of the Alternative History.* Ph.D. diss. University of California–Davis.

Dahl, Danielle. (21 February 2020). "50 Pablo Neruda Quotes Sure to Leave You Questioning Life and Love." *EverydayPower.com*. https://everydaypower.com/pablo-neruda-quotes/.

Drown, Eric Miles. (2001). *Usable Futures, Disposable Paper: Popular Science, Pulp Science Fiction and Modernization in America, 1908-1937.* Ph.D. diss. University of Minnesota.

Fazel Bakhsheshi, Iraj. (2007). *A Message Older Than Time* [زمان فراسوی از پیامی]. Tehran: Ghasidehsara.

Fazel Bakhsheshi, Iraj. (2008). *Guardian Angels* [نگهبان فرشته]. Tehran: Ghasidehsara.

First Iranian SF Novel Republished after 83 Years in 200 Copies. (2017). *Ketab: Iranian Book News*. [online] Available at: http://bit.ly/2LXksRH.

Ghassa, Mohammad. (2014). "Iranian Science Fiction 1971–1991." [online] *Yek Pezeshk*. Available at: http://www.1pezeshk.com/archives/2014/08/science-fiction-in-iran.html.

Hedayat, Sadegh. (1952). "S.G.L.L." In: Sadegh Hedayat, *Saye Roshan* [روشن سایه], 2nd ed. Tehran: Sina: 9–44.

Hellekson, Karen. (2000). "Toward a Taxonomy of the Alternate History Genre." *Extrapolation*, 41(3): 248–256.

Hosseini, Vahid. (2011). "What We Have Done for the Future of Iran? An Interview with Iraj Fazel Bakhsheshi, the SF Writer from Mashhad" [تخیلی-علمی های داستان مشهدی نویسنده بخششی، فاضل ایرج با گفتگو !؟کردهایم چه ایران آینده برای]. [Blog] Halghehaye Dam. Available at: http://vh58.blogfa.com/post-55.aspx.

Jannessari-Ladani, Zahra. (2021). "Eco-Heroines and Saviors in Iraj Fazel Bakhsheshi's *Men and Supertowers* and *The Sun's Sons*." In Douglas Vakoch, *Ecofeminism and Science Fiction*. Lanham, MD: Lexington: 157–170.

Kasravi, Ahmad. (1933). *Aeen* [آیین]. Tehran.

Milani, Abbas. (1992). "Hedayat and the Tragic Worldview" [تراژیک بینی جهان و هدایت]. *Iranshenasi*. 4(3): 554–563.

Mirabedini, Hassan. (2008). "Fantastic and Science Fiction Stories" [تخیلی-علمی و رؤیایی های داستان]. In: Hassan Mirabedini, *A Survey of Development of Persian Fiction and Plays (From the Beginning to 1941)*, 1st ed. Tehran: Academy of Persian Language and Literature: 277–296.

Nooshdaru. (2012-2013). [TV program]. 1: TV Series Group, Seda and Sima's Basij TV Group.

Pedersen, Claus V. (2002). *World View in Pre-revolutionary Iran: Literary Analysis of Five Iranian Authors in the Context of the History of Ideas.* Wiesbaden: Harrassowitz Verlag.

Rieder, John. (2008). *Colonialism and the Emergence of Science Fiction.* Middletown: Wesleyan University.

Sanatizadeh, AbdolHossein. (1934). *Rostam in the 22nd Century* [دوم و بیست قرن در رستم]. Tehran: Ettehadieh.

Suvin, Darko. (1979). *Metamorphosis of Science Fiction: On the Poetics and History of a Literary Genre.* New Haven and London: Yale University Press.

Tooyserkani, Mehrdad. (2005). "A Review of Scientific Imagination in Persian Children's/Young Adults' Literature" [نوجوان و کودک فارسی ادبیات در علمی تخیل تاریخچه بر گذری]. *Pazhuheshnameye Adabiat Kookdak va Nojavan (The Journal of Children's and Young Adults' Literature)*. 40: 63–77.

Vahdat, Farzin. (2001). "The Early Iranian Intellectuals' Confrontation with Modernism: A Dual Approach" [دوگانه رویکرد یک :مدرنیته با ایران روشنفکری اولیه رویارویی]. *Goftegou*. 30: 125–165.

The Family in Time

An Expatriate's Pilgrimage to a Better Future

Ibrahim Al-Marashi

A traveler without knowledge is a bird without wings.

—Saadi

In 2013, commemorating the ten-year anniversary of the Iraq War, Comma Press, a UK publisher, commissioned Iraqi writer Hassan Blasim to edit an anthology, *Iraq + 100*, featuring ten short stories written by Iraqi writers and set in Iraq in the year 2103, exactly a hundred years after the U.S.-led invasion of the country (Blasim, 2016: v).

I saw Blasim's call for contributors just around the time the Islamic State of Iraq and Syria (ISIS) seized Mosul and large swathes of Iraq in June 2014. Contributing to the project appealed to me, given I'm Iraqi-(American), a historian of sci-fi, and a consumer of sci-fi as well. This call provided me with a chance to make my first foray into this genre, as well as to use sci-fi to address the trauma of the ISIS invasion.

Initially I was not sure if they would even entertain my contribution given it asked for pieces from Iraqi writers, and I was part of the diaspora. As the volume came together, it turned out most of the contributors lived outside of Iraq, a sad testimony to the cultural brain drain the country has endured over the last couple of decades. Little did I know that one of the authors, Khalid Kaki, was originally from Kirkuk and now lived in Madrid, where I also lived for several years. We might have passed each other on the streets without realizing it.

As a historian of Iraq and the Middle East, who focuses on past and present events, I think it is still important to speculate about Iraq one hundred years into the future. Collectively, the authors project into Iraq's future, which highlights Iraq's reality in the present. That is what attracts me to speculative fiction. While as a genre it is escapist in nature, yet it simultaneously brings our current reality into greater focus. Sci-fi reveals our anxieties about the convergence between science, automated realities, and what it means to be human. Science fiction is a reflection of our socio-political facts. My story sought to bring our current techno-phobias and combine them with Iraq's real problems that began after the 2003 invasion.

A History in the Making

Once the volume came out, I was intrigued as a historian by Hassan's lament in the introduction that there is not a strong modern science fiction and fantasy literary tradition in the modern Middle East. Al-Mustafa Najjar questions whether this is due to authors refraining from imagining a dystopian future when the present is already dystopian (Al-Najjar, 2014). Blasim writes in a similar vein that it was difficult to persuade many Iraqi writers to write futuristic stories when they were living or have lived with the cruelty and horror of the present.

Blasim states this dearth of sci-fi is surprising given the history of the region. Blasim acknowledges that some would look at *The 1001 Nights* as the beginnings of a proto-SF genre; in Zhraa Alhaboby's story "The Baghdad Syndrome," Scheherazade does make a cameo appearance and Anoud's "Kahramana" refers to Ali Baba's slave girl. Blasim however searches for roots even earlier in the *Epic of Gilgamesh* with elements that invoke "space aeronautics." Blasim (2016: vii), and another author, Muhammad Aurangzeb Ahmad, also cite the work of Ibn Tufail, *Hayy ibn Yaqzan*, composed in what was Muslim Spain (Ahmad, 2017). I would add another work from Spain that exhibits elements of proto-speculative fiction, the work of the Sufi scholar Ibn Arabi from Murcia, in today's Spain. In his *Futuhat al-Makiyya* written around 1238, he describes his travels to "vast cities (outside Earth), possessing technologies far superior than ours" (*Tor Blog*, 2017). Not only did these Spanish-Muslim authors make a contribution to proto-speculative fiction, their example also challenges notions of Western versus Eastern binaries in literature, as they remind us that Spain, facing the Atlantic, is geographically more "Western" than the Britain of Mary Shelley and H.G. Wells.

With that in mind, using sci-fi to deal with real events, as I tried to do, can be traced to Mary Shelley's *Frankenstein*, and the implication of humanity's experimentation with electricity around the time she wrote her work (see Sampson, 2018; D'Anastasio, 2015). Indeed, Frankenstein would inspire Ahmed Saadawi's *Frankenstein in Baghdad,* set in post–2003 Iraq, where the monster is made up of the body parts of the victims of its violence (Dewachi, 2015). H.G. Wells' *War of the Worlds* was a commentary on the British role in the extermination of the local population of Tasmania. In an Asian context, the Godzilla franchise and the post-apocalyptic genre of Japanese manga, such as *Akira,* are imaginative spaces to deal with real trauma: the dropping of the atomic bombs on Hiroshima and Nagasaki.

Even prior to the publication of *Iraq +100,* Iraq had become an imaginative sci-fi space for challenging the 2003 invasion

Hassan Blasim (left) with Comma Press editors Ra Page and Holly Francis (courtesy Dr. Ibrahim Al-Marashi).

A chronicling of the imaginative history of Iraqi thought and literature (courtesy of the artist, Yahya Salah Abul Ghait).

in Western entertainment. Films like *Avatar* critiqued the rise of mercenary companies, where the planet Pandora stands in for Iraq. The reboot of *Battle Star Galactica* portrayed the Cylons as the Americans and the humans resisting them as the Iraqi insurgents, forcing TV audiences to see the conflict from an Iraqi perspective.

My inspirations into this foray came from Philip K. Dick, whose work *Do Androids Dream of Electric Sheep?* was made into the film *Blade Runner*, and the French thinker Jean Baudrillard, whose oeuvre provided the inspiration for the *Matrix* franchise. Without giving away the ending of my story set in Najaf, I found such works raised philosophical issues of how one determines reality in an age of digital and virtual reality. Jalal Hassan's story, "The Here and Now Prison," also invokes the city of Najaf and how it is transformed into virtual reality.

Najufa, a Composite of Past and Present

"Najufa" is a story based on my own family's lineage and experiences, and my first trip to Najaf and Kufa as an adult with my father and mother in 2010. The title of the story assumes both cities are growing at such a fast rate that they will merge into one another.

"Najufa" begins in Baghdad International Airhub, with a passport imbedded in the main character's middle finger, a detail that feels all the more futuristic and impossible in light of Trump's executive order. I wrote the story before Trump's ascendancy to the White House, and that aspect of my story reflects my life where my freedom of movement had been hindered since 9/11. I chose to focus my story on freedom of movement in particular, and the fact that the chip is embedded in one's "middle" finger is an indication of how I feel about modern borders.

I was born in the U.S. and have both American and British nationality and yet still face difficulties travelling. In the U.S., I have been subject to secondary searches well before Trump become president. However, what really angers me is the difficulty I have travelling within the Middle East. For example, while travelling in a country like Jordan or Syria in the nineties, the border officials saw my passports but wanted to know where I was "really" from. They assumed my passports were fake and pulled me to one side, wanting to make sure I was not one of the million Iraqis seeking refuge in their country.

The scene in the Airhub is actually inspired by the arrivals section of Terminal 5 in London's Heathrow Airport. I simply scan my British passport in a machine, it takes my picture, and I am allowed entry into the UK within seconds. However, I am fortunate as an Iraqi in this regard. Blasim himself in 1998 left Baghdad without a passport over fears about a documentary he had made during Saddam Hussein's rule. One of the writers, Anoud, received the inspiration for her story after confusion over her visa at Heathrow, when an immigration officer threatened her with deportation. She wrote, "I had never been so angry in my life and I had never felt so small" (Sharp, 2016). Thus, the Baghdad Airhub is my wish that future travel for everyone would be as seamless as it is for me entering the UK. Of course, with the rhetoric around Brexit, even Britons are becoming more nationalistic in terms of "securing" their borders.

The tensions that drive the relationship between the narrator and his grandfather in my story are based on the tensions I had with my own father during that trip. My father was born in the east African island of Zanzibar, as a result of his father escaping Najaf during the waning days of the Ottoman Empire and the British occupation of southern Iraq. My grandfather took part in an insurgency against British forces, was captured, and then escaped.

My father returned to Iraq in the sixties, went to medical school in Baghdad, and would visit Najaf and his relatives there often. However, my father did not travel to Iraq when Saddam Hussein was in power from 1979 to 2003.

I expected the trip in 2010 to be a nostalgic "home coming" for him, but as an old man in his seventies, he seemed oblivious to the whole place or experience. He was more concerned with drinking tea and relating his life experiences to any random person in the tea house than visiting the shrines there.

His addiction to tea influenced my story, where droids serve the beverage, changing a cherished aspect of Iraqi culture. Droids also guard the shrines, as their advanced technology detects bombs on humans or car bombs. This frees Iraqis from humiliating interrogation and trauma at checkpoints.

In 2010, everyone had to check in the mobile phone outside the shrine complexes, like a coat check, as terrorists used them to detonate explosives remotely. Without phones, the younger pilgrims became fidgety, anxious about missing calls, and wanted to leave after a few minutes of praying. I felt a disconnect between the spirituality of the place and how even I began to think about something as mundane as a missed call. Of course, that phenomenon is no different from life anywhere else in the world. We are living in a techno-addicted world. But in Iraq, whether it is a terrorist or a pilgrim, the phone had become an extension of ourselves, and it was in Najaf that I realized we are essentially cyborgs, human-techno hybrids, where the phone might as well be an extension of ourselves. The droids in the story are a reflection of that phenomenon. In the story I wanted to project the evolution of how we will become the technology a hundred years later, even in an ancient shrine city in Iraq. What separates "Najufa" from other stories in the collection, where religion is deemed no longer necessary or ultimately seen as a destructive force, the Najaf in this story remains a holy pilgrimage site for Muslims, evolving with the technological advancements and outlasting the "Sectarian Wars" that erupted since 2003.

Like Ali Bader's "The Corporal," we also imagine the U.S. in the future. He writes that Iran and Saudi Arabia "are now the vanguard of the civilised world, just like Iraq. The problem is with the West … which has been transformed into an oasis of terrorism, a haven for religious intolerance and hatred" (Bader, 2016: 57). While I refer to ISIS in my story, I also write of CAKA, The Christian Assembly of Arkansas and Kansas, to refer to a similar terrorist group emerging in the American heartland. One reviewer, Christa Blackmon, writes, "After all, does one really need to travel to 22nd Century Baghdad to imagine an American nation run by unhinged, ideological fundamentalists that has devolved into a state of perpetual violence?" (Blackmon, 2017). This was written two months into the Trump administration. Indeed, the Trump administration has prompted commentators to invoke another dystopian classic, Margaret Atwood's 1985 *The Handmaid's Tale*, which was made into a TV series for Hulu (Setoodeh, 2018).

Blackmon, as mentioned earlier, situates her review two months into the Trump administration. She writes of the protests that emerged after his inauguration, using *Star Wars* imagery:

> In these demonstrations, we have continuously seen audiences invoking science fiction and fantasy genres. From posters of Princess Leia/General Organa declaring a "woman's place is in the resistance" to allusions to the authoritarian impulses challenged by the Harry Potter books, the symbols created by imaginative fiction are a shared language and a global rallying cry.
> In this context, *Iraq + 100* is a perfect addition to the cultural resistance package [Blackmon, 2017].

I am a *Star Wars* fan and use the franchise to make my classes on Middle East history a bit more tangible for students first exposed to the region. I see elements of Sufi orders in Obi Wan and the Jedi, or I explain Edward Said's *Orientalism* by telling students to think about the Middle Eastern motifs surrounding Jabba the Hut, who smokes a nargila and maintains a harem that included Princess Leia. Ironically, at the time Blackmon was writing her review, I was also using *Iraq +100* and *Star Wars* as a reference to the Trump administration in an interview for *Warscapes*:

> I do see eerie coincidences between Trump and Chancellor Palpatine, and Steve Bannon is his Darth Vader, a comparison that Bannon apparently relishes. In terms of the rebel alliance, it brought together far ranging planets and galactic groups, like Admiral Ackbar, the squid-like commander from the Mon Calamari, to the Ewoks. And in this regard, today the rebel alliance includes American constituencies ranging from Muslims, Latinos, women, LGBT groups, and just the random American-turned-activist. Not to mention the rallies that have erupted all over the world against the Trump presidency, a galactic wide resistance if you will. These groups in the past would have no reason to come together until the rise of Trump. And that rebel alliance is the new world we have written into existence [Spear, 2017].

Indeed, *Star Wars*, a sci-fi/fantasy hybrid, was an influence in my story's use of "droids," as well as Blasim's apparent use of "tiger droids." Atwood, Blackmon, and I referred to the Women's March in our media engagements, and even in the interview with Atwood, *Star Wars* came up. The George Lucas oeuvre, *Iraq +100,* and the *Handmaid's Tale* all invariably invoke tropes of resistance, again demonstrating that the binary between "Western" and "Eastern" speculative fiction is an artificial one.

The Reception and the Road Ahead

The overall reception of the book was positive and received attention from major media outlets, including the BBC, while *The Guardian* ranked *Iraq + 100* on their list of best sci-fi books of 2016 (Sharp, 2016; Roberts, 2016). Another major American media outlet, *The Atlantic,* covered the book before *Iraq +100*'s release in the U.S. via Tor publishers (Heller, 2017).

The common theme in the articles reviewing the book was their acknowledgment of the anguish expressed in the stories. Amal El-Mohtar's headline, "'Iraq + 100' Is Painful, But Don't Look Away," for National Public Radio in the U.S. writes:

> Underlying these pieces are exhaustion, disgust, contempt, disillusionment, all of which Western readers of speculative fiction will no doubt find alienating; built into our narrative of fiction's usefulness is a sense of healing, catharsis, nourishment that this collection resists [El-Mohtar, 2016].

"Catharsis" remains elusive in these stories, an indication that ten years after the invasion of Iraq, the event which the authors are addressing still remains traumatic for all the writers.

While major media outlets covered the book, there were also thoughtful reviews on the sci-fi fan sites, such as geeksofdoom.com. Gary Makries writes on this site:

> This book defies contemporary concepts of what sci-fi is by adding additional layers of history, laced with emotional turmoil....
>
> Even so, I was ill-prepared for the sheer emotion that this tome evoked ... nay, that it emanated. Beneath these tales are written the pain of people that have known war for so long that many cannot remember a time that death and despair were not a part of it.
>
> You might even discover a new level of compassion or empathy for a war-torn people who stand among the ashes of their forefathers and dare to look up [Makries, 2017].

In this review, the reviewer addresses an American audience, using *Iraq+100* as a means of dialogue, encouraging them to use sci-fi as a way of empathizing, if not sympathizing, with Iraqis.

While the call for this book was issued after the ten-year anniversary of the Iraq War, at the time of this writing, 15 years have now transpired. ISIS has been expelled from all urban centers in Iraq, and the nation had an election where themes of anti-corruption and non-sectarianism triumphed, providing a moment for cautious optimism for the nation.

As for the future, *Iraq +100* will need to be distributed in Arabic to reach Iraqis themselves. Hopefully, it might perhaps be adopted into a graphic novel format, using visual images that can speak to a global audience.

Works Cited

Ahmad, Muhammad Aurangzeb. (27 June 2017). "This Is the Muslim Tradition of Sci-Fi and Speculative Fiction." *Aeon*. https://aeon.co/ideas/think-sci-fi-doesnt-belong-in-the-muslim-world-think-again.

Bader, Ali. (2016). "The Corporal," in *Iraq + 100, Stories from a Century after the Invasion*. Manchester: Comma Press.

Blackmon, Christa. (24 March 2017). "Book Review: 'Iraq + 100' Is Weird, Woeful and Wonderful." *Muftah.org*. http://muftah.org/book-review-iraq-100-weird-woeful-wonderful/#.WNXlRm_yupo.

Blasim, Hassan. (2016). "Foreword," in *Iraq + 100, Stories from a Century after the Invasion*. Manchester: Comma Press.

D'Anastasio, Cecilia. (16 July 2015). "The Earliest Science Fiction." *Motherboard.Vice.Com*. https://motherboard.vice.com/en_us/article/bmj4wv/the-earliest-science-fiction.

Dewachi, Omar. (26 May 2015). "The Wounds of Baghdad's Frankenstein." *Open Democracy*. https://www.opendemocracy.net/opensecurity/omar-dewachi/wounds-of-baghdad%27s-frankenstein.

El-Mohtar, Amal. (10 December 2016). "*Iraq + 100* Is Painful, But Don't Look Away." *NPR: National Public Radio*. http://www.npr.org/2016/12/10/503068002/iraq-100-is-painful-but-dont-look-away.

Heller, Jason. (15 October 2017). "How Sci-Fi Writers Imagine Iraq's Future." *The Atlantic*, https://www.theatlantic.com/entertainment/archive/2017/10/how-sci-fi-writers-imagine-iraqs-future/541512/.

Makries, Gary. (12 September 2017). "Book Review: *Iraq + 100*: The First Anthology of Science Fiction To Have Emerged From Iraq." *Waerloga69*. https://www.geeksofdoom.com/2017/09/12/book-review-iraq-100-scifi-anthology.

Najjar, Al-Mustafa. (9 November 2014). "Arabic Fiction Faces Up to The Future." *Al-Sharq Al-Awsat*. https://eng-archive.aawsat.com/m-najjar/lifestyle-culture/arabic-fiction-faces-up-to-the-future.

Roberts, Adam. (30 November 2016). "The Best SF and Fantasy Books of 2016." *The Guardian*. https://www.theguardian.com/books/2016/nov/30/best-sf-and-fantasy-books-2016-adam-roberts.

Sampson, Fiona. (10 March 2018). "'Frankenstein': An All Too Human Monster." *Financial Times*. https://www.ft.com/content/46233f88-1d4a-11e8-a748-5da7d696ccab.

Setoodeh, Ramin. (10 April 2018). "Margaret Atwood on How Donald Trump Helped *The Handmaid's Tale*." *Variety*. https://variety.com/2018/tv/news/margaret-atwood-handmaids-tale-trump-feminism-1202748535/.

Sharp, Heather. (22 October 2016). "Sci-fi Stories Envisage Iraq in 100 Years." *BBC News*. https://www.bbc.com/news/world-middle-east-37687739.

Spear, Gabrielle. (24 March 2017). "Iraq 2103: Sci-fi Against Empire." *Warscapes.com*. http://www.warscapes.com/conversations/iraq-2103-sci-fi-against-empire.

Tor Blog. (5 September 2017). "Contributors to *Iraq + 100* Reflect on Science Fiction in Arabic Literature." https://www.torforgeblog.com/2017/09/05/two-contributors-to-iraq-100-reflect-on-science-fiction-in-arabic-literature/.

Turning Youthful Curiosity
into an Arab Growth Industry

NOURA AL NOMAN

Science and literature are not two things, but two sides of one thing.
—Thomas Huxley

As a girl in a country that was founded six years after my birth, I was fortunate to be raised in my grandfather's library. In addition to the tomes on history, Arabic language, poetry, and Islam, I found smaller books which awakened my interest in fantasy and science fiction. I still remember Anis Mansour's series of books on the paranormal, *Arwaah Wa Ashbaah* (*Spirits and Ghosts*), *Alatheena Habattou Min'assamaa* (*Those Who Descended from the Heavens*), and *Alatheena Aado Ila'ssamaa* (*Those Who Returned to the Heavens*). But most influential of all, at the age of 12, I saw *Star Wars* when it was released in 1977. It was then that I discovered I had been afflicted with a condition for which there was no name at the time. Decades later I discovered that this condition was "being a geek."

A Fresh Start

After *Star Wars*, I couldn't get enough of SF and fantasy books. With the exception of Stephen King, I read no other genre for almost two decades. SFF fascinated me and transported me to the many worlds and possibilities lacking in Arabic fiction at the time. Sadly, I stopped reading Arabic, and when my children began to use my library, they also read English exclusively (they still do). So, when I started looking for Young Adult (YA) fiction in Arabic and could find nothing for their age, I finally gave in to the urgings of my husband and close friends and began writing a YA novel. In what genre should I write? Well, of course it was going to be SF. This decision was reinforced by the fact that I could see how SF movies attracted young people to cinemas in the UAE, and I was hopeful that they would be interested in reading it in Arabic.

It was a bold step, and had I stopped to think about it at the time, I would probably have given up. How does one write fiction in Arabic? What is the structure, if different than Arabic? How does Arabic handle style? How does one deal with action words which are heavily used in SF? Ironically, SF terminology was not as challenging as I thought it would be, as we are blessed with Arabic subtitles in all the movies and TV shows in the

148

UAE. Yes, they lack a system and were never used in fiction, but that was still not as challenging as using action words in Arabic.

I started writing the synopsis of *Ajwan* in 2009, but the real work started in 2010. Ajwan is a proper female name in some Arab countries. "Jown" is a small sea or a cove, Ajwan is the plural. This was an apt name for a young lady whose race breathed air and water and lived on a water planet. The first pages of the book begin with total emotional devastation, as Ajwan at 19 years of age flees her world hours before it is obliterated by a large asteroid. As a refugee, she symbolizes the 15+ million refugees in the Arab world, faceless and nameless. Her child is then abducted, and over the span of two books she looks for him, pursuing a phantom enemy who has the power to manipulate the minds of the young, the marginalized and the disenfranchised. This enemy promises his private army a home of their own, but to obtain it they must commit atrocities for him, including blowing themselves up "for the cause."[1]

When some of my author friends read the book, they told me it cannot possibly be targeting YA, that it was too mature and political for them. Having seen the types of books my YA children were reading, I know that *Ajwan* speaks to them as equals. As a teen, I used to read novels which were not labeled YA because that classification wasn't available in the late 70s and early 80s. And it was these books which shaped my thinking and perception of the world. This is what I wanted for *Ajwan* to do for our Arab youth, who can see what is happening in their region but don't understand it, nor are interested in understanding it. It was all so old and complicated. I feel that our problems and issues can still be explained to our youth in fiction without having to lecture or pontificate. It is these mysterious issues which trap some youth in a never-ending cycle of ignorance and violence.

From Fiction to Fact

To me, science fiction means putting science at the top of our list of priorities. Science is evidence-based; it demands experimentation and proof. And in a region impacted by so many issues, emotions drive practically all opinions and actions, and there is no demand or room for evidence, for facts. What if our youth were raised on fiction which urges them to demand facts and evidence instead of stoking emotions over age-old grudges? That is why I feel SF is important at this point in time. Needless to say, SF will create more science students and will elevate R&D in this region—a field which has taken a backseat for decades.

Naturally, we need more SF authors and that cannot happen with the handful of books published every year. One cannot become a writer in a genre unless s/he has read extensively in that particular genre. I have not read as many Arabic SF novels as I should, but from what I have read, we have a long way ahead of us before it matures into the role it has achieved in Western literature. Our books are still bound to Earth and are still unable to break free from the dreams of pan–Arabism, etc.

SF is of course misunderstood in the Arab world. People see Hollywood movies and think this is SF literature, which leads them to think that it only revolves around space ships and aliens and is not worthy of respect (or as my mother once asked me: "Why not write proper fiction? Why must you write about creepy crawlies?"). I have met people who have angrily told me that SF is not "literature." Others think that an author has to be a scientist to write SF or that it must contain scientific predictions. This is due to the fact that they have had little exposure to great SF and the many social, political, and even religious issues it has tackled over the past two centuries or more.

Having written three books in the series, with the fourth and final volume[2] on the way, I also started thinking about other writers and how they were faring with Arab publishers who have their own doubts about SF. I decided to start my own publishing house (or as I like to call it, a room). Two years ago, I launched Makhtoota 5229, which focuses on Science Fiction, Fantasy, Horror, and the Paranormal. I knew there were a lot of SF writers out there who cannot sell their books to Arab publishers. And how can we have more authors and more books if there isn't sufficient Arabic content out there? I believe that a person must read heavily in their own genre before they can write in that genre. Or as famous SF author Dr. Nabil Farouk said once, "How can you go take a test, when you haven't studied?"

Since its launch, Makhtoota 5229 has received many applications for publishing, but so far, all the manuscripts have left me with the impression that their writers watched (not read, but watched) a science fiction movie or three and thought that was inspiration enough to write SF. To each applicant I have responded with long emails explaining the difference between a movie and a novel. I have given them advice on the proper structure of a novel, and what they should focus on. One young man's manuscript showed promise, and I wrote to him saying that I can work with him, as an editor, to shape the novel to qualify for publication. His response was, "No, thanks. I like it the way it is." This is because the role of literary editor in the Arab world is non-existent. Whether it is because it is never taught in universities (there are hardly even creative writing courses to begin with), or that the fact that Arab authors refuse for anyone to tell them what is wrong with their text/plot, the fact remains that literary editing is non-existent in the Arab world.

Because of these set-backs, and in order to still contribute to Arabic SF, I chose to create Arabic content by selecting quality SF novels and translating them into Arabic. This way, language will not be a barrier for budding authors. I also chose to translate writing advice books as a means to support the genre.

A Sense of Mission

Which brings me to the latest book whose foreign rights I finally acquired—*Dune* by Frank Herbert. I first read it in my late teens in the 80s and was astounded by the world-building aspects of it. Everything about it was fascinating. And then there were the Arab/Islamic themes, which—before the age of the Internet—were not easily accessible to an American author. This was what impressed me the most about *Dune*.

When I found out a few years ago that this 1965 novel had never been translated into Arabic, I was shocked. Shouldn't Arabic have been the first language it was published in? I sought out the proprietors—with the help of none other than Mr. Alan Dean Foster[3]—and after months of emails and begging on my part, I got the rights. Of course, the Herbert Estate was quite adamant about not changing a single word from the list of "problematic" words I had mentioned to them. Herbert may have picked those "exotic" words to mean something in his world, but when used in Arabic, they have a whole different list of connotations and denotations. It was then that I realized the mess I had put myself in. But there was no turning back.

I chose Mohammed Salama Al Masri[4] to translate *Dune* because he had serendipitously written to me about translating the first chapter about the same time I was in negotiations over the foreign rights. Anyone who has spent time translating *Dune* on his own, without hope for compensation, must be the right person. In addition, there is the way he chose to translate and transliterate some of the terminology and names of the book.

The translation and editing are now done, and I have acquired a new level of respect for *Dune* now that I have dissected it along with Al Masri. How did Herbert get introduced to so many symbols in Arab/Islamic culture? And his use of dialogue to introduce new information and drive the plot forward has influenced my own writing for Book 4 of my series. The translation must have been exhausting for Al Masri, but he wasn't only translating; he was constantly emailing me with articles and ideas and even suggestions for the cover. Needless to say, the man is very passionate about *Dune*.

You have to be very passionate with a novel like *Dune*. It has always been a hard sell, even when translated (in English) to the silver screen; the 1984 film by David Lynch was a flop, and studios have shied away ever since then. Imagine what the Arab reader will have to face reading it in his own language. (John Harrison's miniseries was a commercial success, but how much of the original was retained in the TV version, I wonder?)

The task was no less daunting for me. As an editor, I had to look at the text removed from the source text in order to render fluency to the target text. But above all, I had to look at the text from an Arab reader's perspective and ensure that the "exotic" words that Herbert had used did not confuse the reader with their multiple meanings. Suffice it to say, this will be a very interesting experiment once it is released. Aside from the religious themes, which are bound to raise many hackles, the terminology will be forever debated as no one will have a perfect translation for any of the choices made by Al Masri and myself.

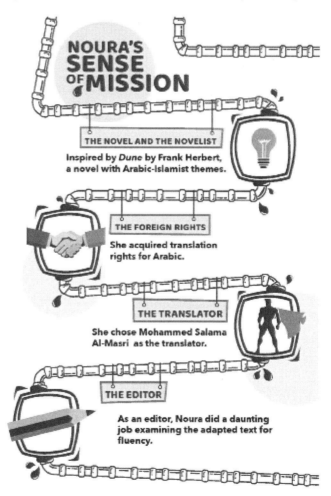

NOURA'S SENSE OF MISSION

THE NOVEL AND THE NOVELIST
Inspired by *Dune* by Frank Herbert, a novel with Arabic-Islamist themes.

THE FOREIGN RIGHTS
She acquired translation rights for Arabic.

THE TRANSLATOR
She chose Mohammed Salama Al-Masri as the translator.

THE EDITOR
As an editor, Noura did a daunting job examining the adapted text for fluency.

An illustration of the hurdles a work of translation goes through in the Arab world, science fiction or otherwise (courtesy of the artist, Yahya Salah Abul Ghait).

If the Arabic of Herbert's classic is a success, think of the potential for the future. There are the remaining Dune novels by Frank Herbert—*Dune Messiah*, *Children of Dune*, *God Emperor of Dune*, *Heretics of Dune*, and *Chapterhouse Dune*—as well as the prequels by Kevin Anderson and Brian Herbert (Frank Herbert's son). It's an industry in the waiting and could be what is called for to ignite the imagination of the Gulf Arab reader towards in-depth SF.

The Way Forward

What I would like to see from the publication of *Dune*, and other similar great works, is a bringing together of SF fans—made easier by social media—to celebrate old authors and encourage new ones.

I'm glad today that I have helped cause a small ripple in the publishing scene here in the Emirates. Two authors have thanked me for the example I set with *Ajwan* and have moved into science fiction themselves since its publication—Shaima Al-Marzooqi,[5] an accomplished children's novelist, literary critic, and now author of the SF new novel *Rayana*, and Mohammed Al Hammadi, author of *The Secret of the Red Planet* and winner of the Emirates Novel Award for his novel *The Last Day*.

Therefore, I can proudly say that in the new Arab world, these genres have only one way to go, UP.

SF is still young in the UAE, younger than in the Arab world at large, but it is gaining momentum (courtesy of the artist, Yahya Salah Abul Ghait).

Translator Biography

Mohammad Salama Al Masri, born in 1986 in Egypt, was originally a translator working for the Center for Western Thought (CWESTT, or مركز الفكر الغربي), in Riyadh, Saudi Arabia—a hub for cross-cultural dialogue between East and West. Next to literary translation, he has translated a documentary movie, *Spin*, a CWESTT book on Western philosophy, and has edited translated works including *Against the Modern World* and *American Paradise*. He's also an accomplished blogger, dedicating himself to combating misconceptions in the Arab media and among Arab intellectuals about the West and other cultures.

NOTES

1. I began writing *Ajwan* in 2009, long before ISIS, but the kind of brainwashing Islamists use on the young and the impressionable was explicitly on my mind. My book is about how the youth and the disenfranchised are used in this way.

2. The tentative title is *Artaziad* (آرتزياد).

3. Alan Dean Foster is an American author of Science Fiction and Fantasy. In addition to his Humanx Commonwealth series of books, he is best known for his fantasy series, *The SpellSinger*. Foster has authored more than forty novels and dozens of novelizations of movies, and recently has been revealed to be the ghost-writer of the novelization of *Star Wars: A New Hope*.

4. Please see his biography below.

5. For a list of her publications please check out her Goodreads page: https://www.goodreads.com/author/show/8426616.

Pursuing the Imagination

One Kuwaiti's Experience with Science Fiction and Other Abnormals

ABDULWAHAB AL-RIFAEE

I'm not interested in how things were, or how we ended up where we are now. What interests me is what we are now and what we will be.
—Ahmed Khaled Tawfik, quoted in Fahmy, 2018.

To me, writing begins with reading, before anything else. I explain this to the young writers we promote through my publishing house. I tell them, "If there is something wrong with your writing, the style in which you write, you must read. Go back home and read, for perhaps a year, and you will find that your writing will improve. It's not a matter of 'fixing' something wrong in a sentence or a story. Not something you can repair in a quarter of an hour. You have to upgrade yourself, and this comes through reading."

Looking at the stories people write, a reader can tell straight away how well read the author is, how *cultured*. One can see it in an individual scene. Every scene has to be studied thoroughly before the author approaches it. The author may describe a place based on the "atmosphere" of the scene. Is it sadness, excitement, fear, fondness? He can take the same situation, the same place, and turn it in one direction or the other. A place where a character meets someone, an old friend, and reminisce about the past, the fond memories this place reminds him of. Alternatively, the author can have the power cut in the middle of the night, in the exact same place, and then a character begins to hear strange sounds and it turns into a horror scene. The more an author reads, the more diverse and detailed his tastes, the more he can do this.

I always say that everyone who reads is a writer, even if he never decides to become a writer. But once he lifts the pen, he knows what to do. He has it in him to be a writer. Reading is the first step.

I had the good fortune of being an avid reader from my earliest days. I have a distinct memory of myself at the tender age of six in 1979, seeing my father coming home with a copy of *Majid*, a famous children's magazine in the Gulf that had just come out at the time. It was the first magazine of its kind in the Gulf, written especially for children. In time, I began to read *The Famous Five* and simplified police stories (detective novels) for young people, and the Superman and Batman comic books. I devoured them! And then the real turning point came when I discovered the Egyptian pocketbook series by Dr. Nabil Farouk and Dr. Ahmed Khaled Tawfik. In their day and

154

age, they were the ones who pioneered the writing of science fiction and horror in the Arab world.

Nabil Farouk wrote science fiction since 1984, and Ahmed Khaled Tawfik began writing horror in 1993. To me, these are the two who laid the foundation of whom I am as a writer. But, as is often the case, making a living got in the way of my youthful interests and ambitions.

It was only in 1998 that I was asked, out of the blue, to write an article for a magazine published by my place of work at the Kuwait Environment Public Authority (1997–2014). I did it as a favor to my friends and colleagues and then found just how popular the article was among fellow employees. As a result, I began writing a continuous stream of articles for the magazine and other publications, such as the youth magazine *Al-Fityan* (*The Young Men*), and also wrote some short stories for family magazines like *Usrati* (*My Family*) and *Al-Yaqaza* (*Awakening*). In 2000, however, I decided to strike out on my own and publish my first book—but that's a whole story by itself!

A Perilous Trek of My Own

Many are surprised that someone with a degree in chemical engineering would go into writing. To be honest, I was surprised at my own decision. The idea of being an author seemed like a flight of fancy to me in the 1990s. Even so, when I look back on it, it makes perfect sense. Almost all of the writers I love to read didn't study literature. When you create something, out of love, you do a much better, a much more creative job, than when you do it because you "have" to, when it's expected from you as part of your job and no more.

Why go far? Look at my two literary heroes, Nabil Farouk and Ahmed Khaled Tawfik. They were medical doctors originally, so they worked outside of their field entirely. If you love something, you excel in it even if you aren't specialized in it and educated in it, and many people specialize in fields but don't *distinguish* themselves in their professions, because they don't love what they're doing. And so, I went into professional writing, not quite knowing what I was getting myself into. It is completely different from writing the odd story or article in a newspaper or magazine. You get a small sum of money, an honorarium, and that is all. But all the work of publishing is done *for* you. Publishing a book is another matter entirely. I suffered at first, because publishers didn't want to take a risk on someone unknown like myself, forcing me to print my first book with my own money. I say "my" money but realize that at the time I was a civil servant and only had my salary, so I actually had to borrow money from friends to afford this reckless decision. And then I realized what a huge mistake I'd made. How was I going to distribute the book? I'd printed 2,000 copies all in one go!

I hadn't thought about that at all, and almost lost hope entirely. I had to take time off from work, carrying the copies with me in plastic sacks. My main customers were charity funds in Kuwait, and I think they bought the book out of-pity, seeing a young, Kuwaiti author trying to make it big, not because they found the work terribly interesting or well written. And the rest of my relatives scolded me for my decision—except for my wife and my grandmother, I should say.

What saved me was the book fair in Kuwait. The man in charge allowed me to have a desk there, something that would never happen now, an individual author with a cubicle promoting himself and explaining what he'd written. But it worked, and my book was a stunning success. I sold half of my printed copies. Even I was surprised. This was *Behind the Closed Door*, a collection of articles explaining phenomenon in our world, including some of the mysteries of the ancient Egyptians.

My story with publishing, beginning in 2011–12, is different. I'd done very well from my first book until 2011, selling in exactly the same way as before: renting a table at the book fair and pitching my books, fiction and non-fiction. Then I found that I was only selling in Kuwait, and no one in the Gulf knew me or any of my works. This was not a financial decision. I was doing well and was very satisfied, selling more and more books year by year. But I wanted to reach a wider audience. At the same time, I found my readers, particularly the young, telling me that they wanted to become writers themselves and wanted my help. My own individual efforts would not be enough. Having a company would solve both problems at once.

On Imaginative Writing and Teaching

I recollect reading a statistic once, published in *Al-Ahram* newspaper in Egypt, I think in 1989, talking about the popularity of science fiction. In America it was 67 percent. In Europe the popularity and acceptance rating was 56 percent. In Russia it was 41 percent. In the Arab world, it was only 9 percent!

But that was in 1989. Now science fiction is at least three or four times more popular in Arabic countries, I am glad to say. Many of the young, both avid readers and authors themselves, are getting bored with realism. It's as if we have only three or four themes, social or political, to write about, a problem we have had for far too long. That said, writing and publishing science fiction is still an uphill battle. There is still a great deal of resistance to it from the literary establishment when it comes to giving out prizes, as well as a lot of miscomprehension about the nature of science fiction itself. And man is the enemy of what he is ignorant of, as the Arabic saying goes. Many have condemned science fiction as something threatening to our culture, a form of *Westernization*.[1] The same criticisms were leveled against satellite television and social media, I should say. (Even in the West, people were afraid of anything new, such as the steam engine, thinking it would kill the babies in the bellies of pregnant women). Another reason entirely that science fiction is *derided* in Arabic countries is that we think that it is pure fancy. We think of *Harry Potter* and *The Lord of the Rings* as science fiction, and they are not, and even when science fiction is identified correctly, we reduce it to alien invasion movies, which we have had our fill of.

Fantasy is about the imagination, but without any boundaries, an imaginary world not grounded in real, cold, hard scientific facts and theories, where you can get away with almost anything. This brand of the imaginary can encompass everything from Mickey Mouse to, again, Harry Potter. The construction of such fantasy worlds is not easy, mind you, and they involve a tremendous amount of mental effort to build, imagining places and people and creatures and a world governed by its own logic. And it is tremendously entertaining and refreshing, there is no doubt. But writing science fiction is even *harder* than that!

Like the fantasy writer, we construct an imaginary world, but we have to back it up with research, facts, and theories, and try and imagine what will come to pass in the future if it becomes possible to implement these facts and theories in the real world, in new and unusual ways. No wonder then there are over twenty subgenres in the world of science fiction. Light sabers belong to only one variety, "Space Opera." "Strangers Among Us" is about life out there in the stars and alien visitations and (yes) invasions. There is "Alternate History" that presumes a change in history and a speculation as to the consequences that follow, good and bad. What if Hitler won the Second World War? What if the Arabs still ruled Al-Andalus? Not to forget alternate worlds and parallel universes, with mankind transferring itself to an alternate location somewhere else after we have used up all our resources here, or mankind stumbling on an identical planet somewhere else during journeys of space exploration. There is the "City of the Future," more commonly known as Utopia (and its opposite, Dystopia), that poses hard questions we need to face about ourselves, about how people will raise their children in the future, education, what our values will be like, and how crime and punishment will be judged. An excellent example of this is *Minority Report*, and also—and this will surprise you—*Planet of the Apes*!

This species of science fiction, as exemplified in these two movies, helps expose cracks in our present day world and flaws in our notions of the ideal society and state. They remind us that chaos, a degree of chaos, is inevitable and perhaps welcome. Wondering about telepathy (mind reading), telekinesis, and seeing the future (precognition) can exist side by side with teleportation and time-travel and discussions about evolution. Science fiction expands our imagination, but also our *scientific vocabulary*. It helps us judge ourselves better. Its serves so many functions, with all these mini-genres in the sci-fi fold serving their own little sets of functions as well.

Not to forget good old-fashioned hard sci-fi, which in some ways is the hardest and the least popular as far as Hollywood is concerned, dealing with the nuts and bolts of scientific discovery and technological application, no different in principle than real-life stories about actual discoveries and inventions that changed our lives and forever. Dazzling people with the value of science is a function not to be trifled with, and something we are sorely in need of here in the Arab world. Even horror, especially the kind I prefer to write, overlaps with these scientific and educational purposes. Horror is a much easier genre than SF, I know, because we all experience fear in our lives and are instinctively attracted to scary stories while growing up. Nonetheless, there are so many realms of fear that are a black box to us, like what is it that a comatose or unconscious person *experiences*? What lies beyond death? What does a person see in the last moments of his life? What does epilepsy *feel* like? What does a split personality feel like? And are all our fears purely supernatural, like genies and evil spells? Or are there other things out there that are worth fearing because they are very real and still unknown to us. Hence, my interest in parapsychology, as well as psychology and mental states and health problems.

My interest in horror has many roots, some scientific, some personal. When it comes to horror, I consider Ahmed Khaled Tawfik to be my godfather. I knew him personally, and we met many times, although sadly I did not have the good fortune to work with him. It was also the trauma of the Gulf War, Iraq's invasion and occupation of Kuwait from 1990–91, that drew me to the genre. I wouldn't lie to you. It had a big impact on my interest in horror. I lived through the whole war. I was 17 at the time. And I have had a taste for horror, and dystopia, ever since.

Some of my most successful series of books, and works especially close to my heart, are in horror—*Unknown Dimensions*, *Rare Cases*, and *The Museum of Souls*. The first is written in the form of a memoir by a young boy, an orphan living with his grandmother, recounting a series of peculiar happenings. The tales have a detective story quality to them and are told from his fragile perspective. The series was in three parts, with the adolescent as the hero. As for the second series, which made me famous, it is told from the perspective of a psychiatrist recounting the strangest cases he has ever encountered. It's in four parts, I've already printed and reprinted it over seven times, and I put a lot of effort into it. It is not just a scary story; research and constructing a narrative were essential for its success. The third book is a special favorite, a novel I even have had translated into English. The story is about a girl who returns to Kuwait from the United States after completing her studies. She ends up having to live with her grandfather who suffers from Alzheimer's. While there, she discovers a fake wall in his house and behind it a room containing statues of key figures from Kuwaiti history. I put a lot of effort into this story, not just in terms of themes, but excitement and intrigue, making the reader wonder about these statues and how they got there and what they represent, and the role of the grandfather—a man almost living in exile from the rest of his family. I've sold 15,000 copies already, and that's just in Arabic.

Finally, talking about writing itself is important too to fine-tune the imagination. One way I help potential authors are the many training courses I teach about how to write a novel, with many lectures about sci-fi literature. People confuse the novel with the short story with the folk tale with the *hikaya* (حكاية). All are stories, technically, but they each have a different logic. It's like saying "vehicle"; a car is a vehicle and a bus and a motorcycle, but riding them demands a different skill. Even cars are not all the same. The short story is anything twenty-five pages or smaller, with a focus on a specific event. A novel is far deeper, with presentations of characters through narrative and character development. A *hikaya*, however, is different even from a short story. The moral of the story is paramount, to the point that it outweighs the story. A *hikaya* can be full of holes, inconsistencies, and the strength of character or plot is not important. And the *hikaya* is often derived from myths and legends, so it looks like science fiction but is not.

These fine distinctions, between fantasy science and horror, and these different modes of writing—short stories, novels, folk stories, and educational stories (*hikaya*), are *not* clear in the minds of authors, let alone the publishers and the readers. It takes a considerable effort to clarify the differences, and it makes our task as writers and publishers much harder. And it brings the critics and many traditional authors down on us as science fiction writers, diluting what we are trying to do and what science fiction can do for us.

Clarifying these distinctions is something I have tried to do through my work with the Kuwaiti Writers Association, but it is hard. Hard work, and I have my commitments as an author, a publisher, and also a husband and father, and a teacher. (I have three children.) The individual can only do so much. The Writers Association has programs to help young authors with their writing skills, but there are only a few of us giving these seminars, and it is a huge effort. And I am already an instructor on novel writing and very proud of the workshops I give, not just in Kuwait but Saudi Arabia, but with universities and companies. I don't just teach; I designed the whole curricula, an extensive syllabus but also simplified and interesting.

I go over such subjects as the history of the novel. How long have novels existed; what were the first novels ever written? I teach how to construct characters, how to construct events that are convincing, how to surprise the reader at the end, how to portray heroes and villains, how to develop stylistics and themes. And then, of course, I discuss genres and subgenres to complete the circle of creativity.

Between Countries and Generations

I was asked once what genre literature, writing like science fiction and horror, can do for the Arabs as a *defeated* people. Defeated psychologically and intellectually. My answer was, if we are defeated as Arabs in these ways, it is because we don't read!

Science and technological invention often begin, are anticipated, by science fiction. H.G. Wells, the great pioneer of SF, was the first to describe time as the fourth dimension, years and years before Einstein. The German V1 and V2 rockets, amazingly, were inspired by Jules Verne's *Journey to the Moon*. Even we have contributed in this way. There was the great Kuwaiti author Tiba Ibrahim who anticipated the cloning of human beings in her novels, a technological possibility that is just around the corner. That is how important and useful science fiction is. You don't have to be a scientist to write SF. You just have to have a vision of the future. It's an admixture of necessity as the mother of invention and the circumstances you are living in.

Sadly, the printing press came late to the Arab world, slowing down our inventiveness. And with the economic problems we all face, reading and culture seem like a luxury to many. Thankfully, things are changing and fast. At one point in time, horror writers in the Gulf could be counted on the fingers of one hand, but their numbers are escalating. The same is true for science fiction. This latest generation, thanks to the internet, is completely different than any before, even my own. This is the first generation in history to have the whole world coming to it without having to go anywhere. There are bad things that come with this access, some irreligious practices and behaviors, but I would say that the benefits of being open to the world far outweigh the disadvantages. Those in the West advanced through reading before anything else. They didn't limit themselves to one set of books or one set of subjects. They didn't just read one genre, but read fantasy and science fiction and horror as well.

The internet has done for us, as Arabs and Gulf Arabs specifically, what the printing press did for Europe in the 16th century. And the young are leading the way. Young authors are always one step ahead of the intellectual elite, the literary elite, in our countries. The internet has allowed young people in my region to understand the value of the book and to read and watch what is produced in the West. You can see this at the book fairs in the Gulf. If the young aren't writing, they are reading. I and publisher and author friends keep meeting young people asking our advice on what to read. Young people are no longer satisfied with just getting their educational certificates. It is no longer their exclusive ambition. They want to read for its own sake. The whole map of book fairs has changed too because of this desire. Now young readers and publishers are established by young people themselves.

For the longest time, in Kuwait, book fairs were mainly for cookbooks and books about magic, thanks to the limited number of novelists writing. This has changed completely. Literature is taking center stage at these events, novels and short story collections, particularly those by young authors. Okay, not everything written by the young is of the best quality, especially compared to classics and the big names in writing, but it has changed things so radically that the overall effect is very positive. And having young authors at these events will help the young improve their writing by interacting with the readers and seeing how publishing works and what else is on display.

I should add here my generation's experiences. You have to understand that I grew up in Kuwait in a time when there was only one TV channel, or two, and only five daily newspapers. I read a lot, but it still did not prepare me for understanding others, understanding how Westerners "think." I didn't know what was going on in the rest of the world. Now, through television and the internet, and social media especially, people go to the West already knowing everything about it beforehand. It was *not* so in my day. I know many people who did their university education in the West, as I did, and came back exactly as they were—learning, or wanting to learn, nothing from the West, even to their own benefit. No culture is without flaws, and no culture is without positive points you can learn from to your own well being. At the other extreme, I know people who came back *more* American than the Americans themselves. I never wanted to do that either!

For me, coming back from the West I realized, again, the importance and value of reading. I wanted to see a book in everyone's hand in the Arab world. That was my intellectual ambition. In the West, in America, they actually have an excuse for not reading. They are working *all* the time. They begin working when they are young, while at college or before. You hear Americans saying that they have to pay for absolutely everything, through taxes. If they could put taxes on the air they breathe, they would. The one thing they get for free is books. They can go to a public library and borrow a book for no charge at all. As a result, I came back with the distinct impression that we Arabs are not doing enough in the area of the intellectual life and writing, and that we have no excuse for this.

In the Gulf, we are all privileged, growing up in oil rich countries that pay for everything for us in terms of education and health and welfare. We say the government doesn't help us, but that's no excuse. Westerners could say the same; look at the taxes they pay. But they don't say this. Social media has also helped us tremendously as authors and publishers. Media in our day did not give authors the kind of attention they need to become known to publishers and even book fairs, as essential as they are, are very limited. Social media fixes many of these older problems. I check my social media sites ever day to see how my titles are doing, what people are saying, for and against. I have become much, much more popular thanks to it.

I enjoy getting posts of comments on which particular work of mine they liked, and why, automatically helping others to find what they are looking for, topics and authors and writing style. Some people were initially afraid that Twitter and Instagram and Snapchat would quench people's thirst for reading, becoming too accustomed to such a tight format to write in. I do not see this at all. Look at the coverage of movies online. People post summaries, a synopsis of a film, and people go and watch it anyway. If anything, it encourages them. Reading these posts is a must, if only to look for bad news that could ruin the reputation of one of your novels. Social media even gives you new ways to express yourself, new genres. Short stories are no longer short enough for the task. I have now posted stories consisting only of two sentences. It's difficult, but that is good in itself. It forces you to be creative and learn how to grab the reader. I did a story about two people, a boy and a girl, who were destined to meet each other and fall in love because they lived in the same neighborhood, but they never did because he used Twitter and she used Facebook! It's as if they live in opposite *dimensions*, I meant.

The catch with this social media genre is copyright. (There is also online slandering and blackmail). Copyright is always a problem in our part of the world, and you may find your stories showing up elsewhere, posted on other online platforms, without your name as author. So, I deleted everything I had posted in the past and saved a copy on my computer for future purposes. And I'd written many such stories, about thirty.

A Final Word

I am optimistic about the next generation for another reason, from my direct experiences here in Kuwait and in my publishing house specifically, and this is because of the number of female writers. They are outnumbering the men, I am glad to say. Specifically, when it comes to young authors, there are names like Husa Abd Al-Razak, Nada Al-Ahmed, Altaaf Al-Blushi, Alaa Jumaa, and Ghadeer Il-Umtari. This is happening in the Gulf too. Batul Kaal. They are doing very well at the book fairs across the region, selling well. Colleagues in publishing are telling me this also.

I am glad to say that my work has born fruit in this regard. At one book fair, a medical doctor thanked me, in front of everybody, for encouraging her daughter to go into medicine through reading my novels and stories!

I was also thrilled to discover that people are reading my works in other languages, and I do not just mean English. The Kuwaiti Writers Association itself was overjoyed that an Iranian student, Fatima Iqbali, has done her MA thesis on my works, seeing this as a promotion and recognition of Kuwaiti literature abroad ("AbdulWahab Al-Rifaee," February 2018). She was particularly happy with how I balanced the craft of writing with my concerns as a genre writer, and added that Kuwaiti artists, writers, and intellectuals were ambassadors for their country and for Arabic culture.

That is where I would like to end this essay, with an eye toward building cultural bridges, not just towards the West, but to the whole world and our own world. We need to be impressed by the West without being awed by it into inaction, and we need to better ourselves as well as being true to ourselves. And science fiction is a big part of this. Hopefully, in the meantime, our movie producers will catch on to its significance and began to make our own sci-fi cinema.

Until then, we have to work harder, write better and, most importantly of all, read more!

NOTE

1. Nada Faris has encountered this criticism in her own studies on science fiction in Kuwait and the Arab world (Faris, April 2018).

WORKS CITED

"AbdulWahab Al-Rifaee… In an Iranian Master's Degree." (7 February 2018). *Al-Rai Digital*. http://www.alraimedia.com/Home/Details?id=0e891f51-be71-42b8-a1a1-40f763e59c34 [Arabic].

Fahmy, Hisham. (2018). "Celebrating the Life of Egyptian author Ahmed Khaled Tawfik." *The Arab Edition*. http://thearabedition.com/blog/celebrating-the-life-of-egyptian-author-ahmed-khaled-tawfik/.

Faris, Nada. (30 April 2018). "Rewriting the Future in Arab Science Fiction: Toward a New Hermeneutic." Talk delivered at the Arab Open University's Knowledge Development Seminar, held on 9 May 2018. *Nada Faris* [personal blog]. http://www.nadafaris.com/arab-science-fiction-aou/.

Interview with Farkhondeh Fazel Bakhsheshi on Publishing Science Fiction in Iran

Egyptian Society for Science Fiction

> Publishing a book is like stuffing a note into a bottle and hurling it into the sea. Some bottles drown, some come safe to land, where the notes are read and then possibly cherished, or else misinterpreted, or else understood all too well by those who hate the message. You never know who your readers might be.
>
> —Margaret Atwood, "American PEN," 28 April 2010

ESSF: Tell us something about yourself. What's your Ph.D. on? Science fiction, by any chance? Good luck, by the way.

Thank you very much. Unfortunately, no, it is about narratology and interactivity. Actually, my MA thesis was about interactive narrative, and it is not known in Iran, and that is why I chose to work on it. The only interactive narration we have in Iran are translations of children's book series called "Choose Your Own Adventure," and I think the best way to enrich our literary knowledge is giving our new generation new styles of literature which are trending in the world. Media is playing a huge role in promoting literature in very different and new ways such as video games and escape rooms, and as a new field they need attention in our country as well. The literature, in its old sense as written books, is losing its audiences and the new forms; it goes through needing promotion in our literary circle. I believe that if we start to update our knowledge on new approaches to literature, we can gain a new look on the old genre as well, the ones that we did not pay attention to earlier such as science fiction.

ESSF: How does Persian literature compare to English literature? And do you speak Arabic?

Unfortunately, no, I don't speak Arabic. If we divide the literature into very general division of old and modern in the comparison between English literature and Persian literature, in the old era Persian literature looks more advanced in form and subject rather than English literature. But, in the recent years, because of English being a universal language and enjoying the larger audience, its literature grows with a very rapid rate, and there are forms of literature that are well known in English literature and practiced for many years while in Iran they are relatively new. Also, as I mentioned earlier, because of the universality of the language, the barriers of translation is already removed, and audience can easily read the English literature in its original language, and the availability of it worldwide is also working in favor of the literature being more well-known and well-read.

ESSF: How long have you been in publishing and why did you choose this profession?

I started when I was twenty. One of my professors at university owned Ahang-e-Ghalam at the time. He saw my enthusiasm about books and literature and as I was looking for a job, he offered me one at his office. I was a quick learner because I enjoyed every second of learning. Soon I got promoted to internal manager and then executive manager. Then the owner decided to retire, and I was finished with university, so I bought the company from him, and now I've run it for ten years. I also owned a book store which, due to economical problems in Iran, I had to close last year. I had it for four years. Because of my passion for literature and books, being a publisher sounds like a good fit for me, so I went to publishing.

ESSF: How long has your company been operating, and how does distribution work in Iran? And what does the name mean?

The company started in 1998, and the name means "song of pen." We won many awards from governmental and private organizations and held exhibitions inside and outside of Iran. Our company has published more than ten books that won the status of "Book of the Year" in different years, and we have also been praised by the ministry of culture and guidance of Iran as the "Publisher of the Year." We publish works from other countries that also speak Farsi such as Afghanistan, Tajikistan, and Uzbekistan as well. Our interest is in promoting new authors who wanted to publish for the first time in the category of literature and history. We are a private publisher, and we are working independently, so we choose the books we publish according to our own interest and the parameters that we value in a good work.

Distribution in Iran works in two different ways, and we are using both. The first way is going through the channel of big distribution companies which are not publishers and usually not only work with publishers, but also work with other artists who create handmade crafts. They have a network of agents all over Iran working with bookstores around Iran; usually they do the job for 40–70 percentage of the book price, depending on the book and its subject. The second channel is composed of publishers themselves, who work independently of the distribution companies. They distribute books with the help of agents using a door-to-door policy, going to bookstores, supermarkets, and gas stations to present books. Of course, this is not a very sufficient method, but it still can help some authors to find their audience.

ESSF: If Ahang-E-Ghalam means "song of pen," then what does Farkhondeh Fazel Bakhsheshi mean?

Farkhondeh in Farsi means happiness. Fazel means someone who knows lots of things. I think it has the same meaning in Arabic, and Bakhsheshi means generous.

ESSF: What range of books do you publish—fiction and non-fiction, academic texts, children's books?

We are focused on literature and history but also published some academic texts based on these subjects.

ESSF: Do you publish "genre" literature—science fiction as well as horror, fantasy and detective fiction? Do you also publish comic books and graphic novels?

We do not publish comic books or graphic novels but we publish science fiction.

ESSF: What are the critics like in Iran when it comes to science fiction? Do they recognize it as worthwhile literature? Do they distinguish between SF and surrealism and magic realism and fantasy?

Science fiction in Iran is more known by translations from other languages, although the Iranian reader is familiar with the genre. There are not many Iranian science fiction authors, and the ones already working in the field are not as famous as foreign writers whose works are translated to Persian. But critics recognize the genre; there are some specific awards contributed to the genre. They distinguish SF from surrealism and magic realism, although the last two are more known and read in critics' circles.

ESSF: Who are the "big names" in Iranian science fiction, other than your brother Mr. Iraj Fazel Bakhsheshi, of course?

Iraj has the highest number of science fiction books written by an Iranian author. Others are not that well published. Of course, there are some names, but I don't know any to consider big names, and there is not much science fiction written by Iranian authors. Most of the science published here is translation. Even Iraj, while keeping the record of the most published Iranian science fiction writer and winning some awards regarding his work in this field, is not a well-known name among Iranian readers. He is mostly famous because his work circulating the academic circles, and thesis and essays are written on his work.

ESSF: Concerning translated science fiction, is this all Western SF—Asimov, Clarke, Philip K. Dick—or do you also have Russian science fiction?

It is not limited to Western writers, although they are the majority. Russian writers are also translated to Farsi. Iranian readers are very familiar with these names, and even more names from other countries as translated literature is very popular in Iran in every genre.

ESSF: Is publishing in science fiction in Iran "profitable"? Is a SF novel or short story collection more likely to bring in money than a children's book or an adventure story or a horror novel?

Unfortunately, as owner of a company that is one of the publishers with the most science fiction books in Iran, I can say that the genre is not profitable. Almost any other genre is more profitable than science fiction. Especially novel translations and romantic novels, if we consider only literature.

ESSF: Who are the main consumers of science fiction books in Iran? Young people, the middle aged, children, university students, etc.? And do you publish electronically as well?

Usually young people, as they are more interested in technology and how it works. Yes, we are online in different websites selling e-books.

ESSF: Is there a large readership for science fiction among girls? Science fiction, everywhere, is perceived as a boy's club. This is certainly a problem in Egypt. Do you try to "encourage" the female readership? If so, how?

It is more popular between boys as the subjects that are dealt with in science fiction are more of boys' interests. Fighting and action, spaceships and monsters. The idea of going to space or the future, it is not so appealing to girls, and I believe it is rooted in the education our children received when they were growing. There are some limitations for girls; they are supposed to be interested in girly things, not wars and machines or flying cars. So, if we want to change these tastes, we need to start a change in our educational system. Of course, in recent years we have a growth in the number of girls interested in science fiction; maybe if a line of a romantic story can be added to the story line of science fiction then it would be more appealing to girls. It sounds a little like a stereotype pattern, but still in the psyche of young girls, a good romantic story is standing above a well written science fiction story.

ESSF: How do you target the readership, and what role do authors play in this?

We hold sessions for readers to meet their favorite authors to ask what they have on their minds. Whenever the author has a new book, we promote it on our social media pages and on our website as well. We participate in book fairs around Iran and any foreign book fair that we can join holding author signature sessions. If there is a chance, we hold circle tables in book fairs concentrating on our new releases. Also, we are in constant relation with newspapers, giving them our list of new books to be promoted by them on their paper or website.

ESSF: Please tell us something about illustration in the book industry in your country. How scientific is publishing in Iran?

We work with a large group of people. The industry in Iran is pretty advanced. We have great artists who work as cover designers or illustrators. We have different kinds of technologies to work on the presentation of our books. We use emboss designs, different styles of cutting shapes and etc. For example, a work named *Coffin* published here, cut like a coffin, is pretty much a normal thing. Cover art is very important in catching the eye of readers in Iran as a bad cover really can ruin a good book. Editing also is very important to correct the grammatical errors or making the language of a book more appealing to the audience. Also, designing the pages is essential as the audience in Iran looks for the whole package in a book. Books with covers made of cloth are pretty popular in Iran. In the field of children's literature, the books are very developed in presentation. We even have books which are waterproof, or books that have parts that can be touched to transfer the feeling of the touching in the story. For example, an animal for children. In Iran there are scented Qurans with silky covers, so I can say that we are pretty advanced in the field.

ESSF: In the West, with bestseller authors, publishers can actually hire them to write a novel about something, like a spy novel or thriller. Does this happen in Iran? Do you sign "exclusive" contracts with authors that cover sequels and translations?

It is more the matter for translators in Iran. We hire them to translate books, but also there are times that we ask an author to write a novel. It happens more with in children's books rather than adult books and in specialized field like psychology rather than literature.

ESSF: Is there an Iranian Tom Clancy?

No, there is not.

ESSF: One of your top authors, needless to say, is Iraj Fazel Bakhsheshi. From his biography he is an engineer, so his chief source of income is not writing. Is this a common pattern in Iran? Do Iranian SF authors have to make a living in other professions? Is this a problem faced by all authors in Iran, or just in new fields like science fiction?

It really depends on the writer, but unfortunately being a writer is not a popular choice for work. Because the market is not stable, many of the writers have another job than writing, and actually this is often a source for having the money to self-publish their works. But there are also writers that make a living out of writing.

ESSF: Are dystopian novels popular in Iran? Are George Orwell, Ray Bradbury, and Aldous Huxley well read in Iran?

Yes, they are. They are all well-known in Iran, and different publishers have published their books with different translations. Orwell is an influential writer in Iran; his *Animal Farm* and *1984* are the books that almost every Iranian has read once or heard about. Ray Bradbury is also popular between different generations. His *Illustrated Man* has two different translations in Iran. Aldous Huxley's novel *Brave New World* was translated to Farsi and republished three or four times. Also, his non-fiction works, collection of essays, were translated to Farsi.

ESSF: Have any of Iraj Fazel Bakhsheshi's novels and stories been translated into English? The website fantasy.ir/ is exclusively in Persian. This is a shame because you have so much talent in the country, you could go global. Does your publishing house employ translators to help get works in Farsi into English, French, or Arabic?

Some of the stories are translated into other languages, but they are not published as books, but they are available on the net. The problem is in contacting and making a contract with a foreign publisher even if there are translations available. Publishing them and then sending them abroad would cost a lot, and it is not profitable. Also, selling the right of the books is not an easy task with lots of rules about doing it that must be followed. We have many talented Iranian writers not only in the science fiction genre, but other genres as well, but with a simple search on the internet, you can see there aren't lots of Iranian books translated and available to non–Iranian readers.

ESSF: Is Ahmed Khaled Tawfik, the Egyptian author of the internationally acclaimed Utopia *(2008), known in Iran? Have you heard of other Egyptian SF authors like Dr. Mustafa Mahmoud and Nihad Sharif?*

Unfortunately, none of them are famous in Iranian market.

Translation from Arabic into Persian is very popular in Iran, but mostly it is done in the field of religious books or academic books.

ESSF: There is modern Iranian literature in Egypt, translated into Arabic, but the translation is often done here in Egypt. And since the books are imported and translated, they are very expensive. Have you thought of translating into Arabic?

We need to do some research on the market before starting to do so, because translating and publishing a book in Iran is also a very expensive process. Adding the shipping and translation fees, it is going to be a huge investment, and it needs a thorough investigation.

ESSF: Where do you see Iranian science fiction in 20 years' time? And would cooperation between Iranian and Arab authors, and publishers and translators, help fulfill your future vision?

These days, boundaries between different medias are vanishing fast, and I hope as in movies and video games, science fiction is absorbing the Iranian young generation. Soon it will lead them to be interested in Iranian science fiction as well. I can't comment on the relation between Arab and Iranian writers as I'm not familiar with them well enough to see the future of this companionship. But as we are close in roots of religion, I can see that our nations would share the same interests, and maybe if there are more ways such as joint conferences or round tables or even conversation sessions between the two groups to close our views together, then it will be a brighter future for our joint literary horizon.

WORK CITED

"American PEN Literary Service Award Speech, New York, April 27." (28 April 2010). *Margaret Atwood: Year of the Flood*. https://marg09.wordpress.com/2010/04/28/.

An Interview from Kuwait

Dr. Naif Al-Mutawa, Creator of The 99,
on Therapy, the Comics Industry,
and Muslim Modernization

EGYPTIAN SOCIETY FOR SCIENCE FICTION

There's a surprising core of fandom that just hates any kind of religion in their science fiction. They really don't want to mix these things together. I'm not quite clear what that's about and why they're so opposed to mixing these things. It becomes a very purist argument. People will say, "If there's any kind of religion in it, it's not science fiction anymore." Well, I don't really buy that. People believe in religions and there are weird, mysterious things that happen in the universe. Why not play with that, too? Why isn't that just as valid as everything else that's part of the human condition, which is theoretically what sci-fi is supposed to be exploring?
—Ronald D. Moore, "You Ask the Q's,
Ronald D. Moore Answers" 2013

ESSF: A brief introduction is called for. Who is Dr. Naif Al-Mutawa, and what is your story with science fiction?

I'm a clinical psychologist who grew up as a bookworm. As a child, I was always reading. I was introduced to science fiction in my early teens with John Wyndham's novels: *The Day of the Triffids*, *The Kraken Wakes*, *Chocky*. I read all his books. I remember when I was on umra [the small pilgrimage], I read *Chocky* there when my mother wasn't looking. I knew I liked science fiction; I looked it up in the Encyclopaedia Britannica, because there was no internet—this was the 1980s—and found that there were big names in science fiction at the time: Robert Heinlein, Isaac Asimov, and Arthur C. Clarke. I picked Heinlein, and read all his books. About 80 or 90 books. I remember when he died, I didn't feel guilty. Now that he was dead, I could move on to another author, but then another book of his came out after he died called *Grumbles from the Grave*. He'd planned for it to come out after he died, so I had to get that too!

That was my introduction to SF, by reading novels.

ESSF: Did reading SF influence your decision to become a clinical psychologist?

Growing up I'd always wanted to become a writer, but my parents told me it's a hobby and not to think of it as a job. And they were right. I was very good at school, so I thought to myself that the right way to get into writing was by understanding character development and personality, which relates a lot to psychology. It helped with English literature too. So, it laid the groundwork for my career later on.

ESSF: Did you grow up in Kuwait or the United States?

Kuwait. But I spent my summers in the United States. From the age of 8 to 18, I spent my summers at a summer camp in New Hampshire, and then four years doing my undergrad, went back to Kuwait for two years, then did three master's degrees and my Ph.D. in the United States.

ESSF: Are you a writer or illustrator or both?

No, a writer. But I illustrated one of my first books. The illustrations were symbolic; the characters were circles and half circles. That's the extent of my ability. I'm not gifted in that way.

I have a series predating *The 99*. One of the books in the series came out after *The 99*, after what happened to me, with all the fatwas and death threats. It came out in Saudi Arabia. It's called *The Bouncy Junior* (حكاية نطوط الصغير) series.[1]

ESSF: Was this an example of children's literature?

That's how it was *perceived*, but not what I originally intended. I won awards for children's literature, ironically. UNESCO awarded me the Tolerance Award in 1997 for the first book in the series.[2] Very flattering, but very amusing, because I'd intended it for adults. A six-year-old would read it one way, a sixty-year-old would read it another. It's full of symbols and hidden hints.

ESSF: Were you exposed to a lot of children's literature while growing up too, English literature?

Only English. I didn't like the Arabic stuff. The reason for this is the Ministry of Information. They banned everything I would have liked, so I only ended up reading it in English. Then I came home with Abd Al-Rahman Al-Manif's book, *Cities of Salt*, in English, and my mother saw it and wouldn't let me read it. I said I'd been reading in English for the past thirty years, to which she said, "How dare you let a translator stand between you and the book. You're reading that one in Arabic." So, she got me the original Arabic, and I *loved* it. I read all his books, and then moved on to Taha Hussein and Naguib Mahfouz, and it was then that I realized it wasn't that I didn't like the Arabic language; it was that I had to buy the books in English.

It was like buying drugs. They weren't accessible. I had to buy them at Madbouli bookshop in Egypt until I was older. They were forbidden in Kuwait. If it hadn't been for that I would have read in Arabic as a child.

So, anything of mine you see in Arabic, know that it's translated because I only write in English.

ESSF: How does doing a comic differ from writing a novel or a story? What are the advantages and challenges of this medium?

Writing a comic is very cinematic. The advantage is that it's communicating with illustrations, which is the oldest means of communication ever, like hieroglyphics, drawings on cave walls. It transcends linguistic barriers.

One of the challenges was learning how collective an enterprise it is.

I wrote the backstory; I wrote the character bible for *The 99*, and the first books. Then I brought in professionals who actually knew what they were doing. They were *way* better than me. I was just experimenting.

What I learned early on is that I was writing the checks, so people were telling me my stories were really great, which they weren't. So, when I took myself out of the writing, the stories became much, much better.

ESSF: Did you grow up reading comics?
Yes and no. I enjoyed them when I got them, but I wasn't really into them. I got them mostly when I was at camp. Batman, Superman, stuff like that.

ESSF: In that case, did you like Superman or Spiderman more?
Batman.

ESSF: But he's not a real superhero. Doesn't have superpowers, just gadgets.
Exactly why I like him!

ESSF: And what about the X-Men and Mutants?
They were the model I followed for *The 99*. If you look at religious models, like the Prophet and the Sahaba [Companions of the Prophet Muhammad] or Jesus and his disciples, you'll notice it's the same used in the X-Men and The Mutants, with Dr. Xavier and his disciples. I used that same model with Dr. Ramzy and his disciples.
That's one way to create a universe, successfully.

ESSF: Do superheroes have a special allure for you? Are you attracted to them?
The reality is I use superhero as a concept for creating the universe. Not so much the superhero himself that concerns me. What happened was I'd written an email to my business school friends, and one of them replied, Constantine Valhouli, who had just done a documentary about comic books called *Sex, Lies and Superheroes* (2003), and he asked me if I'd like to meet the top people at Marvel and DC. That's where I met Neil Adams, who was big in the 1970s with Batman and Robin, and I told him about what I was doing with *The 99*. So, he asked me, "Do you know what 'Shazam' stands for?" I said no, and he told me it's an acronym for six Greek gods! They used Hercules, Aphrodite, etc. It opened up my eyes to the relationship between religion and comics and superheroes. I did my research and found it was really interesting, how these little archetypes manifest in superheroes. That's how the idea started.
It's not so much that I wanted to do superheroes more than having a concept; someone convinced me that superheroes was the genre to tackle that concept.

ESSF: Where do you get your inspiration from?
My life, my reading, and my kids.

ESSF: Do you see therapy and art as one and the same thing?
They can be, and certainly are for me. I always listen to how people *tell* their story. The way their narrative morphs and changes tells me if I've been successful or not in treating them.
And then there are the people who use the creative arts for therapy, art theory, and creative writing. I don't necessarily use that per se, but I certainly listen to the person telling their story: are they the captain of the ship or a passenger? Do they devalue someone else or overvalue another? Do they create a superhero out of someone? Superheroes don't exist in real life, so you need to balance things out, see the people you think are good and are bad, to see that your ideals in real life are not overbearing.[3]

ESSF: What were you trying to do with The 99? *What age group were you targeting?*

I wanted to change how Islam was perceived *by Muslims.* Most people think I was doing it for the West. I wasn't.

I was sick and tired of people who had positioned Islam as about death and murder and killing in the name of God. Our leaders weren't doing enough. Whenever something horrible happens, they say, "This isn't Islam," but they won't say what Islam is. And that's the mission of the people who are terrorizing its name. So, I said that's enough. Islam becomes the average of what just happened, what happened before, and so it keeps going "down" for them. The only thing that beat the Catholic Church was arts and culture in the Renaissance, the ability to interpret and translate works of art that then set down interpretations for the Bible. So, I thought, "Let me get into the Quran and let me lift out values that we share with humanity," but in a very secular way, through superheroes and comic book characters. How Islam was being viewed was very important to me.

As a psychologist, to feed off your previous question, a lot of my work is about perception. How people see themselves, how others see them. Somewhere between the two is where I work. And it wasn't just about how the way the West perceives Islam and how Islam perceives the West, but also how we see ourselves. It became self-defining. Even as Muslims, when something terrible happens, we say, "Oh my God, I hope it wasn't Muslims!"

If you call a child stupid enough times, he'll become stupid. Call someone a terrorist enough times, he'll become a terrorist. I wanted to have an impact there.[4]

And yes, I was deliberately targeting the younger age group with *The 99*, from 6 to 12 year olds, which is the traditional age range for comic books.

ESSF: And why the number "99"?

This alludes to the 99 attributes of Allah subhanahu wa talaa, such as wisdom, foresight, mercy, and other basic human values. Too much discourse focuses on what differentiates us from others, and not what ties us to others. So, I focused on basic human values. When those values are in their absolute form, they are God. Like "the" Mercy. But human beings can be merciful too.

ESSF: How much did it cost to produce? Was your company, Teshkeel Media Group, able to turn a decent profit? Did you sell only in Kuwait or in the Gulf Arab market?

On the comics, no. The TV series did well, but we had political problems. But we're in negotiations now to license *The 99* series elsewhere, inshallah [God willing]. We'll keep you posted.

ESSF: And the production costs?

$40 million, for the TV series. Two series of animation. The comics, not nearly as much. Just about a $1000 per page.

The TV series launched on Netflix in the U.S. and on Cartoon Network throughout Asia. It came out in Mandarin, in Spanish in Mexico and Costa Rica, and came out in parts of Brazil. We become the first IP[5] in history to come out in the Islamic world and go global, and we did it by tapping into basic human values that Islam shares with humanity.

There was a theme park in Kuwait for eight years for *The 99*. It was very, very expensive but worth it. Minus the fatwas, death threats, and law suits!

ESSF: What happened to the TV series exactly? And what were the fatwas about?

Misinformation. The sheikh who condemned me was accurate, correct from a religious perspective, and I'd agree with him. But it didn't *apply* to me. I hadn't done what they said I'd done. If somebody had bothered to ask me, I could have pointed that out.

The sheikh in question said that I could not embody certain attributes. Somebody had told him that I had personified certain attributes that only belong to God. But I had not. That's why I only had 37 characters. I myself refused to personify certain attributes that only belonged to Allah. The person who asked the sheikh mentioned three attributes which I did not use. I actually said that you shouldn't use them!

The guy sued me, and I was in courts in Kuwait for a year and half. I won, was put on trial again, and won again. And now I'm releasing a hypnosis app that I created, which has an Islamic theme to it—the idea of modernizing and introducing Islam as a cultural thing. That's something that they didn't scare me into not doing. But I was uncomfortable for a couple of years after the court cases.

The irony is that HH Sheikh Mohammed Bin Rashid of Dubai gave me the Islamic economy award for media, for the same project I was being tried for! Which is a nice show of support.[6]

ESSF: What did you think of President Obama[7] mentioning The 99 *as a tool of interfaith dialogue?*

One of the proudest moments of my life! But that's also when my problems began starting. I began getting attacked, both here and there. Here I became a Zionist, a mason, Israeli spy. CIA. You name it.

And there, I started getting attacked by ultra right-wing groups, who would say that this proves that Obama is a Muslim and that he's trying to brainwash you with Shariah-superheroes. Anyone watching the show will become radicalized. Can't let the Muslims *brainwash* us like the Mexicans brainwashed us with *Dora the Explorer*!

You can't make this stuff up! And these are the guys who voted for Trump in the end. So, this is real. This is what happened to me, and because of that, *The 99* was never aired on Discovery's channels, which paid a over a million dollars for it, because of the threats from the right-wing in the United States. That's when Netflix aired it for a few years, because of one of my mentors at Disney, Michael Eisner, picked up the phone and called them and said this shouldn't have happened to this guy, look what he's done, it's great work. So, we got on Netflix. Not for the same figure we were hoping for, but the series got aired, which was the important thing.

Then ISIS made a death threat three years ago with a hashtag about who is going to kill Dr. Naif (Akbar, 2015; "Global Reach-Censorship," 2014). My kids were very distressed when they saw it on social media. And ISIS hadn't even watched the series.

When I got taken into the police station for questioning, I was asked why I was insulting God. I laughed. It was nervous laughter but laughter. I said, "How am I insulting God?" For the past ten years, the *only* good thing in the media about Islam was this. It was a very surreal, weird time, and the Islamists got involved in the Arab Spring. It is what it is. But I didn't stop, and I'm still going. And I'm coming back stronger than before.

The new person I'm cooperating with now is very experienced, very involved in media. I was still learning at the time, and getting experience. Inshallah everything will go well.

ESSF: Inshallah. But this was before *the Arab Spring, you say?*

No, the problems came after the Arab Spring. Obama was elected in 2010. The Arab Spring was in 2011, which is when the problems happened.

They called me an infidel, a kafir, in the Friday prayer sermon in Saudi Arabia. It's weird; I'm saying we're not terrorists, and they're saying, yes we are, stop protecting us!

ESSF: The critics, did they have a "position" over The 99?

Look online. You'll find thousands of articles, even dissertations and papers published by professors. One specifically called The Marvel of Islam or Islam Marvellous, two professors analyzed parts of my comic and said, here he is referencing Ibn Sina, here is referencing Ibn Rushd.[8]

That's news to me! I don't remember thinking about them when I was writing, but I have read those books. There have been several conferences on it too. There was the big one at Hedelberg; that's *the* big philosophy conference in the world. And there are papers on Kant and Nietzsche and *The 99*. Look on any academic sources, and you'll find *The 99*.

"Literary" critics, specifically, I don't know. But definitely academicians, with book chapters and documentaries. One on American television called *Wham Bam Islam*.[9] Then there was a documentary where I was one of four creative artists from Islam, which was broadcast on Norwegian television. But I don't keep track of these things. I'm the kind of guy who just does his work.

ESSF: But Kuwaiti critics? Surely they said something for or against?

In Kuwait…. They didn't even know I existed until the uproar. Which is fine. Or else I couldn't have done anything.

In 2009 I was in Turkey at the Alliance of Civilizations, and I won an award there which was cool.[10] Someone there, an official from the Kuwaiti Ministry of Awqaf & Islamic Affairs (religious endowments), actually gave me some advice. The first time a Kuwaiti ever paid me some attention.

At first, I thought he wasn't being honest with me, but he gave me the best advice as I learned later. He said, thank heavens that nobody in his ministry knew what I was doing, or else they would have tried to stop me, from above. They would try to scare me off. It's always good to operate below the radar.

He turned out to be right. So sadly, it is what it is.

When I won the case, I told the judge, I'm going to do this again. Also, the Diwan al-Amiri (office of the Amir of Kuwait) congratulated me *three* times.

You must understand that Kuwait is a monarchy, a hereditary regime, as even in England where you have a monarchy, and you have charges like blasphemy.[11] The law allows for that. But, the government put me in the Kuwait Supreme Education Council (المجلس الأعلى للتعليم), to say to the people, you're afraid he's going to affect the way your children are learning. Well, he is!

ESSF: Well, in that case it's good to see there are people, enlightened people, in power, willing to help science fiction and authors. Not like here.

It's good when you can find those people!

ESSF: Okay. Let's move to a less controversial area. What is the sci-fi scene like in Kuwait?

I honestly can't answer that; I don't know. I'm somebody that works all the time. Fifteen to sixteen hours a day with my patients. I'm going to a restaurant today, Friday, the one day I have off in the week, and I heard about the restaurant from one of my patients. I'm going to a chiropractor tomorrow night, someone I also heard about from one of my patients. And even on Fridays, I'm busy with interviews and meetings.

My world now is very much in the mental health clinic. I practice in Kuwait, Dubai, and Qatar. I'm a professor at the medical school, so I'm not very much in that world anymore.

ESSF: Do you know of Tiba Ahmad Al-Ibrahim, the famous Kuwait sci-fi author? A woman author and a controversial author at that, writing about gender and cloning, cryogenic freezing.

I've heard of her but sadly I haven't read her. Haven't read anything in a while.

ESSF: We know about her in Egypt, which is why we are asking. But don't know what people's reaction was.

Can't tell you more. Sorry.

ESSF: But do the young in Kuwait like science fiction? Are they open to it?

Naturally. Certain kinds of people are wired to like those kinds of stories, wherever they are. Kuwait, Saudi Arabia. And certain kinds of people are more abstract; others are more concrete.

Yes, certainly, there's the Comic Con held here; there's lots of gaming.

ESSF: Are Japanese cartoons still popular on Kuwaiti television?

I don't watch Kuwaiti television anymore. But I'm sure they're still popular. They just launched a children's channel. Not sure who's going to watch it, but they launched it.

ESSF: Is there translation of science fiction in Kuwait? Asimov, Arthur C. Clarke?

Don't know, really. Your best bet is to go to neelwafurat.com (Nile and Euphrates in Arabic). It's the Arabic Amazon.

ESSF: India exerts a big cultural influence on the Gulf, not least in Kuwait. Does that include Indian science fiction and fantasy?

Have no idea.

ESSF: Would that include Indian comics?

There are barely any bookshops left in Kuwait, so have no idea.

ESSF: And why is that? Is this because people aren't reading anymore, or because they are buying all their books online?

A combination, plus random closing down of bookstores by the Ministry of Information as punishment for a particular book being sold. That is why Virgin in Kuwait closed. They closed the whole place down for weeks because of the book *Emarat Yacoubian*.[12] Instead of fining them or taking the book away, they closed the *whole* store down.

ESSF: How "connected" is the sci-fi scene in Kuwait with the rest of the Gulf? Do you know Ashraf Faqih in Saudi Arabia? Do you know Qais Sedk in the UAE?

Again, can't answer on that count. I don't know Ashraf Faqih but I do know Qais Sadek, who did the Japanese manga *Golden Rings*.

ESSF: Kuwait and the UAE are very cosmopolitan countries. Is this a boon for the production of science fiction?

You'd think so. Kuwait has its own bag of tricks. The short answer is I don't know, but Kuwait 30 years ago was leading the Gulf. Not anymore.

ESSF: Kuwait was the first in the Gulf to set up sovereign wealth funds. Everyone else followed suit, even Saudi Arabia.

Kuwait's been the first at everything but the best at nothing!

It's a different metric. Being the first at doing something isn't enough.

ESSF: In that case, do Kuwaitis, in general, not just the young or sci-fi buffs, know Ahmed Khaled Tawfik and Nabil Farouk?

Don't know.

ESSF: Dr. Mustafa Mahmoud then?

Definitely! But again, you have to ask someone not like me. Someone who reads all the time and in Arabic. I only came to Arabic reading late.

ESSF: Can you make a living as an author in Kuwait? Let alone a sci-fi author?

I don't think so. For me to do *The 99*, I couldn't sleep at night. To do this, I had to set up a company and have partners and had to have my own source of income. Otherwise I would not have been prepared to do it. It's very risky.

It's not just the writing. It's *talking* to the Ministry of Information, to get permission. Is it possible? Everything's possible. Is it probable? No!

ESSF: The TV series, it was CGI. Not traditional cartoon. Any particular reason for this?

The producer I worked with at the time recommended it. I'm not much of a technical person. They said this is the way we should do it, and they were right.

ESSF: Is there a good market for comic books and graphic novels in Kuwait?

Not especially. Note that at one point, Teshkeel was the licensee for Marvel and DC comics, and that was probably one of the worst business investments in my life.

ESSF: But why?

Because people didn't buy it! That's why I lost a lot of money. You have to understand that you have limited advertising space in the comic. And it takes months and months to get approval for the titles from the Ministry of Information. In Saudi Arabia, it took nine months to get approval for Spiderman, and 11 months for X-Men. So, unless you're sitting on a lot of money, you don't care. It's a tough, tough business.

ESSF: That information is very disheartening but very insightful. A lot of people didn't know that. Thank you for filling us in.

Well, the big publishers have 100 or 200 titles, so they breakeven or at least make money by virtue of that fact that if one magazine doesn't make money, another one will. Paper will cost me less because I have to buy a million pages, not a hundred pages. But when you're a startup, you're not publishing that much, and distributers aren't always that forthright about numbers, so it becomes very difficult for a small business.

ESSF: You have a degree in business? Did that help you in any way?

Yes, an MBA from Columbia. And yes, it helped tremendously.

ESSF: How important is it for us to produce our own SF movies and TV series? Are comics another way of fighting back, so to speak, against negative stereotypes of Muslims abroad?

Very important. What's the most well-known science fiction story coming out of the Arab world? Aladdin. He can fly a carpet and so on. But, *who* told that story to the rest of the world?

ESSF: Exactly, foreigners.

When foreigners tell your story, you're not the good guy. When Disney started *Aladdin* in the 1990s, in the movie theaters, the opening lyrics [make mention of barbarism and cutting off your ears if they don't like your face].

This is how it started. When protests happened, the video version changed the beginning of it. That's what happens when somebody else tells your story. You have to tell your own story, otherwise you're going to become the bad guy. And then your children are going to believe they're the bad guy, because that's what they hear!

ESSF: Can we, as Arabs and Muslims, take advantage of our common language—Arabic and Islam as a terminology and theology—to create our own market for SF?

Just being in Arabic doesn't necessarily create a single market potentially. But more online than in print. There's other pitfalls though. Classical Arabic is a problem for lots of people; they'd want it more in their own dialect. And adapting it to dialects and local markets will cost more.

ESSF: What is TEDxArabia? You will have to excuse our ignorance here. We're very isolated in Egypt. And would you encourage Arab authors to use such forms as a platform to promote SF?

TED is probably the most well-known conference about the generation of ideas in the world. Lots of talks, lots of people, talking about ideas that impact the world, like Technology, Entertainment, Design.[13] It's a huge brand.

In fact, I spoke at three TEDx events: TEDx Arabia, TEDx Dubai, then at TEDx New York. Basically, like a TED minor league. When TEDx heard my speech, they invited me to speak at TED Global in Scotland and Oxford. TEDx Arabia is a TEDx organized by people in Saudi Arabia. I did mine on *The 99*, an independently organized TEDx.

Yes, it's a good platform. You get a license to do a talk, and you can do on something like Arabic science fiction. It's a *recognized* international brand. You could do a TEDx Masr for Egypt.

ESSF: Would you say the prospects for science fiction are good in the Gulf?

I'd say it's the same as in the rest of the world. It taps into a certain part of the brain, where people like stories like that. Same as anywhere. Nothing special about the Gulf.

ESSF: But the economic prospects surely?

I don't know.

ESSF: Do you know Mrs. Noura Al Noman in the UAE? Do you think her works could be successfully adapted into CGI, cartoons, and comics?

Yes, yes, I know her.

Yes, they can be converted. But I don't know how well they'd do. It all depends on the market. I don't know what the market is like.

Lots of good stories don't end up doing well; lots of very bad stories end up doing very well. Are they convertible? Sure. But that's not enough. One of my mentors in the U.S. told a story about a small dog food company that made the best dog food ever. They had goose liver and I don't know what meat, but the damn dogs wouldn't eat it!

You can have a great product but no market for it.

ESSF: But surely in the Gulf you have marketing companies and PR companies and market research and advertising companies?

But it's a very *limited* market. The idea of doing something for the Gulf is a losing proposition. You have to do something for the world. *The 99* was focused on the world, and the Gulf was just part of it.

ESSF: Any last words of advice to your counterparts and colleagues across the Arab world?

Just good luck and Godspeed. At the end of the day, people don't write because they want to write; they write because they can't not write. Just write; think about the market. If there's censorship, and you're able to deliver the story in a way that doesn't offend the stories, the story is better told than just sitting in the closet because of pride. That happened to me. If I'd changed a few words, it would have been unbanned. I should have done that. But I didn't because of my pride. At least I would have got my story across.

It was *The Bouncy Junior* series, if you must know!

NOTES

1. For a brief summary, in Arabic, see: https://www.goodreads.com/book/show/3127309#.

2. The three books in the series are *To Bounce or Not to Bounce*, *What's in a Color?* and *Triangular Traditions: A Bouncy Junior Story*

3. For the (raging) debate in clinical circles over the therapeutic value of *The 99*, please see (Porta, 2011).

4. For the debate over self-perception and the impact *The 99* has had in this regard, please see (Deeb, 2012; Dünges, 2011; Hansen 2010; Dittmer, 2007).

5. IPTV, Internet Protocol Television.

6. This was the Islamic Economy Award for 2014 (Wolfe, 2015).

7. For the back and forth of comic book portrayals of Muslims following 9/11 and President Obama's comments on *The 99*, please see (Strömberg, 2011). See also (Dittmer, 2014; Obama, 2010; Dar, 2010; Wright, 2009).

8. The academics in question are James Clements and Richard Gauvain (2014).

9. This was a PBS documentary by Isaac Solotaroff broadcast in October 2011.

10. This was the "Marketplace of Ideas" Award the second United Nations Alliance of Civilizations (UNAOC) forum held in Istanbul, 6–7 April 2009. Dr. Naif also received the Eliot-Pearson Award for Excellence in Children's Media from Tufts University, The Schwab Foundation Social Entrepreneurship Award at the 2009 World Economic Forum (WEF) and has been named as one of WEF's Young Global Leaders for 2011.

11. For more details, please see Chapter 4 of *Artists and the Arab Uprisings*, "Nongovernmental Efforts to Engage and Support Artists in the Arab World" (Schwartz, Kaye and Martini, 2013: 45–61).

12. This is Alaa Al-Aswany's controversial (Egyptian) novel *The Yacoubian Building*.

13. Please see Bayrasli (2011) and Al-Mutawa (2010) for additional details.

WORKS CITED

Akbar, Arifa. (11 March 2015). "The all-Islamic super-heroes: Muslim children love *The 99* comics, but hardliners loathe their creator—whose trial for heresy is looming." *The Independent*. https://www.independent.co.uk/arts-entertainment/books/features/the-all-islamic-super-heroes-muslim-children-love-the-99-comics-but-hardliners-loathe-their-creator-10101891.html.

Al-Mutawa, Naif. (22 August 2010). "Islam-inspired comic superheroes fight for peace." *CNN*. http://edition.cnn.com/2010/OPINION/08/22/al-mutawa.islamic.superheroes/index.html.

Bayrasli, Elmira. (13 October 2011). "The Start-Up Man: Naif al-Mutawa." *Forbes*. https://www.forbes.com/sites/elmirabayrasli/2011/10/13/the-start-up-man-naif-al-mutawa/#372879dd10fb.

Clements, James, and Richard Gauvain. (2014). "The Marvel of Islam: Reconciling Muslim Epistemologies through a New Islamic Origin Saga in Naif al-Mutawa's *The 99*." *The Journal of Religion and Popular Culture.* 26(1), Spring: 36–70.

Dar, Jehanzeb. (2010). "Holy Islamophobia, Batman! Demonization of Muslims and Arabs in Mainstream American Comic Books." *Counterpoints*. 346, Teaching Against Islamophobia: 99–110.

Deeb, Mary-Jane. (2012). "*The 99*: Superhero Comic Books from the Arab World." *Comparative Studies of South Asia, Africa and the Middle East.* 32(2): 391–407.

Dittmer, Jason. (2007). "The Tyranny of the Serial: Popular Geopolitics, the Nation, and Comic Book Discourse." *Antipode*. 39(2), March: 247–268.

Dittmer, Jason. (2014). "Towards new (graphic) narratives of Europe." *International Journal of Cultural Policy.* 20(2): 119–138.

Dünges, Petra. (2011). "Arabic Children's Literature Today: Determining Factors and Tendencies." *PMLA*. 126(1), January: 170–181.

"GLOBAL REACH—CENSORSHIP." (2014). *American Libraries*. 45(9/10), September-October: 17.

Hansen, Suzy. (2010). "Super Muslims." *Atlantic*. 305(4), May: 25–26.

Obama, Barack H. (April 26, 2010). "Remarks at the Presidential Summit on Entrepreneurship." *Daily Compilation of Presidential Documents, Special section*: 1–5.

Porta, Miquel. (2011). "*The 99*: A story on health, cross-cultural cooperation and acceptance in times of crisis." *Journal of Epidemiology and Community Health.* 65(4), April: 289–290.

Schwartz, Lowell H., Dalia Dassa Kaye, and Jeffrey Martin. (2013). *Artists and the Arab Uprisings*. Santa Monica: RAND Corporation, https://www.rand.org/content/dam/rand/pubs/research_reports/RR200/RR271/RAND_RR271.pdf.

Strömberg, Fredrik. (2011). "'Yo, rag-head!': Arab and Muslim Superheroes in American Comic Books after 9/11." *Amerikastudien/American Studies*. 56(4), American Comic Books and Graphic Novels: 573–601.

Wolfe, Jennifer. (January 16, 2015). "*THE 99* Creator Honored with 2014 Islamic Economy Award." *Animation World Network*. https://www.awn.com/news/99-creator-honored-2014-islamic-economy-award.

Wright, Robin. (30 March 2009). "Islam's Soft Revolution." *Time*. 173(12): 34–38.

"You Ask The Q's, Ronald D. Moore Answers, Part 2." (3 April 2013). *STARTREK.COM*. https://www.startrek.com/article/you-ask-the-qs-ronald-d-moore-answers-part-2.

SF for a Troubled Nation

An Interview from Yemen
with Wajdi Muhammad Al-Ahdal[1]

EGYPTIAN SOCIETY FOR SCIENCE FICTION

> If I lived in the Caucasus, I'd write fairy tales there.
>
> —Anton Chekhov

ESSF: Please introduce yourself, birth, education, hobbies, your story with reading—and your story with Yemeni literature, let alone Yemeni science fiction.

Wajdi Muhammad Al-Ahdal is a writer and novelist, born in 1973 in Yemen, and holds a Bachelor of Arts from Sana'a University. My hobbies are limited to reading and writing, but as a child I was especially enamored by the *Mickey Mouse* and *Majid* comics and *Superman*. I also read *The 1001 Nights* and the legend of the great Yemeni king Seif bin Zi Al-Yazan and a lot of children's literature from abroad, and many of the classics of literature, but in Arabic and simplified for a young adult audience.

My father played an especial role in fostering my love of reading. He had a tremendous library that covers a whole range of specializations. He always encouraged me to read, and as good luck would have it, he never forced me to read a particular kind of book. I had complete freedom to choose what I wanted to read.

As for writing, I wrote a number of short stories at secondary school, but I began writing in earnest only at university. I began publishing my short stories in the 1990s in newspapers and magazines. In 1998 my first book, *Zahrat Al-Aabir*, was published, an anthology of short stories. So far, I have published 14 books, including five novels, six story collections, a play, and two screenplays. My novel *A Country Without a Sky* was translated into English, *The Donkey Among the Songs* was translated into Italian, and *Mountain Boats* was translated into French. For my experience writing science fiction, I have written six short stories that belong to science fiction literature. I plan to write another six stories, to publish the 12 stories in book form. I have a tentative title for this anthology, *The Blue Egg*.

I should add that my favorite authors are Chekov for short fiction, and Gabriel García Márquez for novels, and Saadallah Wanus in theater, and H.G. Wells in science fiction, Agatha Christie for the detective novel, and Sir Walter Scott for the historical novel.

ESSF: What is the story of Yemeni science fiction itself?

Science fiction literature is rare in Yemen. To my knowledge, there is a single Yemeni novel belonging to science fiction literature entitled *Geography of Water* by the Yemeni novelist (residing in America) Abdulnasser Mugali, which came out in 2009. I read the most famous of his novels and stories and have been following his writings since the nineties of the last century.

I think that the reason why Abdul Nasser wrote a science fiction novel is his presence in a country where science and inventions thrive, and perhaps if he did not emigrate, he would not have dared to write a novel of this kind. Yemen is still a country distant from scientific thinking…. Yemen is not a science-producing country, so it is very difficult for a Yemeni novelist to write science fiction literature.

ESSF: Do you know anything about the works of Habib Abd Al-Rabb Sorouri and Jubran Harmal?

Yes, I know Habib Abd Al-Rabb Sorouri, a dear friend. He is a distinguished Yemeni writer residing in France. I read his novel *The Victim Queen* many years ago. If I remember correctly, cybernetics and mathematics had a powerful presence in it, on account of the presence of a character who is a professor of cybernetics and mathematics—something very new to Yemeni literature.[2]

As for Jubran Harmel, I have not read any of his works, with regret.

ESSF: Does Yemen have a long history of fantastical literature when it comes to folklore and legends? Is it all magic and jinn or is there also technology and prosperity?

Yes, Yemen is rich in myths and folk tales. In the Yemeni countryside, stories of grandmothers are spread about humans being kidnapped by the jinn and travelling to their world, which is completely different from the human world…. It seems that the jinn have a life of their own…. This fantasy is similar to what you read in science fiction literature, where human beings are kidnapped by space beings and moved to the planet they come from.

ESSF: What is your interest in science fiction? Do you see a role for this literature in our Arab society?

Perhaps I am one of the great fans of science fiction, and in my teenage years I would exhaust myself in the search for stories and novels that were in the field of science fiction. I remember reading the same book over and over again to satisfy my passion. I have tried to write several stories that belong to science fiction literature, but I do not know the reactions of readers. As for the role of this type of literature in Arab society, I think it may help to instill the love of science and exploration in the hearts of new generations to come. Reading SF stories and novels makes children and adolescents fall in love with scientific subjects, such as physics, chemistry, engineering, and mathematics.

ESSF: What issues are discussed in Yemeni science fiction? Are they different from the issues discussed in Yemeni literature in general?

Yes, the story of the *Geography of Water* talks about the disappearance of water from the planet because of theft by the population of another planet. It is an environmental novel, and this is not an issue raised in Yemeni literature. And it would not have been raised were it not for Abdulnasser Mugali writing in the science fiction genre.

ESSF: What is the attitude of literary critics in Yemen to science fiction?

Science fiction is not a phenomenon in Yemen for it to be addressed by the critics.

Academic critics often do not believe that a science fiction novel can be an example of serious literature to begin with.

ESSF: Is science fiction literature popular in Yemen? And what are its rivals? Fantasy literature, for example?

Adults do not read science fiction literature. The younger generation strongly loves this type of literature. But the problem in Yemen is its scarcity. What are available in libraries are romantic novels, detective stories, and the classics of world literature. Yemen is a poor country in everything, and this poverty also makes itself felt in the absence of science fiction literature in libraries.

ESSF: Are there any science fiction associations in Yemen? Specialized publishers, specialized magazines?

Unfortunately, there are no associations in Yemen interested in this kind of thing. As for the specialized publishers, the question is a little surprising, because Yemen is already free of publishing houses! The only working publishing house was shut down in 2014. As you can see, a country with a population of 30 million and not even enjoying one publishing house is beyond belief; it smacks too much of science fiction!

ESSF: Are there translations of science fiction literature in Yemen? Are classic writers such as Jules Verne and Isaac Asimov known?

Yemenis unfortunately did not contribute any translations of science fiction literature. For Jules Verne, he is known to some extent because of his famous novel *Around the World in Eighty Days*. Isaac Asimov is known only on a very small scale.

ESSF: Is magic and sorcery more popular than science and knowledge in our Arab world?

I think that the Arab is linked to the past by strong ties, and this makes him believe in magic and sorcery firmly. So, it seems to me that science fiction literature is the right tool for the healing of the Arab from the disease of attachment to the past and make him think about the future and dream of the miracles that science will achieve in the coming years, dreams based on the foundations that are correct and achievable. The problem of the Arabs is that their thinking is all geared towards the past. But how can we make their thinking move towards the future? The solution seems to lie in science fiction and its wide availability to all Arab children.

ESSF: Do Yemeni readers and writers know Tawfik Al-Hakim and Nihad Sharif as authors of science fiction? Do they know that Dr. Mustafa Mahmoud is one of the pioneers of science fiction in Egypt and the Arab world?

Tawfik Al-Hakim is known as a dramatist and novelist of realist literature. Nihad Sharif did not reach Yemen, but the film from his novel *The Lord of Time* achieved a high viewing rate. As for Dr. Mustafa Mahmoud, his books are widely distributed in Yemen, and his sci-fi novel *A Man Under Zero* can be found in almost every bookstore and library.

ESSF: Are the writings of Nabil Farouk and Ahmed Khaled Tawfik famous in Yemen?

Their writings are very popular in Yemen, compared to the very low rates of reading in general, but this popularity is limited to a specific age group, almost from the age of 14–20, and after that the Yemeni reader loses interest in this type of literature.

ESSF: What is the attitude of the new generation towards this type of literature?

The new generation is thirsty for science fiction literature, and there is an amazing demand to read the works of Nabil Farouk and Ahmed Khaled Tawfik. But then a gap occurs. These readers stop reading science fiction after reaching a certain age. The reason is the absence of more mature science fiction stories that accompany their mental development and expanding knowledge.

ESSF: What are the problems faced by the writer in Yemen? Censorship, the economic situation?

First of all, the problems of war, which we have all suffered from since the beginning of the year 2015, and there is no end in sight so far. The currency has collapsed, electricity has been lacking since the beginning of the war, and the state has stopped paying salaries since mid–2016. As for censorship, Yemen is worse off than the idea of censorship itself. There are very dangerous organizations such as Al-Qaeda and ISIS. There are militias of every form and kind, and each imposed its own laws in their area of influence, and no one dares to depart from the ideology that they espouse.

ESSF: Under the current circumstances, are there any novels or articles or stories that have been published recently? What genres?

There are Yemeni novels and stories of many directions published in Beirut and Cairo and other Arab capitals that enjoy a minimal level of stability. But publications in science fiction specifically, I have not heard of any new works.

ESSF: Are authors from the Yemeni Diaspora writing in this area?

The Yemeni writer who lives in the West has a much better opportunity to write science fiction novels by virtue of his knowledge of every new discovery made in the field of science. So, I expect the Yemeni novelists living in Europe and North America to be attracted to the writing of science fiction novels.

ESSF: Do you prefer to live in outer space or in your country?

For me the universe is my country, and I live in it now, in every part of it some way or another.

ESSF: What is your concept of Utopia?

All religions give us a picture of Utopia. Literature is not about creating a picture of Utopia. Literature itself is Utopia.

ESSF: Is realism the most popular kind of literature in Yemen? If so, why? Is it because of poverty, or because of ideological influences, like socialism?

Realism is widespread in Yemen. There is no such thing as detective and science fiction literature in Yemen, actually written here from a Yemeni perspective by our authors. I think that the reason is due to the tyranny of politics over everything, and that Yemen is a country saturated full of problems and in all areas. This is forcing the Yemeni author to write realist literature. So, the literature of science fiction and detective literature and horror literature is perceived to be a kind of luxury in such a poor country and torn apart repeatedly by civil wars.

ESSF: What themes do you explore in your writing, whether science fiction or social drama? Is religion a theme in your science fiction?

I focus on social issues in my stories and novels. For my humble experience in writing science fiction, I try to look at our religious heritage from a different angle, address it by means of science fiction and its techniques.

ESSF: Do you find writing science fiction to be more liberating than regular fiction?

Yes. I tried this in those six stories I wrote and discovered that I enjoyed an amazing space of freedom. Reality restricts you in many ways, and you stay with those limits. But when we write a story that belongs to science fiction literature, it removes many, many obstacles facing your imagination.

ESSF: What are your sources of inspiration? Do you research your science fiction stories?

I do research according to the simple means at my disposal to ensure the validity of the scientific information contained in my stories.

ESSF: Can you give a summary of your favorite SF story in your forthcoming book?

A story entitled "Doma," which talks about a professor in the university's geography department who decides to make a scientific trip to explore the mysterious Barhout well, a pit where no one can get down and in which there are many underground caves. There is a Hadith attributed to the Prophet Mohammad (Peace Be Upon Him) that the well of Barhout is the place where the souls of the infidels settle. The geography professor uses the correct way of going down, and at the bottom he films everything, but when he wanted to take a handful of dirt with him topside, he faces a huge serpent that asks him not to carry the dirt out of the well. Nonetheless, he did not fear the creature and pays its commands no heed. But as soon as he puts his feet on the ground outside of the well, the warning of the serpent begins to come true, and time begins to run backwards, as if it were shrinking.

ESSF: Have you heard of Muhammad Abd Al-Malik Al-Shaibani, a Yemeni science fiction author responsible for Residents of the Galaxy*?*

To be honest, this is the first time I have heard of him. Thanks for informing me of his book. I will search it out with all diligence at the bookshops.

ESSF: Do you know if Yemeni writers living in the Gulf Arab States do any publishing there, whether in science fiction or other genres, including non-fiction? It's a big market and perfect for Yemen. Technically you are a Gulf Cooperation Council (GCC) country.

There are, in fact, Yemeni authors residing in the GCC states. But their numbers, generally speaking, are small. And their publications are of limited impact; it is as if their creativity in penning works about their motherland is what makes their voice unheard. The hurdles between a poor country like Yemen and the wealthy Gulf states are very strict; this makes cultural interaction very low level indeed.

ESSF: The impression one gets now is that there are actually quite a few Yemeni SF writers, but the economic and political situation doesn't allow for them to read and meet each other, so there is no proper sci-fi community in Yemen, which holds things back.

Yes, that about sums it up!

NOTES

    1. Translated by Emad El-Din Aysha.

    2. Sorouri's SF works were a topic of discussion at the "Yemen: Challenges for the Future Conference" held on the 11–12 January 2013 at the Brunei Lecture Theatre of SOAS, University of London (Viviani, 2013). The conference was organized by the British-Yemeni Society.

WORK CITED

Viviani, Paola. (12 January 2013). "Gender and Identity Issues in Yemeni Literature: Habib Abd Al-Rabb Sururi's Fiction." Paper delivered at the "Yemen: Challenges for the Future Conference," Brunei Lecture Theatre, SOAS, University of London. Conference organized by the British-Yemeni Society.

Black Magic and Djinn
in Omani Literature
Examining the Myths and Reality

MANAR AL HOSNI

The deeper the blue becomes, the more strongly it calls man towards the infinite, awakening in him a desire for the pure and, finally, for the supernatural.... The brighter it becomes, the more it loses its sound, until it turns into silent stillness and becomes white.

—Wassily Kandinsky

In Oman, we know them as creatures of the night, creatures of great intrigue and deception, and we know to stay well away from them. "The day belongs to us, but the night belongs to them," were the eeriest words my mother had ever spoken to me as a child the day she forbade me from playing outside past sundown. Apparently, I wasn't the only one to hear those exact words; parents across Oman were reluctant to let their children venture outdoors without adult supervision once the sun set. There has always been much wonder and speculation regarding the existence of the shapeshifting djinn as intelligent creatures opposite and equal—if not superior—to human beings in my home country, the Sultanate of Oman. In this essay, I will attempt to briefly touch upon the appearances, types, abilities and behaviors of the djinn, then I will explore a few Omani legends and stories on the overwhelming djinn presence in Oman as it pertains to the subject of this book. Whereas Western readers are more familiar with the spelling "jinn" or the Anglicized "genie," this essay will use "djinn"; it is the correct spelling translated directly from Arabic to English, meaning the "hidden ones."

Stories of the djinn contained in books like *1001 Nights* have been passed down from generation to generation in Arabia, told to us as scary tales to get us to behave, whispered avidly among groups of gathered friends as spooky "campfire stories," and narrated in the Holy Quran and Sunna (the portion of Muslim law along with the Quran based on the Prophet Muhammed's words and acts). Alas, they are not the wish-granting, joke-cracking, mischievous blue tricksters that movies like *Aladdin* have made them out to be. According to the Holy Quran, the djinn are creatures created from a mixture of fire and smokeless fire whose existence predates mankind, and while djinn can see us, we cannot normally see them (El-Zein, 2009). These powerful creatures exist beyond the realm of our five senses, which may be why we cannot perceive them— unless they want us to. As stated by Dr. Fazlur Rahman (2009), professor of Islam and

A flying mosque is one of the many legends of the Djinn in Oman, a legend worth talking about in literature geared to the international audience (courtesy of the artist, Ammar Al-Gamal).

economics and modernist scholar and philosopher of Islam, the djinn are beings with "much greater physical powers (including invisibility); they are not fundamentally different from men, except for their greater proneness to evil and stupidity" (Rahman, 2009: 122). The djinn marry and procreate just like human beings and will be judged alongside us on Judgment Day. And like the supernatural tales of ghosts and fairies that have captured the imaginations of the West, djinn tales hold an equally sanctified position in Arabian folklore, as well as neighboring regions like Persia and India, and will undoubtedly continue to be passed on to future generations.

Appearances and Traits

There are many types of djinn, each with specialized characteristics. Some have the features of animals like animal heads and body parts, while others have the shapeshifting ability to assume the shape of onagers (a species of wild ass), dogs, serpents, or cats—often black in color (Guiley and Imbrogno, 2011). Serpents are the animal most associated with the djinn in Islamic traditions, as many Islamic narrations tell of a djinn who disguised itself as a serpent. Sunna dictates that serpents and snakes should be killed on sight unless they are found in the home. If so, then they should be warned to leave at least three times before they are killed lest they turn out to be a disguised djinn; Islam values the lives of the djinn just as much as it values the lives of humans (Guiley and Imbrogno, 2011).

More than that, killing a djinn can have serious, perhaps even life-threatening, repercussions. The djinn's most infamous trait is its vindictiveness; they are unforgiving creatures that will not rest until they have had their revenge. Too often, unsuspecting humans will harm a djinn or aggravate them, eliciting their endless wrath (Guiley and Imbrogno, 2011). As children, we are advised to utter the word "Bismillah" (which translates to "in the name of Allah") when discarding waste into dumpsters as a type of djinn loves to nest there, or when urinating in a hole or burrow in the desert or other barren land, because it might turn out to be the home of a certain type of djinn. One tale of the djinn's tendency for vengeance when wronged remains forever etched in my mind. An unfortunate fellow once ventured out at night to dump his garbage, unaware that the neighborhood's communal dumpster was a djinn nesting place. Because he tossed his garbage into the dumpster without saying "Bismillah" and it struck the sleeping djinn, he was haunted and annoyed by the djinn. What happened to him after was never passed on. Nevertheless, I carry this precautionary tale with me everywhere as a reminder to always be cautious around unclean places.

Types and Abilities

The Giant Marids

Stories in the Quran tell of the most powerful and rebellious of the djinn, the Marid. Despite being small in number, Marids are said to be very large, very conceited djinn that possess especially great power even among the djinn. It is this type of djinn that is the inspiration for the djinn or "genie" in *Aladdin*, as Marids can grant wishes, but only after being subdued in battle or through magic rituals. While they have their own free will, they can be compelled by magic to do chores and serve humans, granting them wishes. However, doing so can be quite dangerous; these proud djinn are rebellious and treacherous by nature, and they will twist and distort commands and wishes (Guiley and Imbrogno, 2011). According to the Quran, King Solomon of Israel was granted by Allah the ability to talk to the djinn as well as authority over all djinn, including the rebellious Marids. It was by using this ability that Solomon ordered the Marids to build the First Temple in ancient Jerusalem.

The Infernal Ifrit

Another djinn mentioned only once in the Quran is the infernal Ifrit, the djinn who fetched the Queen of Sheba's throne at the behest of King Solomon. In Arabian folklore, the Ifrit is an enormous, winged creature that is evil and cunning to the point of being difficult to control. Ifrits frequent ruins and live in a society similar to that of Arabs, complete with kings and divided into tribes and clans. The story of the "Fisherman and the Djinn" told by Scheherazade in *1001 Nights* depicts an imprisoned Ifrit rescued from the depths of a lake by a fisherman. Released from a jar, the Ifrit is quick to reveal his true malevolent nature when he demands the fisherman choose which way to die. Luckily for the fisherman, he outsmarts the Ifrit by asking the evil djinn to show him how he'd gotten into the jar. Eager to show off his powers, the Ifrit evaporates into smoke and slips back into the jar and the fisherman quickly reseals it, re-trapping him. Only once the Ifrit promises to not kill him does the fisherman release the djinn. As repayment, the Ifrit sets the fisherman on a course to becoming a rich, well-respected man (Friedman and Johnson, 2014).

The Devil Is a Djinn

In Islam, the devil or Satan is known as Iblis, and we believe that he is a type of infidel, evil djinn who refused Allah's order to bow down to Adam, the first man, because of his hubris and belief that man is a lesser creature. For this act of treason, Iblis was cast down from Heaven and sentenced to live on Earth till the Day of Judgment. As such, all sons and daughters of Iblis—inherently evil in nature—are classified as shaiṭans. A shaiṭan's primary ability is the power to cast evil or malicious thoughts and suggestions into the hearts of mankind and steer them away from the path of righteousness and devotion. Also, they can consort with and assist those who are far from Allah via black magic. An Islamic belief is that every person on Earth is assigned a shaitan by Iblis to whisper evil suggestions into their ears in an attempt to guide us toward evil and blasphemy (Guiley and Imbrogno, 2011).

Al-Jathoom: The Sleep Paralysis Djinn

Science describes sleep paralysis to be the inability of a person to move or speak upon waking up or falling asleep, which may last up to a couple of minutes (Sharpless, 2016). During this episode, a person may hear, feel, or see things—terrifying things that have been depicted in many paintings, such as Henry Fuseli's "The Nightmare" (Palumbo, 1986). Muslims know not to swiftly file away every such occurrence as normal sleep paralysis. Conceptualized as a djinn attack, it is believed that a certain type of djinn known as Al-Jathoom causes sleep paralysis by sitting on the chests of its victims and overpowering them. To counter these disturbing visitations, Muslims are recommended to recite the Quran during and after such incidents, as well as increase daily prayers. While I myself have never seen djinn or had any encounters with them, I know many people who have, my father being one of them. Once over lunch, a question occurred to me about whether or not he had experienced sleep paralysis in his life. In asking, it was clear to the two of us that I was enquiring about whether he had been sat on by the djinn known as Al-Jathoom without actually having to mention this. To my surprise, he confessed to having indeed experienced this bone-chilling experience.

They Can Possess People

One of the djinn's major powers is the ability to possess human beings, be it male or female, young or old. They can completely take over the bodies of their chosen victims either by dominating their thoughts and dreams or by entering their bodies. The djinn are said to have incorporeal bodies or indefinable forms that allow them to slip into the bodies of their victims. As one can imagine, this poses a set of nightmarish consequences for the possessed. A possessed person often exhibits signs of discomfort and pain ranging from tolerable to excruciating, in addition to fits, paralysis, and convulsions. Victims may also experience suicidal thoughts—and many may act upon them. As they are able to take over the functions of a person's body, they can speak through the person's mouth.

In extreme cases, a djinn can take up permanent residence in a person's body, which then requires an exorcism from a skilled sheikh (Guiley and Imbrogno, 2011).

Islam believes that individuals who are far from Allah and are less devout are more susceptible to djinn possession. To ward off possession, much like cases of the evil eye, Muslims are encouraged to recite the Quran on a regular basis and perform their five daily prayers in addition to other rituals. However, it may not always be a question of devotion. Here in Oman, it is not unusual to hear blood-curdling stories where a djinn has fallen in love with a person and possessed them in order to remain close to them—as close to them as possible. It is rooted in an Omani belief that male djinn tend to prefer short, long-haired girls. Once afflicted by a lover djinn, the victim experiences an irregular increase in wet dreams and frequently feels the sensation of being embraced when no one is there. Furthermore, a victim may wake up in the morning to find bruises on their body where there were none the previous night. Possessive and greedy in their nature, the djinn want to keep the possessed to themselves at any cost, even if it means tearing a wife from her husband, or vice versa. These cases of possession are the hardest to exorcise, according to exorcist sheikhs (Guiley and Imbrogno, 2011).

The Djinn Legends of Oman

The Sultanate of Oman is located in the Arabian Peninsula, and the topic of the djinn is one that its people are very familiar with to the point that they opt to refer to the djinn as "Our Good Folk" out of respect and reverence. Even the most sheltered of Omani children have grown up hearing about at least a few djinn stories, for the mountainous country is said to be filled with them. Perhaps it is because of its unique landscape of isolated mountain ranges and vast, empty deserts that Oman finds itself populated by hordes of the djinn, more so than any of its neighbors. Unsurprisingly, this has bestowed Oman with an infamous reputation among its neighboring Gulf countries.

Majlis al Djinn

The presence of the djinn in Oman has undoubtedly influenced its culture and heritage. A famous cave in Oman is called Majlis al Djinn, which literally translates to "gathering place of the djinn," and is the second largest cave chamber in the world as measured by the surface area of the floor (Hanna and Al-Belushi, 1996). Locals claim to see flickering and moving shadows on the walls of the cave, and shouts and cries are constantly heard from it late at night. This has resulted in the firm belief among the locals that the djinn reside in the deep, enormous cave. While the flickering shadows were later determined to be as a result of the light entering the cave through three different holes and openings, the cave remains a center of myths and legends to this day, and no number of geological expeditions has taken away from its magic and mysterious aura. There are many legends from Omani folklore concerning Majlis al Djinn that warn people from setting foot in it or attempt to explain its mysterious geological formations.

One such legend states that whoever dares to enter Majlis al Djinn will never leave it, for the djinn reside in its depths and do not like to be disturbed; they favor their seclusion and privacy above all else. Another legend claims that a good woman by the name of Salma was shepherding by the cave when she fell asleep, and a few of her sheep and cattle wandered into the cave. The djinn of the cave devoured seven of her cattle. Angered by this, Salma called upon the wrath of the heavens and, answering her call, the heavens sent seven meteorites crashing into Majlis al Djinn, creating the seven peculiar holes and openings on its walls. This legend is the reason that Majlis al Djinn is also referred to as Salma's Cave or Salma's Plateau.

Plenty are the legends that surround the Sultanate concerning the mischievous djinn, and they span multiple locations and areas across it. Indeed, it seems that almost every area has a unique djinn story to tell. However, most notorious of them all is the magical, djinn-infested town of Bahla.

Black Magic in Oman

Bahla, a town 200 km from Oman's capital, Muscat, is famous—or rather infamous—among Omanis for its particularly strange occurrences and bone-chilling legends. Some even go as far as to refer to it as the City of Magic. It is not quite clear why Bahla is so afflicted out of all the regions in Oman and the Arabian Peninsula, but the answer may lie somewhere in the annals of its history. Surrounded by open desert on one side and a breathtaking mountain range on the other, Bahla is a town cloaked in mystery and intrigue. An ominous aura drapes itself around the oasis town, one that many have sought to unveil. The town that has been a UNESCO World Heritage Site since 1987 and is also rumored to be the home of many sorcerers and sorceresses—men and women practicing black magic. Using magic, these individuals are able to command the djinn for their personal gains, making them people of ill repute within Omani society. It is even said that some of the djinn being commanded offer their services willingly in exchange for the chance to inflict harm upon mankind; the purposes for which these sorcerers use them are almost always nefarious (Pages, 2019). Legend has it that becoming a practitioner of magic is something that is inherited rather than taught. A father must elect one of his children to follow in his footsteps as continued repayment for having been taught black magic by the djinn and for their continued servitude. In much the same way, once the child has grown up, he will then pass on this "profession" to one of his children. What happens if a sorcerer refuses to give up one of his children has never been revealed. I assume this is because any defiant sorcerer never lives long enough to tell the tale.

The Oasis Wall

The reasons why a sorcerer or sorceress would employ the services of djinn are not always clear. In fact, they can be quite baffling. One particular tale from the folklore in Bahla perfectly illustrates this. A friend of mine was visiting Bahla a few years ago and was shown around the historical town by a tour guide. According to her, the tour guide narrated how a sorceress built the magnificent, fortified wall surrounding the Oasis in Bahla overnight using the djinn to assist her for unclear reasons (Jackson, 2011). This was confirmed by further research I did; no record is able to confirm the true architect behind this renowned wall. Some say that the wall was erected during the Persian presence in the region, while others claim that it was the Nabhani Dynasty who made Bahla their dynasty's capital and built it (Thorpe, 2009). In other words, who is to say that the wall was not constructed by the djinn? If history has taught us anything, it is that there is always a measure of truth from legends and myths.

The Flying Mosque

The building of the wall is not the strangest event to have supposedly happened in Bahla by far. Flying mosques seem to occasionally be in the weather forecast. Bahlawis tell of a mosque that appeared at the edge of the town overnight; the mosque flew and landed there fully intact, much to the residents' shock and horror in the morning. The mosque is believed to have flown all the way from Rustaq, another town in Oman. One version of the legend goes like this: three hermits practicing Sufism, an unorthodox sect of Islam, took refuge in the mosque while it was still in Rustaq. These hermits commanded the power of the djinn, and using this power, flew the mosque to Bahla for reasons unclear. Another narration tells of a woman, a witch, who brought the mosque from Rustaq with the aid of the djinn. Ruins of this mosque can still be found atop a hill outside Bahla known as either the Hill of the Three Saints or the Witch's Hill (Jackson, 2011).

The Tree in the Old Souk

In the oldest section of Bahla's souk sits a lone tree in a brick enclosure said to be thousands of years old. It casts a splendid shade over the market's main square, yet you will find that few are willing to shield themselves from the scorching Arabian sun by standing beneath it. This tree is said to be bewitched by a vengeful sorcerer, and anyone from outside of Bahla will suffer a terrible fate—an untimely death—if they touched it. The old tree was once a frankincense tree whose sap was cultivated and used by the likes of Cleopatra and King Solomon, or so the legend goes. On nights when the moon shines bright, the tree's branches cast gnarly shadows on the ground that are enough to send chills down your spine and, for a moment, you almost sense an ancient, foreboding presence emanating from the tree (Jackson, 2011).

The Djinn in Omani Literature, Research and Media

As can be expected, much of the djinn mythology has integrated itself into Omani literature, be it written or filmed. A simple online search combining the key words "Oman" and "djinn" would bring forth a plethora of newspaper articles, stories, and blogs, each with a unique experience and story to tell. Most of these articles are written by foreigners and visitors to the country who are intrigued by the folklore and the mysterious djinn legends and wish to share it with the West. Interestingly, one can find academic research publications specifically referencing Oman centering on psychotic symptoms and mental health problems attributed to the djinn in Islamic patients. Samir Al-Adawi is an Omani Behavioural Medicine professor at the Sultan Qaboos University who has written about spirit possession in a medical context on a number of occasions. In 2017, he and others published the research paper "Performance of cognitive measures and affective ranges in clients marked with spirit possession in Oman," attempting to explore and assess the cognitive performance in different grades of djinn or spirit possession among Omani citizens (Musharrafi, Al-Kalbani, and Al-Adawi, 2017).

Similarly, a case report co-authored by Dr. Al-Adawi, "Investigation of the cerebral blood flow of an Omani man with supposed 'spirit possession' associated with an altered mental state: a case report," described the clinical case of a possessed 22-year-old Omani patient. In this study, the researchers discussed the case in the context of spirit or djinn possession as a culturally sanctioned idiom of distress, among other things (Guenedi, Hussaini, Obeid, Hussain, Al-Azri, & Al-Adawi, 2009). In addition to research publications, the ever-elusive djinn of Oman have inspired many books and novels internationally. *Of Sea and Sand* by Denyse Woods (2018) features Gabriel Sherlock as the protagonist who arrives in Oman fleeing shame and disgrace in his homeland of Ireland. While in the country, he begins an affair with a woman who might potentially be a djinn.

Despite all of this, when it comes to reading, it might come as a shock that Omanis are rather grounded people with little flare for the supernatural. You will find that few Omanis enjoy fiction and mythological literature, especially our elderly. Most of the time, my parents refuse to watch a supernatural or science fiction movie, and many of my friends confess to much the same. In Oman, a Muslim country, the existence of the djinn is taken as an absolute fact that is not to be questioned; as our faith is interlinked with this belief. One cannot be said to exist without the other. Therefore, any mention of the djinn in media is done so in passing, if ever. I, however, aim to remedy this as a young Omani author with an avid interest in the supernatural and paranormal. And what else to showcase in my stories than the djinn, a race and topic I'm considerably versed in?

My Future Works About the Djinn

Stemming from my deep fascination in the djinn and my desire to shine the light on these mysterious creatures, I'm currently working on a young adult novel about the djinn. Rarely have the djinn been the center of focus in fiction and paranormal novels. Indeed, vampire, werewolf, and fairy books line the fiction section in bookstores and libraries, but you will not find even a third as much about the elusive, magnificent creatures known as the djinn.

While my historical fiction novel *Siren of the Desert* centered in the Arabian Desert, I did not use the djinn as an element in the book; I wanted to showcase them in a book of their own where I could attempt to do them justice. My upcoming djinn novel starts off in Oman, where the female foreign protagonist is visiting the scenic country with her aunt for the first time. While on a tour of one of its historical landmarks, she is abducted by the djinn to their realm of magic and illusions and must carefully make her way back home with the aid of a prince of the djinn. Naturally, I will rely heavily on the local legends and myths that I have cited in this essay; one could not hope to find better content to fill a fiction novel! At the time of writing this essay, I am not yet sure how much or how little of these legends I will use in my book.

Conclusion

Many are the legends that center on the djinn in Oman, and many are those who believe in them wholeheartedly. In some regions like Bahla, it is not hard to see—or *feel*—why. The air is charged with a supernatural aura that transcends human understanding and conception, and the unusual occurrences that happen to ordinary individuals are difficult to dismiss as mere coincidences or anomalies. Foreigners who visit these regions will tell you much the same thing, whether they believe in the djinn or not. It is important to keep an open mind in life because one does not know when they will encounter something extraordinary, something magical, and all at once ominous. As I sit writing this essay in my backyard with a cup of black tea left to chill next to me on the table, a black cat appears at the top of the wall. There is something extraordinary about the cat, something that stares straight at me, if not through me. I rein in the urge to flee and instead stare right back, both mesmerized and terrified. It seems to take me in for a few moments, assessing me, judging me, and then leaps off the wall and out of sight, never to be seen again. I like to think that I passed its test.

Works Cited

El-Zein, Amira. (2009). *Islam, Arabs, and Intelligent World of the Jinn*. Syracuse, NY: Syracuse University Press.

Friedman, Amy, and Meredith Johnson. (19 January 2014). "THE FISHERMAN AND THE JINNI (an Arabian tale), Tell Me a Story." *Uexpress*. https://www.uexpress.com/tell-me-a-story/2014/1/19/the-fisherman-and-the-jinni-an.

Guenedi, Amr A., Ala'Alddin Al Hussaini, Yousif A Obeid, Samir Hussain, Faisal Al-Azri, and Samir Al-Adawi. (2009). "Investigation of the cerebral blood flow of an Omani man with supposed 'spirit possession' associated with an altered mental state: A case report." *Journal of Medical Case Reports*. 3(1). doi:10.1186/1752–1947–3-9325.

Guiley, Rosemary Ellen, and Philip J. Imbrogno. (2011). *The Vengeful Djinn*. Woodbury, NY: Llewellyn Publications.

Hanna, Samir, and Mohamed Al-Belushi. (1996). *Introduction to the Caves of Oman*. Ruwi, Oman: International Printing Press.

Jackson, Baxter. (1 July 2011). "Arabian genies and a flying mosque." *Matador Network*. https://matadornetwork.com/bnt/arabian-genies-and-a-flying-mosque/.

Musharrafi, S., Yahya Al-Kalbani, and Samir Al-Adawi. (2017). "Performance of cognitive measures and affective ranges in clients marked with spirit possession in Oman." *European Psychiatry*. 41. Supplement, April: S516. https://doi.org/10.1016/j.eurpsy.2017.01.676.

Pages, Mar. (22 May 2019). "Visiting Bahla Fort, Oman's only UNESCO fort." *Once in a Lifetime Journey*. https://www.onceinalifetimejourney.com/once-in-a-lifetime-journeys/middle-east/visiting-bahla-fort-omans-only-unesco-fort/.

Palumbo, Donald. (1986). *Eros in the Mind's Eye: Sexuality and the Fantastic in Art and Film*. New York: Greenwood Press.

Rahman, Fazlur. (2009). *Major Themes of the Qur'an*. Chicago: University of Chicago Press. 2nd Edition.

Sharpless, Brian A. (2016). "A clinician's guide to recurrent isolated sleep paralysis." *Neuropsychiatric Disease and Treatment*. 12: 1761–1767. doi:10.2147/ndt.s100307.

Thorpe, Annabelle. (29 August 2009). "Take the high roads to find Oman's hidden treasures." *The Guardian*. http://web.archive.org/web/20171026054247/https://www.theguardian.com/travel/2009/aug/30/oman-travel-hidden-treasures.

Woods, Denyse. (2018). *Of Sea and Sand*. Cairo, Egypt: Hoopoe.

The Codex of Bosnian SF

Raspberries on the Edge of Chaos

HARUN ŠILJAK

…thought can organize the world so well that you are no longer able to see it.

—Anthony De Mello (1985, 113)

In a discussion about non–Western science fiction this week, I made a fairly bad comparison, developing a sandwich theory of science fiction: the two universal slices in the sandwich are (1) science/technology concepts common in the genre, free of all geographical constraints and (2) the fundamental story arcs and messages repeated since the dawn of humanity. The body of the sandwich, I argued, is what defines the taste and makes the local sci-fi communities precious and challenging for the reader from a distant land. This is a story about the taste of Bosnia, and if it has to be one flavor, let it be raspberry jam.

A Town at the Center of the World

The Bosnian capital Sarajevo, as is the case with most of the Balkans, creates more history than it can realistically consume. In the language of time-travelling fiction, it lies in too many fixed points in our universe's timeline. You may remember that the literal trigger of World War I was the one Gavrilo Princip pulled in Sarajevo in 1914, killing Austrian Archduke Franz Ferdinand. Going back in time to Sarajevo on June 28, 1914, could easily be a trope comparable to killing baby Hitler (cf. *Third Doctor* [Doctor Who] audio story "Horrors of War"). The disturbing atmosphere of siege, politics, and the long, bloody chess game with unwilling pieces in the nineties is another fixed point in the timeline (cf. *Seventh Doctor* book *Death and Diplomacy*, by Dave Stone; *Batman: Under the Red Hood*). The nineties put Sarajevo in the media spotlight, which allowed for a context-free use of the name as well (cf. *Star Trek: Deep Space 9* is an example, with the USS *Sarajevo* appearing in the storyline). Sarajevo was in the historical focal point once again, and all of its inhabitants would have been much happier if it were not.

One of the youngsters in the besieged town wanted to change the rules of the game; sure, Sarajevo is now the center of the planet's timeline, but what if it were in that center all along? Not just 1992, not just 1914, but in any random year of our era? Karim Zaimović

194

"The Invisible Man of Sarajevo" (2016)—a mural dedicated to Karim Zaimovic, painted by Boris Stapic, Mensur Demir and Aleksandar Brezar (courtesy of the photographer, Josipa Matkovic).

(1971–1995)[1] wanted big stories to happen in Sarajevo—not necessarily happier than those brought by the war raging all around him, but different. The horror of Zaimović's stories is a controlled one, a safe space for the reader and the writer caught in the uncontrolled horror of reality. Zaimović drew his inspiration from magical realism, from comic books and films; as a knowledgeable reader and author, he wrote numerous newspaper articles and reviews, hosted radio shows, and shared his passion with other Sarajevans while writing the stories of a different Sarajevo, one of the 19th century with vampires, giant Nazi-engineered rats, Nikola Tesla's death ray secrets, and most importantly, genuine inhabitants of the town. When Zaimović wrote of Sarajevo, it is impossible to adapt the story to a different place; it is always the Sarajevo he knew and loved, one of all of its religions and cultural circles, old buildings and neighborhoods, living its life as the world's center. The stories flow as a narration for his radio show, *Joseph and His Brothers*, and he insists on facts, names, dates, documents. Just like Jorge Luis Borges or Danilo Kiš, the Yugoslav incarnation of the great Argentine, Zaimović creates a powerful image of reality that could never be and yet feels more real than any imperfect reality we live in. The names of his characters feel strange, uncanny to the native reader, but the faces and the voices are as real as any other. Zaimović makes an intricate map of the town, full of underground tunnels, secret rooms, and the most important humans that ever walked the Earth because his Sarajevo deserves nothing less than that.

The collection of short stories named *The Secret of Raspberry Jam* is Karim Zaimović's immortal legacy. Karim didn't live to see it: he was killed by a mortar shell in the summer of 1995, months before the war would eventually end. The eponymous story of the Raspberry Jam is a Borgesian parable of Yugoslavia; the secret of peace and harmony in the heart of the Balkans, the holy grail of the divided grounds, is the raspberry jam. Not the cheap, silly thing you can buy in a supermarket, but the secret recipe no one knows today. Miljenko Jergović explained later how Zaimović did not plan for the stories to remain short stories; they were meant to be prose sketches for a graphical novel or film scripts. Zaimović's notebooks were full of great plans and ideas: two unfinished novels, numerous humor pieces, and stories of unmatched originality in the besieged city.

To the best of my knowledge, no translation of Zaimović's "Raspberries" exists in English. However, there is a comic in *Massachusetts Review* 55.3, named "The Secret of Nikola Tesla," drawn based on Karim's story (and another one, "Invisible Man from Sarajevo"). The stories got what they always were supposed to have: masterful drawings that Karim would have loved. The comic and graphic novel scene in Bosnia is small but full of ideas and visions, with brave excursions to fantastic worlds of science fiction, epic fantasy, and horror. Speaking of Bosnia and comics, the war has inspired numerous foreign authors to place powerful stories (many of whom have dedicated their work to Karim, the Sarajevan master connoisseur of the ninth art) on the streets of Sarajevo and other Bosnian towns. From the perspective of science fiction, internationally well-known Bosnian-origins-Belgrade-born-French artist Enki Bilal made a tour de force piece on the breakup of Yugoslavia from a futuristic, apocalyptic perspective, masterfully using Sarajevo as a stage.

Sarajevo's *Fahrenheit 451*

Having mentioned "The Secret of Nikola Tesla," there's a powerful metaphor awaiting in that story: the possibility that the most important discovery in physics, a formula Nikola Tesla derived (yes, the one to end all wars), may have been burned inside a book in besieged Sarajevo, as its inhabitants had to heat themselves during the harsh winters of 1992–1995. The motive of burning books is reinforced by the references to the night of August 25/26, 1992, when the National Library was made a target of a shelling campaign and consequently burned completely. This major act of culturocide remains one of the most striking events of the siege of Sarajevo and features in many works of fiction (and in the case of Zaimović, fantasy). It provides a motif of lost knowledge, often one written in the distant times of the legendary Baghdad caliphs or the first sultans of Istanbul. The war was just beginning, and the ominous Heinrich Heine quote, "Where they burn books, they will also ultimately burn people," came true in the east of the country. Ray Bradbury, the man who made book burning an eternal symbol of science fiction, wrote a letter to Sarajevans:

> Throughout history burning books is an omen that something wicked this way comes. Let me wish for the city and people of Sarajevo to rejoice in the restored library and collection of books; a Phoenix risen from ashes, a treasured abode of art, memory and knowledge. We hope that people everywhere will revel and participate in the reconstruction efforts until the library is restored to its former glory.

The Sarajevo Science Fiction Club "Pulsar" made Ray Bradbury one of its award laureates in 2010, thanking him for his efforts in keeping world peace. Small science fiction communities like Pulsar or small zines like Adnadin Jasarevic's *Prometej* (*Prometheus*) keep the science fiction and fantasy home fires (this time, good fires) burning in the country, supporting young authors and fans. The fact that the Bosnian language, together with Croatian, Montenegrin, and Serbian, is a part of a single polycentric language opens a wider market for writers and readers alike, one that still awaits a boost and establishment of a rich scene.

A Man at the Center of the World

While Zaimović puts the city in the center of the world's time and space, another Bosnian author dived deep into the fantastic to place a man in that same center. Nedžad Ibrišimović's *Vječnik* (2005, English version *The Eternee*, published 2010) is a novel exploring longevity bordering with eternity. It is a novel full of celebrity undead (the Flying Dutchman, the Wandering Jew…) that the protagonist, a scribe by the name of Abdullah Misri el-Bosnawi (a.k.a. Neferti, a.k.a. Imhotep, a.k.a. Juan Sanchez Escobar), meets in his impossibly long life spanning Egypt, Bosnia, and the world. Ibrišimović once again, as many times in his rich novelistic career before *The Eternee*, taps into the unique position of Bosnia, right on the fault line between the East and the West, allowing all religions that have reached the ridges and rivers of Bosnia (primarily Islam, Judaism, Western and Eastern Christianity) to shape the discussion on time, life, eternity, and death. Both the mystical and the plain bring their charm to the story and take the fantasy one step further up the spiritual ladder, making it accessible to those who would otherwise discard fantasy.

Ibrišimović is one of Bosnia's classics,[2] continuing the long tradition of story-telling in the novel form, one that gave us master novelists like Ivo Andrić (1961 Nobel laureate) or Meša Selimović. Writing in this part of the world usually means writing literary fiction, and before novels there were epic poems, little masterpieces of epic fantasy, featuring well-known regional heroes in the constant state of combat. While one could not expect science fiction elements in these old verses written by anonymous epic poets, there's a lot of fantasy, swords, castles, and magic. In the traditional versical narrative, there's another genre flirting with fantasy: the sacral. One such example is the mevlud (mawlid), the poetic rendition of the birth and life of Muhammad, the Messenger of God. The striking visual elements such as the night voyage (Isra) featuring Buraq the flying horse were always challenging parts for the poets creating these stories in verse and a chance to show creativity in fantasy.

The blend of non-fiction, fiction, religion, genre, and fantasy may be surprising to a reader accustomed to bookstore categories, but Bosnian literature has a hard time with the terms one would find in a random bookstore in an English-speaking country. Aleksandar Hemon[3] writes in Richard Lea's 2016 *Guardian* piece "Fiction v nonfiction—English literature's made-up divide,"

> In Bosnian, there are no words for fiction and nonfiction, or the distinction thereof(…). This is not to say that there is no truth or untruth, it's just that a literary text is not defined by its relation to truth or imagination…. Some literary people have bastardised fiction into "fikcija," which makes me cringe, while "ne-fikcija" is even more atrocious. I would never use those words. Your average taxi driver would not understand them.

Similar terminological issues arise at the border of genre and literary fiction; it is as if everything we write aspires to be literature.

A Hill at the Center of the World

The center of the world hypothesis is an attractive one; it is always story worthy. One of those, heavily influenced by alternative history ideas that read like Erich von Däniken's works, crept into the real world with Semir Osmanagić's story of the Visoko pyramids. Long story short, aptly shaped hills near the town of Visoko in central Bosnia are, according to Indiana-Jones-inspired Osmanagić, mighty energy-collecting structures built by an advanced unknown civilization tens of thousands of years ago. As a sci-fi story, the Visoko pyramids would be benign and original, but as a hypothesis pitched to the general audience, they represent an emergent New Age hoax and an attractor for additional pseudoscientific "theories." For a sci-fi fan, that's an uncomfortable thought—exciting sci-fi ideas creeping into the mainstream pretending to be science.

At this point, I have to disclose my lack of credentials: I'm neither a science fiction theorist nor a successful author—my first short story collection was somewhat misaligned with the target audience, reducing the set of readers who would eventually enjoy it to a small, specialized group.[4] But that by no means reduces my passion for writing and reading all things sci-fi, and the ongoing drive for unusual, nonlinear, non-Western approaches to the creation of art. In that regard, I want to conclude this essay with a reflection on my writing.

Sometimes I think that my own fiction reads generically, with most of the local influence removed. I blame my butterfly-chasing nature, running after stories that fly from one place to the other into distant lands and times. Even as such, these "refugee stories" are unmistakably Bosnian, and I don't mean just the annoying lack of definite articles. My characters walked the streets of Sarajevo before they were teleported to my stories, and when they make a decision, it's inspired by what they've heard from the old folks in a farmers' market on a Saturday morning. When they believe in something, it's the belief of the old wise books they exchanged as kids. They find delight in Mondrian's paintings and inspiration in Sufi stories they've heard from their Darwish friends while playing board games. They fear fundamentalism and dangerous rhetorics and find joy in world-building, imagining futures that link their experiences with the world past the rivers that shape the borders of the little Bosnian triangle. Having worked in Bosnian academia, I write fiction that often finds itself in the education and/or research setting, and the culture of the local academic community necessarily shows, with all its virtues and flaws.

Notes

1. Karim Zaimović's legacy is alive and well in Sarajevo. A foundation named after him helps young artists and authors, a mural featuring Karim and his work in a comic book style graces one of Sarajevo's facades, and a play based on his stories is one of the most unusual and most successful productions in Sarajevo.

2. Nedžad Ibrišimović (1940–2011) was often mentioned in the context of potential Nobel laureates from Bosnia at the turn of the 20th to 21st century, with his unique, skilled narration style mirroring the typically Bosnian stories he turned into widely read and critically acclaimed novels which are part of mandatory school literature.

3. Aleksandar Hemon is a celebrated Bosnian American author who is no stranger to fantasy, and even metafantasy; in his novel *The Making of Zombie Wars*, we follow an author writing a zombie fantasy story.

4. My short story collection *Murder on the Einstein Express* (Springer, 2016) tells the stories that range from a strange fairytale about mathematical functions (written under the influence of a calculus exam) to a story about a physics course I always wanted to slip into a curriculum at my institution.

Works Cited

De Mello, Anthony. (1985). *One Minute Wisdom*. New York: Doubleday.
Hemon, Aleksandar. *The Making of Zombie Wars*. New York: Farrar, Straus and Giroux, 2015.
Richards, Justin. "Horrors of War." Perf. Katy Manning. London: BBC Digital Audio, 2018.
Stone, Dave. *Death and Diplomacy*. London: Doctor Who Books, 1996.

Science Fiction in Turkey

Skirting the Edge of a Remembered Future

Gamze G. Özfirat *and* İsmail Yamanol

> It is as if the memory of an entire civilisation and its contribution to the sum of knowledge has been virtually wiped from human consciousness. Not simply in the West but in the Islamic world too, the achievements of Islamic scientists were, until recently, largely forgotten or at least neglected, except by a few diligent specialists such as Harvard University's Abelhamid Sabra, David King, Jamil Ragep and George Saliba.
> —Ehsan Masood (2009: 2)

Although science fiction takes its roots from the fables, myths, and other creations of the vivid imagination of ancient people in the East and West alike, the modern science fiction genre featuring scientific speculation and estrangement from the world as we know it is a latecomer to the global literary scene. The transition from mere fantasy fiction to modern science fiction was so gradual that literary historians as well as the science fiction community worldwide have yet to agree on a point in time when modern science fiction had its dawn. Nevertheless, Mary Shelley's *Frankenstein: A Modern Prometheus* is now widely considered as the groundbreaking novel that sparked the big bang to create the universe of modern science fiction.

The driving force behind this quantum leap in literature was the age of enlightenment and the era of mercantilism/capitalism flourishing in the West. In spite of the previous breakthroughs in the arts and sciences in the Islamic geography from the 9th to the 15th centuries, the Islamic world was initially lagging behind this new literary trend—Turkey included. It was only in the 19th century that the new literary wave hit Turkish intellectual circles and the first examples of the genre—then called *fennî edebiyât* (scientific literature)—were translations of the works by Jules Verne and H.G. Wells, which deeply influenced Turkish writers.

Science of Islamic Progress

The first "scientific" novel was written by Ahmet Mithat Efendi in Imperial Turkey in 1888, and it was about two American doctors in Jefferson City experimenting in galvanoplasty and death. The purpose of the novel was to praise American advances in science, technology and industry while condemning Americans for being even more morally depraved than Europeans, pinning the blame for this depravity on atheism.

Scientific literature in Turkey reached its peak in 1913 and 1914, at a time when the whole country was ravaged by war, and the population was demoralized, fighting for survival day in, day out. The novel as a genre is a late bloomer in Turkish literature. It is possible to observe this stuntedness and novitiate in the early examples of Turkish novels. Nevertheless, pioneers of the Turkish novel, including Semseddin Sami, Ahmet Mithat Efendi, Recaizade Mahmut Ekrem, Sami Pasazade Sezai, Mehmed Murad, Nabizade Nazim, and Namik Kemal during the Tanzimat (reformation) period of the Ottoman Empire, have greatly contributed to the maturation and characterization of the genre in Turkey. Though the traces of Western storytelling on the Turkish novel are barely there, the influence cannot be entirely denied either. Today, the Turkish novel follows the literary norms of the Western novel and aspires to universality. The Nobel Prize in literature being awarded to Orhan Pamuk in 2006 is a milestone on the rising trajectory of the Turkish novel. On the other hand, the influence of traditional Turkish literature on modern Turkish science fiction is rather meager. It is more interesting to see mainstream Turkish writers try their hands in the science fiction genre. *Son Ada* (*The Last Island*) by Zulfu Livaneli and *Bir Sairin Utopyasi* (*A Poet's Utopia*) by Murathan Mungan are two popular works in this regard. Both authors are among the most prominent figures in Turkish literature.

Contrary to the conventional Turkish novel genre, the reflections of ages-old Turkish storytelling in modern Turkish science fiction are much more discernible. Traces of great Turkish storytellers, including Aziz Nesin, Omer Seyfettin, Sebahattin Ali, Sait Faik Abasiyanik, Orhan Kemal, and Memduh S. Esendal, can be followed in modern Turkish science fiction, which is unsurprising considering that Turkish science fiction has evolved and developed over the path paved by storytellers.

Notable examples among the novels and stories published at that time was Molla Davudzade Mustafa Nazim's novel *Ruyada Terakki ve Medeniyet-i Islamiyye-i Ru'yet* (*Observing Islamic Progress and Civilization in a Dream*) depicting an extremely advanced technological society under Islamic law in the 23rd century where men and women are strictly segregated and everyone has to wear the same clothes. Though the novel was clearly inspired by Thomas More's *Utopia*, such a Utopia would of course be a modern day totalitarian Dystopia. *Tarih-i Istikbal* (*History of the Future*, 1913)—another utopian novel by Celal Nuri Ileri—describes an Istanbul in the 152nd century where borders, language differences, and gender discrimination have vanished. Imperialism has not only invaded every remote corner of the world but also spread to other planets, and industrialization has reached a point where the entire Earth is covered by buildings and factories with no patch of soil in sight. Seasons and all the beauties of nature have forever been destroyed, and every trace of grace and elegance has been stripped off humankind. In another scientific story called *Camlar Altında Musahabe* (*Conversing Under the Pines*), published the same year by the famed Turkish poet Yahya Kemal, the hero uses a time machine to travel to 2187 and describes the future Istanbul as a harmonious blend of historical beauty and state-of-the-art technological marvels. In his novel called *Rûsenî'nin Ruyasi—Muslumanlarin 'Megali Ideasi' Gaye-i Hayâliyesi* (*Rûsenî's Dream: The "Grand Vision" and Purpose of Moslems*), Hasan Rûsenî Barkin describes a future where most of the world is either Islamic or Islam-dominated, with the Ottoman Empire as the sole superpower and Turkish as the lingua franca.

This brief spurt in scientific literature was mainly a reflection of the need to rekindle our self-confidence through wishful thinking at a time when everything else was falling apart. As Turkey transformed itself into a republic, this literary genre drifted off into obscurity, and literature became more focused on a realistic treatise of social issues, past or present. The Ottoman school of scientific literature survived for a while through Refik Halit Karay and a few other writers until it slowly petered out.

Risen from the Ashes

In the wake of the Second World War, Turkish scientific fiction was revived in the form of modern science fiction. Though this revival was triggered by the translation of the science fiction classics of the golden age during the 1950s, vigorous science fiction writing began during the 1970s through numerous fanzines and magazines. The longest surviving one among them was *X-Bilinmeyen* (*X-Unknown*) published by Selma Mine from 1976 to 1981. Selma Mine also authored several novels herself, including the well-known *OBI JS 927* published in 1980.

Another pioneer of SF was Orhan Duru, an award-winning, mainstream storyteller who later authored several science fiction stories and novellas. The best known among his works is probably *Yoksullar Geliyor* (*Paupers are Coming*) published in 1982, which describes a future world divided into the rich North and the poor South. He has also coined the term *bilimkurgu* (from *bilim*: science and *kurgu*: fiction) as the Turkish term for science fiction, which was soon embraced by the SF community.

The 1980s heralded the dawn of the golden age of Turkish science fiction with an ever-expanding readership and hundreds of young writers, and nowadays there are more than a hundred published science fiction writers.

Modern Turkish science fiction is generally inspired by the subgenres in the industrialized world including American, European, and Soviet science fiction. Most SF works are secular in character and contain almost no reference to religion. Although the science fiction community in Turkey as a whole is neutral in political matters, the majority of science fiction fans are predominantly secular and progressive. And as Turkey's political environment has evolved towards a more totalitarian system, a striking increase has been observed in the number of the dystopic novels.

Turkish science fiction is as much the child of Apollo and the Space Race as Golden Age American SF (*X-Bilinmeyen Science Fiction Magazine,* printed courtesy Bilimkurgu Kulübü).

Especially since the dawn of the new millennium, the widespread use of the Internet and social media played an important role in the development of sub-cultural groups in Turkey. This dynamism and interaction in the cyber world inevitably paved the way for the science fiction community as well as similar sub-cultural groups in Turkey toward finding a realm of existence in order to appeal to their audiences. Local science fiction enthusiasts, who only had the chance to meet on occasional events before, suddenly had much larger opportunities under their hands. This new environment has in return boosted local creativity in the science fiction genre. New websites, forums, blogs, pages, and groups were created, and ideas were shared and exchanged at a pace never seen before. Now, the created content is just a single click away from enthusiastic audiences. In a sense, the heat of the Internet has brought the ever-simmering cauldron of Turkish science fiction to a massive eruption.

Though the bookracks now offer a larger selection than before, the flow of new works is still inadequate enough to feature a specialized category of Turkish science fiction literature in retail or online bookstores. Still, the increasing number of translated works is also important to offer a larger literary selection to the local readers and writers gathered around this genre. In this respect, the readers play a role as important as the publishers in order to fan the flame of literary production. On the other hand, Turkey is a country in desperate need of scientific and technological progress. Since science fiction is a literary genre nourished by science, and there is a definite interaction between both subjects, the unfortunate lag of Turkey in science and technology is undeniably reflected in science fiction.

It will only be fair to say that science fiction represents the culture of the 21st century in a more characteristic way than the other genres, and this representation is bound to get stronger in the complicated world of our day. We are a civilization developing science and technology at breakneck speed, and the universal popularity of science fiction grows at the same pace. One look around us is enough to see that we are actually living in the world of the science fiction novels written only fifty years ago. In this age of technology, science fiction does not seem such a "crackpot" thing anymore. In a sense, the scope and influence of science fiction has expanded parallel to the transformation in the new world. While once, being a science fiction enthusiast would gather disdain and ridicule, and science fiction meant nothing but UFOs and aliens to the great majority in Turkey, now we can safely assume that this mentality has evolved.

Today, we can talk about extraterrestrial missions, space colonies, virtual reality, cyborgs, robotics, and interstellar voyages in all seriousness. Once the science fiction enthusiasts speaking about these were condemned as half-wits; now scientific gatherings find vigorous and spirited participation from large audiences. Thus, Turkish science fiction literature falls in step with the global pace of the genre. Since literature is and will forever be the greatest inspiration of cinema, this productivity in literature is inevitably reflected also in the seventh art.

Industrializing Science Fiction

When we look at the developmental process of American science fiction in particular, we can promptly observe that it has been greatly fuelled by magazines and fanzines. Indeed, the American science fiction literature went through a historical period called "the age of magazines" from the 1920s to the 1960s. In addition to the contribution of prominent magazine editors including Hugo Gernsback and John W. Campbell, the numerous periodicals published during that period created their own market and readership, increasing the power and influence of American SF on the public. Alas, Turkish science fiction remained devoid of such a driving force. As mentioned above, there were of course certain well-intentioned attempts of science fiction magazines including *Antares, X-Bilinmeyen* (*X-Unknown*), *Atilgan* (*The Enterprise*), *Nostromo,* and *Davetsiz Misafir* (*Uninvited Guest*). However, trying to publish a SF magazine in Turkey was in a sense like running against the wind. Some have given up after a few steps, while some struggled till the last drop of their power. But all was in vain, and they all turned into nostalgic memories on an arid soil.

The inadequate sales numbers, obstacles in distribution, and the low advertising revenues were the greatest factors leading to the demise of these periodicals. Even worse, the market has fallen under the control of certain popular and sectoral magazines published through the years by large trusts. Except for these, it is difficult to reach viable sales numbers, especially if you are trying to survive in a marginal interest area such as science fiction. Consequently, the Turkish science fiction magazines have come to a severe standstill in the new millennium. Thankfully, we have been able to fill this void through the Internet. And e-magazines and websites are especially versatile in fulfilling a similar function in a much faster and practical way.

Thus, science fiction fans in Turkey have gathered under the roof of the Bilimkurgu Kulubu (The Science Fiction Club), the leading organization of the enthusiasts of the genre founded in 1999. The club has a well-organized and regularly updated website at bilimkurgukulubu.com, which is a source of information on science fiction and popular science books and movies containing thousands of short stories as well as interesting and well-researched articles. The club has a Facebook group with almost a hundred thousand registered followers. On the occasion of its 18th anniversary in 2017, the club selected 18 stories by 18 writers and compiled them in an anthology published by Ithaki—a publishing house specializing in science fiction—under the title *Yeryuzu Muzesi* (*The Earth Museum*). This is only the beginning of a tradition which will hopefully continue with new books in the future.

This work has also been endorsed with a message by the legendary sci-fi and fantasy author Ursula K. Le Guin:

I was very happy to learn that Bilimkurgu Kulubu plans an anthology of science fiction stories by Turkish writers. In these troubled times, all artists are strengthened by knowing of other artists working to assert and uphold the creative

More than just a book club, it's an outpost in the gloom of the mundane in literature and business (The official logo of the Turkish science fiction club printed courtesy of designer Serkan Özay).

principle, and of non-profit publishers who support them by freeing their work from the constraints of the market-place. All of us, all over the world, seem to be struggling through a great darkness. Such works are like lamps lighted where we need them most, illuminating what is around them and the way we need to go. The fuel of those lamps is the imagination. Thank you, my Turkish readers and friends and fellow-writers, for keeping the light burning" October 2017.

This message, the Turkish translation of which adorns the back cover of the book, also has historical value as the author's last published words prior to her death on 22 January 2018.

Another circle devoted to SF is a monthly online science fiction magazine called *Yerli Bilimkurgu Yukseliyor* (YBKY) (*Local Science Fiction Rising*). The magazine promotes the works of Turkish science fiction writers and organizes topical short story contests several times a year. Selected topics to date include teleportation, first encounter with an extraterrestrial, colonizing other planets, alternate history, and time paradoxes.

There are various other—some web based—groups interested in themes including science fiction, fantasy, and horror in diverse fields such as literature, graphic arts, comics, movies, computer games, FRP, etc. Writers of science fiction, fantasy, and horror are also brought together under FABİSAD, Fantasy and Science Fiction Arts Association. FABİSAD has been organizing the Gio Awards for best story, best novel, and best illustration of the year since 2013 to honor Giovanni Scognamillo in recognition of his long years of creative service in this field. Since 1998, Informatics Association of Turkey (TBD) has held an annual science fiction short story contest to distribute the prestigious TBD short story awards. And Entropol Books organizes a science fiction micro-story contest every year.

The literary word appeals to the older, and the picture to the younger, an ideal combination to sustain Turkish SF for the future (*Atlgan Science Fiction Magazine*, printed courtesy of Bilimkurgu Kulübü).

A Final Word

We can safely conclude that Turkish science fiction has finally come of age and reached maturity. Both the supply and the demand in this genre are growing. In this day and age, when information gurgles out and cascades in a raging stream, every kind of scientific and technological breakthrough can influence humanity and change lives regardless of its place of origin. So, it is no longer possible to close your eyes and isolate yourself from the rest of the world.

As science and technology progress, science fiction naturally benefits from that progress and gets the chance to appeal to a larger readership. Since science fiction as a literary genre involves reflecting on and questioning the world as we know it, it will only be to the benefit of mankind if it thrives and reaches new audiences. Consequently, science fiction has reached a unique status as a powerful and influential artistic endeavor impossible to resist or ignore.

The Science Fiction Club is an organization striving to render the science fiction genre a respectable cultural interest not only in Turkey, but in the whole world. Thus, the club is also keen on establishing collaborations all over the world, adopting an international attitude parallel to the universality of science fiction. The essence of science fiction encompasses not only individual countries, but the whole world—not just societies, but all humankind. In this respect, we can especially mention our collaboration with the German Science Fiction Club, which is of course spearheaded by the considerable Turkish community in Germany, facilitating communication and allegiance towards common goals. However, the only community from the Islamic world we have been in contact with is the Egyptian Society for Science Fiction. We are ready to contact science fiction clubs all over the world for collaborative projects as long as we share the same goals. In this age of the Internet, we are provided with many means for a rapid and easy communication with the world. And as Turkish science fiction enthusiasts, we love "first contacts."

We are excited because we believe that science fiction is one of the greatest human values in order to subvert the structures deemed indispensable, indestructible, and unchangeable in our world and to open the door to new ideas and actions in the wake of this subversion. The Science Fiction Club has been chasing after this dream for 19 years and invites everyone to share our dream for a freer and happier future worth living. Filling its wings with the winds of this power, Turkish science fiction literature will surely continue its voyage at a greater speed towards the future, the stars, and the dreams of mankind.

WORK CITED

Masood, Ehsan. (2009). *Science and Islam: A History*. London: Icon Books.

A Talk with Shamil Idiatullin

Muslims in the "Contracting" Universe of Post-Soviet SF

EGYPTIAN SOCIETY FOR SCIENCE FICTION

> What else has a journalist to do these days, after all, but report life's miseries?
> —John le Carré (1977:32)

ESSF: Please fill us in on yourself. Who is Shamil Idiatullin? Where did he grow up, what was his education? His parents, language skills, and career? How did he get into science fiction and, more importantly, why?

Shamil Idiatullin is a journalist and novelist, award-winning writer, author of *Brezhnev City* (2017) which received the Big Book Prize. He has been working in journalism since 1988, including being a staff writer for *Kommersant* newspaper since 1994. He was the head of its Correspondent Network, a political columnist for *Kommersant-Vlast* magazine, and is currently the head of the Regional Editions Department. In 2004 Idiatullin published his first novel, *Tatar Hit*.

Now I will allow myself to speak in the first person.

I was born and raised in the Volga region, the historical center of European Islam. The nations who took part in the forming of modern Tatars have been living here for fifteen hundred years, and where Islam became the state religion more than a thousand years ago. I grew up in an ordinary Soviet family—my parents were engineers at the giant KamAZ plant. I studied at school and read a lot. Science fiction was the most favorite part of my reading. It taught me to think, it helped me to look beyond the horizons, it was the most interesting and exciting of what I read, and it gave me a sense of hope which helped me overcome the most boring moments of so-called real life. Almost all teenagers are addicted to SF, but most of them grow out of it, like from old shoes. I fortunately didn't.

As for language, I studied German in school and university. I started learning English a bit too late, however, and by myself which was the only way—without the help of teachers and training courses. My speaking and writing in English are poor; I almost don't understand native talk, but I can read texts.

ESSF: Please give us a brief synopsis of your most distinguished sci-fi novels. What themes animate you when you put pen to paper? Where do you get your inspiration from?

Most of my books can be considered as speculative fiction and only at a stretch. So, my first novel *Руссия*, published under the title *Tatar Hit*, tells about the military conflict

206

A virtuous city above the clouds, proving that the dream of Soviet science fiction is still with us after all that has happened (printed courtesy of the artist, Ammar Al-Gamal).

between the Russian region Tatarstan and, at first, the federal center, finally, the troops of NATO and the USA. Although these conflicts have never happened in reality, I do not consider this novel as a SpecF. *Tatar Hit* is a techno-thriller; a lot of events here are invented, but all assumptions are possible.

My second novel, *USSR™*, is an elegiacal, melancholy, social Utopia about a political conflict over an ambitious project that combines modern high-tech industry with idealized Soviet rhetoric.

The third novel, *Ubyr*, is a mystical, ethnical thriller based on Tatar, Turkic, and Volga folklore. It tells about a teenager who must save his little sister, his family, and the whole world from the evil deadly spirit that has penetrated into the modern city apartment.

My life itself gave me the reasons for these books; made me think about painful topics for me as a person, a citizen, a husband, and a father; and invented the most hard and extreme ways for their development and resolution. I have been happily married for a long time; my son will soon be 25 years old and my daughter will be 18 years old.

ESSF: Who is your chief audience? English speakers or the local audience? The younger readership? Do you feel you voice their concerns?

I write, of course, for the domestic reader. None of my books have been translated into other languages yet, and I find it hard to imagine how a foreign reader might react to them. Probably with some interest. I write books that I like as a reader, and I don't think that I am a significantly different person in comparison with people who live in other countries and speak other languages, but are similar to me in terms of education, the range of international reading, and ideas about the ideals they uphold.

However, my ideas about the main audience are not very trustworthy. Until recently, I thought that if I write tough polyphonic thrillers with a complicated composition and a lot of characters, then my main reader is a techie guy. And then it turned out that the assessment is correct, but still belongs to a minority of the audience. And the majority of my readers are women, 25–55 years old and with a philosophical degree, family and with children! This news shocked me, but I quickly put up with it—after all, this is the top of the main intellectual audience.

For teenagers and children, I wrote only in a small form, but, oddly enough, only these stories and a novella can be considered as a natural SF. The story "This is Just a Game" appeared precisely because of that. I was constantly called an SF-writer, so I wrote a real old-school, fantastic adventure to stop feeling like an intruder. I tried to imagine for what book I would give all my treasures in my childhood: the book that would include an exchange of real and virtual lives, an insidious video game, an exchange of bodies between the boy and the girl, a kingdom with battles, feats of bravery, chases, school intrigues, and the next day's end of the world. So, I wrote such a kind of novella.

ESSF: Is being a journalist different than being an author? Does your education and career as a journalist have any influence on your writing, say, on your usage of language?

In my opinion, these are related things with multidirectional vectors. I became a journalist because I decided that the childhood dream of being a writer is too naive and unfulfilled. But I wouldn't become a writer if I hadn't worked as a journalist for 15 years, if I hadn't got into the habit of every day writing hundreds of carefully thought-out words that contain more than one meaning—and if I didn't understand that a writer should build the completely different buildings from a similar building material. A journalist is a slave of fact: he is the eyes, ears, and nerve endings of society. Just as a writer performs the function of the brain that is directly connected with the eyes, ears, nerves, but is not responsible for the immediate response, but mainly for the comprehension and bizarre ordering of the accumulated material, in short—for dreams. Talking briefly, dreams allow us to fly, to grow, to find the answers to the most important questions, to not go crazy, and to rise every morning ready for the rest of life.

The solution of this task requires the tools which are similar to journalism but are still different, including linguistic and logical ones.

ESSF: Have your concerns and interests as a writer changed since the fall of the USSR in 1991? Are there more opportunities for authors such as yourself in the new, freer environment?

In the USSR I was a schoolboy and a student, so, of course, I could not change as a writer. I don't think that I could become a Soviet writer—my tastes are too specific, my plots are too hard, and my language is too complex compared to the standards that were then considered traditional. And today in Russia, any person, more or less, can publish his book. Another thing is that in most cases, no one will notice such a book, and success is achieved mainly by talented and professionally written books.

In any case, the Soviet era is very important for me as a person, reader, and writer. I was brought up in the works of Soviet writers and among my books the most popular was the realistic Bildungsroman *Brezhnev City*, telling about the tragic decline of the Soviet era.

ESSF: Does the economic situation make life and writing harder for authors?

In Soviet times, writers were the elite; with some luck it was enough to write one book to solve all the material problems for a lifetime. There were few writers, and each book was published in huge circulation—from 100,000 to 500,000 copies—and brought the author a lot of money, fame, and reputation. Today this system does not exist; in Russia thousands of writers publish tens of thousands of books in scanty editions—1,000–3,000 copies. Only a few very popular writers can live by their literary work, without experiencing any problems, thanks to reprints, translations, and adaptations for the screen. The main source of income for the absolute majority of writers, like me, is not related to books. I do not think that the situation will change in the near future.

ESSF: Does Russian literature, especially myths and folktales, exert any influence on your writing? Do the stories, myths, and languages of the non–Russian peoples also exert an influence? Such as the literature of Moldova or the Eskimos or the Uyghurs?

Of course, Russian literature has a huge importance to me. I write in Russian, and most of my favorite writers have always been my contemporaries, who wrote in Russian. I have been loving fairy tales since childhood, including the Russian ones. In adulthood I became seriously interested in the mythology and ethnography of the non–Russian people of Russia, primarily the Tatars to whom I belong, as well as Bashkirs, Altaians, Shorians, Mari, Udmurts, Mordovians, other Turkic and Finno-Ugric people of the Volga region, the Urals and Siberia. The themes and plots that I found there not only helped my preparation for writing the ethnical thriller *Ubyr*, but also became an important motivating factor for starting to work on it.

I have been suspecting for a long time that the work of George Lucas also experienced both Soviet and Turkic influence. Russian SF-fans have a joke that Darth Vader from *Star Wars* is an aged Communist superhero Dar Veter from Ivan Efremov's novel *Andromeda Nebula* (1957). And Han Solo in fact is the name of the hero of the Altai folk tale, recorded in the early 20th century.

ESSF: How exposed were Soviet readers, including yourself, to Western sci-fi? Were Jules Verne and H.G. Wells household names, along with Isaac Asimov, Arthur C. Clarke, and Philip K. Dick? How popular and widely available is Western SF since the fall of Communism?

Jules Verne and H.G. Wells throughout the Soviet period were some of the most published and favorite authors among all kinds of writers. They were known and loved by everyone; individual books and multi-volume collections of their works were published in the USSR even during periods of the most active persecution of science fiction. However, the situation with the rest of Western fiction, as well as foreign literature in general, was much worse. SF and crime writers were published and translated a bit and almost randomly, dividing, as well as other foreign writers, into "progressive," i.e., sympathizing with the USSR, and "reactionary" (all other) authors.

Isaac Asimov, Arthur C. Clarke, Clifford Simak, and Ray Bradbury were considered as progressive ones, but Arthur C. Clarke was exactly the writer who was associated with a great scandal. At the height of the publication of his novel *2010: Odyssey Two* in *Technical—molodezhy* (Technology for Youth) magazine, it turned out that all Soviet cosmonauts in the text bear the names of Soviet dissidents. The publication was cut off, and the editor-in-chief of the magazine was dismissed. A similar scandal was associated with the early termination of the publication of the thriller *The Day of the Jackal* by Frederick Forsyth in the Almaty magazine *Prostor*. Local authorities allegedly saw in the text the step-by-step instruction for preparing an assassination of the leaders of the USSR. As a result, the publication of new books was reduced to a minimum; it was easier to republish the same set of stories by the same authors over and over again. At the same time, any reissued book with the label "SF" was published in huge circulation; it had a great demand and sold on the black market for three to five time the face value. SF-fans reprinted such collections on a typewriter, as well as amateur translations of books not published officially in the USSR, and sold those samizdat-copies under the counter. Those fans could be fired from their jobs for this and even put in prison.

It was very strange situation. The main Anglo-American science fiction writers for the Soviet reader were Harry Harrison and Robert Sheckley, most of the post–World War II classics like Alfred Bester or Robert Heinlein were presented in Russian with just a couple of stories, and the vast majority of big writers like Roger Zelazny, Frank Herbert, John Brunner, and Ursula K. Le Guin were not known to the Soviet reader at all. At the same time, oddly enough, a couple of stories by Philip K. Dick were published in magazines for teenagers, and Stephen King's novels were published in intellectual literary magazines.

After the collapse of the Soviet regime, everything has changed. The reader was immediately attacked by the achievements of world literature, which were held back by the Iron Curtain until now. This attack threw open the horizons of the local reader, but at same time it brought some problems associated with the publication of weak commercial authors and especially with the bad translations. The invasion of SF and crime novels was particularly noticeable and was distinguished by exceptionally poor translations, which were engaged even in inept students with both poor English and Russian. As a result, many readers have stopped reading SF in general, and the reputation of many excellent Western authors was ruined for the mass Russian reader almost for good.

ESSF: A small side query. Is it true that Asimov is actually pronounced (عظيموف) in Arabic?

When I studied at Kazan University, there was a popular legend according to which Isaac Asimov came from an ancient Tatar family and allegedly the writer's grandfather exactly was the man who built the Azimov (Ajem) mosque in Kazan. Of course, the legend had no reason. The Tatar merchant Murtaza Azimov, who built the mosque, had a name that sounds like the name of a famous SF-writer, but he could not be a relative of a Jewish boy from the Smolensk province. The Tatar surname comes from عظيم with the Russian patronymic ending "-ov" added, the Hebrew name derives from azimy (ozim-iye), a word for the winter crops in which Isaac Asimov's great-grandfather was dealing.

ESSF: Are Russian authors aware of what is being written in the Arab world? Have they heard of the leading lights in Arab SF like Ahmed Khaled Tawfik, Taleb Omran, Nihad Sharif, Lina Kilani, or Abd Al-Salam Al-Baqali? Is Naguib Mahfouz more of a household name in literary circles?

Unfortunately, I am completely unfamiliar with the fiction of the Arab world. I hope to catch up on this omission in the foreseeable future.

ESSF: Were you surprised to get an offer from the Egyptian Society for Science Fiction, honestly?
Yes of course. But I was flattered.

ESSF: How "institutionalized" is science fiction in Russia? Are there active policies promoting it from the ministry of education or ministry of culture? Is translation to and from Russian a major priority in the publishing industry? Is there a national sci-fi association? Do you have sci-fi magazines and comic books and sci-fi clubs and conventions, especially for young people?
We are presuming, as Arabs, that such policies did exist in the Communist era, a model to us all.

Russian SF today is experiencing an acute crisis. In the 1990s, science fiction looked like a growing segment with large circulations and loud events (prizes, congresses, etc.). But for the last 15 years, a significant number of publishers and writers have devoted attempts to achieve commercial success with the help of fantasy and action series, games novelizations, and revanchist series in which Stalin managed to crush Hitler with a little help from our contemporary IT-manager, Russian SWAT officer, or even Darth Vader. Gradually, this freaky segment ruined almost the entire niche that is traditionally called "science fiction," washing out from circulation both SF and high-quality literary SpecF. As a result, the mass reader turned away either from Russian authors or from SF in general, while the literary elite, including the part who were associated with book awards, already tried to distance themselves from the "low genre."

The last Russian SF-magazine, *Mir Fantastiki*, announced that its paper issue would be stopped beginning in 2019. The government structures have neither the interest nor the will to support SF. Under these conditions, there is no chance for any program of translation and promotion for Russian SF in foreign markets—only a few commercially successful authors and their agents are doing this on their own.

Reasonable writers and publishers are now looking for a way out of the "SF ghetto." There are some successes, but, unfortunately, today the Russian SF-writer can get serious success only if he pretends that he is not a SF-writer. The best example is the main (in fact) Russian writer Viktor Pelevin, who publishes a completely SpecF novel every year, but for the last twenty years, nobody called him a SpecF-writer.

ESSF: Is publishing in Russia and other former Soviet republics organized the same was as it is in the West? Do you have editors and exhibitions and signing ceremonies and book fairs and marketing strategies?
Yes, today the publishing business in Russia is built according to the Western model, but it has flaws in almost every point: circulation is reduced, bookstores are closing, book fairs collect fewer participants, the primary interest of readers goes to the foreign book, not the domestic one. The state support of literature in Russia cannot be compared with how it is done in Germany, France, Norway, etc.

ESSF: Are there sci-fi series and sagas in Russia, like Asimov's Foundation Saga *or* Star Wars? *And do you have "pocketbook" [paperback] series in Russian SF?*
The last great Russian SF-saga was written by the Strugatsky brothers. There were no figures of comparable scale after them. The number of talented Russian authors is very large: Sergey Zharkovsky, Maria Galina, Andrey Lazarchuk, Andrey Lyakh, Vladimir

Pokrovsky, Vasily Shchepetnev—but they usually do not work in the series format and aren't commercially successful. On the other side, there are many commercial Russian SF-series on the market, both individual and inter-authorial, but in the absolute majority of cases, these are very poorly written military SF or space operas imitating half-a-century-ago books.

In Soviet times, several iconic SF-series, by both Russian and foreign authors, appeared as pocketbooks. Later this format was compromised and was used mainly for cheap, pulp fiction issues. Today, an absolute majority of books in Russia are published in hardcover. Only in recent years have pocketbooks begun to return to the market and attract attention, first of all to young active readers. So far, Western fiction has been reissued in such a standard, but if reanimation of Russian fiction as a class will happen, the paperback will surely be the vehicle to spread.

ESSF: Soviet science fiction has a sterling reputation in the Arab world, as do the classics of Russian literature. Tolstoy, Dostoevsky, Chekov are household names, and not just amongst fellow writers. And you can still find the odd Soviet SF novel, translated into English or Arabic, even in the second-hand book stalls in Cairo including the likes of Aleksey Tolstoy, Arkady, and Boris Strugatsky, Yevgeny Zamyatin, Sever Gansovsky, and Yuri Medvedev, among others.

Are these the SF authors you grew up with in your teens? Or do we have a jaundiced impression of Soviet sci-fi here in Egypt and other Arab countries?

In the history of Soviet fiction, there were two peaks—in the mid–1920s and the 1960s—and a lot of failures and taboos, when SF was under pressure and banned in general or reduced to "popular literature about the atomic tractor that calls young people to technical schools." I grew up in an era of book shortages and a tacit ban of qualitative SF. In those years, only the classics of Russian science fiction were actively republished: Alexey Tolstoy, Alexander Belyaev, Ivan Efremov, and Vladimir Obruchev. The fantastic books of Yevgeny Zamyatin and Mikhail Bulgakov, like many other prominent authors of the 1920s, were banned. The best Soviet science fiction writers, the Strugatsky brothers, as well as their followers and friends (including Sever Gansovsky), were also barely published from 1973 to 1985. Sergey Zhemaytis and Bela Klyueva, chiefs of the SF-department at the Molodaya Gvardiya publishing house and parents of the last Soviet SF-boom, were *fired*. Their department had started to publish high-class SF in the 1950s and created the whole market for the new genre by releasing hundreds of books including the wonderful "Library of Modern SF" in 25 volumes. After 1973 the new editors, Yuri Medvedev and Vladimir Shcherbakov, for almost 15 years had to publish very bad but loyal books, including their own. The situation was a little easier in children's SF, which saved me as a reader. I especially loved books by Vladislav Krapivin and Kir Bulychev. Only at the end of the 1980s did strong authors finally break through to readers—it was the holiday of national SF, which lasted a good 15 years but ended in a rather pitiable manner.

The main reason for the banning was in a legendary phrase by someone official in Communist publishing management: SF is either anti–Soviet or crap. The Strugatskys weren't crap, for sure—so they were considered almost dissidents. *Roadside Picnic* by the Strugatsky brothers, the release of the first book edition, was blocked for almost 10 years.

Gansovsky was very strong and original SF-writer. By the way, he illustrated one of the Strugatsky books, and it was brilliant.

ESSF: You will notice also that there are no Muslims on the aforementioned list. Were there no SF authors in the Communist era, or did they just not receive the international attention they deserved? Could you fill us in on the Muslim names, if any, and what their great achievements were in the genre?

The USSR was a country of militant atheism, so Muslim literature, just like Christian or Buddhist ones, in general, and religious SF in particular, was impossible. The Soviet government actively supported the development of the literature of the people of the USSR in 88 languages, but this literature was strictly structured. A writer with the conditionally Muslim or even non–Russian name had to write on non–Russian topics: Nodar Dumbadze—about Georgians, Fazil Iskander—about Abkhazians, Gabdurakhman Absalyamov—about Tatars, and so on. As a result, Russian-speaking representatives of other nations who wrote on "common Russian themes" preferred to change their names to Russian: Fikret Kamalov became Fyodor, Rinat Sufiyev became Roman Solntsev.

However, when some local literature authors became the stars of all Soviet literature, they could write anything, including science fiction—like aforementioned Fazil Iskander, author of the hard parable "The Rabbits and the Boas," or Chingiz Aitmatov, who used SF and Oriental flavor motifs with comparable strength in his later novels.

Today the situation has changed. On the one hand, the literature in national languages has remained with almost no state support and has become an unobtrusive phenomenon. On the other hand, the number of Russian writers with non–Russian, including Muslim, names, both in the mainstream and in science fiction, has sharply increased. However, I am not ready to call them Muslim writers, since they themselves usually do not profess Islam, and their creative approach can hardly be termed as Islamic.

ESSF: Have you read Xodjiakbar Shaykhov and Begenas Sartov, the great Central Asian SF authors?

In my childhood I was flipping through the book of Shayhov, but it did not seem to be interesting to me. I see the name of Sartov for the first time.

ESSF: What about sci-fi on television and in cinema, Soviet and post–Soviet?

SF on TV and in cinema was much poorer than in books. There were several great philosophical movies like *Stalker* and *Solaris* (both by Andrey Tarkovsky), a few very cool quasi-SF movies with strong satirical background like *Kin-Dza-Dza!* and *Tears Were Falling* (both by Georgy Danelia), and a bunch of teenager adventures about space travels (*Moscow—Cassiopea*), time-travel (*Guest from the Future*), or a humanoid robot in the school (*Adventures of Electronic*).

There was a funny story also with the movie *Planet of the Storms* (1962). Here's a fragment from Wikipedia:

> In 1965, producer Roger Corman acquired rights to the Soviet film and gave it to film student Curtis Harrington to prepare for American release. Harrington added several American-made scenes starring Basil Rathbone and Faith Domergue, which replaced scenes of two of the Russian cast, and dubbed the rest of the material. The dubbed result, under the name *Voyage to the Prehistoric Planet*, went directly to television via American International Pictures. In the cast and credits, Soviet personnel names were removed; only the crew of Harrington's footage and the dubbing cast were identified. were "renamed" with non–Russian names.
>
> In 1968 Peter Bogdanovich (under the name Derek Thomas), again at Corman's behest, created a different American version, adding new scenes involving Mamie Van Doren and several other attractive women in shell brassieres, which was titled *Voyage to the Planet of Prehistoric Women*; the "new" scenes also included minor footage from another Russian SF film, Mikhail

Karyukov's "Sky Is Calling." This version may have had some limited theatrical release on the drive-in circuits in the American south, but primarily also became a "TV movie" through American International Television ["Planeta Bur," 3 May 2020].

And Sever Gansovsky, one of his stories, "Firing Field," was made into the cartoon *Polygon* (1977).

In the post–Soviet era there were a few SF movies that were box-office hits, like the urban fantasy supernatural dualogy *Night Watch*, *Day Watch*, and also *Attraction* (about an alien spaceship that crash-lands in Moscow), but it is hard to talk about the big flow of SF movies and TV-shows, nor about original and high-quality new projects.

ESSF: Concerning post–Soviet SF, can you tell us something about Dmitry Gluhovsky, Boris Georgiev, Ruslan Galeev, Vitaly Sertakov, and Ruslan Melnikov? How is their brand of science fiction different than the Soviet generation of authors?

This name set seems rather random to me. The only star here is Dmitry Gluhovsky, who was glorified by the *Metro-2033* post-apocalyptic franchise—it became a very commercially successful setting involving a dozen authors and was translated into dozens of languages. This is a grand and very successful project but does not have much to do with SF qualitatively. In his recent books, Glukhovsky, again, is trying to get out of a "fantastic ghetto" and join to the mainstream authors.

The rest of the writers on your list, in my opinion, are visible mostly to their not too numerous fans.

The most successful authors who are now associated with the SF-concept are Sergey Lukyanenko (the *Night Watch* series and a few dozen novels and inter-author projects) and Vadim Panov (the urban fantasy cycle *Mystery City* and the cyberpunk-series *Enclaves*), who, in fact, during 20 years have localized standard Western commercial SpecF and fantasy. There is almost no need to talk about the scientific aspect, literary perfection, or originality of such books. Books of pulp-fiction writers like Roman Zlotnikov and Sergey Tarmashev come out comparable and even in large print runs. These authors certainly differ radically from the best Soviet SF-writers, as they write a great deal (preferring a series format) and not very well, and generally do not hold to humanistic principles, but also use the standard commercial trash figure of a strong person in the scenery of gloomy non-stop action.

The duo of the authors who write under the pen name Henry Lion Oldie uses a more original style of highly intellectual fantasy with a rich mythological background.

ESSF: Are Ruslan Galeev and Ruslan Melnikov Muslims?

I don't know, but I doubt it. Ruslan is not a Muslim name; the main Russian writer Alexander Pushkin invented it based on the name of the hero of the Russian remake of the Persian epic "Shahnameh" (Rustam—Arslan—Eruslan—Ruslan). The combination of this name with the Tatar surname usually means that the guy's mother is Russian; the combination of this name with the Russian surname usually means nothing. Galeev—Tatar surname, Melnikov—Russian.

I'm not sure that several other SF-writers with Muslim names consider themselves to be Islamic. Among them is Robert Ibatullin, author of the brightest in recent years hard SF-novel *The Rose and the Worm*, and two authors of female mystical novels: Aliya Yakubova and Albina Nuri, as well as a writer hiding—I mean all of those persons (Ibatullin, Yakubova, Nuri, Al-Atomi) aren't Muslims—under a pen name Berkem Al-Atomi ("Berkem" in Tatar—"Nobody").

The prominent Russian novelist Ildar Abuzyarov, as well as the scientist and writer Professor Renat Bekkin, are obvious Muslims—but the SpecF-element in their books is not dominant. Dmitry Akhtyamov, who took the name Muslim (his official pen name is Muslim Dmitry Akhtyamov) writes absolutely pro–Muslim books, but unfortunately these books are written poorly and ineptly.

ESSF: Is religion a theme in post–Soviet SF? Not just Islam for Muslim authors, but religion in general? Spiritualism and environmentalism certainly seem to have been central themes in the work of Medvedev and Gansovsky.

Islam now and then becomes an object of interest for non–Muslim writers. First of all, of course, in anti–Muslim novels, where the followers of Islam act as terrorists or occupiers. In a positive or neutral way, Muslim realities are used in fantasy or adventure novels about the Eastern Middle Ages. At the same time, there are at least three novels about modern Russia being saved from troubles and enemies by turning to Islam: *Option I* written by Vladimir Mikhailov, who was a well-known SF-author from the Soviet era; *Maskava Mecca* by a large modern novelist Andrei Volos; and *The Rage* by Yuri Nikitin, who has become a living symbol of the prolific author of low-quality military SpecF and fantasy a long time ago.

An illustrative case is associated with the literary prize "Islamic Breakthrough," which was supposed to support pro–Muslim literature. At the first ceremony in 2007, it was awarded to several inconspicuous non–Muslim authors. At this point, the story of the prize was over.

Attempts to promote the concepts of "Muslim literature," "Christian literature," etc., are perceived by most non-committed Russian readers as a deliberately low-quality act of proselytism. I also believe that faith is an intimate thing which nourishes a soul, like blood nourishes the body. When the body is bleeding, the blood instantly loses its vital properties and turns into sticky goo, stinking of copper. Similarly, the faith in the fresh air instantly deteriorates and no longer raises a person; quite the opposite. Therefore, I do not like missionaries, including those who pretend to be writers. Fortunately, in literature, such pretenses are exposed by the text itself, usually on the first page.

ESSF: Is the dialogue of religions and cultural coexistence a concern for Russian authors, not least Muslim authors?

The level of xenophobia and stereotyped thinking in Russian society had become alarming years ago, but, fortunately, the dialogue is still not a problem for most educated and cultured people. The problem is that truly educated, cultured, and empathic people can become an unimportant minority.

ESSF: Is there anything you would like to ask us here at the Egyptian Society for Science Fiction in this regard? Policies you would like us to enact?

Of course, I would definitely like to be convinced of the possibility of the existence of fiction, which at the same time can be scientific, Muslim, and interesting. I really hope to get this chance.

ESSF: To close off, what are your future plans? And are you optimistic about the future of SF penned by Muslim authors?

I am a cautious optimist: I hope for the best; I am preparing for the worst. My immediate plans are connected with the writing of a realistic novel about the modern family, as well as an ethnographic fantasy. I still fight with the desire to write a big, natural, hard

SF-novel, but I hope someday to rise to the possibility of creating such an epic. If at the same time I'll be able to find myself in the good company of Muslim brothers and sisters, I will be happy as well.

الله أعلم (only God knows).

Works Cited

Le Carré, John. (1977). *The Honourable Schoolboy*. New York: Alfred A. Knopf.
"Planeta Bur." (3 May 2020). From *Wikipedia, the free encyclopedia*. https://en.wikipedia.org/wiki/Planeta_Bur.
"Polygon." (1977). *Youtube*. https://youtu.be/zccOrkEaEPI.

Hamid Ismailov on the Remnants of Central Asian Fantasy and Science Fiction

Egyptian Society for Science Fiction

Give a man a car of his own and he leaves humility and common sense behind him in the garage.

—John le Carré (2002: 73)

Strange department, this.
 Their motto was, "The comprehension of Infinity requires infinite time." I didn't argue with that, but then they derived an unexpected conclusion from it: "Therefore work or not, it's all the same." In the interests of not increasing the entropy of the universe, they did not work. At least the majority of them.

—Arkady and Boris Strugatsky (1966: 69)

ESSF: You are the most widely published Uzbek author in the world, and it's an honor to be interviewing you for our book. Please introduce yourself, education, upbringing, career choices. How many languages you speak, and how did you end up in the UK working with the BBC?

I was born in a very religious family; my ancestors were religious figures, either Khodjahs from my mother's side or Sayyids and Khodjahs from my father's side. I was brought up by these very religious people. I met my great-grandfather and great-grandmother. It was quite a traditional family. Because of their faith, a part of the family was killed by the Stalinist repressions. My paternal grandfather was killed in 1938. Also, my maternal grandfather was killed during the Stalinist purges. So, I was brought up mostly by the women of my family, who were also well-educated and well-versed in Islam and in traditional culture. The role of women in passing the traditional culture, to all of us, was enormous because we were brought up mostly by women. My grannies used to tell me stories of 1001 Nights, Uzbek epic stories which were fantastically rich and extremely, extremely elaborate. So, from my childhood, I was embraced with the traditional culture and traditional storytelling. ·

Then my mother died quite early, when I was 12 years old, and I was left with my granny in a traditional family. Then I studied in a Soviet manner, in a way. All my education was in the Soviet time. It was a secular education, not religious, in other fields of life. It

Mr. Hamid Ismailov (right) was our honoured guest in Nasr City (Cairo governorate), during a surprise visit to Egypt. This picture was taken on 16th October 2018 at the ESSF headquarters. He is being greeted by Dr. Hosam Elzembely, director of the ESSF (author photograph).

was well-established and also, for free. So, I graduated from different departments of different universities. I studied biology, I studied law, I studied management. Everything was free of charge. You were able and free to study as much as you wanted, so I studied languages as well. In our family we spoke several languages from early childhood. Most of my family spoke Uzbek. Part spoke Persian. And many spoke Arabic as well because of religious instruction, and quite generally Uzbek is influenced by Arabic. All the abstract words are in Arabic. Russian was there too, and Kyrgyz, Tartar, many languages. Therefore, it was easy for me to study different languages as I grew up, including the European languages.

I became a writer, little by little. When I was 30 years old, I was accepted by the Union of Soviet Writers. I was one of the youngest in the Union. My poetry and writing was not so much Soviet as it "should" be on account of my upbringing—my writing was too *decadent*—therefore I decided to translate classics into Russian and Uzbek instead and was accepted into the Union as a translator.

As for how I ended up in England and working for the BBC, well, during Perestroika I began my own writing, and it was not liked by the authorities of Uzbekistan. Uzbekistan had become independent at that time. My writing was seen as being too honest for them, subversive. They began to file a case against me, especially when I began to work with the BBC making a film about the return to Islamic values in Central Asia, in Uzbekistan, in the Ferghana Valley, searching for traditional roots. I was forced to leave the country under threat of arrest, for three months at first. It has stretched to 27 years now, of me not being able to return to my country. And my work is still banned in Uzbekistan, as well as my name.

ESSF: What are your most internationally acclaimed novels, and which stories are you most proud of personally?

Writing is like giving birth to your children, in a way, so therefore it is very difficult to say I love the youngest child, the eldest child, or my first novel, latest novel. All of them, they are different periods of my life, different interests, aspirations. Therefore, I can't choose between my works.

Luckily, I was fortunate to be translated, unlike other authors from Central Asia. Six novels of mine have been translated into English, and all of them have a certain acclaim. Different occasions, different manners, but all quite widely acclaimed. Different people like different books, of course. Some love *The Railway*, published in 2006; some love longer short stories like "The Dead Lake," voted best read by readers of *The Guardian* and the *Independent*. So, it varies.

ESSF: Your novel The Language of the Bees: A Tale of Hayy ibn Yakzan, *why Hayy ibn Yaqzan? Many consider Ibn Tufail's philosophical story to be one of the earliest examples of science fiction, certainly in Muslim history. What themes do you explore in your many writings and what attracted you to sci-fi specifically?*

And was Hayy *one of those internationally acclaimed novels?*

Unfortunately, it has not been published in English yet (Tilted Axis Press plans to publish it in September 2019), but, funny enough, the Uzbek version of it was published in France. The publishers in France were brave enough to understand to publish it in Uzbek, on the basis of the synopsis I wrote for them in French. They loved it and wanted to make a present out of it to the Uzbek people. It was distributed in Uzbekistan by the offices of the Soros Foundation. Until their offices were shut! Not on account of this distribution, though I cannot say for sure that my book did not play any role in this shutdown.

As to why I wrote the novel, you ask about the choice of Ibn Tufail. Well, the original story was penned by Ibn Sina, my compatriot. A Central Asian from Bukhara, in Afshana near Bukhara. That was my tribute to Abu Ali Ibn Sina, my countrymen and one of the most famous Muslim figures in the West, known as Avicenna. Apart from being a great medical doctor and healer, he was a poet, a philosopher, an excellent philosopher and an excellent writer who wrote Hayy ibn Yaqzan. Then Hayy was taken by Ibn Tufail and many others. To me, the story was a tribute to Ibn Sina. What isn't widely known about him is that in his work as a healer, he searched for the Elixir of Life.

According to legend, his students were not up to the task and didn't follow his instructions and screwed up the fabrication of the elixir of eternal life. In my story, however, his students do follow his instructions and basically, he appears in different moments of history as a "stranger." He appears, for instance, in the Tulip Epoch in Ottoman history; he appears in Japan during the time of geishas and samurais. He appears in Rome at the time of Medici and Savonarola, the geniuses like Leonardo and Botticelli and their works of art. And he appears in Nazi Germany. He travels the world during all the high and low points of human history over the past ten centuries. According to legend, he is now in America, in prison, where they store the UFOs, in Hanger 51, and being experimented on!

So, my protagonist, he goes in search of the Elixir, in search of Avicenna, and he in effect becomes Hayy ibn Yaqzan, travelling west, travelling east. While searching for Ibn Sina, he discovers his own identity, ego, his own essence. That is the parable of Hayy ibn Yaqzan in my novel.

Prisoner name: Ibn Sina
DOB: around 980 A.D
Crime : Immortal

You will notice he has a black eye, from being questioned, and the background in Arabic is from an Ibn Sina manuscript (courtesy of the artist, Ammar Al-Gamal).

ESSF: Is the protagonist you, being forced to travel the world in exile?

Not entirely. It is a much broader novel than that, and I am a character in the novel itself. A *minor* character. The protagonist is much wider and much cleverer than me.

ESSF: People have made comparisons between Hayy ibn Yaqzan to Robinson Crusoe. Are you aware of this and do you have opinions of your own?

Yes, I heard this comparison, though it seems to me that Hayy is about the spiritual quest, whereas Robinson is more about physical survival. That made me search for the lost philosophical work of Avicenna called *Hikmatul Mashriqiyn* (Oriental wisdom or enlightenment wisdom), because apparently it was non-peripatetic, a more illuminating kind of philosophy, which grew up out of his Muslim belief.

The inner space interests me as much as the outer space. Even when I studied biology, I studied neuro-biology!

ESSF: Do you find writing science fiction and fantasy easier or more liberating than regular fiction?

Fiction, any fiction, is much, much better, tells the truth, than any reportage. I discovered this when I was allowed to go to the most notorious prisons of Uzbekistan to report from there. What I discovered is that direct journalistic reportage does not give any understanding of the place. What I learned, for instance, was that people inside this prison, even though it was the most notorious prison in the country, were *safer* than people outside it.

In prison, at least, you had a roof over your head, at least you had three square meals a day, you had torture, you had routines in your life. Whereas outside of this prison, people were thrown out to survive. The prison was in Barsa-Kelmes—the place of no return.

There is a novel, *Soul*, by Russian writer Andrei Platonov, a semi-fantastical story, based on his experiences there, in the 1930s in the early days of the Soviet Union. It's one of the best novels of the 20th century, and it happens exactly there. You can't describe that in a direct reportage. But when you write fiction, even science fiction, you can give the stereoscopic, multi-faceted vision to this reality. Multi-layered vision. Then you can cope with the many sides of the story. Therefore, writing science fiction, fiction, is much more liberating than a straight dealing with the reality.

ESSF: *In that case, a question we were hesitating to ask—do you* miss *it, the Soviet Union?*

Well, the problem is … it is best to tell you metaphorically. My wife went to a memorial of a friend of ours, who had died recently; this was in Berlin. The friend we knew 25 years ago, who lived close to us. At the memorial, there were many pictures on display, and everyone was crying. My wife said afterwards that people were crying not so much for the dearly departed person as crying for themselves, for their lost youth, shown in those pictures.

In those pictures they were young and beautiful, and nowadays, naturally, they were all old and sulky, with another 25, 30 years on their shoulders, so the same with the Soviet Union. Of course, no person chooses what kind of system he is going to live in. Nobody chooses to live in, be born in a totalitarian system like the Soviet Union. But, nonetheless, all my youth, all my first discoveries, my experiences, my first love, all of this was in the Soviet Union. So, how can I not miss it? With age you start to separate what were the "isms," what was the totalitarian side to this society and what was your youth, your life. But, at the time, it was impossible to separate yourself from the times you were living in, your own metaphysical and existential life from the time and space you were obliged to live in.

You can't separate, to follow the Russian saying, the meat and flies buzzing around the meat. As it was said: The fly and the person who tries to capture the fly are the same!

ESSF: *The Soviet Union, it seems, invested a tremendous amount in its people, which is why it had all these great writers. Therefore, it's a great shame the country is gone.*

I will tell you what the deal with all these writers was. You know that the Soviet Union was an ideological state. Marxism was about changing the world; Leninism, however changed it to something completely different. They failed to change the world around them, so they started to change the words around them. They started to rename everything. If you look at the history of the Soviet Union, every single city, every single street, was renamed. They changed the names rather than the world. Therefore, they understood the force of words, a kind of mystical power they had never recognized, but they came to realize the power of suggestion, the power of propaganda, of hypnosis. That is why they came to understand the power of the writers. It was Stalin who said that the writers were the engineers of the human souls.

Therefore, they gave everything to the writers, in order to corrupt them. As a member of the Union of Soviet Writers, I benefited everything. For example, in summer, we used to go, all my extended family, to the best resorts in the country. Every line of poem was paid one ruble, when one dollar was 69 kopeks. They paid you for every line of your poetry one and a half dollars. Can you imagine that? If you wrote a long poem, for instance, on Lenin, say 5,000 lines, in one poem you can earn $7,500. That was why they cared about writers, because it was an empire based on words, on propaganda, rather on the reality and the economics.

ESSF: The two Central Asian SF authors, Xodjiakbar Shaykhov from Uzbekistan and Begenas Sartov from Kirgizia. Were they the first to write science fiction in Central Asia? What were their most distinguished works and what prompted them to try their hand at SF?

Yes, they were. The first to write proper science fiction, they came with scientific background; they were very pure in their commitment to science in their writings. Science fiction, at the time, was very popular. The Strugatsky brothers, Efremov, plus of course Isaac Asimov and Ray Bradbury, who were translated at that time.

Their writings, Shaykhov and Sartov, were in the traditional school of science fiction. They were writing by reading all these books about a scientific future. And the times were like that, Gagarin and the cosmonauts and spaceships, and therefore they were the first two to jump on the trend, and in their languages, one in Uzbek, one in Kirgiz.

ESSF: Did you know them personally?

I knew very well Xodjiakbar Shaykhov. In fact, he was my mentor, because he recommended me to the Union of Soviet Writers. I liked him very much because he was unlike any other writer at the time. This was at the time of Brezhnev, so to be a writer you had to be "engaged," who had to have written about Lenin, about the communist party, about the workers. But he was writing about what he wanted; he was much freer in his spirit than any other writer at the time, the writers around me.

I myself, I found my niche in translation, translating classics from Persian and Uzbek. One particular work I loved, "Beauty and the Heart," was a wonderful Sufi poem, a story with two parents. The father is Reason and the mother is Love, and they give birth to a boy, Fouad, who is Heart. When the boy reaches 16, his mother presents him with a book, and in it he learns of the elixir of life, which comes from the lips of Passion, of Love. He then falls ill and wants to find this elixir, but his mother says to send his slave instead, Nazar, or "sight." The slave follows the lights and goes to the world.

Once again, it is like Hayy ibn Yaqzan, a parable of the microcosm being the macrocosm. He visits the city of Wealth, Wellbeing, Curiosity, etc. … all the other cities that represent the different human capacities, and struggles with the Passion. I had to translate 15,000 lines from Uzbek into Russian, that's how I specialized myself, translating this wondrous literature that is so modern, more modern in fact than post-modern literature.

Shaykhov, he was completely different. He was the proper science fiction writer. That's how we met and liked each other. Both of us were free from the consensual games that writers played at the time.

ESSF: The poem, it sounds like the Epic of Gilgamesh?

Yes, it is, in a way, but more detailed. And very, very elaborate, because Nazar travels through every human capacity. Reasoning, wit, and ultimately, he does find the elixir of life on the lips of Passion, and everything unites in the end.

ESSF: Can you give us a few names of works by Shaykhov to get a feel for the subject-matter and breadth of his writings?

His works: *The Seventh Sir* (1972), *The Mysterious Stars* (1976), "Renee's Mystery" (1977; Russian 1988), "On that unusual day" (1985), "The Brilliance of the Diamond" (1988), and "Demonstration on the Orbit" (1988).

ESSF: Can you tell us a little about Sartov's When the Edelweiss Flowers Flourish *(1969), practically his only SF work to be published in English?*

I didn't know him. I learned about him here in London because one of my friends wanted to publish his book. It was published by Hertfordshire Press, and I read it.

The main character, Melis, meets at the crossroad of the world, Selim; the names are in reverse of each other. And it's about their relationship, and the symbol of Edelweiss, which sorts out all their problems. It's partly science fiction but is also partly Kirgiz folklore, because Kirgiz literature has epics. You have the Manas epic, which is the longest epic of the humankind. It is nearly 2 million verses, and it's bigger than any other epic in the world. Forty times bigger than the Iliad and Odyssey, and therefore Kirgiz writers are very lucky to use all this wealth in their writings. He did the same, because Edelweiss is a flower that grows in the mountains there and has great symbolic power. It is the talisman of love; it is also a healing flower.

ESSF: We can say that, growing up in a fantastical atmosphere, of literature, it helps with science fiction and can be incorporated into the SF and produce something very distinct.

Yes, yes. In the Soviet era, science fiction flourished. It was the way to tell what you want, in a parable. At the same time, science fiction was translated extensively—Asimov, Bradbury, H.G. Wells. They were translated for children.

ESSF: For children, you say?

Yes. It must be understood that it wasn't seen as subversive literature. It was considered as *distractive* literature—literature that "distracted" you from contemporary problems of daily life. So, it was widely promoted. A whole series of books, fantastic books, published by different publishing houses.

ESSF: Was Philip K. Dick ever translated, or Harlan Ellison; the more "subversive" science fiction authors?

No, they were not translated at all.

ESSF: What texts did you grew up with, and were there any SF texts among them?

The 1001 Nights, as I said, told to me by my granny. But, when I was 12, she fell ill, and I had to read her the stories of that book. Over and over again. I hated to do this. I wanted to read Wells or Verne. She insisted. Reading everything, all these volumes, three, four, or five times, to the point that I learnt many of these stories by heart. But, after growing up, I realized the value of the experience. I look back nostalgically to these days. Now, wherever I go, I take these stories with me. The book, to read!

Because, you know, we own *The 1001 Nights* in a way. The stories are happening in Arab lands, in Baghdad, in Damascus, but they are told by Sheherezade to the ruler of Samarkand Shahriyar. So therefore, we do own them.

ESSF: Is fantasy a rival to modernist literature, or a partner to SF?

Unfortunately, nowadays, I can't see anyone writing science fiction. Anyone of stature, whom I know as an established writer in the field of sci-fi either, in Uzbekistan and elsewhere. People are writing parables, once again stories inspired by Muslim literature, Sufi parables, but I can't witness any development of SF in Central Asia.

It is tragic.

ESSF: Tragic, but it's recognizable, unfortunately.

It is, it is, because people are searching for their identity now. The Soviet identity is lost. The space program was part of our identity, the Soviet part. The Soviets were doing all this stuff. It was forgotten, forcefully forgotten. All the propaganda and ideology now, works toward the past. Though they want to sterilize this past, make it less Islamic, more Sufi. Sufi *without* Islam, let us say!

There are parables. For example, if a person writes about freedom, he writes a novella about the wind. How the wind is free to blow here or there, and the whole novella is about wind. An empty novella basically, hollow and full of wind. It is unfortunate, but that is a natural stage of development because the public pressure leads them there, the consensual wisdom, in search of their lost identity.

ESSF: Here is a related question. Uzbeks, do they consider themselves to be Turks or Persians?

They consider themselves Turks, but there is something there. During the previous administration, there was a strong, strong opposition to this concept, that we are Turks. President Karimov *hired* academics to argue that we are not Turks, that we are a separate identity, a much bigger identity than Turkish identity. Nowadays they are playing more Turkish. Under the current president, we are now part of the Union of Turkic people, once again, politically. Therefore, ideologically, they are building their relationship with Turkey.

But, at the same time, Uzbekistan is at the crossroads of Turkish people, where they mix with the Persian tribes. Our language, while Turkish, is heavily Persianized, whereas the Tajik language, which is Persian of Central Asia, is heavily Turkised. A mixed culture. I myself can see that our culture, Uzbek culture, is partly Turkish, partly Persian, partly Arabic. Unlike Turkey which has purified the language, we are left with three words for any one thing: Turkish, Persian, and Arabic. Three versions. With Arabic version we can call the sun "shams" in Arabic and also use the Persian word "oftob," and the Turkish word "kun" or "quyosh." The synonyms are there. We can use all this wealth of languages, although stylistically they are a bit different. If you are using Arabic, it is a bit high brow. If Persian, it is a bit poetic, romantic. If you are using an Uzbek word, it is down to earth. There are sorts of registers for using different words. We also use Arabic words that Arabs don't use so much nowadays, like "alahida."

ESSF: On the topic of language, is it true that Asimov, Isaac Asimov, originally was pronounced (عظیموف)?

Yes. I think so. I think his ancestry was from Bukharian Jews. They apparently moved, then he "became" Isaac *Asimov.*

ESSF: That's a chapter of his history, his personality, most Westerners don't know.

Yes. I never dealt with it myself, but there are claims that he is one of us!

ESSF: The two great Soviet SF writers, Sever Gansovsky and Yuri Medvedev, are surprisingly pro-religious in their stories. Was that odd in the Communist period?

Yes. It was funny, paradoxically funny, because religion was considered by the Marxist definition to be opium for people. But, nonetheless, Soviets used *sci-fi* as opium for people. They used it purposefully to distract people from the problems of the daily life, ordinary life. It was taking a huge part of the book industry. Basically, half of the books published were sci-fi books, and half of the books translated were sci-fi books.

Therefore, what I am discovering, and you might find this interesting, is that the best of the post-modern Russian authors of today—I was thinking about the tradition they come from. I found it and was perplexed by this. Re-reading old Soviet SF of Boris and Arkady Strugatsky—those two great Soviet SF writers—I came to realize that the iconic authors of contemporary Russian post modern literature, like Pelevin or Sorokin, come out of the writings of the Strugatskys!

They are much, much more influenced by Soviet science fiction of the Strugatsky tradition than they are by Solzhenitsyn and other well-known names, like Bulgakov or Pasternak with his *Doctor Zhivago*.

So sci-fi played an *immense* role in forming the post-modern literature of contemporary Russia.

For some examples of what a wonderful resource the Strugatskys are, there are their novels *Trioka* (1968) and *It is Very Difficult to be a God* (1964). In *Troika* you have three people who determine the fate of a planet; the whole population's life is in their hands, about the Stalinist times. Just three people. In *It is Very Difficult to be a God*, you have a Russian spy who plays a god for the people on a planet, which is really about colonial attitudes of Russia in Africa and other places in developing world where the Soviets had influence. Both very well written novels, very funny, and perfect for modern authors to draw on.

ESSF: So, would you say that science fiction, not being labeled subversive literature, afforded Soviet authors a degree of freedom to critique their country, socially and politically?

Yes definitely. The Strugatsky brothers are the classical case.

ESSF: Abdullajon (1991) is an Uzbek sci-fi comedy movie and made after the fall of the Soviet Union. Locally produced SF movies are almost unheard of here in the Arab world. Would it be fair to say that the Central Asians are way ahead of us?

Not really. The movie, while a sensation at the time, was a one-off movie. And it was not real sci-fi. SF for satiric ends, a humorous movie.

But I'll tell you where this tradition comes from, this humorous tradition. It was a defense mechanism. In every totalitarian regime, people are surviving, trying to find protective mechanisms. Totalitarian regimes distort reality to a painful state. Painful and "insane" state. Either you have to commit suicide, if you're in a totalitarian system, or you have to do something painful, like being exiled or becoming schizophrenic, and so on and so forth. So how do normal people protect themselves? Either through laughter or through games, and that was the case with the Soviet Union. The Soviet Union turned everything into an anecdote, into a joke. All the popular jokes are about the politicians, about Brezhnev, about the Communist party, about Stalin. They were laughing at them, privately. That was the way to survive: not taking it seriously. If you did, you would kill yourself or end up in a mental asylum or in exile or in prison.

Therefore, in Uzbekistan in the 1960s, a genre developed known as Lof, which means "hyperbole."[1] (It is not a Turkish word, maybe Arabic, maybe Persian). So, our satiric magazine in Uzbekistan, every issue was publishing dozens of these Lofs. For example, one man says to another, "Last week I was fishing and I caught a fish that was so big that it didn't fit into the lorry." The other man says, "That fish was the child of my fish which I caught, because the picture of *that* fish didn't fit into the lorry!"

So, this genre developed immensely during the Soviet times as a protective mechanism, because everything, the propaganda, was about how well society was developing, while the reality was completely different. So basically, it was repeating the propaganda but in an ironic, sarcastic way. So *Abdullajon* comes from this tradition of telling Lofs. The jokes show the funny side of life, of modern rural life in Uzbekistan, how far it is from Spielberg, how far is from Hollywood, from E.T., and so on and so forth, rather than a sci-fi film.

Soviet science fiction cinema was very well-developed, in contrast. Andrei Tarkovsky famously adapted *Solaris* to the big screen from Stanisław Lem's novel of an intelligent ocean on an alien planet that gives people what they desire. *Solaris*, of course, has been made and remade, even in the West with George Clooney.

Tarkovsky also made *Stalker* (1979) about an alien zone on Earth, restricted and forbidden by the government, again where wishes are granted. Which is similar in a way to this new movie, *Annihilation* (2018), with Natalie Portman.

There is one more science fiction movie made in Central Asia I can think of—*Parizod* (узбекфильм, 2012), about an alien bride and based on the novella by Erkin A'zam.

ESSF: Tell us something about your novel A Poet and Bin-Laden? *Was this on account of 9/11?*

I dealt with the Islamic movement of Uzbekistan and the radicalization of the youth from the very beginning. What I discovered, as an observer, a researcher, was that the authorities had played a certain part in creating the Islamic movement of Uzbekistan. The Islamic movements were originally under the National Front of Uzbekistan, under the secular, democratic opposition, and they were listening to them, during Perestroika, under Gorbachev. Then President Karimov, when Uzbekistan became independent, decided to crush the secular opposition, and by doing this he moved everyone, the National Front and democratic movement, into the mosques, the only place where you could talk freely. He kicked many people out of the country, many writers like myself, and the youngsters moved to the mosques. Not all were religious—many were secular—then the authorities started to crush the mosques. So many young people fled to the mountains, joined the Tajik religious opposition, for a time, then Afghan political opposition, the Taliban. And then bin Laden became one of their leaders.

It was stage by stage, the more they moved, the more persecuted, the more radicalized. In one incident, they were dealing in drugs from the Afghan side of the border, and the security forces were distributing on the other side, playing the same game!

So, the authorities in a way were the authors of this radicalism, like bin Ladenism itself. We know the Americans initially created them against the Soviets, so the same essentially happened in Uzbekistan. That's why I wanted to write the book, since this process was now repeating itself in the West. The book was a case study, basically, of how radical movements are created, how they take over, etc., because we've seen the same with the radical Bolsheviks, and what Lenin writes about radicalizing the Bolsheviks.

All of them, all are of the same nature. Look at it this way: they are fighting the Americans. If you take out the Americans, they will fight the local government. If you take out the local government from the equation, they will start to fight the other party in the some movement. If you take out the party, they will fight in the street. Ultimately, they will fight their brothers and sisters. Radicalism is of the same nature. They want an enemy, basically, to fight against. And their enemy is a shifting enemy.

That was the influence that made me write *A Poet and Bin-Laden*, to show it. It is a novel, but based on the documents. It is so accurate in fact, too documented for its own good, since the fictional character in the novel was then easily identified by the security services!

ESSF: Are there any cultural connections between SF and fantasy in Central Asia and in the Republic of Turkey? Have you heard of Bilimkurgu Kulübü, the main sci-fi club in Turkey?

Not personally. I try to keep myself up to speed with the literary movement in Turkey, but sadly I am not aware enough of the sci-fi movement in Turkey.

ESSF: Living in the United Kingdom, does it affect your style of writing? Does your work as a journalist have any influence on you as a writer?

Some writers are repeating all their lives what they've once discovered. They create and follow their own brand. They write in a certain manner. For me, every book comes with its own style, tone, set up, everything completely different than other books.

To illustrate, my experience with my novel *Underground*. I was writing very quickly, the first 50 pages all in one go. The inspiration was very strong. (*Underground* was my tribute to Moscow). Then I felt that I'd read it before. I found that I was imitating one of my older novels. So, I stopped and tore apart everything, start rewriting, until I got completely different tone and rhythm and language, everything different.

That being said, writing in different languages, I have different palettes at my disposal, a different number of colors in my palette in Uzbek and Russian. Sometimes it interferes and doesn't serve me well. I find I am describing something too closely, in too much detail, in a way that is too beautiful and picturesque. In English, I have fewer colors in my palette, and so I am thinking more about what I'm going to say rather than how I'm going to say it.

Different languages demand different skills; otherwise style comes with the particular work.

Twenty-four years of working with the BBC influenced my approach to the style. In journalism, you are cutting everything to [a] three-minute story; you are becoming very economical.

I have to say that journalism is, up to a point, precision. It helped to crystallize my thinking. But, you have to understand that with literature, you are not after crystal clarity. It is a game; it's a challenge. It's not about the brevity and precision of your message.

ESSF: Political freedom in the West, does it help you write or are restrictions useful? How does the environment impact your writing?

Political freedom in the West helps a great deal. In their homelands, writers are forced to play certain games, certain consensual games, aesthetic games. There is this public pressure to be a certain kind of writer. The people, they listen to the radio, watch television; they are in the process of creating an environment where something is required, where something is not required, something is saluted, hated. Outside pressures force them to write in a certain required manner.

Here I feel no pressure, apart from my aesthetic, ethical, or philosophical aspirations, cultural aspirations. Therefore, I am free. I write. There is the danger of not being relevant to my readers in Uzbekistan, that's true, but it is also a chance that you cannot pass up, being free. To kick the empty space.

The case of Ibn Sina and Al-Farabi, their example, gives me some strength.

ESSF: What advice would you give young authors, Arabs and Muslims? As someone who has extensive experience with the transition to democracy and then back to authoritarianism.

My advice to any writing person is, is like the heavy weight lifters, try to lift to the maximum weight you are trained. Not more. Make 100 percent of yourself, instead of wearing twice as big clothes, in an effort to be more majestic. Try to fit into your natural clothes, your natural weight. Be yourself basically.

The same applies in a political sense, in a cultural sense. To be absolutely brutally honest, I'm a believer, and I think sometimes that it is not my decision and my heroism that made me escape the traps of authoritarianism, because many people are falling into those traps. At least try to be yourself in the situation when you are facing these traps.

ESSF: Are you planning to write any more science fiction any time soon?

I am working on a five-part Russian novel, about so-called Russian soul. It is very much imaginary thing with lots of might-have-beens, what-ifs, subjunctive tenses. Still not decided whether it is pure science fiction. We will see. But I will say this: sci-fi that looks at the past has got the same rights as sci-fi that looks at the future.

Future and past are so interchangeable and interconnected, they flow into another. Our past is an unpredictable as our future.

ESSF: It's interesting that you say that. One of our contributors, an Arab SF author, explained that his entry point into science fiction is qasas Qurani [Quranic stories] because these stories are not about the past at all; they are about lessons for the future. Would you agree with that statement?

Absolutely! The whole idea of the future, I'm looking at the future from a certain manner. For example, 20 years ago I had in front of me several routes, possibilities. When I am looking at my past from that *future*, today, my path is singular. *Something* made me choose that path.

The future always seems to give you so many opportunities, thousands of them, but when you look at your potential future from the point of the "happened" future, the present-day world, you find that there was only really one path in front of you after all. When you come to this point in time, you see that your path to this future was a singular one. That is my interpretation of the future.

ESSF: A final question. What stories do you read your children, and do any of them have inclinations towards writing science fiction themselves?

My son was born in London and therefore his childhood coincided with Harry Potter boom. In fact, everyone called him "Harry Potter." So, my hands were free in that sense; the whole Potter hype went through him due to the books, films, merchandise.

Hamid Ismailov's daughter is just as creative as her father. This is her illustration for *Hayy Ibn Yakzan* (courtesy of the artist, Rano Ismailova).

I didn't play any role apart from buying all Potter stuff and keeping the pace with every new turn and twist in this saga. So, one day all that consumed magic could turn him into a sci-fi writer. Why not?

Editor's Note

Since this interview was conducted, Hamid Ismailov's novel *Of Strangers and Bees: A Hayy Ibn Yakzan Tale* has been published in English and translated by Shelley Fairweather-Vega.

Note

1. http://www.translatos.com/en/uz-en/.

Works Cited

Le Carré, John. (2002). *Call for the Dead*. New York: Simon & Schuster.
Strugatsky, Arkady, and Boris Strugatsky. (1966). *Monday Begins on Saturday*. DAW Books, INC. Translated from the Russian by Leonid Renen, 1977, eBook, https://www.docdroid.net/7slkoaH/monday-begins-on-saturday-arkady-and-boris-strugatsky-pdf.

Perceiving Afghanistan

Abdulwakil Sulamal on Realism,
Translation, and Fantastical Literature[1]

Egyptian Society for Science Fiction

"But I really am like a hallucination. Look at my profile in the moonlight,"
said Behemoth. The cat moved into a shaft of moonlight and was going to
say something else, but was told to shut up and only said:
"All right, all right, I'll be quiet. I'll be a silent hallucination."
— Mikhail Bulgakov, *The Master and Margarita* (1967: 148)

ESSF: First of all, let us thank you for providing us with several of your short stories as well as bio links and interviews. You are a prolific and versatile author and one who is able to get his voice, and the voice of his country, across to an international audience. You have every right to be proud of your writing, and we are proud to have you here with us in our book.

You are clearly an author bursting with energy, going from poetry to short stories to radio and television dramas before you finished school. How do you account for this creative drive? Tell us something about your childhood and your parents. Were you an only child? Aside from bedtime stories, what literature did you grow up with?

Did you have access to other languages and did you read any translated texts early in your life?

I thank you for introducing me and my work to the lovers of literature in your country. I am truly interested in your literature, history, and culture, and I am a big fan of it.

I was in my early youth when I read *Balance in Life and Literature* by Tawfik Al-Hakim and then more of his novels, dramas, and stories. Naguib Mahfouz is also my favorite Arab writer. Recently I have read one of his short story books and after that, the very interesting novel of *The Day the Leader was Killed*.

Like many other Afghan writers, I also started my writing career by writing poems for a short period of time while I was at school. I said my farewells to poetry after finishing school and started to write stories and drama because I really enjoyed listening to stories when I was a child. I was always listening to stories on the radio and watching plays at school.

ESSF: What were television and cinema like when you were growing up? Did radio exert an influence on you as a child?

As a child I lived in poverty. My father was an ordinary shopkeeper and illiterate. I had three sisters and four brothers. We lived in a small, two bedroom rented house. At that time, we were not the only ones who were poor; most Afghans were living in a poverty. In 1978 when I was in the ninth grade, television programs were started in Afghanistan but were limited to Kabul only. Whenever I was going to Kabul for visiting relatives, my biggest enjoyment was to watch TV, and I considered those who lived in Kabul lucky to have a TV. I was the only one from my family who was going to school; my sisters were not allowed to go to school, and afterward I made sure that my younger brother attended school.

I was constantly listening to all the radio series and dramas and was very interested to listen to all radio programs. At the time there was only one newspaper in our city, which I would always buy and read.

Sometimes I was giving my poems to be published in the newspaper. I was in sixth grade when for the first time my poem was published in the newspaper, and I was in tenth grade when I wrote my story "Fire of Revenge" for a radio story series which had gone on-air for three nights. In addition to my mother tongue (Pashto), I have also read some Dari translated literary works. The Pashto language did not have proper international writers nor any translation from any other languages. Therefore, I was obliged to read the works of international writers in Dari language which were published in Iran, but now fortunately we have good writers

Myths are universal the world round, the very language of the soul. Afghanistan now has its version of *The Picture of Dorian Gray*, with a twist (courtesy of the artist, Ammar Al-Gamal).

amongst Pashto speakers, and also we have more and more translated works from other languages. As I said before, TV came to Afghanistan not long ago.

From the day television came to our country, the civil war had also begun. But cinema was the only entertainment in the years when there was no television. Almost every big city had cinema, and they were showing only Indian films, but sometimes there were shows of American or Iranian films. Lots of my peers were going to cinema with or without parents' permission, but I was deprived of the cinema. And my father never allowed me · to see movies in the cinemas. However, many young people learned Indian language from watching cinema. But I was satisfying my thirst for art and literature on radio programs.

ESSF: Are you married and do you have children? Are your children thinking of following in your literary footsteps?

Yes, I am married and I have a son; his name is Tasal. Tasal is 15 years old. He likes films and stories. He is a good story teller and is very talented in acting. It is hard to say that he will follow my footsteps, but if he does, I believe he will be a great writer, and this is my wish too.

ESSF: A great many authors in Egypt, whether in science fiction or mainstream fiction, are medical doctors or journalists, a career path and education chosen for them by their parents. Writing came to them later on as a hobby or a passion.

Is this why you pursued your higher education in military affairs in the Soviet Union instead of going into writing fulltime? Do many Afghani writers have to pursue careers outside of literature?

I think it is true that parents often choose career paths for their children, but in my case, it is a bit different. Ever since my childhood, I was in love with literature, theater, and cinema, and if I had a choice, I would definitely choose one of the above. Unfortunately, as soon as I graduated from school, on the last day of school, I was taken to the army base and was forced to join the army. After a year in the army, they offered me a chance for higher military studies in Soviet Union. I agreed to it reluctantly; I thought after five years of my studies abroad when I am back, the war will end. But unfortunately, when I finished my studies, the situation was even worse. Although I was serving in the army, all my attention and energies were focused on writing.

ESSF: While in the Soviet Union, did you befriend any Soviet authors, whether Russians or Muslims? And what kind of literature did you read—the classics of Russian literature, or their myths and fairy tales, or Soviet science fiction?

I didn't have any writer friends there, but I read Russian writers' works with love and interest.

In my course, we had a specific subject that included international literature in addition to Russian and Eastern European literature. I liked Russian classical literature. To this day I am still reading Leo Tolstoy, Dostoyevsky, Pushkin, Lermontov, Goncharov, Sholokhov, and Genghis Attenborough. My favorite of all is Dostoyevsky, and I cannot compare him with any other writer. To be honest, I have not read any Soviet Union or current Russian Federation science fiction story or novel.

ESSF: Was Soviet literature ever popular in Afghanistan, including Soviet science fiction? Are authors like Alexey Tolstoy, Alexander Belyaev, Ivan Efremov, Vladimir Obruchev, Yevgeny Zamyatin, and Mikhail Bulgakov known to authors and intellectuals like yourself?

Without a doubt, Afghan writers are more familiar with Russian writers compared to other world writers because Russians themselves translated their popular literature into Pashto and Dari languages. There are also Afghan translators who translated Russian literature into Pashto language. The invasion of Afghanistan by Soviet Union and also that it is a country neighboring Afghanistan made a big impact on Afghans to familiarize with Russian literature. Afghan writers are more familiar with the classic Russian literature and writers, but those writers like Boris Pasternak and Vladimir Nabokov are less known to Afghans.

ESSF: Was the literary and cultural atmosphere better in any way during the Communist period? And what challenges and dilemmas do authors and artists face today following the reunification of the country and fall of the Taliban?

Although our literature at that era, you say Communist, was not in a good state, the freedoms of writers were limited, the works of writers were censored, the artworks and literature were under the supervision of the government, but on the other hand, work was also done for the progress and growth of our literature.

We had writers' and artists' associations that were supported financially by the government. The government not only paid the cost of publishing the works of writers, they also paid writers for their work and give them praises.

The growth of our national literature and art was the crucial part of the government's cultural strategy.

Although nowadays the number of our authors has increased compared to the past and every year hundreds of books and articles are published, some of the world's good literature is also translated. But unfortunately, there are still obstacles to the growth and development of our literature.

The current government does not support and encourage writers and poets. The writers are no longer paid for their materials; authors publish their work at their own expense and distribute it for free.

There is no authors' association like before. In the recent years, if there have been some events organized for authors, it has been supported by foreign, non-government organizations such as the Goethe Institute and the British Council, but in the past few years they also stopped their help and support.

ESSF: You have been described as an author in exile and are currently residing in the United Kingdom, and before then the Slovak republic. Have you been barred from returning to Afghanistan?

Did you witness the Soviet occupation and the civil war that came afterwards and with that, the rise of the Taliban and bin Laden? And how did you end up in Slovakia?

I went to Slovakia first and in 2007 arrived in London. I live here now. Although it has been long since I left my country, I am still in contact with my country and my people. Every year I go to Afghanistan; I publish my books there and have an active part in various literary gatherings and meetings. If the civil war ends and the peace is restored, then I would like to return to my country.

Yes, I have witnessed the civil war and Soviet invasion. The painful memories of this great tragedy still remain in my mind and are active in some of my stories such as "Closed Knot" and "Dolay."

I was not in the country during Taliban rule, but I always monitored the situation in the country, and I heard lots of stories about everything those days. I have also written many stories about it.

After the Taliban, I am still monitoring the situation and development in my country, and I am reflecting it in my stories. The "Fifty Million" and "The Slingshot Hit" are the examples of this.

ESSF: The stories you have given us, including "Bed of Thorns," "Fifty Million," "The Wedding Night," "Modern Woman," and "At Gun Point" are all in the realist genre, but they have a satirical and almost surreal feel to them: people shot in the face, people getting their heads chopped off without any effort, and other unpleasantries. A great many of your stories are also about women, and often told from a woman's perspective.

Is it fair to say that Afghani authors feel that it is their responsibility to talk about these real-world concerns more than anything else?

On this point I will not agree with you; my stories do not have one concept. I write in many different formats. My stories often have humor in them, but if you think about it, it will also make you cry too.

Yes, a lot of my stories are about women. At the moment, I might be the only Afghan author who has published two short story books about the sad stories of women, and my third book is ready for publishing.

I consider it my mission and responsibility, as we do not have many women writers, and on the other hand, women writers are not comfortable and often shy to write about those points which are covered in my stories. I believe that writing, making films and theater about women's problems and issues are the historic responsibility of every Afghan writer.

Because Afghan women alongside Afghan men not only take the burden of the ongoing war on their shoulders, but also endure the sin of being a woman in the man-dominated society of Afghanistan. My biggest inspiration to write women's stories was your country's famous author and women's rights activist Dr. Nawal El-Saadawi's writings, especially *The Hidden Face of Eve*. I read this book three times; it made a huge impact on me and inspired me to write women's stories.

ESSF: What would you say are the advantages that come with writing fantastical literature, including science fiction?

Certainly, our literature should develop and move forward parallel to the world's literature and should have different genres. The experience of different formats of literary text is contributing to the enrichment of our literature, but unfortunately in Afghanistan, there is still no diversity of literary forms, and many authors are still attached to realism.

However, there are a number of authors like Akbar Kargar, Emal Pasarlaye, Ajmal Pasarlaye, Hayatulah Zhouand, Nasir Ahmad Ahmadi, and few others who are writing in different formats. Although science fiction is not common in Pashto literature, there are authors like Nasir Ahmad Ahmadi, Zaheer Mahboob, and Emal Pasaralye who wrote science fiction books.

ESSF: Your story "Faces and Thoughts" has a wealthy tyrant living in a mansion with many luxury cars and servants at his beck and call. But he is such an arrogant and evil person, he can't believe that he has turned old and ugly after all these years and was handsome only when he was a young boy, poor and without ambition. When he tears up the portrait made of him when he was a young man, his own face turns ugly until he eventually dies from shock.

Was this scenario influenced in anyway by Oscar Wilde's "The Portrait of Dorian Grey"? And from where do you draw your inspiration?

To be honest, before I wrote this story I did not read Quentin Anderson's "The Imperial Self," Edgar Allan Poe's "The Oval Portrait" or Oscar Wilde's "The Picture of Dorian Gray."

But the odd thing is that [with] my book, commentators think that my story is influenced by these novels. This is a surrealistic, moral story, and its inspiration is from the Afghan warlords. They were ordinary citizens, and war made them strong and mighty people, with whom nobody could compete. Now many such warlords are a legacy of our country.

This story has a great message that power, strength, and wealth can make a man famous and strong, but in addition to this, it can also emphasize the psychological and physical fall of a man. However, if men want to save themselves, they should always return to their simple and real life. But human experience proves that once a man tastes the life of wealth and power, he becomes addicted and finds it extremely difficult to go back to his previous life. This is because of the fear of facing humiliation.

ESSF: Is truth relative in Afghanistan? It certainly seems that way in "The Photograph Trade." Is that what encourages you to write such surrealist satirical snapshots of the country?

This is an image of today's Afghanistan, and it also creates a historic image of the way people felt about pictures. This is a story of the declination of values in our war-dominated country. This story shows that in the society in which values have been obliterated, even ordinary people can be turned into the high status, or sometimes that a person can easily be out of the picture whether he dies or not. Sometimes people who want to use others to their own purposes will flatter and carry them on their shoulders like babies and celebrate them like their idols. But once they fulfill their purposes, they will drop them off their shoulders and break the idols they celebrated.

ESSF: In your Samovar-Strange Horizon *interview (12 April 2017), you say that Pashto short stories are not even a century old and that most Pashto authors write in the realist genre. Do Afghanis read each other's stories from the different language and ethnic groups in the country?*

Yes, it is true that Pashto short stories are not even a century old, and at a time in which the world's literature is experiencing different schools, Afghan writers are still attached to the realist genre. Although there are not many Afghan writers, in the last three decades, there are numbers of authors such as Akbar Kargar, Aubaidulah Mahak, Anwar Wafa Samandar, Ajmal Psarlaey, and Hayatullah Zhound who write in different international literary formats. Afghans, especially Pashtun writers, read the other Afghan writers such as Hazara, Tajik, Uzbik, and other languages with great interest. All Pashtun writers know Dari, but unfortunately Tajik, Hazara, Uzbek, and other Afghans do not read Pashtu writings because most of them do not know Pashtu. Although Pashtu is the formal language of Afghanistan and more than fifty percent of Afghanistan's residents are Pashtuns, other Afghan nations do not know this (Pashtu) language. Fortunately, every literate Pashtun knows Dari language. Dari is [a] very important language for Afghans as it is a formal language of Iran, and Iranians are more advanced than us in translating the world's finest literary works, which is always beneficial for us.

ESSF: In Nigeria, English is very popular as a literary language, not only because it gives their authors an international audience, but also because it allows them to speak to each other with one single language. The same holds true, of course, in India.

Is this a problem in Afghanistan as well, given the diversity of languages and cultures?

Yes, this is a serious problem in our country. We have two formal languages—Pashtu and Dari—although Pashtu is a formal and national language of Afghanistan and Pashtuns are the majority of our country. But Dari language is more widely recognized as Afghanistan's formal language than Pashtu language. Although Pashtuns play a significant role in the formation of modern Afghanistan and Afghan rulers and kings have been mostly Pashtuns, Pashtu has only recently been recognized as a formal language; it has not even been seventy years.

Even now Dari language is more commonly used in most government offices, and although significant numbers of Pashtuns live in Kabul, most educational institutions use Dari language.

ESSF: You also say that Akbar Kargar, Ajmal Pasarlai, and Emal Pasarlaye are no longer following realism. Could you give us an idea of what genres they are writing in? Have they, or any other authors, tried writing science fiction?

Also, are there Afghani time-travel stories, traditional or modern?

Although these authors did not say their farewells to realism, they have written many stories in different forms and subjects. Now they are writing in the internationally recognized forms and genres like Magical Realism, Surrealism and History, etc.

Unfortunately, we do not have science fiction authors. Only few authors such as Mahbobullah Mahboob, Nasir Ahmad Ahmadi, Stana Mirzaheer, and Emal Pasarlaye each wrote only one story in this form. As far as I know, there are no time travel stories written by any Afghan writer.

ESSF: Is Harry Potter popular in Afghanistan? Do Afghani authors read Gabriel García Márquez and Paulo Coelho?

Harry Potter in not translated to Pashto language, and not many people are familiar with it. But García Márquez is known to many authors, and Paulo Coelho's work is translated to Pashtu language. His *Alchemist* novel is translated to Pashtu language by my close friend and translator of my stories Rashed Khatak, who is also a good poet and author.

ESSF: You also draw a contrast between the protagonist in "Thoughts and Faces" and the old kings of Afghanistan, people who weren't democratically elected but who nonetheless knew their limits and were never as powerful, corrupt, and arrogant as this man. (It also seems that only kings had their pictures taken in old Afghanistan, as you say in "The Photograph Trade").

Is nostalgia a theme in your stories, and is the central character in this story a commissar from the Communist period or a warlord from the civil war era?

As I said earlier, mentioning of photos has two angles to it: history and belief. There was a time that religious scholars even reacted to the pictures of the king on the bank notes, and they declared it against the sharia. But when they have been paid with the same notes, the very same day, they announced it permissible. This creates an image of our underdeveloped society. When Taliban were ruling Afghanistan, photos and cameras were forbidden, and also the import of items which had women and other photos displayed on it were banned. Therefore, when the Taliban regime collapsed, there was no photos of Mulla Omar, and up to this date, none has been found by any media company.

The main character of my story is not a communist nor a warlord, but he understands the circumstances of the current situation and wants to benefit from it. He knows he is not doing the right thing, but because the corruption is widespread and accepted, it motivates him to undermine any kind of values and morals.

ESSF: "Thoughts and Faces" is also available in audio as a Pashto Podcast. This is a new technology to many of us here in the Middle East. What advantages does a podcast hold, in your opinion?

Is storytelling in Afghanistan more geared to oral transmission or to a "readership"?

I have many audio stories, and many have been on air from a number of radio stations such as Radio Azadi, Radio Mashal, Radio BBC, and Radio Afghanistan. In my opinion, audio stories are even more effective and interesting; also it is loved by more and more listeners.

Fortunately, presenting audio stories are more common in our country. In Afghanistan it is especially very good as a significant number of Afghans are still illiterate, and the distribution of printed work is also very difficult, almost impossible.

ESSF: One of our contributors, Dr. Taleb Omran, also started out in broadcasting. Would you say that radio is a good medium to change people's tastes when it comes to fantastical literature compared to realism?

Yes, I believe radio is better than reading. Not only do you enjoy to listen to the story, but a talented storyteller and good music make it more interesting. If a story is presented in a contemporary form such as magical realism and surrealism, the desire of listening to stories will be even stronger.

ESSF: Of all the languages your works have been translated in, which would you say is closest to the original written Pashto text? Do you take translation into account while writing in your native tongue?

We ask because of your story "Fifty Million," where you have an old-time Jihadi, Jandad, from the time of the Soviet occupation who is cooperating with the Americans who will pay $50 million to the person who captures or kills bin Laden. Jandad sacrifices his own brother, Zardad, because he looks like bin Laden. There is also Jandad's comrade in arms, Guldad.

Is it a coincidence that their names rhyme? And what do their names mean?

To be honest, I do not like the translation of my stories, and many of my friends who read the translation of my stories told me, "The pleasantness which is your stories cannot be found in the translation." The very good translation of my stories is done by my good friend Rashed Khatak into Urdu language, and many people like it. These names do not have any special meaning. These are common Pashtu names, and it also part of our culture that many families choose names with a slight difference for their children.

ESSF: That's a habit in Egypt too. The late king Farouk, like his father before him, liked the letter "F" and chose names beginning with "F" for his daughters. One more language question then.

Have your stories ever been translated into Arabic, Turkish, Farsi, or Mandarin?

My stories are translated into five languages. It will be an honor for me if my stories are translated to Arabic language, especially the stories I have written about women.

ESSF: In your interview you describe yourself as a "South Asian." Do Afghanis also consider themselves to be Central Asians?

We not only share borders with these countries, we also share cultural and historical heritage with them. In addition to Pashtuns, in our country also live other nations such as Tajiks, Uzbeks, and Turkmens. We have mixed folkloric stories. The great poets of this area such as Ferdowsi, Hafiz, Mulana Jalaluldin Jami, Khoshal Khtak, Saadi, and many others are popular all over this region, and everyone is reading their poems with love. We warm our parties with Mula Nasrudin's jokes, and we enlighten our nights with reading *The Thousand and One Nights.*

ESSF: One of our contributors, Hamid Ismailov, is from Uzbekistan. He grew up reading The 1001 Nights, *along with Central Asian epics. You mention it yourself. Is it widely read in your country, and do Afghani authors and readers have access to the stories and literary traditions of neighboring countries like Uzbekistan, Pakistan, or Iran?*

Yes, we are familiar with the literary and folkloric heritage of each other. Sometimes the questions are raised as to which country belongs this heritage. Each country of the region considers it their own heritage.

ESSF: Hamid Ismailov wrote a documentary novel entitled A Poet and bin Laden. *Have you read this novel or anything by Mr. Ismailov, who is also an author in exile?*

I have read the Pashto translation of Ismailov's novel. I really liked his novel, and also I have learned so much about Islamic extremists in Uzbekistan and Tajikistan. There is also much to be learned about the formation of current governments. It is mostly a political novel.

ESSF: Would you say there is a growing international market for literature from places like Central Asia and Afghanistan and the Arab world? And are labels like Central Asian and South Asian useful when it comes to marketability and winning critical attention?

Although Afghan literature is not as developed as yours and other neighboring countries like Turkey, if these literary works are examined closely, you will discover some of the finest collections of stories that readers would love, and it will have a good market.

I think that, despite [the fact that] there are many fantastic European or American novels and short stories, it will still be different from our culture and will not be easily understood and enjoyed. But if we write good novels and stories in our own Islamic countries, it will be more known to us and liked by everyone. Exchanging our literary work will not only be beneficial for the market, it will also contribute towards the development of our literature.

Not only we should translate our work into each other's languages, we should also organize joint festivals and literary events. There are some events organized by the South Asian Writers community. They will host two to three events every year. I have also been invited twice to these events. If such meetings are held in Egypt and Turkey, it will be very effective and will have a positive impact on the writers of the Islamic countries.

This will bring the authors closer; they will be able to share their experiences and learn from each other. One of the reasons for the internationalization and popularity of Europe's literature, especially for Russia, France and Germany, is that the authors are always in touch. They know each other, and they translate each other's work into their own languages.

Dostoevsky wrote his popular novel *The Gambler* in Germany. Although these countries have been involved in bloody wars in the nineteenth and twentieth centuries with each other, it never affected authors' relationships.

ESSF: In your story "The Solution" (2017), you have a corrupt government minister strong-arming a woman into marrying him, becoming his second wife, in exchange for helping rescue her father who has just been arrested by the security police. A similar scenario unfolds in "Modern Woman." Is it correct to assume that the first story takes place during the Communist period and the second afterwards?

Are the problems of corruption, dictatorship, and "moral hypocrisy" essentially the same in both periods?

Yes, both stories are the two sides of historical facts. It is a picture of corruption in the governments of those periods.

ESSF: You don't give any dates in your stories. It's hard to tell if something is happening in the 1970s or at the time of Taliban or after. Is this deliberate on your part? And is it a common practice in Afghani literature?

I do not think it is necessary that every story or novel should have dates. If stories have dates in them, it will be factorized and documented. It will be in realistic form. From my perspective, the artistic picture of a story should encourage a reader to think during which period of time the events happened.

ESSF: We have two contributors who are the only SF authors in their respective countries—Libya and Mauritania. Are you thinking of moving into science fiction yourself? And from your extensive experience with writing, drama, and publishing, what advice would you give a prospective Afghani sci-fi author?

Few of our writers like Stana Mir Zaheer, Emal Pasarlaye and Mehbobulah Khan wrote few short stories in this form, and also last year Nasir Ahmad Ahmadi published his science fiction novel. But as a whole, we do not have specific science fiction authors. I never thought about it. In addition to special collection of women's stories, I might write some historical stories and also some about musicians.

ESSF: Finally, please tell us about your future plans?

I have two more story collections ready to be published, and when these books are published, I would like to write a theatrical drama. I am also working on a film scenario.

Note

1. Special thanks to Mrs. Palwasha Latif. This interview was conducted before the US withdrawal under President Trump and the subsequent return of the Taliban regime.

Works Cited

Bulgakov, Mikhail. (1967). *The Master and Margarita*. London: Collins and Harvill Press, eBook. Translated from the Russian by Michael Glenny.

"INTERVIEW: ABDUL WAKIL SULAMAL." (12 April 2017). *Samovar*. http://samovar.strangehorizons.com/2017/04/12/interview-abdul-wakil-sulamal/.

Falling in Love with Science Fiction

From Turkey to Tomorrow

MÜFIT ÖZDEŞ

Every one of us is, in the cosmic perspective, precious. If a human disagrees with you, let him live. In a hundred billion galaxies, you will not find another.

—Carl Sagan (1985: 283)

Early Years

I was born in Ankara on May 15, 1943, but grew up and went to school in Istanbul. I would return to Ankara after many years to study electrical engineering and, later, econometrics at Middle East Technical University

I was only 11 years old in 1954 when I first read Heinlein's *Puppet Masters* in my own native tongue. All I had been reading until then had been children's books designed to instill ethical behavior, good manners, and philanthropy in the reader, as well as such literature as would not be considered "harmful" for children. Turkish literature at that time had been an arid desert as far as science fiction was concerned, and I had read no science fiction except for a few scientific romances by Jules Verne.

Heinlein's novel, as well as a handful of recently translated Golden Age classics (from the 1950s), impacted me like a hammer and transformed me into a science fiction fan. However, no more science fiction novels were printed after about ten books because the Turkish readership seemed to be uninterested in the genre. Fortunately, I began to learn English the next year, opening the doors of a vast science fiction universe billions of light years across.

Swept Up by the Times

I was 25 when the revolutionary tide of 1968 hit Turkey. And of course, I was a part of it just like millions of other young people who were disgusted with the pettiness of those who ruled the world. We were trying to form ties for international solidarity against imperialism, so a group of us went to Jordan to join and learn from the Palestinian struggle. We received training and took part in several raids across the Jordan river. When we returned to Turkey, however, we were immediately arrested.

But I am digressing. After my release from prison, a military intervention occurred in Turkey in 1971. I was on the wanted list. So, I had to discontinue my education and flee abroad to Lebanon where I lived in a *mukhayam* (refugee camp) and joined the militia. I was later granted political asylum in Norway. I read science fiction, of course, every chance that I could get, though few such opportunities occurred at the time.

When I returned to Turkey in 1975, I married the love of my life, the fruits of which would be a boy and a girl. My wife and I set up a language service called *Cagdas Translation House* because I had no college degree but was quite proficient in English. This service would later turn into a successful business, though we liquidated it in 2001 when I had to retire due to illness.

There was another military takeover in 1980. I wrote several articles criticizing the government but no one would print them, and neither the internet nor social media existed at the time. I thought I might get around this censorship by writing a science fiction story in 1984 called "Krrcysk" about an insect-like alien being that took control of a boy by invading his nervous system. The boy would go to military school and rise in the military ranks so that he could engineer an army coup and harvest Turkey for meat. But this could not be printed either at the time. That was the first science fiction story that I wrote.

Metis—which is a respectable publishing house—included "Krrcysk" in a selection of antimilitarist science fiction stories in 1991, all of which were translations of stories by masters of the genre, except for mine. Later—in 1996—the same publishing house printed 15 of my stories in a book titled *Son Tiryaki* (*The Last Smoker*). The story that gave the name to the book is about a smoker who flees to a planet in the Alpha Centaurus system rather than give up smoking in a future social welfare Dystopia on Earth. Another popular story in the book is "İki Kısa Bir Uzun" ("Twice Short and Once Long") which is about a very jealous man who falls in love with the co-inventor of a seemingly unsuccessful teleportation system. Another one called "Nostura'nın Öyküsü" ("Nostra's Tale") describes the plight of a deserter from a Capellan space fleet that is secretly waging a climate war against Earth. One story that I particularly like is "Nergisler Kan Kizili" ("Narcissi are Blood Red") about a woman from an alternate reality trapped on this world when the magic box on her mirror breaks down. The book also contains a novelette called *Yeralti Insanlari* (*Subterranean People*) that tells about people living a utopic life ten million years in the future in an underground city below what used to be Istanbul while a hellish climate reigns above, making the surface uninhabitable. But … are they really people?

Another book that I wrote is a novella-sized fantastic fable called *Kimin Agrir O Bagirir* (*Whoever Ails Is the One Who Wails*), which is a satirical love story of the present age as might be narrated by a yarn spinner ten thousand year hence.

I received the prestigious science fiction award of *TBD* (Turkish Cybernetics Society) in 2001 for a short story called "Firar" ("Escape") about a mechanical zookeeper and an infant androgyne in the far future when *Homo Sapiens* has been replaced by *Homo Androgynus*, which has been replaced by *Homo Mechanicus* in turn. This was later printed in an anthology of TBD award-winning tales.

I have contributed science fiction stories and articles to science fiction fanzines and magazines such as *Nostromo* and *Davetsiz Misafir* as well as a number of mainstream magazines such as *Radikal 2, Adali, Esquire,* and *Penthouse.* I also contribute to the monthly online magazine *Yerli Bilimkurgu Yükseliyor* (*Local SF Rising*).

Science fiction is all about broadening horizons and standing outside oneself (courtesy of the artist, Ammar Al-Gamal).

I am a member of Bilimkurgu Kulübü, which is open to writers and fans alike. I am also a member of *FABISAD* (Fantasy and Science Fiction Arts Association), which brings together writers, illustrators, editors, and publishers in science fiction, fantasy, and horror.

Science fiction has always been one of the two important things in my life. College studies and science fiction, falling in love and science fiction, revolution and science fiction … and so forth.

When you are a science fiction fan, limits and boundaries disappear, and wars make no more sense than opposing ant armies quibbling over an anthill. It is only humanity that counts, and maybe not even that, because there are probably countless intelligent alien races throughout the galaxy.

I feel that reading or writing science fiction estranges you from the world and endows you with a state of mind where you have a clear perception of the world precisely because you are estranged from it. I often compare mainstream writers to worms crawling inside an apple, whereas a science fiction writer would be like a worm that dares to break through the surface and observe the apple from an outside perspective as well. This is probably why mainstream readers and writers are inclined to resent the science fiction community.

The Changing Profiles of Turkish SF

Science fiction was shunned until recent years by literary circles in Turkey who associated the genre with trashy works and considered it as escape literature. Remind them of *1984* or *Brave New World* for example, and they would exclaim, "But *that* is not science fiction!" Nevertheless, the genre is now living its golden age in Turkey, which makes me proud to be one of the pioneers. There are now about a hundred writers with books published under their names and hundreds of others contributing to web sites and online magazines.

Most science fiction fans are young people from 15 to 30 years old, and most writers are in the 30- to 50-year bracket. The profile of the science fiction community in Turkey is quite positivistic and secular. Islamic identity and religious faith have never been a key issue in Turkish science fiction, except for the late Ali Nar and a few of his disciples. In fact, the community includes a large number of deists or atheists. Those who are believers mostly adhere loosely to the teachings of Baha al-Din Naqshband and his followers like most Turks do, combined with the tariqs of Sheikh Bedr al-Din, Jalal al-Din al-Rumi, and other sufi leaders. Although I am not a follower of these Sufi orders, the ideas of Hallaj al-Mansur certainly had a great influence on me.

Nationalism does play a role, however, for a minor fraction of the Turkish science fiction community. But these colleagues, including the authors of *Metal Fırtına*—who are also Bilimkurgu Kulübü members—are far removed from xenophobia or chauvinism. The book is obviously inspired by the Iraq war and reflects national anger at the U.S. backing of the Zionist occupation in Palestine as well as resentment of America's pushy attitudes. The intended message is that we are not totally helpless against this imperialist Goliath.

I certainly hope that Turkish science fiction writers will be more concerned in the future with somewhat ignored issues such as climate change and gender equality.

WORK CITED

Sagan, Carl. (1985). *Cosmos*. New York: Ballantine Books.

Girlhood Dreams

An Interview with Funda Özlem Şeran on the Necessity of Turkish Sci-Fi

EGYPTIAN SOCIETY FOR SCIENCE FICTION

Science is the most reliable guide for civilization, for life, for success in the world. Searching for a guide other than science means carelessness, ignorance and heresy.

Religion is an important institution. A nation without religion cannot survive. Yet it is also very important to note that religion is a link between Allah and the individual believer. The brokerage of the pious cannot be permitted. Those who use religion for their own benefit are detestable; it is against just such people that we have fought and will continue to fight. Know that whatever conforms to reason, logic, and the interests and needs of our people conforms equally to Islam. If our religion did not conform to reason and logic, it would not be the perfect religion, the final religion.

—Mustafa Kemal Atatürk

ESSF: Please tell us something about yourself. What does Funda Özlem Şeran mean? It sounds very musical.

Thank you ☺ My first name was given by my aunt, and in Turkish it means "heather," which is a Mediterranean plant of some sort. But recently I found out that in Hindi, Funda means "the basic principle underlying something" which is also the etymon of fundamental ☺.

Özlem is "longing or yearning," and as for Şeran, there are still debates in my family. Some say that it means "according to Sharia" and some suggest that it consists of "şer-an" which can be translated as "bad or evil moment." Depends on your outlook on life I guess ☺.

ESSF: Who were your favorite authors growing up? Did you watch Star Trek *as a child? We couldn't help but notice the* Ghostbusters *T-shirt on your Facebook page.*

Yes, one of my favorite films of all time is *Ghostbusters* ☺. I'd always loved mysterious and bizarre things as a child, so shows like the *Twilight Zone, X-Files, Buffy the Vampire Slayer*, and *Xena: Warrior Princess* were my favorites. I don't remember watching *Star Trek* much, but I was a fan of the *Matrix* trilogy as an adolescent. I also read a lot of Stephen King, whom I still love very much. And I have to mention Douglas Adams' *A Hitchhiker's Guide to the Galaxy*, which had plenty of impact on my writing.

Science fiction affords Turkish women a tremendous opportunity to both empower themselves, on the superhero model, and their country as a whole (courtesy of the artist, Ammar Al-Gamal).

ESSF: What attracted you to science fiction, and how long have you been in the genre?

I think I was like 9 or 10 when I started reading Jules Verne at school. Then in my adolescence I met Arthur C. Clarke's *A Space Odyssey*, which led me to other great sci-fi writers and novels. Sometimes I couldn't really understand the scientific or mechanical aspect of the fiction, but I was and still am fascinated by the possibilities that sci-fi represents to us and our world, suggesting that other worlds and realities are possible through science and imagination. That is sadly a very foreign notion in my society, which is why the genre isn't very popular and well established in Turkey. But recent efforts have started to change that, and fortunately we'll continue to grow in the future.

ESSF: Do you write fantasy, horror, or detective fiction?

Funda Özlem Şeran in the aforementioned *Ghostbusters* outfit (author photograph).

I write horror, fantasy, and science fiction, sometimes even combining them in the same story. I've never tried detective fiction; my fantasy novel *Ecel* has some elements of it, but I really want to try writing a detective story for children someday.

ESSF: Tell us something about your target audience, as an author. Are most of your readers young or from the older generation, boys or girls?

I don't really differentiate between children, young, or older readers; to me, it's all the same as long as you have a good story worth telling. However, that is not the case when it comes to marketing. I can say I have a very wide range of readers starting from 8 [years] of age to 50 or 60. There has been a little gap between the ages of 12–18 that my publisher forces me to write, so it is among the plans ☺. As for gender, again I don't make a difference between boys or girls, men and women. But I want to be able to tell stories that empower women and especially young girls who would find hope and strength for themselves, that they don't need a hero to save them, and they can be their own savior and heroine.

ESSF: That's a very commendable goal, and we wish you the best of luck. Is there a large female readership for SF in Turkey? There isn't here, sadly, although the number of female SF authors is on the rise.

I'm afraid that's the same case in Turkey as well. When we look at the statistics, women buy and read more books than male readers; however, they are more interested in drama/romance and self-help books. So, there aren't many female readers in SF and fantasy/horror; this also affects the level of writing. Most of my colleagues are male, and women writers are so rare. But I can say that our number increases with new generations since little and young girls are being more and more drawn to the alternative genres each day.

ESSF: Where do you get your inspiration from when writing your stories?

Mostly from daily life, small details in the city like the subway or nature, and the relations between people that I find bizarre or funny. I put these things in unconventional atmospheres such as a cyberpunk plot or a horror story. It gives me room to explore new perspectives and twists. I also feed from music a lot, especially while writing. I make playlists to raise motivation. Favorite movies and books are always in the back of my mind, so that I can make references and connections.

ESSF: Do Turkish and Islamic fantasy stories and myths have any influence on your work?

Of course ☺. As a child I grew up with them, and as a writer I try to include my background and culture as much as possible. For one thing, it's what I'm used to, what I know best. And I think there are very essential and beautiful elements that are worth telling in both Turkish and Islamic culture. In my first novel *Ecel*, I tell the story of a young Turkish and Muslim girl named Ece who lives in Istanbul and slays evil djinns using special weapons with sanctified Zemzem water[1] and verses from the Quran like Nâs, Felâk, and the prayer Ayet-el Kürsi. Last year I wrote about the old shamanic rituals of ancient Turks from the Middle Asia in a horror story which was published in the anthology *Anatolian Horror Stories 3*.

ESSF: Is religion an important theme in your writings? Do you believe that science fiction can help the Muslim world advance?

In some of my works, religion is important, like *Ecel*, for example. However, I don't make it the core of my writing or try to deliver a religious or political message through stories; I think it damages the art of things. The same can be said for science fiction as well. In my sci-fi novella *Phobos* for example, I tell the story of an alien who has no notion of humanity, gender, religion, or God, and it discovers all that through classical horror books. To me, religion is like anything in the world: you can make the best of it or you can make the worst, according to your intentions. So, I don't find science and religion as opposites; I think like all aspects of life, they're interrelated and should be used for the wellbeing of humanity, not for the ill intentions or benefits of certain groups. Not just science fiction, but also science and technology that are used for progress and welfare can help the world, Muslim or otherwise.

ESSF: Have you faced any problems in science fiction as a woman? SF has always been perceived as a men's club. Is that the case in Turkey?

I think that is the case all around the world, unfortunately, whereas there are examples of Ursula Le Guin, Margaret Atwood, Octavia Butler, etc. As a thriving female writer, I always had the support and respect of my fellow male writers; I'm so grateful for that. But sometimes male readers can be prejudiced, not knowing your ability and talent as a writer but judging you for your gender. They think just because I'm a woman, I can't write about science or technology. This happened to me recently when I won the first prize in a sci-fi short story contest; people were shocked and a little resentful, but I don't really mind actually, since I've been wrestling with similar, biased views my whole life. It turns out this motivates and sharpens me more, working in my own benefit ☺.

ESSF: Are most of your books sold in paperback or as e-books? Do you have PR firms that promote books or authors in Turkey?

All of my books are sold in paperback; we have clauses in our agreements regarding e-books, but digital publishing in Turkey has not been developed. This is one of the deficits in our sector like the absence of PR firms or agents for writers. Our promotion and publicity are mostly done by ourselves or poorly by publishers, which can cause many strains on both sides. This also affects our representation abroad since there's little or no one that will take the initiative to do so.

ESSF: Metal Fırtına (Metal Storm) was written by two authors: Orkun Uçar and Burak Turna. Is intellectual collaboration like this normal in Turkey, a book with two or more authors?

It isn't very common actually or wasn't so until these two who are also my friends ☺. I remember the time they were talking about and working on the *Metal Storm*; they had a very big success which gave us all hope towards the future of young Turk writers. Later on, Orkun motivated me and my friend Burcu İkizer to write our first published piece *Anne Kız Diyalogları*, which is also a collaboration, a book about the humorous relationship between mothers and daughters. It was very fun and easy to work with a like-minded friend, and I still join that kind of project whenever I have the time and the invitation. Aside from anthologies, we have *Yüksek Doz* novella series that are very well received by the readers. However, publishers and book stores/online selling sites are not quite used to that.

ESSF: Tell us something about Bilimkurgu Kulübü (Science Fiction Club). When was it established, and what does it do? Who are the members? How is it financed?

I don't have vast knowledge about the club's history. I came to meet Bilimkurgu Kulübü quiet recently. About three or four years ago, İsmail Yamanol, one of the founding

Ursula K. Le Guin in one of her last sci-fi outings had words of praise for Turkish SF, along with Funda Özlem Şeran (courtesy Hamdi Akçay and Emre Akgün, book cover designers).

members and the head of the club, contacted me about a sci-fi anthology, which was published this winter with the last words of Ursula Le Guin (*Yeryüzü Müzesi*, or *The Earth Museum* in English). There are over 1,000 members on its Facebook page, but the core team of writers are about 10–15, I guess. Its cause and goals are very important, and the realization of these ends makes me really happy both as a writer and a sci-fi fan.

ESSF: Could you tell us something about the "Turkish Informatics Association" and "Turkish Fantasy Union"?

Turkish Fantasy Union was a short-lived alliance that included various fantasy literature societies in Turkey, I think between 2004–2010. But it was a very influential one and succeeded in promoting young and amateur writers like me, organizing story contests and festivals or panels regarding the genre.

Informatics Association of Turkey, on the other hand, is an older and more professional organization, established in 1971 with the vision of becoming a pioneer civil community to disseminate the culture of informatics [information science and computer technology] in Turkey. Today it has many members, branches, congresses, and organizations that include a SF short story contest. It's one of the most prestigious and important events of the SF society in Turkey that has been held for 20 years.

I forgot to mention Fantasy and Science Fiction Arts Association (FABİSAD) that was formed in 2011. Its members are writers, artists, publishers, editors, etc., that work for the development of fantasy, horror, and SF in Turkey. Some of them, like myself, have been associated with the SF Club as well, so their projects can interrelate sometimes.

ESSF: In Arabic countries, we're used to Turkish soap operas (e.g., Muhanad *and* Sila*) and Turkish period dramas, (*Hareem Al-Sultan *or* Muhteşem Yüzyıl *as it is properly called, and* Resurrection: Ertugrul*) and Sufi-type literature by Elif Shafak. But none of us have ever heard of Turkish science fiction. Would you say that Turkish TV producers and celebrities are not doing enough to promote this new and intriguing cultural export to the Middle Eastern market?*

You're right, even Turkish readers are not aware of the genre in Turkish literature, unfortunately. Let alone markets abroad, we can't even make sci-fi shows or films in our homeland since "this is not what the audience wants" as they say. I don't believe that, and I think if we present real good materials, the readers and audience will receive it with open arms. We just need a little bit of courage and patience; we will prevail ☺.

ESSF: Do you have TV series and movies in the sci-fi genre? Is there a market in Turkey for such productions?

In my childhood, there was a mystery show called *Sır Dosyası*, which was a bit like the *X-Files*. I loved it very much, but other than that, I can't remember one. We can't really say that there's a market for this genre, but with the rise of online networks, bolder productions are being established, so I'm hopeful.

ESSF: Is there a market for comic books and graphic novels in Turkey? It's a great way to get young people involved in sci-fi and helps build an industry of writers, artists, and illustrators. Do you have Turkish comic book superheroes like Superman or Spiderman?

Yes, there's a promising market for comics and graphic novels. We also have very talented artists that work with *Marvel* and *DC*, like Melike Acar, Diren Ayhan, and Özgür Yıldırım. One of them, Yıldıray Çınar, had a Turkish superhero called *Karabasan*, which was a short-lived but phenomenal comic book series. We also had a ten-issue comic book magazine called *Yabani* by Devrim Kunter that combined all these genres in comic book and story form; I had the chance to contribute with a few stories.

ESSF: Is there any coverage of Arabic SF in Turkey? I know for a fact that Turks are very fond of Egypt and that Turkey is now housing many Arabs. Do you also think SF can help bring Turkey and the Arab world closer together?

Yes, we're fond of Egypt as well ☺. But the coverage of sci-fi is limited to Western books and movies, sadly. We try to challenge that fact and would be eager to explore other cultures' take on the genre; I think it would bring our societies together and widen our horizons also.

ESSF: Are there any initiatives to translate Turkish SF into English, French, or Arabic?

Not really, I'm afraid. There are writers who are being translated into other languages, but SF and fantasy aren't among them. Sometimes we talk and argue about making attempts among us writers, although this isn't a writer's job; it's the publishers' or the agents'. And sadly they have been very reluctant about that.

ESSF: What are your plans for the future?

My short-term plans include the continuation of my fantasy novel series *Ecel*. Next year I want to write a children's book in horror or fantasy. There's also a project about post-apocalyptical novellas that is part of *Yüksek Doz* books; I might join them again. I plan to keep writing for both children and grown-ups as well and get published, İnşallah ☺.

ESSF: Finally, any advice for us here in the Arab world?

Imagination and communication are the key to every achievement in human history, I think, so all I can say is keep dreaming and keep in touch with us; together we can accomplish so much. And also thanks so much for this great interview, good questions, and the chance to meet with Egyptian and Arab colleagues. In solidarity! ☺

NOTE

1. This is water from the spring of Zemzem in Mecca.

The Hero in All of Us

Saqib Sadiq on Muslim SF
in the English Language Mirror

EGYPTIAN SOCIETY FOR SCIENCE FICTION

> Look at the evils of the world around you and protect yourself from them.
> Our teachers give all the wrong messages to our youth, since they take
> away the natural flare from the soul. Take it from me that all knowledge is
> useless until it is connected with your life, because the purpose of knowl-
> edge is nothing but to show you the splendors of yourself!
>
> —Muhammad Iqbal

ESSF: Tell us about yourself.

My parents are originally from Pakistan; they migrated to the U.S. in the late 70s in
the hopes of better opportunities. I myself was born in the American city of Indianapolis.
My birth was during the early 80s, so as I came of age, I was exposed to retro cartoons like
He-Man, Transformers, G.I. Joe, Thundercats, etc. I think these early influences had an effect
on my imagination. It certainly helps explain why I so easily slipped into Geek culture.

Another reason could be my inclination towards math and science. I remember
taking computer programming classes in high school (grades 9 to 12) and loving it. As
such, I chose for myself an equally geeky profession, computer science. I graduated with a
bachelor's in science in 2005 from a UK university. After gaining years of industry experience, I now do consulting for a few close clients. I also am currently teaching undergrad
students programming.

Since I am a dual national and I have family in the U.S. as well as Pakistan, I move
between the two countries quite fluidly. These days I live in Karachi, Pakistan, with my
wife. When I am not busy with family matters, I am often found nose deep in a good book,
the genre of which is usually science fiction. Thanks to Kindle and pdfs, I have a huge collection of e-books that I need to get through. Nowadays we are spoilt for choice. There is
so much content! It seems just when I finished one book, another pops up in my queue.

ESSF: How long have you been writing?

My earliest memories of storytelling are at my mother's bedside. The only catch is,
I was doing all the telling! I would regale her with tales of far off lands or how I would
become a pilot so I could take her home to see her dad. Of course, I never became a pilot
but did realize the importance of storytelling. Those early doses of encouragement kept

me going. When my mom saw that I was falling behind in my reading, she took me to the local library; we brought back an armful of children's books. I soon learned about the magic of reading and wanted more.

So, I set out on my own and discovered Roald Dahl, who introduced me to memorable characters; Bruce Coville taught me about aliens, and the Hardy Boys showed me how to craft a good mystery. Somewhere along the line, I got the idea that I could do this too, write stories that is. So, I started writing. I can remember writing at a very early age. My first story was about an android that fought crime. That was something my geeky brain could imagine fully. So, I scribbled it down in a notebook. I really got a kick out of creating that character and the world he inhabited. I guess I haven't stopped doing that! Most of my stories explore the current state of Man. Where are we going as a civilization, as a species? Are we better off now that we have A-Bombs and space stations in the sky? What have we learned and how are we passing that on to the next generation?

ESSF: What do you like about SF?

Previously I had mentioned some authors who catered to children; you can consider them a gateway drug. I soon discovered some stronger themes that have influenced my writing. Isaac Asimov's *I Robot* helped me explore humanity. I enjoyed going to the White Hart with Arthur C. Clarke. Or exterminating giant bugs in Robert Heinlein's *Starship Troopers*. Recently I discovered John Scalzi who is a disciple of Heinlein's. All of these authors tell great stories, but Mr. Clarke takes the cake.

I was able to get my hands on his acclaimed *2001: A Space Odyssey*. My first taste of his writing came from an anthology of his short stories. I really liked his writing style; he always seemed to have a dramatic plot twist in the last few lines of his short stories. So, I was eager to see how he fared in a full-length feature. I am glad to say that I was delighted. Right from the start, the story grips you. The setting is prehistoric times, and the focus

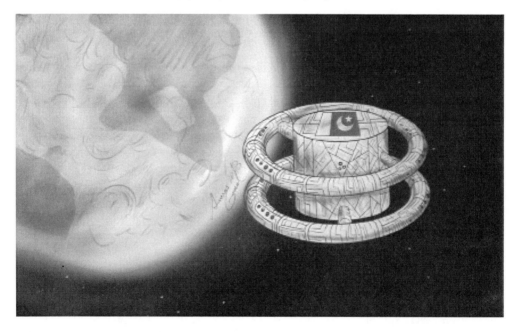

Pakistan meets the space age on the model of sci-fi classic *2001: A Space Odyssey* (courtesy of the artist, Ammar Al-Gamal).

is on a primitive tribe of man apes. Barely surviving in their caves, they have meager defenses against ruthless predators. It isn't until the unlikely arrival of a black monolith that the tide turns. Their minds scanned and enhanced, they soon devise crude weapons to defend themselves. Human nature soon takes root, and they begin to assert their authority on a rival tribe with a severed cougar head mounted on a spike. Most of the opposing foes correctly deduced that man apes now had superior arms by which to attack.

The story jumps to the future, where humans are now exploring space. With a well-established presence on the moon, they soon discover another monolith. What will these unearthly objects teach humanity now? Notice how I make scarce reference to the widely publicized Hal 9000. For me, *2001* wasn't just about a ship's AI going haywire. It was more about the spirit of discovery and reaching man's potential.

ESSF: Which subgenres are your favorites?

Military SF is my favorite sub-genre. These stories blatantly portray conflict. It requires fortitude and discipline on part of the protagonist to make it through. This is inspiring to me. I like learning about comradery and discipline. I like to get into the psyche of the fighting man. What compels someone to take arms and defend his family, his country? Or even why a mercenary would kill and die just for money. If you are interested in getting into Military SF, do check out John Steakley's *Armour*. Also, I really liked John Scalzi's *Old Man's War* series of books. I have also been meaning to read Joe Haldeman's *Forever War*.

Alien invasion stories are also interesting. If done right, humanity has to set aside its differences and fight a common enemy; think *Independence Day*. Of course, if you are a believer, you already know that we have a common enemy which we must fight constantly. I'll give you a hint; he is closer to us than our jugular vein and loves to misguide us with whispered temptations.

Dystopia is also fascinating. It is an examination of a future world that has been taken over by our greed, giving birth to a nightmare world. Think *Hunger Games*. I read all three books and loved it. It actually helped me understand how the ruling elite can become so disconnected from the suffering masses. How we can become so self-absorbed we forget to ask our neighbors and relatives if they are okay, if they have enough to eat. Our lack of empathy these days is not unlike the world described in these stories.

I myself write in this genre. If you want an example of what it is like to be living in the fictitious universe I have created, check out "Sidra's Story": https://www.smashwords.com/books/view/759507

I am particularly proud of this short story because I had to challenge myself. You see, up to now I never had a female protagonist. Writing from a female perspective was particularly hard. I had to push myself and think like a different person. I think I did a good job capturing the main protagonist's mannerisms. But of course, that is for you the reader to decide.

ESSF: Can you give an account of your personal experiences with SF as a Muslim?

I recently moved back to Pakistan, where I decided to use a popular ride sharing app. When the car pulled up, I wanted to sit up front; you have better access to the air conditioning that way. As is custom, you greet the driver and inform him of your destination. Once we were underway, he got to talking as to why he's driving a taxi these days. It was a typical story of hard times and using the driving service as a safety net. But what was different was him relating his childhood experiences, which included watching *Star Trek.*

As a child, he was mesmerized by the future. He was eager to have communicators and view screens and starships. The best part was when he reached adulthood, he didn't let the world bring him down. He continued believing, continued being optimistic. I think we as Muslims have lost this optimism; we have suffered so many failures, we feel like there is no hope in sight. But my driver was the exception; he still hung on to the vision of a hopeful future. He could relate to those far-off explorers and their mission to find strange new worlds.

Although we don't have starships just yet, we do have video communication. And although most of us might take it for granted, he knew better. He knew how far we had come and how these technologies were marvels. I couldn't agree with him more.

But what fascinated me and got me thinking was how shows like *Star Trek* and SF in general have a message of inclusion. Its themes are universal and relate to the human condition at a primordial level. I was never really sure if this held up in non–Western cultures. But now, here was proof of this phenomenon. Here was a guy halfway around the world who got it; he was not hopeless but was eagerly ready to embrace the future.

In this day and age, we are constantly being bombarded with new ideas. It takes wisdom and insight to weed out the bad ones from the good ones. As Muslims, we have a rich tradition to refer to, to help us filter the world around us. With its emphasis on seeking knowledge and unraveling the mysteries of the cosmos, SF is most certainly a good idea.

ESSF: How did you get into the field?

I got serious in my writing when I reached university. I was in the library when I came upon an article describing how asteroid mining will become practical in the years to come. The reason being that the payoff was huge enough for companies to invest in the necessary research to give us the tools to perform this type of feat.

Well, that was just so inspiring. With all the wars we are fighting over resources, our appetites still won't be satisfied. We will need to harvest the stars themselves! I couldn't wait for the research, so I started to imagine the devices for myself. Then I begin to think about who would operate this kind of machinery. How would they live? And on and on. Soon enough I was drafting my first novel.

I pitched the finished manuscript to a few publishers. All of them rejected me. One, however, got back to me with a reason for rejecting me, which was nice of them. So, I decided to self-publish. I had heard great things about Smashwords and decided to upload my manuscript as an e-book on their site. I promoted my book on social media and my website, and soon enough people began downloading the free sample; some of them even purchased the entire novel outright!

As mentioned, you can grab this novel from my Smashwords profile. It is called *Reapers of the Damned*: https://www.smashwords.com/books/view/21238

In it I take readers to a far-flung asteroid on which a mining space station has been established by the mega corp, Gemcore. Since they are extracting more than they need, strange occurrences begin happening around the station. This is all witnessed by a young miner by the name of Raza. He must ultimately decide if he wants to continue serving the corp or reclaim his soul.

ESSF: SF authors are struggling over here. They think "self-publishing" will get them recognized internationally. Any advice?

Well, it's possible to be recognized internationally. Thankfully, there are many open-minded people around the world who want to hear a balanced perspective. If you speak with an authentic voice and present your side of the story in an appealing manner, people will listen. My suggestion would be to start small. Focus on yourself first; ensure you hone your craft. Then develop a following. My experience has been that this is an organic process. It all depends on who notices you and where you hang out, either online or offline.

With regard to self-publishing, I wholeheartedly endorse this approach. I myself do so. I have had some success in this area. But if you want to study a truly successful case, take a look at Andy Weir. Here was a regular guy who had a day job as a computer programmer and was writing a sci-fi novel in his spare time (reminds me of myself!). He had a website where he would upload chapters. Once fully uploaded, people asked for an e-book. He made one, and it soon became a bestseller on Amazon. From there he got noticed by a traditional publisher who offered him a contract. He even got noticed by Hollywood, who turned his novel in to a movie starring Matt Damon. I am of course talking about *The Martian*.

ESSF: Can social media help?

Naturally Andy's rocket ride to success is exceptional. It isn't this way for everyone. Most of us will need to work hard to establish ourselves. In this regard, social media can help, especially Twitter. As I said, the readers are out there. People want to hear from you, and those people can be found on Twitter. If you have never been on Twitter, this may seem like a daunting task. But believe me, it couldn't be easier. Just use the right hashtags.

For example, if you put #MuslimShelfSpace in the search bar, you will be given a ton of resources to look through. #DiverseBookBloggers; #WeNeedDiverseBooks; #MuslimsInLit; #MuslimSquadWL are also good hashtags to skim through. When you tweet, try reaching out to the writing community. They will help you along in your journey. #amwriting; #writerslife and #WhyIWrite are great for this purpose.

ESSF: Is there a local SF industry in Pakistan, now that you're living there? Is the genre popular?

Well, I get mixed reactions. If I want to talk about science, how we are pushing to go to Mars, I get pessimistic responses because Pakistanis don't see themselves doing that. I think there needs to be a sense of optimism if you are going to be writing about something as fantastic as the universe.

Having said that, there is always an exception. Take for example this cartoon, "Teetoo and Tania Promo": *https://youtu.be/lEtOvjzAuTs*. It is an attempt at getting Pakistanis interested in SF, at least the little ones.

As far as writers go, I have been absorbing Ziauddin Sardar's YouTube videos; he isn't a SF writer but can be thought of as a Muslim Futurist: http://ziauddinsardar.com/books-1/.

ESSF: How do you think SF is relevant to Muslims?

Orientalists have always given caricatures of Arabs and Muslims to Western media. However, in recent years, the volume and ferocity has increased. Especially in Hollywood where it is given that the villain will be a Muslim. This makes it harder for us to have a dialogue with Muslim youth and curious non–Muslims. We need to share our stories, humanize ourselves. Drive the fear away; replace it with love.

We as a society can no longer remain invisible. We need more and more individuals who are media savvy. This requires good communication skills and the ability to present our case in a pleasing manner. All of these skills can be acquired by learning to tell stories. Creative writing is simply a medium to tell these stories.

No one can doubt the power of storytelling. Just look at the work being done at Marvel. Although I don't belong to the African-American community, I can appreciate the impact *Black Panther* has had. It has broken stereotypes, shown that dark-skinned people can be noble and intelligent. This was something that was lacking. It seemed every gangster and drug pusher happened to be Black. Very few positive role models were offered. We need to do the same for ourselves.

That's why I was so ecstatic when I met Saladin Ahmed at Columbia University. Its chapter of the MSA had organized an event called the Muslim Protagonist. The idea was to teach participants how to create stories with Muslim characters as the heroes/heroines. I learned from Ahmed how writing is a craft and crafting a story is similar to how an engineer designs a machine. That analogy really clicked for me and helped me to approach my writing in a more professional manner.

I also got to meet G. Willow Wilson who gave an excellent lecture on the Hero's Journey, which is a ready-made template to use when outlining your stories. Wilson was already involved with Marvel at the time thanks to the *Kamala Khan* comics, but now Ahmed has also joined the Marvel ranks too. We should all be very proud of both of them.

That's not to say other studios are not putting out great works. Teshkeel's *The 99* has made waves. It's a spin on *X-Men*, but instead of mutants, we have humans who have been endowed with supernatural abilities thanks to Noor stones. Essentially, this ensemble cast is a vehicle to impart morals to children, which have universal appeal.

Of course, we need not limit ourselves just to comics. Well-produced dramas can also have a positive impact. By now everyone has heard of the historical drama *Resurrection: Ertugrul*. I can't tell you how relevant this drama series is to our times. During the life and times of Ertugrul, the Ummah [Muslim nation] was going through a crisis. Enemies invading from all sides. It seemed the end was near. But through perseverance, hard work, and above all faith, we as a people survived.

As a sci-fi writer, I have drawn inspiration from this series. I recently tweeted how I have been binge watching and how I love the relationship between the hero and his mentor. This relationship was instrumental in guiding him on the true path. Therefore, I have given my novel's main character a mentor he can turn to when he is confused and not sure how to move forward.

But to be clear, not everything depicted in *Resurrection: Ertugrul* is historically accurate. Rather than attributing that to creative liberties, in my mind I imagine we are reliving our past in an alternate timeline. Thus, giving the series some SF creds. You may or may not agree with my theory, but it certainly works for me.

ESSF: Also, can you tell us the story of your relation with IslamScifi.com?

I had grown fascinated with Geek culture and how it intersected with Muslim culture. And so, I started curating a growing list of stories and characters on my Facebook page, the unique feature of which is stories with Muslim heroes. Essentially it was a combination of my two greatest passions: Islam and Science Fiction. After going it alone for many years, I finally stumbled across like-minded people when I came across the *Islam SciFi* blog.

I was a lurker for quite a while, admiring the work being done from afar. I never imagined I would be involved, but as fate would have it, Aurangzeb, the founder of Islam-Scifi, put out a call for volunteers. I jumped at the opportunity. I felt like I belonged here and could make a unique contribution. From what I know about bloggers, all of us have been bitten by the writing bug. We brew stories either consciously or subconsciously. When life allows it, we get a chance to type up our thoughts and unburden ourselves.

So, I sent some writing samples for review. They were screened and appeared to be a cultural fit, and before I knew it, I was in! I planned a series of articles focused on writing SF in general and ISF (Islamic Science Fiction) in particular. One piece I wrote ties into this article's theme; in it I propose an archetype for a Muslim hero.

As we know, we can't help emulate our heroes, especially children. Parents trying to raise pious children often times feel frustrated when their kids start misbehaving after watching questionable content on TV. Unplugging your cable service doesn't help because they can pick up bad ideas from school, the neighborhood, marketplace etc. So how do we get them hooked on proper role models?

Well that's where writers come in. Studying the biographies of luminaries from our past, such as scholars, just leaders, and even the Companions [of the Prophet Muhammad] can be a weighty task for a child. But as writers, we can make this research part of our process. Once we find admirable characteristics, we give those attributes to our characters. We can then have them portray noble deeds, good behavior, etc. Through our stories, not only will children be entertained, but they just might realize that there is a hero inside them!

I am planning another series of articles for the blog, the theme of which will be combating Islamophobia. This is a huge problem; not only is it causing a crisis of faith for Muslims, but it is also spreading hate and suspicion in the hearts of non–Muslims. This becomes an issue when we must interact not only on the international stage, but also on a day to day basis. I can't tell you how many times I've shocked people when I board a domestic flight in the U.S. A bearded, brown-skinned face sets their fear factor into overdrive, which doesn't help anybody.

ESSF: Does living in a Muslim country affect your writing? Were the stories you wrote in America different?

As I had mentioned earlier, the way I imagined fictitious worlds was largely influenced by my exposure to pop culture in my childhood. It was the catalyst from which I began writing my stories. We are living in an increasingly interconnected world, a global village as it's called. Therefore, kids all over are watching the same programming (I'm referring, of course, to the Cartoon Network), with a few regional shows mixed in. In this context, I don't think living in a Muslim or non-Muslim country would have an effect on my writing.

Having said that, I do believe the act of traveling and experiencing different cultures does have a positive effect. Mainly you become much more broadminded. When I was working in the U.S., one of my colleagues wondered if the places they showed on the news were real. Which was amazing, because of course they are real places, but you would never know that if you never left your country. This is also evidence of how Americans are becoming increasingly isolated from the world, but that is a separate discussion.

ESSF: Do you only write in English?

Unfortunately, yes. My schooling was in the U.S. So, I learned how to read, write, and do research in the English medium. My mother, however, had taught me how to read Urdu and of course Arabic so that I could read the Quran. But I never learned how to write in Urdu or Arabic, although learning these other languages certainly helped me think differently. My father was a fan of Urdu poetry, especially the works of Allama Iqbal. Iqbal was inspired by Rumi and often wove Islamic themes into his verses. My father would explain these poems to me, which also shaped my thinking. Unconsciously these thoughts surfaced in my writings. So much so that my English teacher noticed and pointed out how me being bilingual set me apart from the other students. No one else was thinking and writing like me.

ESSF: What can we expect next from you?

To answer that, I need to share how I think. My belief is that God has endowed you with life. He reminds us of this each and every time we wake up from a deep sleep, each time we take a breath. This revival is courtesy of him alone. It wasn't due to your family or your boss and certainly not society. So why be enslaved to them? Your energy is your birthright; only you choose how to spend it. Plan your day according to your priorities. What do YOU want to accomplish today? What others want you to accomplish should be secondary. Only in this way can we find inner peace and happiness.

However, these days people are not being taught this. Rather there is an agenda to promote worldly matters. It seems like we are nothing more than consumers. It is a life that fails to recognize the inherent nature of man, that he must have a close relation to his creator in order to sustain himself.

I want to explore this theme further. That's why I am expanding on my first novel and planned out a trilogy. Through this medium, I will take a look at a dystopic future where consumerism has run amok, so much so that our greed has given rise to mega corporations. These corporations have effectively supplanted Earth's governments and rule the masses with an iron fist, draining resources from the Earth and the heavens like a plague. Thankfully, there is a small group of resistance fighters known as the sovereigns. They must battle the mega corps or risk losing their way of life.

Works Cited

Sadiq, Saqib. "Ar-Raan." (29 July 2016). https://www.smashwords.com/books/view/654815.
Sadiq, Saqib. "Ishan." (18 July 2010). https://www.smashwords.com/books/view/19240.
Sadiq, Saqib. *Reapers of the Damned.* (10 August 2010). https://www.smashwords.com/books/view/21238.
Sadiq, Saqib. "Sidra's Story." (16 November 2017). https://www.smashwords.com/books/view/759507.

The Indian Recipe
for Good Science Fiction

Technology, Politics, and Religion

SAMI AHMAD KHAN

ESSF: You have a PhD in science fiction. What was your thesis statement?

I worked on Indian Science Fiction (written in English) at Jawaharlal Nehru University's Centre for English Studies. I focused on how extrapolations/projections/speculations (in Indian-English SF) were responses to specific historical events, and how the themes of these narratives drew attention to the contemporary material realities of a developing India. In a nutshell, after studying the socio-political aspects of select SF texts, I located how Indian English SF writers—through their narratives—reinterpreted, reworked, and addressed maladies prevalent today. For example, Shovon Chowdhury's *The Competent Authority* satirizes multiple social evils such as communalism, casteism, red-tape, corruption, xenophobia, etc. Rimi Chatterjee's *Signal Red* and Priya Sarukkai Chabria's *Generation 14* paint dystopias borne out of political/genetic/religious fundamentalism and highlight not just the suffering of individuals under repressive regimes but also how resistance to such exploitative power structures is universal and intrinsic to human nature.

ESSF: How long have you been writing?

Everyone feels and thinks, whether consciously or not. If one can think, imagine or feel it, then one wants to express it. Some sing, some dance, some paint, and some write. Although there are multiple modes available for such expressions, I write simply because the act makes me happy. It always has. I started writing stories in school itself. As a child, I remember staring at the star-studded skies for hours at a stretch. I used to squint at the distant planets in the hopes of finding any movement. My earliest SF memory is from primary school, when I read about a space battle in a Hindi comic book I got my hands on while visiting my grandmother's village during the summer vacations. It changed the way I saw the world. Suddenly the home-school-home-playground-home-school routine started looking so mundane, so insignificant to me. We're such tiny specks in the universe, *ashraful makhluqat* or not.[1] I started creating worlds in my head where life—as we didn't know it—existed. Thus began a journey which continues till today.

While I wrote a few pieces in school, my first (major) SF publication was a one-act play about time-travel I wrote in my first year of BA: it was published in *Science Reporter*,

259

India's leading science magazine brought out by the government. After a few other short stories over the next few years, my first novel *Red Jihad* came out in 2012. It was a political thriller set in India's troubled red-corridor and questioned the menace of terrorism. I kept writing SF—and on SF—since I am a researcher on this genre/mode. This led me to *Aliens in Delhi*.

A long time ago, I was driving around Raisina Hill (India's Capitol Hill) on a rather balmy evening. As the fierce sun set, traffic personnel, yellow police barricades, and security forces lined the streets in order to facilitate the top brass returning home after a hard day at work. Red-beaconed convoys slipped past me, and frenetic police whistles burrowed in my ears. I saw Rashtrapati Bhawan (President's House) and Sansad Bhawan (Parliament House) in the distance, and a web of interconnected questions immediately sprang to my mind. Why is the security beefed up like this? I got my answer in one word: terrorism. Half-jokingly, I started to ponder over threats worse than the usual terrestrial 'others'. Why don't, I asked myself, aliens visit India? What if Jadoo (the happy, helpful alien from *Koi…Mil Gaya*) landed in India one day—except this time, it wanted us all dead? What would India do to when aliens attack? *Aliens in Delhi* emerged out of such a speculative exercise, fusing SF with genre thriller. Interestingly, in much of 'western' SF, the hostile/invading alien is a thinly veiled representation of the 'menace from the Orient', that is, the geographical location I write out of, and I was curious to know who would constitute the other/alien for those who *themselves* are regarded as aliens—at least by western pulp SF.

ESSF: What drew you to science fiction specifically?

Perhaps because SF is a genre/mode that ideates, interrogates and speculates about the problematic interfaces between technology, humanity and social realities, and this becomes all the more pivotal in our times where, for example, a cell phone not only makes phone calls but can as easily incite a riot or a revolution. SF emerges as a software that recalibrates the readers' mind so as to counter fundamentalism, extremism and parochialism by portraying the existence of a plurality of voices and viewpoints, and by showcasing dystopian futures. I am intrigued by the infinite possibilities of SF. That being said, I don't just write SF to make this world a better place. Maybe that will happen later. I write it because it's *fun*. That's why pulp speaks to me the most—both as a reader and a writer. Since it's the act of writing that gives me the kicks, it's empowering to think that the ice-cream joint you visit weekly might soon have an ominous UFO poised over it. What will happen then? How would the ice-cream guy react? What would I do? What would a kid next-door do? How would the constable at the corner react? I then proceed to think along similar lines, and conjure up a narrative that is impossible, but extremely thrilling to envision!

ESSF: What kind of SF did you grow up with?

I didn't read any local SF writers while growing up, sadly. A major influence when I was in high school was popular western SF, primarily French and American. The only Indian SF I remember till my BA was Satyajit Ray's unforgettable Professor Shonku. However, I realized in post-graduation that fantastic (SF) work has already been done in Indian regional languages for over a century now. India is a country of a billion people and a thousand languages. The fault was mine—I was limited by English, the medium of instruction in school, and had unwittingly neglected other languages: a colonial hangover. It was only much later I realized that Indian SF has had a substantial creative and critical corpus, one that can be termed even richer and deeper than (present) Indian English SF. For example, Sujatha in Tamil, Jayant Narlikar in Marathi, DC Goswami in Assamese, Ray in Bangla, are just a few iconic writers who are revered across many Indian states, cultures and languages. I finally read English translations of some of them in university, and realized the SF scene in India had been thriving for a long time—it was I who was ignorant of the situation, thanks to the language barrier. Here, I must concede right away that this conversation is about Indian SF written in English, and acknowledges its limitations of not being able to engage with SF in other Indian languages. That being said, I must point out that SF in Indian English still doesn't have the same critical mass as it has in other Indian languages despite notable work in it, and that's something I want to work upon—as a writer and researcher both. Returning to your question, I am a huge fan of *Star Trek, Star Wars, Doctor Who,* and *The Hitchhiker's Guide to the Galaxy.* These were the texts that made me fall in love with SF in the first place. I respect how SF, while being full of space battles and laser guns and experiments gone wrong etc., somehow also ends up commenting on the world we live in, thereby indirectly telling us to take better care of the world around us. We've got just one planet. Fighting injustice, standing up for human rights, exploring strange new worlds to initiate peaceful contact—these are some of the themes which drive the abovementioned texts forward. Writing SF, as I earlier said, is also fun, even if politically catatonic! After all, who wouldn't want to read about evil bug eyed monsters from outer space trying to seize your popular haunts?

ESSF: Are the readers, critics and publishers in India cordial to the genre? Is writing SF a challenge?

I would say yes, writing SF is a challenge—just as reading it is, with its absent paradigms (Angenot)[2] and Subjunctivity (Delany)[3]. Many see SF as a genre imported from the "West." I don't. Indian SF has had its own history and tradition, and isn't 'new' here. As I have argued elsewhere (*Star Warriors of the Modern Raj*): the question whether SF is a recent import to India or if it has a long history of adoption and adaptation that predates its currently presumed 'westernised' avatar, ravels more strands than it unravels. To locate an unbiased evolutionary history of Indian SF, one has to be equidistant from two separate approaches. The first perceives Indian SF as a recently imported form that has started to be used by our writers of late, a form that merely imitates western SF (for example, viewing *Koi… Mil Gaya* as mere copying of *ET*). The second believes that SF has been present in India since times immemorial: it regards SF as a fairly old mode in India, one whose examples can be found in Indian classical/mythological texts (the approach that sees *brahmastras* as nuclear weapons). I differ from them both. SF may not be as old as the Indian classics, but it is also not as new; it is not a reflection of its western counterpart, nor is it a direct import from the west. Indian SF may be a relatively new form, but it is indigenous, and most scholars today regard SF to have been available in Indian articulation for some time now. Though I concede that Indian SF in English has not had the same share of critical and creative successes that SF enjoys in other regional languages. While this situation is fast changing, Indian SF in English still has a lot of uncharted space to explore. It is also true that getting an SF text (in English) out is relatively more difficult than, say, romance/mythology in these times. Constrained by prevailing market forces, publishers are often a bit reluctant about SF since they feel it will not 'sell'. Sometimes escaping the limitations imposed by market forces becomes imperative. Also, as Indians turn to yet more forms/modes of writing, SF is on the rise. Moreover, good stories always have a market (irrespective of their genre). The time is ripe for Indian SF in English getting more visibility and acceptance. This is also manifest in the rise of *Mithila Review* and *Kalpabiswa*, two important SFF magazines from India. Two more organisations dedicated to SF in India are the Indian Science Fiction Writers' Association (ISFWA) and the Indian Association for Science Fiction Studies (IASFS): both are doing stellar work. They also organize conferences, etc., on SF, and seek to popularize the writing and critical reading of SF.

ESSF: Can SF face up to fantasy?

Here I would like to use an example I often cite: it involves *Star Trek*, *Harry Potter* and *Thor*. Speculative Fiction (SpecFic) can be seen as an umbrella term for the literatures of "What if" and includes genres such as Science Fiction, Fantasy, and Mythology etc. All these genres construct alternate realities which deviate from realist narratives (hence categorized under speculative fiction, which "speculates", worlds which are not real in nature, and only their operating mechanisms make them different from each other despite having similar narratives themes and phenomena. A person might travel from point A to point B in an instant in a SpecFic text. In Fantasy, this might be due to "floo power/apparition" (*Harry Potter*), in SF this might be explained by teleportation (*Star Trek*), and in mythology this might be the result of the will of a divine being (Bifröst in *Thor*). While events remains the same (instantaneous travel between two points), the *way* they are described determine whether the text is classified as SF or F. I see them both as twins. Both SF and Fantasy can be viewed as falling under the umbrella term of Speculative Fiction, and I don't perceive them as locked in a perpetual battle of binary opposition. In fact, they meet more than they differ, as the growing SFF in the world exhibits.

ESSF: Even in the marketplace and among the critics?

Critics judge a text by its literary merit, not genre—at least that's what I'd like to believe. So yes, SF can face up to fantasy in the eyes of the critics (whether it has to is a different question since I don't think we need to see SF and F as existing at opposite poles, engaged in an antagonistic relationship). As for the marketplace, it all depends on the prevailing mood of the readership, and shaping this mood are various factors—what's being produced, how is it being marketed, what about the target audiences, what are the existing spaces for "growth," what contours the demand-supply chain, etc. Writing, especially popular writing, is being shaped not merely by the merit of the text, but by how it is deployed in the market, and to what effect. I personally feel this is precisely why SF must strive to escape the clutches of such market forces but at the same time use the market to carve a space for itself.

ESSF: How receptive is the English-language market to an Indian SF writer?

Gollancz has recently come out with two volumes of South Asian Science Fiction—the first volume has my story "15004" and the second has "Biryani Bagh". However, the market is receptive to SF but perhaps not as much as romance, mythology or other genres. Even a casual reading of Indian SpecFic writers reinforces the belief that SF isn't just a pulp form: Indian SF in English can also be layered, aesthetic, politically-conscious, and aware of the paradigms of oppression and exploitation. Many Indian writers in English use SF to highlight social evils. To cite four examples: Vandana Singh's *The Woman Who Thought She Was a Planet and Other Stories* critiques, among other things, India's patriarchy, gender violence, and regressive perspectives towards women. Mainak Dhar's

Zombiestan indicts terrorism, mindless violence and religious fundamentalism; Manjula Padmanabhan's *Escape* questions patriarchy, totalitarianism and male chauvinism; and Anil Menon's *The Beast with Nine Billion Feet* interrogates the ramifications of profit-driven, nature-bending global capitalism. In short, the kind of SF that is worthy of being canonized, and one which commands the English-language market to receive it with open arms. However, at the other end of the spectrum, Indian English SF also has pulp narratives which have no pretensions of aesthetic or political superiority and unabashedly celebrate the pulp nature of SF. Both these variants end up enriching the scope and nature of Indian English SF.

ESSF: How important is "religion" as a theme and backdrop to your writing?

It isn't for me. While I have studied how *other* Indian SF writers in English are conscious of religious paradigms in their works, I don't really ponder over the "religion vs. science" question in my creative writing. I do that in my critical writing. I have, for example, authored two research papers on religion/gods in Indian SF which are presently hosted by *Fafnir* and MOSF's *Journal of Science Fiction*; they are titled "Goddess Sita Mutates Indian Mythology into Science Fiction" and "*Gods of War Toke* While Riding a *Vimana*" respectively. In essence, this is a question that I have asked of others, but not of me, since personally, I am happy delinking my writing till now from religion, though this may change in the future.

ESSF: Would you say that this pitting of religion against science is a Western construction and not necessarily something evident in the experiences of other cultures?

I would say that Indian SF breaks away from the conception of pitting science against religion. Even the west has its own Lords of Light, a la Roger Zelazny. In Indian SF, science usually complements religion, not counters it—though there are no hard and fast rules. I'd like to mention *Joker* (2012) here as an example, a Bollywood film which features an Indian space scientist (Agastya) who seeks to locate ET life in an US lab. Agastya is forced to return to his village (Paglapur) in India because of his father's ill-health; the village itself has been forgotten by various state governments, and is plagued by scarcity of water, electricity etc. Agastya comes up with a development plan to transform his village into a tourist destination and builds crop-circles in the nearby fields. Some villagers even dress as aliens and roam in the nearby jungle to corroborate the alien story. While the deception is successful at first, it is ultimately caught, and Paglapur and Agastya face ridicule. Shorn of all hope, the villagers pray and seek divine intervention. In a deus ex machina, an *actual* ET lands in Paglapur in a UFO that is shaped like a Shiva-Linga (a Hindu religious symbol and a manifestation of God). Paglapur becomes the centre of attention once again. I'd like to quote from a research paper of mine:

Joker …is the only contemporary film to bring back aliens and takes the fusion between science and divinity to a whole new level… *Joker* depicts the failure of socio-economic developmental models that focus on urban industrialization at the expense of rural consolidation. Not only is the alien-ship based on a mythological shape (no wonder the manifestation of mythological in Bollywood SF films has now become an important axis around which contemporary analysis revolves), the movie has political underpinnings too, thereby uniting Indian materiality and mythology (Khan, 2014: 198).

I then proceed to utilize Prof. Rick Altman's frame of reference in the paper and conclude that perhaps Bollywood SF films (and Indian SF, where faith/belief is always as important as science) have all the semantic elements of SF (aliens, spaceships, hi-tech

Could the Taj Mahal be a target for alien invasion like the White House? SF from the Global South poses these neglected questions (courtesy of the artist, Ammar Al-Gamal).

laboratories etc.), but they are arranged in a syntax that is not always regarded as SF by producers in other cultural, linguistic and geographical locations. This hybridization ensures discrete structures (of mythology) are perused to create a space-ship that looks like a Shiva-Linga (*Joker*), a separate form of communication devised to emit an "Om" which then aids in First Contact (*Koi… Mil Gaya*), and an alien invasion (modelled on aliens invasions in Hollywood) is turned on its head when the invaders turn out to be from a neighbouring country, not planet (*Wahan Ke Log*). It seems as if Bollywood is comfortable with a science that is either rooted in a mythological past, or is derived from it.

ESSF: Is the kind of SF you wrote in America different than the kind you write in India? Basically, is where you live have an effect on your imagination?

Geography always gives a local tinge to the narrative being produced, apart from, of course, providing different target audiences. Even while writing SF, one would think about how the society one lives in responds to science, and how science permeates the minds of the people. Geography and cultural context were of paramount interest in my head when I was writing my second novel. Why didn't, I asked myself, aliens visit India? Why did they always go to the US or Europe? A repressed, post-colonial angst raged within me. India is a thriving democracy, a rising superpower, and a country of more than a billion people. Are we not *good* enough to deserve being invaded by aliens? Moreover, how *exactly* would a hostile alien race proceed to conquer earth? Lastly, how would the Indian state apparatus respond to such a horrifying eventuality? It all began as a joke in my mind—and became a military-SF-thriller with the passage of time. As of now, I am working on a zombie story set in Oslo.

ESSF: Those are the exact same sentiments of Neill Blomkamp's District 9. *Do you believe that science fiction can help put the Third World on the global agenda?*

That's precisely my point. Or perhaps its exact opposite. The Third World doesn't need to be intentionally hoisted to the global stage—it already *is* the global stage by the virtue of its people. The developing world doesn't need to play according to anyone else's tune on any stage. We're writing for ourselves, and we surely don't need any external validation from anyone else. If we think we do—then we're still colonized mentally.

ESSF: Bollywood is bigger than Hollywood. Is there a thriving SF movie industry in India and can locally made SF cinema help popularise SF in Third World countries?

The qualitative and quantitative presence of SF in Bollywood is negligible when compared to Hollywood. Despite massive film production, not many SF films have been produced by Bollywood[4]. The fact that it is the voice of a nation that is increasingly viewing science as the panacea to all issues merely deepens this paradox, as I argue in *Bollywood and its Other(s)*. The whys of it are interesting, and I'll briefly skim over a few reasons to explain this dearth of SF in Bollywood here (though it would require a full-fledged PhD thesis to answer them fully, perhaps not even then): SF films are expensive to produce as they need special effects and CGI. They may not always be cost-effective. They require advanced technologies to produce. Also, Indian audiences already have a taste of Fantasy and Mythology in their (cultural) lives and Bollywood films utilise this already existing immersion rather than create a new kind of entertainment that SF films provide. However, as I said, things are changing, and with a rising middle-class with more contact with popular western SF, and a desire to try something new, indigenously produced SF is on the rise, and the future looks bright.

ESSF: Do you think SF can play an important role in helping the Muslim world?

I think SF can play an important role in helping the entire world, not just Muslims. We are all human beings, and are driven by the same hopes, dreams, aspirations, fears, and emotions. India, just like the Arab world, has its own ancient civilisation with developments in mathematics, science, astronomy, navigation etc. taking place millennia ago: the precursors to modern-day science. But since SF talks about what it is to be human, and how to retain that humanity in the midst of chaos, it belongs to us all—for all times. That's why I am wary of labels such as Muslim/Christian/Hindu/Right/Left/Hard/Soft SF. Very often these labels, coined to explain and categorise, start distorting what SF really is. James Gunn established SF as a literature of more than the individual since it talked about threats to humanity, and in doing so, united it. SF emerges as a genre that, unlike others, portrays the whole of civilisation in danger. To top it all, SF becomes mankind's search for itself. This is why it has the potential to help the entire human race. Though yes, SF has the potential to fight against radicalism, extremism, parochialism, and actually does so. I still think SF's larger political goals are directed towards creating a better world and a more conscious human species, and are not just limited to singing paeans to technologically-advanced civilisations, (though even when it does, it is well within its rights to do so).

ESSF: Your story "Operation Mi'raj" got the third prize in the Islamicate SF Short Story Contest (2016). We're all fans of Gandhi, and Nehru, here in the Arab world. Would you say that science fiction creates a space for cross-cultural dialogue?

SF is all about building bridges, about creating a shared tomorrow, about speculating—and then acting—for a better world. However, that being said, the story you mention is about a military operation that is driven by realpolitik rather than humanitarian betterment. It's not as innocuous—it's what happens when you fuse SF with political and war thrillers. It has its dose of (ultra)nationalism too! I engage with SF as someone who loves the pulp-roots of the genre, someone who embraces it, someone who knows SF crawled out of the sewers, and someone who understands that SF's political correctness needn't always be visible—or even present. It all depends on who's writing, why, when, and for whom. That's the beauty of SF: that's why we've even invented labels for all kinds of SF. The ultimate aim is to tell a good story. And what is "good"? To each his own!

ESSF: Is writing SF a science or an art? How much is research, how inspiration—and where do you get your inspiration from?

It's both—25% science, and 75% art, as Gernsback also put it. It requires extensive research, yes, but also tremendous amounts of inspiration. I usually get my inspiration from the (depressing) news we see/hear/read every day—daily happenings are much more dystopian than we could have imagined. Not only are we killing each other, we are also killing ourselves with the air we breathe, the food we eat, and the water we drink. We are killing our flora and fauna; and we are killing our planet. It is, sadly, this dystopia in our daily lives that ensures SF is here to stay, for it is in this precise genre/mode that a solution to our problem lies. Extrapolating such future(s) from our (dystopian) today is an exercise that keeps me on my toes: for if we can predict the apocalypse, maybe we can stop it.

ESSF: What do you hope to accomplish when you write?

The act of writing itself gives me the maximum amount of happiness. I don't write for good reviews or commercial success—I hope to get the creative kicks from writing when I'm building up a narrative. I may have had the honor of being bestowed with a few awards, and the privilege of securing a decent readership and encouraging reviews in the process, but I still think the best compliment is when you read something you wrote years ago, and as you do that, a faint smile tugs at the corners of your lips. You want to read more, and remember what you wrote years ago since it still sounds interesting, crazy—and readable.

ESSF: Advice for us here in the Arab world?

The Arab world has an extremely rich history and boasts of a cultural heritage that spans back to the dawn of man. I look forward to reading more from the Arab world. The universal nature of science meets the local tenor of fiction in SF.

As for promoting SF from an academic perspective: well, not many universities in India offer MA-level courses in SF, but I am happy to share that I taught a course on SF at GGSIP University, Delhi (2020-2021). Let's see what happens in the future! I sincerely hope there is more cross-cultural engagement with each others' SF. Reading about SF from various national, cultural and linguistic paradigms can be extremely enriching and enlightening.

ESSF: Future plans?

The intersection of religious and political ideologies in Science Fiction fascinates me. My latest book (*Star Warriors of the Modern Raj*) comes up with an "In situ model" that advances three nodes vis-à-vis the space, time and being of India's SF: the "transMIT thesis" evidences how Indian SF transmits (emergent) technologies, (sedimented) mythologies and (mutating) ideologies across/through its narratives; the "antekaal thesis" interrogates the ruptured temporalities of Indian SF; and the "neoMONSTERS thesis" approaches marginalisation-monsterization as contingent on specific material realities. Presently, I am on a Marie Skłodowska-Curie Actions Fellowship at the University of Oslo, Norway, where I work towards evolving the neoMONSTERS—mutating/mutagenic ontological narratives in space-time echoing realistic situations–thesis. I hope to comprehend how monstrosity/alterity are deployed in India's SF, and how these others/monsters become about the demons within and without. Perhaps this might help, in its own insignificant way, towards vanquishing the ghouls of violence, fanaticism, xenophobia and bigotry that plague our world today.

ESSF: A science fiction question. If you could go backwards in time and meet Rudyard Kipling and EM Forster, what would you tell them?

Kim, the Indian SF machine will *not* stop![5]

Acknowledgment

This chapter is a part of a project that has received funding from the European Union's Horizon 2020 research and innovation program under the Marie Skłodowska-Curie grant agreement No 101023313.

Notes

1. This is an Islamic religious expression meaning the "most noble of creation."
2. See Angenot.
3. Quoted in Landon, page 8.
4. Bollywood is the Hindustani-language (Hindi+Urdu) contributor to the Indian film-industry. Indian cinema is equally represented by film industries in other Indian languages, which have their own thriving film cultures such as Kollywood (Tamil), Tollywood (Telugu/Bangla) and Mollywood (Malyalam) etc.
5. E. M. Forster wrote "The Machine Stops"; it was published 1909.

Works Cited

Angenot, Marc. "The Absent Paradigm: An Introduction to the Semiotics of Science Fiction," *Science Fiction Studies*, vol. 6, no. 1 (1979), 9–19, https://www.jstor.org/stable/4239220.

Khan, Sami Ahmad. (2021). *Star Warriors of the Modern Raj: Materiality, Mythology and Technology of Indian Science Fiction in English*. University of Wales Press.

Khan, Sami Ahmad. (2016). "Goddess Sita Mutates Indian Mythology into SF: How Three (SF) Stories from *Breaking the Bow* Reinterpret the *Ramayana*." *Fafnir—Nordic Journal of Science Fiction and Fantasy Research*.

Khan, Sami Ahmad. (2016). "*Gods of War Toke* While Riding a *Vimana*: Hindu Gods in Three Indian Science Fiction Novels." *MOSF Journal of Science Fiction*, vol. 1, no. 1 (2016), https://publish.lib.umd.edu/?journal=scifi&page=article&op=view&path%5B%5D=442.

Khan, Sami Ahmad. (2014). "Bollywood's Encounters with the Third Kind: A Critical Catalogue of Hindi Science Fiction Films". In Vikrant Kishore, Amit Sarwal and Parichay Patra (eds.), *Bollywood and Its Other(s): Towards New Configurations*. New York: Palgrave Macmillan: 186–201.

Landon, Brooks. (1997). *Science Fiction After 1900: From Steam Man to the Stars*, Twayne Publishers.

Muhammad Aurangzeb Ahmad

An Interview on Islam and Sci-Fi, AI Ethics,
and Sustainable Development

EGYPTIAN SOCIETY FOR SCIENCE FICTION

Machinic desire can seem a little inhuman, as it rips up political cultures, deletes traditions, dissolves subjectivities, and hacks through security apparatuses, tracking a soulless tropism to zero control. This is because what appears to humanity as the history of capitalism is an invasion from the future by an artificial intelligent space that must assemble itself entirely from its enemy's resources.

—Nick Land (1993: 479)

ESSF: Please introduce yourself: your background and education and early exposure to SF and why you fell in love with it? Who are your favorite authors and which language do you read SF in predominantly?

I am Muhammad Aurangzeb Ahmad, the founder and editor of the Islam and Science Fiction project. I grew up in Pakistan and moved to the U.S. right after high school. I have a Ph.D. in Computer Science from the University of Minnesota, where my thesis was on using machine learning to model human behavior in massive online games. I have been interested in the big questions of life since childhood, e.g., What is the origin of the universe? What is the nature of reality? Why are we here, etc. I have always thought of science fiction as an important mode of inquiry to explore such questions. My grandfather started a book company in Pakistan in 1949 where my father worked, and thus while growing up, I had access to a lot of books. Sci-fi opened up access to imagined worlds that were fascinating in their own regard. In addition to sci-fi, I already read a lot of science-related texts when growing up, and I can see the connection between the two. I must have been thirteen or fourteen when I got fascinated with the idea of thinking machines and started reading about Artificial Intelligence. My penchant for this subject has stayed with me for the subsequent two decades as it guided me though my choice of Ph.D. and subsequent career. Even in my work, there is an element of AI, e.g., when my father passed away a few years ago, I set out to create a simulation of my father which could interact with my kids. Among the classic sci-fi authors, my favorites are Philip K. Dick, Ursula K. Le Guin, Isaac Asimov, Arthur C. Clarke, and Roger Zelazny. Among the contemporary authors are Kim Stanley Robinson, Ted Chiang, Robert Charles Wilson, Cixin Liu, and Chris Beckett. I mostly read in English but also try to read widely in translations from other languages.

ESSF: Isaac Asimov began writing science fiction early in his career, before he had a career in fact, writing when he was still at university. In your case, you began promoting science fiction while still an undergrad. Please fill us in on the details and how, and when, you dreamed up the "Islam & Sci-Fi" website?

During my undergrad years, I became fascinated with the idea of the religious and spiritual dimensions of science fiction. Works like Roger Zelazny's *Lord of Light*, Walter M. Miller Jr.'s *Canticle for St. Lebowitz*, Issac Asimov's *The Last Question*, James Blish's *Case of Conscience, etc.*, left a lasting impression on me. Many of the science fiction stories that I loved had Buddhist influences, which made me look for science fiction with Islamic themes or Islamic influences. Around 2005, after searching the internet and the university library, both offline and online, I realized that there was not much information on this subject. I said to myself that I might not be the only person who is looking for this information and that I should research this subject and bring it all together under a single umbrella—this is how the "Islam and Science Fiction" project was born.

ESSF: How has the retinue of "Islam & Sci-Fi" grown and changed over the years? Please give us a list of contributors and how you approached them and attracted them to your project.

And how did you get to know Ahmed A. Khan, Saqib Sadiq, and Rebecca Hankins?

The roster of contributors to "Islam & Sci-Fi" has varied over the years and is also currently in flux. The first person to approach me to further the cause of the project was Ahmed A. Khan, who promulgated the idea of the anthology around the subject. I connected with Professor Rebecca Hankins in a similar context where we got connected via her work on Islamic sci-fi, and lastly the connection with Saqib Sadiq happened because of a similar reason. Most of the people who have contributed have come to the project via two routes, either they directly connected with me in order to contribute to the project or via a call for contribution.

ESSF: What does it feel like being the co-editor of the first ever Muslim SF anthology?

The anthology came out in 2008; Ahmed A. Khan and I felt that even though there were numerous scattered works of

By a strange quirk of fate both Dr. Elzembely (left) and Dr. Muhammad Aurangzeb Ahmad were participating in the "A2K4D" conference, which explains this fortuitous occasion to meet, talk and get an endorsement of our efforts at the ESSF (author photograph).

science fiction written by Muslims or sci-fi inspired from Islamic cultures, there was literally no collection which brought this theme together or was focused on it. The *Mosque Among the Stars* was thus created to address this deficiency. I feel fortunate to have co-edited the anthology as it has inspired many to pursue this genre over the years.

ESSF: The director and founder of the Egyptian Society for Science Fiction, Dr. Hosam Elzembely, has designated four "waves" of Egyptian science fiction: the early exploratory phase, the phase when full time, specialized SF writers entered the field, the popularization phase, and finally the phase where the ESSF enters the picture and young authors begin to produce their own distinctive variety of Arab SF.

This gradual process of growth and transformation doesn't always apply to other Arab countries, sadly. What is the case with Pakistan? Who are the early pioneers of the genre in your country and how do younger authors differ from them? Has the history of Pakistani SF been cumulative?

There are definitely echoes of the waves that Dr. Hosam has identified in Pakistan sci-fi, but each country has its own peculiarities that limits comparisons. Additionally, Pakistan has a distinct literary history of fantasy fiction that connects it with larger literary currents in South Asia, that pre-dates its creation as a nation-state. Authors like the Bengali physicist Jagadish Chandra Bose were writing science fiction in South Asia as early as 1896; Begum Rokeya Sakhawat Hossain arguably wrote the first example of feminist science fiction in 1905. After the inception of Pakistan, the genre of adventure fiction with elements of science fiction can arguably be said to have a large following among the youth, especially in the works of Ibn-e-Safi, Mazhar Kaleem, M.A. Rahat, etc. While it would be a stretch to say that their works constitute true science fiction, they have enough elements of proto-sci fi to warrant a special mention of any discussion on sci-fi in Pakistan. More recently, the editorial work of Mahvash Murad in *The Djinn Falls in Love* and SFF stories by Usman Malik, etc., are trailblazing the way. Additionally, the Salam Awards for Science Fiction has helped kickstart the genre in Pakistan. That said, I would summarize that while science fiction has made inroads in Pakistan in the last decade or so, it has still not come up to a point to be a major genre in its own right, but that may change in the future.

ESSF: Are there sci-fi clubs or associations in Pakistan? Is there a writer's union or syndicate in Pakistan that helps represent authors and promote genre literature in general? What are the big sci-fi contests in your country?

To the best of my knowledge, such an organization is still lacking with respect to genre literature in general, including science fiction. The closest thing that I can think of is the Salam Award for Speculative Fiction, which has been given annually since 2017. The award is given as part of a contest on speculative genre writing including science fiction and has a rotating jury comprising of internationally renowned authors like Jeff VanderMeer, Anil Menon, Jeffrey Ford, etc.

ESSF: What other Pakistani authors and academics are promoting Pakistani sci-fi, and what different approaches are they taking? We're eager to learn from our counterparts and colleagues across the Global South.

The name of Usman Malik comes to the fore, as he was the main person behind starting the Salam Award. In addition to publishing in the speculative fiction genres, he has held seminars, invited internationally renowned authors to talk to aspiring writers in Pakistan online, and in general encouraged the community of aspiring writers to be more active. Mahvesh Murad is an editor based in Pakistan who has edited a few well noted anthologies of speculative fiction and whose work has been inspirational for many authors in the country.

ESSF: Next to "Islam & Sci-Fi," you also have a planned SF magazine Takwin. *Please tell us more. Who's involved with project, what is your target audience, and what do you hope to accomplish through this publication?*

Yes, the SF magazine is in the works. The magazine is tentatively titled *Takwin*, which refers to the creation of synthetic life by humans in the lab setting. This was one of the stated goals of many Muslim alchemists in the medieval era. It is also meant to high-light the fact that concepts like artificial life are not a modern sci-fi concoction but rather have precedents in past civilizations including the Islamic civilization. The details are being finalized, and it may take a very different form in the end, so the details are hard to share right now. That said, there are few things that I can share at the moment, e.g., the goal of the project is to establish a vehicle for the dissemination of science fiction inspired by Islamic cultures and civilization and to advance the scholarly study of this new genre.

ESSF: Have you considered writing SF stories yourself? Please list some of your favorite story ideas.

I have thought about writing science fiction stories for almost two decades but never got a chance to sit down and write something. This is something on my perpetual to do list. I am interested in writing about either the big questions in life, e.g., the origin and nature of life or rather the mundane. Hopefully, one of these days I will actually sit down and write down a story myself.

ESSF: Almost all of us have a career outside of writing, in journalism or academic life, so we never have enough time to actually put pen to paper. Would it be a good idea to list story ideas and get other *authors to transform them into actual stories?*

You could even set up a contest and have several authors working on a single-story idea and then pick the best resulting story. Could this be a model to promote SF for young and struggling authors, especially those writing on Islamic themes or with a Muslim background?

Yes, limitations imposed by external careers and other responsibilities are definitely a limitation that pretty much everyone in this genre has to deal with, including myself. The idea that you have outlined is definitely an intriguing one. I have thought about this myself and realized that asking people to write specific stories may not yield the required results. However, I do like the model of focusing on certain themes via contests. This is the approach that I took with the second sci-fi anthology that I edited called *Islamicates*. I am in the middle of planning a sequel to the anthology, which would be focused on cer-tain subjects.

ESSF: Science fiction often prefaces actual discoveries and inventions. There is a "quantum computer" in the indie sci-fi flick The Machine *(2013), for instance. It's described this way: "Electrons floating on superfluid helium." But now there actually is a quantum computer. How does it work and how does it differ from regular computers, and is it anything like the computer in* The Machine?

The idea of quantum computing has been around since at least the 1980s. The well-known physicist Richard Feynman even speculated almost forty years ago that a quantum computer could do things that classical computers could not do. Peter Shor, a professor of mathematics at MIT, came up with an algorithm in 1994 that could factor integers that would take classical computers millions of years to do. Classical computers, the computers all of us use, are based on the principle of using bits—1s and 0s to represent data—but a bit can either be 1 or 0 at a given time. Quantum computers, on the other hand, use qubits to represent information, i.e., a bit can be in a superposition of 1s and 0s at the same time in contrast to bits. This allows novel ways to do computation and implement algorithms that are far beyond the capabilities of classical computers.

ESSF: Is it true that the first computer virus was invented by a Pakistani? That's what we heard in the Arab world in the 1980s.

The early history of the first computer virus is a bit complicated—there are a few examples of viruses that infected a handful of computers that predate the virus that was created in Pakistan. The first virus that infected many computers was Elk Cloner by Rich Skrenta that infected the Apple II computers in 1981. However, in January 1986, brothers Basit Farooq Alvi and Amjad Farooq Alvi released the first IBM-PC compatible virus, which went on to be responsible for the first computer virus epidemic. The virus was called Brain, and it infected the PC by replacing the boot sector of a floppy disk with a copy of the virus. Unlike almost all viruses today, the Brain computer virus was written by the Alvi brothers not to cause mischief, but rather to protect their medical software, used for a heart monitoring system, from piracy. To summarize, it would be correct to say that *one* of the first computer viruses, although not the first virus, was created by Alvi brothers from Pakistani, but the first virus pandemic was because of the virus created by the Pakistani brothers.

ESSF: Do you think genre literature can help in the process of development itself? India is the second largest exporter of software in the world, and they invested in R&D and centers of excellence before anyone else in the Third World.

The software industry in India as well as the general competency of Indian engineers and scientists has its roots in educational reforms that were done shortly after the independence of India by Nehru's government. The Indian Institutes of Technology were set up in the 1950s, and it is after many decades that India is reaping the benefits. Genre literatures can definitely be an impetus for development. A large number of technologies have antecedents in science fiction or the genre itself was inspirational in development of new technologies, e.g., communicators from *Star Trek*, submarines from Jules Verne's work, Edward Bellamy came up with the idea of credit cards in the late 19th century, self-driving cars, etc. At the very minimum, sci-fi inspires people to pursue careers in STEM.[1] The long-term effects of promoting a sci-fi culture can certainly help in development by impacting the wider society to fostering a culture of learning and curiosity in the sciences.

ESSF: A number of Arabic countries, like the UAE and Qatar, are promoting science through multiple projects involving astronomy and aeronautics and space exploration. Could this be a conduit to promote science fiction?

It would be a shame if they did *not* use this opportunity to promote science fiction. While initiatives in science and technology can help spread awareness and inspiration in the populace, more often than not it is narratives which inspire the population to create a lasting scientific culture. Science fiction is one aspect of creating such narratives.

ESSF: On the topic of artificial intelligence, your field of expertise, the UAE has its own AI Minister now. Is the world finally catching up with the sci-fi imagination? And would you say we need such government agencies and regulations to insure both the success and proper usage (ethical constraints) of such path-breaking scientific applications?

The speed at which many technologies are being developed and deployed is unprecedented, which is creating a regulation gap since it is next to impossible for governments to legislate against. That said, there is definitely a need for the general population to be educated about the impact of technologies like machine learning, artificial intelligence, etc., on their lives to ensure proper regulation and ethical usage. In this regard, government regulation is important, but scientific literacy of the populace is a prerequisite. The Islamic world has a long history of deep philosophical debates on moral and ethical questions, and it should focus some of its energies on trying to address questions related to ethical conundrums facing AI right now, e.g., how does one engineer a moral system in a machine? What does it mean for an algorithm to be fair? Addressing questions like these not only require technical expertise but also a deep understanding of society and the consequences of technology.

ESSF: Please tell us something about the paper you presented at the "Artificial Intelligence, Innovations and Inclusion: What Prospects for the Middle East and Africa?" at the American University in Cairo? Dr. Elzembely himself gave two papers at the conference.[2]

What are the economic prospects for artificial intelligence? People often mistakenly assume that just because something can be done properly in a laboratory that it will automatically sell and be adopted in real life. We need a more realistic picture both to promote technology in our countries and to help shelter against backlashes against science and technology, and science fiction.

Science fiction has a long and illustrious history of helping us think about the present and how technology has the potential to transform society. In this respect, the goal of science fiction is not to make predictions about the future, but rather it is to guide the present. The same goes for science fiction in the Islamic world. Firstly, with the great deal of technological advancements and social transformation going on in the world right now, there is a need to assess how economically, socially, and even ideologically Muslim societies will be transformed. Science fiction is a great tool to explore such questions. Secondly, it is important for Muslims to be at the forefront in narrating their own stories because if they do not tell their stories, then someone else will, and that narrative may not be positive or adhere to the lived reality of the vast majority of Muslims in the world.

I have experience with implementing Artificial Intelligence models in both an academic setting as well as in the industry, so I know the divide between creating AI in the sanitized setting of a lab versus deploying a production level industrial grade model. The real world has constraints that one has to think about when thinking about implementation of AI models, e.g., the quality of data is not always great, scalability and usage are important factors, unforeseen consequences of technology is ever-present, etc. What science fiction enables us to do is to think about not just technology but also its potential impact on society. It is the difference between envisioning a technology like Twitter versus thinking about its social impact on society viz election meddling. Alternatively, think about how it would have been relatively easy to predict the invention of cars in the late 19th century but still very difficult to envision traffic jams. What I call the science fiction imagination can help us address some of these challenges, e.g., think about how Google has de facto become the source of religious knowledge for a large percentage of Muslims in the world, even though that was never Google's intent. One of the traditional roles of *ulema* or scholars in the Muslim community was to ensure that the average lay Muslim has access to correct information and not be swayed by extremist ideas. It turns out that many extremist organizations are good at search engine optimization but traditional schools are not. From a legal Islamic perspective, an interesting implication is that search engine optimization becomes *fard kifaya* or mandatory at the community level on the *ulema*. This is not how Muslims traditionally conceive the role of their scholars, but this is the new reality. Speculative thinking and science fiction can help us think through these problems.

ESSF: How is the market for sci-fi and genre literature and movies changing globally? Is the non–Western world, a country the size of China for instance, having an effect on the market?

Many cultures and civilizations have antecedents to science fiction in what can be described as proto sci-fi, however as a distinct literary genre, science fiction was traditionally a Western phenomenon with some notable exceptions. However, what is happening in the last decade or so is that science fiction is evolving into a truly global phenomenon. China has come into its own as a viable market separate from the West. The case of the *Warcraft* movie illustrates this where the movie performed poorly in the U.S. but did really well outside the U.S., especially in China. As the relative economic power of the West declines and new economic centers emerge in the East, a polycentric global pop culture is emerging where genre literature, television series, and movies outside the West have much greater possibility to go global. The recent global success of the German series *The Dark*, *Onisciente* and *3%* from Brazil, *Osmosis* from France, etc., to name just a few. I reckon and hope that by the end of the decade, international sci-fi may be something that we take for granted.

ESSF: Could this portend well for Arabic and Muslim countries if we begin producing SF movies and TV series[3] and publish or translate increasingly in English?

This is definitely an opportunity that Arab and Muslim countries should capitalize on. The cultural moment is definitely ripe for producing SF movies and TV series that can reach a global audience, but it needs to be capitalized. This, however, has to be done without losing the cultural context and soul of the works involved. A case in point is the poetry of Rumi in the U.S. where even though he is one of the most well-known poets in the U.S., being quoted by celebrities and the layperson alike, his work has been purged of its Islamic content. Translation of *Frankenstein in Baghdad* and Ahmed Khaled Tawfik's *Utopia* have received wide acclaim in the English-speaking world. The wordsmithing in novels and stories needs to be complemented with creations in the television and movie genre fiction to make a truly global impact.

ESSF: Finally, an idea we are working on at the ESSF, one of our long-term goals since the founding of the society in 2012, is to establish a global Arab and Muslim SF association.

Do you think this is a viable idea, from your own personal experiences? And how would you go about promoting Arab and Muslim SF?

I think it is a good idea to work towards such a goal; there are many scattered efforts in various countries around science fiction and speculative fiction, and it would be great to have them under a single umbrella so that people in different countries can not only learn from each other's experience, but also build upon what has already been done in other countries. In term of what strategies may be viable in promoting Arab and Muslim

SF, I think greater cooperation and participation in global events is the way of the future. It is only a matter of time before a work of global significance in science fiction comes out of the Muslim world.

NOTES

1. An acronym for science, technology, engineering, and mathematics.

2. The conference was organized by the aptly titled *Access to Knowledge for Development Center—A2K4D* at the AUC's Business School and held on 13–14 October 2019, at the old AUC campus in Tahrir Square.

3. Following this interview, a pioneering Arab sci-fi series was broadcast on satellite television in Egypt in the holy month of Ramadan in 2020—*Al-Nihaya (The End)*, produced by Egyptian movie star Youssef El Sherif. The story takes place in a post-apocalyptic world, in the year 2120, after the Arabs have reunited and even liberated Palestine, at variance with most if not all Arabic SF; but corruption and the police state still predominate.

WORK CITED

Land, Nick. (1993): "Machinic Desire." *Textual Practice*. 7:3: 471–482. http://dx.doi.org/10.1080/0950236 9308582177.

The Expanse of Mauritanian SF

Tuning French to a Future Informed by the Past[1]

MOUSSA OULD EBNOU

> There is only one way left to escape the alienation of present day society: *to retreat ahead of it.*
>
> —Roland Barthes (1975: 40)

From where do I draw inspiration for the science fiction that I write? In a word, from *myself.*

I draw from the many layers of my identity, as a Mauritanian, as an Arab and Muslim, an African, as a well-travelled speaker of French, and as a student of philosophy and Greek tragedy. Mauritania is the land of a million poets, as we proudly proclaim, and so poetry and the proper usage of Arabic and the music of the words and names I deploy are always a key issue with me when I put pen to paper. Less well known about Mauritania, however, is our music, another source of inspiration. My writings, to me, are a symphony, and they have to be choreographed to our musical traditions.

As an Arab and Muslim, the Quran is a great source of inspiration for me, the qasas (stories) in the Quran and the knowledge and implications herewith. To me they are more than tales about bygone times and people who are dead and gone. They are studies of the future, history lessons on the human condition and what we are capable of as a species, warnings about what we could do to ourselves if we are not careful, taking heed from those before us. The Quran itself is replete with de facto time-travel stories, and I refer to more than one in my novels, and there is no greater epic than the story of Adam and Eve and the journeys of the living and the dead. Other than the Quran, I am also inspired by a second religious source, namely, the philosophical story, such as Ibn Sina's story "Salman and Absaal," and "Hayy ibn Yaqzan" of course, in all its four manifestations—the original text by Ibn Sina and Sahrawardi and Ibn Tufail and Ibn al-Nafis.

These are Islamic stories, true enough, but they also represent differing intellectual currents and genres in Muslim history—Islamic parables, Sufism, neo-Platonism, and neo-Aristotelianism. There is no doubting the relationship between philosophy and science fiction. Philosophy has always been preoccupied with the fantastical to test the limits of the possible, of speculating on other states of being and existence. The philosophical parable's chief concern is to imagine a parallel world to the one we are now living in, the phenomenal world that is obvious to our senses, imagining a world that is different. And as Philip K. Dick explained, if you don't like this world, search for another one!

This ambition to make things anew, however, needs to be tempered by another facet of our philosophical heritage bequeathed to us by the ancient Greeks. Namely, tragedy.

As someone who speaks and publishes in French, and someone who has studied the literary and philosophical traditions of the West quite extensively, I incorporate more than I was born with into my art. I write my novels in French first, then translate them into Arabic, then return to the French text. And even while writing in French, I am always thinking about the appropriate Arabic word. Not just translating in a literal manner but searching out the right tone of voice and verbal pleasure of the Arabized text, while utilizing French to escape the too tight conventions of Arabic.

But first my story, of how I became a writer, and a science fiction writer at that.

A Story of Intersecting Stories

It is best to introduce myself through my positions on life and literature, to peel away the layers of my identity and the identity of Mauritania. My life story and my love of literature are intertwined, and with that comes my history with politics and my education, both at home and abroad.

When my first novel in French, *L'Amour Impossible*, came out, the publisher (L'Harmattan, Paris) insisted on describing it as an example of "African" science-fiction. As I later explained to the French sci-fi publication *Galaxies*, while I had not labeled the novel as an African SF novel myself, I was perfectly happy with this designation.[2] Mauritanians are proud to be Arabs, but we have a long and deep relationship with the African continent that I am equally proud of. (We are technically North Africans, but if you look at the map, you will see we have no outlet to the Mediterranean. We are instead on the Atlantic Ocean.) Our identities as Africans and Arabs overlap, and in more than one way. We have all equally had to face colonialism, we have all equally learned from the French language as a consequence, and we have our long history of interactions before then. African culture, for me, is always a source of fertile inspiration, and as I like to remind my Arabic brethren, nearly two-thirds of us live on the African continent, so bilingualism extends beyond speaking Arabic and French to speaking *African* Arabic.

My African identity is also constitutive of my sense of mission as an author of science fiction. As I informed *Galaxies*, it is my belief that science fiction can produce a true Copernican revolution in African thought and harmonize their development models. The more important thing is that it can foment a change of perspective, to lead to a transformation of the way we think, our ideas, and the methods we employ to reach them. It must be understood that in Africa, we tend to look to the past to illuminate our present. What science fiction can do is help us look to the future to understand our present, to break out of the retrospective way of thinking of things. The stakes of the future are *already* existent in the present, making science fiction with its future focus an ideal tool to illuminate the present-day world that is always clouded in uncertainty and obscurity, of which direction we should turn and what impasses we face and the backlog from the negative aspects of the past. Another world is being built, and science fiction can help Africans both comprehend and inhabit it. Not that there isn't something to be said for the past, a point I highlight in my latest work, the three part series about the Hajj (pilgrimage) to Mecca from the perspective of the past, to be followed by an account set in the contemporary world, and then attaining its completion with the story of pilgrimage in the future, to see how much has changed and how much has not, and why and what we can learn from this.[3]

As a French-speaking African author, I also want to *reposition* French-speaking African SF, put it on the literary map of the world, and change the very perception of African SF in the francophone world. In its current state, French-speaking African SF is on the margins of the genre. Nigerian, Kenyan, South African, and English-speaking African SF is far more well-established and internationally popular—English is the lingua franca of the world, a French term ironically. At the same time, francophone African SF is seen as "exotic" in the French-speaking world itself, a mere annex to French SF. This is unacceptable and must change if we are to have a genuine intercultural dialogue on the African continent itself, to converse on an equal footing not only with the West but also with the African speakers of Portuguese and Spanish and, of course, English. If French-African SF was recognized in France itself, and in the educational system in francophone Africa, it could take off and attain the respectability—and sustainability—it needs.

I am enamored by Jules Verne, like everybody else, but I am sad to say that French science fiction itself has fallen behind. The so-called Golden Age of science fiction, following the Second World War, was exclusively in the world of English-language SF.

Perhaps a little African input can revive the ghost of Verne to the benefit of all!

Now for my story with reading and politics and philosophy, assuming such polarized distinctions can actually hold in real life.

I spent the cream of my childhood in the village of Boutilimit, living in the customary Mauritanian way, with all the members of my extended family in one tent. That is, 4 by 4 meters, with uncles and aunts and cousins and all the necessities of life that we had to carry with us. Not much room for privacy. Nonetheless, I was able to chart my own course even in these quarters. I found an innovative way to plug my ears and read and read, for hours on end, keeping the noise of the world out and swimming in the world of words where there is no shoreline in sight!

Then my family moved to the capital, Nouakchott, in 1965 where my father gave up his original work as a merchant and became a guard at the football stadium of the capital. We pitched our tent *inside* the stadium. But I, through a stroke of luck, and a little determination, was able to get a room all to myself, to stash the books I had accumulated over the years and resume reading in more earnestness. (The stadium belonged to the ministry of youth and culture, but only in the daytime.) Better still, there was a storehouse of books in the stadium, in a locked room without a roof. I scaled the walls every chance I got, reading day and night with the aid of a candle, until I had to succumb to the power of sleep. It was a veritable treasure-trove of literature on everything and anything.

I vaguely remember a period in my adolescence where I read a lot of space operas, in translation of course, along with epic and dramatic adventures. But I found the geopolitical settings to be deeply disappointing, simplistic, and clichéd. Perhaps that is what drew me to politics, beginning with my formal schooling.

I enlisted in school, primary education, in 1965. My education had been exclusively in the tent prior to that. By 1968 I was in secondary education, and that is when I became politically active. I participated in student protest marches despite the fact that I was related by bonds of blood to the president of the time, Moktar Ould Daddah, God rest his soul. My generation criticized him severely, seeing in him the new face of imperialism and protesting his one-party state. We charged him and his clique with ignoring the plight of the Third World, focusing on narrow material matters alone. Our heroes were Che Guevara, Ho Chi Minh, and Fidel Castro, the civil rights movement in the United States, the Chinese revolutionary youth, and the hippie movement across the world.

Sadly, the youth of Mauritania today are only interested in the prospect of stability; they no longer dream. My generation was different. Unemployment had not reared its ugly head at the time, and so we placed politics above all other considerations. We voiced our concerns and complaints with no thought for the morrow.

A small proviso for the reader. When I say student protests, I mean "pupils," since there were no universities in the country at the time. I myself was only 14. It did not dent our enthusiasm, however. We were rebelling against society itself, our traditional mode of life, and wanted to build an ideal society. We were adherents of the singer Johnny Hallyday!

People laugh and say this is youthful exuberance. I say this is part of growing up and part of being a patriot. That is what citizenship means, being *involved*. And to think, we were living in palaces at the time. A palace, for a Mauritanian of my generation, meant a room with no furniture. But they were spacious enough for us to hold our meetings in and plot and plan for our country's future. In my case, I joined the Arab National-ists, the automatic response of the Arab world to the defeat of 1967 and the loss of Pales-tine. We were also opposed to the Westernization of our world, the loss of Arabic, forcing us to work underground. I was charged with the organizational responsibilities for the National Democratic Movement, of the Baath Party, in the good old days of the Baath party, I should say. I established a whole Marxist wing in the movement, in a desperate attempt—with my colleagues and friends—to reconcile Arab nationalism with Marxism. We wanted socialism true enough, but that did not mean floating away into the worlds of internationalism while traditional pan–Arabism itself had been for too long negligent of the plight of the poor. We tried to insert ourselves into social and political life, everything from the schools to public speaking and popular debate.

Things began to come to fruition in 1972 and 1974, when President Ould Daddah showed his customary political acumen and implemented a swathe of policies meant to revise our relationship with France. He issued a national currency of our own and nation-alized French assets in the country, finally putting to an end to France's long arm in our lands, a veritable state within a state. This was a blessing in disguise, sucking the life out of the opposition as the politically active flocked to the ruling party, giving the president the green light to throw his lot in with Morocco and push Mauritania into an unneces-sary war with the Western Desert. This sank the country into an economic recession, something we had never experienced before, perpetuating the coup of 1978, and the rest is history.

Luckily, I'd attained my bachelor's degree and was able to make it to France to study journalism, and by 1978 I began to study philosophy at the Sorbonne alongside my jour-nalism studies. But, true to form, it was in France that I befriended Dominique Bouya-hia, an activist on the furthest of the French left-wing, who in turn introduced me to René Lefeuvre, a man in his seventies and the founder of the SPARTACUS publishing house (in 1934), a severe critic of Stalinism and the whole Soviet bloc. I became one of the SPARTACUS de Amis Les, the young friends of the movement, so to speak, dedicating ourselves to reviving the older, purer form of non–Leninist Marxism.

After attaining my doctorate, I moved to the United States to work with the UNDP in New York as a cultural adviser on behalf of my country and got engrossed in left-wing politics there too. Once I'd finished my two-year tour of duty in New York, I returned to my homeland, intent on changing the way things are done through the instruments of the mind, which is why I helped establish Nouakchott University, heading its philosophy department.

Coming up against a brick wall, I decided to try my hand at writing—and the situation has only gotten worse with the current military regime in power. The next chapter in my life began, and with that more political trials and tribulations for my beloved country. Initially I wanted to do anthropology in reverse, dissecting Western societies I'd lived in through works of fiction. Alas, globalization put an end to that minor quest since the modern is *here*, right in front of us, in our homelands, raising all these technological and ethical and environmental issues that science fiction as a genre is ideally suited for.

As said above, I am someone who is not satisfied with the world as it is, and not only in my country, which now resides under a military dictatorship. Changing the way things are is the vocation of the philosopher and the journalist, but more often than not, it is the vocation of the author of fiction and science fiction specifically, a field of writing that overlaps with philosophy more than any other.

But writing fiction and science fiction is better. It's either that or writing philosophical treatises that nobody will read!

The Greatest Tales Ever Told

That being said, I also write because I'm a Muslim. I don't just mean that I write from a Muslim perspective, which is true enough given how well-travelled I am, but writing *because* I am a Muslim.

We are commanded in the holy Quran itself to write: "…So *recount* these narratives, so that they may reflect." (7: 176).[4] And it must be understood that these stories strewn throughout the holy book are not so much about the past—the follies of peoples dead and gone—as they are about the *future* and the secrets of things to come. That is the fulcrum of my employment of the Quran in my science fictional stories since the task of SF is to draw us to speculate about our surroundings, our current reality, to lay bare its machinations before our very eyes. My novel, *The Impossible Love*, for instance, is in truth inspired by the sin of Adam and the fall, whereby mankind has to leave the Earth in the future, after it has become uninhabitable thanks to the technological world we have created. From there things only become worse, as artificial insemination leads to too many males in society, the age-old preference for boys in our communities as Arabs and Africans, and then a rejoinder with a society tipped too much in the favor of females, eventually collapsing into a segregated standoff between the two sexes, and a love story of an Adam and Eve duo who are trying desperately to break these boundaries and reassert the Godly balance of the past.

The novel is also, in part, inspired by the Quranic account of the burden placed on the shoulders of man, the trust that God offered the heavens and earth and the hills and that the heavens, earth, and hills refused to take, but that man in his infinite folly assumed upon himself (verse 33.72). To me, man's renouncing of the covenant he made with God is the direct result of technological advance and technological arrogance, and the Quran is in effect prophesizing this through these stories of events in the so-called bygone past. To quote another verse from the holy Quran: "Corruption doth appear on land and sea because of (the evil) which men´s hands have done, that He may make them taste a part of that which they have done, in order that they may return" (3:41).[5]

Impossible Love, however, was a pure novel of science fiction, with space-travel and technology and genetics and social systems by design. In my second novel, *Barzach* (*Madinet Al-Riyah* in Arabic), I relied more heavily still on the Quran, at the level of the initial inspiration for the story, the construction of characters and storyline, and even the naming of the characters themselves. I rely on the Quranic figure of Al-Khidr, the mysterious figure who was wiser even than the Prophet Moses (PBUH). Here the equivalent character named Al-Khudair allows the protagonist to journey through time, to see the future world himself and pass judgment on it, to see if it was worth all the trouble. *Barzach* is a work of science fiction but also a work of historical fiction. I toyed with the idea, at first, to rely on the relativity theory in physics as a means of explaining how static time is in the isolated bubble that the protagonist resides in when traveling between the ages, centuries at a time, but decided against this option. It was not aesthetically pleasing to someone with my religious and philosophical sensibilities. Then I recollected the Quranic story of The People of the Cave, a band of freedom seekers who took refuge in a cave from persecution, who were made to sleep by the Almighty for three hundred and nine years.

That was the trick: how to extend the life of the hero. It was by divine will. Al-Khudair is the lord of time, allowing the hero to be a witness on men's deeds on the so-called march of human progress.

Also pressing on my mind was the need for a key moment in the storyline where time *folds* in on itself, in circular fashion, and all things become clear to the protagonist, the truths he's been searching for, allowing him to pass judgment on history, himself, and time itself. Again, I found the solution to this narrative hurdle in the Quranic storytelling mode, with these words of wisdom: "And the agony of death cometh in truth. (And it is said unto him): This is that which thou wast wont to shun." (50.19).[6] It is at the point of death that time extends and becomes circular, allowing one to see one's past, no matter how many years you lived, and see your beginnings till everything is laid bare before your very eyes.

To further elaborate, here is a passage from my novel:

"I am in a new world, in which I am assaulted by memories, strange and facile memories of life that has never left me…. The pangs of death have brought me the Truth…. Nothing eludes me any longer…. My gaze is as sharp as steel…. The throes of death illuminated the details of my life that appeared magnified a thousand fold, as if a thousand desert suns were directed at the dark corners…. The barriers between the apparent and the hidden, the visible and the secluded, the known and the unknown were removed…. Consciousness is made from beyond the realm of consciousness. I am present in the area after life, and before death, that in-between place where I recollect the reel of my life…. I hear it, I see it, I realize it, all in detail. There is no before or after…. I, the one who wasted his days trying, to no avail, to tie my life to my dreams, tie my feelings to the unconscious, my awareness to the awareness of others, to pass judgment on others and myself and on the times, all in vain, attempts failed and betrayed…. Here I witness what I failed to achieve all my life, accomplished of its own accord, passing before my very eyes at the hour of my death…. Now, after I have left the field, I see the outcome of the decisive battle between my life and my dreams, embodied in front of me with infinite precision, everything taking its proper size, before being swallowed whole by the sinkhole of nothingness. I see the whole world through the lens of the beholder, no riddles remain, no more secrets…. All are at the same level of clearance…. Time has reduced itself to the one dimension, the past and the future no longer exist … only the present…. I have found my beginning…" [pages 9–10].

Now witness these verses from the holy Quran:

50.19. And the stupor of death will bring Truth (before his eyes): "This was the thing which thou wast trying to escape!"

50.20. And the Trumpet shall be blown: that will be the Day whereof Warning (had been given).

50.21. And there will come forth every soul: with each will be an (angel) to drive, and an (angel) to bear witness.

50.22. (It will be said:) "Thou wast heedless of this; now have We removed thy veil, and sharp is thy sight this Day!"[7]

It is clearer in the original Arabic, of course, but you will see that the very phrasing I use, not just the scaffolding of the storyline and themes, is all taken from our holy book.

French … to a Mauritanian Beat

You are free to ask why someone like me, who protested for the protection of Arabic and for nationalizing foreign assets, would go about writing in French. Partly it is to reach a wider audience, as explained above, but in part also because writing in a foreign tongue is a *tool* for self-exploration. It allows me to perceive myself and my surroundings in a way that my mother tongue cannot facilitate. Facts, supposedly self-evident, appear in a different light entirely to me when you express them in another language. Arabic then plays the role of authenticator, grounding what I have written in my cultural experiences.

By writing first in French, I try to get away from what is familiar to me by taking my distance from my language. French, the foreign language, is a necessary tool to get rid of the rhetoric of the Arabic language and escape the conventions, automatisms, and expressions of the mother tongue. According to Derrida, the mother tongue is only the first of the foreign languages that one learns. Derrida believes that monolingualism is an impossibility. There is a kind of pre-language in which people draw and from which they translate to express their thought. Therefore, the translation would be inherent to the speech act, always a first operation rather than, as commonly accepted, second. Our mother tongue is, so to speak, our first foreign language.

Derrida asserts that one never possesses the language one speaks, that one is in fact always foreign to it. And so, the self-translated version gives me the opportunity to *find* my mother tongue. Through translation, I become more spontaneous in Arabic anyway, and so the finished Arabic version includes the supreme degree of recovery of authenticity.

At first, I wrote and published what I wrote straight away in French, then translated the published text in Arabic. Now I am cannier and more patient and more observant. I keep the French manuscript in draft form and began to edit and modify the French text in light of my concerns and considerations when I begin to Arabize my story. That is precisely what I did with my third novel, the first of my Mecca trilogy (Hajj Al-Farraj), cataloging the experiences of Mauritanians on pilgrimage to Mecca, in the past, the present, and then in the future. I wrote it, in French, during the period of 2001–2003, then Arabized it from 2003–2004, and then published it in 2005, although the "French" edition—this time—did not come out till 2016!

This balancing act between French and Arabic comes out in many guises. One is the act of naming. The significance of a character's name is intimately tied up with the subject of the narrative. My choice of names is not haphazard and encapsulates within it the subject of the narrative. In fact, the names can often impose themselves on the narrative and from their starting point. The protagonist in *The Impossible Love* is named Adam, after all, and Adam is not just the name of the first man but a symbol of the "complete" man, from whom was created women. And then man fell into sin, thanks to woman, and with that the violation of the covenant man made with God, and these blunders and this rupture with the divine order of things are the central theme of the novel.

The heroine of *Impossible Love*, however, is not named Eve. Instead she is called "Manikè," derived from the classical Greek word for the act of prophesying. It is meant to signify that womankind is in charge of determining man's fate. And the fate of Adam in the novel is to *become* a woman, so he can live out the rest of "his" days with his sweetheart in the segregated world of the future. And this is a segregation that the men are chiefly responsible for. No wonder then that you have the character of Androgyne who represents the confusion of the roles of male and female and the breaking down of these once clear gender boundaries, a feature of modern-day society. There is also Riman, a name that dredges up satanic imagery, and the character stands in for the devilish qualities of modern technology.

I am also very fond of amalgamations of words for my characters, taking heed from how this happens in spoken languages all the time, not to mention my own personal history with word games. (My mother named me Moussa, after the Prophet Moses [PBUH] because of a dream she had while pregnant with me, and it involved a scripture belonging to the daughter of Shuayb, the wife of the noble Prophet Moses). As an infant I called my mother Makdayah (مَكّدَايَه). Little did I know at the time that this was a combination of the word Mak (مَك), a reference to suckling from the breast of the mother, and Dayah (دَايَه), the Arabic for midwife or nanny; I learned this when I decided to choose Makdayah as a name for one of my female characters. If you look at the historical figure of Sibawayh (سيبويه), for instance, you will find that this is actually a nickname given to him by his mother, and means—in Persian—the "scent of apples." His literal name, however, was Omar bin Uthman bin Qanbar, not nearly as colorful a name and even we, as Arabs, use his amalgamated nickname.

Again, language is a resource, and the more languages you speak, the more raw materials you have at your disposal and, critically, the more aware you are of these resources.

Any one language has limitations, and you tend to take a straightforwardly literal interpretation of words and names in your language if you speak no others, especially when writing and constructing a narrative and set of characters. It also opens up the opportunity to combine words *across* languages, something that does in fact happen throughout history when people interact from different cultures, something to be cherished and employed to the fullest in literature.

The female character of Solima, in *Madinet Al-Riyah*, is in fact a cross between three words: Soleil (the French word for "sun"), Libya (not on Earth but on the human map of the planet Mars), and Mars, the red planet itself. Solima herself isn't human but takes on a human form to make her job easier, traveling across space and time—journeying through black holes—to harvest souls in a vampiric but nonetheless benign fashion, soaking up the words spoken by endangered species like humankind for posterity's sake. And to better prepare herself for her job, she enrolls herself in the "Human Languages and Civilizations Teaching Centre" in Libya, so to speak, on the planet Mars. (The astronomers of the West used these labels, not me.)

There is the city of Oudaghust, the legendary Mauritanian caravan city that was buried under the sands and forgotten by time, and "Ghostbuster," the name of the head of the archaeological team that is sent out to locate this buried city. Oudaghust sounds like Ouda "Ghost," as in Ghostbusters. And "Buster" itself means a searcher after, hence, the archaeologist Ghostbuster, someone who pursues phantasms and *mythical* cities.

This is as far as word games go, tapping into the histories and languages of both Arabs and Europeans. The overarching structure of my novels, however, is thoroughly homegrown, I can assure you.

Madinet Al-Riyah in particular is arranged in the form of a musical session, in three parts or phases, led as it in Mauritanian practice by the Tidnit, the Mauritanian oued (lute). The Tidnit ensemble is arranged to signify, to match, the phases of rise and decline of life itself. The first is the first flowering of life, the second maturity and the reaching of completion, the very zenith of life, while the third and last phase symbolizes decay, decline, and eventual extinction. And so, the first part of the text corresponds to the black method (the first of the Tidnet session), the second part corresponds to the white method, and the third to the Liknidi method. The last part of the narrative deals with the future technological society that has lost its humanity and so matches the Liknidi method, which symbolizes the music that was not written by man but written by *death*; something beyond this world reaches to it. Or as we say in our Baydani dialect of Arabic, Al-Ghoul Anufl (الغول انْوَفْل), since anything that leads to man's *demise* is a Ghoul, a macabre, otherworldly beast.

Liknidi is in the text itself, but in disguise, under the label (برج التبانة), the Milky Way Galaxy. Or at least the tower-like part that we can see at night; (برج) means tower in Arabic. And I use the Liknidi as a reference to another world, as the musician who plays these tunes does not belong to this world, the human world of the living, but to the world of the afterlife. It is in this third act of the novel that mankind must vacate the Earth to other worlds in the galaxy. In parallel, there is the alien race Solima belongs to who land on Earth in search of fragments of humanity's lost golden age.

More than this, you actually *hear* the music of man's demise. As one character describes it: "Heavy, noisy, sharp, in sequence, speedy, falling on your ears to pierce the body, entering through every pore, its tunes are dense and obscene" (page 162). And where is this music heard? The storehouse of the toxic wastes, the very symbol of the technological society and how they laid the Earth to waste. corrupting the land and the water, and the air and the soul. (It is even worse than that, with our planet becoming the storehouse for nuclear wastes for the entire system, and Mauritania being singled out by Earth authorities to get the lion's share of this toxicity!)

The music is described by a human character in this sequence as rancid and *hellish*, resulting from an orchestra of metallic dooms, the clicking and clanging of computers, erratic sounds that slice into you like a knife and burst your ear drums, accompanied by rabid screams that make you feel ill (page 164), all testaments to man's stubbornness in the face of his own arrogance, a stain on his conscience forever and ever. And it is this man who has befriended Solima; she explains her mission and her true nature, setting everything in perspective for him as a human being, almost as much as the music does. (You will also notice my Meccan epic is likewise divided into "three" parts).

It is also here that Solima and her human friend chance onto a peculiar character, bald and ugly and potbellied and dressed much like the mad dervishes you see walking the streets, portending doom and salvation to a neglectful audience of passers-by. He is a character who has emerged before in my novels. Who is he, pray tell? None other than Socrates, in Muslim garb!

I should add here that my negative attitudes towards modern technological society do not stem exclusively from my Mauritanian upbringing or Quranic injunctions. They also come from my studies in France, which afforded me the opportunity to explore the writings of Martin Heidegger, whose criticism of the world of technology profoundly affected me.

But first let me preface my concerns, and *technique*, with reference to the philosophy and theater of the ancients, which was always far more eloquent.

Every era has its own Socrates, and every nation. And so Muslims may suffer the same fate as humanity in a future where people continue to ignore the lessons of history (courtesy of the artist, Ammar Al-Gamal).

Philosophy in the Flesh of a Novel

I always love to squeeze themes and techniques from my heritage into my novels, whether they be of a particularistic Islamic origin or from our shared human heritage, and this is certainly the case with my love of Greek philosophy and Greek tragedy. A case in point is *Oedipus the King* by Sophocles, a playwright who wrote a tragedy about the failure of man's *vision*, so to speak. (In Arabic we distinguish between *basar*, the act of seeing, and *baseera*, noticing and understanding what is right in front of you and seeing beyond it to the values evident in a particular situation. Straight away there is a lesson in language here, since the Arabic captures the classical Greek notions better than many a European language.)

No wonder then that Oedipus pokes his own eyes out by the end of the tragedy and that a "blind" man was the one who warned him at the beginning. As Karl Reinhart and Heidegger argue, what breaks off the glorious exploits of the King in his early days from his later, and what leads to his downfall at the end, is specifically his inability to distinguish between appearance and reality. He could only stand to see the truth after blinding himself.

Likewise, in *Madinat Al-Riyah*, Oudaghust is informed by a soothsayer that he will be murdered by his own grandson. The only difference is that Oudaghust doesn't poke his eyes out since he is the techno Oedipus of our day and age. Instead he is seduced by appearance, the technological affluence of the future world that spells its own doom.

Remember also that the story of Al-Khidr and the Prophet Moses (PBUH) was a story of *humility*, since Al-Khidr did things that were inexplicable to Moses (PBUH). Even with his foreknowledge as a prophet and messenger of God, even with his education in the house of Pharaoh and the glories of ancient Egypt, he still could not fathom Al-Khidr's actions and condemned them only to learn afterward how wrong he was. He was judging from mere appearances and suffered limitations like anyone else, a warning call to modern civilization and its self-indulgence at the behest of modern science and technology.

This puts Quranic stories and Islamic parables on an equal footing with Greek tragedy and philosophy. But there is also the motif of "vision," of clarity only coming during the final pangs of death. This recollects, on purpose, the legacy of Oedipus. This is also why I insist in my novel, in imitation of the Greek oracles, to state explicitly that one cannot judge the future by the standards of the present.

All men, and not just kings blinded by power and success, think they can see things as they are, pursuing what they take to be noble ends, through appropriate means. But, more often than not, we are blind, and our pursuits backfire on us in more terrible ways, spelling our ultimate doom. Stripping away the appearance to witness the underlying realities is the only salvation; we must learn God's hidden wisdom behind the way things are. To quote from the Quran again, and in Surat Al-Kahf—which recounts the story of the People of the Cave—no less: "Those whose striving goes astray in the present life, while they think that they are working good deeds" (18:104).[8]

Not that the Greek heritage is far off, in my way of thinking. Philosophy and religion, to me at least, work hand in hand. Hence my sneaking in of the figure of Socrates, the ugly person of great stature in *The Impossible Love*. More appropriately, I use him as an opposite to the devil, symbolizing the eternal struggle between good and evil. But also, the dualism of knowledge and "ignorance," of people who pursue vile self-interest and personal glory while thinking that they are helping everybody. It is the same in *Madenat Al-Riyah*, but in Muslim guise, predicting the coming of our savior the Mahdi, without specifying the exact date!

Finally, there is Androgyne in *The Impossible Love*. The name is not just a play on words and modern society—it comes straight out of Plato's *Symposium*, the Platonic myth of Aristophanes about the three original races of humankind: male, female and the third sex consisting of both male and female parts and the punishment meted out to them by Zeus through forceful separation.

A Final Word

To me, *Impossible Love* is merely a scientific version of this myth, of the origin of the craving of human beings for their opposites who complete them and make them whole again, much as in holy scripture Eve was extracted out of the substance of Adam, the first man, the complete human.

Like the Platonic myths, science fiction can save us. The myths of SF show us what was hidden from our vision. My fiction is rooted in the anxieties of man in the face of his techno-scientific present, but also in his hopes and his sense of wonder, such distinctly Greek proclivities we should cherish in the world of today.

Writing is a risky business, a leap into the unknown, and perhaps more so in the case of science fiction when contrasted to the other genres. Fortunately, in today's world, the borders between SF and the mainstreams of literature are not so precise anymore.

I believe that SF exceeds the available knowledge on technological realities and gives us a speculative look at the future of these realities, which can confirm or refute our apprehensions as non-specialists. It is a guide in the intellectual wilderness of tomorrow, but I still say that it needs grounding in older forms of artistic and philosophical experience and in our culture and religion as Arabs and Muslims and Africans. It is a guide in need of a guiding hand itself.

That is what I do with my novels, using French to spread the word of Mauritanians to the four corners of the Earth, and Arabic to make sure I don't lose myself in my speculations!

NOTES

1. Translated by Emad El-Din Aysha.
2. Please see "Interview with Moussa" (2017) and Ryman (2018) for more on my classification as an African novelist.
3. To date, only the first part of the novel has been published, and both in Arabic (حج الفجار) and French (La Mecque païenne).
4. http://al-quran.info/#7.
5. https://www.sahih-bukhari.com/Pages/Quran/Quran_english_arabic_transliteration.php?id=30.
6. http://www.alim.org/library/quran/ayah/compare/50/19.
7. https://www.quran411.com/surah-qaf.asp.
8. http://www.alquranenglish.com/quran-surah-al-kahf-104-qs-18-104-in-arabic-and-english-translation.

WORKS CITED

Barthes, Roland. (1975). *The Pleasure of the Text*. New York: Hill and Wang. Translated by Richard Miller.
"Interview with Moussa Ould Ebnou (Mauritania)." (March 2017). *Galaxies: SF Africa*. 46.88: 96–99 [French].
Ryman, Geoff. (31 March 2018). "African SFF 2017 by Geoff Ryman." https://locusmag.com/2018/03/african-sff-2017-by-geoff-ryman/.

From Arrakis to Senegal

The Science Fiction of Interfaith Dialogue and Spiritual Coexistence

MAME BOUGOUMA DIENE

Bless the Maker and all His Water. Bless the coming and going of Him,
May His passing cleanse the world. May He keep the world for his people.
—Frank Herbert, *Dune*[1]

My first encounter with Islam and science fiction, or rather Islamized science fiction, which I wouldn't be remiss in thinking was the first encounter for most of the Western world, was with Frank Herbert's speculative fiction classic *Dune* and its sequels and prequels and movie and miniseries.

By this point thirty years have gone by, and the young starry-eyed boy who lost himself in the deserts of Arrakis and lost sleep over the Guild of Navigators' spice-induced mutations has grown... a bit. Yet the fascination is still there, and this fascination has grown beyond fandom as a writer with an Islamic background, to creating my own worlds and begging for more. For a more authentic vision of Islam in science fiction, for a vision that takes the religion we have now and looks at what it can become, possibly even questioning its very existence and validity.

Right there I am stepping into dangerous territory.

Nigh *haram*.[2]

Who am I to question God? Everything in Islam is predetermined. *Inch'Allah*[3] is reminding ourselves of the will of God in all things, so how could people second guess his creation and propose an evolution to what should, by definition, be perfect?

Never mind that these are exactly some of the questions that Frank Herbert asked. But since he is not a Muslim, he is free to critique whatever he wants, and question whatever he wants, and postulate upon the unfathomable. It is the vision of an outsider—a powerful, galaxy spanning vision, but that of an outsider still.

But shouldn't this be the prerogative of every *Muslim*? To question. To reinvent. To demand more than what they are given?

This article is not an attempt to answer these questions, nor is it, unfortunately, to create an authentic vision of Islam in the future. I am an outsider myself. Part of my family is Senegalese Muslim and Sufi, part of it is French and Roman Catholic, I myself am a child of the Great Satan.[4] I don't believe in God as strictly monotheistic and as most religions define it, and you will have to wrestle a salami sandwich from my cold dead hands. And even then...

Dr. Elzembely (left) pictured with a colleague from Senegal and the U.S., Mame Diene, who graced ESSF's humble headquarters and added his name to its list of international dignitaries (author photograph).

Buddha driven to tears by the false confrontation between East and West, and East and East (courtesy of the artist, Ammar Al-Gamal).

Rather, I will look at:

* Buddislam and the treatment of Buddislamics in the *Legends of Dune* prequels (*The Butlerian Jihad*, *The Machine Crusade*, and *The Battle of Corrin*).
* The likelihood or unlikelihood of Islam and Buddhism merging in a contemporary context, and,
* How I, as a writer, and a diasporic African, relate to the above and would like to see the literary scene become more cognizant, understanding and embracing of its diversity.

Herbert's Religious Vision

It should come as no surprise that religion is an essential part of Frank Herbert's *weltanschauung*.

Many argue that the economic competition between the Landsraad, the Bene Gesserit, and the Spacing Guild over the spice mélange, reminiscent of the reality of oil in our societies and our dependence on it, is Herbert's central theme in *Dune*. This theory is superficially supported by the fact that the Fremen are a post–Islamic society, living on a giant desert planet that could be compared to the Arabian Peninsula and the deep roots of Islam in the desert and the early Arabic culture that birthed them. They are nomads who control access to the finite resource.

I humbly suggest otherwise.

Dune is—beyond a reflection on politics, economics, environmentalism, and the pitfalls of advanced technology—at its heart, a ten-thousand-year experiment to recreate God. A failed experiment for those who have read the books to their completion, including the two final chapters written by Brian Herbert and Kevin J. Anderson (*Hunters of Dune* and *Sandworms of Dune*) that will be analyzed here as part of the larger *Dune* canon.

Again, there is nothing surprising here; the evolution of man into the Godhead is not just present in *Dune*. In Frank Herbert's other less well-known classic, *The God Makers*, the storyline takes place following a galaxy-shattering war, as a man takes the three following steps towards becoming God:

1. Coming upon the awareness of secret aggression.
2. Coming upon the discernment of purpose within the animal shape.
3. Experiencing death.

Several religions appear in *Dune*, mostly in the prequels, as hybrids of religions we have today: Buddislam, Nava Christianity, Mahayana Christianity, and Zen Hakigenshu. Many of them are ritualistic and an excuse to cover excessive hedonism, but Buddislam stands out as being the most central to Herbert's world building.

Buddislam, as the name suggests, is a hybrid of Zen Buddhism and Islam, the two dominant religions of the Eastern Hemisphere today. Buddhislamics worship Buddallah, with an approach very similar to contemporary Islamic practice.

Buddhislam itself is the result of a schism within Third Islam, and divided into three sects that reflect the major schisms of modern-day Islam:

* Zensunnis
* Zenshias
* Zensufis

Zensunnism

Zensunnism is a religious belief combining principles of Zen Buddhism and Sunni Islam, and the variation of Buddhislam that is most developed in the *Dune* series.

While the origins of the religion itself are murky, and Zensunnis are believed to have wandered before settling on Arrakis, going through different planets on a quest for a homeland. While this is part of the Zensunni mythos, it is also a consequence of the war against the thinking machines.

Zensunnis are defined as followers of a schismatic sect that broke away from the teachings of Maometh (the so-called "Third Muhammed") about 1381 B.G (Before Guild). The Zensunni religion is noted chiefly for its emphasis on the mystical and a reversion to "the ways of the fathers." Most scholars name Ali Ben Ohashi as leader of the original schism, but there is some evidence that Ohashi may have been merely the male spokesperson for his second wife, Nisai.

The emphasis on the mystical, and the traditionalism of "the ways of the fathers" suggests that Zensunnism is partly influenced by Sufism.

Further elements of Zensunni religion are directly borrowed from Islamic culture and the Arabic and Persian languages:

Dune	Islam
• Auliya: In the Zensunni Wanderers' religion, the female at the left hand of God; God's handmaiden • Fiqh: knowledge, religious law; one of the half-legendary origins of the Zensunni Wanderers' religion • Ilm: theology; science of religious tradition; one of the half-legendary origins of the Zensunni Wanderers' faith • Misr: the historical Zensunni (Fremen) term for themselves: "The People" • Shah-Nama: the half-legendary First Book of the Zensunni Wanderers • Ulema: a Zensunni doctor of theology	• Auliya (Arabic: أولياء) the Arabic word for saints • Fiqh (Arabic: فقه) Islamic jurisprudence • Ilm (Arabic: علم) the Arabic word for theological knowledge, theology • Misr (Arabic: مصر) the Arabic word for a settlement and also the Arabic name for the nation of Egypt (providing a play on the "gypsies" who were thought incorrectly by Europeans to have come from Egypt) • Shahnameh (Book of Kings [Persian: شاهنامه]) a Persian epic account of the Persian Shahs through the 12th century • Ulema (Arabic: علماء) Muslim doctors of the science of religious law

Despite all the above, Fremen culture, which is originally Zensunni, has been adulterated by the manipulations of the Bene Gesserit over millennia. More than that, Fremen Zensunnism is dramatically affected by the very fact of being on Arrakis, the psychic and physical effects of the Spice Mélange, and above all, Shai Hulud, The Maker, the giant worm whom the Fremen worship as God, and who, when Leto II embraces the Golden Path, *is* God.

Zenshiism

Zenshiism is a hybrid of the religious principles of Zen (a school of Mahayana Buddhism) and Shia Islam.

Zenshiism is not referred to directly in the original *Dune* series, but in the *Legends of Dune* by Brian Herbert and Kevin J. Anderson. There is less detail available about the actual principles and values inherent to Zenshiism.

Despite the absence of a theological model to draw from, Zenshias are represented as being a more violent sect than Zensunnis, who are considered to be sheep-like pacifists.

This last bit probably reflects on international politics and the "enmity" between the United States of America and the Islamic Republic of Iran. (Remember the "Great Satan" from above?) The breakdown in the relationship between America and Persia has had the pervasive effect of painting Shias as more violent than other Islamic sects.

In the *Dune* canon, on planet Poritrin where Zensunnis and Zenshias were both enslaved, Zenshias led the slave rebellion despite advice from Zensunni slaves, and when purchased on the market, their implicit difference in "philosophy" is downplayed by a greedy slaver when asked what separates the two groups.

Even ten thousand years in the future, it seems that the Ahl Al Bayt[5] can't get a break!

Zensufism

Zensufism is a hybrid of Zen and Sufism, a form of Islamic mysticism, which seeks a direct connection with God. The most famous philosopher and poet of which, Rumi, spoke of love as the pathway to connecting with God—more on this below.

Oddly enough, the abhorrent Tleilaxu geneticists (Bene Tleilax) have adopted a hybrid of Zensunnism and Zensufism, although they have clearly taken a path of their own in regards to their highly xenophobic and misogynistic culture, antagonistic to the core with Sufism's peaceful preaching.

Zensufism is also referred to very little and only in *Chapterhouse: Dune*, the last book written by Herbert where the Bene Gesserit turn their planet (Chapterhouse) into a desert to recreate the conditions on Dune and bring Shai Hulud back to life.

Islamophobia Now and in the Future

It seems that no matter how far into the future we travel, how many hybrids of our contemporary religions we develop, or who the real enemy is (in this case Thinking Machines), someone will find a reason to despise Muslims, or Zenmuslims as the case may be.

Ironically, the reasons why people portray Islam in a negative light today and in the *Dune* prequels couldn't be more diametrically opposed.

Islamophobia, the fear of Islam as a religion and by extension Muslims as a people, is a contemporary political and cultural reality. It is seen by many as a religion that preaches the murder of the infidel and a rejection of modernism. While this couldn't be farther from the truth, thanks to some minor groups preaching exactly those values, the image is an easy sell to a Western audience for whom Islam has been the enemy since the Crusades. This includes *de-Islamizing* the identity of Western allies such as the Kurds and the "Northern Alliance" in the United States–led contemporary invasion of Afghanistan. Never mind that 85 percent of Kurds are Muslim and fighting against organizations that pervert the image of Islam, such as the Islamic State. Never mind that the

Northern Alliance's real name is the "United Islamic Front for the Salvation of Afghan-istan." Only enemies of the West are labeled Islamic with solely religiously motivated goals; allies are stripped of any reference to their religion and portrayed in a conveniently secularized light. Is it that surprising, then, that people only think the worst about Islam?

In *Dune*, Buddislamists are despised for another reason entirely. They are pacifists who refuse to take part in the war against the Thinking Machines; damned if you do, damned if you don't. They are enslaved wholesale as a consequence and contribute to the war effort through toil rather than tempest. In fact, the Zensunni population of Dune, the Arrakis Fremen, are marooned slaves who fled the oppression of a society that made them the scapegoat for not all, but most of its ills thousands of years in the past.

Zensunnism regains popularity with the advent of the failed messiah Paul Muadib, who upon conquering Arrakis, embarks upon a Jihad that changes the known universe, bringing the legacy of Fremen Buddislamic culture to the forefront of intergalactic governance, if only for a time.

Buddhism and Islam Today

Given the significance of Buddislam to the *Dune* series, let's give a quick look at how Islam and Buddhism fare today.

How likely is it that Buddhism and Islam would ever merge into a cohesive spirituality, taking our present-day, 21st century world as a starting point?

Peace generates less press than conflict. It seems like such an obvious maxim, but it is crucial to remember this bias when looking at the depiction of modern and historical relations between Buddhism and Islam.

If one were to zero in on the epicenter of turmoil between Buddhist and Muslim populations, Myanmar's staggering humanitarian crisis with the displacement of Burmese Rohingya populations to neighboring Bangladesh is a case in point in both religious and racial intolerance.

The Burmese monk Wirathu, whom the *New York Times* painted as the face of Buddhist terror, heads the Organization for the Protection of Race and Religion and has been vocal in his incitement of hatred against the Rohingya minority, claiming they present a double threat, both religious and racial. He claims that Muslims pose a demographic and thus cultural threat to the country's integrity and denies their right to citizenship in Myanmar, claiming that the Rohingya are illegal Bangladeshi immigrants.

His fiery speeches led to riots in 2012, the burning of a mosque, and over a hundred casualties. The current crisis led to the displacement of an estimated 700,000 people, most of them across the border into Bangladesh.

This position appears to be supported by the vast majority of the Burmese population. Even the world-renowned former political prisoner and rights activist Aung San Suu Kyi has remained eerily silent on the issue.

I would be remiss not to mention violence on the part of Rohingya extremists that has fed into the pre-existing hatred and made the Rohingya cause less sympathetic to the few in the country who support their right to equality. Muslims represent barely 5 percent of the 54 million Burmese. While the number is still relatively significant, it does not in any way pose the demographic and cultural threat Wirathu and his supporters claim it to be.

The destruction of the Buddhas of Bamiyan by the Taliban in Afghanistan in 2001 shocked the world, deepening the sentiment that Islam and other cultures are incompatible. While the loss of the statues is a cultural and historical tragedy, this is where the bias introduced earlier plays in.

There have been Muslims in Afghanistan for *twelve hundred* years. For those twelve hundred years, no one destroyed the statues. The Taliban did. And just like that, it became a reflection not of the Taliban's intransigent ways, but of Islam and all Muslims, ignoring the simple fact that it is about terrorism, not Islam. I grew up in the eighties; my terrorists were blue-eyed and blond Eastern and Central Europeans. Make of that what you will.

To truly appreciate the depth of the divide that was created between Islam and Buddhism, one has to go back to the 1200s and the purported destruction of the Buddhist University in Nalanda in Northeast India.

Founded in the 5th century as a monastery, Nalanda over time became the prime institution of higher learning in Asia, boasting a student body of three thousand.

One day in the fall of 1202 CE, or so the story goes, Muslim soldiers rode in on horseback, slaughtered students and teachers alike and destroyed the university, leaving it in ruins, a trail of bodies in their wake.

This last event has become the symbolic marker of the incompatibility of Islam and Buddhism, of the enmity between the two religions that culminates in the examples above.

The reality, however, is much more nuanced.

I'm not naïve; such a tall tale has a basis in reality. I'm perfectly willing to believe that Muslim warriors (I do not use the term Mujahidin here, as there is no evidence that the conquest was a strictly religiously motivated Jihad) engaged in the killing of students and staff and that there was severe damage to the infrastructure. Such is the way of conquest, regardless of political, racial or religious motivations. Have any of you heard about Benin City? (Koutonin, 18 March 2016).

Nalanda did not vanish from history in 1202. It kept on functioning as a Buddhist university for another century, albeit in a much-diminished capacity. Chinese monks sought Buddhist texts in India late into the 14th century. Buddhism, despite numerous clashes with its mother religion, Hinduism, remained alive in India until the 17th century.

Nalanda did not signal the death of Buddhism in South Asia; the decline began five centuries earlier and is unrelated to Islam. When Chinese Buddhist scholar and traveler Xuanzang visited India in the 7th century, he already noted the religion's decline and made some dire predictions about Nalanda's future. Yet the image lingers on, an existential threat posed by Umma to the Sangha.

The present seems grim, but then again peace doesn't sell, and if it does, who is buying? The headlines will pick and choose.

Just as I have done here.

A more astute person would point to a thousand years of connections, parallels, historical moments of true cohabitation and rule, and love, and bring them together.

My simple point is this: all the above means nothing. Two or three thousand words that you might as well forget because however Buddhislam occurred in our speculative future, it wasn't the Buddhist or Muslim extremists who pulled it together; it was people who saw truth through the rituals and divisive rhetoric, who preserved through adversity, the bad press the threats, the ostracism.

I remember Captain Carrot from Terry Pratchett's *Discworld* series being asked which religion he believed in. He said that he believed that every religion held an element of an essential truth, thus dodging a casus belli between Ankh Morpork and somewhere on the Disc. May we be so lucky, but it does send a simple and positive message: there is always room for unity and room for truth. May you find your own…with a little help from the SF profession.

Islam, Africa, and Speculative Fiction

My parents introduced me to *Dune*. I remember their excitement when it popped up on TV around the time I was eight or nine years old. Both were and are still fascinated by the depth of philosophy and mysticism apparent throughout the series. Both were fascinated by how the novel and its sequels infuse Islamic elements into a future society and subvert them as part of a larger whole.

As an adult, having finished the tale of the Kwizats Haderach and looking back on my childhood, I came to understand why and how this fantastic vision of an Islamized future was very much reminiscent, in my mind at least, of the elements of Sufi Islam that were familiar to me as a child.

As I was growing up, we used to visit Senegal every year or every other year. We would stay in Saly, the beach resort outside what used to be the small town of Mbour, now one of the country's major economic centers by virtue of tourism alone. Every day at twilight my father would round up my brothers and me and direct us to our room until it was time for dinner.

I didn't understand it at the time, but to my father, a Senegalese man of the coastal, fisherman ethnic group called the Lebou, this was a special time. Some might call it the Witching Hour.

Every Lebou community along the coast has a protective spirit attached to it. The spirit can be kind or not, playful or vindictive, but it helps guide the community through communication with the local marabout—a Muslim religious leader and teacher in West Africa and (historically) in the Maghreb—and protects its people against external aggression. They are known as Rab and can possess you at their whim.

Those spirits have different names: Leuk Daour Mbaye in Dakar, Mame Coumba Lambaye in Rufisque, among others. Some of these spirits are connected. I've heard that Leuk Daour and Mame Coumba are an item. Perhaps they are the embodiment of one single spirit taking on different forms.

To my father, twilight meant that it was the Rab's time to walk the beach, not humans, and while the spirit may not be malevolent, who knew how it would take to our presence on its beaches in those fleeting moments when night and day tease each other on the horizon.

The time of the unseen. In between calls to prayer.

To me this was what Sufi Islam was, an attempt to bridge the gap, to bring cultures together outside of any normative framework, a free-flowing torrent, connecting the past with the present and looking into the future.

As an author, this is still one of the most striking elements of my upbringing and a very influential part of my writing. A Muslim country where the religious and the spiritual met, where the modern religion of Islam did not clash with tradition, the zensunni way of the fathers, you could say. Instead, they somehow seemed to embrace, creating something new, unique, and beautiful.

I refer to Leuk Daour, the Rab of Dakar, in several of my stories. In "The Broken Nose," a science fiction short story published by *Omenana* magazine, a young dealer allows Leuk Daour, whose colors are red and black, to possess him and start a revolution. In my recent collection *Dark Moons Rising on a Starless Night*, a horror collection published by Clash Books, the story "Black & Gold" follows a young boy who devours the white horse that sometimes symbolizes Leuk Daour and becomes the Rab at a time when the forces of post-colonialism are set to wreck more havoc in Senegal than ever before.

While the world has its eyes turned on T'Challa of Wakanda in *Black Panther*, and the mash-up of Africana it delivers in a beautifully empowering vision of the continent, people still overlook the rich African tradition of fantastic storytelling, the reaching back to ancient Egypt, of astrology, of looking at the stars for answers to present and future conundrums.

The Dogon people of Mali in many ways epitomize this clash of cultures. A people who, without any technological advances, nonetheless knew of the existence of distant stars hundreds of years before telescopes were precise enough to pinpoint them. Their knowledge is gleaned from two brothers, known as Nommos, aliens who take the form of fish walking on their tails that came to earth to teach them.

Nommo is also the name of the seminal award given now for the second year running by the African Speculative Fiction Society, a point of origin, if you will.

The Dogon were pushed into the mountainous regions of Mali, the Bandiagara cliffs, when Islam expanded in West Africa, and they didn't want to lose their traditions to this new faith that took much of the world by storm. Today, a large number if not most Dogon are Muslim, but they are still Dogon; they still practice their traditional rites, and they still look towards Sirius, the star nearest to our solar system, full of knowledge that we outsiders have no understanding of, awaiting what's coming next.

My story "Ogotemelli's Song," in the *AfroSFv3* anthology by Ivor Hartmann and StoryTime, refers symbolically to one of their elders as a central character.

Speaking of Nommos, beyond the award, the African Speculative Fiction Society provides an invaluable resource in the form of Nigeria's Wole Talabi's list of published African SFF, an updatable roster keeping track of African speculative publications starting in 1952. It is a work in constant progress that readers here are invited to add to ("List of Published," 27 May 2020). In addition to the list of published authors, another resource is the list of publishers of African speculative fiction.[6] There are two lists, African and International venues, but the African list is the most important. African authors supporting African publishers, and vice versa, is a fundamental step towards developing the genre where it should be developed, *in Africa*.

There have been other attempts to capture the breadth of publications from Africa and the Middle East over the past few years ("RESSOURCES SUR LA," 25 June 2018). Identifying whether the stories are written by Muslims or not isn't as easy as it would seem. Some names and geographies are obviously of Muslim heritage, but does the author claim that heritage or not? A Kinshasa friend and former colleague, Sefu, told me his name was Muslim, derived from Saifu, Saif Ullah. Even the name Zaire is of Arabic origin in the lion's roar Zair.

Several Francophone African countries have large Muslim populations and authors of the speculative. As the francophone spokesperson for ASFS, I'm having a harder time identifying them. Perhaps because the francophone scene of magazines, e-zines, and reviews, predominantly in France and Quebec, is not as large and "lucrative" as the more established and older Anglophone scene (Porte-plume, 23 August 2016). Perhaps because francophone literary culture tips towards classical publications as opposed to a more entrepreneurial and dynamic online and pulp originated scene in the larger Anglo world. And that becomes truer even for smaller language groups like lusophone countries such as Angola, who've had waves of Muslim immigrants from West Africa that they call "Mamadu."[7]

Regardless of the reason, they are out there. *Galaxies SF*, a French speculative review, recently published an edition focused on Africa. One of my stories is in that edition, but I particularly liked Moussa Ould Ebnou's story "Dreg Dreg," about the lingering psychological effects of colonialism against the backdrop of the everyday life of a Mauritanian village. It is a story both humorous and profound.

I like to go to old wolof folktales for inspiration sometimes (Copans and Couty, 1988). The characters are Muslims by and large, but their daily life is very much local and often irreverent and hilarious. Some of them definitely have fantastical elements, but Africa is a place where the real world and the spirit world are one. Many Africans would take offense at labeling their traditions and spiritual and ancestral worship as "speculative." It is not a matter of speculation. It is a matter of *awakening*. Perhaps you see it, perhaps you don't, but it is real nonetheless.

Award-winning Canadian SFF author Geoff Ryman, one of African speculative fiction's strongest supporters and one of the minds behind the African Speculative Fiction Society, coined the term Traditional Belief Realism to explain the continuous stream between the living and spirit world in African story telling.

Africa is a natural breeding ground for stories and tales of the speculative, the imaginative, the groundbreakingly refreshing in a world dominated by recycled visions of European monsters, formulaic super heroes, and horror movies where the black man dies first. It's such a stiff world, so utterly predictable and so completely bland, where the supernatural is always evil and has nothing to tell us of value about ourselves. The material reigns supreme, with all that means in terms of selfishness and greed and lust—the very things that drove imperialism and still drive neo-colonialism.

African science fiction and fantasy is more than just a vision of a technologically advanced and economically prosperous Africa, judging progress by *Western* standards. It is Africans deciding for themselves what counts as being advanced, where you don't lose your soul in the world of machines where man becomes a machine—one of the things a Westerner like Frank Herbert did in fact get spot on. In Africa, our ghosts don't haunt our houses; they guide us intimately, until we become ghosts ourselves, ancestors in turn. That is our contribution as Africans to the sci-fi world, questioning the very boundaries of what counts as science and superstition, a ballsier breed of the "speculation" in fiction.

History is written on the sands of Arrakis, on the beaches of Dakar, on the dunes of Agadez, and carved in the Matobo hills of Zimbabwe. The vision of the future set in *Dune* asks all the right questions and postulates amazing things. Perhaps, just perhaps, when we actually step foot into a better future, that vision will be *African*.

NOTES

1. Quote taken from "Dune," *WIKIQUOTE*, https://en.wikiquote.org/wiki/Dune.
2. Haram is Arabic for forbidden.
3. A Muslim incantation meaning God willing.
4. United States of America.
5. This is a reference to the family and descendants of the Prophet Muhammad (PBUH).
6. "Publishers of Speculative Fiction by Africans," http://www.africansfs.com/resources/africansfpublishers.
7. "BILLY B—MAMADU OFICIAL VIDEO," https://www.youtube.com/watch?v=IOCiyimPLq8.

WORKS CITED

Copans, Jean, and Philippe Couty. (1988). *Contes wolof du Daol*. eBook. http://horizon.documentation.ird.fr/exl-doc/pleins_textes/divers07-10/27124.pdf.

Koutonin, Mawuna. (18 March 2016). "Story of cities #5: Benin City, the mighty medieval capital now lost without trace." *The Guardian*. https://www.theguardian.com/cities/2016/mar/18/story-of-cities-5-benin-city-edo-nigeria-mighty-medieval-capital-lost-without-trace.

"List of Published African SFF." (27 May 2020). *African Speculative Fiction Society*. http://www.africansfs.com/resources/published.

Porte-plume, Damien. (23 August 2016). "Quelles sont les revues de l'imaginaire?" *Skōp*. https://www.skop.io/a/quelles-sont-les-revues-de-l-imaginaire [French].

"RESSOURCES SUR LA SCIENCE-FICTION AFRICAINE." (25 June 2018). *ReS Futurae*. https://resf.hypotheses.org/ressources/ressourcessfafricaine [French].

Rafeeat Aliyu

*Identity, Islam, and Women's Writing
Meet in Afro-Futurism*

EGYPTIAN SOCIETY FOR SCIENCE FICTION

> You were born with wings, why prefer to crawl through life?
>
> —Rumi

ESSF: What drew you to science fiction, and how do you distinguish it from "speculative" fiction?

I was a huge fan of all the science fiction shows on TV growing up, in particular *Star Trek: Deep Space Nine, Voyager,* and *Stargate SG-1.* I didn't start reading science fiction until I was much older, in university. I think what drew me to science fiction is the world-building. When I wrote as a young girl, I never set stories in places I knew but preferred setting them in imagined worlds. Eventually, I realized that the most interesting imagined worlds could be found in the science fiction and fantasy genre.

As for what distinguished science fiction from speculative fiction, to me speculative fiction covers a wider array of genres and styles than the science fiction umbrella. I find that a good number of the African science fiction I read blends other genres such as fantasy; that's why I'm more comfortable with the speculative fiction tag.

ESSF: What are your favorite subgenres and which authors exerted the most influence on you during your career?

I enjoy many subgenres! From apocalyptic to cyberpunk…. I've also enjoyed some military science fiction. I consider alternate history, parallel worlds, and space western to be among my favorite subgenres as well.

Two authors that exerted the most influence on me at the start of my career were Octavia Butler and Nalo Hopkinson. That list has grown as I delved into the works of other writers, but I credit Butler and Hopkinson with really showing me that people who look like me can have their science fiction stories. Reading Octavia Butler's "Kindred" was an eye-opener for me; it's about an African-American woman who travels back in time to the antebellum South where she has to ensure that her ancestry survives. *Lilith's Brood,* another collection of books by Butler, imagines a future after a nuclear war has left the Earth uninhabitable. A race of aliens appears to start the project of genetically modifying and training humans to repopulate the Earth that they've rebuilt. I still remember the joy I felt reading Nalo Hopkinson's *Salt Roads* and *Brown Girl in the Ring. Salt Roads*

299

mixes in several genres, from speculative to historical to magic realism, to tell the story of three women across time and history intertwined with the water deity Lasirén.

ESSF: You mention the Star Trek *world and* Stargate. *Is it hard to find SF in bookstores and libraries in Nigeria? Is it the language barrier?*

It was a bit hard to find SF books. We had places where we bought second-hand books, and if you looked hard enough, you'd find SF books after the Jackie Collins, Tom Clancy, Sidney Sheldon, and John Grisham books. When it came to genre books, we'd often only get them if someone was going abroad (that way we could ask them to buy the books we wanted for us). As an adult, I've seen some SF books in stores in Abuja and Lagos, but these tended to be the very popular books like *Lord of the Rings* or the Harry Potter series. Cassava Republic has published some of SF writer Nnedi Okorafor's books, which have made SF with Nigerian characters more accessible here. It's not a language barrier but may be linked to the stereotype that Nigerians don't read/don't have a reading culture.

ESSF: Did you have an especial soft spot for Avery Brooks, aka Captain Sisko, and Captain Janeway?

I loved Captain Janeway!

ESSF: What is your focus on when you write? Science, politics, women, the environment?

Out of those four, I'd have to pick women as I'm deliberately focused on telling women's stories. Then environment and politics will tie at second place.

ESSF: What is Afro-futurism?

There are so many ways to define Afro-futurism. Recently I've come to see that everyone has their own definition of Afro-futurism. I have no idea who coined the term Afro-futurism, but I believe the earliest example of it was from Sun Ra, the American musician known for his cosmic outlook and cutting-edge fashion. Today, examples of Afro-futurism are everywhere, from the *Black Panther* movie to Janelle Monae's music. Within the continent, I've found works from South African musician Simphiwe Dana (the video for the song "Ndiredi") and the Kenyan collective Just a Band to have elements of Afro-futurism.[1]

For me it's a work of art, literature, or concept that draws from a re-imagined future (or past) of Africa and people of African descent the world over.

ESSF: Do you like setting your stories in the distant reaches of outer space or back home on Mother Earth?

Most of my stories are set in alternate universes because I like to play around with world-building. So, it'd be set on Mother Earth but not the one that's familiar to us. I've considered setting stories in the distant reaches of outer space, but I think I prefer reading stories set here.

ESSF: What is your idea of paradise on Earth? What would an African "Utopia" look like?

An African utopia would be one that is completely and totally free and fair. Where there wouldn't be any structural inequalities. Goodbye to poverty and also to sexism, misogyny. There will be no subjugation of people along the lines of ethnicity or tribe and sexuality. This utopia will be one that embraces and makes room for the huge variety of people that are African and includes the Diaspora. For family life, maybe it'd go back to the days where the village raised the child, so there'll be less emphasis on the nuclear unit, and children will be protected by the community. Needless to say, young people will have more opportunities. I don't know how that will manifest, but if it's a utopia, every sector needs to have opportunities. I imagine people living both in villages and cities. Everyone shouldn't have to move to the city to have a better life or access to infrastructure. Villages should have the same access to running water, electricity, sanitation, technological development, etc. For food, it'll probably be a combination of both homegrown and synthetic; the kinds of food we eat will very likely change, especially when you consider that we aren't eating the exact same foods our ancestors did. I have a hard time picturing the whole continent united, but I do see a redrawing of the colonial lines/borders to make more accommodation for ethnic similarities.

ESSF: How popular is science fiction in Nigeria? Do the critics and publishers like it or just the readers? How long has there been SF in Nigeria and Africa?

I think science fiction is growing in popularity here, especially with the advent of the *Omenana* magazine. More and more people are interested in these stories, however I'm not seeing as much science fiction from Nigerian publishers as I'd like… there's always room for more. There is a lot of ground for critics to cover. Still, organizations like Okadabooks have made an impact with their "Literally What's Hot" column (which featured my flash fiction story about a robot's attempt to rescue a child, "Debug") on BellaNaija, for example (OkadaBooks, 2016).

Nigerian SF has a long history that few know about. There's a science fiction book with a man who travels to a parallel world from colonial Nigeria published in 1934. Incidentally, it was written by a Muslim writer in Northern Nigeria, Muhammadu Bello Kagara. Then our folktales have so many elements of science fiction, whether time travel or the discovery of new worlds…. I strongly believe there are other science fiction writers from Nigeria's past that have faded into obscurity and that we no longer remember.

ESSF: Are African legends and myths an important influence on science fiction in Africa? If so, can you give us some examples from your own writings or those of others?

This links to my answer to the question above! The examples I can give to my own writing fall under the banner of fantasy. My story "Yoyin of the Enchanting Form in Expound" is a direct retelling of a folktale. When I write science fiction, I am heavily influenced by the history that I use as a template to build on and imagine futuristic worlds.

I've been very fascinated by tales of people living underwater in rivers and lakes and would like to sit down and craft an Atlantis-like story sometime in the future. That is still in the making though.

ESSF: How important is poetry to your writings and the writings of your fellow SF authors?

I don't read as much poetry as I'd like, and at the moment it's not a big influence on my writing.

ESSF: Would you say that Muslim SF authors like yourself are making a major contribution to modern African literature?

Sadly, I wouldn't. When I think of top Nigerian writers, I can only think of a few that are Muslim. And then when I think of the smaller circle of SF writers here, there are even fewer Muslims. I wonder if they are writing in languages other than English.

ESSF: Chinua Achebe insisted on writing in English as a way of getting around national divisions in Nigeria. Are you of the same opinion when it comes to writing in English? Do you speak Arabic?

I'm half and half on this. While I agree with Chinua Achebe that English can bypass national divisions and make literature accessible to more people, at the same time I'd love to have my books published in local Nigerian languages too.

I was taught to read and write the Arabic of the Quran as a child; that's the extent of my Arabic.

ESSF: Can science and speculative fiction help mend bridges between Muslims and non–Muslims?

It can widen horizons and encourage readers to consider different ideas and perspectives, so yes, it is possible that it could mend bridges. I don't think that it'll mend them completely or change how people feel deeply. But it could be the start of something positive.

ESSF: How aware are writers in sub-Saharan Africa of what's being done in North Africa in the field of speculative fiction? (I can tell you straight off that we in North Africa are completely unaware of what goes on down South). Would pooling resources help us both reach a wider international audience?

There is definitely a lack of awareness. However, for SF fans looking online for books from African writers to read, it's very likely that they will come across recommendations of works by North African writers. Speaking personally, I have come across lists of SF works by North African writers but tended to skip them over for something closer to home.

A pooling of resources will be a great place to start; I imagine going further too. For example, just think about the amazing stories compiled in an anthology of fiction from Muslim SF writers across Africa.

ESSF: What is the "Book Sprint method"?

Oh, the Book Sprint method involves sitting down to write a book within a week (five days). It usually brings together a bunch of writers, editors, etc., to start and finish a book on a chosen theme within a very short period of time. I had the great pleasure of taking part in a Book Sprint to write *Nameless* with seven other Nigerian writers; it's a collection of several stories drawing from different aspects of Nigerian society (2014).

ESSF: Is the internet changing the way books are being sold in Nigeria? Can e-books help African SF authors reach a wider audience? Is self-publishing an option for struggling African authors writing in English?

A publisher will be better placed to answer whether the internet is changing the way books are sold in Nigeria. However, I believe that e-books can help us reach a wider audience. I mentioned above that there's a general belief that Nigerians don't like reading or have a reading culture. A number of start-ups are rising to challenge that. One of them is Okadabooks, which provides smartphone-friendly e-books through its app. I was surprised to learn that people are reading my short stories through the Okadabooks app. I'm not sure they'd have come across my work otherwise.

I have friends who have tried self-publishing, often using Okadabooks, so it's definitely an option. I personally prefer the traditional route, so I'm trying my hand at that first.

ESSF: In addition to being an author, you're a media consultant, amateur photographer, and filmmaker. That's quite a toolkit to help promote science fiction.

Haha, yes, it is. I'm just trying to diversify my skills because Nigeria can be a tough place to succeed in.

ESSF: That's a lot of career tracks. On your webpage, you describe yourself as a "content creator" too. When do you get time to write? And would this indicate that it is difficult for an SF author to make a living just from writing?

Content creator is a blanket term for all the things I do, listed above. I typically write when I have the time off work, but I don't write as much as I'd like. For example, the last time I wrote anything this year was February and before that, maybe October last year. I don't know any young Nigerian SF authors that make a living just from writing, so it does indicate that it's difficult.

ESSF: How long before we see African science fiction movies on the silver screen?

Which silver screen? Nigerian cinema industries have made several attempts at science-fiction movies (even though many of them have had bad reviews). I just learned that there's apparently even a Hausa science fiction movie, *Aduniya* (Lere, 2013).

Of course, there's still a long way to go in terms of effects and moving storylines, but I'll be optimistic and believe things will improve.

ESSF: Your plans for the future, for yourself, and African SF?

More books, more stories. I'm working on publishing a collection of short stories set in an alternate futuristic Nigeria devastated by climate change and desertification.

I'd love to curate a collection of African SF when I have the time. It'd be great to have voices from North Africa in that; interestingly this is something I hadn't considered before.

NOTE

1. Nderedi—SIMPHIWE DANA, https://youtu.be/gRm74OwziZ4.

WORKS CITED

Lere, Mohammed. (4 September 2013). "Kannywood to Release First Science Fiction Movie 'ADUNIYA.'" Premium Times. https://www.premiumtimesng.com/entertainment/144148-kannywood-release-first-science-fiction-movie-aduniya.html.

Nameless. (26 November 2014). "HEINRICH-BÖLL-STIFTUNG: The Green Political Foundation." https://ng.boell.org/2014/11/26/nameless.

OkadaBooks. (28 June 2016). "Literally What's Hot! OkadaBooks Analyzes Rafeeat Aliyu's 'DEBUG.'" Bella Naija blog. https://www.bellanaija.com/2016/06/literally-whats-hot-okadabooks-analyzes-rafeeat-aliyus-debug/.

A Bird's-Eye View of the Comic
Book Scene in Nigeria

Ashiru Muheez Afolabi

When the neutral observer thinks about comics and comic books, the first thing that comes to mind is the superhero genre where fan favorites like Batman, Superman, X-Men, Spiderman, Incredible Hulk, and other heroes from the DC and Marvel comics roster reign supreme. These aspects of comic books are so dominant that they have spun into TV shows and movies, creating their own universe in other mediums and raking in billions of dollars in the process. According to the statistics portal, statista.com:

> As of January 2020, the superhero movies "Avengers: Endgame," "Spider-Man: Far from Home," and "Joker" among others collected a combined box office revenue of nearly 3.2 billion U.S. dollars. This figure includes the box office revenues generated by four "Batman" re-releases, as well as the 2019 revenues for "Aquaman" and "Spider-Man: Into the Spider-Verse." Superhero movies have grown immensely popular in the last few years, not just in the United States but on a global level. DC's "Aquaman" grossed almost 1.15 billion U.S. dollars worldwide in 2018, and movies from the X-Men series continued to perform well in theaters across the world ("Superhero movies," 2020).

This is from movies alone. TV shows and video games are also other mediums American comic books have inspired. Outside America, Japan is another comic book powerhouse. The Japanese Manga comics are a vast empire of comic books. The unique drawing style of Manga comics has also been the inspiration behind cartoons, movies, TV shows, and video games like *Alita*, *Crying Freeman*, *Dragon Ball Z*, *Naruto*, and *Bleach* to name a few. Factsanddetails.com values the annual sales of Manga at $10 billion, which is a *third* of total Japanese publishing revenue.

Outside of these two, the French and British also have good comic industries. However, one country with a diverse and exciting comic book industry which is often ignored or not reckoned with when comics are discussed is Nigeria. The Nigerian comic book industry is blessed with unique material and well-crafted stories. The artwork in some of these comics is as good as the best in any part of the world. The stories range from sci-fi and fantasy stories to superheroes as well as politically motivated stories.

Backdrops to an African Case Study

The first concerted attempt to promote African comics and superheroes was actually in Ghana in the 1970s. This began with pamphlets depicting Marvel Comics superheroes teaming up with local folk heroes from Twi legends like the Anansenem, legends that have a tremendous geographical expanse extending from Ghana and west Africa to the Caribbean and the United States. What is also interesting about this hybrid mix of heroes is that the storylines are hybrid too, breaking many conventions in Western and African storytelling. To quote Karin Barber's "Popular Arts in Africa":

> In the stories, there were ordinary Ghanaian people who reminisced about the glorious past and complained about contemporary issues, such as corrupt soldiers and politicians. Marvel comic book heroes, Ananse and other folktale figures would discuss these issues, hide among ordinary Ghanaian people, and use their superhuman strength or lead a popular revolt to seek justice, showing the corrupted Ghanaians the error of their ways. These superheroes were generally described as having special powers due to otherworldly connections or a connection to the past beyond that of the everyday African. These powers gave them the possibility to change the world and cause political transformation [Barber, quoted in Pijnaker, 2018].

In the 1980s Nigeria became the next African torchbearer for such culturally distinctive superhero comics with the launching of the Captain Africa magazine in 1987, thanks to Ghanaian Andy Akman in Nigeria and Mbadiwe Emelumba of African Comics Ltd. More specifically, this model of superhero was there to "displace the white Captain Africa who featured in a 1950s Hollywood serial in which he stumbled upon conflict and saved an African nation" (Pijnaker, 2018). Citing James Brooke's 1988 feature in the *New York Times*, Tessa Pijnaker argues that "Captain Africa was characterised as part of a trend among a new generation of illustrators across Africa to decolonize comics, especially as a reaction against white saviour stories such as Tarzan and The Phantom" (Pijnaker, 2018). African modernity was at stake, as well as colonial independence—a continent staking its claim to the future.

Even so, many of these early attempts came to nothing, and they were muffled by other attempts to promote black superheroes by foreign publishers that placed restrictions on the political and cultural content of many of their own comics—such as *Powerman* and *Mighty Man*. Now, to examine my country's experience in the here and now.

Nigerian Comics, Promise and Peril

In terms of sales and market value, it is difficult to say exactly how much creators of comic books work in Nigeria. Like almost everything else in Nigeria, it is difficult to get accurate statistics for sales and income generated from this potentially lucrative subsection of publishing and entertainment. Also, the struggling economy in the country does not encourage the production and distribution of comics in hardcopy. Add piracy to the mix, and it becomes difficult to see how the traditional model of printing and selling will make a profit. Most producers in the Nigerian comic industry resort to selling digital copies of their works. To make ends meet, a lot of them usually go into related industries like advertising, animation, screenwriting, and movie and music production. In these areas, they can channel their creativity to put food on the table and keep their businesses running.

It is not uncommon to be able to get free copies and samples of Nigerian comics in digital and hard copy formats. This is because creators usually put up free sample chapters online as a way to attract customers. They also partner with big name brands in other industries who acquire comics and distribute them along with their products. A good example of this practice is the football-themed comic *Supa Strikas*. It was originally developed in Nigeria but was bought by a South African company ("Supa Strikas," 2020). The comics were sold in Texaco outlets and fast food companies like Mr. Biggs. These companies sometimes included samples of the comics along with their products to customers. Big name South African brands and international brands like Nike and Chevron also came on board as the South African owners spread the comics to different parts of the world.

Going back to the content, back in the day (if you were not lucky enough to have them sent from abroad), comic book fans in Nigeria had to make do with comic sections in the daily newspapers. These ranged from satires to action to pure comedy. Some stories were serialized. Others, especially the ones for comic relief, were one offs. Then, there was the popular comic character, Papa Ajasco. Papa Ajasco, a bald, bespectacled man with a pot belly, also had a comedy TV show. Both the comics and the show were produced by Wale Adenuga, who also produced *Binta*, a comic for school-aged kids. There were also the adult themed comics *Benbela* and *Lulu, Lolly*. They were mainly funny, sexual escapades of the characters in the comics. Most of these were printed in black and white. Wale Adenuga also produced the magazine *Ikebe Super*, which featured a lot of comic book works. It was much later, when the aforementioned *Supa Stryka* hit the shelves, that things took a different turn.

Today, you can't talk of comics in Nigeria without mentioning Comic Republic. The online multimedia company was founded by Jide Martin and made its publishing debut in 2013. The stories and characters are indigenous. A visit to the website has the caption "Welcome to a World of Heroes!" Clicking "Enter" takes the reader into a world of heroes of different varieties.

The flagship character is Guardian Prime, who some have dubbed the "Nigerian Superman." He is the fifth element (fire, water, air, earth, and man) created by God in his own image to be the perfect man with extraordinary abilities. The backstory is that every two thousand years, a guardian for humanity is born. Tunde Jaiye, aka Guardian Prime, is this generation's guardian.

A relatively new addition to the comic industry is Revolution Media. The production company boasts of artists/writers like Sewedo Nupowaku and Hanu Afere. Their debut comic in 2018 was titled *Trinity Red October*. The 8-part, award-winning comic has been described as a high octane political thriller that traces the history of Nigerian politics to the present day. Corruption and political scheming are interwoven with tradition and culture in this critically acclaimed comic. Revolution also has a number of comics in the works.

Youneek Studios is another producer of Nigerian content. The amazing art work and diverse characters the company has on its books create a comic book reader's dream. Characters like EXO (an impatient and reckless but brave character who has an Ironman-type suit combined with ability-,enhancing chemicals called nanites flowing in his bloodstream) and Queen Malika (empress and military strategist with deadly sword fighting abilities) are just two of the characters from Youneek. Through a combination of history, culture and mythology, Youneek Studios uses comics and other forms of media to tell African stories that are easily relatable, regardless of the reader's background.

Vortex Comics has a diverse array of stories and comic productions. The titles produced by Vortex include *Secret Society*, *Orisha*, *Ekun*, and *Local Champions*. Productions on this imprint range from toy-like art to very realistic drawings. The stories are diverse and will leave a reader dizzy with options.

Some content producers use social media to push out their works. These are web artists that use their Twitter, Facebook, Instagram, and other social media to put out works and have garnered a strong following over the years. They include Awele Eneli (producer of I.Journal), Justin Irabor (Obaranda), KRO Onimole (Crasher Comics), and St. Wosh. Themes produced here mainly focus on everyday life and sometimes give readers a weekly dose of comic relief.

Other comic producers to watch out for are Epoch Comics, Mad Comics, Collectible Comics, Spoof Comics, Peda Comics, Awonda Comics, Linebugs Comics, Panaramic Entertainment, Wildfire Comics, Taniarts Concepts, Kolanut Productions, and Shadowblack Comics.

The diverse array of stories and artwork means that the Lagos Comic Con, the biggest comic convention on the African continent, has continued to expand since it first launched in 2012 with 300 attendants, growing to over 4,000 in 2018!

A Concluding Word

The comic book industry in Nigeria has much to offer the world. In the areas of science fiction and fantasy, there is a lot of mind-blowing content and innovative ideas. Though mostly influenced by stories from the Western world, content producers have come up with stories and artwork that are uniquely Nigerian and African and cannot be mistaken for anything else. With the right investment, the sector will bring unique and distinct stories into the limelight.

To round off this article, I will shamelessly promote my writing for comics. I am working with my friends Oluwole Aina and graphic artist Scot Mmobuosi to produce a comic book series titled *Tales of Conquest*. Our stories for the series are based on events that happened in ancient times. The stories are stories of African origin. In the future, we plan to work on other non-African stories that fit the concept. The stories are based on the past with a focus on the socio-cultural and political interaction between and within ancient empires. This interaction often led to war and conflict. Through a combination of fictitious and sometimes real characters and events, the stories are told with a healthy dose of humor, suspense, and intricate twists. You can check out our works at www.talesofconquest.com.

The important thing to highlight is that this has been a long time coming. A large and thriving comic industry and dedicated readership, especially among the young, means rising stars in the future with new heroes and new comics and new adventures and new approaches to old and new themes. More African authors, readers, superheroes, and comics mean more and more that Africa can make its voice heard and gets its message across, and with that, Muslim African voices, themes, and storylines.

It means, we hope, a growing audience for science fiction and a growing *legitimacy* for our brand of science fiction both on the African continent and internationally. It is a financially feasible brand if the history of statistics is anything to go by.

I hope you enjoy what you see.

Works Cited

Pijnaker, Tessa. (11 June 2018). "African Superheroes in the 1970s and 1980s: A Historical Perspective." *AFRICA IN WORDS.* https://africainwords.com/2018/06/11/african-superheroes-in-the-1970s-and-80s-a-historical-perspective/.

"Supa Strikas." (5 May 2020). *Wikipedia.* https://en.wikipedia.org/wiki/Supa_Strikas.

"Superhero Movies: Box Office Revenue 2019." (10 January 2020). *Statista.* https://www.statista.com/statistics/311931/superhero-movies-box-office-revenue/.

The Sudan and Genre Literature

Between Historical Speculation,
Magic Realism, and Science Fiction

AMIR TAG ELSIR

> I want to take my rightful share of life by force, I want to give lavishly, I want love to flow from my heart, to ripen and bear fruit. There are many horizons that must be visited, fruit that must be plucked, books read, and white pages in the scrolls of life to be inscribed with vivid sentences in a bold hand.
>
> —El-Tayeb Saleh (1969: 5)

First, a brief description of myself. I am a physician. I worked for a few years in the east of Sudan, particularly in my city Portsudan, then in the border areas with Eretria, where I got ideas for many, many stories and novels. I have been an expatriate in Qatar since 1993, working and writing there, and although the medical field is difficult, I could find a good measure of time to write. My rituals in writing are very simple. When I have an idea. I go to my writing corner, which is a small space in the Radisson Blu Hotel Doha. It is in the lobby, but I can separate myself from the surroundings and just work on my computer. This is usually during the day, and I change my duties in the hospital to the evening shift. I stay there around four or five hours, writing about a thousand words, and no more, then I go to my duties and come next day to continue, until I finish the work. There's no previous planning, just an idea, and I find myself writing until the end. After finishing, I read the manuscript and add or remove some parts but usually no major things. The work stays a little with me, before I send it to my publisher. This ritual I described is, of course, when I have an idea to write, but most of the year I never go to the corner. My weekly articles in newspapers and other things like interviews and surveys are usually written in the house. In that corner I wrote most of my known works. I am writing in Arabic, of course, and have never tried to write in English. I believe that any writer can create well in his mother language.

Second, let me explain that what I am writing is not science fiction as people know it, but some writing could be fantasy or magic realism, and some of them including new things created by me, things like objects, drugs, diseases, names, and even organ functions that are not really present in reality. I will explain later how this is the case by reviewing two or three of my important novels.

I have been writing for a long time. I started writing poems at a very young age, when I was a student in primary school, and continued with poetry until university. By that time, I had begun publishing my work in great magazines and newspapers. In 1988, when I was in the last year of university in Egypt, I started to write novels. From that time, I have been in the field, and my novels now number 25 or 26; I cannot remember. And in the last few years, I write and publish a book every year, so I have a large number of readers and appear in annual Arabic prizes lists like the Sheikh Zaid Book Award, the International Prize for Arabic Fiction ("the Arabic Booker"), and others.

My first novel is very short, about 90 pages; its name is *Karmakol*, which is the name of the village in Sudan in which I was born. The novel is very concise and full of poetry, and you can consider it a long poem; this is normal for me because I came from a poetry background.

It was very difficult to find a publisher at that time with my completely unknown name, but finally and after a great effort, I found one: a publishing house called Alghad. The owner Kamal Abdelhalim was a great Egyptian poet and also an active leftist. He agreed to publish the book and keep my expensive watch (a Rolex), which was a gift from my father, with him. I also had to distribute and sell my own book. Once I brought a satisfactory sum of money with me, then I could get my Rolex back. This is what happened, and it was about three months before all the copies of the book were sold to students.

The book actually found a great readership and started a new type of writing, and many major critics in Egypt wrote about it positively. However, my literary ambitions were stopped when I travelled to Sudan to work as a doctor and was completely immersed in the field. That was the case until I travelled to Qatar to work in primary health care. In 1996, after three years of being there, I started to regain my love of writing. I started to work on a book, then next year another, and so on. Because I practice medicine on a regular schedule, after that I can find some good hours to write. Besides novels, I have written biographies, poetry, and collections of my articles in newspapers—there are now five non-fiction books.

As for my genre preferences, you could always say that there is a dissatisfaction with social realism in Sudan, particularly among the younger writers and readers. However, from my experience, I would say that I believe that any writer has his own style that he can use to write. This of course suits his thinking and capabilities. Also, the process of reading is very similar because readers prefer one style to another and so on, although I have thousands of readers in the Arab world and across the glove. Still, some readers don't like my style; some critics also keep on criticizing my works. I don't care about all this and just keep on writing.

As for my sources of inspiration, there is definitely Sudanese folklore. My writing depends on that rich subject, and if you read any of my books, you will find some information about Sudanese rituals in marriage, death, children's circumcision and deliveries, war, and many things. These things appear clearly in novels like *Ishtiha*, *Maher Al Sayah*, and *Ebola 76*.

I can't mention all my novels but will mention some of the important ones;

- *Maher AL Sayah*: first edition Dar Ward Syria–2002–4th edition Dar Al Sagi Lebanon. It appeared in English with two titles: *The Korak Council* and *The Yelling Dowry*. This is a historical novel about an imaginary Sultanate in the west of Sudan in the 17th century. In this novel I built a complete fantastic world; you will find people, streets, markets, magic, food, transportation, and every other thing. In this world, I put my own creation of some diseases not present in reality like a sclerotic fever that causes penile erection, Haboob disease that causes recurrent abdominal pain, and many others. Also, I created some drugs or elixirs prepared by the Sultanate Hakeem [doctor] called Dobagi. I tried in this book to speak about dictatorship and terror and how people may lose their dignity by transforming men to women and also to animals.

- *Tawtrat Al Qibti* or *Cots Worriers*. This book is important but unlucky. It has been published three times but never translated to any language. It was written in 2009 and speaks about a religious revolution that occurred in Sudan. The rebels killed people, destroyed the town, and took women as captives to be used by the Mujahedeen. The book was actually written before the appearance of the Islamic Khilafa state, or ISIS, which appeared later in Iraq and Syria. If you read the book, you will find what the imagination can do for a writer, as it became a real thing in those poor places. Later in 2016, I wrote a second part of the novel called *Flowers in Flames*, which speaks about the captives and women. Fortunately, it became widespread and reached the short list of the Arabic Booker prize.

- *The Grub Hunter*: 1st edition 2010, Thagafa publishing, Emirate, and 4th edition Dar Alsagi. This book was short listed for the Arabic Booker prize in 2011 and was translated into English, Italian, Farsi, and Turkish. It is the first book that made my name very well known, and thousands of people know it and write about it. It is about an intelligence agent that retired after an accident and decided to write a novel. The story is very clear and written simply, so it gained a lot of popularity.

- *Ebola 76*: Dar Alsay. This is one of my famous books and gained a huge popularity, especially after the appearance of the COVID-19 virus. The first outbreak of hemorrhagic fever caused by the Ebola virus happened in Congo and the south of Sudan in 1976. I wrote about it after I heard about the disaster from a colleague who was a doctor there at that time and survived while all the hospital staff died. The book contains human tragedies and a very sad story about the disease and the fighting of people to live, exactly like what is happening today. The book was translated into six languages and is a best seller today.

- *French Perfume*: first edition, ASP Lebanon 2009. It was also translated into many languages. It is mainly a psychic novel about imagination and madness, with many fantastic points as usual in my style. The hero Ali Jarjar loves a French woman. He has heard that she will come to live in his neighborhood, and he spends his time waiting for her until he decides to create an imaginary woman and say she is the French lady.

- *Telepathy*: an important psychic novel published in Arabic and English 2015— Bloomsbury. It is about a writer who wrote a story about a schizophrenic person and discovered that he was a real person and tried to change his fate in the novel as he was killed by cancer.

- For an example of a biographic novel, we can speak about *Qalam Zayneb* or The Pen of Zayneb, one of the most successful books ever. Three years ago, it was added to the Syllabus of Baccalaureate (secondary-education) in the UAE and is studied each year by fifty thousand students. There are many activities about the book like films, theatre sketches, etc. It is simply about my life when I was working as a doctor in Obstetrics and Gynecology, where I met many people that inspired me with stories.

There are a lot of other books, but I think these examples are enough to give an idea about my style in writing which, as I mentioned, is a mixture between reality and fantasy with the creation of things never found in the world.

Now to talk about literary life in Sudan. Actually, I have never tried publishing in Sudan; from the start I published in Egypt and Beirut, and now my publisher is Hachette Antoene, a major Arabic publisher based in Lebanon. However, according to my information, there are new publishers in Sudan that have now started to follow good, technological ways to produce books. I saw some of their books; they looked fine but still need improvement to reach the standard way of publishing and distributing.

There is, of course, also the problem of censorship in Sudan, the most famous case being El-Tayeb Saleh's *Season of Migration to the North*. Of course, this was during the past regime, that of Omer Bashir, who was thrown out by a massive popular revolution. Now nothing is banned in Sudan. My new novel was published two months ago and is about this revolution. Its name is *Anger and Kandakat*. Kandakat is a title brought from history; it is given to strong women that help in war near men.

Finally, about my future plans, now I am planning to write a complete SF novel. This subject is important, and I think I can do it, although it is difficult and demands a big effort.

About science fiction in Sudan, I think there is no writer of SF in Sudan. In general, this subject is rare in Arab literature as we are not creators of science itself, but consumers of what the West manufactures. Crime literature is also rare; in 2018 I wrote a historical crime novel, which succeeded and introduced me to readers as a writer of this type of book. Its title is *A Painful Part of a Story*, and it is undergoing English translation.

I think people want to know the names of the writers I enjoyed during growing as a writer and how I gained from reading their work. I was very influenced with Latin American style, especially Gabriel García Márquez, but later on I created my own style which I update usually with every book I write. I think the act of writing is a training lesson. You write more; you gain more. Writing my first science fiction novel will be this way as well, a lesson on how to write more SF. And I hope a lesson for all aspiring Sudan authors who want to enter this field.

Work Cited

Saleh, El-Tayeb. (1969). *Season of Migration to the North*. Oxford: Heinemann. Translated by Denys Johnson-Davis.

Science Fiction

A Living Reality for Every Malaysian

AZRUL BIN JAINI

The new world is as yet
behind the veil of destiny
In my eyes, however
its dawn has been unveiled
—Muhammad Iqbal

While we are relaxing with our families at home, in front of the TV set, we are also catching up with our favorite hi-tech and futuristic series or films. Then commercial breaks appear so we can see spectacular imaginary of a photocopy machine or a car transforming into a robot. Or, there are scanners which enlarge images of what we assume to be harmful bacteria that are 99.9 percent obliterated by a single sweep of powerful soap. Or, there are hilarious, hungry aliens looking through a telescope, eager to get delicious chocolates from earth.

Science fiction. Two words that people don't recognize, yet they live with them in their daily lives. These are the symbols of science fiction manifested in our lives in the form of drama, cinema, animation, books, novels, magazines, comics, games, toys, or even advertisements. We live in an advanced modern world compared to people of the past.

A few decades back, television was a luxury, and only the few wealthy could afford a black-and-white set. But nowadays, almost everyone could afford small gadgets for watching their favorite YouTube videos. Home appliances get smarter and more complex. Authorities hunt criminals down with the aid of sophisticated technologies and forensic sciences. In the battlefield, war is increasingly fought by robotic warriors. Humanity's dependence on its own creations deepens day by day.

Global Cultural Phenomenon

Yet when asked "What is science fiction?" probably most people don't know what to answer. In fact, it is a cultural global phenomenon we have become all too familiar with. Simply we recognize these items: robots, cyborgs, space ships, rockets, planets and stars, aliens, hi-tech weaponry, the apocalypse, etc., all imagined through the media we mentioned before. We can take a simple definition from prominent figure in science fiction, Ben Bova. He explains that science fiction:

… stories are those in which some aspect of future science or high technology is so integral to the story that, if you take away the science or technology, the story collapses [Bova, 1981: 6].

Science fiction, or sci-fi as we call it, is popular across the world. P.W. Singer (2009) in his *Wired for War: The Robotics Revolution and Conflict in the 21st Century* stated that of all books published in the United States, 10 percent belong to sci-fi and fantasy genres. He also mentioned that six of the top-ten grossing movies of all time are science fiction, led by *Star Wars* (Singer, 2009). Every year we see many films with sci-fi themes increasing and received by a greater audience.

I myself was exposed to many works of science fiction since my childhood. I was 9 years old when I watched Luke Skywalker piloting the Rebel Alliance X-Wing, the agile space fighter that released the last proton torpedo that eventually annihilates the Galactic Empire's Death Star in *Episode IV: A New Hope*. I also watched Japanese and American superhero series like *Kamen Riders* and *Power Rangers*. My friends and I laughed at the heroes looking so illogical, talking through a wrist watch. But who is having the last laugh now with cell phones and wrist watches with digital cameras?

During my teen age years, I preferred the more civilized Protoss than the bloodthirsty, mindless Zerg in the PC game StarCraft. Meanwhile the Tiberium conflict in *Command and Conquer*, the elusive antagonist Brotherhood of NOD was more dynamic than Global Defense Initiative (GDI). I love watching science fiction movies, especially *Star Wars* during their comeback with Episodes I–III in the early 2000s. Indeed, the long "radiation" of science fiction's exposure and experience helped me with completing my first space opera novel in the Malay Language entitled *Galaksi Muhsinin*.[1] I believe there are people in other parts of the world who share common experience during these times.

From Imagination to Reality

> If science fiction is escapist, it's escape into reality.
> —Asimov (quoted in Bova, 1981: 6)

Undeniably sci-fi has influenced scientists and engineers to realize their imagination into reality. Through their imagination, authors speculate about the possibilities of "what if" questions into the future. Jules Verne penned a visionary work *Paris in the Twentieth Century* (1863) that went unpublished during his lifetime. Eighty-nine years after his death, his great-grandson discovered the manuscript locked in a safe and published it as a bestseller in 1994. Verne was able to imagine a future of skyscrapers made of glass, automobiles powered by gasoline, calculators, worldwide communications, and even electronic music almost precisely as we find them in our life today (Verne, 2011: xvi).

Verne's influential novel of space travel was read by Konstantin Tsiolkovsky (1857–1935), who schemed proto-space rockets. Verne's problematic space travel mechanism in his *From the Earth to the Moon and Around the Moon* (1865) prompted Tsiolkovsky to come up with the idea of multi-staged liquid fuelled rockets. In fact, that idea did come true decades later.

In *How it Works Book of Robots* magazine (2016), we can see the spectacular advancement of robotic engineering, especially in Japan; robots had been in their culture. Post-war generations were exposed with visionary ideas of science fiction through mangas and television series. When they grow up, they are the ones who make their dreams in reality. One of them is Kogoro Kurata, a Japanese engineer. He realized his dream of building the first human single-pilot super-robot in 2012. It is an impressive machine powered by diesel-powered hydraulics and also equipped with advanced cockpit systems, a fully functioning hand, and operational weaponry (White, 2016: 12).

The counterpart to Kurata is America's *Megabot Mark II*. Although it is not the first of its kind in the U.S., the Mark II made its debut in a science fiction-inspired colossal fight of *Battlebots* in 2016 (White, 2016: 39).

Another device created with sci-fi inspiration is the revolutionary Sakakibara-Kikai's Land Walker bipedal exoskeleton. It was an effort to replicate battle mech of Galactic Empire's All Terrain Scout Transport (AT-ST) in *Star Wars* (White, 2016: 56). Enryu Robotic Rescue Dragon was deployed during the 2011 nuclear disaster of Fukushima, Japan. An advanced robot, it is designed to be capable of going into hazardous areas and withstand severe conditions (White, 2016: 57).

Meanwhile, *Star Trek* sparked Martin Cooper's idea of the cell phone. While watching a scene in *Star Trek*, John Adler of Stanford Medical School was inspired to invent a cyberknife that performs surgery by sending a beam into cancer tumors.

Donna Shirley, the director of the Science Fiction Museum and Hall of Fame in Seattle, Washington, is another example. She graduated in aeronautical engineering from the University of Oklahoma and became one of the first female engineers at NASA's Jet Propulsion Lab in 1966, pursuing her career for 32 years. The key factor in her success story was inspiration from science fiction (Singer, 2009: 152).

Back to Origin

> … sf begins at the time that science, as we understand the term today, begins.
>
> —Bould et al. (2009: 4)

Researchers vary in tracing back the origin of sci-fi. Some of them mark Mary Shelley's gothic tale *Frankenstein* (1818) as the pioneer of this genre. Some of them trail it as far back as the ancient Mesopotamian epic of *Gilgamesh*. Others turned to the 16th century Copernican Revolution as its beginning.

Nevertheless, it was in the background of the 19th century Industrial Revolution that sci-fi was popularly received by readers. This was the age considered as the "Classical Age" of sci-fi. The period was shaped by the strong influence of the "Father of Sci-fi," the prolific French author Jules Verne (1828–1905) who wrote "extraordinary voyages" popularizing science and travel. Meanwhile contemporary to Verne was Herbert George Wells (1866–1946). Wells' "scientific romances" brought this genre to its "full maturity" during his own day and age (Bould et al., 2009: 20).

However, after their deaths, sci-fi plunged into stagnation and decline. Especially during this "Pulp Age" or comic age, from the 1920s till the 1940s, the themes of their predecessors were timelessly repeated. Little breakthroughs of novel ideas only resulted in qualities that were still very far from being satisfying. Sci-fi recovered at the hands of Isaac Asimov in the 1930s, and this genre expanded rapidly with the new "dominant mode" of the silver screen in the 1970s (Roberts, 2000: 85).

Infinite Boundaries of Definition

> I suppose it is a measure of the richness of the field of science fiction that no two of its practitioners are liable to agree on even something as fundamental as its definition.
>
> —Asimov (1982: 3)

The wide expansion of sci-fi since its birth somehow troubled its researchers to define it. Science fiction had established itself as a distinct breed, integrating the scientific scheme with its own characterization.

As noted in *The Routledge Companion to Science Fiction*, the genre has expanded into numerous themes and subgenres such as space opera, time travel, utopia, dystopia, apocalyptic, postcolonialism, posthumanism and cyborg, virtuality, environmentalism, ethics and alterity (Bould et al., 2009: vii–ix).

Adam Roberts (2000) in his *Science Fiction: The New Critical Idioms* generally defines sci-fi as:

> … as a genre or division of literature distinguishes its fictional worlds to one degree or another from the world in which we actually live: a fiction of the imagination rather than observed reality, a fantastic literature [2000: 1].

His definition focuses the criteria on dealing with "Otherness," which makes it distinct from other fiction. "Otherness" brings a new meaning of something, or the world setting is different from what we have today. It might be in outer space or on another planet. Sometimes the setting is here on Earth but with a different background setting and environment, or has some situation in simulation like of those in the *Matrix* trilogy.

Another criterion is the presence of "Novum" (or "new things," as Adam Roberts uses the term). It is an important particular in sci-fi as these new things "distinguish the SF tale from a conventional literature." The novum might be anything, such as a tangible object (gadgets, spacecraft, a time machine) or something more conceptual (Roberts, 2000: 190–191).

Roberts summarized his study of this genre through the lens of three influential sci-fi critics: Darko Suvin, Robert Scholes and Damien Roderick. He wrote:

> … implicit within these three definitions is a sense of SF as *symbolist genre*, one where the novum acts as symbolic manifestation of something that connects it specifically with the world we live in [Roberts, 2000: 16; italics in original].

At the end of his study he summarized sci-fi, again, as a symbolist genre but:

> … one distinguished from other symbolist modes of literature by the fact that its symbols are deployed within rationalised and materialist discourse, most usually that of "science" and "pseudo-science." The point of this symbolic medium is to connect the exploration of the encounter with difference to our experience of being-in-the-world [Roberts, 2000: 181].

Further key criteria he discussed in the scope of sci-fi's definition:

1. The key feature is requiring either the "novum" or the "otherness" explained with physical rationalization (Roberts, 2000: 5). It must be sound and rational in its explanation, balanced between the cognitive and estrangement of the difference encountered. The rationalization might be in the sphere of adherence with scientific and technological principles (Roberts, 2000: 8). Sometimes there are involved novum

outside of the boundaries of science. Which means that the novum or technology does not yet exist in the present, but it is possible in future. But it is rationalized soundly (Roberts, 2000: 9–10).

2. Sci-fi takes it roots from the materialism of the scientific outlook (Roberts, 2000: 5). Roberts further mentions, "It is this materialism, once again, that distinguishes the effectiveness of the SF use of symbol from the widespread use of symbolism in other literatures."

3. Although Roberts took positive accounts on sci-fi, he also criticizes the phenomenon of sci-fi in his "prediction versus nostalgia" discussion (Roberts, 2000: 30–36). He argues that sci-fi should be visionary and look forward into the future. But in fact, according to his study, most sci-fi texts "are more interested in the ways things have been." He considers that this phenomenon as "counter-intuitively, SF is a historiographic mode, a means of symbolically writing about history" (Roberts, 2000: 36).

Unfolding the Truth

> Science fiction is … time and again, accordingly, a revolutionary mode of writing.
>
> —Roberts (2000: 182)

We have discussed sci-fi as a cultural phenomenon that came into being along with science. Throughout the timeline of its existence, sci-fi novums indeed inspired and sparked the inventions of brilliant devices. It is a literature of wonders that challenges our minds to the limit. To add to this thought, we quote its positive impact on literature:

> Science fiction most effectively addresses the questions that have defined the age we live in: technology, gender, race, history. As a literature of ideas, where the emphasis is less on literary technique, SF has been able to trade in the concepts of philosophy, theory, history and politics in vivid and popular ways. More than this, there is a fundamental vigour and energy to SF fabulation that is invigorating and energising for the readers or viewers [Roberts, 2000: 182].

On the surface, the audience is certainly awed with amazing ideas of the novums and Otherness, particularly outstanding with the aid of special effects in movies. But deep in the inner reaches of sci-fi, we particularly as Muslims observe something that we must be mindful of.

Sci-fi was forged in the crucible of "Western" literature which reflects *their* secular worldview, civilization, character, and personality. Regarding this origin, we correlate with Prof. Seyyed Hossein Nasr in his *A Young Muslim's Guide to the Modern World*, that:

> Literature, especially in the form of the novel, began to create an ambience to compensate many readers for the loss of God in Western society… [Nasr, 2007: 225].

Sci-fi is about stories of how people might interact with technology. Technology comes from the application of science. Science in the light of today's understanding is being interpreted through the prism of Western secular philosophy. Secular philosophy, mainly dependent on pure rationalism and empiricism, rejects revelation and spiritual intuition as sources of knowledge (Al-Attas, 2013: 114–116). Certainly, their perception, thought, actions, and characters will exert this influence on the storyline.

Prof. Dr. Syed Muhammad Naquib Al-Attas[2] wrote his influential book on *Islam and the Philosophy of Science* in 1990. His disciple, Dr. Ugi Suharto, made his summary review on this matter. It is stated that science, according to Prof. Al-Attas, is not "neutral." Truly science is determined by its interpretation. Today, modern philosophy "has become the interpreter of science, and organizes the results of the natural and social sciences into a worldview. It is this interpretation of the statements and general conclusions of science and the direction of science along the lines suggested by the interpretation that must be subjected to critical evaluation…" (Al-Attas, 2013: 113–114). The worldview of Islam has an important role in confronting Western philosophy that interprets science with secularistic interpretation "whereby nature [is] devoid of spiritual significance" (Al-Attas, 1978: 35). Science in its evolution in Western philosophy not only departed from religion; indeed it has been deployed as an instrument *against* religion (Suharto, 2012).

For example, the novel *Dune* (1965) by Frank Herbert is considered to be a masterpiece and the very pinnacle of science fiction. A fantastic novel in terms of its novum and Otherness, no doubt, Herbert made a sound and clear picture we could imagine as if we are part of the story. But one thing is sure is that he imagined a *corrupted* Islam "synthesized" with other religions. Or more accurately, syncretism in Islam. This is a phenomenon called pluralism, which reflects the perception of Islam being a cultural product of human beings through the process of historical change, even syncretism like the other main religions throughout history (Suharto, 2012: 7–10). Islam is portrayed as being syncretized with other religions such as Christianity and Buddhism. We can see in the glossary the religious terms redefined and reinterpreted in a corrupted and deviant form.[3] For Muslims, this is unacceptable and clearly directed against Islam. Because of this, Muslims who love conventional sci-fi should be aware of such symbolic meanings, some of which might be harmful to their creed.

Into the Orbit of Islamic-Oriented Sci-Fi Literature

We emphasized earlier that sci-fi has been a new, foreign element introduced from the West, and now it has been part of our life in the Muslim world. Some Muslim novelists have ventured into this mode of writing.

We have gone through the positive and negative aspects of sci-fi. Outwardly, it resembles the symbol of advancement of humanity. Inwardly it seems to be, ironically, a darkness lurking behind the veil of shadows. There are beliefs, creeds, conceptual understandings of science interpreted again through the prism of Western philosophy in sci-fi. Muslims must critically filter these dangerous elements.

In my opinion, even though sci-fi is imbued with those things, it still contains valuable yet significant elements which can be counterproductive. If we tackle them properly and carefully, sci-fi would be a potentially beneficial instrument in encountering the cultural and scientific philosophy of the West. Of course, we should not be too apologetic and merely reactionary in this regard, putting more of an alternative than merely complaining to the benefit of all.

How?

From my study of sci-fi, there are similarities we encountered with philosophy as encountered by our illustrious scholars in the past. I was inspired by this idea through reading Dr. Adi Setia Adi Dom, who wrote an article "The theologico-scientific research program of the mutakallimun: Intellectual historical context and contemporary concerns with special reference to Fakhr al-Din al-Razi" in the journal *Islam & Science*, (Dom, 2005). Put concisely, he argues in this article that:

1. Ancient Greek philosophy was introduced to the Muslim world by means of translation into Arabic. It went into full swing in the 8–9th centuries. Muslim intellectuals whose reception with philosophy, called falasifah (Muslim peripatetic or mashsha'i), were responsible in discussing and disseminating philosophy (Al-Attas, 2010). It was a new yet foreign element fluxed into the Muslim intellect.

2. Those falasifah (plural for philosophers) not only inherited Greek philosophy but also made commentaries of their own: criticisms, modifications, and replacements of key concepts in Greek philosophy (Ismail and Wan Abdullah, 2012: 170). They were also trying to interpret philosophy "through the eyes of the worldview of Islam" (Al-Attas, 2010: 6). But the thoughts written down in their books brought confusion and have been controversial enough that scholars attempted to answer their arguments. Al-Kindi (d. 866), Al-Farabi (d. 950), and Ibn Sina (d. 1037) were the prominent figures of falasifah (Al-Attas, 2010: 172).

3. There were scholars who accepted and there were also those who rejected philosophy. It was because there were thoughts incompatible with the creed, beliefs, and worldview of Islam. Generations of theologians or *mutakalimun* constantly resisted but to no avail. There was deadlock between these two factions (Al-Ghazali, 2005).

4. Then came Imam Al-Ghazali (d. 505H / 1111), a versatile Persian scholar in the 11th century. He was aware of the acute hostility between the falasifah and mutakalimun, deadlocked in their arguments. Before

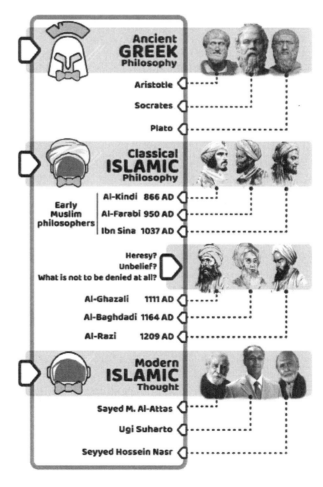

A brief history of Islamic thought, a legacy worth living up to in the era of science fiction (courtesy of the artist, Yahya Salah Abul Ghait).

he engaged with philosophy, he studied it over three years until he wrote four books in encountering falasifah. The most famous one was his *Tahafut al-Falasifah* or the *Incoherence of the Philosophers* (Al-Ghazali, 1989: xiv).[4] During his engagement on philosophy, he carefully distinguishes philosophical elements into three:

(a) What must be counted as unbelief
(b) What must be counted as heresy
(c) What is not to be denied at all (Al-Ghazali, 2005: 20).

Prof. Dr. Alparslan Açikgenç in his foreword to Dr. Syed Ali Tawfik al-Attas' *A Guide to Philosophy: The Hidayat al-Hikmah of Athir al-Din al-Mufaddal ibn 'Umar al-Abhari al-Samarqandi*, stated that Imam Ghazali actually did not attack philosophy *per se*. He mainly directed his arguments on the Aristotelian metaphysical elements as discussed by falasifah (Al-Attas, 2009). In his autobiography *Munqidz al-Dalal* (*Deliverance from Error*), Imam Ghazali excluded logic (Shahran, 2013: 91) and natural science or physics[5] from his criticisms, focusing instead on attacking metaphysics.

5.   Scholars such as Dr. Adi Setia Adi Dom mentioned that at the end of the engagement of Imam Al-Ghazali against the philosophers, he *filtered* their works and appropriated those beneficial yet harmless elements into the realms of Muslim intellectual tradition. His footsteps would be followed by Imam Abu Barakat Al-Baghdadi (d. 1164) and accomplished by another distinguished scholar, Imam Fakhruddin Al-Razi (d. 1209) (Dom, 2005: 131–132).

I'm inspired by the works of these honorable Imams. They engaged philosophy in equal terms. They studied carefully with their utmost intellectual capacity. They did not simply reject; instead they critically engaged with what they encountered. They "cleaned out" the heretical elements in philosophy and accepted anything beneficial into the intellectual realms of the Muslim world. I think the same goes for sci-fi. We engage by identifying and examining the worldview, history, thoughts, ideologies, secular philosophy, and of course the sciences; we reject whatever is incompatible with the principles of Islam underlining its core as symbolized in sci-fi. Then on the basis of this framework, Islamic values would be infused in it.

Islamic-Oriented Sci-Fi

By Islamic-oriented sci-fi, I mean sci-fi which does not violate or assault Islam and is integrated with the values of Islam. From what we have gone through in our discussion, I would suggest few ideas which I hope especially Muslim authors or directors involved in sci-fi will consider. The realm of Islamic sci-fi should be in the orbit of:

Neutralization and Filtration of Sci-Fi

Within the framework of Islamic-oriented sci-fi, enlightened authors or directors should be able to identify, engage, and neutralize concepts, perceptions of secular philosophy, and the science of Western civilization within conventional sci-fi. The engagement should be directed critically towards the inward aspects that involve their worldview about God, the universe, and man. The neutralization and filtration are essential because it will serve as the crucible in forging our further work in writing or directing, which is on the basis of Islamic literature.[6]

Mapping Islamic-Oriented Sci-Fi

Once the norms and symbols of conventional SF have been "cleaned" of harmful elements, the works should then be mapped within the ground structure of Islamic literature. Muslim authors especially have to be observant of the basic tenets and principles of Islam. The endless boundary of conventional sci-fi should be watchful within the parameters of the creed of Islam. Transgressing it would be risky to our faith.

Islamic-oriented sci-fi should be focused on aligning the storyline and characters in accordance with our worldview regarding God, the universe, and man. It is about the journey of spiritual and intellectual acknowledgment of the existence of the majestic attributes of God that are symbolized through His open book: the universe.[7] Man should be aware of his humbleness, thus serving his true purpose as His viceregent of the world.

Malaysia's SF in Brief

Fadli Al-Akiti, one of the leading SF authors in Malaysia, states that the first pure SF appeared in the Malay language in 1989. To this day, Al-Akiti has counted about 84 sci-fi novels that were written, according to his blog.[8] There are many short stories still uncounted. Some of them are compiled in several anthologies, 12 recorded to date (Al-Akiti, 2018). The names include Lokman Hakim, Ahmad Patria, Nisah Haron, Fadli Al-Akiti, Ted Mahsun, Nor Azida Ishak, Dali Fazuri, and Sri Rahayu Mohd Yusop. All are dedicated SF novelists. We are lucky to have many talented writers competing in contests like "Sayembara Novel Fiksyen Sains dan Teknologi" held by University Technology Malaysia (UTM) and Kumpulan Utusan Publications. The big sci-fi novel publishers in Malaysia include Penerbit X, FIXI, Buku Hitam Press, Lejen Press, and Dewan Bahasa dan Pustaka.[9]

Not to forget the many short story contributors, like Muzaf Ahmad, Rosli Muhammad Ali, Ahmad Muzaffar Baharuddin, and Idris Boi. Outlets for short SF include *Dewan Kosmik* magazine, published by Dewan Bahasa dan Pustaka. Many anthologies contain Malaysian SF such as *Pistol Laser Lisa* (2013) by Sindiket Sol-Jah, *Biohazard* (2014) by Simptomatik Press, and *IMAGIKATA* (2016) by Penerbit X.

Generally, sci-fi in Malaysia is unique. Many Muslim authors are involved in sci-fi in their own language. Commonly, local authors have the conscious feeling of the incompatibility of some elements of Western SF with either Islam or our local values as Malaysians and Asians.

Although not all of the works published by Malay authors are apparently Islamic-oriented, there are strong tendencies to instill good values in their works. Some of them even infuse Islamic values implicitly by layering meanings that readers need to interpret. This is a particularly positive way of going about things. Not only does it engage the reader's intellect and avoid a didactic mode of writing, but it also allows Malaysian sci-fi authors to observe the sensitivity of norms and culture in a multi-religious and multi-ethnic atmosphere such as Malaysia. Though in particular, Muslim authors should

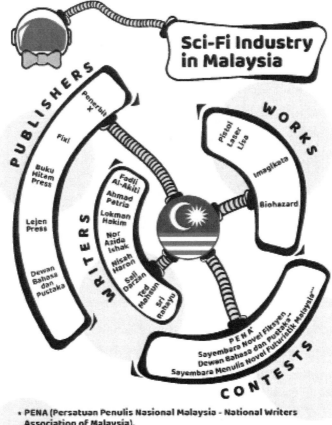

Sci-Fi Industry in Malaysia

PUBLISHERS
Penerbit X
Fixi
Buku Hitam Press
Lejen Press
Dewan Bahasa dan Pustaka

WRITERS
Fadli Al-Akiti
Ahmad Patria
Lokman Hakim
Nor Azida Ishak
Nisah Haron
Safi Oazran
Ted Mahsun
Sri Rahayu

WORKS
Pistol Laser Lisa
Imagikata
Biohazard

CONTESTS
PENA
Sayembara Novel Fiksyen,
Dewan Bahasa dan Pustaka
Sayembara Menulis Novel Futuristik Malaysia

• PENA (Persatuan Penulis Nasional Malaysia - National Writers Association of Malaysia).
•• Dewan Bahasa dan Pustaka (Institute of Language and Literature).
••• Sayembara Menulis Novel Futuristik Malaysia (Malaysia's Futuristic Novel Writing Competition) which is sponsored and organized by GAPENA (Gabungan Persatuan Penulis Nasional - Federation of National Writers Associations of Malaysia).

A representative cross section of the creative minds and publishing muscle behind science fiction in Malaysia (courtesy of the artist, Yahya Salah Abul Ghait).

be continuously wary and vigilant towards secular elements imbued within the vast framework of sci-fi.

Galaksi Muhsinin

In the light of Islamic-oriented sci-fi, Fadli recorded that there are 13 published novels listed in this sphere. One example is the space opera entitled *Galaksi Muhsnin,* written in the Malay language.

Its story presents a projection of a "space version" of Islamic civilization with a diverse, multi-ethnic community living in harmony and standing unified around Islam. The core inspiration and mission of the people is *Rahmatan lil Alamin* as depicted in the Quranic verse of Surah al-Anbiya' (verse 107), that Allah sent the Prophet Muhammad

(PBUH) as a mercy [rahma] to the worlds. Under the leadership of a caliph, they vigilantly protect the peace they inherited against enemies lurking for them over a century. The world is in their hands, but their heart burns with faith.

The author adopts the novums and Otherness of space opera: galaxies, planetary systems, space stations, spacecraft, space travels, robots, etc. Meanwhile from the point of view of the story and the characters, the Universe of Islamic values, their traditions and civilization, are strongly inculcated. On the other hand, the cosmos is indeed viewed in the novel as a manifestation of the wonder of God Almighty, to be contemplated, preserved, and respected. Finally, the epic struggles of characters totally reliant on their God are symbolic to us today in preserving our faith despite the restlessness of the encounters with the modern world.

Torch of Hope

With this article, I have hopefully presented a beneficial basic guide, especially for Muslim sci-fi authors. Islamic-oriented sci-fi provides an exceptional channel in inspiring a new Muslim generation. They face sci-fi almost every second of every day. Everywhere they look, they are somehow familiar with it. Albeit it is the science fiction of the modern world we face today, so it is hoped that we could educate them into the Islamic teachings and values in creative and true ways. We must never allow ourselves to slip into despair. With the invaluable richness of our history, our intellectual traditions and civilization of the past we inherited, they seem to me to be a tremendous resource for stories to be told … in a sci-fi style.

NOTES

1. Published in 2008 and reprinted in 2016.

2. Born on 5 September 1931, in Bogor, Java, Syed Muhammad Naquib bin Ali bin Abdullah bin Muhsin al-Attas has spent a lifetime in the pursuit of knowledge rooted in the traditional Islamic sciences. He is competent in diverse academic fields such as philosophy, metaphysics, Kalam, history, and literature. He has developed a goal-oriented philosophy and methodology of education, to "Islamize the mind, body and soul" of the student. He extends this focus to its effects on the personal and collective lives of Muslims as well as others, including the spiritual and physical non-human environment. He has authored twenty-seven authoritative works on various aspects of Islamic thought and civilization, particularly on Sufism, cosmology, metaphysics, philosophy, and Malay language and literature. He was the founder of International Institute of Islamic Thought and Civilization (ISTAC). Source: Adi Setia Adi Dom (2003). "Al-attas' Philosophy of Science: An Extended Outline," *Islam & Science Journal*, Vol. 1 (December 2003) No. 2.

3. Please see Frank Herbert (1990: 513–533) and the prequel by Brian Herbert and Kevin J. Anderson, *Dune: The Butlerian Jihad* (2002: 609, 615).

4. Al-Ghazali, Ahmadie Thaha and Kamariah Mohd. Ali (trans.) (1989). *Tahafut al-falasifah: Kekacauan para filsuf.* Dewan Bahasa dan Pustaka: Kuala Lumpur

5. As mentioned in *Tahafut*, Imam Ghazali argued that natural phenomenon that are not conflicting tenets of Islam although described by philosophy should be accepted. He argued that it is unwise because it is not useful. Tahafut (Al-Ghazali, 1989: 7).

6. For the characteristics of Islamic Literature I refer to the work of Prof. Emêritus Dr. Muhammad Bukhari Lubis, in his inaugural lecture at Universiti Pendidikan Sultan Idris or Sultan Idris Education University (UPSI) entitled *Kesusasteraan Islami Bandingan: Menyingkap Tabir Mengungkap Fikir* (2017).

7. In Islamic thinking we see that there are two books to guide us, the Quran and the world itself.

8. Fadli al-Akiti, *Kubu Buku.* Retrieved from http://fadliakiti.blogspot.com/p/senarai-novel-sai-fai.html on 1st August 2018.

9. For a website showcasing the latest Malaysian genre publications please see "Malaysian Science Fiction," https://penasaifai.com/.

WORKS CITED

Al-Akiti, Fadli. (Accessed 1 August 2018). "Senarai Antologi Cereka Sai-Fai." *Kubu Buku.* http://fadliakiti. blogspot.com/p/senarai-antologi-cereka-sai-fai.html.

Al-Akiti, Fadli. (Accessed 1 August 2018). "Senarai Novel Sai-Fai." *Kubu Buku.* http://fadliakiti.blogspot.com/ p/senarai-novel-sai-fai.html.

Al-Attas, Syed Ali Tawfik. (2009). *A Guide to Philosophy: The Hidayat Al-Hikmah of Athir Al-Din Al-Mufaddal ibn 'Umar Al-Abhari Al-Samarqandi.* Selangor: Pelanduk Publications.

Al-Attas, Syed Ali Tawfik. (2010). *The Mashsha'i Philosophical System: A Commentary and Analysis of the Hidayat Al-Hikmah of Athir Al-Din Al-Mufaddal ibn 'Umar Al-Abhari Al-Samarqandi.* Selangor: Pelanduk Publications.

Al-Attas, Syed Muhammad Naquib. (1978). *Islam and Secularism.* Kuala Lumpur: Angkatan Belia Islam Malaysia (ABIM).

Al-Attas, Syed Muhammad Naquib. (2013). *Prolegomena to the Metaphysics of Islam: An Exposition of the Fundamental Elements of the Worldview of Islam.* Kuala Lumpur: Centre for Advanced Studies on Islam, Science and Civilization (CASIS).

Al-Ghazali, Abu Hamid. (1989). *Tahafut Al-Falasifah: Kekacauan Para Filsuf.* Translated by Ahmadie Thaha. Kuala Lumpur: Dewan Bahasa dan Pustaka.

Al-Ghazali, Abu Hamid. (2005). *Deliverance from Error and the Beginning of Guidance.* Translated by W. Montgomery Watt. Kuala Lumpur: Islamic Book Trust.

Asimov, Isaac. (1982). *Asimov on Science Fiction.* New York: Avon Books.

Bould, Mark, Andrew M. Butler, Adam Roberts, and Sherryl Vint, eds. (2009). *The Routledge Companion to Science Fiction.* New York: Routledge.

Bova, Ben. (1981). *The Craft of Writing Science Fiction That Sells.* Cincinnati: Writer's Digest Books.

Dom, Adi Setia Adi. (2005). "The theologico-scientific research program of the mutakallimun: Intellectual historical context and contemporary concerns with special reference to Fakhr Al-Din Al-Razi." *Islam & Science: Journal of Islamic Perspectives on Science, Civilization and Intellectual History*, 3(2), Winter. http://www.cis-ca.org/jol/vol3-no2/adi.pdf.

Herbert, Brian, and Kevin J. Anderson. (2002). *Dune: The Butlerian Jihad.* Great Britain: Herbert Limited Partnership.

Herbert, Frank. (1990). *Dune.* New York: Ace Books.

Ismail, Mohd Zaidi, and Wan Suhaimi Wan Abdullah. (2012). *Adab dab Peradaban: Karya Pengi'tirafan untuk Syed Muhammad Naquib al-Attas.* Petaling Jaya: MPH Publishing.

Nasr, Seyyed Hossein. (2007). *A Young Muslim's Guide to the Modern World.* Kuala Lumpur: Islamic Book Trust.

Roberts, Adam. (2000). *Science Fiction: The New Critical Idiom.* London: Routledge.

Shahran, Mohd Farid bin Mohd. (2013). *Akidah dan Pemikiran Islam: Isu dan Cabaran.* Kuala Lumpur: Institut Terjemahan & Buku Malaysia.

Singer, P. W. (2009). *Wired for War: The Robotics Revolution and Conflict in the 21st Century.* New York: Penguin Books.

Suharto, Ugi. (Accessed 13 August 2018). "Ulasan Buku: Prolegomena to the Metaphysics of Islam." *Penuntut Ilmu.* http://hanputra.blogspot.com/2012/08/prolegomena-to-metaphysics-of-islam.html.

White, Jon, ed. (2016). "Top 10 Robots." *How it Works Books of Robots.* 2nd ed. Bournemouth, UK: Imagine Publishing.

Verne, Jules. (2011). *From the Earth to the Moon and Around the Moon.* London: Wordsworth Editions.

Raising the Elements of Locality and the Moral Story in SF

An Attempt to Make SF a Classy Genre in Indonesia

RIAWANI ELYTA

> And (remember) when your Lord said to the angels: "Verily, I am going to place (mankind) generations after generations on earth." They said: "Will You place therein those who will make mischief therein and shed blood,— while we glorify You with praises and thanks (Exalted be You above all that they associate with You as partners) and sanctify You." He (Allah) said: "I know that which you do not know."
>
> —Surat Al-Baqarah 2:30, Holy Quran (Muhsin Khan translation, quoted in "Al-Baqarah: THE COW," 2016)

Indeed, when a representative of the Egyptian Society for Science Fiction (ESSF) offered this "project" to me, I was filled with doubts. I'm not an easily trusting person, especially with someone that I only know via social media, even though he said he got a recommendation about me from Dr. Jörg Matthias Determann, a historian at Virginia Commonwealth University in Qatar who had previously brought my novel, *The Trinil Gate*, into one of his seminars for discussion.

When the ESSF mentioned the names of science fiction (SF) writers from various countries who are participating in this project, and unfortunately I know none of them, I felt doubtful again, as I felt unworthy to participate with such esteemed names. I'm a writer and novelist, but I'm not a specialist in the SF genre. The only SF novel I have ever written is the *Trinil Gate*. (In bahasa Indonesia, it is *Gerbang Trinil*.) I wrote it with my friend Syila Fatar, who contributed most of the SF ideas in our novel.

Even when I agreed to join in the end, it was none other than Syila's encouragement that was responsible. Although she did not participate, she convinced me to write this essay. Besides that, I think, maybe this is my only chance to write about the phenomenon of SF in my country, together with such writers from so many other countries.

The Overview of SF in Indonesia

Science fiction, called "fiksi ilmiah" (fiction scientific) in my country, is a speculative genre usually associated with imaginative concepts such as futuristic science and technology, space travel, time travel, travel faster than the speed of light, parallel universes, and extraterrestrial life. Science fiction often explores the potential consequences of scientific innovation and other innovations and is called the "idea" literature in Indonesia. So, if you refer to this definition, SF should be a genre with a very wide range, as far as the expanse of knowledge that God has devoted to the whole universe and contained in the Quran.

The SF novel talks about the universe, life on planets other than Earth, galaxies and space, natural phenomena, and so on. But it is also very possible to combine it with imagination and fantasy elements, as long as it can still be accepted logically.

No ape man is an island. The future may hold the secrets of the past in store for us, as Indonesian science fiction says (courtesy of the artist, Ammar Al-Gamal).

However, the extent of SF literature turned out to not necessarily open up great opportunities in my country. Not many SF genre novels are produced by local writers here. Even if there are, they are less popular than SF novels from Western countries. Before writing this essay, I conducted a survey among my Facebook friends about their knowledge of SF—this was in February 2019. Ninety percent of them are more familiar with SF novels from Western countries such as novels by Dan Brown and Michael Crichton than by Indonesian authors like Djoko Lelono and Arief Rachman. I myself have only read work by these authors and then a long time ago.

While there are those who know local SF novels, it turns out there are no more than five titles that they know and have read. Most of them know the Supernova serial by Dee, and fortunately they still recognize our novel, *The Trinil Gate*. When I looked at the SF community in goodreads, I also found a reality that was not much different. The community members were busy asking their friends about local SF novels that had been published as their reference to read. And I am grateful that our novel, *The Trinil Gate*, was also mentioned in the conversation. At least, even though this novel is not very in demand, it successfully shows its identity as a SF novel.

About *The Trinil Gate*

Perhaps you want to know what *The Trinil Gate* is all about. Here is a summary of this story.

This is a novel about Areta. Areta is not an ordinary girl. She is obsessed with the ancient human fossils of Pithecanthropus erectus, until one day she discovers that these ancient humans were *not* extinct. Her search brings Areta to Trinil, East Java. She tries to find the truth and reveal the secrets that her grandmother kept. But curiosity actually takes her on a dangerous adventure. She discovers that the Pythe nation is not only still around, but they returned to Earth with a mission to rule the Earth and create a new generation on Earth, even though for that, humans must be eliminated and extinct.

Areta has no choice but to fight furiously because this is not only about her life, but there is something more important: about the future of planet Earth.

I would also like to write down here an interview by Dr. Jörg Determann (JG) about *Trinil Gate* (Determann, October 2018):

> (JG): What inspired you to write *Gerbang Trinil*?
>
> (ME): This novel was written by me and my friend, Syila Fatar. *Gerbang Trinil* was inspired by our wishes to write a novel based on Indonesian culture and history combined with something futuristic. We thought this was a rare combination of themes in this genre, and we hope this novel can also relate the young reader to the history of ancient humans (homo sapiens) in Indonesia: pythecanthropus.
>
> (JG): What other special elements of Indonesian culture and history did you include in the book?
>
> (ME): The other special elements is about the mysticism surround the life and figure of Maheswari, Areta's grandma. Although we live in a modern era, some old Indonesian people still have strong belief in mysticism. And the unique thing here, there is a relation between Maheswari's mystic ritual with the aliens who trapped Areta and many women on their "planet" beyond the Earth. The story ending was also quite shocking, that a kind-charm guy in this story, was one of the aliens.
>
> (JG): Is the mystic ritual you are describing an Islamic ritual?
>
> (ME): The mystic ritual isn't an Islamic ritual. It's describing an old traditional mysticism that is contrary to and against the Islamic fundamental. Through this part about mysticism, we tried to send a message: something against religion and our belief in God (Allah) will destroy our life and the world.
>
> (JG): Do you see your *Gerbang Trinil* as part of such a trend in Indonesian literature to emphasize women's rights and to condemn men's power over women?
>
> (ME): Feminism is a little part of it, but more importantly, the message is to inspire teenagers, including young girls, to be heroes in their environment and in their own way. This message is represented by Areta's struggle to save the trapped women and the world from pythe's attack.
>
> (JG): You mentioned the word "environment." I felt environmentalism is as much part of your book as feminism. Would you agree? One of the reasons that the Pithe want to take over the world is because humans have destroyed forests. The Pithe need the forests to live. Am I understanding this correctly?
>
> (ME): Yes, it's a hidden message too. The destruction of the environment will come if humans don't keep the Earth well. In this story, pythe aliens symbolize the threat if the environment was destroyed. In the real life, the pythe (threat) is a huge disaster: flood, forest fire, landslide, etc., as the impact of destroying the environment. We hope readers can perceive this message through this story.

Note above that the word "Pithe" is spelled and capitalized inconsistently. This is a faithful reproduction of the interview in print. The proper spelling is "Pithe."

The Survey About SF

OK. Now we go back to the topic of this essay, which is the phenomenon of SF in Indonesia. The level of popularity for SF by local writers in Indonesia is not very encouraging.

This is evidenced by the limited number of local SF novels published in this country which are less able to reach market tastes that have been dominated by SF from Western countries. My writing partner, Syila Fatar, said that the lack of publication of local SF in Indonesia is equal to technological developments in this country. Syila told me she had written a story about a giant bird that was used as a vehicle in a country, but the story was stagnant once the film *Avatar* appeared with more sophisticated technology.

Before I wrote this essay, I conducted a survey among readers and writers about their opinions on SF. I'll put the results of the survey here. First of all, I will present the results of a survey to readers, about why local SF is of less interest.

1. The western SF novel is more detailed, complete, has real descriptions, the scientific references are amazing, and the imagination is still connected with human logic, while the local SF, on the other hand, is still *floating*, it has not dared to do maximum exploration, and there is a *fear* of making mistakes.

2. Many local SF novels experience holes in the plot and have more elements of fantasy, which are more prominent than scientific analysis.

3. The Western SF novel has expanded the domestic market so that the local fans of SF have made it a reference standard.

4. The scientific element in the local SF novel is more like a *patch*, not like the Western SF novel where the scientific element is really strong and becomes the very "spirit" of the story

5. The Western SF novels are convincing in presenting the imagination of future technological developments that are sophisticated and futuristic, especially those that are visualized in a movie.

6. Hollywood cinema has succeeded in convincing that the setting of SF is indeed happening there, not elsewhere. This can be seen from the comparison of SF with Western backgrounds, especially USA as compared to other countries' backgrounds.

Furthermore, I surveyed several authors about the major obstacles and challenges faced by local SF writers.

1. Local publishers seem to always give less space to local SF novels. Due to market considerations, local publishers prefer to publish Western SF novels which have become world best sellers.

2. Publishers and readers tend to neglect local SF novels, even though some of them have good qualities, while some of Western SF novels turn out to be just average in terms of quality.

3. The writing of the SF novel requires serious scientific and research references, sometimes requiring large costs. At the same time, the marketing of SF local novels is not encouraging. Only popular writers usually get a large number of readers. This fact makes many local writers reluctant to write in the SF genre.

I should add, from personal experience, the job situation faced by Indonesian authors, even in popular genres like Young Adult. I work for a regency government. I'm the head of the case management division at my office. Most authors in my country have regular jobs. Even if a writer writes full time, an average author does many kinds of writing jobs.

Conclusion: Suggestions and Opinions

From some articles that the ESSF shared with me, I saw at a glance that the obstacles and problems about SF in Middle Eastern countries and Muslim countries were not much different. Maybe this is also one of the factors that drives the writing of this book. A form of struggle of SF writers in countries with a Muslim majority is to make SF's work more recognized in their own lands.

Actually, I also do not directly justify that this only happens in Muslim-majority countries, because so far, I have not studied what has happened in Asian countries compared to European countries.

However, in order to make the discussion in this book more focused, we should indeed only talk about the development of SF in Muslim countries.

From my analysis of the survey above, and glimpsing the development of SF in my country as well as other Muslim countries, here are some of my opinions that hopefully can contribute to the increase of SF publication in the future, both in number and quality.

1. SF in Muslim countries and the Middle East needs to *present something different* from Western SF novels. I am sure that every country has its own peculiarities and localities. We have tried this in *Trinil Gate*. This novel raises elements of locality about the existence of Pithecanthropus and mystical rituals conducted by Areta's grandmother.

2. SF in Muslim countries should also incorporate *religious elements and messages*. And this will also be an extra value because SF readers will get the moral and positive message that they rarely get from Western SF novels. Even this we have traversed through the *Trinil Gate*. As I told Dr. Determann in an interview, *Trinil Gate* contains a message about the importance of preserving nature and the environment from damage because if damage has already occurred, the consequences will be on humans who inhabit the Earth.

3. Publishers need to give *more space and opportunity* to local SF, *not* to make Western SF a comparison, because as one of my friends, the author Maya Lestari, said, publishers sometimes still underestimate local SF even though the quality can match that of the Western SF novel.

4. There needs to be a solid force to *introduce* local SF; perhaps a *special strategy is needed* to make local SF viral, so that it will attract readers to start paying attention and respecting local SF.

5. There need to be *special awards* for the SF novel. In my country there is now a national award for the best literary novels and the best Islamic novels. Maybe in the future, it can be planned to give awards to SF genre novels as a trigger for the motivation of SF writers to produce quality novels.

6. By forming a community of readers for SF novels, namely those who are very fond of SF novels, publishers and writers can invite them to work together to promote the SF novel. Unique and classy *promotional activities* need to be made, so that the SF novel will also be considered a *classy* novel.

As a Moslem, I believe that the Quran is the most complete and perfect source of scientific reference. So, I think SF writers in Muslim countries will not suffer from any lack of ideas to add scientific elements and make it an amazing novel.

I hope this book will contribute positively to the development of SF, especially in

Muslim countries. I am sure there is always an opportunity to look stunning and display something that the existing Western SF novels do not have.

Finally, I want to quote the wisdom words I included in *Trinil Gate*, hopefully representing my hope for SF's work in Muslim countries in the future:

> "We cannot change the past to improve the future. But we have the present to change anything" (*Marry Him If You Dare*).

Author's Note

Syila Fatar is the pen name of Amalia Dewi. She was born in Probolinggo, East Java. In addition to *Trinil Gate*, she has written short fiction anthologies and children's works. Her most recent novel is *Tibu, Syifa's Lovely Cat*.

She is the exception to the rule in Indonesia in that she is a full-time author who does not hold another job elsewhere. Pray that we should all be so lucky.

WORKS CITED

"Al-Baqarah: THE COW." (2016). Quran.com. https://quran.com/2/30?translations=17,101,22,21,19,20,18,95

Determann, Jörg Matthias. (8 October 2018). "Imagining Extraterrestrial Life in the Muslim World." Second paper presented at the "Roman' The Stars" event of the Qatar Faculty Forum, Fall 2018. Liberal Arts Lecture Series, Texas A&M at Qatar.

The Writer's Prerogative

An Interview from the Philippines
with Kristine Ong Muslim

EGYPTIAN SOCIETY FOR SCIENCE FICTION

Poets need be in no degree jealous of the geologists. The stony science, with buried creations for its domains, and half an eternity charged with its annals, possesses its realms of dim and shadowy fields, in which troops of fancies already walk like disembodied ghosts in the old fields of Elysium, and which bid fair to be quite dark and uncertain enough for all the purposes of poesy for centuries to come.

—Hugh Miller

ESSF: You have a very impressive CV, and that's putting it mildly. It's an honor to have you with us here in this project. So, when did you start writing exactly and what drew you to the profession?

Thank you so much! The honor is mine. I've been writing since I was a teenager, although nothing publishable then. I love reading. I love books and the long-obsolete local comics. Printed on cheap newsprint with the ink bleeding off each time pages are turned, Philippine comics such as *Hiwaga*, *Nightmare*, *Kilabot*, and many other Tagalog comics, their adult contents of sex and gore notwithstanding, were my childhood reading staples. I don't see my writing as a profession. I am also aware of how my latter statement reeks of privilege. Writing is something I love doing. It would have been different, I suppose, if I viewed this as a profession, a profession with its own regimentation and maintenance requirements. I think writing would have been less fulfilling.

ESSF: What appeals to you about science fiction specifically? Did having a degree in chemical engineering influence your career choice?

I grew up reading and loving science fiction, so I was naturally drawn to it when writing. The choice of an engineering degree—because I love the sciences, too.

ESSF: Who were your favorite authors growing up? Which subgenres do you write in?

I don't really think of subgenres when I write. That only comes much later when I have to send works for publication. I tend to end up writing non-realist fiction most of the time. My favorite authors growing up include Ray Bradbury, Stephen King, many American pulp writers. Thomas Disch's *The Brave Little Toaster*, the Disney version, is one notable favorite.

331

ESSF: How old is science fiction in the Philippines? Did the Cold War play a role in the genre?

Seven decades old, give or take. Victor Fernando Ocampo, a contemporary Filipino writer based in Singapore, uncovered a Tagalog [an indigenous language in the Philippines] work published in 1945 by Mateo Cruz Cornelio. That work was the first known SF by a Filipino. I don't know of the role played by the Cold War.

ESSF: Was the fear of nuclear annihilation a concern for Filipino SF? And was the presence of American G.I.s in the country an influence?

The nuclear apocalypse is one of the go-to doomsday scenarios. I'm sure it has infiltrated Filipino SF to a certain extent. The same is true for American GIs, as well as many Western genres and subgenre tropes, which are mangled and abused by some Filipino writers. There are, of course, able Filipino writers who do intelligently revitalized takes on familiar tropes, even ones that blur subgenre borders. Examples of the latter include Mia Tijam, Paolo Enrico Melendez, and Adam David.

ESSF: Is there a difference between the kind of SF written by Muslims in the Philippines and the kind written by non–Muslims? Is religion a theme in your own writings?

I wouldn't know the difference as I've only read science fiction by non–Muslim Filipinos. I don't even know if there is a Muslim Filipino SF writer out there. Religion may be a theme in my writing, because Philippine culture is steeped in it and is choked to death by its influence, but I don't consciously incorporate it. I don't like to talk about religion, but I *want* to talk about it. Filipinos are generally religious, not spiritual, thus the gross amount of importance placed on the superficial, on material and consumerist excesses. My father is an orthodox Islam practitioner, while my mother is in one of those Christian denominations. My name is a misnomer as its etymological equivalent means a Christian Muslim. I do not believe in and cannot be made to accept anything even remotely monotheistic, and this strong inclination finds its way into my writing.

ESSF: You live in the countryside, a rural town in Maguindanao. Does the peace and quiet help you write better, or is being close to nature the source of your inspiration?

I think so. There's a difference between the writing I've produced when I was still working in cities and my writing now, which is more introspective.

ESSF: Do you face any problems in science fiction as a woman?

No, no difficulties that I'm aware of, thanks to other writers (like Nalo Hopkinson, Nisi Shawl, and Joanne Merriam, among many other names in international SF) who had made this so. In the Philippines, we have the feminist small press called Gantala Press.

ESSF: Science fiction and poetry seem worlds apart. How do you reconcile the two?

I don't reconcile them. I think that's the beauty of it—that the form, the structure, their combined baggage are turning out to be receptive to efforts at mixing and matching.

ESSF: Could you give us a sample poem?

These two poems were from my book, *Meditations of a Beast*, which was published by a student-run university press in the University of Wisconsin–Stevens Point.

The Oil Spill

Men in hazmat suits try to put out
the intractable black fire. They lug snakes
that spurt fire-retardant polymer beads.

The ocean heaves, a centimeter or two
deeper than last year. There is now a sickly
sweet undertone to the smell of brine.

The spill is all over the beach, scalding
the lithe juggernauts of the deep
and the fragile ones in shells.

The spill blinds, burns seabirds,
grows pustules and canker sores
on the skins of everything that lives.

The spill is cackling lunacy gushing,
enfolding the continental crust.
The spill is slick on the surface of the dead.

The Village of Fog

The spill is slick on the surface of the dead.
Then it seeps into porous clay, taints the aquifer.

Here is the local cemetery, where some of us
stop bristling at the possibility of decay.

In the west, the orchard. Wait for it to bloom.
In January, the frigid vastness can be spanned

with arms outstretched. Elsewhere is the sea,
where some of us break the surface, backs and flanks

against the squall. Beyond is the beleaguered
calm. A village is nothing but suffocating fog,

nothing but cogs, subsoil, oblivion.
A dirt road lurks inside every house.

ESSF: Does being multilingual help you when you write? As Arabs, we think of Arabic as a supremely musical language. Does the same hold of Filipino and Spanish?

Yes, absolutely. Switching between multiple languages all the time enhances cognition and memory. I write in English, read in English and in Filipino. And my day-to-day language is a combination of both, plus the vernacular. Filipino and Spanish—well, I'm not so sure of its musical quality (relative to English) but I do find Filipino and Tagalog are more poised in conveying a heightened sense of drama.

ESSF: Tell us something about SFPA, the Science Fiction and Fantasy Poetry Association?

I am not a member. It publishes a journal called *Star*Line*, which published some poems in the past. It also gives out three annual awards: the Elgin award for best book of speculative poetry, the Rhysling for best poem published in a year, and the Dwarf Stars award for best short poem. I have been nominated for these three awards. The only ones who can nominate are SFPA members.

ESSF: Would you say they do a good job coupling poetry and SF together and that they help promote Asian and Third World authors?

Absolutely.

ESSF: Please tell us about your book The Drone Outside. *How influenced are you by current events in your writings?*

Very much influenced. The bulk of *The Drone Outside* was written in the weeks-long siege and aerial bombing resulting from the terrorist attack of Marawi, a city that's a four- or five-hour drive from where I live. I had no internet connection at that time, and the lack of distraction helped the writing, a fact I'm sharing here sans any celebratory sense as that time period involved horrible loss of life and property. *The Drone Outside* is, in many ways, slanted to reflect the clinical distance afforded by the scrutiny of reality through a remote-controlled viewing device, the dissolution of moral boundaries, and the sociopathy of war.

ESSF: Are you a fan of Philip K. Dick?

Definitely. And J.G. Ballard.

ESSF: It's always good to see that the weirder brand of SF has made its way to the Philippines. We ask because of your story "Day of the Builders," which sounds reminiscent of Dick's story "The Builder," about a suburbanite American wasting his time building a boat when it's really a wooden box, a nuclear fallout shelter.

No. The builder in my story is different.

ESSF: Is the science fiction you write different from that produced in the West? Are your concerns and subject-matter different, or is it a matter of stylistics? Is there a distinctive East Asian school of SF?

On the surface, no, my work is not all that different because my formative influences were Western writers. But of course, it is infused by my unique personal touch, which is grounded on my cultural upbringing and my environment. I wouldn't know of any East Asian SF that distinctively brands itself as such.

ESSF: Does Japanese science fiction, whether anime, manga, or written literature, have an influence on Filpino SF? You will be surprised to learn that Japanese works are very popular, and very influential, all the way over here in the Middle East.

Absolutely! And I didn't know it went as far as Middle East! From graphic novels to novelty items, Japan's anime and manga have carved its solid place in Filipino pop culture, literature, and art.

ESSF: How do you reach an international audience, from the Philippines? Is writing in English enough? (We can use every piece of advice we can get here in the Arab world).

In my case, yes. My decision to use English and the fact that I've always sent the majority of my works out to foreign publishers (compared to domestic ones) has helped a lot in reaching an international audience. And I should point out that, in a way, my writing in English has contributed to pushing English-language Filipino literature's perception in world literature as something that's representative of Filipino literature. It's not. English-language Filipino literature is a slap in the face of authenticity; it is an inadequate subset of Filipino literature and should be viewed as such—the literature of the Filipino elite. Also, I am disappointed by Anglophone Filipino writers and editors who cannot be bothered to acknowledge and even knowingly support this notion.

ESSF: Are you a fan of the late Edward Said?

Unfortunately, I did not have the honor of being acquainted with his work. That is something I must remedy.

ESSF: What was the secret to the success of People of Colo(u)r Destroy Science Fiction, *winner of the 2017 British Fantasy Award for Best Anthology? Can you give us some background on your contribution to this special issue of* Lightspeed Magazine?

My role in that award-winning anthology: I helped select the pieces that went into the original fiction section. *People of Colo(u)r Destroy Science Fiction's* critical and commercial success can be attributed to how easily—and in style—the anthology fills the non–Caucasian void in the SF world.

ESSF: You were a long-time editor with LONTAR: The Journal of Southeast Asian Speculative Fiction, *a publication coming out of Singapore. Tell me about your experience there. Are such literary platforms an effective way of changing people's perceptions about Asians and art coming out of the Third World? Could you envision such a journal in a region like the Middle East?*

LONTAR: The Journal of Southeast Asian Speculative Fiction is all Jason Erik Lundberg's laudable vision to carve literary space for Southeast Asian voices. We've had an incredible run, ten beautifully packaged issues offering a selection of fine speculative fiction, poetry, and art by Southeast Asian creatives—so yes, initiatives such as LONTAR are effective vehicles in changing perceptions about contemporary Asian art and literature. The only challenge is, of course, money. There is no shortage of interesting and original material to fill the issues. LONTAR was pretty much funded by a grant-giving body of the Singaporean government. As for the Middle East, I am saying this with complete awe, that's where Sumer is and that's where ancient Egypt is. The Middle East is so way, way ahead of the rest of the world because it has the earliest known human civilizations and has writing preserved on clay tablets. Something like a Middle Eastern *LONTAR* equivalent? Why not! For one, there's *The State*, a journal based in Dubai that has put out themed issues. Speculative fiction is not *The State's* focus but I just want to point out its outstanding curation.

ESSF: How does being an editor differ from being an author? Does it help you write better? Are you harsher in your judgments of the author you review as an author yourself?

Being an editor is being a reader while staking one's reputation and credibility. Yes, being an editor, as well as a translator, helps my writing by providing continuous mental exercise. Both require critical traction, attention to details. Writing can be a passive affair at times, but not editing and translating.

ESSF: Future projects? (And thanks for the compliment on Middle Eastern history).

I'm working on several manuscripts, including a linked story collection that should read like a novel. It is about the weird ins and outs of people in an apartment building.

Aditya Nugraha Wardhana on Indonesia's New Wave SF

Comics, Cartoons, and Leveraging Literature Between the East and West

EGYPTIAN SOCIETY FOR SCIENCE FICTION

> The measure of a man is not his intelligence. It is not how high he rises in the freak establishment. The measure of a man is this: how swiftly can he react to another person's need? And how much of himself can he give?
> —Philip K. Dick (2013: 52–53)

ESSF: Beast Taruna is an alternative history work. How did you get into the genre and who were your favorite authors growing up?

The background of my interest in the genre of alternate history started in my school days with the video game *Red Alert 2*. It actually sparked the idea of a world where history went in a different path, in this case, the disappearance of Hitler. This extraordinary event, since it was caused by Einstein's time machine, gave way to an expansionist Soviet Union led by Joseph Stalin, who immediately invaded Europe before the Allies launched a counterattack. The spark was there, but the main inspiration for putting myself into the alternate history genre was the legendary novel *The Man in the High Castle* by Philip K. Dick, which I read during high school. As it was a novel, the details regarding the alternate world where the Nazis and Japanese won World War II was amazing for me.

ESSF: You also write in the superhero subgenres. Would Japanese SF have anything to do with this? Did you grow up watching Japanese cartoons (giant robots, space battles, educational cartoons)? Is Japanese science fiction influential in Indonesia?

I grew up in '90s Indonesia where the prevalence of Japanese science fiction TV series was huge. Like most of my generation, I grew up watching *Super Sentai* (or *Power Rangers* as the American adaptation) or other Japanese tokusatsu superhero shows. This of course affects the superhero elements of my novel, culminating in a five-person team who use armor suits to fight evil.

ESSF: Talking to authors in Indonesia who have been "identified" as science fiction writers, you discover they write in magic realism or dark fantasy or horror. Is there no market for SF in Indonesia? And why are people confusing these different genres?

Make no mistake, there is a *huge* market for science fiction in Indonesia, but this issue is delicate. As a whole, Indonesian people tend to take pride in themselves and their culture. Any genre, be that dark fantasy or horror or SF, will be more popular if they are relatable to Indonesian people or their culture. For example, American-styled but Indonesian-made superheroes like Volt will be popular here, but their image will be eclipsed once someone used the characters from old Indonesia mythology or *wayang* shadow puppet stories, albeit remodernized. This of course can be countered by massive promotion efforts via networking.

ESSF: How old is science fiction in Indonesia? Did it begin in the 1950s, after the Second World War, or much more recently? Are the classics of SF—H.G. Wells, Jules Verne, Isaac Asimov, Arthur C. Clarke, Robert Heinlein—popular there?

The SF genre in Indonesia is not as old as that in United States. From what I know, the earliest original Indonesian science fiction novel is *Jatuh ke Matahari* (*Falling into the Sun*) by Djoko Lelono in 1976. There was a surge of SF, mainly in the superhero subgenre, during the Soeharto years between 1970s and 1990s when there were many both translated and original Indonesian works, but it went bust in a way since the economic collapse of 1998.

The writers you have mentioned are not so popular in Indonesia nowadays, mainly because there aren't many translated novels by them here. This also worsened by the preference of Indonesian readers for the romance or fantasy genre.

ESSF: Who are the big names in Indonesian SF, the pioneers and the new generation?

Djoko Lelono is surely one of the big names of the SF genre in Indonesia with themes mainly about space exploration. Dee Lestari is also one, with her novel about aliens combined with philosophical discussions. There are some other writers, but I can't recall their names since most made only one SF novel, not a series.

Djoko Lelono's main SF series, *Penjelajah Antariksa* (*Space Explorers*), is set in alien worlds across the galaxy, mainly in the world of Poa. I think he was mainly inspired by Western SF writers such as Arthur C. Clarke and Heinlein, etc.

I have never read Mr. Djoko's work myself, unfortunately. I was more influenced by Arief Rachman, the author of the post-apocalyptic *Everyday Adventures*.

Most of the writers of this generation are light novel authors, as is *Everyday Adventures*.

ESSF: Were his works translated?

Not to my knowledge. Distributed regionally only.

ESSF: Is there an online directory for Indonesian writers? There is for Malaysian SF authors.

No, there is not. There are some efforts in making Indonesian writers come together in one media such as Ciayo Comics, but it is more for comic writers.

ESSF: Is there any cooperation between genre authors in Indonesia and Malaysia? Do you have a SF association or fan clubs in Indonesia?

I have no knowledge about Malaysia, but there is some cooperation with Singaporean writers and comic artists.

There are some science fiction associations and fan clubs in Indonesia, but they are more about comics. On the other hand, the LCDP group on Facebook is a general group with several SF authors and editors.

ESSF: Is all SF in Indonesia written in the local language?

Yes, as our market is still the local market in Indonesia. This doesn't include the imported SF books that are sold in various bookstores such as Kinokuniya.

ESSF: Tell us about your book Beast Taruna. *Is this a novel or comic book series? And please tell us about the demographics of the age-groups you target? Do Indonesian girls read SF too?*

Beast Taruna is a "light novel" series, basically a compromise between novel and comic book. The term itself is the variation of the illustrated novel from Japan. Each chapter contains one or more illustrations depicting certain scenes. *Beast Taruna* tells the story of five high school friends who live in an alternate Indonesia where Nazi Germany and the Japanese Empire won the Second World War. They live a normal life until they are appointed as superheroes to fight coming evil. The setting presents a moral dilemma and paradox as the definition of "evil" itself becomes blurry since the heroes are defending a world where the horrors of Nazi and Japanese atrocities are alive and well.

My target reader demographic is mainly generations who have nostalgia for the '90s, back to the somewhat golden age of Japanese superhero TV shows in Indonesia. But I also want to hook younger young adults and the teen generation just to tell them that a superhero story is not always so light and perfect. Some of my readers are females, although they tend to pay closer attention to the fit male characters of the story.

ESSF: Do you find superheroes to be empowering for the young? Are Spiderman and Superman and Wolverine popular in Indonesia?

With the launch of Marvel Cinematic Universe, Spiderman and other Marvel superheroes are popular in Indonesia. This is supported by various TV shows on cable TV channels and comics in import book stores. They are empowering for young adults and teens since the stories are simple and easier to digest to them.

ESSF: Have you read The 99 *comic book series, coming out of Kuwait?*

I have read the first issue of *The 99*. It was good, but the large magazine format is not suitable for Indonesian readers who are already accustomed to smaller novel-sized and Japanese manga-sized reading materials.

ESSF: How different is your novel from Philip K. Dick's masterpiece? There is a nuclear war brewing in The Man in the High Castle *too between Germany and Japan, the victorious axis powers.*

The Man in the High Castle is the main inspiration for *Beast Taruna*. The main difference is that while there is a Cold War–like tension situation in *High Castle*, peace and cooperation are visible between the new superpower nations of Nazi Germany and the Japanese Empire in *Beast Taruna*. Visible since there is a "secret" war and conflicts behind the scenes.

ESSF: How did you construct the storyline? Did you model it on the actual occupation of Indonesia by European powers in the past? Was the Cold War and what happened to Sukarno and the non-aligned movement an influence?

I based the setting of Bumiseruni on various inspirations. Yes, the main source is the real-life Japanese occupation of Indonesia in the Second World War. But I also used several references to their post-war plans if they won the war. This includes several colonies and puppet states such as the in-story Empire of Indonesia akin to Empire of Manchukuo in our world.

The first draft actually used the global situation similar to the Cold War with Nazi Germany and the Japanese Empire taking the place of the superpower nations. But the revision changed this to be more subtle, with the nations appearing to work together while conflicting in the back.

ESSF: Kazuki Yudhistira, the protagonist of your novel, what does his name mean? And the setting for the action-adventure, the city of Bumiseruni, what does it signify? What does the name itself mean?

Kazuki Yudistira is actually not his real name; it is Kazuki Miura. The family name comes from his Japanese background. But this heritage is challenged by his own father who married an Indonesian woman, something not so common in Japanese-dominated Asia. This is caused by the toxic relationship he had with his family in the Home Islands. He chose Yudistra for his son since the name was based on a heroic character from old Indonesian *wayang* (or Indian Hindu depending on the source) mythology.

Bumiseruni is a fictional city down on the western coast of Borneo, close to the real-life location of Pontianak. I chose to have a fictional setting since most superhero stories are based in one. The backstory for Bumiseruni is that it was constructed by the Japanese colonists to support Pontianak and mimic the Japanese panorama, complete with artificial steep hills. The name itself comes from "Bumi," which means earth or land, and "Seruni," which is the name of a beautiful flower commonly found in Indonesia.

ESSF: Is Bumiseruni an ecofriendly city? Is the environment a theme in your works and in the works of other Indonesian SF authors?

Environment is actually a huge part of the *Beast Taruna* world setting. This is based on my research of various eco-friendly policies made by Nazi Germany in our real world, ranging from banning animal testing, extensive greening projects, and the prohibition of smoking. This is extended into the world of *Beast Taruna* with the presence of more efficient hypersonic aircrafts and zeppelins, the prevalence of a mass transport system such as Bumiseruni's own monorail, and crazy things such as an atomic-powered motorcycle owned by one of the main characters. On the darker side, there is a passing scene where the Nazi and Japanese delegates meet in Paris to talk about climate change, which results in more eco-friendly methods used in their concentration camps.

Regarding the environmental theme in other SF stories in Indonesia, I don't have knowledge of it.

ESSF: Is religion a theme in the novel? Is Sufism popular in Indonesian literature?

Religion is not the main theme of the novel itself since I want it to be enjoyable for everyone from different religious backgrounds.

Sufism is almost unheard of in Indonesian literature as far as I can recall.

ESSF: Does the category "East Asian" sci-fi or "Southeast Asian" SF attract you personally? If so, why?

It attracts me since it can counterbalance the prevalence of Western and Western-styled SF stories out there both in Indonesia and the world in general.

ESSF: Indonesia participated in the making of Beyond Skyline *(2018) and has its own very well-developed brand of martial arts, Pencak Silat, and martial arts movies. How long before Indonesia starts making its own SF movies?*

There are already some original Indonesian SF projects, mainly in the superhero genre. Gundala, a 1970s Indonesian speedster superhero akin to The Flash, was rebooted as a major film in 2019.

ESSF: What are your future plans? Are you hoping your novel will be made into a cartoon series or even a live-action movie? What did you think of the live-action version of Ghost in the Shell *(2018)?*

My future plans for now is to expand the *Beast Taruna* series into new books and spin offs. Regarding adaptations, honestly it is still far from my goals, but anything is possible.

Ghosts in the Shell was a long-running anime series back in the '80s and '90s. As any adaptation will show you, to compact that into a two-hour movie will cause you to lose most of the trademark ideas, especially with a story accessible to common American audiences. The story was too simple and predictable for me, but the atmosphere of the city setting was amazing.

ESSF: Any advice for us in Egypt and fellow Muslim countries?

As I am also growing, this advice can be applied to myself as well. We should expand our works into the English language so that we can disperse them into a broader market, not just confined to our local one.

Work Cited

Dick, Philip K. (2013). *Our Friends from Frolix 8*. Boston: Mariner Books.

Archiving the Future

A Conversation with Rebecca Hankins on the
Fictional Frontiers of Muslim and African SF

EGYPTIAN SOCIETY FOR SCIENCE FICTION

> Education is the passport to the future, for tomorrow belongs to those who prepare for it today.
> —Malcolm X (quoted in Parham et al., 2016: 137)

ESSF: Please give us a very personal introduction. How did you get into sci-fi and how did you get into the Obama administration?

PERSONAL INTRODUCTION

In many ways my life has been a SF drama, with a little fantasy and magical realism thrown in for good measure! I was born in Pontiac, Michigan, 20 miles outside of Detroit, a bastion of Black power where the Nation of Islam (NOI) and Malcolm X were mainstays of the African American communities. Although I never belonged to the NOI, I admired their discipline, cleanliness, and the respect shown women. After graduating high school and starting my undergraduate education at Eastern Michigan University in Ypsilanti, Michigan, I dropped out to start a family and live the life of mundane existence. As Shakespeare writes in *Twelfth Night*, "Some are born great, some achieve greatness, and some have greatness thrust upon 'em." I never believed I would eventually travel to Jordan, Jerusalem, Singapore, Malaysia, Indonesia, or even England; these were my SF/fantasy dreams. When I stood before the Dome of the Rock in Jerusalem, it was like science fiction. I had an out of body experience! Who would have thought this little Black girl from the *sleepy bedroom* suburb of Pontiac, with middle class parents, the youngest of four girls, would ever visit these amazing historical places. It was truly a life altering experience!

I became a librarian and archivist actually by happenstance. I was living in New Orleans, Louisiana, a city considered, at that time, prior to Hurricane Katrina, a largely African American city with a strong Catholic influence. I was trying to find work, but at the time I had no degree, but I did have a few hours of undergraduate education. I enrolled in and had just finished a free business skills program sponsored by the Urban League of New Orleans and was starting the interview process for potential jobs. I interviewed at a number of places and often times I was met with suspicion and sometimes outright hostility. I'm a visibly Muslim, African American woman; this means I wear the Muslim headscarf or khimar, so most employers weren't used to seeing someone that looked like me. I was getting very frustrated and wanted to give up, but then I interviewed for a position at The Amistad Research Center at Tulane University, the premiere archival institute that documents the history and culture of Africans and African Americans. Before I arrived home from the interview, the director, who eventually became my mentor and good friend, Dr. Clifton H. Johnson, offered me the job that launched my career as an archivist and librarian. He took a chance on me, this person without a degree of any kind, and a person-of-color who also looked different; this has had a profound impact on me and has sustained me through difficult times. Throughout my academic career, it has been essential that I provide a voice, space, and presence for those communities victimized, ignored, or marginalized within academia and society. These principles have been woven throughout my 30-year career and undergird my commitment to the work I do.

My SF History

I come from a family of nerds and geeks; we love our SF, fantasy, comic books, and video games, from our earliest love of the 1960s *Star Trek* to the fanatical worship of the franchise, my favorite being *Deep Space 9*, to all of the *Star Wars*, *Dune* (books and films), and our current Marvel/DC Comics superheroes. This interest and love for science fiction grew when I was hired as an assistant professor/archivist at Texas A&M University's Cushing Memorial Library & Archives. Texas A&M University's library has the third largest science fiction, fantasy, and comic book collection in the world. If you are a *Game of Thrones* fan, we have the George RR Martin papers at Cushing and numerous other writers. I saw major gaps in what they were collecting in terms of people of color, so I started buying materials to fill that gap.

When I started my position, I first began to survey our holdings, and it was apparent that there was a lack of representation of Muslims in Cushing's science fiction collections, but I knew about books such as *Arabian Nights* and movies such as *Dune* and *Star Wars,* storylines that borrowed heavily from Islam. I started to notice that the influence of Islam and Muslims had been ignored, marginalized, or unacknowledged. I have worked to infuse the collections with the works and solicited papers from these groups of people. I decided that I would write about this problem while also showing where Islam and Muslims fit into the larger picture of that influence.

I've contributed information on science fiction to Dr. Muhammad Ahmad's website *Islam and Science Fiction* over the years, and in March 2015, I interviewed well-known author G. Willow Wilson (of *Ms. Marvel* fame). This was before she published that series. The interview with Wilson has been quoted in a thesis and translated into the Indonesian language, Bahasa. I used that interview to inquire about her papers; although she is not ready to let them go, I am on her radar. I have personally met her, so we remain connected. I've also shared the website with others far and wide, nationally and internationally.

Muhammad and I presented at conferences such as the Southwest Texas Popular Culture Conference (SWTXPC) in Albuquerque, New Mexico, on 11 February 2012, and the Popular Culture Assn/American Culture Assn Conference, in Boston, Massachusetts, on 14 April 2012. We also hosted a very successful, Islamic science fiction short story contest with prize money, and we are working on a book.

This work has also led to my making connections with writers and scholars all over the world such as Yasmin Khan, Naomi Foyle, and Yusuf Nuruddin. I have had writers ask me to read their works and write reviews. UK journalist Alexander Jones of *Stylist Magazine* asked me to contribute a paragraph on Octavia Butler for an essay titled *Sci Fi: The Feminist Frontier-Parallel Universe*, May 2017. I'm also working on an essay with Muhammad for the *Bloomsbury Handbook of Islam and Popular Culture*.

Probably my most impactful work was a co-authored essay with my colleague Joyce Thornton titled "Influence of Muslims and Islam in Science Fiction, Fantasy and Comics" for the book *Muslims and American Popular Culture* (Hankins and Thornton, 2014). This essay led to a request for me to develop and lead a two-day workshop for infusing Islamic popular culture into the curriculum for K-12 and undergraduate students at Kennesaw State University for 14 faculty from the English and Africana Studies Department. I created a number of digital tools and a website.

Another important essay that deals with SF is titled "The Peculiar Institution: The Depiction of Slavery in Steven Barnes's *Lion's Blood* and *Zulu Heart*" published in *Africana Islamic Studies* (Hankins, 2016). I heard from the author Steven Barnes who wrote me, "Loved your essay. I feel that you understood what I was trying to do with those books." This article's incubation was originally given at the University of Houston's symposium titled New Approaches to Research on African American Islam. This is another essay that has established my work as an expert in the area of Islamic SF.

I have also written a review of the book *Where No Black Woman Has Gone Before: Subversive Portrayals in Speculative Film and TV* published in spring 2019 for the *Science Fiction Research Association Reviews of Non-fiction Books*. I've also presented my work internationally in both South Korea (Sogang University), London (Tottenham Palestine Literature Festival), and Bogor, Indonesia (high school students), that was covered in the Bogor Cibinong, Indonesia newspaper (Sastrawijaya, 2015). I've also written articles that have been published in the UK titled "The Case for Fictional Islam" (Hankins, July–August 2015) and "Fictional Islam: A Literary Review and Comparative Essay on Islam in Science Fiction and Fantasy" (Hankins, 2009).

OBAMA ADMINISTRATION

As noted above, my long career, research and publishing, archival expertise, commitment, and advocacy culminated with the president of the United States, Barack Obama, appointing me to a three-year term (2016–2019) to the National Historical Publications and Records Commission (NHPRC), the funding arm of the National Archives and Records Administration (NARA), and one of the most prominent research funding agencies in the USA. NHPRC is a body of 14 Commissioners, where two of us have the distinction of being Presidential Appointees. In his announcement, President Obama said, "I am confident that these outstanding individuals will serve the American people well, and I look forward to working with them." Our mandated charge is to review hundreds of proposals that provide $5–$10 million dollars annually to projects documenting America's history. I have had many people tell me that no one deserved this honor more than me, but I know too many archivists who work in the trenches and are never recognized. These women and men who do their jobs in anonymity. So yes, I deserved this honor, but there are so many others that deserve it too. You never know how your name gets in front of the president of the United States and he says her not him. It is a mystery, the stuff of SF and fantasy!

ESSF: A brief history of African/American Muslims in the U.S.?

Africans have been in the Americas prior to the founding of the United States. The first Africans to encounter the Americas were a combination of merchants, serfs, or slaves. Scholars such as Ivan Van Sertima, Sylviane Diouf, Michael Gomez, and Allan D. Austin have written extensively on African Muslims, a combination of Arabs and Africans, in the Americas, both free and enslaved. Austin's book contains information about the life of about 80 African Muslims enslaved in America between 1730 and 1860. Because education and literacy were widespread and encouraged amongst Muslim peoples throughout the Continent, all of these Muslims were educated and left some record of their presence. These scholars and many others are starting to document their lives and history. Dr. Diouf notes that Muslims, who had a love for freedom, were at the center of many of the uprisings, rebellions, and fights against slavery. There was such a concern about some of these rebellions that many countries tried to ban the importation of Muslim Africans, but scant attention was paid to this as the slave trade continued, as the case of the Amistad Africans attest. One of the most significant historical African Muslim figures that we should all know about is Sengbe Pieh (Cinque), the hero of the Amistad Revolt. As someone who was the senior archivist at the Amistad Research Center at Tulane University in New Orleans where the papers of the Amistad Revolt are held, I didn't discover that he was Muslim until I had worked there for two years. Even Steven Spielberg's film *Amistad* has one shot, after Cinque and the other Africans had taken over the ship, where you see them in prayer.

It must be remembered that Muslims have had a long association with this country. Muslim-led Morocco was the first country to acknowledge the then-fledgling project that was the United States, in 1777; these two countries maintain one of the longest-enduring peace treaties in American history. Such facts are indisputable, but we learn very few of these positive stories from the national or international media or from the products of popular culture. Muslims have been here for generations. They are your neighbors, your friends, your soldiers, your doctors, your teachers, your grocers, your students, your librarians, your archivists!

Enslaved African Omar ibn Said (1770–1864), one of the most well-known Muslims and the first to write his biography in Arabic, was brought to North Carolina as a slave. Just before Omar's death, a North Carolina newspaper published a photo of what it called "The Lord's Prayer," written in Arabic by him. However, when one reads the Arabic, it is Sura An Nasr (Chapter 110) of the Quran. As Diouf notes in her book, *Servants of Allah: African Muslims Enslaved in the Americas,* slave narratives recorded as late as the 1940s relate how Islam was practiced by some African American descendants of slaves in the islands of the Carolinas. Diouf asserts that the impact of the Islamic past survives in many things African Americans do today, including jazz music.

Some contemporary figures we all know well are converts to Islam. Elijah Muhammad was the founder of the Nation of Islam, one of the largest and most recognizable groups of Black Muslims in the U.S., and his son Warith Deen Muhammad, who took over the organization after his death. Malcolm X was, according to the scholar Sohail Daulatzai, who spoke at the Global hip-hop and the New Muslim Culture Event at Temple University in 2018, "...maybe the most important man to come out of this land we call

America…. Malcolm was saying we can't confine ourselves to being Americans" (Santan-gelo, 2018). There are a number of Black Muslims in the music and entertainment fields who are well known: Akon, Q-Tip and Ali Shaheed from A Tribe Called Quest, Lupe Fiasco, Mos Def, Eve, Dave Chapelle, Jermaine Jackson, and the first Muslim to win an Academy Award, Mahershala Ali.

We now regularly see and hear of Muslims who are adding to the richness of our multi-cultural and pluralistic United States stories. More Muslims are throwing their hats into the political arena, resulting in the election of Muslim females and males to political office. including Missouri State Representative Yaphett El-Amin, Minnesota Congress-woman Ilhan Omar, Detroit Congresswoman Rashidah Talib, former Congressman Keith Ellison, now Minnesota's Attorney General, and Indiana Congressman Andre Carson.

We note that scholars are using their research to touch upon issues within the Mus-lim community, such as Harvard Law School professors Intisar Rabb, Drs. Jamillah Karim, Khalil Abdur Rashid, and Amina McCloud, to name a few notables. Muslim men and women have always had a presence in sports, such as Hakeem Olajuwon, Olympic fencer Ibtihaj Muhammad, with the first khimar (headscarf) wearing Barbie doll created in her likeness, and football players and brothers Hamza and Hussain Abdullah. And of course, Muhammad Ali, who was considered the personification of strength in the face of adversity. His faith is what kept him strong throughout his life. He has been the recipient of the highest civilian award, the Medal of Freedom.

There are over 1.6 billion Muslims in the world today, with the Continent having a sizable number of these adherents. The late scholar Ali Mazrui noted that there are more Arabic-speaking Africans than Arabic-speaking Arabs. African American Muslims rep-resent about 30–35 percent of the approximately 4–6 million Muslims in America. Not all African American Muslims are converts, particularly 3rd and 4th generations. Although Christianity remains the dominant faith tradition in America, there are 20 states where the next largest faith community is Islam, and North Carolina is one of those states. You will find Muslims in every aspect of our history in America. Muslims are the second larg-est religious population in the world today, and the Pew Research Forum estimates that the number of Muslims will "increase by about 35% in the next 20 years. In the United States, for example, the population projections show the number of Muslims more than doubling over the next two decades" ("The Future of the Global Muslim Population," 2011). According to a recent *Washington Post* article, Islam is the second most followed religion after Christianity in 20 states (Wilson, 2014). They include the state of Texas where I live and the state of Michigan where I was born, where there have always been significant populations.

ESSF: What is the nature of your work as an archivist? Do you see any contradiction between cataloguing the past and imagining the future?

At the Amistad Research Center at Tulane University (mentioned above), I became the chief acquisitions archivist, responsible for all acquisitions to the institution in the areas of manuscripts and art. Before departing Amistad, I was the senior archivist with knowledge of the holdings, history, and structure of the Center. This knowledge was invaluable in assisting researchers, faculty, and students who used Amistad's resources. It enabled me to serve as a consultant for movies, screenplays, books, documentaries, con-ferences, art exhibitions, archives, and schools. I learned years later that the person who was responsible for accepting people into the Urban League program did not want me

The Archivist of the United States Dr. David Ferriero swearing in Rebecca Hankins as one of two presidential appointees at the NHPRC Meeting (author photograph).

because, in her words, "We would never be able to place her in a job." My career has definitely proved her wrong! There are too many times to count of the shock and surprise when I show up to teach classes or meet with people; it's priceless. All of these reactions motivate me to do this kind of work, influence what I research and publish, and just as importantly, determine where my advocacy lies.

There are no contradictions in my work as an archivist who preserves history because you collect, preserve, and make accessible history, not for those who are dead and gone, but for future generations. Providing access to history is what we do as archivists, and that is always in the forefront of my work. We must have an accurate accounting of everyone's history in America, an accounting of a holistic past that represents intentional cataloguing of this past that allows for the imagining of the future. Archivists who do this work understand there is no contradiction; on the contrary, it is necessary that we make every attempt to collect the known and unknown, the prominent and the obscure. One of the most pressing issues is ensuring that we do have diverse representation within these institutions, and that includes diversity in both collections and people. I am constantly lecturing groups and individuals: if you don't save your history and documents that chronicle that history, then anyone can write whatever they want about you and your activities. Preserving and donating your papers, records, and history ensures that your voice, life, and work can't be distorted or changed. In short, if you don't see this as important, anyone can tell your story from a perspective that doesn't reflect your issues, interests, or voice. This is especially true for marginalized populations, so it is my mission to make sure they are represented in the archives, research, presentations, publications, and teaching.

It is essential to introduce a diverse array of writers and documentation to students. I have also worked with students to present their work on Islamic science fiction and encourage teachers/professors to structure a course around science fiction, fantasy, and/or comics that draws on creative writing at the high school level and at the undergraduate level. Speculative fiction that encompasses SF, fantasy, and comic books can be used to study research methods, astronomy, literature, gender roles, sexuality, mathematics and almost any subject using *Muslims and American Popular Culture* as a textbook for assignments. The workshop I gave at Kennesaw State University in Georgia and my article, "The Case for Fictional Islam," specifically addressed ways to infuse Islamic SF, fantasy, and comic book literature into the curriculum.

ESSF: How does sci-fi written by Muslims in the United States differ, if at all, from science fiction written by Muslims in the Muslim world?

If you examine the works by Muslims internationally, there is a tendency to be negative, pessimistic, and fatalistic. Ahmed Saadawi's *Frankenstein in Baghdad* and Ali Mazrui's *The Trial of Christopher Okigbo* are examples of this view. U.S. writers Ian Dallas's *The Book of Strangers* (1972), G. Willow Wilson's *Cairo*, and Donald Moffitt's *Crescent in the Sky* (1990) and *A Gathering of Stars* (1990) are much more positive, heroic, and optimistic works that paint Muslims in much more favorable storylines. Of course, there are more works by non–Muslims about Muslims that are both positive and negative. There is no shortage of books, short stories, or films that use Islam as a negative plot device. With the terrorists' attacks of 9/11 and the *War on Terror*, science fiction writers have jumped on the "all-things Arab/Muslim-are-terrorists" bandwagon. Unfortunately, this is not a recent phenomenon. Science fiction and fantasy writers have a long history of treating Islam and Muslims as backward, evil, and intolerant from G.K. Chesterton's *The Flying Inn* (1914) to Brian Aldiss' *H.A.R.M* (2008).

ESSF: How eager are Muslim authors, and advocates like yourself, to network with Arab and Muslim authors and establish Arab Muslim science fiction on the global literary map? What initiatives are you working on specifically?

History has shown that African Americans have consistently worked with Arab writers, scholars, and activists, but much of that history needs to be uncovered. There have been recent studies such as that by Sohail Daulatzai (*Black Star, Crescent Moon*, 2012) that discuss Malcolm X's trip to Egypt in 1964 where he met with writers, activists, and scholars and called for African/Arab unity. *The Bandung Conference* of 1955, held in Bandung, Indonesia, pushed for Afro/Arab unity, an historic conference that included many African Americans from the United States, although one of the greatest advocates of this unity, the renowned scholar W.E.B. Du Bois, was not allowed to attend by the U.S. government. Interestingly, it was Du Bois' son, David Graham Du Bois (*Malcolm X: On Islam, U.S., Africa*, 1964), who lived for years in Egypt and wrote about Malcolm X's visit to Egypt. The scholar and writer Radwa Ashour, Ph.D., whose 1991 novel, *Siraaj: An Arab Tale* is an account of Arab involvement in a slave rebellion on a fictional East African island in the late 19th century, is someone who recognizes the synergy and connection between African American experiences and Arab history. She studied African American literature at the University of Massachusetts at the suggestion of Shirley Graham Du Bois, her mentor, another connection to W.E.B. Du Bois. Her 1975 dissertation, *The Search for a Black Poetics: A Study of Afro-American Critical Writings*, reflects the influence of African American literature.

The Tottenham Palestine Literature Festival, an annual literary festival held in London, has featured science fiction writers, including a panel I was on in 2014 with author/scholar Naomi Foyle and curator/advocate Yasmin Khan, both well-known for their work promoting Arab/Islamic science fiction. I was also asked to submit a short essay in the

London magazine *Stylist* for an article on feminist science fiction writers. I wrote about the author Octavia E. Butler, a prolific writer of SF. I've also written reviews, and my first article on SF was published in the British journal *Foundation*. My most recent publication on SF was published in the UK publication *Critical Muslim,* edited by a group of Arab scholars.

ESSF: What is Afro-futurism and how does it link in, if at all, with advocacy politics and Third World causes? Do you believe that Muslim authors from the African continent can make a unique contribution to this burgeoning genre?

Afro-futurism is defined as speculative fiction, SF, fantasy, futuristic literature that is written about and by Africans and African Americans. These works often are critical writings that focus on race, gender, and sexuality. Afro-futurism is a term that has gained attention in the last 10–15 years, but it actually has been around for a while. Some early writers of Afro-futurism include W.E.B. Du Bois' *The Comet* (1920) and George S. Schuyler's *Black No More* (1931). Its popularity is growing, with about 10–11 books written about the subject from 2013–2018. There are websites dedicated to the subject including Afro-futurism.com and BlackScienceFictionSociety.com and the AfroFuturism Festival, now an annual event. Some other writers of this genre include Africans and African Americans such as Steven Barnes (*Zulu Heart* and *Lion's Blood*), Tananarive Due (*Blood Colony*), Nalo Hopkinson, N.K. Jemisin (*The Fifth Season*), Colson Whitehead (*The Underground Railroad*), Octavia Butler (*Kindred),* and others.

ESSF: We are inexcusably ignorant of African authors of SF here in the Arab world, as you can imagine. How well recognized is Afro-futurism on the literary scene? What do the critics think? Have Afro-futurist authors faced any problems getting published?

There is the late Kenyan economist and scholar Dr. Ali Mazrui (mentioned earlier) whose book *The Trial of Christopher Okigbo* is his only work

Malcolm X's trip to Egypt not only broadened his mind as a Muslim but broadened all our minds to the possibilities lying beyond our borders, in space as well as time (courtesy of the artist, Ammar Al-Gamal).

of SF/fantasy. Nnedi Okorafor (*Binti*) has received wide-spread acclaim including profiles in *The New York Times* (Alter, 2017). There are the films by Wanuri Kahiu, *Pumzi* (2014) and *From a Whisper* (2008), both Afro-futuristic films with some Islamic elements. There are a number of American writers that write African SF, including the late Octavia Butler, Jalaluddin Nuriddin (poetry and music *Beyonder*), and Steven Barnes (*Lion's Blood* and *Zulu Heart*). We now have a core group of African Americans whose works are acknowledged and recognized. Sheree R. Thomas's book, *Dark Matter: A Century of Speculative Fiction from the African Diaspora*, and Vanessa E. Jones' article, "Race, the final frontier: Black science-fiction writers bring a unique perspective to the genre," include many of the Islamically influenced writers and writings.

One of the oldest websites featuring Black writers is the Black Science Fiction Society that focuses on Black people from all over the world. Every Friday there is a new interview online with SF authors, artists, and comic book creators. The site serves as a clearing house for events, conferences, and seminars that focus on Afro-futurism. There's also the symposium held at Northwestern University on Black Feminist Futures that looks, critically, at the state of Afro-futurism and women. Finally, the Schomburg Center for Research in Black Culture in New York hosts an annual Black Comic Book Festival, now in its tenth year.

ESSF: How influenced is Utopia, in Afro-futurism, by African folklore and myths and how much by modern utopian literature? And what is their idea of Utopia?

Afro-futurism, contrary to some of the Muslim American writers of SF, often depicts dystopian futures with bleak and post-apocalyptic storylines. Many of the origin stories are steeped in folklore or folk tales, a popular genre in African storytelling. These folk stories are often morality tales that provide life lessons. Many Afro-futurist writers are not looking at morality or providing lessons; they tend to reflect current issues of race and gender that often require their audiences to question humanity and the status quo. They often include very unsatisfactory endings that are often cautionary tales for humanity. This is a subject that has been tackled by an increasing number of scholars from a multitude of perspectives, including an entire special issue of the Oxford University journal *Critical Muslim* in 2014. I will note that the controversial Muslim leader Sayyid Qutb (Al-Qaida and other extremist groups cite his work as a major influence on their ideology) also influenced his followers in Egypt to write utopian works such as Ahmad Ra'if's popular play titled *Al-bu'd al-khamis* in 1987. This essay can add another layer to the ongoing discussion on the impact of the concept of utopianism within an Islamic discourse.

ESSF: Tell us about your history with the Islam Sci-Fi website? How does it work, who dreamed it up, and how can someone contribute? How many non–Muslims are involved?

My mentor and the now retired curator of the Cushing Science Fiction collection, Prof. Hal Hall, pushed me to research and write about this genre. While conducting research for my first foray into writing about Islamic SF, I discovered a website titled *Islam and Science Fiction* (http://www.islamscifi.com/contributors/) created by Dr. Muhammad Aurangzeb Ahmad at the University of Minnesota. I contacted him in 2009 about my interest in working with him on his website. I joined as a contributor in 2010. He has invited Muslims and non–Muslims to contribute to the site. He has published interviews with Muslim and non–Muslim writers of SF, fantasy, and other popular culture literature. The website is the most comprehensive place for information on the influence that Islam has and continues to have on speculative fiction. We also have created a portal on the Texas A&M University's OakTrust, our institutional repository, for adding some of our works. We hope to eventually move much of our writings and presentations to the OakTrust for safe housing since the Islamic Science Fiction website has been hacked in the past.

ESSF: Have your efforts faced any resistance, whether from the academic establishment or from Muslims themselves?

I posed a similar question to the Muslim SF/fantasy writer G. Willow Wilson (writer of the *Ms. Marvel* comic books) in an interview for the Islam and Science Fiction website that would resonate with some of what I wrote above. She noted that most of her works are in English, limiting her audience, but she continued, "Living in Egypt for example, there's been a new wave of young authors that are producing more novels that are becoming more popular" (Hankins, 15 March 2015). I agree with Wilson; there is less resistance now than in the past, where now this work is finding wider audiences.

Scholarly criticism, the type of writing I do, is not as prevalent as producing and creating literature. Critical reviews are becoming more mainstream with journals and scholarly conferences. Universities are encouraging academic programs, especially within the humanities, to infuse their courses with the study of SF, fantasy, and other speculative fiction. Texas A&M has a number of courses and a literary competition for the best short stories based on SF and fantasy. Science fiction is also being taught in the Science, Technology, Engineering, and Math (STEM) fields as a way to inspire innovation and creativity. In 2016 the Islamic SF website sponsored a short story competition, where I served as a judge, for the best stories based on Islamic themes. We received 39 entries and had 12 winners! Each winner received monetary prizes and was published in an anthology.

Conclusion

In conclusion, something I noted in my article titled "The Case for Fictional Islam" that is very pertinent to the longevity of this genre: "We must continue to emphasise the connection between science fiction and scientific inquiry in the Muslim world: an interest in science fiction will spark an interest in science, and vice versa. An education that exposes Muslim societies to fictional Islam can shape a positive and viable future for Muslim societies" (Kareem, n.p.).

Works Cited

Alter, Alexandra. (6 October 2017). "Nnedi Okorafor and the Fantasy Genre She Is Helping Redefine." *The New York Times.* https://www.nytimes.com/2017/10/06/books/ya-fantasy-diverse-akata-warrior.html.

"The Future of the Global Muslim Population." (27 January 2011). *Pew Research Forum.* http://www.pewforum.org/2011/01/27/the-future-of-the-global-muslim-population/.

Hankins, Rebecca. (2009). "Fictional Islam: A Literary Review and Comparative Essay on Islam in Science Fiction and Fantasy." *Foundation: The International Review of Science Fiction and Fantasy.* F105, Spring: 73–92. [An electronic copy can be found at: http://islamscifi.com/Foundation-Fictional%20Islam%20article.pdf].

Hankins, Rebecca. (15 March 2015). "Islam Sci-fi Interview of G. Willow Wilson (Part 1)." *Islam and Science Fiction.* http://www.islamscifi.com/islam-sci-fi-interview-of-g-willow-wilson-part-i/.

Hankins, Rebecca. (2016). "The Peculiar Institution: The Depiction of Slavery in Steven Barnes's *Lion's Blood* and *Zulu Heart.*" In James L. Conyers, Jr., and Abul Pitre (eds.), *Africana Islamic Studies.* Lanham: Lexington Books: 111–116. [An electronic copy can be found at: https://oaktrust.library.tamu.edu/bitstream/

handle/1969.1/156312/Rebecca%20Hankins-African%20American%20Islam%20manuscript-pre-pub.
pdf?sequence=1&isAllowed=y].

Hankins, Rebecca, and Joyce Thornton. (February 2014). "Influence of Muslims and Islam in Science Fiction, Fantasy and Comics." In Iraj Omidvar and Anne R. Richards (eds.), *Muslims and American Popular Culture.* Santa Barbara: ABC-CLIO Imprint-Praeger Publications: 323–348.

Kareem, Ruqayyah [Rebecca Hankins]. (July–August 2015). "The Case for Fictional Islam." *Critical Muslim.* Issue #15.3: Educational Reform. https://www.criticalmuslim.io/the-case-for-fictional-islam/.

Parham, Thomas A., Adisa Ajamu, and Joseph L. White. (2016). *Psychology of Blacks: Centering Our Perspectives in the African Consciousness.* London: Routledge.

"Pumzi is Brilliant Kenyan Sci-Fi." (25 March 2014). *Shine.* http://shine.forharriet.com/2014/03/pumzi-is-brilliant-kenyan-sci-fi.html#.

Santangelo, Nick. (18 April 2018). "How Muslim Culture Inspired Hip-Hop." *Temple University, College of Liberal Arts.* https://liberalarts.temple.edu/news/how-muslim-culture-inspired-hip-hop.

Sastrawijaya, A. (6 January 2015). "Professor Origin US Inform Islam in American." *Bogor Online news.* http://bogoronline.com/berita-profesor-asal-as-informasikan-islam-di-amerika.html.

Wilson, Reid. (4 June 2014). "The second-largest religion in each state." *Washington Post Online.* http://www.washingtonpost.com/blogs/govbeat/wp/2014/06/04/the-second-largest-religion-in-each-state/.

Under the Microscope

An Academic Appraisal
of the Evolving Milieu of Arab SF

Barbara K. Dick

> Science fiction is the search for a definition of man and his status in the universe which will stand in our advanced but confused state of knowledge (science), and is characteristically cast in the Gothic or post–Gothic mould.
>
> —Brian W. Aldiss (1973: 8)

Recent years have witnessed an increasing interest, in both academia and the general media, in science fiction that is written by Arab authors in their own tongue. The nascent canon of Arabic SF is now large enough to be considered as a legitimate field of study, led mainly by Egyptian authors, though with significant contributions also from Syria, Morocco, Saudi Arabia, Kuwait, and the UAE. Beginning in the 1940s with Tawfik al-Hakim and still in its formative stages compared to the vast output of SF in the West, the Arabic-language genre is gaining greater publicity, including a recent month-long SF translation event in Jordan, the Sindbad Sci-Fi events held at the British Library in London, and the formation of the Egyptian Society for Science Fiction, circa 2012. Academics, journalists, and translators are starting to view what was for many years a somewhat marginalized literary genre in the Arab world and asking questions not only about the practical aspects of translation and publication, but also about the reasons behind this increased interest.

Where does Arab SF begin? Many critics view SF as an essentially modern literature, arriving in the vanguard of real-world scientific discovery, then continuing in its wake. SF is seen as an outworking of the modern age's literary response to the technological drivers of modernity. The literature runs side by side with technological progress, taking inspiration from the invention of the Mechanical Turk—whose inventors presented a technology alien to its contemporary audience as an Orientalist exoticism—and the social upheavals of the industrial revolution, medical advances extending human life, the exploration of space (replacing the shrinking terra incognita of the Earth), robot labor, advanced weaponry, and mass surveillance, to mention a few of the popular tropes.

Some scholars of Arabic SF are romantically inclined to draw out a tenuous but unbroken literary thread between the fanciful moon-voyages of the second-century writer Lucian of Samosata to the earliest modern texts of Arabic SF, the plays of Tawfik al-Hakim in 1950s Egypt. Choosing Lucian, a Syrian of the classical world, as a starting point on a purely territorial basis leaves a rather long interlude, even before Al-Farabi's tenth-century *Opinions of the Residents of a Splendid City*, or Al-Qazwini's *Awaj bin Anfaq* (1250), and Ibn Tufail's twelfth-century *Hayy Ibn Yaqzān*.

The matter can perhaps best be resolved if we agree that SF must have some (even *soi-disant* or imaginary) relationship with science, thereby classifying Lucian's moon-voyage as magical or fantastical, and including the Arabian Nights and *mirabile* literature and folk-tales of the Arabian Nights and Sindbad in this fantastical genre; science fiction, in the modern sense, begins with scientific discoveries, the awareness of which is not confined only to an elite cadre of scientists and policymakers, but existing, even in a poorly-understood state, in the consciousness of the literary and general public. In any case, part of the charm of the genre is the unveiling by science of possibilities previously considered to be fantasy: Arthur C. Clarke's Third Law famously stated, "Any sufficiently advanced technology is indistinguishable from magic."

Critical awareness of the genre can be traced back to the 1960s in a few academic journals, but interest was sparked afresh in 2006, when the German-Iraqi engineer Achmed Khammas published an essay entitled "The Almost Complete Lack of the Element of 'Futureness' (Science Fiction in Arabic Literature)," the first of a steadily-growing trickle of articles questioning in general the lack of home-grown science fiction written in Arabic. Khammas' essay was a response to the first symposium on Arabic science fiction and literature that took place in Casablanca in 2006. According to Khammas, the consensus of attendees was that there should be more SF written in Arabic, but for children, with the specific purpose of encouraging Arab children's interest in science and with the ultimate aim of creating elite Arab scientists practicing in Arab laboratories and universities, supporting political independence and economic development in the Arab world (without, it is implied, having to buy expensive licensed technology from other countries).

This question of whether or not SF's main purpose is didactic is an interesting one, and the assumption that reading SF fosters an interest in science that will inspire future ground-breaking research can to some extent be supported by the experience of scientists who do affirm that their interest was first piqued by reading SF (subject of course also to inherent ability, funding, and opportunity). However, this downplays the fact that the science in SF is only one facet of an essentially futurist literature, one that often exposes the reader to alternative ideas about social and political aspects of the imagined future. Technology may provide the backdrop to the action of an SF novel and may be an important plot driver, but it is also a human drama, and technological progress also has profound effects on social and political reality.

Khammas does not dismiss the importance of the science element in science fiction, although Muhammad Azzam's 1994 Arabic language study of SF, *Al-Khayal al-Ilmi fi al-Adab,* gives this aspect of the literature greater prominence. Khammas is far more interested in how the Arab reader processes the alternative social and political worlds presented by Western SF. Writing in 2006, he perceived the failures of nationalism, pan–Arabism, the dominance of clan structures, and reliance on imported technology, as well as religious strictures and even a lack of familiarity with scientific vocabulary in Arabic, as militating against widespread public interest in science fiction, which has rightly been called the "literature of change." Therefore, his conclusion was broadly pessimistic, as he did not foresee the situation changing in the near future, although he wished for a more "colorful" or varied Arab literary world that includes a place for SF.

Others have since asked similar questions; in 2009 the British journalist Nesrine Malik attributed the lack of interest in futuristic literature to "…malaise … fatalism and helplessness inculcated by years of social and political stagnation" (*Guardian*, 30.7.2009), while in 2012, Yazan Al-Saadi, writing in *Al-Akhbar*, characterized Arabic SF texts as essentially feeble imitations of Western SF, inferior because of an alleged inherent inferiority complex among Arab SF writers. Reuven Snir suggested in the German academic journal *Der Islam* in 2000 that the perception of SF as an essentially foreign, imported genre could have impacted negatively on its acceptability, while more recently, the late Ahmed Khaled Tawfik, a prolific and popular Egyptian author of medical horror and SF as well as professor of tropical medicine at Tanta University, opined that it would be many years before SF was as popular and accepted as it is in the Western world (interview with Cheryl Morgan for the [now defunct] World SF blog in June 2012):

> … science fiction is a relatively new innovation in Egypt. People there have only been writing novels for just over 100 years, starting with Francis Fathallah in Syria or Haikal in Egypt. Before that we had very little fantastical literature, except for the *Arabian Nights*. Sophisticated new inventions such as science fiction are very rare. Most people still are not aware of it, or don't understand it. It will take 50 to 100 years before it is respected [Morgan, 2012].

There is a small body of academic Arabic SF criticism, notably former Egyptian government minister Yusuf Al-Sharuni's book *Al-Khayal al-Ilmi fi al-adab al-arabi al-mu'asir* (2000), Syrian astronomer Taleb Omran's *Fi al-Khayal al-Ilmi* (1989), Mahmoud Qasim's *Al-Khayal al-Ilmi—Adab al Qurn al-Ashrin* (2006), and a handful of Ph.D. theses including those by 'Azza Ghanem (Ain Shams, 1988) and Maha Mazlum Khadr (Cairo, 1999). Most of these studies are not wide-ranging in terms of covering the whole corpus of literature, devote many pages to tracing the ancient and mediaeval folkloric heritage of fantasy, or concentrate heavily on the Western genre, and when they do address Arabic SF, are excessively iterative in terms of plot repetition at the expense of analysis. More recently, in Tunisia, Kawthar Ayed has written on dystopian literature in Arabic, and in the U.S., Gary Boutz wrote his doctoral thesis on generic features of SF in the novels of Kassem. In Israel, Isam Asaqilah has written on character construction in Arabic SF novels, and in Italy, Ada Barbaro published a full-length Italian-language study entitled *La fantascienza nella letteratura araba* (Science Fiction in Arabic Literature) (2013).

Origins

In the West, SF's origins are often traced to early romances of other worlds, but the first European texts to achieve true mass popularity were the dystopian romances of the British author H.G. Wells and the explorers' fantasies of the French writer Jules Verne. The literary passions of certain editors also played a part—Hugo Gernsback and John Campbell's cheap "pulp" journals of the 1930s helped the genre to reach a large audience, capitalizing on the public interest in technological developments and launching the careers of writers such as Isaac Asimov, E.E. "Doc" Smith, and Robert Heinlein. The popularity of these magazines reflected the public interest in the space race between the USA and Russia, as well as developing the public discourse about the directions in which scientific discovery was driving social, political, and environmental change.

In the Arab world, translation was the first fertilizer that began the germination of the indigenous literature in the Arabic language. Following the Napoleonic invasion of

Egypt, often figured as the date of the first encounter of the Arab world with modernity, the 19th century saw the establishment of the Schools by the rulers of Egypt, and translations of Verne and Wells and of Aldous Huxley's *Brave New World* quickly appeared—of questionable quality, but conveying the basic idea. The first real flowering began in the late 1940s. Matti Moosa notes that the public appetite in the popular Egyptian fiction journals (the nearest equivalent to Gernsback's and Campbell's pulp novels in the U.S.) was for mystery and detective fiction, but the fashions of literary taste were actually more similar to Britain's at the time, when Kingsley Amis identified 22 SF magazines in the U.S., and only two in Britain.

The playwright Tawfik al-Hakim is most commonly agreed to be the first modern Arab writer to experiment with SF. His 1950 novel *Lū 'Arif Al-Shabāb* (*If the Young Men Knew*), his 1957 play *Riḥlat illa al-Ghād* (*Journey to Tomorrow*) and 1958 plays *Fi-Sinnat Malayūn* (*In the Year One Million*) and *Al-Ikhtirā'a Al-Ajīb* (*The Amazing Device*), followed by his 1970 plays *Taqrīr Al-Qamr* (*Moon Report*), and *Shā'ar 'ala Al-Qamr* (*Poet on the Moon*) (1971), clearly embodied SF tropes, in particular post-moon landing interest in lunar travel. Both Khammas and Sharuni mention the popular 1950s radio plays of Yusuf Ezzedine Issa as among the first Arabic SF texts, although these do not appear to be in print, and Sharuni says that many were published in an abridged format only.

The 1960s saw the publication of Moustafa Mahmoud's *Al-'Ankabūt* (*The Spider*) (1965), *Al-Khorūj min al-tābūt* (*Rising from the Coffin*) (1965), and *Rajul taḥt al-Ṣifr* (*Man Below Zero*) (1966). Mahmoud was intensely interested in spiritual experiences, having made something of a long spiritual journey in his own life, flirting with Buddhism before returning to Islam in his later years. The somewhat shaky scientific premise of *The Spider* rests upon the function of the brain's pineal gland as a doorway to the "spirit," which is eternal and reincarnated. The spirit is independent of the body, existing outside time, and the physical brain, the *mokh*, is merely a machine operated by this "ghost," or *rūh*. His protagonist speculates that human psychic abilities are merely poorly understood, and we are like blind, deaf worms that would not believe it if they were told that one day their descendants would grow eyes and ears.

The Spider and *Man Below Zero* are cautionary tales about scientists who go too far, who commit themselves to discovery at the price of their own lives and transgress moral boundaries. In *The Spider*, the villain murders his experimental subjects in his quest for the elixir, and the hero loses his humanity during his successive reincarnations. In *Man Below Zero*, the scientist anti-hero abandons humanity and his pregnant wife in favor of incorporeal space travel. The reader is being invited to make a judgment that excessive passion for knowledge leads to moral transgression.

The 1970s began with Yusuf al-Siba'i's *Laystu Waḥdak* (*You Are Not Alone*) (1970), although the SF output in this decade was dominated by Nihad Sherif, beginning with 1973's *Qāhir al-Zaman* (*Conqueror of Time*), *Raqm 4 Ya'omrikum* (*Number 4 Commands You*) (1974), and *Sukkān al-'ālam al-thānī* (*Inhabitants of the Second World*), an SF romance set underwater that was predicated upon the world's need to exploit the inexhaustible resources of the sea, continuing with *Ash-Shay* (*The Thing*) (1988) and *Ibn Al-Nujūm* (*Son of the Stars*) (1997).

According to Khammas, two Moroccan SF novels, *Iksīr al-Ḥiyāt* (*Elixir of Life*) by Mohammed Aziz al-Habbabi and *At-Ṭawfān al-Azrāq* (*The Blue Flood*) by 'Abd Al-Salām Al-Baqqāli, appeared in 1974 and 1979 respectively. Sharuni mentions two texts that are the sole SF output of their authors: Mohammad Hadīdī's *Shakhs Ākher fi al-Mir'āt* (*The

Other Person in the Mirror) (1975) and *Hurūb illa al-Faḍa'* (*Escape to Space*) by Hussein Qadry (1981). Khammas places Taleb Omran's first SF novel, *Planet of Dreams*, in 1978, the same year as Ra'ūf Waṣfī's *Space Invasion*; Omran has since published more than forty novels and collections of short stories.

Nabil Farouk, the highly prolific author of the *Milaff al-Mustaqbal* (*Future File*) series, made his debut in 1979 with "The Prophecy," a short story that won him the Tanta Cultural Palace Prize, and in 1984 began the first of the *Future Files* novels; the series now numbers 150 novellas. The action of the *Future Files* revolves around a team of four Egyptian scientists: Nur, Ramzy, Mahmoud, and Salwa. Nur does not have a specialty but leads a team of three who do: Mahmoud, the "ray" scientist; Ramzy, the psychologist; and Salwa, the communications expert. Nur is an all-round hero; in No. 6 *Zā'ir min Al-Mustaqbal* (*Visitor from the Future*), the Egyptian intelligence chief compliments Nur, saying that he has "the body of a fighter, the mind of a scientist, the heart of an artist and the morals of a knight":

تحمل جسد مصارع ,و عقل فنان ,و اخلاق فارس

Nur blushes modestly, as he prefers to give credit to his team, but his genius is presented as tempered by humility (as well as religious faith), and humanity; in No. 15 *Muthallath Al-Ghumūḍ* (*Triangle of Mysteries*), the villain Ra'uf says that Nur has a scientific mind, but it is nothing compared to his (evil) genius, because Nur's mind is affected by human emotions and instincts.

The first thirty *Milaff* novellas are set mostly on Earth, but at the end of No. 30 *Al-Nār Al-Bārida* (*The Cold Fire*), following a diplomatic imbroglio with the Israelis, the Chief transfers Nur to the Space Police. Space in the *Milaff* is almost always populated by hostile aliens, although they are always ultimately mastered by Nur for whom all space falls under the *khilāfah* of God.

Farouk makes enthusiastic use of the familiar tropes of science fiction, such as aliens, advanced weaponry, interplanetary travel, mind control, robots and flying saucers, as well as riffling on the "ancient aliens" theories beloved of Erich von Daniken, and which underline the nationalist agenda by showing both Atlantis and ancient Egypt to be originators of advanced technology long before the West. However, he also plays with the genre, throwing in monsters from Greek mythology and making some of his novellas detective novels where there is a rational explanation for the mystery rather than an advanced scientific or supernatural plotline.

Relations between the team members in the *Milaff* revolve around marriage. Nur and Salwa's romantic interest in each other is apparent from the beginning, and by No. 6 *Zā'ir min Al-Mustaqbal* (*Visitor from the Future*), Salwa is quick to take the "visitor" aside to ask him what the history books have to say about Nur's marriage. A rival for Nur's affections is introduced in the form of an attractive and worldly presenter of *Video News*, Moushira Mahfouz, but Nur's relationship with Salwa is safely sanctioned by marriage very early in the series. In No. 15 *Muthallath Al-Ghumūḍ* (*Triangle of Mysteries*), Salwa is absent from the mission because she is pregnant with their first child, a daughter called Nashwa.

In the *Milaff*, while Salwa is regularly abducted by monsters or human villains and in need of rescue, this is not her sole function as a female character, as it would be in the classic tradition of Western pulp SF where the heroine is a helpless creature. Farouk takes care to show that Salwa's skills and knowledge are valuable to the team, and that she is a respected scientist whose work is recognized by other characters in the series. In No. 8

Al-Irtijāj Al-Qātil (*The Deadly Tremor*), the scientist Hussein recognizes Salwa because of her academic reputation, and she often invents communications devices that save the lives of the team.

Ṣabrī Mūsa's *Al-Sayyid min Ḥuql al-Sabānkh* (*Lord of the Spinach Field*), an accomplished futuristic dystopia that was clearly heavily influenced by Soviet writer Yevgeny Zamyatin's *We* (1924), was first published in 1982. The world of Homo, the hero, is a post-apocalyptic future where the Earth has been destroyed in an "electronic war," and the inhabited regions are sheltered beneath glass domes that protect them from the toxic atmosphere. Homo works as a manual laborer in a spinach field from which rocket ships export bales of spinach to the rest of the world, and his wife Layla works in a climate control station. Interrogated upon his return home, Homo starts to question the government and joins a rebel, Baruf, to demand access to the poisoned outside world, away from the control of the government and its machine masters. A public debate in the brain-shaped Hanging Hall grants his wish; the purpose perhaps is to show that life outside this controlled society is so difficult that the government can afford to let one or two rebels go as examples, as they present no threat, and the government can continue to offer its citizens a highly controlled yet comfortable life.

Science fiction is often used as an arena in which to explore alternative models of relationships between the sexes, and this is particularly true in the dystopian future of *Lord of the Spinach Field*, where husbands and wives are not expected to be faithful to each other, and relations with other partners, or in government-run love shops, are expected. Children are raised in vats in child-factories so as to avoid normal family bonding with parents. While the hero Homo and his wife the heroine Layla have a tender relationship, Layla's relationship with Homo's friend David is shown to be deeply troubling to both Homo and Layla, as they have formed an emotional bond with each other.

The most frequently-used phrase in the *Lord of the Spinach Field* is "عصر العسل," the "age of honey," in which the characters refer to themselves as living. It is repeated twenty-one times and has the strong feel of a mantra imposed by the regime, which is constantly listening to all of the population at all times through universal surveillance devices. The rebel Barūf inverts its use in his first appearance in the conversation parlor after Homo's release, when he talks of the freedom of the human spirit: "But this truth has drowned, gentlemen, in the honey of this age!" ("تلك الروح أيها السادة ...فى عسل هذا العصر!") "لقد غرقت"; 1987: 65).

Khammas also mentions the first Iraqi SF novel *The Green Stain* (1984) by Kassem al-Khattat and the collections of short stories *She Pulsates with Life* by Muwaffaq Uays Mahmud and *The Green Planet* by Ali Karim Kathem (both 1987) among the Arabic SF literature of the 1980s.

In the 1990s, Khammas writes that:

> …the number of writers taking an interest in the genre grew, with the likes of Kassem in Lebanon, Mustafa al-Kailani in Tunisia, Abdallah Khalifa in Bahrain and Mussa Oald Ibno in Mauretania. The female Syrian writer Lina Kailani wrote forty texts, the Jordanian Sulaiman Mohammed al-Khalil dealt with cloning with a black humour all too seldom seen in Arabic literature and in Saudi Arabia, the short story collections *Ghosthunters* (1997) and *Yearning for the Stars* (2000) by Ashraf Faqih found their way into the book stores [2006].

The Kuwaiti mathematician and parliamentary candidate Tiba Al-Ibrahim published the first in her genetic/cryogenic dystopian trilogy, *The Pale Man*, in 1985, followed by its successors *The Multiple Man* and *The Extinction of Man* in 1992, the same year as the Egyptian geneticist 'Omayma Khafāji published her genetic engineering horror/SF text *Jarīmat Al-'Alam* (*Crime of a World*) in Moscow. The Egyptian geologist Muḥammad al-'shrī published three SF novels from 2007 to 2009, and most recently Ahmed Khaled Tawfik published *Ūtūbiā* (*Utopia*) (2010), while Emirati writer Noura Al Noman released *Ajwān* (*Gulfs*) in 2013.

Factors such as literacy, pricing, prevailing literary preference, and the possibility of censorship of progressive literatures, especially in countries where religious conservatism is a dominant social force, continue to shape access to literature in general, despite recent translation initiatives in the Arab world. Although the rate of adult literacy has improved since the 1960s, it is still worth considering Fabio Caiani's point made in his 2007 study *Contemporary Arab Fiction: Innovation from Rama to Yalu* that lack of literacy need not necessarily mean that writers are without agency; in the early 20th century, it has been suggested that journals flourished in Egypt, despite a high rate of illiteracy, because of the impact of orality in street culture. While oral literary café culture may now be becoming obsolete, having been replaced to a large extent by internet communication, lending and samizdat publishing or copying of texts continues to allow a wider circulation than that afforded by publishing. However, the number of full-length novels in the genre remains very small, with only a few new texts of note appearing each year.

The recent popularity of Tawfik's best-selling Egyptian horror/SF novellas including *Ūtūbiā* (*Utopia*), and public interest in Noman's debut *Ajwān* (*Gulfs*), as well as the determination of Ayed and Omran, and more recently Sindbad Sci-Fi, among others, to promote the genre actively, show that at this time of social and political turmoil and increased public debate on the role of Islam in public life, a literature of the future, and of alternative possibilities to the status quo, is now needed more urgently than ever.

Science in Science Fiction

SF is an Enlightenment literature; its emphasis on science and rationality is the most important differential marker between SF and fantasy, with its frequently retrograde Tolkeinesque mediaeval settings and mythical beasts. SF has at least a notional rational basis and a heuristic, potentially iconoclastic, ethos, meaning that it is able to interrogate social, political, and religious norms; in the words of astrobiologist Mark Blake and his co-author, Anglican priest Neil Hook, in their 2008 critical study *Different Engines: How Science Drives Fiction and Fiction Drives Science:* "Science fiction began with the scientific revolution. It marks the paradigm shift of the old Universe into the new" (2008: 14).

All countries face the challenges of modernity, and the discourse around the benefits and drawbacks of scientific progress is universal. The public discourse on science versus religion, the rational versus the supernatural, is no less fiercely contested in the Arab world than it is in the West. There is a strand of thought in cultural criticism that somewhat provocatively pitches a scientifically pre-eminent West against a less developed Middle East, measured through numbers of Nobel prizes and money spent on space exploration programs (for an account of Arab space exploration, see Jörg Matthais Determann's *Space Science and the Arab World: Astronauts, Observatories and Nationalism in the Middle East* [2018]), and commonly figuring the enlightenment of the Arab world as having taken place eight hundred years ago in the thirteenth-century House of Wisdom in Baghdad. This approach is described in Edward Said's account in *Orientalism* of Kissinger's view of the Arab world as being preserved in a pre–Newtonian state. The same dichotomy between a backwards, mystical East and a technically-advanced West is mocked in Amin Al-Rihani's poem *Ānā al-Sharq*, published in 1922, quoted in Khaled Kishtainy's *Arab Political Humour* (1985): "I am the Orient: I have philosophies, I have religions. Is there anyone who might buy them from me for aircraft?" (1985: 69).

In reality, cutting-edge research science anywhere is a highly elite and expensive activity, and few consumers in the West, or anywhere else, have any real grasp of how their everyday technological devices work. The previous lack of advanced research facilities, and even a space program, are rapidly being remedied in the Arab world with the funding of institutions such as the Qatar Science and Technology Park, KAUST in Saudi Arabia, SESAME in Jordan, and many other university departments.

Religious or cultural ambivalence or hostility about scientific enquiry that potentially presents a challenge to religious authority is also a real concern. Marwa Elshakry addresses the 19th century reaction to Darwin in the Arab world in her 2013 study *Reading Darwin in Arabic 1860–1950*. Pakistani nuclear physicist Pervez Hoodbhoy, in *Islam and Science: Religious Orthodoxy and the Battle for Rationality* (1991), remarked upon Egyptian Muslim Brotherhood ideologue Sayyid Qutb's opposition to science and the perceived disconnect between the Saudi love of technology and dislike of heuristic enquiry. Hoodbhoy further suggested that it was lack of support for Arab scientific development that allowed Arab territories to become dominated by the colonialist powers, a conceptual position shared by C.P. Snow in his "Two Cultures" lecture, during which he reminded Britain that it was its own lack of technological know-how that made the fortune of Prussian signals officer Siemens.

American political scientist Aaron Segal, writing over twenty years ago in the *Middle East Quarterly* in 1996, asked, "Why does the Muslim world lag in science?" and argued that, far from the rationalist agenda of the Enlightenment being off-putting to a devout Muslim world, the Enlightenment's very detachment of science from Christianity actually made it more acceptable to Islam. He identified import substitution as the main factor removing the imperative for indigenous research and development: "The prevailing mentality continues to be that of buying science and technology rather than producing it." Segal also identified demographic factors, language barriers, poor educational systems, lack of research provision, statism, lack of professional societies, lack of resources, authoritarianism, lack of regional co-operation, and government incompetence as the main contributing factors to this state of affairs at the time.

In a 2006 article in the *Socialist Review*, Neil Davidson suggested that mediaeval Islam was actually more accepting of scientific innovation than the socially static Christian empire and that the oppositional element crept in much later, when the Arab world was re-introduced to scientific progress from countries where it flourished under Marxist regimes. Davidson's view is that the Enlightenment was possible in Christian Europe, despite opposition from both Protestant and Catholic sources, precisely because of the oppositional energy generated; whereas, in the Islamic world, the fear of science as a challenge to Islamic religious authority was not active to the same degree, in part due to the lack of centralization and hierarchy of religious authority. This subject is explored more fully by Christopher de Bellaigue in *The Islamic Enlightenment: The Modern Struggle between Faith and Reason* (2017). There is nonetheless a particular school of thought that claims that the Quran foresaw many scientific discoveries, the dissolution of the popularly perceived impermeable barrier between science and religion expounded in Bucailleism. Of course, the idea of "Islamic" or "Arab" science is nonsensical, as Jim Al-Khalili points out (*Pathfinders: The Golden Age of Arabic Science*, 2012). Science has no religion or nationality; neither East nor West can set a heavy paternalistic or proprietorial hand on "science," and the very universality of "science" facilitates its transfer between East and West (subject, of course, to the real limiting factors, economic and political controls). Claiming a particular discovery or invention on behalf of an ethnicity, nationality, or in the case of "Islamic science," religion, is a chauvinistic attempt at ownership, a territorial marking of ethnic or spiritual one-upmanship.

Yet the heuristic spirit and willingness to question is a key part of scientific success and of good SF. Achmed Khammas cites this remark: "A scientific novel which is connected with phantasy cannot fall on fertile ground in an environment of preprepared answers and rejection of a culture of knowledge" (Dr. Omar Abdelaziz, quoted in Khammas, 2006). Nationalism nonetheless plays a part in the generation of Arabic SF: the futuristic Egypt of Farouk's *Milaff al-Mustaqbal* series for teenagers is full of nationalist pride. ʿAzza Ghānim notes that making Cairo a center of international meetings about world crisis is a wishful idea also seen in Nihad Sherif's *Qāhir al-Zaman* (*Conqueror of Time*), while Al-Sharuni's study of Arabic SF finds multiple examples of textual dreams of an Egypt being a leader in the scientific world.

Despite the benefits of technological development, scientific advancement is much more often the subject of profound ambiguity, if not actual fear. Apprehension surrounding automation and the fear of the "rogue" computer or robot are embodied in Al-Baqqāli's *At-Ṭūfān al-Azraq* (*The Blue Flood*). A group of scientists has retreated from the world after the Second World War to a hidden mountain in Morocco and puts their knowledge into a supercomputer ("عقل اليكتروني") called معاذ, a word meaning "SANCTUARY," an acronym in Arabic for "Collective of Automatic Electronic Intelligences" ("مجمع العلاقات الإلكترونية الذاتية") to keep the secrets of science safe if there should be a Third World War. One of the conflicts in the book is the wish of the now-rogue SANCTUARY to take up the scientists' "third option" for the future of mankind: a deadly flood of blue rays that will wipe out humanity, allowing the scientists to build a new, better world.

In a text already ridden with SF clichés, SANCTUARY's actions are driven by jealousy of the human ability to love; it wistfully asks the hero Dr. Nādir, "Can I, a machine … love?" Its longing for human or spiritual experience is its eventual undoing, when Nādir persuades it to give him the power to switch it off. The plot of the novel, constructed around the common SF premise of the robot longing for humanity, while simultaneously very much concerned with Nādir's emotional and sexual development, is ultimately driven by the human fear of putting the destiny of mankind under the control of a machine intelligence.

In the *Milaff*, Farouk's team makes friends with an Atlantean robot who becomes obedient to Nur, but in No. 158 *Ḥarb Al-Ghad* (*Tomorrow's War*), during an exposition on binary code and machine intelligence, Nashwa says that machine intelligence cannot learn by trial and error (which is not true) or have that spark of feeling that she says only Allah can create. While robots may have physical strength and machine intelligence, they are put in their place as inferior to humans made by God.

In *Lord of the Spinach Field*, the classic SF theme of manufactured robot intelligence achieving self-awareness and becoming a threat is superseded by the robots actually becoming god-like. When Homo stumbles upon a room in the Hanging Hall filled with banks of computers, he realizes that he is in the Temple of the Electronic Minds; robot intelligence takes on an additional, priestly function, as a computer shows Homo the history of his world, including millions of years of evolution, the purpose of which is for the robot to show that robots are simply another step in the evolutionary process. The computer asks him:

> Why do you fear robots, Homo, and resist them, when men made them? Without the making of the robot, you would remain on the ladder of development, sliding back down to the ground to your nearest relatives, the mammals?!
>
> الآلة...و بغير الأداة و الآلة، لبقيت على درج التطور متلصف بالأرض الى جوار أقربائك من الثدييات؟
>
> فلماذا تخشى الآلة يا هومو و تتراجع أمامها، و قد صرت انسانا بالأداة و [1987: 190].

When the regime defends the robot overlords, Homo responds with a passionate appeal for the inherent supremacy of the organic human. He tells the regime that these are "false geniuses, artificial savants, cold minds, not human ("صناعية مختلقة، و باردة، و لا انسانية"), and that "flesh and blood are both necessary, humanity is necessary..." ("ان الدم و اللحم ضروريان...ان البشرية ضرورية..."; 1987: 40); the language is almost exactly the same as that used by Rosita, Shāhīn's neglected wife, when she pleads for humanity to prevail over scientific advancement at the end of Mahmoud's *Man Below Zero.*

Immortality, or the artificial extension of life, is a frequent theme in SF and speculative literature, as a literary response to the universal fear of death and oblivion. The idea of eternal life requires a scientific development that is plausible at least within the fictional world of the text and may also allow the text to challenge or reinforce religious dogma on the question of life after death, the existence of the spirit as separate from the body and immortal, as well as the permissibility and practical aspects of artificially extending the lifespan beyond the naturally experienced maximum.

There is a strong tendency in Western literature to present immortality or indefinite extension of lifespan or artificial creation of life as a moral fable about its dangers. From *Frankenstein* onwards, immortality is almost always framed as an ultimately unsatisfactory and futile desideratum, whether due to the resultant inherent separation from humanity, or decrepitude, selfishness, and disturbance of the natural balance of life.

The question of how to reconcile respect for Allah's creation and human scientific interference with the natural world is explored in *Milaff* No. 17 *Nabḍ Al-Khulūd* (*Pulse of Eternity*) and No. 46 *Al-Kawkab Al-Mal'ūn* (*The Cursed Planet*). In the former, when Nur and the Intelligence Chief are talking about eternal life, the Chief says that the natural law set by the Creator decides the time of death and birth, referring to a natural balance, and that the scientist's work threatens this balance:

> , و إلا أتت فترة تضيق فيها الأرض بمن عليها, و أصبح حتمًا اللجوء إلى القتل لإعادة هذا التوازن الطبيعة الطبيعة الذى أبدعه الخالق (عز و جل), يحتّم حدوث حالات الوفاة, المقابلة الزيادة التى تصنعها المواليد. إن قانون.

Nur says that he agrees with Yūsuf, but finds the idea of eternal life hard to believe. At the end, Salwa asks Nur if he would take eternal life if it was offered. Nur says no; the real eternal life is being remembered for what one did. He would prefer a short life of fighting crime to an eternity of spreading destruction across the universe and would rather protect "my faith and my country" ("ديني و وطني"). The team also quotes the Quran, though infrequently, and they pray in times of trouble. It is clearly important to Farouk to make sure that his characters set a good example to their young readers, showing them that they can be both religious and scientists.

Mustafa Mahmoud's fascination with Eastern philosophy and reincarnation touches on the theme of immortality; it also reinforces the idea as seductive but, ultimately, fundamentally inhuman and therefore transgressive. The plot of *Man Below Zero* revolves around Dr. Shāhīn's wish to transform his body, as he has already transformed mice, into pure wave energy, a kind of teleportation that is irreversible. Although his wife tries to prevent the transformation, his jealous assistant, who is in love with his wife, gives him the means to escape imprisonment and effect the transformation. Although he wins the admiration of the watching world as he relays his impressions from space, his decision is characterized as selfish. While immortality in folk-tales is traditionally shown to be compromised by the burden of physical decrepitude, here even incorporeal immortality is shown to be pointless in the absence of humanity and love.

Shāhīn cannot see why immortality is not a good thing; however, his assistant 'Abd Al-Karīm's darker, nihilistic view of death as a desideratum is rooted in his unrequited passion for Shāhīn's wife, Rosita. 'Abd Al-Karīm calls death a respite; without it, he says, life would turn into a nightmare, without the hope of release:

راحة...نهاية...و بدون هذه الراحة تتحول الحياة إلى كابوس لا أمل في الخلاص منه
لأن الموت—(Mahmud, 2009: 47)

The question of who should be allowed to be immortal is raised at the end of *The Blue Flood*, when the regime Chief warns that it should not be made available to all, just to special individuals who are of benefit to the human race; immortality is to be the preserve of a social and scientific elite.

Elixirs and the ambivalences around their use also appear frequently in the texts. In *Min mufakkirah Rajul lam yūlad* (*Diary of a Man Not Yet Born*), the narrator, writing in the year 2567, tells of the recent invention of a drug that makes the user happy all the time, although he disapproves of enhancing the brain in an artificial way that does not lead to true happiness. He adds that many scientists opposed this drug and made fun of it; philosophers argue that true happiness comes from being in harmony with one's environment.

In *The Spider*, the hero Dāūd watches in secret as Damiān cuts open a giant spider to extract the silk from its spinnerets. He then finds evidence that he had been trying to make an elixir out of this silk, a fertilized egg, a plant bud, and some hormones, these being the life-generating parts of each living thing; the mixture also includes an extract from the pineal gland. The purpose is to achieve immortality, but not corporeal immortality; this elixir allows the user to experience past lives, although on a descending ladder of sentience, as during the process of past life regression Dāūd first experiences various past lives in the Arab world. During his first trip under the influence of the elixir, he finds himself in old Basra, then in Deir Balah in the Sinai desert, then in a Cordoba market, then at the siege of Acre and the battle at Qal'at al-Ḥuṣn. While on his second trip, he becomes a slave, an ox, and finally a tree. The final dose, that he cannot resist, kills him.

These primitivist references have a faint echo in the trance experienced by the teenage anti-hero of *Utopia* under the influence of "Phlogiston," the new fashionable hallucinogen, where he associates its scent with the perfume of ancient swamp forests, Cleopatra's sweat, dervishes' incense, Parisian belles, flowers, and ambergris. Also in *Lord of the Spinach Field*, the hero Homo imagines breaking free from his slavish existence and running naked with his wife and children in a primitive forest.

At the end of *The Spider*, the pathologist who examines the burnt-out laboratory speculates about the scientific plausibility of the elixir, but dismisses it, and the idea of eternal life, as irrational. His deputy has the last word, adding, "Who knows?" "هذه دنيا كلها طلاسم"—"In this world, everything is a cryptic code" (Mahmoud, 1989: 98). The titular spider is only present for a few pages, to be dissected to provide an elixir ingredient, and seems to have been intended as an emblem of horror and revulsion. The title was surely also meant to suggest the web-like nature of the hero's seduction and entrapment by the drug and the temptation to eternal life. The villain Damiān pleads with Dāūd that he is not a murderer (having killed a number of people in his experimental phase) because all of the people were ultimately immortal, as reincarnation is implied to be the true fate of each soul. The fable is the typical cautionary tale regarding immortality; the hero's descent from human being to animal to plant in successive incarnations is the price.

The brave new world of Mahmoud's *Man Below Zero* has its own version of Huxley's *soma*; in 2062, the Egyptian chemist Badran invented *Sa'ādūl*, a popular opiate developed from oasis grass. This drug is made from herbs with anesthetic properties and is used not only recreationally but also in the manufacture of milk, chocolate, and the citizens' daily bread. A student who starts to disrupt the lecture is given a forcible injection of *Sa'ādūl*, showing that the drug is used for the purposes of social control by the regime in the same way as the beer pills of *Lord of the Spinach Field*. *Sa'ādūl* is a control mechanism and also a clear marker of a totalitarian society.

Mahmoud viewed science as neutral in itself, writing in *Reading the Future*, "Science is a neutral weapon, like a knife you can use to cut an apple to offer to your friend, or to cut his throat" (*Qirāt Lil-Mustaqbal*: 58). He was enthusiastic about its possible benefits and passionate about the need for Arab countries to develop alternative energy sources to oil. However, his concern was not only that technology would be misused, but that dependence upon it would somehow erode humanity. In *Al-Ahlām* (*Dreams*), he frets that "modern scientific advances have turned the human being into a giant without a heart" (2004: 99). It is perhaps significant that in his foundation hospital linked to his mosque in Dokki, Mahmoud liked to offer both traditional and modern remedies. This persistent, conservative affection for the old ways, for folk tradition interwoven within the interstices of orthodox Islam, irresistibly recalls the symbolic smoking lamp of Yaḥya Haqqi's *Qindīl Umm Hāshim*, a fable about the complex relationship between tradition and modernity in Egypt.

Mahmoud was not opposed to the importation of Western technology but strongly objected to the importation of Western morals. He berated his fellow Arabs as degenerate, for allowing Americans to develop their oil wells for them while they wasted their money on palaces and at the gambling tables of Monte Carlo and Las Vegas, calling for an Arab scientific awakening, and an age of enlightenment and reform. At all stages of his "spiritual journey," his agenda remained deeply conservative as well as suspicious of the West. In *Reading the Future*, we find him variously blaming the Freemasons, socialism, crack cocaine, and heroin for Egypt's problems, as well as Israel and America. Mahmoud's fascination with Eastern philosophy and reincarnation meshes well with his views on the direction that Egypt's foreign relations should take; politically, he viewed an alliance with the Far East as preferable to collaboration with the West. In 1992, he called for a single

Arab market modeled on the then-EEC, and proposed a simple exchange of resources: "They need our oil, and we need their technology" (Riḍwān, 2010: 38).

Despite the tension in the popular public discourse between the "two cultures" of science and religion—transcendence versus materialism, irrational versus rational, revelation over reason—Robert Scholes, following his definition of fabulation, says that allegorical tales (stories characterized by discontinuousness from reality, but which take a realistic approach in the actual narrative) are used often by religions precisely because they believe in an alternate reality. Robert Matthew, in his 1989 study of Japanese science fiction, figures religion as a kindly partner to science: "Religion and ethics play a significant part (some would say a crucial part) in underpinning a society's willingness to work productively, its attitude towards important social relationships, and its degree of readiness to accept change" (149).

For Mahmoud, science takes second place to the supernatural in his novels; the religious reader is in a safe literary space with others who share his beliefs. In *Rising from the Coffin*, he speaks through his characters: "Faith is truth, it does not contradict science; rather, true faith is the highest level of science":

تذكر أن الدين الحق, لا يناقض العلم, لأن الدين الحق هو منتهى العلم (2005 :55).

As the sun's gravitational force draws Shāhīn towards it, he says that he has a feeling of "returning to the wellspring"—"شعور العائد إلى المنبع"—comparing himself to an arrow fired from a hunter's bow, that fires human beings through time and space, travelling with longing towards the absolute:

نحن السهام الصغيرة من قيودنا ويرسلنا محلقين في اللازمان واللامكان مهاجرين في شوق إلى المطلق... هناك يتوتر القوس بأقصى طاقته... ليطلقنا

Shāhīn, travelling in bodiless form through the solar system towards the sun, actually sees Allah as physically present, although he does not describe Allah:

أرى الآن في يقين أن الله موجود...بل هو الحقيقة الوحيدة التي غابت عنا جميعاً في غرور التقدم المادي.... نعم فأنا

"Yes, I can see now with certainty that God exists ... that he is actually the only truth that is hidden from us all by the illusion that materiality offers us" (Mahmoud, 2005: 91–92).

Again, there is the clear wish on the part of the author to maintain the mystery of the workings of the Universe, and respect belief in God.

Conclusion

Most of the texts from the 1950s onwards show Arab characters undertaking scientific research and fantastical journeys, inspired by Western SF and by real-life developments such as space travel. While there is a clear longing in many of the texts for a scientifically pre-eminent Arab world, this is not the only or main feature of Arabic SF; the texts also deal in detail with utopian, dystopian, religious, political, gender, and social themes.

Tawfik's dystopian *Utopia* is not just the literature of change, but the literature of revolution, as it shows an economically polarized society that is not only showing signs of becoming a reality in Egypt, but in many other countries, not just in the Arab world.

Although the Slovenian SF critic Darko Suvin in his *Metamorphoses in Science Fiction* (1979) famously believed that the act of reading SF actually sublimated and wasted the imaginative energy of change needed for revolution, SF, like all literature carefully read, changes the way we think about the world, and this is not necessarily an immediate process.

In *The Genesis of Arabic Narrative Discourse* (1993), Sabry Hafez observed that genres tend to emerge as a response to public need, and that translations help to ease the strangeness and enable audiences to become adjusted to new ideas. How much better can home-made SF, written in Arabic, interrogate the changes currently facing the Arab world.

While it is important that those of us who love Arabic SF do not overstate its influence, it still being a fairly marginal literature, the fact that interest in the literature and the discourse around it is continually growing is a positive sign, and we look forward to many more future Arabic SF classics yet to be written.

WORKS CITED
Texts in Arabic

Al-Baqqāli, Aḥmed Abd Al-Salām. (2012). *At-Ṭūfān al-Azraq*. Edition printed on-demand by Amazon as *Al Tufan Al Azraq* by Ahmad A Al Baqali. USA (sic): Hasan Yahya Publishers.
Al-Quwīrī, Yūsuf. (1997). *Min mufakkirat Rajul lam Yūlad*. Benghazi: Dār Al-Rūwād.
Farouk, Nabil. *Milaff Al-Mustaqbal* series. Cairo: Al-Mu'assassa Al-'Arabiya.
Farouk, Nabil. No. 6 *Zā'ir min Al-Mustaqbal* (Visitor from the Future).
Farouk, Nabil. No. 8 *Al-Irtijāj Al-Qātil* (The Deadly Tremor).
Farouk, Nabil. No. 15 *Muthallath Al-Ghumūḍ* (Triangle of Mysteries).
Farouk, Nabil. No. 17 *Nabḍ Al-Khulūd* (Pulse of Eternity).
Farouk, Nabil. No. 30 *Al-Nār Al-Bārida* (The Cold Fire).
Farouk, Nabil. No. 46 *Al-Kawkab Al-Mal'ūn* (The Cursed Planet).
Farouk, Nabil. No. 158 *Ḥarb Al-Ghad* (Tomorrow's War).
Mahmoud, Mustafa. (1989). *Al-'Ankabūt*. 5th Edition. Cairo: Dār Al-M'ārif.
Mahmoud, Mustafa. (2004). *Al-Ahlām*. Akhbār Al-Yawm.
Mahmoud, Mustafa. (2005). *Al-Khurūj min al-tābūt*. Cairo: Dār Akhbār Al-Yawm.
Mahmoud, Mustafa. *Rajul taḥt al-Ṣifr*. (2008). Cairo: Dār Akhbār Al-Yawm.
Mahmoud, Mustafa. *Qirāt Lil-Mustaqbal*. Cairo: Dār Akhbār Al-Yawm, no date
Mūsa, Ṣabrī. *Al-Sayyid min Haql al-Sabānikh*. (1987). Cairo: Al-Hay'a al-Miṣriyya al-'Āmma lil-Kitāb, first published 1982.
Riḍwān, Muhammad. (2010). *Muṣṭafa Mahmūd: Mishwār Al-'Umr*. Cairo: Dār Al-M'ārif.
Tawfik, Ahmed Khaled. (2010). *Ūtūbiā*. Doha: Bloomsbury Qatar Foundation Publishing.
Tawfik, Ahmed Khaled. (2011). *Ūtūbiā* (Utopia), tr. Chip Rossetti. Doha: Bloomsbury Qatar Foundation Publishing.

Books in English

Aldiss, Brian Wilson. (1973). *Billion Year Spree: The True History of Science Fiction*. Garden City, NY: Doubleday.
Al-Khalili, Jim. (2012). *Pathfinders: The Golden Age of Arabic*. London: Penguin.
Amis, Kingsley. (1962). *New Maps of Hell: A Survey of Science Fiction*. London: The Science Fiction Book Club by arrangement with Victor Gollancz Ltd.
Brake, Mark L., and Neil Hook, Eds. (2008). *Different Engines: How Science Drives Fiction and Fiction Drives Science*. Basingstoke: Macmillan Science.
Caiani, Fabio. (2007). *Contemporary Arab Fiction: Innovation from Rama to Yalu*. London and New York: Routledge.
Determann, Jörg Matthias. (2018). *Space Science and the Arab World: Astronauts, Observatories and Nationalism in the Middle East*. London: I.B. Tauris.

Hafez, Sabry. (1993). *The Genesis of Arabic Narrative Discourse*. London: Saqi Books.

Hoodbhoy, Pervez. (1991). *Islam and Science: Religious Orthodoxy and the Battle for Rationality*. London and New Jersey: Zed Books.

Kishtainy, Khalid. (1985). *Arab Political Humour*. London: Quartet Books.

Matthew, Robert. (1989). *Japanese Science Fiction: A View of a Changing Society*. London: Routledge and Nissan Institute of Japanese Studies, University of Oxford.

Moosa, Matti. (1997). *The Origins of Modern Arabic Fiction*. Boulder and London: Lynne Rienner. (2nd edition).

Said, Edward. (2003). *Orientalism*. Reprinted with a new Preface. London: Penguin.

Scholes, Robert. (1975). *Structural Fabulation*. Notre Dame, Indiana: University of Indiana Press.

Snow, C.P. (1998). *The Two Cultures*. Cambridge: Canto, Cambridge University Press.

Suvin, Darko. (1979). *Metamorphoses of Science Fiction: On the Poetics and History of a Literary Genre*. New Haven, CT: Yale University Press.

Articles and Blog Posts

Al-Saadi, Yazan. (3 June 2012). "Arabic Science Fiction: A Journey Into the Unknown." *Al-Akhbar*. http://english.al-akhbar.com/node/7995.

Davidson, Neil. (March 2006). "Islam and the Enlightenment." *Socialist Review*. 304. http://socialistreview.org.uk/304/islam-and-enlightenment.

Khammas, Achmed A.W. (10 October 2006). "The Almost Complete Lack of the Element of 'Futureness': Science Fiction in Arabic Literature." *Telepolis*. https://www.heise.de/tp/features/The-Almost-Complete-Lack-of-the-Element-of-Futureness-3408243.html.

Malik, Nesrine. (30 July 2009). "What Happened to Arabic Science Fiction?" *The Guardian*. http://www.theguardian.com/commentisfree/2009/jul/30/arab-world-science-fiction.

Morgan, Cheryl. (11 June 2012). "Ahmed Khaled Towfik Interview." *The World SF Blog*. Permanent URL: http://worldsf.wordpress.com/tag/ahmed-khaled-towfik/.

Segal, Aaron. (June 1996). "Why Does the Muslim World Lag in Science?" *Middle East Quarterly*: 61–70.

Snir, Reuven. (2000). "The emergence of science fiction in Arabic literature." *Der Islam*. Vol. 77, No. ii: 263–285.

Between Two Traditions

A Testimonial on Translating
Arabic Science Fiction Stories

Areeg Ibrahīm

> Every language is a world. Without translation, we would inhabit parishes
> bordering on silence.
>
> —George Steiner[1]

Science Fiction (SF) is challenging to translate. I was immersed in the experience of translating from Arabic into English four of Hosam Elzembely's SF short stories: "Parallel Universes," "Facebook Ghosts," "Coma," and "Sama and Mercury." Going through the experience, I was constantly caught between two traditions of SF writing (Western and Eastern) and the two different cultures of the Arabic source text (ST) and the English target text (TT). My account analyzes some of the problems I faced, along with the strategies and procedures I followed, in order to translate Elzembely's SF stories.

Growing up in Egypt during the 1980s, SF was not quite a prevalent genre in modern Arabic literature. However, for some reason, I had developed an interest in reading SF works, fuelled by a window of SF episodes and series that had opened up to me when my family lived in the UK for a while. At that time, the British television was airing episodes from *Star Trek* as well as from a discontinued show that I recall was called *Monkey Magic*. Representatives from the TV once visited our home in London to survey the spectators' views of their famous shows. I had chosen these two. One of them, *Star Trek,* continued to be aired and the other one was discontinued.

Going back home to Egypt, my fascination with SF continued, and I was eager to devour amounts of literature in the genre. At that time, only works of Egyptian writers Mustafa Mahmoud (1921–2009) and Nihad Sharif (1932–2011) fit that category. I preferred the work of Sharif, and I recall being swept away by one of his stories: *Al-Masat Al-Zaitoniah* (*Olive Diamonds*), published in 1979. Interestingly, one of his stories was later turned into a movie, entitled *Qaher Al-Zaman* (*Time Conqueror*) in 1987, starring Noor Al Sharif and Athar Al-Hakim. Later on, Nabil Farouk started publishing an intriguing series of young adult stories entitled *Malaf Al-Mustaqbal* (*Future Files*).

I must admit that I stopped following SF works in Arabic literature in the millennial years, especially since Hollywood was providing me with my full share of SF movies. However, recently, I was introduced to the activities of a nascent group called the Egyptian Society for Science Fiction, founded by ophthalmologist Dr. Hosam Elzembely in

2012. The society held seminars and meetings, and even published SF works. It has published six anthologies of SF stories so far. It even wanted to publish a SF magazine, and I was invited to translate one story from Western literature into Arabic. I came across a short story, "Silence of the Asonu,"[2] by American writer Ursula Le Guin (1929–2018). I wanted to introduce Arab readers to her works. I had decided to translate the whole story but changed my mind for fear of copyright issues. So, the best solution was to only translate an excerpt, and I do not recall if it got published or not. This was the excerpt:

ST (Source Text)

The Silence of the Asonu
   The silence of the Asonu is proverbial. The first visitors believed that these gracious, gracile people were mute, lacking any language other than that of gesture, expression, and gaze. Later, hearing Asonu children chatter, the visitors suspected that among themselves the adults spoke, keeping silence only with strangers. We know now that the Asonu are not dumb, but that once past early childhood they speak only very rarely, to anyone, under any circumstances. They do not write; and unlike mutes, or monks under vows of silence, they do not use any signs or other devices in place of speaking.
   This nearly absolute abstinence from language makes them fascinating.

TT (Target Text)
(مقتطف) الأسونو صمت (١٩٩٨) قصة قصيرة بقلم أورسولا لاجوين ترجمة :د.أريج إبراهيم إن صمت الأسونو مضرب للمثل. لقداعتقد الزوار الأوائل لمستوى الأسونو أن أولئك الناس الكيسون الناحلون هم أيضاً بكمّ، و يفتقرون أية لغة أخرى عدا لغة الاشارة، و التعبير، و النظرة. و لكن، و فى وقت لاحق، و حين سمع الزوار ثرثرة أطفال الأسونو، ظنوا أن البالغين يتحدثون أيضاً فيما بينهم، و يحتفظون بصمتهم مع الغرباء فقط. و نحن نعرف الآن أن الأسونو ليسوا خرساً، و لكنهم بعد تخطى مرحلة الطفولة المبكرة، من النادر جداً أن يتحدثوا مع أى شخص، و تحت أى من الظروف. و هم لا يكتبون؛ و على عكس البكم، أو الرهبان الملتزمون بوعود الصمت، هم لا يستخدمون يستخدموا أية اشارات اشارة، أو أجهزة أخرى بدلاً من التحدث. و فى هذا الامتناع المطلق تقريباً (الظاهري / او المجازي؟؟!!) عن اللغة ما يجعلهم رائعين.

Now getting to the actual work of translating, I realized that this was not an easy task, and I was happy it was not a long work. First of all, I was torn between two urges: it is a creative work, and I want to be engaged in this act of creation, but it was not my work, and as a researcher, I was bound by a certain code of honor of faithfulness to the original. Also, I realized, it was not easy to translate SF and recreate a whole world that exists in the mind of another SF author. I can try to reproduce the descriptions, but in the end, it is my imagination that will interpret the work, and no two imaginations are alike, I assume. In addition to the difficulty of maintaining a style of literariness, there were of course technical issues that any translator encounters, and these include lexical and syntactic issues, as well as cultural references. One lexical issue is proper names. I first wondered whether or not "Asonu" was a proper name. There is one more complication in SF, and that is the creation of new worlds that make the translator unsure about many things. In such a short excerpt, there were also cultural and religious references. The source text's culture mainly consists of readers with a Biblical background who know about the monks' vows of silence vis-à-vis the target text audience who are mostly Muslim readers. I faced a dilemma of whether or not to use paratexts such as the translator's notes. I abstained from that and kept it to a minimum because as a literary text, I wanted the reader to enjoy a certain amount of smoothness in reading. Now this was one example of trying to translate a foreign text into an Arabic text and how I was caught between two cultures and two traditions of writing.

I was in a similar bind when I started translating Hosam Elzembely's SF short stories from Arabic into English. I specifically refer to the four short stories I translated: "Parallel Universes," "Facebook Ghosts," "Coma," and "Sama and Mercury." Now I was trying to translate an Arabic ST into an English TT, bearing in mind that my native language is Arabic, and it would have been easier to go the other way around. However, I wanted the non–Arabic speaker to learn about SF writings in another culture.

SF writings, even though they are created worlds most of the time, do not exist in a vacuum but are very much influenced by the writer's background and frames of reference. When I first read some of the earlier works by Elzembely, especially his novel *America 2030*, I realized that his work carried an Islamic frame of reference. As suggested by T.S. Eliot, it is better to understand the works of a writer by reading his previous works. To apply, it was important to learn about some of the earlier works of Elzembely. In *The Planet of the Viruses* (2001), *The Great Space Saga* (2001), and *America 2030* (2001), the writer was envisioning a future with a unified Muslim nation, not unlike the European Union. I learned about his overall oeuvre in order to be able to clearly transfer his work into a different language and culture. This knowledge came in handy because, for example, in "Parallel Universes," the author refers to a future where there is a "United Arab Country."

When I started approaching SF as a translator, I had to do a different kind of research. I was no longer a reader but a researcher, and I needed to know about the field I was going to translate into, to choose the best approach for translation, and to consider both traditions of the source text (ST) and target text (TT). Science fiction has usually been regarded as existing in a liminal space between science and literature. Thus, a translator of SF can encounter the dilemma of which method of translation to follow and whether to treat the text as literary or scientific. I must say that the background of each translator also plays a role. I was myself an avid reader of SF, with some background in science education, a writer of literature in Arabic, and an academic in the field of comparative literature with some experience in translation. As I immersed myself in the world of the writer and the text, I was not only held between the two forces of science and literature, but also the disparate traditions of SF in the source and target texts, as well as the different Eastern and Western cultural and religious backgrounds. My account as a practitioner shows some of the linguistic, and cultural issues I encountered and the strategies I followed in accomplishing the translation.

Translation Problems

Lexical and Stylistic Problems

When I first translated the first short story, "Parallel Universes" (published in Arabic in 2012 in *Anthology 1*; published in English in 2013 in *Anthology 2*), first of all I was conscious of the genre I was translating. SF is a complex genre; it is a mix of literature and science. I tried to maintain the relatively scientific style of the writer and endow it with a sense of literariness, since the story had a unique literary style in the original Arabic. So, the first issue I encountered pertained to the genre. It was present right from the title. The literal translation would have been "Parallel Worlds," but the genre-specific translation made it a better choice to go for "Parallel Universes." This problem can also be considered a lexical problem as it pertains to word-choice between synonyms.

Another example of choosing between synonyms that was informed by the story's genre was of the word "sphere." It could have been translated as "ball," but the first choice sounded more genre-appropriate and gave it a sense of gravity and scale.

As for "Facebook Ghosts" (published in Arabic in 2013 in *Anthology 2*; published in English in 2013 in *Anthology 3*), a similar problem was faced in the title. Synonyms included spooks, specters, etc. "Spooks" sounded slightly informal. "Specters" may have been suitable, and it has a literary sound to it, however, since the whole story revolves around characters who think that Facebook is haunted, I preferred to use the more common term of "ghosts."

As for "Coma" (published in Arabic in 2013 in *Anthology 3*; published in English in 2013 in *Anthology 4*), most lexical issues pertain to technical terms. This particular story uses a lot of medical terminology. I had to search many of them such as coma, diabetes, insulin, hypoglycemia, hyperglycemia, hemorrhage, Magnetic Resonance Imaging (MRI), Electroencephalography (EEG), and Electrocardiogram (ECG).

"Sama and Mercury" was published both in Arabic and English in *Anthology 6* in 2018. I chose to leave the girl's name as Sama, but this caused some translation loss. The name in Arabic means "Sky," and this name was relevant to a story about planets. However, such translation loss was minor, and the level of loss was inevitable and did not affect the main meaning of the story.

In terms of the style of the writer, I tried to be as faithful as possible as to when the writer uses narration and when he uses dialogue. In terms of dialogue, I was faced with the diglossia problem pertaining to the Arabic language. The author was using a register of the language that is closer to the spoken or colloquial Egyptian accent. That was not too informal, rather, very close to MSA (Modern Standard Arabic). In order to recreate the same effect, I tried to make the dialogue more conversational and informal like spoken English. For instance, in the story "Sama and Mercury," there was a part in the dialogue when the daughter addresses her father as "Baba," or the short Arabic word for father. Since it was meant as informal, in order to recreate the same intimate feeling, I resorted to translate it as "Daddy" and sometimes "Papa." There was no need to use the same Arabic word as the English-speaking reader would not have understood it, and there was no need for paratexts to explain.

Culture-Specific Problems

One of the cultural-specific issues that also pertains to the style of the writer was the culture that is portrayed. As I explained earlier, I was aware that the author is trying to envision a unified and advanced Islamic civilization. Therefore, it was important for me to try to recreate such culture. For example, in "Parallel Universes," I did not revert to the strategy of adaptation, for example, of proper names but kept the names of the main character as Dr. Mohamed Abdel-Hady, his wife, Nurulhoda, and Colonel Hatem Seifudin from the Scientific Intelligence. Such an approach may have provided some sense of for-eignization for the target reader, but it was necessary to capture the feeling of the story. However, when it came to military ranks, I preferred in this case to go for the domesti-cation approach by finding the foreign equivalent for the rank because I did not feel the target audience will understand the equivalent Arabic rank. In "Facebook Ghosts," the same approach was used, especially when the author tried to use names that are particu-lar to the region of Upper Egypt, specifically Luxor, such as Haggag (who is named after a famous Sheikh). I felt no need to use a note to explain this information because the meaning of the name has no relevance to the action of the story. In "Coma," the Arabic names were also retained as Dr. Fadel Nur al-Din and Dr. Shugaa' Mahmoud.

Also, the author does not refer to the Georgian calendar but to the Hijri calendar as characteristic of this unique Islamic civilization. Again, these features needed to be included in the translation and not domesticated into the target culture; doing so would have lost the translation the essence of the author's ideology.

Names of places were also transliterated. For example, the laboratory of Dr. Abdel-Hady was set in the Mokattam district in Cairo. Keeping the name would allow the reader to get a feeling of the locality of the story. The same happened with names of cities because the writer was referring to real cities in Egypt: Cairo, Alexandria, Ismailia, and Port Said. In "Facebook Ghosts," the same approach was used. The author prefers to situate his stories in real places in Egypt but in the future. For example, this story happens in the neighborhood of El-Karnak in Luxor. As a translator, I wanted the reader to have a feel of the local color of the stories, so I kept the names of places and locations as they were and did not attempt to find a Western equivalent. A similar sit-uation happened while translating "Coma"; the cultural references in this story per-tain to street names, such as the Autostrade, and residential neighborhoods, such as Nasr City, in Cairo. The translator needed to be familiar with these places so as not to mistranslate.

There were also religious references. For instance, in "Facebook Ghosts," there is a reference to the afternoon prayer. The procedure used was also transliteration along with expansion. I wrote the 'Asr Prayer, as it is known to Muslims, but also explained that it was the afternoon prayer. In "Sama and Mercury," there was a reference to the weekly Fri-day sermon. I preferred not to use paratexts since it is not so difficult to search the inter-net and know that Muslims go to prayers every Friday just as Christians go to church every Sunday.

Translation Approaches and Procedures

Generally, my strategy was a mix of foreignization and domestication, but I was mostly leaning towards foreignization in order to transfer to the target reader a feel of this different culture: a unified Muslim civilization. There were instances when I did not need to recreate a certain cultural atmosphere, so I preferred to lean more towards domestication and find equivalence in the target culture. As for instance, when I used the word "Daddy" or "Papa" in "Sama and Mercury" instead of "father" or "baba."

In terms of procedures, there were minor instances of omission; adaptation was spo-radically used, as in the case of "Colonel" in "Parallel Universes." There was also expan-sion to explain culture-specific or religious terms, as with the 'Asr prayers in "Facebook Ghosts."

Conclusion

In short, translating Hosam Elzembely's SF short stories was an informative experience. It was a journey through which I learnt to navigate many aspects about the SF genre itself and about the special style of Elzembely's stories. The experience required me to mediate between two cultures and between two traditions of writing SF stories. I had to explore strategies to problem solve the difficulties I encountered, whether they pertained to the lexis, style, or culture.

Notes

1. Quote taken from "George Steiner Quotes," *BrainyQuote*, https://www.brainyquote.com/quotes/george_steiner_581451.
2. Le Guin (2010). The original story was published in 1998.

Works Cited

Elzembely, Hosam. (2013). "Coma." Trans. Areeg Ibrahīm. In *Anthology 4*. Cairo: Ibda'.
Elzembely, Hosam. (2013). "Facebook Ghosts." Trans. Areeg Ibrahīm. In *Anthology 3*. Cairo: Ibda'.
Elzembely, Hosam. (2013). "Parallel Universes." Trans. Areeg Ibrahīm. In *Anthology 2*. Cairo: Ibda'.
Elzembely, Hosam. (2018). "Sama and Mercury." Trans. Areeg Ibrahīm. In *Anthology 6*. Cairo: Al-Said for Publishing and distribution.
Le Guin, Ursula. (December 2010). "The Silence of the Asonu." *Lightspeed: Science Fiction & Fantasy*. Issue 7, http://www.lightspeedmagazine.com/fiction/the-silence-of-the-asonu/.
Sharif, Nihad. (1979). *Al-Masat Al-Zaitoniah* (*Olive Diamonds*), Cairo: Dar Al-Maeref.

Conclusion

HOSAM A. IBRAHIM ELZEMBELY

The story of the writing of this book is a book in its own right. The book evolved with every new set of contributors, going from a collection of essays by authors from Arabic and Muslim countries giving their firsthand accounts of their individual country experiences, to a mixture of personal essays, academic-length articles, and interviews by a range of contributors, many of whom were neither Arabs or Muslims or were headquartered outside of the Arab and Muslim world.

We learnt to adapt through rapid accretion. Contributors, writers of fiction, made it clear to us that writing an essay was a very different proposal than penning a story, a very different discipline that demanded a different set of aptitudes. One of our contributors turned a set of questions for an essay into an interview, and in the process, we had an entirely new format to tackle the complex topics at hand—country experiences of individual authors—as well as a new way with which to engage and attract new contributors to our project. Not only authors but translators and publishers and members of book clubs and sci-fi associations were giving us little known details about the book markets in their respective countries. With a growing number of contributors, we were able to enlist academics, both locals and experts from abroad, and went from our initial model of personalized essays to proper, full-length academic articles. The more names we accumulated, the easier it became to approach the bigger names in the literary world. We listed our existing set of contributors in any message we sent out, whether via email or Twitter or Facebook. The book grew and grew and grew until it surpassed our wildest expectations.

We received a phenomenal amount of support at almost *every* juncture, and in real-time. We would post a comment or request on Facebook or Twitter, on the pages of various advocates of science fiction whether individuals and groups, and instantaneously we would get references and advice and potential names to contact. But special mention must go to four names that have marshaled us in our efforts from the very beginning—Marcia Lynx Qualey, James E. Gunn, Rebecca Hankins, and Jörg Matthias Determann. They had the academic and literary experience with science fiction, publishing, editing, and the English language to point us in the right direction and teach us how to approach prospective publishers and what pitfalls to watch out for, as well as suggesting contributors and putting in a good word for us with them.

The only remaining question then is where do we go from this point on? Translation of the finished published text from English to Arabic, Turkish, Farsi, and multiple other languages in the nations surveyed here is the obvious first step, including Malaysia

373

and Indonesia, not to forget the continental Europeans. From there the sky is the limit. We may follow up this book with an anthology translated into English of young, aspiring Arab authors. We may turn the book into a study text replete with questions and answers and open-ended exercises. We may engage in online, real-time, audio-visual discussions with like-minded individuals and groups over the book and our premier organization, the ESSF, or launch a newer, larger organization that will pull together all those who participated in the birthing of our book to the benefit of the global audience. We may publish a series of specialized studies on such unexplored topics as Sufism in Arabic and Muslim science fiction or artificial intelligence in Arab-Muslim sci-fi or comparative studies with other bodies of SF produced in the Global South.

The trick is sustainability, so that the international reader never loses interest and always craves more and more from us. The reader of our book will ultimately decide the critical and commercial reception and the contribution we can make to further the knowledge and concern with Arabic and Muslim science fiction. It is to the reader that we owe our ultimate debt of gratitude, and we hope in earnest we have met his expectations.

I would like to save my last words of the book to spotlight my coeditor Dr. Emad El-Din Aysha. Without this man's perseverance, organization, and dedication, this book would never have seen the light.

About the Contributors

Ashiru Muheez **Afolabi** is an author from Lagos, Nigeria, who started writing in 1996 after finishing secondary school, beginning with comic stories followed by *Curse of the Kings* (2004) and *My People's Past* (2005). His short story "Amphibian Attack" came out in the sci-fi anthology *Lagos 2060*. He has a BA in sociology (University of Lagos) and a master's in international relations and strategic studies (Lagos State University). He has worked as a management consultant and trainer.

Muhammad Aurangzeb **Ahmad** is an internationally recognized expert on artificial intelligence and an affiliate associate professor in the Department of Computer Science at the University of Washington. He earned his Ph.D. from the Center for Cognitive Science at the University of Minnesota. Long an advocate of science fiction, he edited the first anthology of short science fiction stories for the *Islam and Science Fiction* website in 2008 with Ahmed A. Khan entitled *A Mosque Amongst the Stars*.

Wajdi Muhammad **Al-Ahdal** is a novelist, short-story writer, screenwriter, and dramatist. He received a degree in literature from Sanaa University, has won scores of Arab literary and theater prizes, and works at the National Library in Sanaa. His novel *Mountain Boats* drove him into exile, thanks to an extremist campaign against the book, and it took German Nobel Laureate Günter Grass and the former Yemeni president to help get him back into the country.

Manar **Al Hosni** is an Omani law graduate from the University of Manchester. She is the author of the historical romance novel *Siren of the Desert* and an upcoming novel centering on the djinn of Oman. She is the first-place winner in the Oman's Ambassadors Award 2019, in the Literature category.

Rafeeat **Aliyu** is a horror and speculative fiction writer based in Nigeria. Her short stories have been published in *Strange Horizons, Nightmare, Expound,* and *Omenana* magazines as well as the *Queer Africa 2* and the *AfroSF Anthology of African Science Fiction* anthologies. She is a Clarion West Graduate (2018).

Ahmed Salah **Al-Mahdi** is an author (young adult, fantasy, science fiction), graphic designer, and literary translator. He is a graduate in Arabic literature from the Faculty of Arts, Cairo University, and his novels include *Reem: Into the Unknown, Malaaz: The City of Resurrection, The Black Winter,* and *The Brave Rabbit*. He is also involved in translating graphic novels and Lovecraftian fiction and is planning translations of his own novels into English.

Ibrahim **Al-Marashi** is an associate professor of Middle East history at California State University San Marcos (CSUSM). He is a co-author of *Iraq's Armed Forces: An Analytical History, The Modern History of Iraq* with Phebe Marr, and *A Concise History of the Middle East* with Arthur Goldschmidt, Jr. He was also a distinguished contributor to the *Iraq + 100* anthology.

Naif **Al-Mutawa** is a distinguished clinical psychologist from Kuwait. He is also a member of the Kuwait Supreme Education Council, Kuwait SME Fund Investment Committee, and winner of the UNESCO Tolerance Award for 1997. His most distinguished contribution to Arabic science fiction is the comic book series *The 99* and the internationally recognized TV series of the comic, which earned him praise from President Obama and condemnation from extremist right-wingers, Muslims and non–Muslims alike.

Noura **Al Noman** started writing when she turned 45. Noting the huge deficit in books for young Arabs, she wrote *Ajwan*, one of a handful of science fictions novels set in the Arab world. Winner of the Etisalat Best YA Novel Award in 2013, it was followed by a sequel, *Mandaan*, in 2014, and another, *Saydounia* in 2016. She is working on the fourth and final book in the series.

Abdulwahab **Al-Rifaee** is an author, publisher, and literary coach. He earned his degree in chemical engineering from the University of Tulsa in Oklahoma in 1997 and worked as a civil servant in the Kuwait Environment Public Authority (1997–2014). Since then he has become one of Kuwait's most acclaimed writers, with 17 novels to his name and in genres frowned upon for the longest time in Arabic literature, including science fiction, horror, psychology, and parapsychology.

Mohammed Abdullah **Alyasin** is a Syrian school teacher, librarian, and aspiring SF author residing in the United Arab Emirates. He is a member of the Arab Science Fiction Writers Union and has numerous publications on science fiction in magazines and in book form in the Arabic language. His master's in Arabic literature was on the topic of Arabic SF from a comparative perspective, and he is completing his Ph.D. on Abbasid literature.

Kawthar **Ayed** is an assistant professor of modern literature at the University of Tunis. She completed her thesis in 2008 in France, at the University of Aix–Marseille I, under the title: "Dystopian Anticipation Literature and the Expression of the Crisis in the Western and Arab World." Her Ph.D. supervisors were Roger Bozzetto and Guy Larroux. She first studied SF at the academic level at Sousse University in Tunisia.

Emad El-Din **Aysha** holds a Ph.D. in international studies (2001) from the United Kingdom and has taught at numerous English-language universities in Egypt where he lives, and is also a freelance journalist and translator. He is a SF author and member of the Egyptian Society for Science Fiction and the Egyptian Writers Union. He has also published numerous interviews, reviews, and academic articles on genre literature and has one published online course on SF in the MENA region.

Farkhondeh Fazel **Bakhsheshi**, owner of Ahang-e-Ghalam Publishing House, is an English literature critic, one of the leading publishers of science fiction in Iran, and an author of fiction herself. Her essays on different approaches to literature have been published in conferences and journals, and she is a Ph.D. candidate in English literature pending the approval of her dissertation.

Azrul **Bin Jaini** is a graduate of the faculty of Mechatronics Engineering, International Islamic University Malaysia. He is the author of the space opera novel *Galaksi Muhsinin*, published in 2008 in the Malay language and reprinted in 2016. He has written his blog since 2008, discussing sci-fi in the light of Muslim issues as well as exploring ideas and frameworks of sci-fi infused with Islamic elements.

Mouad **Bouyadou** graduated from the Scientific Institute of Technology (IST) and the Central School of Computing and Management (ECIG), and lives in Switzerland. He is a novelist, short story and flash fiction writer in the sci-fi genre. He specializes in military SF, adventure stories, and spy and detective-type SF fiction. He writes only in Arabic, although he speaks fluent English and French.

Barbara K. **Dick** studied classics at University College, Oxford, and worked as a political risk broker before returning to university to study Arabic under the UK's CASAW (Centre for the Advanced Study of the Arab World) program. Her doctoral thesis at Durham University (2016), supervised by Professor Paul Starkey, was entitled "Modern Arabic Science Fiction: Science, Society and Religion in Selected Texts."

Mame Bougouma **Diene** is a Franco-Senegalese American and the francophone/U.S. spokesperson for the African Speculative Fiction Society. He is published in *AfroSFv2* and *v3*, *You Left Your*

Biscuit Behind, Myriad Lands Volume II, This Book Ain't Nuttin to Fuck Wit: A Wu Tang Tribute Anthology, Omenana, Brittlepaper, Truancy, Fiyah Magazine, Strange Horizons, Galaxies Magazine, Edilivres, Sunspot Jungle, and *EscapePod. Dark Moons Rising on a Starless Night* was nominated for the 2019 Splatterpunk Awards.

Moussa Ould **Ebnou** is a professor of philosophy at the University of Nouakchott and the country's only SF author. He completed his Ph.D. in philosophy at the Sorbonne in 1983, worked as an advisor at the UNDP (1983–85), and later became an advisor to the Mauritanian presidency on cultural affairs from 1992–2007. All of his published works of fiction are in the sci-fi genre, beginning with *L'Amour Impossible* (1990) and *Barzakh* (1993).

The Egyptian Society for Science Fiction (ESSF) was launched in 2012 by a group of Egyptian sci-fi enthusiasts. The founder and president is Hosam A. Ibrahim Elzembely, a professor of ophthalmology and a sci-fi writer. The ESSF convenes a regular cultural salon catering to Egyptian and Arabic literary audiences. Its second most distinguished activity is publishing the Shams El-Ghad anthologies, with nine issues so far. The ESSF cultural salon celebrated its golden jubilee in 2021, completing 50 events since its launch in 2012.

Riawani **Elyta** is an author, civil servant, blogger, and content writer. She was born in Tanjungpinang, Riau Island Province, Indonesia, and earned a bachelor's degree in public administration. She has authored a total of 26 books, with 17 novels in the genres of romance, inspiration, and also SF, and nine nonfiction works on the themes of teen motivation, parenting and marriage, and has won multiple awards as a novelist and blogger.

Hosam A. Ibrahim **Elzembely** is an Egyptian medical doctor, university professor, human development expert, and author (fiction and nonfiction). He is the founder of the Egyptian Society for Science Fiction (ESSF). He is also a member of the Egyptian Writers' Union (head of its Scientific Committee), has edited all the volumes of the ESSF anthology series, and wrote *The January 25th Revolution: Lessons and Examples for Human Development* and *Simplifying Medical Sciences for Children.*

Ziane **Guedim** is an Algerian author (fiction and nonfiction), blogger, freelance writer, and translator. He has a bachelor's degree in English studies from the Faculty of Arts and Languages at Blida University. He writes in Arabic, English, and French. Two of his most notable short stories are "The Moon Is Always Full" (published in *The Lorelei Signal*) and "A Slice of Heaven" (*The Worlds of Science Fiction, Fantasy and Horror Volume 2* anthology).

The late James E. **Gunn**, from the Golden Age of science fiction, was an emeritus professor of English at the University of Kansas, winner of the SFWA Grand Master award, SFRA Pilgrim Award, and member of the Science Fiction and Fantasy Hall of Fame. He was also the editor of the six-volume *Road to Science Fiction, The Science of Science-Fiction Writing,* and *Isaac Asimov: The Foundations of Science Fiction.*

Rebecca **Hankins** holds the Wendler Endowed Professorship and is a certified archivist at Texas A&M University. Her teaching, scholarly research, and service intersects with her professional work that centers on the African Diaspora, women and gender studies, and the use of popular culture as a pedagogical method that offers new approaches to the study of Islam.

Areeg **Ibrahīm** is a professor of English and comparative literature, Helwan University. She obtained both her BA and MA from the American University in Cairo and her Ph.D. in comparative literary and cultural studies from the University of Connecticut. She is also a distinguished literary translator and co-translated into Arabic a series of books on theater (*Theatre and Human Rights*). She is on the editorial board of the new *Arab Stages Journal.*

Shamil **Idiatullin** is a journalist, editor, and writer. He graduated from Kazan State University with a degree in journalism and has served as head of the Regional Editions Department at the Kommersant newspaper in Moscow. He published his first book in 2004, and since then has written seven more. In 2017, his novel *Brezhnev City* received the Big Book Prize.

Hamid **Ismailov** is a world acclaimed Uzbek writer living in exile in the UK. He writes in Russian and English and is the author of dozens of novels in different languages. His books include *The Railway, The Dead Lake, The Underground, A Poet and Bin-Laden, The Devils' Dance, Language of Bees: Hayy ibn Yakzan* (speculative fiction), among others.

Zahra **Jannesari-Ladani** is an assistant professor of English language and literature at the University of Isfahan. She has published extensively and presented conference papers on American and British science fiction (on John W. Campbell, Robert Heinlein, post-humanism). She is also a Farsi translator and a member of the Science Fiction Research Association and her own country's Fantasy Academy.

Sami Ahmad **Khan** is an author (*Red Jihad, Aliens in Delhi*), documentary maker and an academic. He completed his master's at Jawaharlal Nehru University, and then went to the University of Iowa on a Fulbright grant. He holds a Ph.D. in SF and has taught at IIT Delhi, Jawaharlal Nehru University, JGU and GGSIPU, Delhi. He is currently a Marie Skłodowska-Curie Actions Fellow at the University of Oslo, Norway. His latest book is *Star Warriors of the Modern Raj*.

Faycel **Lahmeur** is a writer, translator, and critic who lives in Algeria. His books include the novel *Amin Ialawani* and the short story collection *Chroniques D'outre Monde*.

Kristine Ong **Muslim** is the author of nine books including the fiction collections *Age of Blight, Butterfly Dream,* and *The Drone Outside,* and editor of two anthologies—the British Fantasy Award–winning *People of Colo(u)r Destroy Science Fiction* (with Nalo Hopkinson) and *Sigwa: Climate Fiction Anthology from the Philippines* (with Paolo Enrico Melendez and Mia Tijam). Her short stories have appeared in *Conjunctions, Tin House,* and *World Literature Today.*

Taleb **Omran** is one of the most distinguished science fiction writers in Syria. He has a Ph.D. in differential geometry and astronomy from the University of Aligarh, India, and is a professor on the faculty of civil engineering at the University of Damascus, having taught previously at universities in Algeria, India, and Oman. He is also a member of the Arab Writers' Union and founder of the Syrian educational satellite TV channel and the science fiction magazine.

Müfit **Özdeş** has had his stories published in *Son Tiryaki* (*The Last Smoker*). He became a dedicated consumer of science fiction in elementary school and a writer in 1983. He was a student in Middle East Technical University in 1968 and joined in the global action for a better world, resulting in several years in prison and exile. He now lives in Istanbul where most of his stories take place in the present or the future.

Gamze G. **Özfırat** is a linguist and polyglot with BA degrees in English literature and classical philology and an MA in English literature. Introduced to science fiction at an early age, her undying enthusiasm for the genre has grown over the decades. She is working as a translator and editor and is also a prominent member of the premier SF club in Turkey, Bilimkurgu Kulübü.

Marcia Lynx **Qualey** is a translator, literary editor, freelance journalist, and blogger who works at promoting Arabic literature. An American now residing in Morocco, she had been living in Egypt when she launched *Arab Literature* (in English), which won the 2017 "Literary Translation Initiative" award at the London Book Fair. She also teaches writing and is involved with the Kitab Sawti and the Library of Arabic Literature projects.

Saquib **Sadiq** consults as a business analyst and teaches computer programming to university students. After years of reading from the sidelines, he began writing. He has one SF novel and three short stories to his name. His mission statement in life is to explore the intersection of Geek culture with Islam and to counter the Islamophobic narratives.

Funda Özlem **Şeran** graduated with a degree in political science and international relations from Marmara University, completed her MA in the same department with her thesis on political science fiction, comparing utopian and dystopian literature. Being also interested in horror and fantasy genres, she is an award-winning writer and has publications in both children's and adult literature.

Harun **Šiljak** is a complexity and control scientist based at Dublin's Trinity College where he investigates the complexity of future communications networks. His sci-fi work includes a short story collection, *Murder on the Einstein Express and Other Stories*. He organizes Stranger Fictions workshops for researchers and artists in Ireland and has an unpublished novel in the state of perpetual editing.

Abdulwakil **Sulamal** received his master's degree in military pedagogy from the then Soviet Union in 1989 and later joined the Writers Union of Free Afghanistan (1994). He speaks Russian and Slovak in addition to English, Dari, and his mother tongue Pashto and has published nine short story collections, a mixture of surrealism and speculative fiction.

Jeremy **Szal** writes about galactic nightmares, wide-screen futures, and characters fighting for hope in dark worlds. He is author of the dark space-opera novel *Stormblood*, published in February 2020, the first of a trilogy. His short fiction has appeared in *Nature, Abyss & Apex, Lightspeed, Strange Horizons, Tor.com, The Drabblecast*. He is the fiction editor for the Hugo-winning *StarShipSofa*.

Amir **Tag Elsir** is a Sudanese doctor, poet, and novelist. He gained his medical degree from Egypt, University of Tanta, and now practices medicine in Qatar. He has won several awards and written numerous successful novels and biographies translated into ten languages including French, English, Polish, Spanish, and Italian. He has written magic realism and historical novels, and is planning a SF novel.

Abdulhakeem Amer **Tweel** is a blogger, tourist guide, historian, civil society activist, nuclear engineer, and author (fiction and nonfiction). He is Libya's only living science fiction writer with two published anthologies to his name to date. His bachelor's project in nuclear engineering has since been listed as a patented invention, and he is a founding member of the Saraya Forum for Literature and Arts (2011) and the Law 88/1975 Victims Assemblage (2012).

Aditya Nugraha **Wardhana** attained his bachelor's degree in science (majoring in biology) at the University of Indonesia in 2013. He is a high school biology teacher, as well as a graphic designer and author of light novels. His two main publications to date are *Beast Taruna: Episode 1* (2016) and *Red Rose for Heroes* (2019).

İsmail **Yamanol** is a Turkish science fiction writer and founder of the Turkish Science Fiction Club. An amateur student society during its initial years, the club was transformed into a subcultural platform in the new millennium when access to the internet became more widespread in Turkey. He continues his career in Istanbul as an advisor, editor, and proofreader for publishing houses and contributes to periodicals with his articles on science fiction.

Fadi **Zaghmout** is a gender activist, blogger, and author from Jordan. He holds an MA in creative writing and critical thinking from University of Sussex in the UK. He has one published sci-fi novel, *Heaven on Earth*, a best-seller in Jordan along with his first novel *The Bride of Amman*, a feminist novel that deals with homosexuality. His third novel, *Laila and the Lamb* (non–SF), was released but was swiftly banned in Jordan.

Index